Revised and Updated

TERRORISM AND COUNTERTERRORISM

UNDERSTANDING THE NEW SECURITY ENVIRONMENT

READINGS & INTERPRETATIONS

About the Authors

Colonel Russ Howard, a career Special Forces officer, is now a professor and department head at the United States Military Academy. As a Special Forces officer, Colonel Howard served at every level of command, including: A Detachment Commander in the 7th Special Forces Group to Group, B Detachment Commander in the 1st Special Forces Group, Battalion Commander in the Special Warfare Center and School, and Commander of the 1st Special Forces Group. In preparation for his academic position, Colonel Howard earned degrees from San Jose State University, the University of Maryland, the Monterey Institute of International Studies, and Harvard University. Presently, he is finishing a Ph.D. in international security studies at the Fletcher School of Law and Diplomacy. During the course of his career Colonel Howard has had antiterror and counterterror responsibilities, and has taught and published articles on terrorism subjects.

Major Reid Sawyer, a career Military Intelligence officer, is an instructor of political science at the United States Military Academy. As an Intelligence officer, Major Sawyer served in counternarcotics and special operations assignments. Major Sawyer earned his undergraduate degree from the United States Military Academy and holds a master's degree from Columbia University. Major Sawyer has lectured on terrorism to various groups and is currently working on a research project for the Institute of National Security Studies on the efficacy of counterterrorism measures. Major Sawyer is the current director of terrorism studies at West Point.

Revised and Updated

TERRORISM AND COUNTERTERRORISM

UNDERSTANDING THE NEW SECURITY ENVIRONMENT

READINGS & INTERPRETATIONS

RUSSELL D. HOWARD
COLONEL USA

REID L. SAWYER
MAJOR USA

FOREWORD BY
BARRY R. MCCAFFREY
GENERAL USA (RET.)

The **McGraw·Hill** Companies

Book Team

Vice President and Publisher   *Jeffrey L. Hahn*
Managing Editor   *Theodore Knight*
Director of Production   *Brenda S. Filley*
Developmental Editor   *Ava Suntoke*
Copy Editors   *Robin N. Charney, Cynthia Goss*
Designer   *Charles Vitelli*
Typesetting Supervisor   *Juliana Arbo*
Typesetting   *Jocelyn Proto, Cynthia Powers*
Proofreader   *Julie Marsh*
Permissions Editor   *Rose Gleich*

McGraw-Hill/Dushkin

A Division of The **McGraw-Hill** Companies

530 Old Whitfield Street, Guilford, Connecticut 06437

Library of Congress Control Number 2002106286

ISBN 0-07-287301-9

Printed in the United States of America

10 9 8 7 6 5 4 3 2 1

Visit the Online Learning Center With PowerWeb at

http://www.dushkin.com/terrorism/

Contents in Brief

Contents

Foreword

On September 11, 2001, the United States was confronted with the stark reality of modern terrorism. The brutal murder of thousands of innocent lives stripped away our ability to ignore the threat posed by the emergence of transnational terrorist organizations. The terrorism we witnessed on September 11 was a giant escalation of an evolving threat. Prior to these tragic attacks, Americans had witnessed a steadily growing series of violent attacks culminating in more than 5,000 casualties in the terrorist bombings of our East African embassies in 1998. Now the question is not *if* further terrorist attacks will occur in the United States, but *when* and to what magnitude. One thing is certain, terrorists will continue to try to adapt to the changing counterterror security environment.

Terrorism, at its very roots, centers on fear and targets our liberal democratic values. The fear generated by terrorism speaks to our vulnerabilities and the government's apparent lack of ability to stop further attacks. The current proliferation of lethal technologies, combined with radical ideologies, potentially presents truly horrific scenarios. We will continue to witness new forms of terrorism, be they viruses that selectively attack target populations or suicide bombers attempting to slaughter our children in our nation's schools. It is imperative for all of us to study and learn about these new threats. We will be driven to understand why terrorism occurs and how best to counter terrorism's driving forces. The goal of this superb collection is to heighten the reader's awareness of the critical issues related to the threat of terrorism. Although it is impossible for any single work to address the entire breadth of the terrorism field, this volume captures the most salient pieces on the subject.

There are many terrorism experts in academia. However, there are only a handful of individuals who combine impressive academic credentials with extensive special operations combat and training experience. The editors of this compilation, Colonel Russ Howard and Major Reid Sawyer, are two distinguished scholars who have also spent careers on the cutting edge of U.S. military special operations. Their combined experience of over 30 years in the front lines of the struggle to prevent terrorism provides them with a distinct and uniquely informed perspective on the current war on terrorism. Together they have gathered and edited the best works of more than 15 of the leading commentators on terrorism at a critical time in our nation's history.

This superbly researched book also reflects their experience in teaching security-related courses in the Department of Social Sciences at West Point. Colonel Howard and Major Sawyer have refined their thinking on the topic by their experimentation with the curriculum in these national security courses. We suggest that students of national security polity will find this book to be a unique combination of well-known and astute thinkers who have articulated the current and future policy implications of terrorism. The relevant experience of both Howard and Sawyer as editors places them in the best position to "connect the dots" of this wide-ranging material.

There is much uncertainty about the future. However, we are sure that only through diligent and creative study can America effectively address this very real asymmetrical threat to our national security. We are challenged to develop a conceptual framework to re-evaluate the security environment. Clearly we must craft flexible and effective counterterrorism strategies. The policy solutions to this complex threat of terrorism do not lie solely with our military, or even our government. Instead, we must create cooperative efforts to find a national solution to manage the terrorist threat that involves a partnership with the international community combined with an integrated and coherent strategy, which unites community, state, and federal authorities supported by business, the health professions, and academia. We also cannot allow ourselves to become trapped in overly simplistic views of the threat. Our challenge is to dramatically embrace our domestic security while carefully preserving our precious freedoms guaranteed in the Bill of Rights, as well as the safety and dignity of foreigners living among us.

Through the thoughtful study of the definitions, issues, and recommendations provided by these accomplished authors and the editors, we can hopefully move toward a better understanding of terrorism and its causes.

Barry R. McCaffrey

Preface

The haunting image of New York's falling twin towers defined for the world the reality of the "new terrorism." Americans had faced terrorism before September 11. However, terrorism's previous incarnations, were not nearly as organized, deadly, or personal as the attacks inflicted on New York City and Washington, D.C., or on that remote Pennsylvania field.

In 1984 when I first became involved in the antiterrorism and counterterrorism efforts, most international and national terrorism was ideological. It was part of the East versus West, left versus right confrontation—a small but dangerous side-show to the greater, bipolar, Cold War drama. In the past, terrorism was almost always the province of groups of militants that had the backing of political forces and states hostile to American interests. Under the old rules, "terrorists wanted a lot of people watching, not a lot of people dead."[1] They did not want large body counts because they wanted converts. They wanted a seat at the table. Today's terrorists are not particularly concerned about converts and don't want a seat at the table, "They want to destroy the table and everyone sitting at it."[2]

What is new to me and my generation, but not to Reid Sawyer and his, is the emergence of terrorism that is not ideological in a political sense. Instead it is inspired by religious extremism and ethnic-separatist elements, who might be individuals such as the Unabomber, or like-minded people working in cells, small groups, or larger coalitions.[3] They do not answer completely to any government, operate across national borders, and have access to funding and advanced technology.[4] Such groups are not bound by the same constraints or motivated by the same goals as nation-states. And, unlike state-sponsored groups, religious extremists, ethnic separatists, and lone Unabombers are not susceptible to traditional diplomacy or military deterrence. There is no state with which to negotiate or to retaliate against. And, today's terrorists are not concerned about limiting casualties. Religious terrorists, such as al Qaeda in particular, want casualties—lots of them.[5]

The new terrorism is not an ideological ism like communism or capitalism whose value can be debated in the classroom or decided at polls. It is an ancient tactic and instrument of conflict. Terrorism today has a global reach that it did not have before globalization and the information technology revolution. It can ride the back of the Web, use advanced communications to move immense financial sums from Sudan to the Philippines, to Australia, to banks in Florida.[6] And, for $28.50, any Internet surfer can purchase *Bacteriological Warfare: A Major Threat to North America*, which shows how to grow deadly bacteria that could be used in a weapon of mass destruction.

Clearly, the United States and its citizens are favored targets of the new terrorists. Many wonder why. "Why do They Hate Us?" was the banner headline in *Newsweek* and the *Christian Science Monitor* soon after 9/11. Why should Islamic extremists hate us? After all, was it not United States that saved those who follow the Islamic faith in Kuwait, liberated them in Iraq, and continues to protect them in Bosnia and Kosovo? Is it a Jihad, a war of faiths between Christians and Muslims as some suggest? Or is the United States a target because of the resentment it has spread through societies demoralized by their recent history. As one knowledgeable journalist put it, "A sense of failure and injustice is rising in the throats of millions," because Arab nations have lost three wars against Israel, their arch-foe and America's ally.[7]

Many also believe that globalization is not only a technological tool for terrorists, but that it is a root cause of terrorism either separately or in conjunction with religious extremism. Extreme Muslim fundamentalists and others who have missed the rewards of globalization worry that unbridled globalization exploits workers and replaces ancient cultures with McDonald's and Mickey Mouse.[8] According to some, globalization is based on the American economic system, and because the United States is the dominant world power, it has succeeded in expanding the reach of its version of globalization to more and more areas of the world. As the gap between the rich and poor has grown wider during the last twenty years of U.S.-led globalization the poor have watched American wealth and hegemony expand, while they, themselves, have received little or no benefit.[9]

There are other theories about rising terrorism and future targets, many of which will be covered in this book. One thing is certain however, America is a target. It has been attacked and will be again unless the attacks can be prevented or preempted. Rudi Giuliani made this very clear to West Point's 2002 graduating class when he was the guest speaker at their final dinner banquet. He theorized that America was attacked for a number of reasons: it prizes political and economic freedom, elects its political leaders, and has lifted people out of poverty; it also has religious freedom, respects human rights as well as the rights of women. America's adversaries do not, and they are threatened by the freedoms we have. "We are right and they are wrong," Giuliani said to thunderous applause. "There is no excuse and no justification for these attacks," he said. The mayor told the cadets that America has already won the war on terrorism. "We still have a lot of battles to win, but we have actually won the war on terrorism because the terrorists tried, but could not break our spirit."

This book, edited at West Point, will address those "battles to win"—how to fight and win them, and why America and the free world are in the dubious position of having to fight the battles in the first place. Why edit the book at West Point? More importantly, why have two career soldiers edit the book? Brigadier General Dan Kaufman, West Point's dean, answered these questions in a Los Angeles Times interview. "Suddenly, now the world is a much more dangerous place," he said. "The nation is at risk again. The notion that the American homeland is vulnerable is new to all of us. Given where West Point sits—fifty miles from ground zero—there is a sense of immediacy here."[10]

Organization

Terrorism and Counterterrorism: Readings and Interpretations, is in two parts. Part I analyzes the philosophical, political, and religious roots of terrorist activities around the world and discusses the national, regional, and global effects of historical and recent terrorist acts. In addition to material on the threats from suicide bombers, as well as from chemical, biological, radiological, and nuclear weapons, there are also important contributions analyzing new and growing threats: narcoterrorism, cyberterrorism, and genomic terrorism.

Part I

Part I contains six chapters. *Chapter 1* consists of articles by Bruce Hoffman, Paul Pillar, and Eqbal Ahmad, who define terrorism and address several specific questions, in some cases from very different perspectives: What is terrorism? What is counterterrorism? Who is a terrorist? Who are terrorists? And, why do these questions matter? Hoffman's "Defining Terrorism" emphasizes the changing nature of terrorism. He succinctly defines its past and present, explains its evolution, and predicts where it might be headed in the future. His offering is an important primer that will prepare the reader for the rest of the book. In his article, "The Dimensions of Terrorism and Counterterrorism," Paul Pillar considers what terrorism is and why it is a real problem. As the title suggests, however, Pillar goes further and identifies the necessary elements and limitations of any counterterrorism policy. Pillar, a CIA veteran, believes counterterrorism policy should not stand alone but be part of a broader effort to maintain national security and that it needs to be integrated into all foreign policy decision-making. Ahmad's "Terrorism: Theirs & Ours," like Hoffman's article, also emphasizes change. "To begin with," writes Ahmad, "terrorists change. The terrorist of yesterday is the hero of today, and the hero of yesterday becomes the terrorist of today." His example is Osama bin Laden, who was once an American ally in the fight against the Soviet Union and is now public enemy number one.

What motivates people to turn to terrorism is examined in *chapter 2*. Articles by professional colleagues Martha Crenshaw and Louise Richardson look at more than the traditional psychological, cultural, and socioeconomic reasons for terrorism. Addressing terrorism in a greater globalization context in "The Logic of Terrorism: Terrorist Behavior as a Product of Strategic Choice," Crenshaw shows that terrorism is a perfectly rational and logical choice for some individuals and groups: "The central problem is to determine when extremist organizations find terrorism useful.... Terrorism is not the only method of working toward radical goals, and thus it must be compared to the alternative strategies available to dissidents."

Louise Richardson's "Global Rebels" also helps the reader distinguish between terrorism and other forms of violence, especially political violence. In so doing she also analyzes the different types of terrorist-sponsored relationships between terrorists and "axis of evil" states.

Chapter 3 explores the rise and impact of new terrorism in greater depth and then looks at some of the technological and control mechanisms that make today's ethnonationalist terrorists more difficult to detect and defeat than the left-wing and right-wing terrorists of earlier eras.

I begin the dialogue in "Understanding al Qaeda's Application of the New Terrorism" by outlining the six ways today's terrorism differs from that of the Cold War. Specifically, the new terrorism is more violent, and better financed than in the Cold War era. The new terrorists operate globally, are better trained, more difficult to penetrate, and have access to and say they will use weapons of mass destruction. My article discusses the advantages present-day terrorists, particularly al Qaeda, have over their counterparts in the 1960s, 70s, and 80s.

A trio of RAND specialists, John Arquilla, David Ronfeldt and Michele Zanini, suggest in "Networks, Netwar, and Information-Age Terrorism" that a new type of enemy and warfare will be the product of the information revolution, including the rise of new, more complex forms of terrorism. New systems and organizations and modes of conflict used by modern-day terrorists will inevitably affect the nature and styles of warfare. Using "netwar" and "cyberwar" as weapons, these terrorists will attack modern societies' vulnerabilities. The authors recommend that new organizations, strategies, technologies, and doctrines will be required to defeat this new form of enemy.

Brent Ellis's article, "Countering Complexity: An Analytical Framework to Guide Counter-Terrorism Policy-Making," ends *chapter 3*. True to its title, Ellis provides an analytical framework for assessing the new terrorism. He agrees with Hoffman that policy makers must have a more comprehensive understanding of terrorism in all its dimensions, including an understanding of the nuances of specific terrorist groups. The framework presented in Ellis's article assesses terrorist groups according to the nature of their motivation, their level of organization and of technological sophistication. He is optimistic and believes that countering the terrorist threat is not beyond our capabilities.

An old saying I learned as a child is that "More people have been killed in the name of God than for any other reason." Things have not changed. Indeed the articles in *chapter 4* argue that religious terrorism is on the rise and is unprecedented in its militancy and activism. "Between the mid-1960s and the mid-1990s," writes Magnus Ranstorp, "the number of fundamentalist movements of all religious affiliations tripled worldwide." In his article, "Terrorism in the Name of Religion," Ranstorp explores the reasons for the dramatic increase of religious-motivated terrorism and identifies the causes and enemies that promote violence out of religious belief in both established and newly formed terrorist groups. The post-Cold War security environment figures prominently in his analysis. Mark Juergensmeyer's "Logic of Religious Violence" uses the struggle of the Sikhs in India as a case study to suggest why some religions "propel the faithful rather easily into militant confrontation" while others do not. "The pattern of religious violence of the Sikhs could be that of Irish Catholics, or Shi'ite Muslims in Palestine, or fundamentalist Christian bombers of abortion clinics in the United States." He argues that violence associated with religion is not an aberration but arises from the fundamental beliefs of all the world's major religions.

The final article in *chapter 4*, Adam Dolnik's "All God's Poisons: Re-evaluating the Threat of Religious Terrorism," takes issue with the common assertion that religious terrorist groups are more likely to use weapons of mass destruction (WMD) than their secular counterparts. Unfortunately, writes Dolnik, the logic of the assertion is greatly simplified and inaccurate. In his view, religious terrorists are essentially very similar to other secular terrorists: narrow-minded individuals who fail to see alternative perspectives on the issues they are fighting for. Dolnik reaches the conclusion that conducting a "superterrorist" attack with biological, chemical, nuclear, or radiological weapons would be extremely difficult for any terrorist group, religious or secular, and asserts the likelihood of a successful mass-casualty attack remains low.

Chapter 5 explains why (WMD)—chemical, biological, radiological, and nuclear— are becoming the weapons of choice among terrorist organizations and some governments. Jessica Stern's "Getting and Using the Weapons" shows how chemical and biological weapons, along with a simple nuclear device that spews radioactive isotopes, are ideal terrorist tools. She argues, however, that "despite the evidence of such weapons as instruments of terror, terrorists have seldom used them" because the technical obstacles of acquiring the weapons and disseminating or exploding them are considerable.

The contributors to this chapter agree that lumping all WMD weapons in one category is probably a mistake. MacArthur Foundation Fellow Christopher F. Chyba makes this point in his post-September 11 article, "Toward Biological Security." A former member of the National Security Council in the Clinton administration, Chyba points out that WMD weapons differ greatly: "Put simply, biological weapons differ from nuclear or chemical weapons, and any biological security strategy should begin by paying attention to these differences." According to him, "An effective strategy for biological security will encompass nonproliferation, deterrence and defense, but the required mix of these components will be very different from those in strategies for nuclear or even chemical weapons."

In "The Bioterrorist Threat in the United States," Richard Pilch formalizes the way to assess the current bioterrorism threat to the United States by using a simple formula: Threat = Vulnerability x Capability x Intent. Pilch emphasizes the major technical hurdles involved in acquiring, producing, and delivering a potential biological warfare agent. The article uses a crop-duster scenario for a case study and concludes that while the likelihood of a bioterrorist attack is small, policy makers must take a worst-case scenario seriously.

Chapter 6 identifies nontraditional forms of terrorism and potential terrorist weapons that could be used with deadly results. In "Narcotics, Terrorism, and International Crime: The Convergence Phenomenon," which has been updated for this book, General Barry McCaffrey and Major John Basso use case studies from different world regions to illustrate the insidious and debilitating nature of narcoterror. McCaffrey, former drug czar in the Clinton administration, is the ideal person to address this issue and is still passionate about halting the flow of drugs into America and stopping drug production in the less developed world.

Martha Crenshaw's article defines the "logic of terrorism" in strategic terms. Bruce Hoffman's complimentary piece "The Logic of Suicide Terrorism," in this chapter, describes how the tactics of terrorists, particularly suicide bombing, are also very logical. Written in easily understood, cost-benefit terms, Hoffman explains that "the fundamental characteristics of suicide bombing, and its strong attraction for the terrorist organizations behind it, are universal: Suicide bombings are inexpensive and effective." Hoffman's syntax forces one to rethink modern warfare's technological jargon. According to him, suicide bombers are the ultimate smart bomb. They guarantee media coverage and are less complicated and compromising than other kinds of terrorist operations. Hoffman uses Israel, which has more experience with suicide bombers than any other place, as the case study for his article. Hoffman notes that Israel is not the United States, but says Americans can take precautions to substantially reduce the threat of suicide bombing in America based on Israel's experience.

In "Terrorism and IT: Cyberterrorism and Terrorist Organizations Online," Maura Conway asserts that the information revolution is driving dramatic changes in political, diplomatic, military, economic, social and cultural affairs, which can be both good and bad. Conway, points out that just as the ability of the Internet to communicate words, images, and sounds underlies the power to persuade, inform, witness, debate, and discuss, it also underlies the ability to slander, propagandize, disseminate bad or misleading information, and engage in mis-information and/or disinformation. Terrorists understand this and are availing themselves of the opportunity to connect. In particular, says Conway, "both substate and non-state actors are said to be harnessing—or preparing to harness—the power of the Internet to harass and attack their foes."

Madeleine Gruen reminds us that not all terrorism is inflicted on the United States by Islamic extremists and that the homegrown variety is as adept at using information technology as their Middle East counterparts. In "White Ethno-Nationalist and Political Islamist Methods of Fundraising and Propaganda on the Internet," Gruen explores three main uses of the Internet by domestic and international terrorist groups: propaganda, furthering resistance, and fundraising. Perhaps the greatest cause for concern in the article is her description of the exponential growth in "hate sites" on the Internet. According to Gruen in 1995 there was only one problematic hate site on the Internet; now there could be as many as 300,000. She concludes by offering "some solutions for change." Like many of the authors featured in this book, Gruen believes the solutions for control and change must be multilateral, and that both state and private agencies have an important role in limiting terrorists' ability to further their agendas via the Internet.

"Terrorism in the Genomic Age," by John Ellis paints a frightening picture of the possible misuse of the human genome. Breaking the DNA code has many positive possibilities writes Ellis, a biological terrorism expert and Pulitzer Prize nominee for his work at the *Boston Globe*. It also has many liabilities. Consider narcotics. Shortly after the attacks on the World Trade Center and the Pentagon, the *New York Times* reported that Osama bin Laden had funded an effort to develop a genetically modified "super heroin." In theory, genetically modified poppy plants could lead to the development of an instantly addictive and wildly potent heroin product that could be introduced to a much broader market segment. If the number of junkies doubles or triples, narcoterrorism becomes seriously destabilizing. Ellis also argues that breaking the DNA code will allow terrorists to identify racial vulnerabilities and to attack them.

Part II

Part II of this book deals with past, present, and future national and international responses to terrorism and defenses against it. Organized into three chapters, the essays and articles in Part II analyze and debate the practical, political, ethical, and moral questions raised by military and nonmilitary responses, including preemptive actions outside the context of declared war. In addition, two detailed appendices—"Background Information on Designated Foreign Terrorist Organizations" and "Significant Terrorist Incidents, 1961–2001"—are provided at the end of Part II.

Chapter 7 examines the challenge to democratic and human rights norms that democracies must contemplate when facing terrorist threats. It also examines the "just war" theory as it might apply to protracted warfare with nonstate actors.

Laura Donohue explains in "Fear Itself: Counterterrorism, Individual Rights, and US Foreign Relations post 9-11" that public sentiment generally supports counterterrorism measures. However, she notes, "Following a significant terrorist attack, a liberal, democratic government, forced to respond and yet also forced to balance the tension between liberal democratic values and the possible security threat faced by the state and the population, will often introduce 'temporary' counterterrorist measures." "The difficulty," she says, "is that in the face of terrorism, it can be extremely difficult to repeal temporary provisions." They risk becoming permanent and counter to liberal democratic values.

In his final article in this book, "A Nasty Business," Bruce Hoffman notes the difficulty intelligence organizations in democracies have in collecting intelligence against terrorists: "Gathering 'good intelligence' against terrorists is an inherently brutish enterprise, involving methods a civics class might not condone." Hoffman also advances the question asked by many after September 11: How much of their civil rights, liberties, and freedoms are Americans willing to give up in order to prosecute the war on terrorism?

In his speech to West Point's 2002 graduates, President George W. Bush spoke of preemption as a means of dealing with terrorists. "Our security," said President Bush, "will require all Americans to be forward-looking and resolute, to be ready for preemptive action when necessary to defend our liberty and to defend our lives." Historically, Americans have been leery of using military force for preemptive purposes, because "just war" doctrine justifies the use of force only after one is attacked.

Two just war articles clarify the doctrine when applied to terrorism, non-state actors, and weapons of mass destruction. "Terrorism and Just War Doctrine," by Anthony Clark Arend concludes that "the nature of terrorists and terrorist actions raises a number of critical challenges for just war doctrine, and that doctrine offers a great deal of guidance for counterterror operations." At the same time, Arend also seems to support President Bush's "preemptive action" comments by suggesting a state has the right to preempt terrorist actions if it can show that an attack is imminent, and if its response is proportionate to the threatened attack.

In "NBC-Armed Rogues: Is there a Moral Case for Preemption?" Brad Roberts supports the notion of "preemptive action," particularly if it would stop a nuclear, chemical, or biological attack. However, while agreeing that there is a moral case for preemption, Roberts asserts that "it is not quite as tidy as policy-makers might desire."

The selections in *chapter 8* discuss grand strategies (or the lack thereof) executed by the United States and its opponents in terrorism and counterterrorism warfare. In "The Soft Underbelly of American Primacy: Tactical Advantages of Terror," Richard Betts asserts that a strategy of terrorism "flows from the coincidence of two conditions: intense political grievance and gross imbalance of power." Says Betts, terrorism "may become instrumentally appealing by default—when one party in conflict lacks other military options." "This is why terrorism is the premier form of 'asymmetric warfare,' the Pentagon buzzword for the type of threats likely to confront the United States in the post-Cold War world."

Jim Robbins agrees and further explains in "Bin Laden's War" that bin Laden fully understood that the United States was not a weak adversary—it was powerful, too much so to be attacked frontally." In fact, says Robbins, bin Laden's 1996 Declaration of War against the United States "explicitly stated the need for asymmetric engagement." Robbins masterfully lays out bin Laden's strategy to defeat the United States before explaining that bin Laden's fatal error was misperceiving America's courage and the willingness of Americans to fight. Robbins also argues that Bin Laden "allowed his capabilities to outpace his strategy." "He discovered and exploited seams in American security to conduct a brilliant, innovative and stunning act of violence, but in so doing deviated from the long-term strategy necessary to pursue a successful guerrilla struggle."

"The Real Intelligence Failure on 9/11 and the Case for Doctrine of Striking First" by Richard Shultz and Andreas Vogt argues—unsurprisingly—that the events of 9/11 were partly the result CIA and FBI intelligence and coordination failures. Information concerning the attacks was in the hands of both agencies before 9/11, say Shultz and Vogt, but the two organizations failed to share the information and put "two and two together." However, the authors also maintain that the intelligence failures went well beyond simple analysis and coordination problems. They contend that the FBI, CIA, and the Pentagon did not understand terrorism as a strategy for a new type of "fourth generation" warfare. Before 9/11, "terrorism was seen as a secondary national security challenge—not a clear and present danger—even after the deadly 1998 East Africa embassy bombings." Fortunately, the authors believe that President Bush and Secretary of Defense Rumsfeld understand what fourth generation warfare is and have a doctrine to fight it. The new "Bush Doctrine," first articulated by Bush at West Point, emphasizes preemption over deterrence and containment, two key components of Cold War doctrine and thinking.

In "The Struggle Against Terrorism: Grand Strategy, Strategy, and Tactics," Barry Posen asserts that the United States should pursue a comprehensive strategy of selective engagement to prosecute its campaign against terrorism. Posen introduces the idea that special operations forces are the ideal for executing a selective engagement strategy. "Flexible, fast, and relatively discriminate forces are essential," Posen argues, and "the United States has large special operations forces well suited to the counterterror mission."

Wyn Q. Bowen argues in "Deterring Mass-Casualty Terrorism" that there is still a role for deterrence in a counterterror strategy. Unlike some contributors to this book who believe deterrence has nothing to offer as an element of a broader, comprehensive strategy for preventing mass casualty terrorism, Bowen believes deterrence still works, and that credible deterrent strategy requires knowing enemy motives, worldview, resolve, capabilities and vulnerabilities. It also requires the capability to deliver on the deterrent message.

Organizing to fight is the topic of *chapter 9*. Specifically, which organizations should be charged with fighting the terrorist threat and how must they adapt for the fight? Although written before 9/11, Martha Crenshaw's "Counterterrorism Policy and the Political Process" describes how difficult it is for any president, including George W. Bush, to implement a coherent counterterrorism policy. "Due to pressures from Congress," says Crenshaw, "the president will not be able to set the agenda for counterterrorism policy with as much freedom as he can in other policy areas." Crenshaw also contends that implementing counterterrorism policy decisions will "also be affected by controversy, due to rivalries among agencies with operational responsibilities." Thus, she correctly predicted before 9/11 that "it will be difficult for any administration to develop a consistent policy based on an objective appraisal of the threat of terrorism to American national interests."

Dick Betts does not necessarily disagree, but he is not sure reorganizing America's intelligence apparatus will alleviate interagency rivalries. In "Fixing Intelligence," Betts argues that reorganizations usually prove to be three steps forward and two back, because the intelligence establishment is so vast and complex that the net impact of reshuffling may be indiscernible. Reforms that can be undertaken now will make the intelligence community a little better," writes Betts however, "equal emphasis must go to measures for civil defense, medical readiness, and 'consequence management,' in order to blunt the effects of the attacks that do manage to get through."

Jeff H. Norwitz, author of "Combating Terrorism: With a Helmet or a Badge?" believes the Bush administration not only needs to rethink (and reorganize) its intelligence-gathering capabilities, but must also rethink its approach to defeating terrorism. Norwitz's essay examines old terrorism paradigms and offers a perspective on how "criminal approaches" have not grasped the nature of the war on terrorism. According to Norwitz, "terrorism challenges the categories of what is legal and illegal," so that the normal rules of evidence are difficult to apply. "Good intelligence is the cornerstone for dealing effectively with terrorism," says Norwitz, "and the U.S. intelligence community, heavily dependent on technical collection means, is almost omniscient." Nowritz advocates a greater role for the Department of Defense in the war on terror, particularly in the American homeland: "Only the military can truly deal with catastrophic evens such as biological, chemical, and radiological attacks and consequence management."

In "The Limits of Military Power," Rob de Wijk states that "the West's armed forces are fundamentally flawed. Conceptually, the focus is still on conventional warfare, but the new wars will be unconventional." "The West needs special forces to confront unconventional irregular fighters such as terrorists, and those forces are not available in large quantities." Nevertheless, de Wijk contends that the military, including special forces, cannot win the war on terrorism alone. There also must be a "campaign to win the hearts and minds of the Islamic people."

David J. Rothkopf also believes that the military, particularly special forces, cannot win the war on terror alone. In "Business versus Terror," he explains that an alliance of doctors, venture capitalists, and corporate project managers—the private-sector army—is the United States not-so-secret weapon and best hope. "Its best troops," says Rothkopf, "will be regiments of geeks rather than the special forces that struck the first blows against the Taliban in Afghanistan."

About three-quarters of the offerings in this eclectic reader on terrorism were written after September 11 and because of that terrible event. The others were obviously written before the event. Interestingly, and eerily, almost all of the pre-September 11 articles either predict, or speak about the likelihood or possibility of a catastrophic terrorist event occurring on American soil. No one paid attention. Let's hope some pay attention to the insights in this book and the others like it that are sure to come.

—Russell D. Howard

Notes

1. Brian Michael Jenkins, "Will Terrorists Go Nuclear?" RAND Paper P-5541 (1975), p. 4.
2. James Woolsey, 1994.
3. Stephen A. Cambone, *A New Structure for National Security Policy Planning*, Washington D.C.: Government Printing Office, 1996, p. 43.
4. Gideon Rose, "It Could Happen Here—Facing the New Terrorism," *Foreign Affairs*, March-April, 1999, p. 1.
5. Bruce Hoffman, *Inside Terrorism*, New York: Columbia University Press, 1998, p. 205.
6. Paul Mann, "Modern Military Threats: Not All They Might Seem?" *Aviation Week & Space Technology*, April 22, 2002, p. 1. (Gordon Adams quote)
7. Peter Ford, "Why Do They Hates Us," *Christian Science Monitor*, September 27, 2001, p. 1.
8. http://globalization.about.com/library/weekly/aa100101a.htm
9. http://discuss.washingtonpost.com/wp-srv/zforum/02/nation_christison0410.htm
10. John Hendren, "At West Point a New Breed of Cadet," *Los Angeles Times*, May 31, 2002, p. 17.

Part 1

Defining the Threat

Chapter 1

Terrorism Defined

Chapter 1 introduces the problems inherent in defining a topic as complex as terrorism. In the news everywhere, used to describe events from the Philippines to Central America, from the Middle East to the United States, we "think we know what it is when we see it." But is that enough? Bruce Hoffman does not think so. In his reading "Defining Terrorism" he struggles to come up with a definition of the term that avoids the "promiscuous" and imprecise labeling of a range of acts. He provides dictionary definitions but finds them to be "unsatisfying" because ultimately a society's definition is a reflection of the political and social tenor of the times. Hoffman traces the historical use of the term "terrorism" from the reign of terror that followed the French Revolution; to the communist and fascist movements in Russia, Italy, and Germany; to the narco-terrorism of the 1990s. He concludes with a definition that seeks to distinguish terrorists from guerrillas, ordinary criminals, and assassins.

Paul Pillar, because of his years of experience in the U.S. Army and Central Intelligence Agency, approaches terrorism from a practical, problem-solving vantage point. As such, his primary intention is to provide sound counterterrorism policy. Pillar feels that arguing the semantics of a precise definition is "confusing" and "cumbersome" and that it does not ultimately help one to determine good policy. He begins his study of terrorism and counterterrorism from a working definition used by the U.S. government, "as good a definition as any." The reading that follows examines the effects, both direct and indirect, of terrorism and outlines the four elements of good counterterrorism policy. The selection concludes with Pillar's reflections on the evolving nature of the world order, and the need for policy that adapts to change.

Eqbal Ahmad, in contrast to Paul Pillar, finds the official definition of and approach to terrorism to be an extremely limiting one, which stirs up emotion without "exercising our intelligence." Ahmad maintains that we do need to know what terrorism is before we can determine how to stop it. Most important, we must first study the motives of the terrorists. Throughout his reading, Ahmad uses Osama bin Laden and his transformation from U.S. ally to terrorist as a case study. His reading concludes with three recommendations to the United States for dealing with terrorism, which, although written in 1998, are remarkably prophetic in light of the events of September 11, 2001.

Bruce Hoffman, 1998

Defining Terrorism

What is terrorism? Few words have so insidiously worked their way into our everyday vocabulary. Like 'Internet'—another grossly over-used term that has similarly become an indispensable part of the argot of the late twentieth century—most people have a vague idea or impression of what terrorism is, but lack a more precise, concrete and truly explanatory definition of the word. This imprecision has been abetted partly by the modern media, whose efforts to communicate an often complex and convoluted message in the briefest amount of air-time or print space possible have led to the promiscuous labelling of a range of violent acts as 'terrorism'. Pick up a newspaper or turn on the television and—even within the same broadcast or on the same page—one can find such disparate acts as the bombing of a building, the assassination of a head of state, the massacre of civilians by a military unit, the poisoning of produce on supermarket shelves or the deliberate contamination of over-the-counter medication in a chemist's shop all described as incidents of terrorism. Indeed, virtually any especially abhorrent act of violence that is perceived as directed against society—whether it involves the activities of anti-government dissidents or governments themselves, organized crime syndicates or common criminals, rioting mobs or persons engaged in militant protest, individual psychotics or lone extortionists—is often labelled 'terrorism'.

Dictionary definitions are of little help. The pre-eminent authority on the English language, the much-venerated *Oxford English Dictionary [OED]*, is disappointingly unobliging when it comes to providing edification on this subject, its interpretation at once too literal and too historical to be of much contemporary use:

> **Terrorism:** A system of terror. 1. Government by intimidation as directed and carried out by the party in power in France during the revolution of 1789–94; the system of 'Terror'. 2. *gen.* A policy intended to strike with terror those against whom it is adopted; the employment of methods of intimidation; the fact of terrorizing or condition of being terrorized.

These definitions are wholly unsatisfying. Rather than learning what terrorism is, one instead finds, in the first instance, a somewhat potted historical—and, in respect of the modern accepted usage of the term, a uselessly anachronistic—description. The second definition offered is only slightly more helpful. While accurately communicating the fear-inducing quality of terrorism, the definition is still so broad as to apply to almost any action that scares ('terrorizes') us. Though an integral part of 'terrorism', this definition is still insufficient for the purpose of accurately defining the phenomenon that is today called 'terrorism'.

A slightly more satisfying elucidation may be found in the *OED*'s definition of the perpetrator of the act than in its efforts to come to grips with the act itself. In this respect, a 'terrorist' is defined thus:

> 1. As a political term: a. Applied to the Jacobins and their agents and partisans in the French Revolution, esp. to those connected with the Revolutionary tribunals during the 'Reign of Terror'. b. Any one who attempts to further his views by a system of coercive intimidation; *spec.* applied to members of one of the extreme revolutionary societies in Russia.

This is appreciably more helpful. First, it immediately introduces the reader to the notion of terrorism as a *political* concept. As will be seen, this key characteristic of terrorism is absolutely paramount to understanding its aims, motivations and purposes and critical in distinguishing it from other types of violence.

Terrorism, in the most widely accepted contemporary usage of the term, is fundamentally and inherently political. It is also ineluctably about power: the pursuit of power, the acquisition of power, and the use of power to achieve political change. Terrorism is thus violence—or, equally important, the threat of violence—used and directed in pursuit of, or in service of, a political aim. With this vital point clearly illuminated, one can appreciate the significance of the additional definition of 'terrorist' provided by the *OED*: 'Any one who attempts to further his views by a system of coercive intimidation'. This definition underscores clearly the other fundamental characteristic of terrorism: that it is a planned, calculated, and indeed systematic act.

Given this relatively straightforward elucidation, why, then, is terrorism so difficult to define? The most compelling reason perhaps is because the meaning of the term has changed so frequently over the past two hundred years.

The Changing Meaning of Terrorism

The word 'terrorism' was first popularized during the French Revolution. In contrast to its contemporary usage, at that time terrorism had a decidedly *positive* connotation. The system or *régime de la terreur* of 1793–4—from which the English word came—was adopted as a means to establish order during the transient anarchical period of turmoil and upheaval that followed the uprisings of 1789, as it has followed in the wake of many other revolutions. Hence, unlike terrorism as it is commonly understood today, to mean a *revolutionary* or anti-government activity undertaken by non-state or subnational entities, the *régime de la terreur* was an instrument of governance wielded by the recently established revolutionary *state*. It was designed to consolidate the new government's power by intimidating counter-revolutionaries, subversives and all other dissidents whom the new regime regarded as 'enemies of the people'. The Committee of General Security and the Revolutionary Tribunal ('People's Court' in the modern vernacular) were thus accorded wide powers of arrest and judgement, publicly putting to death by guillotine persons convicted of treasonous (i.e. reactionary) crimes. In this manner, a powerful lesson was conveyed to any and all who might oppose the revolution or grow nostalgic for the *ancien régime*.

Ironically, perhaps, the terrorism in its original context was also closely associated with the ideals of virtue and democracy. The revolutionary leader Maximilien Robespierre firmly believed that virtue was the mainspring of a popular government at peace, but that during the time of revolution must be allied with terror in order for democracy to triumph. He appealed famously to 'virtue, without which terror is evil; terror, without which virtue is helpless', and proclaimed; 'Terror is nothing but justice, prompt, severe and inflexible; it is therefore an emanation of virtue.'

Despite this divergence from its subsequent meaning, the French Revolution's 'terrorism' still shared at least two key characteristics in common with its modern-day variant. First, the *régime de la terreur* was neither random nor indiscriminate, as terrorism is often portrayed today, but was organized, deliberate and systematic. Second, its goal and its very justification—like that of contemporary terrorism—was the creation of a 'new and better society' in place of a fundamentally corrupt and undemocratic political system. Indeed, Robespierre's vague and utopian exegeses of the revolution's central goals are remarkably similar in tone and content to the equally turgid, millenarian manifestos issued by many contemporary revolutionary—primarily left-wing, Marxist-oriented—terrorist organizations. For example, in 1794 Robespierre declared, in language eerily presaging the communiqués issued by groups such as Germany's Red Army Faction and Italy's Red Brigades nearly two centuries later:

> We want an order of things… in which the arts are an adornment to the liberty that ennobles them, and commerce the source of wealth for the public and not of monstrous opulence for a few families… In our country we desire morality instead of selfishness, honesty and not mere 'honor', principle and not mere custom, duty and not mere propriety, the sway of reason rather than the tyranny of fashion, a scorn for vice and not a contempt for the unfortunate…

Like many other revolutions, the French Revolution eventually began to consume itself. On 8 Thermidor, year two of the new calendar adopted by the revolutionaries (26 July 1794), Robespierre announced to the National Convention that he had in his possession a new list of traitors. Fearing that their own names might be on that list, extremists joined forces with moderates to repudiate both Robespierre and his *régime de la terreur*. Robespierre and his closest followers themselves met the same fate that had befallen some 40,000 others: execution by guillotine. The Terror was at an end; thereafter terrorism became a term associated with the abuse of office and power—with overt 'criminal' implications. Within a year of Robespierre's demise, the word had been popularized in English by Edmund Burke who, in his famous polemic against the French Revolution, described the 'Thousands of those Hell hounds called Terrorists… let loose on the people'.

One of the French Revolution's more enduring repercussions was the impetus it gave to anti-monarchial sentiment elsewhere in Europe. Popular subservience to rulers who derived their authority from God through 'divine right of rule', not from their subjects, was increasingly questioned by a politically awakened continent. The advent of nationalism, and with its notions of statehood and citizenship based on the common identity of a people rather than the lineage of a royal family, were resulting in the unification and creation of new nation-states such as Germany and Italy. Meanwhile, the massive socio-economic changes engendered by the industrial revolution were creating new 'universalist' ideologies (such as communism/Marxism), born of the alienation and exploitative conditions of nineteenth-century capitalism. From this milieu a new era of terrorism emerged, in which the concept had gained many of the familiar revolutionary, anti-state connotations of today. Its chief progenitor was arguably the Italian republican extremist, Carlo Pisacane, who had forsaken his birthright as duke of San Giovanni only to perish in 1857 during an ill-fated revolt against Bourbon rule. A passionate advocate of federalism and mutualism, Pisacane is remembered less on this account than for the theory of 'propaganda by deed', which he is credited with defining—an idea that has exerted a compelling influence on rebels and terrorists alike ever since. 'The propaganda of the idea is a chimera,' Pisacane wrote. 'Ideas result from deeds, not the latter from the former, and the people will not be free when they are educated, but educated when they are free.' Violence, he argued, was necessary not only to draw attention to, or generate publicity for, a cause, but to inform, educate and ultimately rally the masses behind the revolution. The didactic purpose of violence, Pisacane argued, could never be effectively replaced by pamphlets, wall posters or assemblies.

Perhaps the first organization to put into practice Pisacane's dictum was the Narodnaya Volya, or People's Will (sometimes translated as People's Freedom), a small group of Russian constitutionalists that had been founded in 1878 to challenge tsarist rule. For the Narodnaya Volya, the apathy and alienation of the Russian masses afforded few alternatives to the resort to daring and dramatic acts of violence designed to attract attention to the group and its cause. However, unlike the many late twentieth-century terrorist organizations who have cited the principle of 'propaganda by deed' to justify the wanton targeting of civilians in order to assure them publicity through the shock and horror produced by wholesale bloodshed, the Narodnaya Volya displayed an almost quixotic attitude to the violence they wrought. To them, 'propaganda by deed' meant the selective targeting of specific individuals whom the group considered the embodiment of the autocratic, oppressive state. Hence their victims—the tsar, leading members of the royal family, senior government officials—were deliberately chosen for their 'symbolic' value as the dynastic heads and subservient agents of a corrupt and tyrannical regime. An intrinsic element in the group's collective beliefs was that 'not one drop of superfluous blood' should be shed in pursuit of aims, however noble or utilitarian they might be. Even having selected their targets with great care and the utmost deliberation, group members still harboured profound regrets about taking the life of a fellow human being. Their unswerving adherence to this principle is perhaps best illustrated by the failed attempt on the life of the Grand Duke Serge Alexandrovich made by a successor organization to the Narodnaya Volya in 1905. As the royal carriage came into view, the terrorist tasked with the assassination saw that the duke was unexpectedly accompanied by his children and therefore aborted his mission rather than risk harming the intended victim's family (the duke was killed in a subsequent attack). By comparison, the mid-air explosion caused by a terrorist bomb on Pan Am flight 103 over Lockerbie, Scotland, December 1988 indiscriminately claimed the lives of all 259 persons on board—innocent men, women and children alike—plus eleven inhabitants of the village where the plane crashed.

Ironically, the Narodnaya Volya's most dramatic accomplishment also led directly to its demise. On 1 March 1881 the group assassinated Tsar Alexander II. The failure of eight previous plots had led the conspirators to take extraordinary measures to ensure the success of this attempt. Four volunteers were given four bombs each and deployed along the alternative routes followed by the tsar's cortege. As two of the bomber-assassins stood in wait on the same street, the sleighs carrying the tsar and his Cossack escort approached the first terrorist, who hurled his bomb at the passing sleigh, missing it by inches. The whole entourage came to a halt as soldiers seized the hapless culprit and the tsar descended from his sleigh to check on a bystander wounded by the explosion. 'Thank God, I am safe,' the tsar reportedly declared—just as the second bomber emerged from the crowd and detonated his weapon, killing both himself and his target. The full weight of the tsarist state now fell on the heads of the Narodnaya Volya. Acting on information provided by the arrested member, the secret police swept down on the group's safe houses and hide-outs, rounding up most of the plotters, who were quickly tried, convicted and hanged. Further information from this group led to subsequent arrests, so that within a year of the assassination only one member of the original executive committee was still at large. She too was finally apprehended in 1883, at which point the first generation of Narodnaya Volya terrorists ceased to exist, although various successor organizations subsequently emerged to carry on the struggle.

At the time, the repercussions of the tsar's assassination could not have been known or appreciated by either the condemned or their comrades languishing in prison or exiled to Siberia. But in addition to precipitating the beginning of the end of tsarist rule, the group also deeply influenced individual revolutionaries and subversive organizations elsewhere. To the nascent anarchist movement, the 'propaganda by deed' strategy championed by the Narodnaya Volya provided a model to be emulated. Within four months of the tsar's murder, a group of radicals in London convened an 'anarchist conference' which publicly applauded the assassination and extolled tyrannicide as a means to achieve revolutionary change. In hopes of encouraging and coordinating worldwide anarchist activities, the conferees decided to establish an 'Anarchist International' (or 'Black International'). Although this idea, like most of their ambitious plans, came to nought, the publicity generated by even a putative 'Anarchist International' was sufficient to create a myth of global revolutionary pretensions and thereby stimulate fears and suspicions disproportionate to its actual impact or political achievements. Disparate and uncoordinated though the anarchists' violence was, the movement's emphasis on individual action or operations carried out by small cells of like-minded radicals made detection and prevention by the police particularly difficult, thus further heightening public fears. For example, following the assassination of US President William McKinley in 1901 (by a young Hungarian refugee, Leon Czolgocz, who, while not a regular member of any anarchist organization, was nonetheless influenced by the philosophy), Congress swiftly enacted legislation barring known anarchists or anyone 'who disbelieves in or is opposed to all organized government' from entering the United States. However, while anarchists were responsible for an impressive string of assassinations of heads of state and a number of particularly notorious bombings from about 1878 until the second decade of the twentieth century, in the final analysis, other than stimulating often exaggerated fears, anarchism made little tangible impact on either the domestic or the international politics of the countries affected. It does, however, offer an interesting historical footnote: much as the 'information revolution' of the late twentieth century is alleged to have made the means and methods of bomb-making and other types of terrorist activity more readily available via the Internet, on CD-ROM, and through ordinary libraries and bookstores, one of anarchism's flourishing 'cottage industries' more than a century earlier was the widespread distribution of similar 'how-to' or DIY-type manuals and publications of violence and mayhem.

On the eve of the First World War, terrorism still retained its revolutionary connotations. By this time, growing unrest and irredentist ferment had already welled up within the decaying Ottoman and Habsburg Empires. In the 1880s and 1890s, for example, militant Armenian nationalist movements in eastern Turkey pursued a terrorist strategy against continued Ottoman rule of a kind that would later be adopted by most of the post–Second

World War ethno-nationalist/separatist movements. The Armenians' objective was simultaneously to strike a blow against the despotic 'alien' regime through repeated attacks on its colonial administration and security forces, in order to rally indigenous support, as well as to attract international attention, sympathy and support. Around the same time, the Inner Macedonian Revolutionary Organization (IMRO) was active in the region overlapping present-day Greece, Bulgaria and Serbia. Although the Macedonians did not go on to suffer the catastrophic fate that befell the Armenians during the First World War (when an estimated one million persons perished in what is considered to be the first officially implemented genocide of the twentieth century), IMRO never came close to achieving its aim of an independent Macedonia and thereafter degenerated into a mostly criminal organization of hired thugs and political assassins.

The events immediately preceding the First World War in Bosnia are of course more familiar because of their subsequent cataclysmic impact on world affairs. There, similar groups of disaffected nationalists—Bosnian Serb intellectuals, university students and even schoolchildren, collectively known as Mlada Bosnia, or Young Bosnians—arose against continued Habsburg suzerainty. While it is perhaps easy to dismiss the movement, as some historians have, as comprised of 'frustrated, poor, dreary and maladjusted' adolescents— much as many contemporary observers similarly denigrate modern-day terrorists as mindless, obsessive and maladjusted—it was a member of Young Bosnia, Gavrilo Princip, who is widely credited with having set in motion the chain of events that began on 28 June 1914, when he assassinated the Habsburg Archduke Franz Ferdinand in Sarajevo, and culminated in the First World War. Whatever its superficially juvenile characteristics, the group was nonetheless passionately dedicated to the attainment of a federal South Slav political entity—united Slovenes, Croats and Serbs—and resolutely committed to assassination as the vehicle with which to achieve that aim. In this respect, the Young Bosnians perhaps had more in common with the radical republicanism of Giuseppe Mazzini, one of the most ardent exponents of Italian unification in the nineteenth century, than with groups such as the Narodnaya Volya—despite a shared conviction in the efficacy of tyrannicide. An even more significant difference, however, was the degree of involvement in, and external support provided to, Young Bosnian activities by various shadowy Serbian nationalist groups. Principal among these was the pan-Serb secret society, the Narodna Obrana ('The People's Defence' or 'National Defence').

The Narodna Obrana had been established in 1908 originally to promote Serb cultural and national activities. It subsequently assumed a more subversive orientation as the movement became increasingly involved with anti-Austrian activities—including terrorism—mostly in neighbouring Bosnia and Hercegovina. Although the Narodna Obrana's exclusionist pan-Serbian aims clashed with the Young Bosnians' less parochial South Slav ideals, its leadership was quite happy to manipulate and exploit the Bosnians' emotive nationalism and youthful zeal for their own purposes. To this end, the Narodna Obrana actively recruited, trained and armed young Bosnians and Hercegovinians from movements such as the Young Bosnians who were then deployed in various seditious activities against the Habsburgs. As early as four years before the archduke's assassination, a Hercegovinian youth, trained by a Serb army officer with close ties to the Narodna Obrana, had attempted to kill the governor of Bosnia. But, while the Narodna Obrana included among its members senior Serbian government officials, it was not an explicitly government-controlled or directly state-supported entity. Whatever hazy government links it maintained were further and deliberately obscured when a radical faction left the Narodna Obrana in 1911 and established the Ujedinjenje ili Smrt, 'The Union of Death' or 'Death or Unification'—more popularly known as the Crna Ruka, or the 'Black Hand'. This more militant and appreciably more clandestine splinter has been described by one historian as combining

> the more unattractive features of the anarchist cells of earlier years—which had been responsible for quite a number of assassinations in Europe and whose methods had a good deal of influence via the writings of Russian anarchists upon Serbian youth—and of the [American] Ku Klux Klan. There were gory rituals and oaths of loyalty, there were murders of backsliding members, there was identification of members by number, there were distributions of guns and bombs. And there was a steady traffic between Bosnia and Serbia.

This group, which continued to maintain close links with its parent body, was largely composed of serving Serbian military officers. It was led by Lieutenant-Colonel Dragutin Dmitrievich (known by his pseudonym, Apis), himself the chief of the Intelligence Department of the Serbian general staff. With this key additional advantage of direct access to military armaments, intelligence and training facilities, the Black Hand effectively took charge of all Serb-backed clandestine operations in Bosnia.

Although there were obviously close links between the Serbian military, the Black Hand and the Young Bosnians, it would be a mistake to regard the relationship as one of direct control, much less outright manipulation. Clearly, the Serbian government was well aware of the Black Hand's objectives and the violent means the group employed in pursuit of them; indeed, the Serbian Crown Prince Alexander was one of the group's benefactors. But this does not mean that the Serbian government was necessarily as committed to war with Austria as the Black Hand's leaders were, or that it was prepared to countenance the group's more extreme plans for fomenting cross-border, anti-Habsburg terrorism. There is some evidence to suggest that the Black Hand may have been trying to force Austria's hand against Serbia and thereby plunge both countries into war by actively abetting the Young Bosnians' plot to assassinate the archduke. Indeed, according to one revisionist account of the events leading up to the murder, even though the pistol used by Princip had been supplied by the Black Hand from a Serb military armoury in Kragujevac, and even though Princip had been trained by the Black Hand in Serbia before being smuggled back across the border for the assassination, at the eleventh hour Dmitrievich had apparently bowed to intense government pressure and tried to stop the assassination. According to this version, Princip and his fellow conspirators would hear nothing of it and stubbornly went ahead with their plans. Contrary to popular assumption, therefore, the archduke's assassination may not have been specifically ordered or even directly sanctioned by the Serbian government. However, the obscure links between high government officials and their senior military commanders and ostensibly independent, transnational terrorist movements, and the tangled web of intrigue, plots, clandestine arms provision and training, intelligence agents and cross-border sanctuary these relationships inevitably involved, provide a pertinent historical parallel to the contemporary phenomenon known as 'state-sponsored' terrorism (that is, the active and often clandestine support, encouragement and assistance provided by a foreign government to a terrorist group), which is discussed below.

By the 1930s, the meaning of 'terrorism' had changed again. It was now used less to refer to revolutionary movements and violence directed against governments and their leaders, and more to describe the practices of mass repression employed by totalitarian states and their dictatorial leaders against their own citizens. Thus the term regained its former connotations of abuse of power by governments, and was applied specifically to the authoritarian regimes that had come to power in Fascist Italy, Nazi Germany and Stalinist Russia. In Germany respectively, the accession to office of Hitler and Mussolini had depended in large measure on the 'street'—the mobilization and deployment of gangs of brown- or black-shirted thugs to harass and intimidate political opponents and root out other scapegoats for public vilification and further victimization. 'Terror? Never,' Mussolini insisted, demurely dismissing such intimidation as 'simply... social hygiene, taking those individuals out of circulation like a doctor would take out a bacillus'. The most sinister dimension of this form of 'terror' was that it became an intrinsic component of Fascist and Nazi governance, executed at the behest of, and in complete subservience to, the ruling political party of the land—which had arrogated to itself complete, total control of the country and its people. A system of government-sanctioned fear and coercion was thus created whereby political brawls, street fights and widespread persecution of Jews, communists and other declared 'enemies of the state' became the means through which complete and submissive compliance was ensured. The totality of party control over, and perversion of, government was perhaps most clearly evinced by a speech given by Hermann Goering, the newly appointed Prussian minister of the interior, in 1933. 'Fellow Germans,' he declared,

> My measures will not be crippled by any judicial thinking. My measures will not be crippled by any bureaucracy. Here I don't have to worry about Justice; my mission is only to destroy and exterminate, nothing more. This struggle will be a struggle against chaos, and such a struggle I shall not conduct with the power of the police. A bourgeois State might have done that. Certainly, I shall use the power of the State and the police to the utmost, my dear Communists, so don't draw any false conclusions; but the struggle to the death, in which my fist will grasp your necks, I shall lead with those there—the Brown Shirts.

The 'Great Terror' that Stalin was shortly to unleash in Russia both resembled and differed from that of the Nazis. On the one hand, drawing inspiration from Hitler's ruthless elimination of his own political opponents, the Russian dictator similarly transformed the political party he led into a servile instrument responsive directly to his personal will, and the state's police and security apparatus into slavish organs of coercion, enforcement and repression. But conditions in the Soviet Union of the 1930s bore little resemblance to the turbulent political, social and economic upheaval afflicting Germany and Italy during that decade and the previous one. On the other hand, therefore, unlike either the Nazis or the Fascists, who had emerged from the political free-for-alls in their own countries to seize power and then had to struggle to consolidate their rule and retain their unchallenged authority, the Russian Communist Party had by the mid-1930s been firmly entrenched in power for more than a decade. Stalin's purges, in contrast to those of the French Revolution, and even to Russia's own recent experience, were not 'launched in time of crisis, or revolution and war... [but] in the coldest of cold blood, when Russia had at last reached a comparatively calm and even moderately prosperous condition'. Thus the political purges ordered by Stalin became, in the words of one of his biographers, a 'conspiracy to seize total power by terrorist action', resulting in the death, exile, imprisonment or forcible impressment of millions.

Certainly, similar forms of state-imposed or state-directed violence and terror against a government's own citizens continue today. The use of so-called 'death squads' (often off-duty or plain-clothes security or police officers) in conjunction with blatant intimidation of political opponents, human rights and aid workers, student groups, labour organizers, journalists and others has been a prominent feature of the right-wing military dictatorships that took power in Argentina, Chile and Greece during the 1970s and even of elected governments in El Salvador, Guatemala, Colombia and Peru since the mid-1980s. But these state-sanctioned or explicitly ordered acts of *internal* political violence directed mostly against domestic populations—that is, rule by violence and intimidation by those *already* in power against their own citizenry—are generally termed 'terror' in order to distinguish that phenomenon from 'terrorism', which is understood to be violence committed by non-state entities.

Following the Second World War, in another swing of the pendulum of meaning, 'terrorism' regained the revolutionary connotations with which is it most commonly associated today. At that time, the term was used primarily in reference to the violent revolts then being prosecuted by the various indigenous nationalist/anti-colonialist groups that emerged in Asia, Africa and the Middle East during the late 1940s and 1950s to oppose continued European rule. Countries as diverse as Israel, Kenya, Cyprus and Algeria, for example, owe their independence at least in part to nationalist political movements that employed terrorism against colonial powers. It was also during this period that the 'politically correct' appellation of 'freedom fighters' came into fashion as a result of the political legitimacy that the international community (whose sympathy and support was actively courted by many of these movements) accorded to struggles for national liberation and self-determination. Many newly independent Third World countries and communist bloc states in particular adopted this vernacular, arguing that anyone or any movement that fought against 'colonial' oppression and/or Western domination should not be described as 'terrorists', but were properly deemed to be 'freedom fighters'. This position was perhaps most famously explained by the Palestine Liberation Organization (PLO) chairman Yassir Arafat, when he addressed the United Nations General Assembly in November 1974. 'The difference between the revolutionary and the terrorist,' Arafat stated, 'lies in the reason for which each fights. For whoever stands by a just cause and fights for the freedom and liberation of his land from the invaders, the settlers and the colonialists, cannot possibly be called terrorist.... '

During the late 1960s and 1970s, terrorism continued to be viewed within a revolutionary context. However, this usage now expanded to include nationalist and ethnic separatists groups outside a colonial or neo-colonial framework as well as radical, entirely ideologically motivated organizations. Disenfranchised or exiled nationalist minorities—such as the PLO, the Quebecois separatist group FLQ (Front de Libération du Québec), the Basque ETA (Euskadi ta Askatasuna, or Freedom for the Basque Homeland) and even a hitherto unknown South Moluccan irredentist group seeking independence from Indonesia—adopted terrorism as a means to draw attention to themselves and their respective causes, in many instances with the specific aim, like their anti-colonial predecessors, of attracting international sympathy and support. Around the same time, various left-wing political extremists—drawn mostly from the radical student organizations and

Marxist/Leninist/Maoist movements in Western Europe, Latin America and the United States—began to form terrorist groups opposing American intervention in Vietnam and what they claimed were the irredeemable social and economic inequalities of the modern capitalist liberal-democratic state.

Although the revolutionary cum ethno-nationalist/separatist and ideological exemplars continue to shape our most basic understanding of the term, in recent years 'terrorism' has been used to denote broader, less distinct phenomena. In the early 1980s, for example, terrorism came to be regarded as a calculated means to destabilize the West as part of a vast global conspiracy. Books like *The Terror Network* by Claire Sterling propagated the notion to a receptive American presidential administration and similarly susceptible governments elsewhere that the seemingly isolated terrorist incidents perpetrated by disparate groups scattered across the globe were in fact linked elements of a massive clandestine plot, orchestrated by the Kremlin and implemented by its Warsaw Pact client states, to destroy the Free World. By the middle of the decade, however, a series of suicide bombings directed mostly against American diplomatic and military targets in the Middle East was focusing attention on the rising threat of state-sponsored terrorism. Consequently, this phenomenon—whereby various renegade foreign governments such as the regimes in Iran, Iraq, Libya and Syria became actively involved in sponsoring or commissioning terrorist acts—replaced communist conspiracy theories as the main context within which terrorism was viewed. Terrorism thus became associated with a type of covert or surrogate warfare whereby weaker states could confront larger, more powerful rivals without the risk of retribution.

In the early 1990s the meaning and usage of the term 'terrorism' were further blurred by the emergence of two new buzzwords: 'narco-terrorism' and the so-called 'gray area phenomenon'. The former term revived the Moscow-orchestrated terrorism conspiracy theories of previous years while introducing the critical new dimension of narcotics trafficking. Thus 'narco-terrorism' was defined by one of the concept's foremost propagators as the 'use of drug trafficking to advance the objectives of certain governments and terrorist organizations'—identified as the 'Marxist-Leninst regimes' of the Soviet Union, Cuba, Bulgaria and Nicaragua, among others. The emphasis of 'narco-terrorism' as the latest manifestation of the communist plot to undermine Western society, however, had the unfortunate effect of diverting official attention away from a bona fide emerging trend. To a greater extent than ever in the past, entirely criminal (that is, violent, *economically* motivated) organizations were now forging strategic alliances with terrorist and guerrilla organizations or themselves employing violence for specifically political ends. The growing power of the Colombian cocaine cartels, their close ties with left-wing terrorist groups in Colombia and Peru, and their repeated attempts to subvert Colombia's electoral process and undermine successive governments constitute perhaps the best-known example of this continuing trend.

Those who drew attention to this 'gray area phenomenon' were concerned less with grand conspiracies than with highlighting the increasingly fluid and variable nature of subnational conflict in the post–Cold War era. Accordingly, in the 1990s terrorism began to be subsumed by some analysts within the 'gray area phenomenon'. Thus the latter term came to be used to denote 'threats to the stability of nation states by non-state actors and non-governmental processes and organizations'; to describe violence affecting 'immense regions or urban areas where control has shifted from legitimate governments to new half-political, half-criminal powers'; or simply to group together in one category the range of conflicts across the world that no longer conformed to traditionally accepted notions of war as fighting between the armed forces of two or more established states, but instead involved irregular forces as one or more of the combatants. Terrorism had shifted its meaning again from an individual phenomenon of subnational violence to one of several elements, or part of a wider pattern, of non-state conflict.

Why Is Terrorism So Difficult to Define?

Not surprisingly, as the meaning and usage of the word have changed over time to accommodate the political vernacular and discourse of each successive era, terrorism has proved increasingly elusive in the face of attempts to construct one consistent definition. At one time, the terrorists themselves were far more cooperative in this endeavour than they are today. The early practitioners didn't mince their words or hide behind the semantic camouflage of more anodyne labels such as 'freedom fighter' or 'urban guerrilla'. The nineteenth-century anarchists, for example, unabashedly proclaimed themselves to be terrorists and frankly proclaimed their tactics to be terrorism. The members of Narodnaya Volya similarly displayed no qualms in using these same words to describe themselves and their deeds. However, such frankness did not last. The Jewish terrorist group of the 1940s known as Lehi (the Hebrew acronym for Lohamei Herut Yisrael, the Freedom Fighters for Israel, more popularly known simply as the Stern Gang after their founder and first leader, Abraham Stern) is thought to be one of the last terrorist groups actually to describe itself publicly as such. It is significant, however, that even Lehi, while it may have been far more candid than its latter-day counterparts, chose as the name of the organization not 'Terrorist Fighters for Israel', but the far less pejorative 'Freedom Fighters for Israel'. Similarly, although more than twenty years later the Brazilian revolutionary Carlos Marighela displayed few compunctions about openly advocating the use of 'terrorist' tactics, he still insisted on depicting himself and his disciples as 'urban guerrillas' rather than 'urban terrorists'. Indeed, it is clear from Marighela's writings that he was well aware of the word's undesirable connotations, and strove to displace them with positive resonances. 'The words "aggressor" and "terrorist"', Marighela wrote in his famous *Handbook of Urban Guerrilla War* (also known as the 'Mini-Manual'), 'no longer mean what they did. Instead of arousing fear or censure, they are a call to action. To be called an aggressor or a terrorist in Brazil is now an honour to any citizen, for it means that he is fighting, with a gun in his hand, against the monstrosity of the present dictatorship and the suffering it causes.'

This trend towards ever more convoluted semantic obfuscations to side-step terrorism's pejorative overtones, has, if anything, become more entrenched in recent decades. Terrorist organizations almost without exception now regularly select names for themselves that consciously eschew the word 'terrorism' in any of its forms. Instead these groups actively seek to evoke images of:

- freedom and liberation (e.g. the National Liberation Front, the Popular Front for the Liberation of Palestine, Freedom for the Basque Homeland, etc.);
- armies or other military organizational structures (e.g. the National Military Organization, the Popular Liberation Army, the Fifth Battalion of the Liberation Army, etc.);

- actual self-defence movements (e.g. the Afrikaner Resistance Movement, the Shankhill Defence Association, the Organization for the Defence of the Free People, the Jewish Defense Organization, etc.);

- righteous vengeance (the Organization for the Oppressed on Earth, the Justice Commandos of the Armenian Genocide, the Palestinian Revenge Organization, etc.);

—or else deliberately choose names that are decidedly neutral and therefore bereft of all but the most innocuous suggestions or associations (e.g. the Shining Path, Front Line, al-Dawa ('The Call'), Alfaro Lives—Damn It!, Kach ('Thus'), al-Gamat al-Islamiya ('The Islamic Organization'), the Lantero Youth Movement, etc.).

What all these examples suggest is that terrorists clearly do not see or regard themselves as others do. 'Above all I am a family man,' the arch-terrorist Carlos, 'The Jackal', described himself to a French newspaper following his capture in 1994. Cast perpetually on the defensive and forced to take up arms to protect themselves and their real or imagined constituents only, terrorists perceive themselves as reluctant warriors, driven by desperation—and lacking any viable alternative—to violence against a repressive state, a predatory rival ethnic or nationalist group, or an unresponsive international order. This perceived characteristic of self-denial also distinguishes the terrorist from other types of political extremists as well as from persons similarly involved in illegal, violent avocations. A communist or a revolutionary, for example, would likely readily accept and admit that he is in fact a communist or a revolutionary. Indeed, many would doubtless take particular pride in claiming either of those appellations for themselves. Similarly, even a person engaged in illegal, wholly disreputable or entirely selfish violence activities, such as robbing banks or carrying out contract killings, would probably admit to being a bank robber or a murderer for hire. The terrorist, by contrast, will *never* acknowledge that he is a terrorist and moreover will go to great lengths to evade and obscure any such inference or connection. Terry Anderson, the American journalist who was held hostage for almost seven years by the Lebanese terrorist organization Hezbollah, relates a telling conversation he had with one of his guards. The guard had objected to a newspaper article that referred to Hezbollah as terrorists. 'We are not terrorists,' he indignantly stated, 'we are fighters.' Anderson replied, 'Hajj, you are a terrorist, look it up in the dictionary. You are a terrorist, you may not like the word and if you do not like the word, do not do it.' The terrorist will always argue that it is society or the government or the socio-economic 'system' and its laws that are the *real* 'terrorists', and moreover that if it were not for this oppression, he would not have felt the need to defend either himself or the population he claims to represent. Another revealing example of this process of obfuscation-projection may be found in the book *Invisible Armies*, written by Sheikh Muhammad Hussein Fadlallah, the spiritual leader of the Lebanese terrorist group responsible for Anderson's kidnapping. 'We don't see ourselves as terrorists,' Fadlallah explains, 'because we don't believe in terrorism. We don't see resisting the occupier as a terrorist action. We see ourselves as *mujihadeen* [holy warriors] who fight a Holy War for the people.'

On one point, at least, everyone agrees: terrorism is a pejorative term. It is a word with intrinsically negative connotations that is generally applied to one's enemies and opponents, or to those with whom one disagrees and would otherwise prefer to ignore. 'What is called terrorism', Brian Jenkins has written, 'thus seems to depend on one's point of view. Use of the term implies a moral judgement; and if one party can successfully attach the label *terrorist* to its opponent, then it has indirectly persuaded others to adopt its moral viewpoint.' Hence the decision to call someone or label some organization 'terrorist' becomes almost unavoidably subjective, depending largely on whether one sympathizes with or opposes the person/group/cause concerned. If one identifies with the victim of the violence, for example, then the act is terrorism. If, however, one identifies with the perpetrator, the violent act is regarded in a more sympathetic, if not positive (or, at the worst, an ambivalent) light; and it is not terrorism.

The implications of this associational logic were perhaps most clearly demonstrated in the exchanges between Western and non-Western member states of the United Nations following the 1972 Munich Olympics massacre, in which eleven Israeli athletes were killed. The debate began with the proposal by the then UN Secretary-General, Kurt Waldheim, that the UN should not remain a 'mute spectator' to the acts of terrorist violence then occurring throughout the world but should take practical steps that might prevent further bloodshed. While a majority of the UN member states supported the Secretary-General, a disputatious minority—including many Arab states and various African and Asian countries—derailed the discussion, arguing (much as Arafat would do two years later in his own address to the General Assembly) that 'people who struggle to liberate themselves from foreign oppression and exploitation have the right to use all methods at their disposal, including force'.

The Third World delegates justified their position with two arguments. First, they claimed that all bona fide liberation movements are invariably decried as 'terrorists' by the regimes against which their struggles for freedom are directed. The Nazis, for example, labelled as terrorists the resistance groups opposing Germany's occupation of their lands, Moulaye el-Hassen, the Mauritanian ambassador, pointed out, just as 'all liberation movements are described as terrorists by those who have reduced them to slavery'. Therefore, by condemning 'terrorism' the UN was endorsing the power of the strong over the weak and of the established entity over its non-established challenger—in effect, acting as the defender of the status quo. According to Chen Chu, the deputy representative of the People's Republic of China, the UN thus was proposing to deprive 'opposed nations and peoples' of the only effective weapon they had with which to oppose 'imperialism, colonialism, neo-colonialism, racism and Israeli Zionism'. Second, the Third World delegates argued forcefully that it is not the violence itself that is germane, but its 'underlying causes': that is, the 'misery, frustration, grievance and despair' that produce the violent acts. As the Mauritanian representative again explained, the term 'terrorist' could 'hardly be held to apply to persons who were denied the most elementary human rights, dignity, freedom and independence, and whose countries objected to foreign occupation'. When the issue was again raised the following year, Syria objected on the grounds that 'the international community is under legal and moral obligation to promote the struggle for liberation and to resist any attempt to depict this struggle as synonymous with terrorism and illegitimate violence'. The resultant definitional paralysis subsequently throttled UN efforts to make any substantive progress on international cooperation against terrorism beyond very specific agreements on individual aspects of the problem (concerning, for example, diplomats and civil aviation).

The opposite approach, where identification with the victim determines the classification of a violent act as terrorism, is evident in the conclusions of a parliamentary working group of NATO (an organization comprised of long-established, status quo Western states). The final report of the 1989 North Atlantic Assembly's Subcommittee on Terrorism states: 'Murder, kidnapping, arson and other felonious acts constitute criminal behavior, but many non-Western nations have proved reluctant to condemn as terrorist acts what they consider to be struggles of natural liberation.' In this reasoning, the defining characteristic of terrorism is the act of violence itself, not the motivations or justification for or reasons behind it. This approach has long been espoused by analysts such as Jenkins who argue that terrorism should be defined 'by the nature of the act, not by the identity of the perpetrators or the nature of their cause'. But this is not an entirely satisfactory solution either, since it fails to differentiate clearly between violence perpetrated by states and by non-state entities, such as terrorists. Accordingly, it plays into the hands of terrorists and their apologists who would argue that there is no difference between the 'low-tech' terrorist pipe-bomb placed in the rubbish bin at a crowded market that wantonly and indiscriminately kills or maims everyone within a radius measured in tens of feet and the 'high-tech' precision-guided ordnance dropped by air force fighter-bombers from a height of 20,000 feet or more that achieves the same wanton and indiscriminate effects on the crowded marketplace far below. This rationale thus equates the random violence inflicted on enemy population centres by military forces—such as the Luftwaffe's raids on Warsaw and Coventry, the Allied firebombings of Dresden and Tokyo, and the atomic bombs dropped by the United States on Hiroshima and Nagasaki during the Second World War, and indeed the countervalue strategy of the post-war superpowers' strategic nuclear policy, which deliberately targeted the enemy's civilian population—with the violence committed by substate entities labelled 'terrorists', since both involve the infliction of death and injury on noncombatants. Indeed, this was precisely the point made during the above-mentioned UN debates by the Cuban representative, who argued that 'the methods of combat used by national liberation movements could not be declared illegal while the policy of terrorism unleashed against certain peoples [by the armed forces of established states] was declared legitimate'.

It is a familiar argument. Terrorists, as we have seen, deliberately cloak themselves in the terminology of military jargon. They consciously portray themselves as bona fide (freedom) fighters, if not soldiers, who—though they wear no identifying uniform or insignia—are entitled to treatment as prisoners of war (POWs) if captured and therefore should not be prosecuted as common criminals in ordinary courts of law. Terrorists further argue that, because of their numerical inferiority, far more limited firepower and paucity of resources compared with an established nation-state's massive defence and national security apparatus, they have no choice but to operate clandestinely, emerging from the shadows to carry out dramatic (in other words, bloody and destructive) acts of hit-and-run violence in order to attract attention to, and ensure publicity for, themselves and their cause. The bomb-in-the-rubbish-bin, in their view, is merely a circumstantially imposed 'poor man's air force': the only means with which the terrorist can challenge—and get the attention of—the more powerful state. 'How else can we bring pressure to bear on the world?' one of Arafat's political aides once enquired. 'The deaths are regrettable, but they are a fact of war in which innocents have become involved. They are no more innocent than the Palestinian women and children killed by the Israelis and we are ready to carry the war all over the world.'

But rationalizations such as these ignore the fact that, even while national armed forces have been responsible for far more death and destruction than terrorists might ever aspire to bring about, there nonetheless is a fundamental qualitative difference between the two types of violence. Even in war there are rules and accepted norms of behaviour that prohibit the use of certain types of weapons (for example, hollow-point or 'dum-dum' bullets, CS 'tear' gas, chemical and biological warfare agents), proscribe various tactics and outlaw attacks on specific categories of targets. Accordingly, in theory, if not always in practice, the rules of war—as observed from the early seventeenth century when they were first proposed by the Dutch jurist Hugo Grotius and subsequently codified in the famous Geneva and Hague Conventions on Warfare of the 1860s, 1899, 1907 and 1949—not only grant civilian non-combatants immunity from attack, but also

- prohibit taking civilians as hostages;
- impose regulations governing the treatment of captured or surrendered soldiers (POWs);
- outlaw reprisals against either civilians or POWs;
- recognize neutral territory and the rights of citizens of neutral states; and
- uphold the inviolability of diplomats and other accredited representatives.

Even the most cursory review of terrorist tactics and targets over the past quarter-century reveals that terrorists have violated all these rules. They not infrequently have

- taken hostage civilians, whom in some instances they have then brutally executed (e.g. the former Italian prime minister Aldo Moro and the German industrialist Hans Martin Schleyer, who were respectively taken captive and later murdered by the Red Brigades and the Red Army Faction);
- similarly abused and murdered kidnapped military officers—even when they were serving on UN-sponsored peacekeeping or truce supervisory missions (e.g. the American Marine Lieutenant-Colonel William Higgins, the commander of a UN truce monitoring detachment, who was abducted by Lebanese Shi'a terrorists in 1989 and subsequently hanged);
- undertaken reprisals against wholly innocent civilians, often in countries far removed from the terrorists' ostensible 'theatre of operation', thus disdaining any concept of neutral states or the rights of citizens of neutral countries (e.g. the brutal 1986 machine-gun and hand-grenade attack on Turkish Jewish worshippers at an Istanbul synagogue carried out by the Palestinian Abu Nidal Organization in retaliation for a recent Israeli raid on a guerrilla base in southern Lebanon); and
- repeatedly attacked embassies and other diplomatic installations (e.g. the bombings of the US embassies in Beirut and Kuwait City in 1983 and 1984, and the mass hostage-taking at the Japanese ambassador's residence in Lima, Peru, in 1996–7), as well as deliberately targeting diplomats and other accredited representatives (e.g. the British ambassador to Uruguay, Sir Geoffrey Jackson, who was kidnapped by leftist terrorists in that country in 1971, and the fifty-two American diplomats taken hostage at the Tehran legation in 1979).

Admittedly, the armed forces of established states have also been guilty of violating some of the same rules of war. However, when these transgressions do occur—when civilians are deliberately and wantonly attacked on war or taken hostage and killed by military forces—the term 'war crime' is used to describe such acts and, imperfect and flawed as both international and national judicial remedies may be, steps nonetheless are often taken to hold the perpetrators accountable for these crimes. By comparison, one of the fundamental *raisons d'être* of international terrorism is a refusal to be bound by such rules of warfare and codes of conduct. International terrorism disdains any concept of delimited areas of combat or demarcated battlefields, much less respect of neutral territory. Accordingly, terrorists have repeatedly taken their often parochial struggles to other, sometimes geographically distant, third party countries and there deliberately enmeshed persons completely unconnected with the terrorists' cause or grievances in violent incidents designed to generate attention and publicity.

The reporting of terrorism by the news media, which have been drawn into the semantic debates that divided the UN in the 1970s and continue to influence all discourse on terrorism, has further contributed to the obfuscation of the terrorist/'freedom fighter' debate, enshrining imprecision and implication as the lingua franca of political violence in the name of objectivity and neutrality. In striving to avoid appearing either partisan or judgemental, the American media, for example, resorted to describing terrorists—often in the same report—as variously guerrillas, gunmen, raiders, commandos and even soldiers. A random sample of American newspaper reports of Palestinian terrorist activities between June and December 1973, found in the terrorism archives and database maintained at the University of St. Andrews in Scotland, provided striking illustrations of this practice. Out of eight headlines of articles describing the same incident, six used the word 'guerrillas' and only two 'terrorists' to describe the perpetrators. An interesting pattern was also observed whereby those accounts that immediately followed a particularly horrific or tragic incident—that is, involving the death and injury of innocent persons (in this instance, the attack on a Pan Am airliner at Rome airport, in which thirty-two passengers were killed)—tended to describe the perpetrators as 'terrorists' and their act as 'terrorism' (albeit in one case only in the headline, before reverting to the more neutral terminology of 'commando', 'militants', and 'guerrilla attack' in the text) more frequently than did reports of less serious or non-lethal incidents. One *New York Times* leading article, however, was far less restrained than the stories describing the actual incident, describing it as 'bloody' and 'mindless' and using the words 'terrorists' and 'terrorism' interchangeably with 'guerrillas' and 'extremists'. Only six months previously, however, the same newspaper had run a story about another terrorist attack that completely eschewed the terms 'terrorism' and 'terrorist', preferring 'guerrillas' and 'resistance' (as in 'resistance movement') instead. The *Christian Science Monitor*'s reports of the Rome Pan Am attack similarly avoided 'terrorist' and 'terrorism' in favour of 'guerrillas' and 'extremists'; an Associated Press story in the next day's *Los Angeles Times* also stuck with 'guerrillas', while the two *Washington Post* articles on the same incident opted for the terms 'commandos' and 'guerrillas'.

This slavish devotion in terminological neutrality, which David Rapoport first observed over twenty years ago, is still in evidence today. A recent article appearing in the *International Herald Tribune* (a Paris-based newspaper published in conjunction with the *New York Times* and *Washington Post*) reported an incident in Algeria where thirty persons had been killed by perpetrators who were variously described as 'terrorists' in the article's headline, less judgementally as 'extremists' in the lead paragraph and as the still more ambiguous 'Islamic fundamentalists' in the article's third paragraph. In a country that since 1992 has been afflicted with an unrelenting wave of terrorist violence and bloodshed that has claimed the lives of an estimated 75,000 persons, one might think that the distinctions between 'terrorists', mere 'extremists' and ordinary 'fundamentalists' would be clearer. Equally interesting was the article that appeared on the opposite side of the same page of the newspaper that described the 'decades of sporadic *guerrilla* [my emphasis] warfare by the IRA' in Northern Ireland. Yet fifty years ago the same newspaper apparently had fewer qualms about using the word 'terrorists' to describe the two young Jewish men in pre-independence Israel who, while awaiting execution after having been convicted of attacking British military targets, committed suicide. Other press accounts of the same period in *The Times* of London and the *Palestine Post* similarly had no difficulties, for example, in describing the 1946 bombing by Jewish terrorists of the British military headquarters and government secretariat located in Jerusalem's King David Hotel as a 'terrorist' act perpetrated by 'terrorists'. Similarly, in perhaps the most specific application of the term, the communist terrorists against whom the British fought in Malaya throughout the late 1940s and 1950s were routinely referred to as 'CTs'—for 'Communist terrorists'. As Rapoport warned in the 1970s, 'In attempting to correct the abuse of language for political purposes our journalists may succeed in making language altogether worthless.'

The cumulative effect of this proclivity towards equivocation is that today there is no one widely accepted or agreed definition for terrorism. Different departments or agencies of even the same government will themselves often have very different definitions for terrorism. The US State Department, for example, uses the definition of terrorism contained in Title 22 of the United States Code, Section 2656f(d):

> premeditated, politically motivated violence perpetrated against noncombatant targets by subnational groups or clandestine agents, usually intended to influence an audience,

while the US Federal Bureau of Investigation (FBI) defines terrorism as

> the unlawful use of force or violence against persons or property to intimidate or coerce a Government, the civilian population, or any segment thereof, in furtherance of political or social objectives,

and the US Department of Defense defines it as

> the unlawful use of—or threatened use of—force or violence against individuals or property to coerce or intimidate governments or societies, often to achieve political, religious, or ideological objectives.

Not surprisingly, each of the above definitions reflects the priorities and particular interests of the specific agency involved. The State Department's emphasis is on the premeditated and planned or calculated nature of terrorism in contrast to more spontaneous acts of political violence. Its definition is also the only one of the three to emphasize both the ineluctably political nature of terrorism and the perpetrators' fundamental 'subnational' characteristic. The State Department definition, however, is conspicuously deficient in failing to consider the psychological dimension of terrorism. Terrorism is as much about the threat of violence as the violent act itself and, accordingly, is deliberately conceived to have far-reaching psychological repercussions beyond the actual target of the act among a wider, watching, 'target' audience. As Jenkins succinctly observed two decades ago, 'Terrorism is theatre.'

Given the FBI's mission of investigating and solving crimes—both political (e.g. terrorism) and other—it is not surprising that its definition focuses on different elements. Unlike the State Department, this definition does address the psychological dimensions of the terrorist act described above, laying stress on terrorism's intimidatory and coercive aspects. The FBI definition also identifies a much broader category of terrorist targets than only 'noncombatants', specifying not only governments and their citizens, but also inanimate objects, such as private and public property. The FBI definition further recognizes social alongside political objectives as fundamental terrorist aims—though it offers no clearer elucidation of either.

The Department of Defense definition of terrorism is arguably the most complete of the three. It highlights the terrorist threat as much as the actual act of violence and focuses on terrorism's targeting of whole societies as well as governments. The Defense Department definition further cites the religious and ideological aims of terrorism alongside its fundamental political objectives—but curiously omits the social dimension found in the FBI's definition.

It is not only individual agencies within the same governmental apparatus that cannot agree on a single definition of terrorism. Experts and other long-established scholars in the field are equally incapable of reaching a consensus. In the first edition of his magisterial survey, *Political Terrorism: A Research Guide*, Alex Schmid devoted more than a hundred pages to examining more than a hundred different definitions of terrorism in an effort to discover a broadly acceptable, reasonably comprehensive explication of the word. Four years and a second edition later, Schmid was no closer to the goal of his quest, conceding in the first sentence of the revised volume that the 'search for an adequate definition is still on'. Walter Laqueur despaired of defining terrorism in both editions of his monumental work on the subject, maintaining that it is neither possible to do so nor worthwhile to make the attempt. 'Ten years of debates on typologies and definitions', he responded to a survey of definitions conducted by Schmid, 'have not enhanced our knowledge of the subject to a significant degree.' Laqueur's contention is supported by the twenty-two different word categories occurring in the 109 different definitions that Schmid identified in his survey (see Table 1).

At the end of this exhaustive exercise, Schmid asks 'whether the above list contains all the elements necessary for a good definition. The answer', he suggests, 'is probably "no".' If it is impossible to define terrorism, as Laqueur argues, and fruitless to attempt to cobble together a truly comprehensive definition, as Schmid admits, are we to conclude that terrorism is impervious to precise, much less accurate definition? Not entirely. If we cannot define terrorism, then we can at least usefully distinguish it from other types of violence and identify the characteristics that make terrorism the distinct phenomenon of political violence that it is.

Distinctions as a Path to Definition

Guerrilla warfare is a good place to start. Terrorism is often confused or equated with, or treated as synonymous with, guerrilla warfare. This is not entirely surprising, since guerrillas often employ the same tactics (assassination, kidnapping, bombings of public gathering-places, hostage-taking, etc.) for the same purposes (to intimidate or coerce, thereby affecting behaviour through the arousal of fear) as terrorists. In addition, both terrorists and

Table 1.1

Frequencies of Definitional Elements in 109 Definitions of 'Terrorism'

	Element	Frequency (%)
1	Violence, force	83.5
2	Political	65
3	Fear, terror emphasized	51
4	Threat	47
5	(Psychological) effects and (anticipated) reactions	41.5
6	Victim–target differentiation	37.5
7	Purposive, planned, systematic, organized action	32
8	Method of combat, strategy, tactic	30.5
9	Extranormality, in breach of accepted rules, without humanitarian constraints	30
10	Coercion, extortion, induction of compliance	28
11	Publicity aspect	21.5
12	Arbitrariness; impersonal, random character; indiscrimination	21
13	Civilians, noncombatants, neutrals, outsiders as victims	17.5
14	Intimidation	17
15	Innocence of victims emphasized	15.5
16	Group, movement, organization as perpetrator	14
17	Symbolic aspect, demonstration to others	13.5
18	Incalculability, unpredictability, unexpectedness of occurrence of violence	9
19	Clandestine, covert nature	9
20	Repetitiveness; serial or campaign character of violence	7
21	Criminal	6
22	Demands made on third parties	4

Source: Alex P. Schmid, Albert J. Jongman et al., *Political Terrorism: A New Guide to Actors, Authors, Concepts, Data Bases, Theories, and Literature.* New Brunswick, Transaction Books, 1988, pp. 5-6.

guerrillas wear neither uniform nor identifying insignia and thus are often indistinguishable from noncombatants. However, despite the inclination to lump both terrorists and guerrillas into the same catch-all category of 'irregulars', there are nonetheless fundamental differences between the two. 'Guerrilla', for example, in its most widely accepted usage, is taken to refer to a numerically larger group of armed individuals, who operate as a military unit, attack enemy military forces, and seize and hold territory (even if only ephemerally during daylight hours), while also exercising some form of sovereignty or control over a defined geographical area and its population. Terrorists, however, do not function in the open as armed units, generally do not attempt to seize or hold territory, deliberately avoid engaging enemy military forces in combat and rarely exercise any direct control or sovereignty either over territory or population.

It is also useful to distinguish terrorists from ordinary criminals. Like terrorists, criminals use violence as a means to attaining a specific end. However, while the violent act itself may be similar—kidnapping, shooting, arson, for example—the purpose or motivation clearly is not. Whether the criminal employs violence as a means to obtain money, to acquire material goods, or to kill or injure a specific victim for pay, he is acting primarily for selfish, personal motivations (usually material gain). Moreover, unlike terrorism, the ordinary criminals' violent act is not designed or intended to have consequences or create psychological repercussions beyond the act itself. The criminal may of course use some short-term act of violence to 'terrorize' his victim, such as waving a gun in the face of a bank clerk during a robbery in order to ensure the clerk's expeditious compliance. In these instances, however, the bank robber is conveying no 'message' (political or otherwise) through his act of violence beyond facilitating the rapid handing over of his 'loot'. The criminal's act therefore is not meant to have any effect reaching beyond either the incident itself or the immediate victim. Further, the violence is neither conceived nor intended to convey any message to anyone other than the bank clerk himself, whose rapid cooperation is the robber's only objective. Perhaps most fundamentally, the criminal is not concerned with influencing or affecting public opinion: he simply wants to abscond with his money or accomplish his mercenary task in the quickest and easiest way possible so that he may reap his reward and enjoy the fruits of his labours. By contrast, the fundamental aim of the terrorist's violence is ultimately to change 'the system'—about which the ordinary criminal, of course, couldn't care less.

The terrorist is also very different from the lunatic assassin, who may use identical tactics (e.g. shooting, bombing) and perhaps even seeks the same objective (e.g. the death of a political figure). However, while the tactics and targets of terrorists and lone assassins are often identical, their purpose is not. Whereas the terrorist's goal is again ineluctably *political* (to change or fundamentally alter a political system through his violent act), the lunatic assassin's goal is more often intrinsically idiosyncratic, completely egocentric and deeply personal. John Hinckley, who tried to kill President Reagan in 1981 to impress the actress Jodie Foster, is a case in point. He acted not from political motivation or ideological conviction but to fulfil some profound personal quest (killing the president to impress his screen idol). Such entirely *apolitical* motivations can in no way be compared to the rationalizations used by the Narodnaya Volya to justify its campaign of tyrannicide against the tsar and his minions, nor even to the Irish Republican Army's efforts to assassinate Prime Minister Margaret Thatcher or her successor, John Major, in hopes of dramatically changing British policy towards Northern Ireland. Further, just as one person cannot credibly claim to be a political party, so a lone individual cannot be considered to constitute a terrorist group. In this respect, even though Sirhan Sirhan's assassination of presidential candidate and US Senator Robert Kennedy in 1968 had a political motive (to protest against US support for Israel), it is debatable whether the murder should be defined as a terrorist act since Sirhan belongs to no organized political group and acted entirely on his own, out of deep personal frustration and a profound animus that few others shared. To qualify as terrorism, violence must be perpetrated by some organizational entity with at least some conspiratorial structure and identifiable chain of command beyond a single individual acting on his or her own.

Finally, the point should be emphasized that, unlike the ordinary criminal or the lunatic assassin, the terrorist is not pursuing purely egocentric goals—he is not driven by the wish to line his own pocket or satisfy some personal need or grievance. The terrorist is fundamentally an *altruist*: he believes that he is serving a 'good' cause designed to achieve a greater good for a wider constituency—whether real or imagined—which the terrorist and his organization purport to represent. The criminal, by comparison, serves no cause at all, just his own personal aggrandizement and material satiation. Indeed, a 'terrorist without a cause (at least in his own mind)', Konrad Kellen has argued, 'is not a terrorist'. Yet the possession or identification of a cause is not a sufficient criterion for labelling someone a terrorist. In this key respect, the difference between terrorists and political extremists is clear. Many persons, of course, harbour all sorts of radical and extreme beliefs and opinions, and many of them belong to radical or even illegal or proscribed political organizations. However, if they do not use violence in the pursuance of their beliefs, they cannot be considered terrorists. The terrorist is fundamentally a *violent intellectual*, prepared to use and indeed committed to using force in the attainment of his goals.

By distinguishing terrorists from other types of criminals and terrorism from other forms of crime, we come to appreciate that terrorism is

- ineluctably political in aims and motives;

- violent—or, equally important, threatens violence;

- designed to have far-reaching psychological repercussions beyond the immediate victim or target;

- conducted by an organization with an identifiable chain of command or conspiratorial cell structure (whose members wear no uniform or identifying insignia); and

- perpetrated by a subnational group or non-state entity.

We may therefore now attempt to define terrorism as the deliberate creation and exploitation of fear through violence or the threat of violence in the pursuit of political change. All terrorist acts involve violence or the threat of violence. Terrorism is specifically designed to have far-reaching psychological effects beyond the immediate victim(s) or object of the terrorist attack. It is meant to instil fear within, and thereby intimidate, a wider 'target audience' that might include a rival ethnic or religious group, an entire country, a national government or political party, or public opinion in general. Terrorism is designed to create power where there is none or to consolidate power where there is very little. Through the publicity generated by their violence, terrorists seek to obtain the leverage, influence and power they otherwise lack to effect political change on either a local or an international scale.

Bruce Hoffman is an authoritative analyst of terrorism and a recipient of the U.S. Intelligence Community Seal Medallion, the highest level of commendation given to a nongovernment employee. He is currently the director of the Washington, D.C., office of the RAND Corporation, where he heads the terrorism research unit, and he regularly advises both governments and businesses throughout the world. This reading is a chapter from his book *Inside Terrorism*.

Paul R. Pillar, 2001

The Dimensions of Terrorism and Counterterrorism

Delimiting a subject is the first step in dealing with it intelligently, and this is especially true of terrorism and counterterrorism. Terrorism has often been conceived in intractably broad ways, while the costs of terrorism and the ways to combat it tend to be construed too narrowly.

What Terrorism Is

Efforts to define terrorism have consumed much ink. A recent book on terrorism, for example, devotes an entire chapter to definitions; the chapter documents previous definitional attempts by earlier scholars, some of whom gave up the effort.[1] Many students of terrorism clearly consider its definition an important and unresolved issue.[2] The concern about definitions, besides reflecting any scholar's commendable interest in being precise about one's subject matter, stems from the damage done by the countless twisted and polemical uses through the years of the term "terrorism." The one thing on which every user of the term agrees is that terrorism is bad. So it has been a catch-all pejorative, applied mainly to matters involving force or political authority in some way but sometimes applied even more broadly to just about any disliked action associated with someone else's policy agenda.

The semantic quagmire has been deepened not only by indiscriminate application of the term terrorism but also by politically inspired efforts *not* to apply it. This was most in evidence in the 1970s, when multilateral discussion of the subject in the United Nations General Assembly and elsewhere invariably bogged down amid widespread resistance to any condemnation—and hence any labeling as terrorism—of the actions of groups that had favored status as "national liberation movements" or the like. Variations on this pattern have continued to frustrate efforts to arrive at an internationally accepted definition of terrorism.

Another, less frequent, tendentious approach to defining terrorism is to define it in ways that presuppose particular policy responses. For example, define it as a crime if you want to handle it mainly as a law enforcement matter, define it as war if you intend to rely on military means, and so on. Arguing semantics as a surrogate for arguing about policy is a confusing, cumbersome, and ultimately poor way to arrive at a policy.

A reasonable definition of terrorism would capture the key elements of what those leaders and respondents to opinion polls who have expressed concern about terrorism probably have in mind, without being so broad as to include much else that is not in fact the concern of those whose job descriptions mention terrorism. As good a definition as any, given some clarification and minor modification, is the statutory one that the U.S. government uses in keeping statistics on international terrorism: terrorism, for that purpose, means "premeditated, politically motivated violence perpetrated against noncombatant targets by subnational groups or clandestine agents, usually intended to influence an audience."[3] This definition has four main elements.

The first, premeditation, means there must be an intent and prior decision to commit an act that would qualify as terrorism under the other criteria. An operation may not be executed as intended and may fail altogether, but the intent must still be there. The action is the result of someone's policy, or at least someone's decision. Terrorism is not a matter of momentary rage or impulse. It is also not a matter of accident.

The second element, political motivation, excludes criminal violence motivated by monetary gain or personal vengeance. Admittedly, these latter forms of violence often must be dealt with in the same fashion as terrorism for purposes of law enforcement and physical security. Criminal violence can also have political consequences if it is part of a larger erosion of order (as in Russia). And ordinary crime is part of the world of many terrorists, either because they practice it themselves to get money or because they cooperate with criminal organizations.[4] Terrorism is fundamentally different from these other forms of violence, however, in what gives rise to it and in how it must be countered, beyond simple physical security and police techniques. Terrorists' concerns are macroconcerns about changing a larger order; other violent criminals are focused on the microlevel of pecuniary gain and personal relationships. "Political" in this regard encompasses not just traditional left-right politics but also what are frequently described as religious motivations or social issues. What all terrorists have in common and separates them from other violent criminals is that they claim to be serving some greater good.[5]

The third element, that the targets are noncombatants, means that terrorists attack people who cannot defend themselves with violence in return. Terrorism is different from a combat operation against a military force, which can shoot back. In this regard, "noncombatant" means (and has been so interpreted for the government's statistical purposes) not just civilians but also military personnel who at the time of an incident are unarmed or off duty (as at Khubar Towers or at the U.S. Marine barracks in Beirut).

The fourth element, that the perpetrators are either subnational groups or clandestine agents, is another difference between terrorism and normal military operations. An attack by a government's duly uniformed or otherwise identifiable armed forces is not terrorism; it is war. The requirement that nongovernmental perpetrators be "groups" is one point, however, on which the statutory definition could usefully be modified. A lone individual can commit terrorism. Mir Aimal Kansi's shooting spree outside the Central Intelligence Agency was politically motivated, and the four-year manhunt for him was always rightly regarded as a counterterrorist operation. Because there was no indication that he had acted at anyone else's behest, however, his attack never counted in the government's statistics on terrorism. For the present purposes, Kansi and any others like him may be considered one-person terrorist groups.

There is one other respect in which terrorism must be conceived somewhat more broadly than the statutory definition above. Terrorism as an issue is not just a collection of incidents that have already occurred; it is at least as much a matter of what might occur in the future. The threat of a terrorist attack is itself terrorism. Moreover, the mere possibility of terrorist attacks, even without explicit threats, is a counterterrorist problem. Indeed, one of the most vexing parts of that problem concerns groups that have not yet performed terrorist operations (or maybe have not even yet become groups) but might conduct terrorist attacks in the future. There is no good way to record this potential or to quantify it, and it would be pointless to manipulate formal definitions to try to embrace it. But counterterrorist specialists must worry about it. It is part of the subject at hand.

The conception of terrorism given above excludes some things that have occasionally been labeled as "terrorism" and are themselves significant national security issues—in particular, certain possible uses by hostile regimes of their military forces, such as ballistic missiles fired at civilian populations. To be sure, there are some similarities to terrorism, involving the motivations of the perpetrators, the impact on the target populations, and even the identity of some of the governments involved. These other security issues, however, have their own communities to deal with them, both inside and outside government. The relationships between different security issues must be noted and analyzed, but that does mean expanding the concept of an issue beyond workable limits. Counterterrorist specialists have enough on their plates without, say, weighing into debates on ballistic missile defense.

The concept of terrorism delineated here is not just reflected in a U.S. statute. It is also in the mainstream of what most students of terrorism seem to have in mind, despite their collective definitional angst. Moreover, it also is in the mainstream of what modest international consensus has evolved on the subject, at least the farther one gets from large multilateral debating halls and the closer to rooms where practical cooperation takes place. The latter point is important, given the necessarily heavy U.S. dependence on foreign help for counterterrorism. It is also important that whatever concept of terrorism the United States uses not be capable of being twisted to apply to actions the United States itself may take in pursuit of its security interests.

About the latter point, two distinctions are critical. The first is the one between terrorism and the overt use of military force. As the world's preeminent military power, it is in the United States' interest to keep that distinction clear, but this is not just a unilateral U.S. interest. The distinction has a broader moral and legal basis, as reflected in international humanitarian law on armed conflict and its rules requiring combatants to identify themselves openly.[6] The second key distinction is between actions that are the willful result of decisions taken by governmental or group leaders, and actions that result from accidents or impulsive behavior by lower-ranking individuals. The latter are bound to happen, and have happened, in incidents involving the United States, just because of the number of circumstances in which U.S. personnel find themselves in which it could happen. One's concept of terrorism must distinguish clearly—as the definition above does—between, for example, the alleged bombing by Libyan agents of Pan Am 103 and the accidental shooting down of Iran Air 655 in the Persian Gulf by the U.S. cruiser *Vincennes*. Despite the similarities of these incidents (290 people perished in the downing of the Iranian flight in July 1988; 270 people died in the Pan Am incident in December of the same year), and even though Tehran was still calling the Iran Air incident a "crime" more than a decade later, these were fundamentally different events. One was a government's deliberate use of its agents to murder scores of innocent travelers; the other was a tragic case of mistaken identity by a warship's crew that believed itself to be in a military engagement.

The place of clandestine agents and subnational groups in the definition of terrorism requires a bit more reflection, because the United States has used many of both. Not only that, but such use has sometimes involved lethal force, and some of that force has caused civilian casualties. But the real question is whether the intentional (that is, premeditated) infliction of civilian casualties through agents or sponsored groups—say, to undermine a hostile regime—is an option that the United States can safely forswear. It is. For one thing, the irregular use of lethal force against civilians would likely be counterproductive, by enabling the targeted regime to rally popular support in the face of a presumed external threat. Just as important, such methods are contrary to what the American public would support as being consistent with American values (a key test to be applied to any proposed covert action, even ones never likely to become public knowledge). Recent operations such as air strikes against Yugoslavia or Iraq have shown the great emphasis the United States has come to place on *avoiding* civilian casualties, even as collateral damage in a conventional military campaign.[7]

The conceptual lines between terrorism and other forms of politically driven violence are blurry. They would be blurry under any definition. The definition given above is at least as clear as any other, but it still leaves uncertainty as to whether certain specific incidents are acts of terrorism. The U.S. government has an interagency panel that meets monthly to consider such incidents (for the sake only of keeping accurate statistics, not of determining policy). The panel debates such questions as whether a particular target or intended target should be considered a noncombatant. Split votes are not unusual.

Good policy on terrorism does not, however, require hand-wringing about how exactly to define it. For the great majority of counterterrorist activities, the late Justice Potter Stewart's approach toward pornography will suffice: that it is unnecessary to go to great lengths to define it, because one knows it when one sees it.[8] Even though the U.S. government itself has several other definitions of terrorism written for different purposes, definitional discussions are seldom part of intragovernmental deliberations on the subject, beyond the statistic-keeping panel just mentioned. Lawyers do sometimes have to inject precision about whether certain statutory criteria have been met. This usually revolves around not the meaning of terrorism itself, however, but rather, for example, whether certain conditions (such as U.S. citizenship of the victims) are present that would permit a criminal prosecution. In most situations in which a counterterrorist response may be required, government officials simply recognize terrorism when they see it and do what they need to do. Any uncertainty about whether a given incident is terrorism is due not to semantics but rather to incomplete information.

The blurriness of the definitional lines is a salutary reminder that terrorism is but one form of behavior along a continuum of possible political behaviors of those who strongly oppose the status quo. Alternative forms include other types of violence (such as guerrilla warfare), nonviolent but illegal actions, regular partisan or diplomatic activity, or simple expressions of opinion that never even crystallize into something as specific as a political party, resistance movement, or terrorist group. Sound counterterrorist policy does not focus narrowly only on terrorism itself (however defined) but instead takes into account that terrorists have a menu of other tactics and behaviors from which to choose, and that the conflicts underlying terrorism invariably have other dimensions that also affect U.S. interests.

The distinction between terrorism, as defined here, and other forms of violence by subnational groups is apt to be faint in the eyes of some of the people directly involved. The Muslim fight against Indian control of Kashmir, for example, has been a blend of terrorist attacks against civilians and guerrilla warfare against Indian military forces. At least some of the insurgent leaders recognize the distinction publicly and deny attacking civilians. "We are a legitimate freedom movement," said a leader of one of the larger groups, "and we do not want to be stigmatized with the terrorist label."[9] But attacks in Kashmir against cinemas and parliamentary candidates continue, along with ambushes of Indian army patrols. The course of the conflict in Kashmir, and how each side privately views it, will not depend on the exact proportion of attacks against civilian rather than military targets. Both kinds of attack are unjustified in Indian eyes; both kinds are part of an overall struggle for self-determination, in the eyes of the militants. The selection of targets has probably depended in large part on such tactical factors as the physical vulnerabilities of the targets and the local capabilities of the groups.

For most Americans, however—and for many others—the distinction between terrorism against civilians and warfare (including guerrilla warfare) against an army entails an important moral difference. The warrior who dons a uniform is understood to be assuming certain risks that the civilian does not, and the guerrilla who fires at someone who is armed and can fire back is not regarded as embracing the same evil as one who kills the helpless and the unarmed. While the United States must be cognizant of the tendency of many to gloss over such distinctions, it should not let the distinctions be forgotten. Its message should be that terrorist techniques, in any context, are unacceptable.

Which gets to the most important point to remember about definitions: terrorism is a *method*—a particularly heinous and damaging one—rather than a set of adversaries or the causes they pursue. Terrorism is a problem of what people (or groups, or states) *do*, rather than who they are or what they are trying to achieve. (If Usama bin Ladin, for example, did not use or support terrorist methods, he would be of little concern to the United States—probably receiving only minor notice for his criticism of the Saudi government and his role in the Afghan wars.) Terrorism and our attention to it do not depend on the particular political or social values that terrorists promote or attack.[10] And counterterrorism is not a war against some particular foe; it is an effort to civilize the manner in which any political contest is waged.

Why It Matters

Terrorism has many different costs. The direct physical harm inflicted on people and property is the most obvious, but it is by no means the only, or even the most important, cost. It is the most measurable ones, in that deaths and injuries can be counted and property damage can be assessed. The significance of even these direct physical costs can be a matter of debate, however, involving disagreements over exactly what should be measured and against what standard the measurement should be compared.

Start with the question of whose casualties to count. In any discussion of U.S. policy, U.S. citizens are clearly the primary concern. Six hundred and sixty-six American citizens died from international terrorism in the 1980s and 1990s.[11] During the same period 190 Americans died from domestic terrorism within the United States, for a total of 856 American deaths from terrorism during the past two decades.[12] Going beyond U.S. citizens, however, greatly expands the numbers. Deaths of all nationalities from international terrorist incidents during the same twenty years totaled 7,152. (There were also more than 31,000 wounded.) The scale of death and suffering expands yet another order of magnitude if one takes account of terrorism that is not "international" because it takes place within a single nation's borders and directly involves only that country's nationals. There are no statistics on this type of terrorism worldwide, but consider just one of the bloodier examples:

Algeria. Most published estimates of the number killed in Algeria by the extremist violence that broke out in 1992 are around 100,000. Many of these deaths were not from terrorism, but many others were, including particularly gruesome mass throat-slittings in villages. Even without U.S. citizens being involved, and even without considering the indirect effects that might be more significant for U.S. interests, this scale of bloodshed warrants attention. The death toll has certainly been at least comparable to that of many natural disasters to which the United States has felt obliged to respond. The deaths in Algeria did, in fact, lead the counterterrorism community in the U.S. government to examine ways in which it might help.

Returning to the more direct U.S. concern with American casualties, what is the right frame of reference for assessing their magnitude? To any contention that the victims of terrorism are many—or few—one is entitled to ask, "compared with what?" Against some possible standards of comparison, such as highway deaths (more than 40,000 annually in the United States), the number of victims of terrorism seems tiny. And the number is less than the bathtub drownings, lightning strikes, and some other standards that critics have used. A more appropriate basis for comparison might be other deaths from foreigners committing political violence—that is, warfare. Even there, American fatalities from terrorism are minuscule compared with such major efforts as World War II (291,557 U.S. battle deaths), Korea (33,651) or Vietnam (47,378).[13]

U.S. military activity since Vietnam, however, provides a different perspective. U.S. deaths from nonterrorist hostile action in military operations during the 1980s and 1990s (including the Iranian hostage rescue attempt, peacekeeping in Lebanon, the bombing of Libya, the escorting of Kuwaiti tankers, and Operations Urgent Fury in Grenada, Just Cause in Panama, Desert Storm in the Persian Gulf, Restore Hope in Somalia, and Uphold Democracy in Haiti) totaled 251. Even adding the 263 deaths from nonhostile causes (most of which were incurred in Desert Shield and Desert Storm) yields a total of 514, less than the number of Americans killed by terrorists during the same period. The biggest single inflictor of casualties on the U.S. military during this period was a terrorist attack: the bombing of the U.S. Marine barracks in Beirut in 1983, which killed 241. Besides, some of the other military deaths (the eight who died in the attempt to rescue hostages in Iran in 1980, and the two who were lost during the air strikes against Libya in 1986) were casualties of U.S. responses to terrorism. The nature of the hazard that Americans face in carrying out official duties overseas has evolved over the past quarter century to the point that a commission studying the U.S. overseas presence could state in 1999 that "since the end of the Vietnam War, more ambassadors have lost their lives to hostile actions than generals and admirals from the same cause."[14]

There has been an underlying evolution in how U.S. policymakers view casualties, and this also affects how the consequences of terrorism are likely to be viewed. Since Vietnam, the United States has expended lives, or put them in harm's way, more reluctantly than before. The casualties that the U.S. military suffered in Somalia in 1993 (and their graphic and wrenching coverage in the media) appear to have accentuated this trend. Survey research suggests that policymakers and other civilian and military elites may be overestimating the American public's aversion to casualties in military operations incurred in performance of missions that have at least the potential to be successful.[15] Whether or not that is true, policies and strategies, including warfighting strategies, now place very high priority on minimizing casualties. The remarkable phenomenon of a major military campaign without any U.S. battle casualties—the air war against Yugoslavia in 1999—was the apotheosis of this trend. The trend can only accentuate the significance that Americans will place on whatever American lives are lost to terrorism in the future.

Two other dimensions of what terrorists have been doing lately, or appear poised to do in the future, bear on how to think about the direct physical costs of terrorism. One is that terrorism in recent years has become increasingly lethal. More terrorist attacks than before are designed to inflict high casualties. Deaths from international terrorism more than doubled from the first half of the 1990s to the latter half of the decade, even though the number of incidents declined 19 percent. This trend is associated... with the nature of some of the terrorist groups that have come to the fore during this time, and there is no reason to expect a reversal of the pattern anytime soon.

The other dimension is the much-ballyhooed danger of chemical, biological, radiological, or nuclear (CBRN) terrorism inflicting mass casualties. There are some legitimate reasons for concern about this to be greater now than a few years ago. The just-mentioned increased lethality of international terrorism is one reason; the more that terrorists use conventional means to kill large numbers of people, the less of a conceptual leap it is that they would use unconventional means to try to accomplish the same objective. Related to that is the increased role of small, religiously driven groups like the World Trade Center bombers, who are less likely than many larger groups (or states) to be deterred by the consequences of their own escalating violence—because they have no constituent populations to abhor their methods and no fixed assets to be the target of retaliation. The availability of materials and expertise relevant to CBRN weapons is another basis for concern. The focus has been on what might come out of the former Soviet Union (not just "loose nukes" but also substances related to biological or chemical weapons, as well as the knowledge and skills of displaced Soviet weapons scientists) and on weapons-related information that is now readily available on the Internet. Intelligence that shows some terrorist groups to be interested in CBRN capabilities is another concern. So is the precedent set by Aum Shinrikyo's attempt in 1995 to use sarin in a Tokyo subway to inflict mass casualties. Finally, the enormous public attention given to the danger of CBRN terrorism has itself probably increased the danger by pointing out to terrorists some of the possibilities—not only how such weapons might be used but also how much they frighten people.

Public discussion of CBRN terrorism has tended to stress many of these concerns—and the vulnerabilities of the United States to conceivable mass-casualty CBRN attacks—but given less emphasis to reasons that such attacks may still be unlikely. The General Accounting Office [GAO] has noted this pattern and emphasized the important distinction between conceivable terrorist threats and likely ones. The GAO observes that some of the public statements of U.S. officials about the CBRN threat have omitted important qualifications to the information they have presented.[16] The qualifications can be found not only in the classified material that the GAO reviewed but also in what is now a sizable scholarly literature on CBRN terrorism.[17] Experts who have studied the subject in depth have found numerous reasons to doubt whether CBRN terrorism is as much a wave of the future as is widely perceived.

Some of those reasons involve technical and other difficulties that any terrorist would face in acquiring the capability to inflict mass casualties with CBRN devices or agents. Some of the substances in question (for example, virulent forms of pathogens that would be needed to make biological weapons, as distinct from other forms that might be used in the production of vaccines) are not as easy to obtain as is commonly supposed.[18] Even with raw material in hand, there are formidable challenges in converting it into an effective and deployable device. Some toxic agents are difficult to keep both potent and stable. Dissemination is a major challenge, with both biological and chemical agents. Airborne particles containing anthrax, for example, can easily be either too large or too small to infect people through inhalation. Chemical agents need to be produced in large quantities and dispersed over wide areas to have hope of causing large numbers of casualties. Given such challenges, development of a CBRN capability to cause mass casualties would require a major, sophisticated program that is well beyond the reach of the great majority of terrorist groups. Aum Shinrikyo demonstrated this point. Despite being unusually well endowed in money and technical talent and going to great lengths to develop CBRN capabilities, Aum's biological program failed completely, and its attempt to use sarin to kill hundreds or thousands on the Tokyo subway instead killed only twelve.

Other reasons for doubt involve terrorist intentions. Terrorists have generally been tactically conservative and have favored proven methods. The hazards and uncertain effects of using CBRN materials are not likely to be attractive to many of them, particularly given the proven effectiveness of old-fashioned truck bombs—in places as diverse as Beirut and Oklahoma City—in causing casualties numerous enough to be considered "mass." The fear-inducing aspect of an unseen killer like a biological pathogen may have appeal to some terrorists, but the theatrical aspect of an event that makes a loud explosion is apt to appeal to even more. Moreover, the large and well-organized groups that have the best chance of obtaining a CBRN capability are also the ones that—because they have the most to lose by outraging their constituencies or inviting forceful retaliation—are most likely to be deterred from using such a capability. Aum Shinrikyo was an exception, but what may be most significant (with more than five years having passed since the incident in the Tokyo subway) is that Aum did not start a trend.

The foregoing leads to the following conclusions about CBRN terrorism. First, it is a legitimate cause for concern; it represents one more way in which terrorism can entail major costs, and one more reason to be serious about countering it. Second, the actual threat of CBRN terrorism—which is impossible to gauge with anything approaching precision—has probably risen somewhat over the last few years but is much less than the alarmist treatment of the subject in the United States would lead one to believe. Third, actual CBRN attacks would (as with such attacks in the past) be more likely to cause few, rather than many, casualties. Their impact would be less a matter of the direct physical effects than the indirect psychological effects on the target population. How a government conditions its public to think about such an attack... is thus critical in determining what the impact will be.

A fourth conclusion (bearing in mind the preceding two) is that the specter of CBRN terrorism should not be the main basis for shaping thinking about terrorism overall or for organizing efforts to confront it. It would be a mistake to redefine counterterrorism as a task of dealing with "catastrophic," "grand," or "super" terrorism, when in fact these labels do not represent most of the terrorism that the United States is likely to face or most of the costs that terrorism imposes on U.S. interests. A CBRN incident that causes very many casualties is the sort of high-impact, low-probability event that, because of the high impact, policy must take into account. The potentially high consequences may be reason enough to devote more attention and resources to preparing for such an event. But the low-probability aspect of the scenario should also be remembered, and the scenario should not be allowed to distort or downgrade the attention paid to more probable forms of terrorism.

Similar considerations apply to cyberterrorism, about which high concern is even more recent, and the uncertainties even greater. Some terrorist groups have indeed demonstrated considerable sophistication with computers and computer networks. Presumably some groups that lack the necessary expertise for conducting electronic sabotage could purchase it from venal and adventurous individuals. Electronic attacks to date that have been associated with terrorist groups have been few and simple, such as "spam" attacks in which large numbers of messages overload a government's server. The capability of terrorist groups to conduct electronic attacks more damaging than these incidents, or than the nonterrorist sabotage that has occasionally disabled major web sites, is more questionable. Terrorist intentions regarding cyberterrorism are even more problematic. Linking the objectives of actual terrorist groups to scenarios of electronic sabotage that would serve those objectives is conjecture.

To express such skepticism is not to deny the worth of security measures that would protect against unconventional terrorism, not only because of the potentially high consequences of such terrorism but also because many of those measures would also guard against other dangers. Almost all of the steps being taken to safeguard the nation's electronic infrastructure from terrorist groups, for example, would also help to protect it against attacks from the sources that, based on recent experience, seem to pose the main threat of electronic sabotage: individual hackers, and perhaps others driven by nonterrorist motives. This last point is true as well of some measures to defend against biological terrorism, which might include a strengthening of the public health system (including, perhaps, the additional acquisition of vaccines or antidotes) that would be needed anyway to deal effectively with natural or accidental outbreaks of disease.[19]

Terrorism in general, even when conducted with conventional means, tends to have greater psychological impact relative to the physical harm it causes than do other lethal activities, including warfare. In this regard, the earlier comparisons with casualties from past military operations understate, in a sense, the significance of terrorism. The distinction between the fair fight of an open military engagement and the unfair one of a terrorist attack on helpless victims comes into play. Ask the average American if the life of a soldier who dies in battle is worth the same as the life of a countryman who has died from terrorism, and the answer will be yes. But ask after each type of event how much shock and revulsion that American is feeling, and the reaction will be stronger after the terrorist incident. That the felt impact of terrorism tends to be disproportionate to the material damage has led some to argue that if government (and others who comment on terrorism) would only play down its significance and treat it more like ordinary crime, its actual importance and usefulness to the terrorist would lessen.[20] How government publicly portrays terrorism does indeed matter. But however much one might try to talk down the subject, some of the special shock of a terrorist attack will always be there; it is in the nature of the event.

The indirect costs of terrorism are, overall, significantly greater than the direct physical ones. The indirect costs are many and varied. They start with the fear instilled in individual citizens, and what it leads those citizens to do. The fear itself—the sheer mental discomfort—is a cost. So is the economic effect of fearful citizens not taking trips or not patronizing certain businesses. And so is the social effect of those citizens arming themselves or ostracizing fellow citizens of particular ethnic backgrounds that are associated with terrorism, or doing any of a number of other dysfunctional things that less fearful citizens would not do.

Countermeasures against terrorism are also a major indirect cost. Price tags can be placed on some of them but capture only part of the expense. What was labeled as the terrorism-related portion of the Clinton administration's budget for fiscal year 2000, for example, amounted to about $10 billion, although that is a malleable figure depending on what one includes under the counterterrorist label. To take a single type of expense as a more tractable example, the panel chaired by retired Admiral William Crowe that studied the bombings in East Africa estimated that $14 billion would be required over ten years to implement its recommendations for improving the security of U.S. diplomatic missions.[21] Federal expenditures are only part of the picture, because many security countermeasures against terrorism are expenses of state or local governments or of the private sector. And the cost of many measures cannot realistically be estimated at all, although they have innumerable second- and third-order effects that, aggregating them over the entire nation, are surely huge. Every time someone empties his pockets and takes a detour through a metal detector to gain access to a public building, there are costs—which may include not only inconvenience to an individual but also the time and thus the expense involved in transacting a piece of business.

The expenditures made in responding to a problem beg the question, of course, of how many of those expenditures have been necessary and effective. Most of the success stories about countermeasures against terrorism are fragmentary and anecdotal, and it is impossible to calculate how much trouble would have occurred in their absence. But the very fact that so many resources are consumed—however necessary or unnecessary, effective or ineffective, any particular countermeasure may be—is itself a reason for the subject to command policy attention.

With some antiterrorist programs—including some big, expensive ones—past effectiveness and the future need to spend substantial resources are easier to see. Aviation security is an example. A major success story over the past quarter century has been a drastic reduction in skyjackings. Although some other factors affecting terrorists' choice of methods have been involved, the chief reason for this welcome development has been a comprehensive security system that has made it much harder to bring on board an aircraft the wherewithal to hijack it. This system is costly, including the visible costs of x-ray machines, metal detectors, and the staff to operate them, as well as less visible costs such as lengthening the time required to make business trips. The Federal Aviation Administration is now endeavoring to reduce the vulnerability of civil aviation in the United States to the other terrorist threat it faces—in-flight bombings—by enhancing procedures for screening checked baggage on domestic flights. The FAA estimates that this single change would cost $2.8 billion over ten years.[22]

Finally, the costs of terrorism embrace a host of other political and policy effects. They include the governmental equivalent of fear among individual citizens—that is, the government does not do certain things (which could be anything from a trip by a VIP to the holding of a New Year's celebration), or does them in a more gingerly or less effective manner, than it otherwise would because of fear of terrorist attacks. Costs also include the shaping of the political environment in unfavorable ways. Any challenge to government's monopoly on the use of force (which terrorism and other politically motivated violence necessarily entails) affects citizens' views toward government itself, including the trust they place in it to meet their needs for order and security.[23]

The costs of terrorism also include major effects on U.S. foreign relations and foreign interests, especially the following.

First, the possibility of terrorist attacks inhibits, or at least complicates, a wide range of U.S. activities overseas and the maintenance of an official U.S. presence abroad. This includes the necessary concern that almost any official American working overseas must have with security (and in some places it is a high concern), which means a distraction from that official's primary job. It also includes major security-driven operational decisions having significant impact on other missions. For example, the United States vacated its embassy in Sudan in February 1996 (without formally breaking diplomatic relations) because of terrorism. The specific concerns were not only with the terrorism-related policies of the Sudanese government but also with whether U.S. officials living and working in Khartoum would be safe, given the presence in Sudan of a rogue's gallery of international terrorist groups.[24] The absence of a resident diplomatic mission in Sudan, which has the largest territory of any African country and touches on numerous conflicts in the unstable northeastern and East Africa regions, unavoidably hinders support for U.S. interests in the area. One of the things it has hindered is collection of intelligence, including intelligence on terrorist threats that could materialize elsewhere. (It is worth remembering that most of those arrested in June 1993 for plotting to bomb the Hudson River tunnels and other landmarks in New York City were Sudanese.)

A similar security-driven redeployment was the move, following the bombing of Khubar Towers in 1996, of nearly 4,000 U.S. troops in Saudi Arabia from the urban areas of Dhahran and Riyadh to the isolated (and hence less vulnerable to terrorism) Prince Sultan Air Base. The move itself cost $200 million (which the U.S. and Saudi governments agreed to split). Perhaps more costly was the impact on morale, training, and readiness of the isolation and accompanying changes in deployment policy, including the withdrawal of command sponsorship for dependents and the cutting in half (from ninety days to forty-five) of the tours of the fighter pilots who overfly Iraq.[25]

Besides the impediments to official U.S. activity, there are also security-related complications for the private sector. If a U.S. business decides to brave the risk of terrorism in making a direct investment in a hazardous area, it will have expenses for security that will be an added cost of doing business. If the risk dissuades it from making the investment, then an opportunity for making and repatriating profits, and for enhancing employment in the local economy, will have been lost.

A second cost of terrorism in terms of foreign policy is the undermining of peace processes, including ones in which the United States has invested heavily and which, absent the disruption of fresh terrorist attacks, might otherwise be ripe for progress. The series of suicide bombings in Israel by Hamas and the Palestine Islamic Jihad in early 1996, for example, caused popular support for the Labor Party's peace policies to crumble, paved the way for Benjamin Netanyahu's upset election victory, and retarded progress toward further Arab-Israeli accords. In Northern Ireland, attacks in August 1998 by the republican splinter group calling itself the "Real IRA" (especially a car bomb in Omagh that killed 29 and injured at least 330) led to an unraveling of the Good Friday peace accord to the point that, later in the year, the agreement seemed close to collapse. More recently, it has been the main IRA's retention of its means of terror (the issue of "decommissioning of arms") that has been the principal reason for setbacks in the Northern Ireland peace process, such as the temporary suspension of the provincial government in February 2000.

Third, terrorism risks enflaming other regional conflicts that are already closer to war than to peace. (The spark that ignited World War I—the assassination of Archduke Francis Ferdinand—was a terrorist act.) The hijacking by Kashmiri militants of an Indian airliner in December 1999, for example, led to a new round of recriminations between India and Pakistan and raised the temperature of their dispute. Neither this incident nor most others like it have led to a war, but they at least temporarily increase the danger of one breaking out.

Fourth, the concern of an otherwise friendly government that it will become a target of terrorism may dissuade it from cooperating with the United States. Sometimes it fears being perceived as doing Washington's bidding. Sometimes what Washington asks it to do is unpopular for other reasons. In either case the specific fear is that extreme opponents of the requested cooperation will strike back with violence. The cooperation in question may range from diplomatic support to the hosting of a military deployment.

And fifth, terrorism can destabilize friendly governments. This is much less common than merely influencing the policies of such governments, and terrorism itself seldom topples regimes. It has sometimes caused major damage to the social or economic fabric of important countries, however, and as a result has called regimes' political stamina into question. This was true of Peru at the height of Sendero Luminoso's campaign of violence, and to a lesser degree of Egypt when terrorist attacks devastated that country's economically vital tourist industry in the early 1990s.

None of these costly consequences for U.S. foreign relations results *only* from terrorism. Numerous other political, economic, military, diplomatic, and cultural dimensions of the global environment (or regional environments) also affect them. Many of these dimensions involve the United States directly or are subject to U.S. influence. This is part of why counterterrorist policy must be considered and formulated as an integral part of U.S. foreign policy. Counterterrorism is one means by which to pursue the objectives implied above—stable and cooperative allies, effective regional peace processes, and so forth—and others as well. The means, including counterterrorism, used to pursue these objectives must be employed as part of a consistent, well-integrated strategy. And in the judgment of history, whether these objectives are achieved is likely to be at least important as the means used to achieve them.

Of course, the basic counterterrorist goal of saving lives and property from terrorist attack is a worthy end in its own right and not just a means. Indeed, some of the objectives posited above, such as effective regional peacemaking, could just as appropriately be viewed as means toward, among other things, the end of reducing violence, especially terrorist violence. The permutations of ends and means relationships between counterterrorism and other foreign policy goals are innumerable. That is the point. Counterterrorism is part of a larger, complicated web of foreign policy endeavors and interests, with numerous trade-offs and unintended consequences that should not be ignored.

The Elements of Counterterrorist Policy

No single approach makes an effective counterterrorist policy. The policy must have several elements. In that respect, counterterrorism is similar to many other policy problems, including other ones that involve the physical well-being of the public.

Consider, for example, highway safety. Highway deaths and injuries are a function of the highways themselves, the vehicles that travel them, the traffic laws, the enforcement of those laws, and the drivers. Government can reduce deaths and injuries somewhat through action on each of these fronts (for example, installing guard rails, raising crash resistance standards for cars, lowering speed limits, putting more police on patrol, tightening licensing requirements for drivers). Each type of measure addresses only part of the problem. Each has diminishing returns. Each entails compromises with other interests, such as competing demands for use of tax dollars, ease and efficiency in getting people where they want go, or environmental concerns. So some measures are taken in all of these areas, rather than concentrating safety efforts in only one of them.

The major fronts on which the problem of terrorism can be addressed are the root conditions and issues that give rise to terrorist groups in the first place and motivate individuals to join them; the ability of such groups to conduct terrorist attacks; the intentions of groups regarding whether to launch terrorist attacks; and the defenses erected against such attacks. Each of these corresponds to a phase in the life cycle of terrorism, from simmering discontent to the conduct of an actual terrorist operation. As with the example of highway safety, important and useful work can be done on each front. But also like that example, efforts on any one front are insufficient to manage the problem and are necessarily limited by competing objectives and equities. Effective counterterrorism requires attention to all four areas.

Roots

Cutting the roots of terrorism is not commonly thought of—or officially expressed as—an element of U.S. counterterrorist policy, for a couple of reasons. One is that it is farther removed than any of the other elements from the here-and-now worries of imminent threats, actual attacks, and what to do about them. It is not as pressing a concern as other counterterrorist work, the links between roots and people actually getting killed or maimed are often tenuous and twisted, and cause-and-effect relationships are difficult to prove. The other reason is that doing something about roots involves the management of numerous foreign policy matters that are not primarily the responsibility of people who call themselves counterterrorist officials. In fact, it embraces a huge swath of U.S. foreign policy on such things as regional and local conflicts, political instability within states, and social and economic conditions in countries in which terrorist groups have arisen or could arise.

Just because a cause-and-effect relationship is difficult to measure, however, does not make it nonexistent. Conditions do matter. Terrorists and terrorist groups do not arise randomly, and they are not distributed evenly around the globe. Scholars who have examined the origins of subnational political violence in general have pointed to the need to consider the perceived deprivation and other grievances that provide motives for violence, as well as the calculations and political opportunities of dissident leaders who mobilize such discontent, to understand better when and where violence breaks out.[26]

Two types of antecedent conditions are germane to the emergence of terrorists. One consists of the issues expressed directly by the terrorists and those who sympathize with their cause: political repression, a lack of self-determination, the depravity of their rulers, or whatever. People who are angry over such issues are more likely to resort to extreme measures, including terrorism and other forms of violence, than ones who are not.

Palestinian support for violence against Israeli targets, for example, has to some extent varied inversely with progress in the peace process aimed at realizing Palestinian self-determination. This is true even though most Palestinians realize that Islamist terrorism against Israel has been counter-productive in the sense of retarding the peace process itself, boosting electoral support for harder-line Israeli leaders, undermining the economy of the Occupied Territories, and causing the Palestinian Authority to be preoccupied with security rather than with political development.[27]

The other type of root condition includes the living standards and socioeconomic prospects of populations that are, or may become, the breeding stock for terrorists. Terrorism is a risky, dangerous, and very disagreeable business. Consequently, few people who have a reasonably good life will be inclined to get into that business, regardless of their political viewpoint. Those who have more desolate lives and little hope of improving them will have fewer reservations about getting into it. The majority of terrorists worldwide are young adult males, unemployed or underemployed (except by terrorist groups), with weak social and familial support, and with poor prospects for economic improvement or advancement through legitimate work. To take the Palestinian example, most members of the extremist Palestine Islamic Jihad are of low social origin and live in poverty in the bleak neighborhoods or refugee camps of the Gaza Strip.[28] Hamas also does its most successful recruiting in Gaza.

The connection between lifestyles and proclivity for terrorism has been the basis for a technique that has been used successfully to get low-level members of certain terrorist groups to leave the terrorist business and to stay out of it. Tell the young man that if he cuts all ties with his current organization he will receive assistance in finding a job and a new place to live. Tell him also that the financial assistance he receives will depend partly on his getting married (and, preferably, having children). Settling down into a stable family life with some means of supporting it makes a return to terrorism very unlikely. For such reclamation cases, the principal roots of terrorism have been severed.

Obviously not every terrorist or potential terrorist can be bought off in this way. Policy initiatives on a larger scale do affect the roots of terrorism, however. Peace processes that lead to some measure of self-determination may do so. Political reforms that open up peaceful channels for dissent may do so. And economic development that improves prospects for a better standard of living may do so. The possibilities for snipping away at the roots of terrorism in these and similar ways should be noted and made part of the policy deliberations. But there are three major constraints on what can be done by focusing on roots alone.

The first constraint is the complexity of the relationship between antecedent conditions and the emergence of terrorists. It is not nearly as simple a matter as giving disgruntled people votes or a higher income. No one has produced a good algorithm for the many variables that, in combination, breed terrorists. In the nineteenth century, terrorism frequently emerged in direct response to repression, but the correlation between political grievances and terrorism in more recent times is less obvious.[29] In fact, terrorism today appears more often in free than in unfree societies.[30] Peace processes that realize the aspirations of a majority may, at least in the short term, enflame a minority that opposes a settlement for other reasons. As for economic conditions, one must take account of cases such as the emergence of Islamic terrorist groups in some wealthy Muslim societies like Kuwait but not in some poor ones like Niger.[31] The tearing of traditional social fabrics by economic development may have actually encouraged terrorism in some places.

The second constraint is that counterterrorism can never be the only consideration, or sometimes even the chief one, in determining U.S. policies that affect the economic well-being of certain foreign populations or self-determination for certain ethnic groups. Resource limitations obviously weigh heavily on decisions regarding economic assistance. On the political side, U.S. support for even so long-standing a principle as self-determination has always been limited by a variety of interests and concerns.[32] Some things that an unhappy, potentially terrorist-breeding, population may consider unjust may be viewed by the United States, for politically and ethically sound reasons, as not unjust and in no need of major change. The likely effect on emergent terrorism should be one factor, but only one of many, that is brought to bear on policies that affect these sorts of political and economic conditions overseas.

And third, no matter how much effort is expended on cutting out roots of terrorism, there will always remain a core of incorrigibles—and these will include the terrorists about whom the United States must worry the most. They will remain because for some individuals (even though they are sane and political, not pathological), terrorism also serves personal needs—self-fulfillment, making a big mark, or following some other inner demon—that have little to do with the order of the outside world.[33] They will also remain because the viewpoints of some are simply too extreme to be accommodated. And they will remain because once terrorist groups and terrorist leaders emerge, they develop their own goals and dynamics that go beyond the causes that may have bred them in the first place. The second and third of these factors, and probably the first, apply, for example, to Usama bin Ladin and his inner circle. As former State Department counterterrorism coordinator L. Paul Bremer has put it: "There's no point in addressing the so-called causes of bin Ladin's despair with us. We are the root cause of his terrorism. He doesn't like America. He doesn't like our society. He doesn't like what we stand for. He doesn't like our values. And short of the United States going out of existence, there's no way to deal with the root cause of his terrorism."[34]

Capabilities

Reducing the ability of terrorist groups to conduct attacks—conduct them effectively, or in many different places—is at the heart of U.S. counterterrorist programs (especially in the narrow sense of counterterrorism as offensive efforts against terrorists, as distinct from defensive antiterrorism programs). This work involves a variety of intelligence, legal, and other counterterrorist instruments....

Attacking terrorist capabilities has been an effective way of reducing many brands of terrorism. Most of the successes have been unpublicized, piecemeal acts of disruption—a cell rolled up here, a terrorist operative arrested there. A more visible and dramatic example of how effective even a single blow against a group can be was the Peruvian raid in April 1997 at the Japanese ambassador's residence in Lima, which had been seized four months earlier by the Tupac Amaru Revolutionary Movement (MRTA). The raid not only freed all but one of the seventy-two remaining hostages; it also crippled the MRTA's capability to conduct future terrorism. Several of the group's most able operational leaders died in the raid.

As with the other elements of counterterrorist policy, however, a focus on degrading the capabilities of groups has inherent limitations. One limitation, as the bombing in

Oklahoma City demonstrated, is that even the infliction of mass casualties does not always require much capability. That horror was accomplished with two men, a truck, and home-made fertilizer-based explosives. A prior detention (or just investigation) of Timothy McVeigh and Terry Nichols conceivably could have prevented the bombing, but there was nothing else that authorities could have done before the incident to reduce terrorist capabilities to conduct it. Infrastructures and networks of cells—which are critical to the ability of many foreign terrorist groups to conduct attacks—were not present in the case.

Too little capability for U.S. authorities to go after is one limitation; too much capability is yet another one. A major transnational terrorist group such as Lebanese Hizballah is simply too large and widespread an organization to wipe out with a few well-conceived counterterrorist operations. Using such operations to chip away at Hizballah's capabilities is, and should remain, a priority task for U.S. counterterrorism. Such operations can be effective at least in curtailing the group's ability to strike in certain regions. But such a group is not as vulnerable as a smaller one like the MRTA. It must be assumed that, even in the face of vigorous counterterrorist operations, the group will retain a capability that must be negated through the other elements of counterterrorist policy.

Intentions

There is indeed an enormous amount of terrorist capability around the world, in the hands of groups as well as hostile states, which could inflict major harm on the United States (or others) if those who control that capability decided to do so. This includes not only avowedly anti-American groups such as Lebanese Hizballah (which has not directly carried out a confirmed terrorist attack against a U.S. target since at least 1996) but also highly capable groups (such as Hamas or the Tamil Tigers) that have directed their violence elsewhere. Having less rather than more terrorism is thus a function not only of degrading terrorist capabilities but also of terrorist leaders *choosing*—for whatever reason—not to use what capabilities they have to attack. In short, terrorist intentions matter.

The intentions of terrorist groups (what the leaders of groups that already exist choose to do) raise some of the same motives and issues that are related to terrorism's roots (why terrorist groups arise in the first place and people join them). The status of the Arab-Israeli peace process, for example, affects Palestinian terrorism through its influence on intentions (decisions by Hamas's leadership on whether, when, and against what targets to stage attacks) as well as on roots (the emergence of Hamas and the Palestine Islamic Jihad in the first place and the willingness of young Palestinians to be recruited for suicide missions). Again, the issues involved go well beyond counterterrorism, and policy decisions on them necessarily also reflect other objectives and equities.

Measures that are more commonly regarded as counterterrorism also affect terrorist intentions. Punishing terrorists through prosecution or retaliatory strikes, for example, might have some deterrent effect…. The posture that the United States takes toward the political aspirations of groups it has officially branded as terrorist affects the intentions of those groups. The same could be said of state sponsors of terrorism.

One of the longest standing and most frequently expressed tenets of U.S. counterterrorist policy also has to do with terrorist intentions: that the United States will make no concessions to terrorists. The principle is simple: that not rewarding terrorism will give terrorists less incentive to try using it again. It would be difficult to prove that the principle always works in practice, but some analysis has pointed to past patterns of how terrorists have attempted to coerce different states at different times to suggest it has some validity.[35]

The U.S. part of the record is clouded by the fact that the United States has at times made concessions to terrorism. The most notorious instance was the Iran-Contra affair, in which the United States secretly sold arms to Iran in 1986 as part of an effort to gain release of hostages held by Iranian-backed terrorists in Lebanon. That episode certainly tarnished the U.S. image of steadfastness against terrorism, but in some respects terrorists still have good reason to view the United States as one of their most obdurate opponents. Even Israel—despite being a famously hard-line fighter against terrorism that has refused to make concessions while hostages were held—has struck deals with extremist opponents, including ones in which large numbers of prisoners were released in return for much smaller numbers of Israeli nationals. It is with regard to the classic type of terrorist coercion—holding the target country's citizens hostage to obtain a release of prisoners—that the United States has stood most firm. Even Iran-Contra did not involve opening any U.S. jail cells.

A benefit of that firmness was seen after the MRTA's capture of the Japanese ambassador's residence in Lima. The six U.S. officials who were at the reception when the terrorists struck were among the first to be released. The kidnappers let them go five days after the incident began while keeping 140 other hostages, including many foreign officials as well as Peruvians. The MRTA probably calculated (correctly) that to the extent the United States stayed directly involved, it would counsel a harder line to the Peruvian leadership than would many of the Asian and Latin American governments whose officials the MRTA had also seized.

An obvious limitation to firmness in any hostage incident is the immediate risk to the lives of the hostages. No government, the United States included, can promise itself or anyone else that it would never, under any circumstances, make concessions to save the lives of its citizens. Its management of the incident would have to take into account the magnitude and credibility of the harm being threatened, along with its own longer-term credibility and reputation. Accordingly, the rhetorical emphasis of this aspect of U.S. counter-terrorist policy perhaps should be less on "no concessions" and more on the slightly more flexible "terrorism will not be rewarded." A concession made in the face of an immediate threat of great harm need not constitute a reward unless the terrorists were demanding some irreversible act, and there are few of those (even released prisoners can be recaptured).[36] Once the immediate peril is over, the terrorists can be hunted to the ends of the earth and appropriate action taken to ensure that when the books on the incident are closed, it will not count as a reward for terrorism.[37] Certainly no government need feel obliged to observe commitments made under duress. Consider the repatriation of the crew of the USS *Pueblo*, a U.S. Navy ship that North Korea seized in 1968; the United States repudiated the "admission" (of violating territorial waters) demanded by the North Koreans even as it was signing it.

A broader limitation on how much can be expected from this kind of firmness is that the classic hostage-and-specific-demand incident is simply not as big a part of international terrorism as it used to be. Although U.S. citizens have been bit players in a few such incidents in recent years (such as the Lima event and the hijacking of the Air India jet), U.S. crisis managers have not for a long time had to wrestle directly with dramatic, well-publicized, hostage situations in which lives are staked against a need to stay tough on terrorism. The great majority of terrorist attacks today (and most of the best-known recent incidents) involve terrorists going right out and killing people, rather than making specific demands and putting themselves in a position to kill people if the demands are not met. The very U.S. firmness discussed above (and stronger backbones grown by some other governments) probably has had something to do with this, and to that extent it is another endorsement for a policy of firmness....

Terrorists who suddenly detonate a bomb may still be looking for a concession, even though there are no apparent hostages and no explicit negotiations. Hizballah's bombings of the U.S. and French embassies in Beirut in April 1983, for example, and its attacks later that year on the U.S. Marine barracks and a French military base, were aimed largely at expelling from Lebanon the multilateral peacekeeping force of which the U.S. and French contingents were a part. In such circumstances, the United States is in a sort of bargaining relationship with the terrorists, whether or not it wants to be or says it is. It cannot ignore the public demands of the terrorist group, and its own policies regarding the subject matter of those demands are in effect part of the negotiation.[38] So there is yet an opportunity to demonstrate firmness, but one with even more potential problems and complications than in the traditional hostage incident. Refusal to act the way the terrorists want not only risks further attacks along the lines of what has already occurred (which was certainly an implicit threat in Lebanon) but also may mean continuing a policy that is unwise or unsustainable for other reasons. The alternative is to do what the terrorists would wish (which the United States and its allies did in Lebanon, pulling their troops out in early 1984), which—regardless of how the move is billed and the other reasons for it—may be seen as a concession to terrorism.

Other terrorist attacks are conducted without any particular concessions in mind; the destruction is more of an end in itself, motivated by hatred or revenge. With those who would wage this brand of terrorism (exemplified by the bombing of the World Trade Center by Ramzi Yousef's group), there is no way to influence intentions over the long term—whether by being steadfast in not rewarding terrorism, or being forceful in punishing it, or through any other means. The incorrigibility of such people is the main limitation of this element of counterterrorism. An ad hoc terrorist such as Yousef, who was not part of any permanent organization, is particularly unlikely to be deterred for long or to be coaxed on to a less violent path. Yousef was out to kill as many Americans as he could, he and his colleagues did not have fixed assets that could be bombed in retaliation, and he showed no sign of caring about his cohorts being caught and prosecuted.

Defenses

The one way in which the bin Ladins and Yousefs can be deterred is at the short-term, tactical level, by erecting security countermeasures that persuade them that a contemplated attack would fail. Some security measures that the United States has used overseas have had this effect. In at least one recent instance, a plot to attack a U.S. embassy was called off in the planning stage because the terrorists concluded that the security they had observed there could not be overcome. Antiterrorist defenses, therefore, are another way to influence terrorist intentions.

Physical defenses are also an element in their own right in saving lives from terrorism, even where they do not deter. And lives are saved even when attacks are not defeated entirely. The security measures at Khubar Towers, which kept the explosive-laden truck from penetrating the perimeter of the compound, prevented a death toll that would have far exceeded the nineteen U.S. servicemen who were killed. Similarly, in both Nairobi and Dar es Salaam in 1998, physical barriers and the refusal of guards to admit onto embassy grounds the trucks used by the terrorists greatly minimized U.S. casualties. Besides, the bigger the bomb the terrorists have to build, and the larger and more complex their operation has to become to defeat the defenses, the greater the chance that their operation will be compromised and discovered.

Antiterrorist defenses constitute a very large proportion of the U.S. fight against terrorism, certainly in resources but also in leadership attention. At the state and local level and in the private sector defenses are virtually the entire effort. Efforts at the federal level include defensive measures at both home and abroad. The two major overseas defensive programs—protection for U.S. diplomatic and military installations—have each received renewed emphasis in response to attacks in recent years.

On the diplomatic side, the bombings in Nairobi and Dar es Salaam highlighted the failure to meet standards for embassy security that had been established after earlier tragedies in Lebanon (the so-called Inman standards, after Admiral Bobby R. Inman, who chaired an Advisory Panel on Overseas Security in 1985). As of mid-1999, 229 of the 260 U.S. diplomatic posts worldwide still lacked the 100-foot setback (from the compound perimeter) specified in the Inman standards.[39] The funding level that the Crowe panel recommended is unlikely to be reached, but the Clinton administration in its last year budgeted more than $1.1 billion for embassy security in fiscal year 2001 and requested $3.4 billion in advance appropriations for fiscal years 2002 through 2005.[40]

Protection for military forces received a comparable fillip from the attack at Khubar Towers. In September 1996, Secretary of Defense William Perry issued a fresh directive on defending against terrorism (DoD Directive 2000.12) and initiated numerous enhancements to U.S. force protection efforts. A new section, headed by a general officer, within the Joint Staff was given responsibility for coordinating and promoting the military's antiterrorism efforts, promulgating doctrine on the subject, implementing a comprehensive training program, and conducting vulnerability assessments of installations around the world. The annual military antiterrorist budget is now about $3.5 billion.

The cost of defensive measures—particularly in dollars but also in restrictions on freedom of movement—is their main limitation. Comprehensive protection for everything in the terrorists' sights would be prohibitively expensive. As the Crowe panel acknowledged, "We understand that there will never be enough money to do all that should be done. We will have to live with partial solutions and, in turn, a high level of threat and vulnerability for quite some time."[41] A related limitation is that terrorists sometimes respond to security countermeasures by shifting their attention to more vulnerable targets. In some cases this means—given the terrorists' own limitations on where and how they can operate—that no attack occurs. But in others it means that a target with less robust defenses gets hit. The shift can be from one specific target to another (for example, from military bases to private businesses).[42]

Another limitation is that some terrorists are remarkably resourceful in adapting to, and overcoming, antiterrorist defenses. The Irish Republican Army (IRA), for example, has cleverly changed its methods for detonating bombs, using devices ranging from radar guns to photographic flash equipment, to stay ahead of the British use of electronic measures to prevent detonations.[43] Yousef demonstrated comparable operational cleverness with the method he devised for bombing U.S. airliners over the Pacific (and which he successfully tested, with a small amount of explosive, on a Philippine Airlines plane in December 1994). The technique involved bringing on board innocuous-looking items (including a prepared digital watch and a bottle for contact lens solution that really contained a liquid explosive), assembling them in a lavatory, and leaving the assembled device hidden on the aircraft when the terrorist got off at an intermediate stop.

Such ingenuity points to the limitations of using technology to defend against terrorism. It is not as if good minds have not been put on the problem. The federal government has a Technical Support Working Group that oversees a vigorous program of research, development, and rapid prototyping of antiterrorist technologies; the program has grown rapidly in recent years to reach an annual budget of close to $40 million. The Defense Science Board, an advisory body that includes some of the nation's leaders in applying technology to problems of national security, devoted its 1997 summer study to transnational threats, including terrorism, and how to respond to them.[44] The threat itself is not, at bottom, technological. Technology is useful in limited ways in defending against it but is not itself a solution.

All counterterrorist work—regardless of the instruments employed, the particular partners enlisted, or the specific enemies confronted—involves one or more of the elements just described. The limitations of each are patent; the need to address all of them together is strong. But the challenges facing U.S. counterterrorist policy reflect not just the limitations of counterterrorism itself. That policy must be adapted to a real world in which both the terrorist threat and the place of the United States as a terrorist target have evolved in important ways.

A former U.S. Army officer and executive fellow at the Brookings Institution, **Paul R. Pillar** has been a member of the Central Intelligence Agency (CIA) since 1977. In 2000 he was appointed the national intelligence officer for the Near East and South Asia of the National Intelligence Council of the CIA. His particular areas of interest include terrorism, negotiation, and counterterrorist policy. This reading is from his book *Terrorism and U.S. Foreign Policy*.

Notes

1. Bruce Hoffman, *Inside Terrorism* (Columbia University Press, 1998), chap. 1. Another recent chapter-length discussion of definitions is in David Tucker, *Skirmishes at the Edge of Empire: The United States and International Terrorism* (Praeger, 1997), chap. 2, pp. 51–69.
2. See, for example, the several articles on the subject in the autumn 1996 issue of the journal *Terrorism and Political Violence*, particularly Andrew Silke, "Terrorism and the Blind Men's Elephant," vol. 8 (Autumn 1996), pp. 12–28.
3. 22 U.S.C. 2656f (d).
4. For an argument that terrorism and crime should be kept conceptually distinct, see Phil Williams, "Terrorism and Organized Crime: Convergence, Nexus, or Transformation," in Brad Roberts, ed., *Hype or Reality: The "New Terrorism" and Mass Casualty Attacks* (Alexandria, Va.: Chemical and Biological Arms Control Institute, 2000), pp. 117–45. A contrasting view is in Roger Mead and Frank Goldstein, "International Terrorism on the Eve of a New Millennium," *Studies in Conflict and Terrorism*, vol. 20 (July-September 1997), p. 301.
5. Hoffman, *Inside Terrorism*, p. 43.
6. The discussion in chapter 4 on multilateral diplomacy addresses further what these rules, and recent modifications to them, imply for counterterrorism.

7. Assassination as a possible counterterrorist tactic is discussed in chapter 4.

8. Concurring opinion by Justice Stewart in *Jacobellis v. Ohio*, 378 U.S. 184, 197 (1964).

9. Quoted in Pamela Constable, "Kashmiri Rebels Pressure Pakistan," *Washington Post*, October 20, 1999, p. 23.

10. As Brian Jenkins has pointed out, this conception of terrorism does involve one value judgment: that an end does not justify the means. Brian M. Jenkins, "Terrorism: A Contemporary Problem with Age-old Dilemmas," in Lawrence Howard, ed., *Terrorism: Roots, Impact, Responses* (Praeger, 1992), p. 14.

11. International terrorism includes any incident that is terrorism under the statutory definition given above and that involves two or more nationalities when one considers the perpetrators, the victims, and the location of the incident.

12. Statistics are from unpublished FBI data.

13. Statistics on U.S. military casualties are Department of Defense data (web1.wbs.osd.mil/mmid/m01/sms223r.htm (November 2001).

14. Overseas Presence Advisory Panel, *America's Overseas Presence in the 21st Century* (Washington, November 1999), p. 38.

15. Peter D. Fravet and Christopher Gelpi, "How Many Deaths Are Acceptable? A Surprising Answer," *Washington Post*, November 7, 1999, p. B3.

16. General Accounting Office, *Combating Terrorism: Issues in Managing Counterterrorist Programs*, T-NSIAD-00 145 (April 6, 2000), pp. 3–4.

17. The most comprehensive study is Richard A. Falkenrath, Robert D. Newman, and Bradley A. Thayer, *America's Achilles' Heel: Nuclear, Biological, and Chemical Terrorism and Covert Attack* (MIT Press, 1998). Despite the somewhat ominous title, this is a well researched work that lays out arguments both for and against the idea that terrorists are likely to employ unconventional weapons. A useful survey is Roberts, *Hype or Reality*, especially the chapter by Brian Jenkins, which summarizes points on which there appears to be consensus among most specialists. A recent book that touches on diverse aspects of the subject is Jessica Stern, *The Ultimate Terrorists* (Harvard University Press, 1999). Jonathan B. Tucker, ed., *Toxic Terror: Assessing Terrorist Use of Chemical and Biological Weapons* (MIT Press, 2000), examines several past cases of attempted or reported terrorists' use of chemical or biological substances. Reasons to be skeptical about the magnitude of an unconventional terrorist threat are discussed in David C. Rapoport, "Terrorism and Weapons of the Apocalypse," *National Security Studies Quarterly*, vol. 5 (Summer 1999), pp. 49–67; Ehud Sprinzak, "The Great Superterrorism Scare," *Foreign Policy*, no. 112 (Fall 1998), pp. 110–24; Jonathan B. Tucker and Amy Sands, "An Unlikely Threat," *Bulletin of the Atomic Scientists*, vol. 55 (July-August 1999), pp. 46–52; Brian M. Jenkins, "The Limits of Terror: Constraints on the Escalation of Violence, " *Harvard International Review*, vol. 17 (Summer 1995), pp. 44–45, 77–78; Henry Sokolski, "Rethinking Bio-Chemical Dangers," *Orbis*, vol. 44 (Spring 2000), pp. 207–19; the exchange on "WMD Terrorism" in *Survival*, vol. 40 (Winter 1998–99), pp. 168–83; and part 1 of the *First Annual Report of the Advisory Panel to Assess Domestic Response Capabilities for Terrorism Involving Weapons of Mass Destruction*, December 15, 1999.

18. This is all the more true of acquiring a usable nuclear device or the fissile material necessary to make one, both of which—despite the breakdown of many of the controls in the former USSR—are still protected by significant safeguards. Partly for this reason, use of a device producing a nuclear yield is the least likely CBRN terrorist event. Use of radioactive material as a containment to be dispersed by a conventional bomb is more probable.

19. W. Seth Carus, "Biohazard," *New Republic*, vol. 221 (August 2, 1999), pp. 14–16.

20. See, for example, John Mueller and Karl Mueller, "Sanctions of Mass Destruction," *Foreign Affairs*, vol. 78 (May-June 1999), p. 44.

21. *Report of the Accountability Review Boards on the Bombings of the US Embassies in Nairobi, Kenya and Dar es Salaam, Tanzania on August 7, 1998* (January 8, 1999), Key Recommendations, sec. 1.A.12 (www.terrorism.com/state/accountability_report.html [November 2000]).

22. FAA Notice 99-05, "Security of Checked Baggage on Flights Within the United States," *Federal Register*, vol. 64 (April 19, 1999), p. 19230. This cost estimate is a maximum, assuming a combination of profiling of passengers and matching passengers with their bags. Greater use

of explosives detection machines (which are hardly inexpensive themselves) might reduce the cost.

23. Philip B. Heymann, *Terrorism and America: A Commonsense Strategy for a Democratic Society* (MIT Press, 1998), p. 16.

24. Barbara Crossette, "Fearing Terrorism, U.S. Plans to Press Sudan," *New York Times*, February 2, 1996, p. A6.

25. Steven Lee Myers, "At a Saudi Base, U.S. Digs In, Gingerly, for a Longer Stay," *New York Times*, December 29, 1997, p. A1.

26. See, for example, the research on ethnically based conflict reported in Ted Robert Gurr, *Minorities at Risk: A Global View of Ethnopolitical Conflicts* (Washington: U.S. Institute of Peace Press, 1993).

27. Khalil Shikaki, "The Politics of Paralysis II: Peace Now or Hamas Later," *Foreign Affairs*, vol. 77 (July-August 1998), pp. 35–36.

28. Ziad Abu-Amr, *Islamic Fundamentalism in the West Bank and Gaza: Muslim Brotherhood and Islamic Jihad* (Indiana University Press, 1994), p. 96.

29. Walter Laqueur, "Reflections on Terrorism," *Foreign Affairs*, vol. 65 (Fall 1986), p. 91.

30. Leonard B. Weinberg and William L. Bubank, "Terrorism and Democracy: What Recent Events Disclose," *Terrorism and Political Violence*, vol. 10 (Spring 1998), pp. 108–18.

31. Daniel Pipes, "It's Not the Economy, Stupid: What the West Needs to Know about the Rise of Radical Islam," *Washington Post*, July 2, 1995, p. C2.

32. Richard N. Haas, *Conflicts Unending: The United States and Regional Disputes* (Yale University Press, 1990), p. 53.

33. See Martha Crenshaw, "How Terrorists Think: What Psychology Can Contribute to Understanding Terrorism," in Howard, *Terrorism: Roots, Impact, Responses*, pp. 71–93; Jerrold M. Post, "Terrorist Psycho-logic: Terrorist Behavior as a Product of Psychological Forces," in Walter Reith, ed., *Origins of Terrorism: Psychologies, Ideologies, Theologies, States of Mind* (Cambridge University Press, 1990), pp. 25–40; Robert S. Robins and Jerrold M. Post, *Political Paranoia: The Psychopolitics of Hatred* (Yale University Press, 1997), chaps. 4 and 6; and Laqueur, *The New Terrorism*, pp. 93–96.

34. *The NewsHour with Jim Lehrer*, Public Broadcasting System, August 25, 1998.

35. See, for example, Richard Clutterbuck, "Negotiating with Terrorists," in Alex P. Schmid and Ronald D. Crelinsten, eds., *Western Responses to Terrorism* (London: Frank Cass, 1993), p. 285.

36. Thomas C. Schelling, "What Purposes Can 'International Terrorism' Serve?" in R. G. Frey and Christopher W. Morris, eds., *Violence, Terrorism, and Justice* (Cambridge University Press, 1991), pp. 31–32.

37. See Heymann, *Terrorism and America*, pp. 40–46; and Tucker, *Skirmishes at the Edge of Empire*, pp. 74–80.

38. Schelling, "What Purposes Can 'International Terrorism' Serve?" p. 25.

39. Fact Sheet on Funding for Embassy Security, Department of State, August 4, 1999 (www.usinfo.state.gov/topical/pol/terror/99080404.htm [October 2000]).

40. White House Fact Sheet on Embassy Security Funding, February 10, 2000 (www.usinfo.state.gov/topical/pol/terror/00021004.htm [November 2000]).

41. *Report of the Accountability Review Boards*, Introduction.

42. Walter Enders and Todd Sandler in "The Effectiveness of Anti-Terrorism Policies: A Vector-Autoregression-Intervention Analysis," *American Political Science Review*, vol. 87 (December 1993), pp. 829–44, analyze statistics on terrorist incidents to conclude that the fortification of diplomatic installations has reduced attacks on those installations but has led terrorists to conduct more assassinations instead. They reach a similar conclusion about the installation of metal detectors in airports.

43. Hoffman, *Inside Terrorism*, pp. 180–82.

44. Defense Science Board 1997 Summer Study Task Force, *DoD Responses to Transnational Threats*, volume 1: Final Report (October 1997).

Eqbal Ahmad, 1998

Terrorism: Theirs & Ours

Eqbal Ahmad was one of the major activist scholars of this era. He was born in India prob-ably in 1934. He was never quite sure. He left with his brothers for the newly created state of Pakistan in 1947. In 1996, the BBC did a powerful and moving TV documentary chron-icling Ahmad's trek in a refugee caravan from his village in Bihar to Pakistan. The film, not shown on PBS in the U.S., is remarkable not just as an historical document but also for providing insight into the dangers of sectarian nationalism. Ahmad's secular thinking was surely shaped by the wrenching communal and political violence he experienced as a youngster. Even before the subcontinent was engulfed in the homicidal convulsions of 1947, Ahmad witnessed his own father murdered before him.

Ahmad came to the United States in the 1950s to study at Princeton. Later he went to Algeria. It was there that his ideas about national liberation and anti-imperialism crystallized. He worked with Frantz Fanon, author of The Wretched of the Earth, *during the revolt against the French. Returning to the U.S., he became active in the civil rights and anti-Vietnam War movements. It was during his involvement in the latter that I first heard his name. He was ac-cused of plotting to kidnap Henry Kissinger. The trumped-up charges were dismissed.*

I did my first interview with him in the early 1980s in his apartment on New York's Upper West Side. It was memorable. I had just gotten a new tape recorder. I returned home think-ing, Wow, I've got a great interview. I hit play and discovered the tape was blank. I had failed to turn the machine on. With considerable embarrassment I explained to him what happened. He said, "No problem." He invited me over the next day and we did another in-terview. This time, I pressed the right buttons. Whenever I tell that story, his friends would nod and say, "That's Eqbal."

Ahmad's radical politics and outspoken positions made him a pariah in academic circles. After years of being an intellectual migrant worker, Hampshire College in Amherst, Mas-sachusetts, hired him in the early 1980s as a professor. He taught there until his retirement in 1997. He spent most of his final years in Islamabad where he wrote a weekly column for Dawn, *Pakistan's oldest English-language newspaper. His political work consisted chiefly of trying to bridge differences with India on the issues of Kashmir and nuclear weapons. He was also speaking out against the rise of Islamic fundamentalism and was concerned about the possible Talibanization of Pakistan.*

Eqbal Ahmad died in Islamabad, Pakistan, on May 11, 1999. His close friend Edward Said wrote, "He was perhaps the shrewdest and most original anti-imperialist analyst of the postwar world, particularly of the dynamics between the West and postcolonial Asia and Africa; a man of enormous charisma, dazzling eloquence, incorruptible ideals, unfailing generosity and sympathy.... Whether on the conflict between Israelis and Palestinians or

India and Pakistan, he was a force for a just struggle but also for a just reconciliation....
Humanity and genuine secularism... had no finer champion."

"Terrorism: Theirs & Ours" was one of Eqbal Ahmad's last public talks in the United
States. He spoke at the University of Colorado at Boulder in October 1998. It was broad-
cast nationally and internationally on my weekly Alternative Radio program. Eqbal Ah-
mad's near prophetic sense is stunning. After the September 11 terrorist attacks, I aired the
speech again. Listeners called in great numbers requesting copies. They almost all believed
that the talk had just been recorded.

—David Barsamian

Until the 1930s and early 1940s, the Jewish underground in Palestine was described as
"terrorist." Then something happened: around 1942, as news of the Holocaust was spreading, a certain liberal sympathy with the Jewish people began to emerge in the Western
world. By 1944, the terrorists of Palestine, who were Zionists, suddenly began being described as "freedom fighters." If you look in history books you can find at least two Israeli
prime ministers, including Menachem Begin,[1] appearing in "Wanted" posters saying, TER-
RORISTS, REWARD [THIS MUCH]. The highest reward I have seen offered was 100,000 British pounds for the head of Menachem Begin, the terrorist.

From 1969 to 1990, the Palestine Liberation Organization (PLO) occupied center
state as a terrorist organization. Yasir Arafat has been repeatedly described as the "chief of
terrorism" by the great sage of American journalism, William Safire of *The New York*
Times. On September 29, 1998, I was rather amused to notice a picture of Yasir Arafat and
Israeli prime minister Benjamin Netanyahu standing on either side of President Bill
Clinton. Clinton was looking toward Arafat, who looked meek as a mouse. Just a few years
earlier, Arafat would appear in photos with a very menacing look, a gun holstered to his
belt. That's Yasir Arafat. You remember those pictures, and you'll remember the next one.

In 1985, President Ronald Reagan received a group of ferocious-looking, turban-
wearing men who looked like they came from another century. I had been writing about the
very same men for *The New Yorker*. After receiving them in the White House, Reagan
spoke to the press, referring to his foreign guests as "freedom fighters." These were the
Afghan mujahideen. They were at the time, guns in hand, battling the "Evil Empire." For
Reagan, they were the moral equivalent of our Founding Fathers.

In August 1998, another American president ordered missile strikes to kill Osama bin
Laden and his men in Afghanistan-based camps. Mr. bin Laden, at whom fifteen American
missiles were fired to hit in Afghanistan, was only a few years earlier the moral equivalent
of George Washington and Thomas Jefferson. I'll return to the subject of bin Laden later.

I am recalling these stories to point out that the official approach to terrorism is rather
complicated, but not without characteristics. To begin with, terrorists change. The terrorist
of yesterday is the hero of today, and the hero of yesterday becomes the terrorist of today.
In a constantly changing world of images, we have to keep our heads straight to know what
terrorism is and what it is not. Even more importantly, we need to know what causes terrorism and how to stop it.

Secondly, the official approach to terrorism is a posture of inconsistency, one which evades definition. I have examined at least twenty official documents on terrorism. Not one offers a definition. All of them explain it polemically in order to arouse our emotions, rather than exercise our intelligence. I'll give you an example which is representative. On October 25, 1984, Secretary of State George Shultz gave a long speech on terrorism at the Park Avenue Synagogue in New York City. In the State Department Bulletin of seven single-spaced pages, there is not a single clear definition of terrorism. What we get instead are the following statements. Number one: "Terrorism is a modern barbarism that we call terrorism." Number two is even more brilliant; "Terrorism is a form of political violence." Number three: "Terrorism is a menace to Western moral values." Do these accomplish anything other than arouse emotions? This is typical.

Officials don't define terrorism because definitions involve a commitment to analysis, comprehension, and adherence to some norms of consistency. That's the second characteristic of the official approach to terrorism. The third characteristic is that the absence of definition does not prevent officials from being globalistic. They may not define terrorism, but they can call it a menace to good order, a menace to the moral values of Western civilization, a menace to humankind. Therefore, they can call for it to be stamped out worldwide. Anti-terrorist policies therefore, must be global. In the same speech he gave in New York City, George Shultz also said: "There is no question about our ability to use force where and when it is needed to counter terrorism." There is no geographical limit. On the same day, U.S. missiles struck Afghanistan and Sudan. Those two countries are 2,300 miles apart, and they were hit by missiles belonging to a country roughly 8,000 miles away. Reach is global.

A fourth characteristic is that the official approach to terrorism claims not only global reach, but also a certain omniscient knowledge. They claim to know where terrorists are, and therefore, where to hit. To quote George Shultz again, "We know the difference between terrorists and freedom fighters and as we look around, we have no trouble telling one from the other." Only Osama bin Laden doesn't know that he was an ally one day and an enemy another. That's very confusing for Osama bin Laden. I'll come back to him toward the end; it's a real story.

Fifth, the official approach eschews causation. They don't look at why people resort to terrorism. Cause? What cause? Another example: on December 18, 1985, *The New York Times* reported that the foreign minister of Yugoslavia—you remember the days when there was a Yugoslavia—requested the secretary of state of the U.S. to consider the causes of Palestinian terrorism. The secretary of state, George Shultz, and I'm quoting from *The New York Times*, "went a bit red in the face. He pounded the table and told the visiting foreign minister, "There is no connection with any cause. Period." Why look for causes?

A sixth characteristic of the official approach to terrorism is the need for the moral revulsion we feel against terror to be selective. We are to denounce the terror of those groups which are officially disapproved. But we are to applaud the terror of those groups of whom officials do approve. Hence, President Reagan's statement, "I am a contra." We know that the contras of Nicaragua were by any definition terrorists, but the media heed the dominant view.

More importantly to me, the dominant approach also excludes from consideration the terrorism of friendly governments. Thus, the United States excused, among others, the terrorism of Pinochet, who killed one of my closest friends, Orlando Letelier, one of Chilean President Salvador Allende's top diplomats, killed in a car bombing in Washington, DC in 1976. And it excused the terror of Zia ul-Haq, the military dictator of Pakistan, who killed many of my friends there. All I want to tell you is that according to my ignorant calculations, the ratio of people killed by the state terror of Zia ul-Haq, Pinochet, Argentinian, Brazilian, Indonesian type, versus the killing of the PLO and other organizations is literally, conservatively 1,000 to 1. That's the ratio.

History unfortunately recognizes and accords visibility to power, not to weakness. Therefore, visibility has been accorded historically to dominant groups. Our time—the time that begins with Columbus—has been one of extraordinary unrecorded holocausts. Great civilizations have been wiped out. The Mayas, the Incas, the Aztecs, the American Indians, the Canadian Indians were all wiped out. Their voices have not been heard, even to this day. They are heard, yes, but only when the dominant power suffers, only when resistance has a semblance of costing, of exacting a price, when a Custer is killed or when a Gordon is besieged. That's when you know that there were Indians or Arabs fighting and dying.

My last point on this subject is that during the Cold War period, the United States sponsored terrorist regimes like Somoza in Nicaragua and Batista in Cuba, one after another. All kinds of tyrants have been America's friends. In Nicaragua it was the contra, in Afghanistan, the mujahideen.

Now, what about the other side? What is terrorism? Our first job should be to define the damn thing, name it, give it a description other than "moral equivalent of founding fathers" or "a moral outrage to Western civilization." This is what *Webster's Collegiate Dictionary* says: "Terror is an intense, overpowering fear." Terrorism is "the use of terrorizing methods of governing or resisting a government." This simple definition has one great virtue: it's fair. It focuses on the use of violence that is used illegally, extra-constitutionally, to coerce. And this definition is correct because it treats terror for what it is, whether a government or private group commits it.

Have you noticed something? Motivation is omitted. We're not talking about whether the cause is just or unjust. We're talking about consensus, consent, absence of consent, legality, absence of legality, constitutionality, absence of constitutionality. Why do we keep motives out? Because motives make no difference. In the course of my work I have identified five types of terrorism; state terrorism, religious terrorism (Catholics killing Protestants, Sunnis killing Shiites, Shiites killing Sunnis), criminal terrorism, political terrorism, and oppositional terrorism. Sometimes these five can converge and overlap. Oppositional protest terrorism can become pathological criminal terrorism. State terror can take the form of private terror. For example, we're all familiar with the death squads in Latin America or in Pakistan where the government has employed private people to kill its opponents. It's not quite official. It's privatized. In Afghanistan, Central America, and Southeast Asia, the CIA employed in its covert operations drug pushers. Drugs and guns often go together. The categories often overlap.

Of the five types of terror, the official approach is to focus on only one form— political terrorism—which claims the least in terms of loss of human lives and property. The form that exacts the highest loss is state terrorism. The second highest loss is created by religious terrorism, although religious terror has, relatively speaking, declined. If you are looking historically, however, religious terrorism has caused massive loss. The next highest loss is caused by criminal terrorism. A Rand Corporation study by Brian Jenkins examining a ten-year period (1978 to 1988) showed fifty percent of terrorism was committed without any political cause. No politics. Simply crime and pathology. So the focus is on only one, the political terrorist, the PLO, the bin Laden, whoever you want to take.

Why do they do it? What makes terrorists tick?

I would like to knock out some quick answers. First, the need to be heard. Remember, we are dealing with a minority group, the political, private terrorist. Normally, and there are exceptions, there is an effort to be heard, to get their grievances recognized and addressed by people. The Palestinians, for example, the superterrorists of our time, were dispossessed in 1948. From 1948 to 1968 they went to every court in the world. They knocked on every door. They had been completely deprived of their land, their country, and nobody was listening. In desperation, they invented a new form of terror: the airplane hijacking. Between 1968 and 1975 they pulled the world up by its ears. That kind of terror is a violent way of expressing long-felt grievances. It makes the world hear. It's normally undertaken by small, helpless groupings that feel powerless. We still haven't done the Palestinians justice, but at least we all know they exist. Now, even the Israelis acknowledge. Remember what Golda Meir, prime minister of Israel, said in 1970: There are no Palestinians. They do not exist.

They damn well exist now.

Secondly, terrorism is an expression of anger, of feeling helpless, angry, alone. You feel like you have to hit back. Wrong has been done to you, so you do it. During the hijacking of the TWA jet in Beirut, Judy Brown of Belmar, New Jersey, said that she kept hearing them yell, "New Jersey, New Jersey." What did they have in mind? She thought that they were going after her. Later on it turned out that the terrorists were referring to the U.S. battleship New Jersey, which had heavily shelled the Lebanese civilian population in 1983.

Another factor is a sense of betrayal, which is connected to that tribal ethic of revenge. It comes into the picture in the case of people like bin Laden. Here is a man who was an ally of the United States, who saw America as a friend; then he sees his country being occupied by the United States and feels betrayal. Whether there is a sense of right and wrong is not what I'm saying. I'm describing what's behind this kind of extreme violence.

Sometimes it's the fact that you have experienced violence at other people's hands. Victims of violent abuse often become violent people. The only time when Jews produced terrorists in organized fashion was during and after the Holocaust. It is rather remarkable that Jewish terrorists hit largely innocent people or U.N. peacemakers like Count Bernadotte of Sweden, whose country had a better record on the Holocaust. The men of Irgun, the Stern Gang, and the Hagannah terrorist groups came in the wake of the Holocaust. The experience of victimhood itself produces a violent reaction.

In modern times, with modern technology and means of communications, the targets have been globalized. Therefore, globalization of violence is an aspect of what we call globalization of the economy and culture in the world as a whole. We can't expect everything else to be globalized and violence not to be. We do have visible targets. Airplane hijacking is something new because international travel is relatively new, too. Everybody now is in your gunsight. Therefore the globe is within the gunsight. That has globalized terror.

Finally, the absence of revolutionary ideology has been central to the spread of terror in our time. One of the points in the big debate between Marxism and anarchism in the nineteenth century was the use of terror. The Marxists argued that the true revolutionary does not assassinate. You do not solve social problems by individual acts of violence. Social problems require social and political mobilization, and thus wars of liberation are to be distinguished from terrorist organizations. The revolutionaries didn't reject violence, but they rejected terror as a viable tactic of revolution. That revolutionary ideology has gone out at the moment.

In the 1980s and 1990s, revolutionary ideology receded, giving in to the globalized individual. In general terms, these are among the many forces that are behind modern terrorism.

To this challenge rulers from one country after another have been responding with traditional methods. The traditional method of shooting it out, whether it's with missiles or some other means. The Israelis are very proud of it. The Americans are very proud of it. The French became very proud of it. Now the Pakistanis are very proud of it. The Pakistanis say, Our commandoes are the best. Frankly, it won't work. A central problem of our time: political minds rooted in the past at odds with modern times, producing new realities.

Let's turn back for a moment to Osama bin Laden. *Jihad*, which has been translated a thousand times as "holy war," is not quite that. *Jihad* in Arabic means "to struggle." It could be struggle by violence or struggle by non-violent means. There are two forms, the small *jihad* and the big *jihad*. The small *jihad* involves external violence. The big *jihad* involves a struggle within oneself. Those are the concepts. The reason I mention it is that in Islamic history, *jihad* as an international violent phenomenon had for all practical purposes disappeared in the last four hundred years. It was revived suddenly with American help in the 1980s. When the Soviet Union intervened in Afghanistan, which borders Pakistan, Zia ul-Haq saw an opportunity and launched a *jihad* there against godless communism. The U.S. saw a God-sent opportunity to mobilize one billion Muslims against what Reagan called the Evil Empire. Money started pouring in. CIA agents starting going all over the Muslim world recruiting people to fight in the great *jihad*. Bin Laden was one of the early prize recruits. He was not only an Arab, he was a Saudi multimillionaire willing to put his own money into the matter. Bin Laden went around recruiting people for the *jihad* against communism.

I first met Osama bin Laden in 1986. He was recommended to me by an American official who may have been an agent. I was talking to the American and asked him who were the Arabs there that would be very interesting to talk with. By *there* I meant in Afghanistan and Pakistan. The American official told me, "You must meet Osama." I went to see Osama. There he was, rich, bringing in recruits from Algeria, from Sudan, from Egypt, just like Sheikh Abdul Rahman, an Egyptian cleric who was among those convicted for the 1993 World Trade Center bombing. At that moment, Osama bin Laden was a U.S. ally. He remained an ally. He turned at a particular moment. In 1990 the U.S. went into Saudi Arabia with military forces. Saudi Arabia is the holy place of Muslims, home of Mecca and Medina. There had never been foreign troops there. In 1990, during the build-up to the Gulf War, they went in in the name of helping Saudi Arabia defend itself. Osama bin Laden remained quiet. Saddam was defeated, but the American foreign troops stayed on in the land of the kaba (the sacred site of Islam in Mecca). Bin Laden wrote letter after letter saying, Why are you here? Get out! You came to help but you have stayed on. Finally he started a *jihad* against the other occupiers. His mission is to get American troops out of Saudi Arabia. His earlier mission was to get Russian troops out of Afghanistan.

A second point to be made about him is that he comes from a tribal people. Being a millionaire doesn't matter. His code of ethics is tribal. The tribal code of ethics consists of two words: loyalty and revenge. You are my friend. You keep your word. I am loyal to you. You break your word, I go on my path of revenge. For him, America has broken its word. The loyal friend has betrayed him. Now they're going to go for you. They're going to do a lot more. These are the chickens of the Afghanistan war coming home to roost.

What is my recommendation to America?

First, avoid extremes of double standards. If you're going to practice double standards, you will be paid with double standards. Don't use it. Don't condone Israeli terror, Pakistani terror, Nicaraguan terror, El Salvadoran terror, on the one hand, and then complain about Afghan terror or Palestinian terror. It doesn't work. Try to be even-handed. A superpower cannot promote terror in one place and reasonably expect to discourage terrorism in another place. It won't work in this shrunken world.

Do not condone the terror of your allies. Condemn them. Fight them. Punish them. Avoid covert operations and low-intensity warfare. These are breeding grounds for terrorism and drugs. In the Australian documentary about covert operations, *Dealing with the Demon*, I say that wherever covert operations have been, there is a drug problem. Because the structure of covert operations, Afghanistan, Vietnam, Nicaragua, Central America, etcetera, have been very hospitable to the drug trade. Avoid covert operations. It doesn't help.

Also, focus on causes and help ameliorate them. Try to look at causes and solve problems. Avoid military solutions. Terrorism is a political problem. Seek political solutions. Diplomacy works. Take the example of President Clinton's attack on bin Laden. Did they know what they were attacking? They say they know, but they don't know. At another point, they were trying to kill Qadaffi. Instead, they killed his young daughter. The poor child hadn't done anything. Qadaffi is still alive. They tried to kill Saddam Hussein. Instead they killed Laila bin Attar, a prominent artist, an innocent woman. They tried to kill bin Laden and his men. Twenty-five other people died. They tried to destroy a chemical factory in Sudan. Now they are admitting that they destroyed a pharmaceutical plant that produced half the medicine for Sudan.

Four of the missiles intended for Afghanistan fell in Pakistan. One was slightly damaged, two were totally damaged, one was totally intact. For ten years the American government has kept an embargo on Pakistan because Pakistan was trying, stupidly, to build nuclear weapons and missiles. So the U.S. has a technology embargo on my country. One of the missiles was intact. What do you think the Pakistani official told the *Washington Post*? He said it was a gift from Allah. Pakistan wanted U.S. technology. Now they have the technology, and Pakistan's scientists are examining this missile very carefully. It fell into the wrong hands. Look for political solutions. Military solutions cause more problems than they solve.

Finally, please help reinforce and strengthen the framework of international law. There was a criminal court in Rome. Why didn't the U.S. go there first to get a warrant against bin Laden, if they have some evidence? Enforce the United Nations. Enforce the International Court of Justice. Get a warrant, then go after him internationally.

Eqbal Ahmad was born in India but moved to the newly created state of Pakistan in 1947. His theories about national liberation and anti-imperialism developed over years of involvement in radical causes worldwide. Ahmad spent the last years of his life addressing the conflict between India and Pakistan regarding Kashmir and speaking out against the rise of Islamic fundamentalism and the influence of the Taliban in Pakistan. This reading is a transcript of a public talk he gave at the University of Colorado in October 1998. Ahmad died in 1999.

Note

1. Yitzhak Shamir is the other.

Chapter 2

Why Terrorism?

The psychology behind the motivation and behavior of terrorists has been examined extensively, but the public, as well as many specialists, have often been content to write off terrorists as irrational fanatics. Rather than see terrorism as an unintended outcome or the last resort of pathological individuals, Martha Crenshaw examines the use of terrorism as a deliberate strategy. She describes a framework of rational decision making, examining the calculations of cost versus benefit that go into the choice of terrorism as a weapon. Crenshaw concludes that neither the psychological nor the strategic explanation alone is adequate for examining terrorist behavior, but offers the strategic choice framework as an "antidote" to the persistent psychological stereotypes that she believes are nonproductive and potentially dangerous.

In the second selection, Louise Richardson examines the different levels of state sponsorship of terrorism, ranging from complete state control, such as in the case of Iran, to state financial support with no hope of control, such as Muammar al-Qaddafi's support for the Irish Republican Army. The U.S. government has tended to focus on state-sponsored terrorism as an instrument of foreign policy, reflected in the State Department's required annual list of state sponsors. But Richardson focuses here on terrorist movements as transnational connections among nonstate actors, and she encourages those responsible for directing counterterrorist strategy to examine the many possible levels of interaction between state and nonstate actors.

Martha Crenshaw, 1998

The Logic of Terrorism: Terrorist Behavior as a Product of Strategic Choice

This [selection] examines the ways in which terrorism can be understood as an expression of political strategy. It attempts to show that terrorism may follow logical processes that can be discovered and explained. For the purpose of presenting this source of terrorist behavior, rather than the psychological one, it interprets the resort to violence as a willful choice made by an organization for political and strategic reasons, rather than as the unintended outcome of psychological or social factors.[1]

In the terms of this analytical approach, terrorism is assumed to display a collective rationality. A radical political organization is seen as the central actor in the terrorist drama. The group possesses collective preferences or values and selects terrorism as a course of action from a range of perceived alternatives. Efficacy is the primary standard by which terrorism is compared with other methods of achieving political goals. Reasonably regularized decision-making procedures are employed to make an intentional choice, in conscious anticipation of the consequences of various courses of action or inaction. Organizations arrive at collective judgments about the relative effectiveness of different strategies of opposition on the basis of abstract strategic conceptions derived from ideological assumptions. This approach thus allows for the incorporation of theories of social learning.

Conventional rational-choice theories of individual participation in rebellion, extended to include terrorist activities, have usually been considered inappropriate because of the "free rider" problem. That is, the benefits of a successful terrorist campaign would presumably be shared by all individual supporters of the group's goals, regardless of the extent of their active participation. In this case, why should a rational person become a terrorist, given the high costs associated with violent resistance and the expectation that everyone who supports the cause will benefit, whether he or she participates or not? One answer is that the benefits of participation are psychological....

A different answer, however, supports a strategic analysis. On the basis of surveys conducted in New York and West Germany, political scientists suggest that individuals can be *collectively* rational.[2] People realize that their participation is important because group size and cohesion matter. They are sensitive to the implications of free-riding and perceive their personal influence on the provision of public goods to be high. The authors argue that "average citizens may adopt a collectivist conception of rationality because they recognize that what is individually rational is collectively irrational."[3] Selective incentives are deemed largely irrelevant.

One of the advantages of approaching terrorism as a collectively rational strategic choice is that it permits the construction of a standard from which deviations can be measured. For example, the central question about the rationality of some terrorist organizations, such as the West German groups of the 1970s or the Weather Underground in the United States, is whether or not they had a sufficient grasp of reality—some approximation, to whatever degree imperfect—to calculate the likely consequences of the courses of action they chose. Perfect knowledge of available alternatives and the consequences of each is not possible, and miscalculations are inevitable. The Popular Front for the Liberation of Palestine (PFLP), for example, planned the hijacking of a TWA flight from Rome in August 1969 to coincide with a scheduled address by President Nixon to a meeting of the Zionist Organization of America, but he sent a letter instead.[4]

Yet not all errors of decision are miscalculations. There are varied degrees of limited rationality. Are some organizations so low on the scale of rationality as to be in a different category from more strategically minded groups? To what degree is strategic reasoning modified by psychological and other constraints? The strategic choice framework provides criteria on which to base these distinctions. It also leads one to ask what conditions promote or discourage rationality in violent underground organizations.

The use of this theoretical approach is also advantageous in that it suggests important questions about the preferences or goals of terrorist organizations. For example, is the decision to seize hostages in order to bargain with governments dictated by strategic considerations or by other, less instrumental motives?

The strategic choice approach is also a useful interpretation of reality. Since the French Revolution, a strategy of terrorism has gradually evolved as a means of bringing about political change opposed by established governments. Analysis of the historical development of terrorism reveals similarities in calculation of ends and means. The strategy has changed over time to adapt to new circumstances that offer different possibilities for dissident action—for example, hostage taking. Yet terrorist activity considered in its entirety shows a fundamental unity of purpose and conception. Although this analysis remains largely on an abstract level, the historical evolution of the strategy of terrorism can be sketched in its terms.[5]

A last argument in support of this approach takes the form of a warning. The wide range of terrorist activity cannot be dismissed as "irrational" and thus pathological, unreasonable, or inexplicable. The resort to terrorism need not be an aberration. It may be a reasonable and calculated response to circumstances. To say that the reasoning that leads to the choice of terrorism may be logical is not an argument about moral justifiability. It does suggest, however, that the belief that terrorism is expedient is one means by which moral inhibitions are overcome....

The Conditions for Terrorism

The central problem is to determine when extremist organizations find terrorism useful. Extremists seek either a radical change in the status quo, which would confer a new advantage, or the defense of privileges they perceive to be threatened. Their dissatisfaction with the policies of the government is extreme, and their demands usually involve the displacement of existing political elites.[6] Terrorism is not the only method of working toward radical goals, and thus it must be compared to the alternative strategies available to dissidents. Why is terrorism attractive to some opponents of the state, but unattractive to others?

The practitioners of terrorism often claim that they had no choice but terrorism, and it is indeed true that terrorism often follows the failure of other methods. In nineteenth-century Russia, for example, the failure of nonviolent movements contributed to the rise of terrorism. In Ireland, terrorism followed the failure of Parnell's constitutionalism. In the Palestinian-Israeli struggle, terrorism followed the failure of Arab efforts at conventional warfare against Israel. In general, the "nonstate" or "substate" users of terrorism—that is, groups in opposition to the government, as opposed to government itself—are constrained in their options by the lack of active mass support and by the superior power arrayed against them (an imbalance that has grown with the development of the modern centralized and bureaucratic nation-state). But these constraints have not prevented oppositions from considering and rejecting methods other than terrorism. Perhaps because groups are slow to recognize the extent of the limits to action, terrorism is often the last in a sequence of choices. It represents the outcome of a learning process. Experience in opposition provides radicals with information about the potential consequences of their choices. Terrorism is likely to be a reasonably informed choice among available alternatives, some tried unsuccessfully. Terrorists also learn from the experiences of others, usually communicated to them via the news media. Hence the existence of patterns of contagion in terrorist incidents.[7]

Thus the existence of extremism or rebellious potential is necessary to the resort to terrorism but does not in itself explain it, because many revolutionary and nationalist organizations have explicitly disavowed terrorism. The Russian Marxists argued for years against the use of terrorism.[8] Generally, small organizations resort to violence to compensate for what they lack in numbers.[9] The imbalance between the resources terrorists are able to mobilize and the power of the incumbent regime is a decisive consideration in their decision making.

More important than the observation that terrorism is the weapon of the weak, who lack numbers or conventional military power, is the explanation for weakness. Particularly, why does an organization lack the potential to attract enough followers to change government policy or overthrow it?

One possibility is that the majority of the population does not share the ideological views of the resisters, who occupy a political position so extreme that their appeal is inherently limited. This incompatibility of preferences may be purely political, concerning, for example, whether or not one prefers socialism to capitalism. The majority of West Germans found the Red Army Faction's promises for the future not only excessively vague but distasteful. Nor did most Italians support aims of the neofascist groups that initiated the "strategy of tension" in 1969. Other extremist groups, such as the *Euzkadi ta Akatasuna* (ETA) in Spain or the Provisional Irish Republican Army (PIRA) in Northern Ireland, may appeal exclusively to ethnic, religious, or other minorities. In such cases, a potential constituency of like-minded and dedicated individuals exists, but its boundaries are fixed and limited. Despite the intensity of the preferences of a minority, its numbers will never be sufficient for success.

A second explanation for the weakness of the type of organization likely to turn to terrorism lies in a failure to mobilize support. Its members may be unwilling or unable to expend the time and effort required for mass organizational work. Activists may not possess the requisite skills or patience, or may not expect returns commensurate with their endeavors. No matter how acute or widespread popular dissatisfaction may be, the masses do not rise spontaneously; mobilization is required.[10] The organization's leaders, recognizing the advantages of numbers, may combine mass organization with conspiratorial activities. But resources are limited and organizational work is difficult and slow even under favorable circumstances. Moreover, rewards are not immediate. These difficulties are compounded in an authoritarian state, where the organization of independent opposition is sure to incur high costs. Combining violent provocation with nonviolent organizing efforts may only work to the detriment of the latter.

For example, the debate over whether to use an exclusively violent underground strategy that is isolated from the masses (as terrorism inevitably is) or to work with the people in propaganda and organizational efforts divided the Italian left-wing groups, with the Red Brigades choosing the clandestine path and Prima Linea preferring to maintain contact with the wider protest movement. In prerevolutionary Russia the Socialist-Revolutionary party combined the activities of a legal political party with the terrorist campaign of the secret Combat Organization. The IRA has a legal counterpart in Sinn Fein.

A third reason for the weakness of dissident organizations is specific to repressive states. It is important to remember that terrorism is by no means restricted to liberal democracies, although some authors refuse to define resistance to authoritarianism as terrorism.[11] People may not support a resistance organization because they are afraid of negative sanctions from the regime or because censorship of the press prevents them from learning of the possibility of rebellion. In this situation a radical organization may believe that supporters exist but cannot reveal themselves. The depth of this latent support cannot be measured or activists mobilized until the state is overthrown.

Such conditions are frustrating, because the likelihood of popular dissatisfaction grows as the likelihood of its active expression is diminished. Frustration may also encourage unrealistic expectations among the regime's challengers, who are not able to test their popularity. Rational expectations may be undermined by fantastic assumptions about the role of the masses. Yet such fantasies can also prevail among radical undergrounds in Western democracies. The misperception of conditions can lead to unrealistic expectations.

In addition to small numbers, time constraints contribute to the decision to use terrorism. Terrorists are impatient for action. This impatience may, of course, be due to external factors, such as psychological or organizational pressures. The personalities of leaders, demands from followers, or competition from rivals often constitute impediments to strategic thinking. But it is not necessary to explain the felt urgency of some radical organizations by citing reasons external to an instrumental framework. Impatience and eagerness for action can be rooted in calculations of ends and means. For example, the organization may perceive an immediate opportunity to compensate for its inferiority vis-à-vis the government. A change in the structure of the situation may temporarily alter the balance of resources available to the two sides, thus changing the ratio of strength between government and challenger.

Such a change in the radical organization's outlook—the combination of optimism and urgency—may occur when the regime suddenly appears vulnerable to challenge. This vulnerability may be of two sorts. First, the regime's ability to respond effectively, its capacity for efficient repression of dissent, or its ability to protect its citizens and property may weaken. Its armed forces may be committed elsewhere, for example, as British forces were during World War I when the IRA first rose to challenge British rule, or its coercive resources may be otherwise overextended. Inadequate security at embassies, airports, or military installations may become obvious. The poorly protected U.S. Marine barracks in Beirut were, for example, a tempting target. Government strategy may be ill-adapted to responding to terrorism.

Second, the regime may make itself morally or politically vulnerable by increasing the likelihood that the terrorists will attract popular support. Government repressiveness is thought to have contradictory effects; it both deters dissent and provokes a moral backlash.[12] Perceptions of the regime as unjust motivate opposition. If government actions make average citizens willing to suffer punishment for supporting antigovernment causes, or lend credence to the claims of radical opponents, the extremist organization may be tempted to exploit this temporary upsurge of popular indignation. A groundswell of popular disapproval may make liberal governments less willing (as opposed to less able) to use coercion against violent dissent.

Political discomfort may also be internationally generated. If the climate of international opinion changes so as to reduce the legitimacy of a targeted regime, rebels may feel encouraged to risk a repression that they hope will be limited by outside disapproval. In such circumstances the regime's brutality may be expected to win supporters to the cause of its challengers. The current situation in South Africa furnishes an example. Thus a heightened sensitivity to injustice may be produced either by government actions or by changing public attitudes.

The other fundamental way in which the situation changes to the advantage of challengers is through acquiring new resources. New means of financial support are an obvious asset, which may accrue through a foreign alliance with a sympathetic government or another, richer revolutionary group, or through criminal means such as bank robberies or kidnapping for ransom. Although terrorism is an extremely economical method of violence, funds are essential for the support of full-time activists, weapons purchases, transportation, and logistics.

Technological advances in weapons, explosives, transportation, and communications also may enhance the disruptive potential of terrorism. The invention of dynamite was thought by nineteenth-century revolutionaries and anarchists to equalize the relationship between government and challenger, for example. In 1885, Johann Most published a pamphlet titled *Revolutionary War Science*, which explicitly advocated terrorism. According to Paul Avrich, the anarchists saw dynamite "as a great equalizing force, enabling ordinary workmen to stand up against armies, militias, and police, to say nothing of the hired gunmen of the employers."[13] In providing such a powerful but easily concealed weapon, science was thought to have given a decisive advantage to revolutionary forces.

Strategic innovation is another important way in which a challenging organization acquires new resources. The organization may borrow or adapt a technique in order to exploit a vulnerability ignored by the government. In August 1972, for example, the Provisional IRA introduced the effective tactic of the one-shot sniper. IRA Chief of Staff Sean MacStiofain claims to have originated the idea: "It seemed to me that prolonged sniping from a static position had no more in common with guerrilla theory than mass confrontations."[14] The best marksmen were trained to fire a single shot and escape before their position could be located. The creation of surprise is naturally one of the key advantages of an offensive strategy. So, too, is the willingness to violate social norms pertaining to restraints on violence. The history of terrorism reveals a series of innovations, as terrorists deliberately selected targets considered taboo and locales where violence was unexpected.

These innovations were then rapidly diffused, especially in the modern era of instantaneous and global communications.

It is especially interesting that, in 1968, two of the most important terrorist tactics of the modern era appeared—diplomatic kidnappings in Latin America and hijackings in the Middle East. Both were significant innovations because they involved the use of extortion or blackmail. Although the nineteenth-century Fenians had talked about kidnapping the prince of Wales, the People's Will (Narodnaya Volya) in nineteenth-century Russia had offered to halt its terrorist campaign if a constitution were granted, and [although] American Marines were kidnapped by Castro forces in 1959, hostage taking as a systematic and lethal form of coercive bargaining was essentially new....

Terrorism has so far been presented as the response by an opposition movement to an opportunity. This approach is compatible with the findings of Harvey Waterman, who sees collective political action as determined by the calculations of resources and opportunities.[15] Yet other theorists—James Q. Wilson, for example—argue that political organizations originate in response to a threat to a group's values.[16] Terrorism can certainly be defensive as well as opportunistic. It may be a response to a sudden downturn in a dissident organization's fortunes. The fear of appearing weak may provoke an underground organization into acting in order to show its strength. The PIRA used terrorism to offset an impression of weakness, even at the cost of alienating public opinion: in the 1970s periods of negotiations with the British were punctuated by outbursts of terrorism because the PIRA did want people to think that they were negotiating from strength.[17] Right-wing organizations frequently resort to violence in response to what they see as a threat to the status quo from the left. Beginning in 1969, for example, the right in Italy promoted a "strategy of tension," which involved urban bombings with high numbers of civilian casualties, in order to keep the Italian government and electorate from moving to the left.

Calculation of Cost and Benefit

An organization or a faction of an organization may choose terrorism because other methods are not expected to work or are considered too time-consuming, given the urgency of the situation and the government's superior resources. Why would an extremist organization expect that terrorism will be effective? What are the costs and benefits of such a choice, compared with other alternatives? What is the nature of the debate over terrorism? Whether or not to use terrorism is one of the most divisive issues resistance groups confront, and numerous revolutionary movements have split on the question of means even after agreeing on common political ends.[18]

The costs of terrorism. The costs of terrorism are high. As a domestic strategy, it invariably invites a punitive government reaction, although the organization may believe that the government reaction will not be efficient enough to pose a serious threat. This cost can be offset by the advance preparation of building a secure underground. *Sendero Luminoso* (Shining Path) in Peru, for example, spent ten years creating a clandestine organizational structure before launching a campaign of violence in 1980. Furthermore, radicals may look to the future and calculate that present sacrifice will not be in vain if it inspires future resistance. Conceptions of interest are thus long term.

Another potential cost of terrorism is loss of popular support. Unless terrorism is carefully controlled and discriminate, it claims innocent victims. In a liberal state, indiscriminate violence may appear excessive and unjustified and alienate a citizenry predisposed to loyalty to the government. If it provokes generalized government repression, fear may diminish enthusiasm for resistance. This potential cost of popular alienation is probably least in ethnically divided societies, where victims can be clearly identified as the enemy and where the government of the majority appears illegal to the minority. Terrorists try to compensate by justifying their actions as the result of the absence of choice or the need to respond to government violence. In addition, they may make their strategy highly discriminate, attacking only unpopular targets.

Terrorism may be unattractive because it is elitist. Although relying only on terrorism may spare the general population from costly involvement in the struggle for freedom, such isolation may violate the ideological beliefs of revolutionaries who insist that the people must participate in their liberation. The few who choose terrorism are willing to forgo or postpone the participation of the many, but revolutionaries who oppose terrorism insist that it prevents the people from taking responsibility for their own destiny. The possibility of vicarious popular identification with symbolic acts of terrorism may satisfy some revolutionaries, but others will find terrorism a harmful substitute for mass participation.

The advantages of terrorism. Terrorism has an extremely useful agenda-setting function. If the reasons behind violence are skillfully articulated, terrorism can put the issue of political change on the public agenda. By attracting attention it makes the claims of the resistance a salient issue in the public mind. The government can reject but not ignore an opposition's demands. In 1974 the Palestinian Black September organization, for example, was willing to sacrifice a base in Khartoum, alienate the Sudanese government, and create ambivalence in the Arab world by seizing the Saudi Arabian embassy and killing American and Belgian diplomats. These costs were apparently weighed against the message to the world "to take us seriously." Mainstream Fatah leader Salah Khalef (Abu Iyad) explained: "We are planting the seed. Others will harvest it.... It is enough for us now to learn, for example, in reading the *Jerusalem Post*, that Mrs. Meir had to make her will before visiting Paris, or that Mr. Abba Eban had to travel with a false passport."[19] George Habash of the PFLP noted in 1970 that "we force people to ask what is going on."[20] In these statements, contemporary extremists echo the nineteenth-century anarchists, who coined the idea of propaganda of the deed, a term used as early as 1877 to refer to an act of insurrection as "a powerful means of arousing popular conscience" and the materialization of an idea through actions.[21]

Terrorism may be intended to create revolutionary conditions. It can prepare the ground for active mass revolt by undermining the government's authority and demoralizing its administrative cadres—its courts, police, and military. By spreading insecurity—at the extreme, making the country ungovernable—the organization hopes to pressure the regime into concessions or relaxation of coercive controls. With the rule of law disrupted, the people will be free to join the opposition. Spectacular humiliation of the government demonstrates strength and will and maintains the morale and enthusiasm of adherents and sympathizers. The first wave of Russian revolutionaries claimed that the aims of terrorism were to exhaust the enemy, render the government's position untenable, and wound the government's prestige by delivering a moral, not a physical, blow. Terrorists hoped to paralyze the government by their presence merely by showing signs of life from time to time. The hesitation, irresolution, and tension they would produce would undermine the processes of government and make the Czar a prisoner in his own palace.[22] As Brazilian revolutionary Carlos Marighela explained: "Revolutionary terrorism's great weapon is initiative, which guarantees its survival and continued activity. The more committed terrorists and revolutionaries devoted to anti-dictatorship terrorism and sabotage there are, the more military power will be worn down, the more time it will lose following false trails, and the more fear and tension it will suffer through not knowing where the next attack will be launched and what the next target will be."[23]

These statements illustrate a corollary advantage to terrorism in what might be called its excitational function: it inspires resistance by example. As propaganda of the deed, terrorism demonstrates that the regime can be challenged and that illegal opposition is possible. It acts as a catalyst, not substitute, for mass revolt. All the tedious and time-consuming organizational work of mobilizing the people can be avoided. Terrorism is a shortcut to revolution. As the Russian revolutionary Vera Figner described its purpose, terrorism was "a means of agitation to draw people from their torpor," not a sign of loss of belief in the people.[24]

A more problematic benefit lies in provoking government repression. Terrorists often think that by provoking indiscriminate repression against the population, terrorism will heighten popular disaffection, demonstrate the justice of terrorist claims, and enhance the attractiveness of the political alternative the terrorists represent. Thus, the West German Red Army Faction sought (in vain) to make fascism "visible" in West Germany.[25] In Brazil, Marighela unsuccessfully aimed to "transform the country's political situation into a military one. Then discontent will spread to all social groups and the military will be held exclusively responsible for failures."[26]

But profiting from government repression depends on the lengths to which the government is willing to go in order to contain disorder, and on the population's tolerance for both insecurity and repression. A liberal state may be limited in its capacity for quelling violence, but at the same time it may be difficult to provoke to excess. However, the government's reaction to terrorism may reinforce the symbolic value of violence even if it avoids repression. Extensive security precautions, for example, may only make the terrorists appear powerful.

Summary. To summarize, the choice of terrorism involves considerations of timing and of the popular contribution to revolt, as well as of the relationship between government and opponents. Radicals choose terrorism when they want immediate action, think that only violence can build organizations and mobilize supporters, and accept the risks of challenging the government in particularly provocative way. Challengers who think that organizational infrastructure must precede action, that rebellion without the masses is misguided, and that premature conflict with the regime can only lead to disaster favor gradualist strategies. They prefer methods such as rural guerrilla warfare, because terrorism can jeopardize painfully achieved gains or preclude eventual compromise with the government.

The resistance organization has before it a set of alternatives defined by the situation and by the objectives and resources of the group. The reasoning behind terrorism takes into account the balance of power between challengers and authorities, a balance that depends on the amount of popular support the resistance can mobilize. The proponents of terrorism understand this constraint and possess reasonable expectations about the likely results of action or inaction. They may be wrong about the alternatives that are open to them, or miscalculate the consequences of their actions, but their decisions are based on logical processes. Furthermore, organizations learn from their mistakes and from those of others, resulting in strategic continuity and progress toward the development of more efficient and sophisticated tactics. Future choices are modified by the consequences of present actions.

Hostage Taking as Bargaining

Hostage taking can be analyzed as a form of coercive bargaining. More than twenty years ago, Thomas Schelling wrote that "hostages represent the power to hurt in its purest form."[27] From this perspective, terrorists choose to take hostages because in bargaining situations the government's greater strength and resources are not an advantage. The extensive resort to this form of terrorism after 1968, a year that marks the major advent of diplomatic kidnappings and airline hijackings, was a predictable response to the growth of state power. Kidnappings, hijackings, and barricade-type seizures of embassies or public buildings are attempts to manipulate a government's political decisions.

Strategic analysis of bargaining terrorism is based on the assumption that hostage takers genuinely seek the concessions they demand. It assumes that they prefer government compliance to resistance. This analysis does not allow for deception or for the possibility that seizing hostages may be an end in itself because it yields the benefit of publicity. Because these limiting assumptions may reduce the utility of the theory, it is important to recognize them.

Terrorist bargaining is essentially a form of blackmail or extortion.[28] Terrorists seize hostages in order to affect a government's choices, which are controlled both by expectations of outcome (what the terrorists are likely to do, given the government reaction) and preferences (such as humanitarian values). The outcome threatened by the terrorist—the death of the hostages—must be worse for the government than compliance with terrorist demands. The terrorist has two options, neither of which necessarily excludes the other: to make the threat both more horrible and more credible or to reward compliance, a factor that strategic theorists often ignore.[29] That is, the cost to the government of complying with the terrorists' demands may be lowered or the cost of resisting raised.

The threat to kill the hostages must be believable and painful to the government. Here hostage takers are faced with a paradox. How can the credibility of this threat be assured when hostage takers recognize that governments know that the terrorists' control over the situation depends on live hostages? One way of establishing credibility is to divide the threat, making it sequential by killing one hostage at a time. Such tactics also aid terrorists in the process of incurring and demonstrating a commitment to carrying out their threat. Once the terrorists have murdered, though, their incentive to surrender voluntarily is substantially reduced. The terrorists have increased their own costs of yielding in order to persuade the government that their intention to kill all the hostages is real.

Another important way of binding oneself in a terrorist strategy is to undertake a barricade rather than a kidnapping operation. Terrorists who are trapped with the hostages find it more difficult to back down (because the government controls the escape routes) and, by virtue of this commitment, influence the government's choices. When terrorists join the hostages in a barricade situation, they create the visible and irrevocable commitment that Schelling sees as a necessary bond in bargaining. The government must expect desperate behavior, because the terrorists have increased their potential loss in order to demonstrate the firmness of their intentions. Furthermore, barricades are technically easier than kidnappings.

The terrorists also attempt to force the "last clear chance" of avoiding disaster onto the government, which must accept the responsibility for noncompliance that leads to the deaths of hostages. The seizure of hostages is the first move in the game, leaving the next move—which determines the fate of the hostages—completely up to the government. Uncertain communications may facilitate this strategy.[30] The terrorists can pretend not to receive government messages that might affect their demonstrated commitment. Hostage takers can also bind themselves by insisting that they are merely agents, empowered to ask only for the most extreme demands. Terrorists may deliberately appear irrational, either through inconsistent and erratic behavior or unrealistic expectations and preferences, in order to convince the government that they will carry out a threat that entails self-destruction.

Hostage seizures are a type of iterated game, which explains some aspects of terrorist behavior that otherwise seem to violate strategic principles. In terms of a single episode, terrorists can be expected to find killing hostages painful, because they will not achieve their demands and the government's desire to punish will be intensified. However, from a long-range perspective, killing hostages reinforces the credibility of the threat in the next terrorist incident, even if the killers then cannot escape. Each terrorist episode is actually a round in a series of games between government and terrorists.

Hostage takers may influence the government's decision by promising rewards for compliance. Recalling that terrorism represents an iterative game, the release of hostages unharmed when ransom is paid underwrites a promise in the future. Sequential release of selected hostages makes promises credible. Maintaining secrecy about a government's concessions is an additional reward for compliance. France, for example, can if necessary deny making concessions to Lebanese kidnappers because the details of arrangements have not been publicized.

Terrorists may try to make their demands appear legitimate so that governments may seem to satisfy popular grievances rather than the whims of terrorists. Thus, terrorists may ask that food be distributed to the poor. Such demands were a favored tactic of the *Ejercito Revolucionario del Pueblo (ERP)* in Argentina in the 1970s.

A problem for hostage takers is that rewarding compliance is not easy to reconcile with making threats credible. For example, if terrorists use publicity to emphasize their threat to kill hostages (which they frequently do), they may also increase the costs of compliance for the government because of the attention drawn to the incident.

In any calculation of the payoffs for each side, the costs associated with the bargaining process must be taken into account.[31] Prolonging the hostage crisis increases the costs to both sides. The question is who loses most and thus is more likely to concede. Each party presumably wishes to make the delay more costly to the other. Seizing multiple hostages appears to be advantageous to terrorists, who are thus in a position to make threats credible by killing hostages individually. Conversely, the greater the number of hostages, the greater the cost of holding them. In hijacking or barricade situations, stress and fatigue for the captors increase waiting costs for them as well. Kidnapping poses fewer such costs. Yet the terrorists can reasonably expect that the costs to governments in terms of public or international pressures may be higher when developments are visible.

Furthermore, kidnappers can maintain suspense and interest by publishing communications from their victims.

Identifying the obstacles to effective bargaining in hostage seizures is critical. Most important, bargaining depends on the existence of a common interest between two parties. It is unclear whether the lives of hostages are a sufficient common interest to ensure a compromise outcome that is preferable to no agreement for both sides. Furthermore, most theories of bargaining assume that the preferences of each side remain stable during negotiations. In reality, the nature and intensity of preferences may change during a hostage-taking episode. For example, embarrassment over the Iran-*contra* scandal may have reduced the American interest in securing the release of hostages in Lebanon.

Bargaining theory is also predicated on the assumption that the game is two-party. When terrorists seize the nationals of one government in order to influence the choices of a third, the situation is seriously complicated. The hostages themselves may sometimes become intermediaries and participants. In Lebanon, Terry Waite, formerly an intermediary and negotiator, became a hostage. Such developments are not anticipated by bargaining theories based on normal political relationships. Furthermore, bargaining is not possible if a government is willing to accept the maximum cost the terrorists can bring to bear rather than concede. And the government's options are not restricted to resistance or compliance; armed rescue attempts represent an attempt to break the bargaining stalemate. In attempting to make their threats credible—for example, by sequential killing of hostages—terrorists may provoke military intervention. There may be limits, then, to the pain terrorists can inflict and still remain in the game.

Conclusions

This essay has attempted to demonstrate that even the most extreme and unusual forms of political behavior can follow an internal, strategic logic. If there are consistent patterns in terrorist behavior, rather than random idiosyncrasies, a strategic analysis may reveal them. Prediction of future terrorism can only be based on theories that explain past patterns.

Terrorism can be considered a reasonable way of pursuing extreme interests in the political arena. It is one among the many alternatives that radical organizations can choose. Strategic conceptions, based on ideas of how best to take advantage of the possibilities of a given situation, are an important determinant of oppositional terrorism, as they are of the government response. However, no single explanation for terrorist behavior is satisfactory. Strategic calculation is only one factor in the decision-making process leading to terrorism. But it is critical to include strategic reasoning as a possible motivation, at a minimum as an antidote to stereotypes of "terrorists" as irrational fanatics. Such stereotypes are a dangerous underestimation of the capabilities of extremist groups. Nor does stereotyping serve to educate the public—or, indeed, specialists—about the complexities of terrorist motivations and behaviors.

Martha Crenshaw is the John Andrus professor of government at Wesleyan University, where she has taught international politics since 1974. She is the editor, with John Pimlott, of the *International Encyclopedia of Terrorism* and the author of countless articles and texts on the subject of political terrorism.

Crenshaw currently serves on a task force concerning foreign policy toward the Islamic world at the Brookings Institution.

Notes

1. For a similar perspective (based on a different methodology) see James DeNardo, *Power in Numbers: The Political Strategy of Protest and Rebellion* (Princeton, N.J.: Princeton University Press, 1985). See also Harvey Waterman, "Insecure 'Ins' and Opportune 'Outs': Sources of Collective Political Activity," *Journal of Political and Military Sociology* 8 (1980): 107–12, and "Reasons and Reason: Collective Political Activity in Comparative and Historical Perspective," *World Politics* 33 (1981): 554–89. A useful review of rational choice theories is found in James G. March, "Theories of Choice and Making Decisions," *Society* 20 (1982): 29–39.

2. Edward N. Muller and Karl-Dieter Opp, "Rational Choice and Rebellious Collective Action," *American Political Science Review* 80 (1986): 471–87.

3. Ibid., 484. The authors also present another puzzling question that may be answered in terms of either psychology or collective rationality. People who expected their rebellious behavior to be punished were more likely to be potential rebels. This propensity could be explained either by a martyr syndrome (or an expectation of hostility from authority figures) or intensity of preference—the calculation that the regime was highly repressive and thus deserved all the more to be destroyed. See pp. 482 and 484.

4. Leila Khaled, *My People Shall Live: The Autobiography of a Revolutionary* (London: Hodder and Stoughton, 1973), 128–31.

5. See Martha Crenshaw, "The Strategic Development of Terrorism," paper presented to the 1985 Annual Meeting of the American Political Science Association, New Orleans.

6. William A. Gamson, *The Strategy of Social Protest* (Homewood, Illinois: Dorsey Press, 1975).

7. Manus I. Midlarksy, Martha Crenshaw, and Fumihiko Yoshida, "Why Violence Spreads: The Contagion of International Terrorism," *International Studies Quarterly* 24 (1980): 262–98.

8. See the study by David A. Newell, *The Russian Marxist Response to Terrorism: 1878–1917* (Ph.D. dissertation, Stanford University, University Microfilms, 1981).

9. The tension between violence and numbers is a fundamental proposition in DeNardo's analysis; see *Power in Numbers*, chapters 9–11.

10. The work of Charles Tilly emphasizes the political basis of collective violence. See Charles Tilly, Louise Tilly, and Richard Tilly, *The Rebellious Century 1830–1930* (Cambridge: Harvard University Press, 1975), and Charles Tilly, *From Mobilization to Revolution* (Reading, Mass.: Addison-Wesley, 1978).

11. See Conor Cruise O'Brien, "Terrorism under Democratic conditions: The Case of the IRA," in *Terrorism, Legitimacy, and Power: The Consequences of Political Violence,* edited by Martha Crenshaw (Middletown, Conn.: Wesleyan University Press, 1983).

12. For example, DeNardo, in *Power in Numbers*, argues that "the movement derives moral sympathy from the government's excesses" (p. 207).

13. Paul Avrich, *The Haymarket Tragedy* (Princeton: Princeton University Press, 1984), 166.

14. Sean MacStiofain, *Memoirs of a Revolutionary* (N.p.: Gordon Cremonisi, 1975), 301.

15. Waterman, "Insecure 'Ins' and Opportune 'Outs'" and "Reasons and Reason."

16. *Political Organizations* (New York: Basic Books, 1973).

17. Maria McGuire, *To Take Arms: My Year with the IRA Provisionals* (New York: Viking, 1973), 110–11, 118, 129–31, 115, and 161–62.

18. DeNardo concurs; see *Power in Numbers*, chapter 11.

19. See Jim Hoagland, "A Community of Terror," *Washington Post*, 15 March 1973, pp. 1 and 13; also *New York Times*, 4 March 1973, p. 28. Black September is widely regarded as a subsidiary of Fatah, the major Palestinian organization headed by Yasir Arafat.

20. John Amos, *Palestinian Resistance: Organization of a Nationalist Movement* (New York: Pergamon, 1980), 193; quoting George Habash, interviewed in *Life Magazine*, 12 June 1970, 33.

21. Jean Maitron, *Histoire du mouvement anarchiste en France (1880–1914)*, 2d ed. (Paris: Société universitaire d'éditions et de librairie, 1955), 74–5.

22. "Stepniak" (pseud. for Sergei Kravshinsky), *Underground Russia: Revolutionary Profiles and Sketches from Life* (London: Smith, Elder, 1883), 278–80.

23. Carlos Marighela, *For the Liberation of Brazil* (Harmondsworth: Penguin, 1971), 113.

24. Vera Figner, *Mémoires d'une révolutionnaire* (Paris: Gallimard, 1930), 206.

25. *Textes des prisonniers de la "fraction armée rouge" et dernières lettres d'Ulrike Meinhof* (Paris: Maspéro, 1977), 64.

26. Marighela, *For the Liberation of Brazil*, 46.

27. Schelling, *Arms and Influence* (New Haven, Conn.: Yale University Press, 1966), 6.

28. Daniel Ellsburg, *The Theory and Practice of Blackmail* (Santa Monica: Rand Corporation, 1968).

29. David A. Baldwin, "Bargaining with Airline Hijackers," in *The 50% Solution*, edited by William I. Zartman, 404–29 (Garden City, N.Y.: Doubleday, 1976), argues that promises have not been sufficiently stressed. Analysts tend to emphasize threats instead, surely because of the latent violence implicit in hostage taking regardless of outcome.

30. See Roberta Wohlstetter's case study of Castro's seizure of American Marines in Cuba: "Kidnapping to Win Friends and Influence People," *Survey* 20 (1974): 1–40.

31. Scott E. Atkinson, Todd Sandler, and John Tschirhart, "Terrorism in a Bargaining Framework," *Journal of Law and Economics* 30 (1987): 1–21.

Louise Richardson, 1998

Global Rebels: Terrorist Organizations as Trans-National Actors

The widespread usage of the term terrorism, in many contexts, has rendered the word almost meaningless. Today, its only universally understood connotation is so pejorative that even terrorists don't admit to being terrorists anymore. A glance at current usage reveals child abuse, racism, and gang warfare all incorrectly described as terrorism. Thus, if terrorism is to be analyzed in any meaningful way, it must be readily distinguishable from other forms of violence, especially other forms of political violence. In this article, terrorism is defined as politically motivated violence, directed against non-combatant or symbolic targets and designed to communicate a message to a broader audience. The critical feature of terrorism is the deliberate targeting of innocents in an effort to convey a message to another party. This particular characteristic differentiates terrorism from the most proximate form of political violence: the irregular warfare of the guerrilla. While it could certainly be argued that states engage in terrorism, this article focuses on non-state actors: terrorist movements.

Although terrorism is most often targeted against domestic political structures to effect political change, this article focuses on the international connections between terrorists. Political scientists coined the term trans-nationalism when they realized that the prevailing state-centric paradigm could not adequately explain the extent and impact of international interactions. Trans-nationalism denotes the interplay between non-state actors—international interactions not directed by states. On the other hand, trans-governmentalism refers to relations between sub-units of governments not controlled by the national executives.

US Perceptions of Terrorism

The United States tends to see terrorism less as a trans-national force and more as an international one. More specifically, the United States generally perceives international terrorism as deliberately directed by governments, usually against US targets. In the 1980s, the notion of an extensive, covert Soviet conspiracy to undermine the West prevailed. Today, the prevailing image is that of the radical Islamic fundamentalist following instructions from Middle Eastern capitals. International terrorism, therefore, is seen as state-sponsored terrorism, and state-sponsored terrorism, like terrorism more generally, is something only the bad guys do.

In response to public concern about state-sponsored terrorism, the US State Department is required to report annually to Congress on the patterns of global terrorism and to list the states considered sponsors of terrorism. Congress then imposes trade sanctions on the designated states. Currently, there are seven states on the list: Cuba, Iran, Iraq, Libya, North Korea, Sudan and Syria. This list, of course, is a political instrument and reflects far more than the extent of state-sponsored terrorism. The economies of Cuba and North Korea, for example, ensure that neither government is in any position to promote, much less fund, international terrorism. Indeed, in 1995, the North Korean government repudiated terrorism and any support for it. The two governments remain on the list, ostensibly for providing a safe haven to terrorists, but more likely because domestic pressure from Cuban voters in Florida and alliance relations with South Korea make their removal politically difficult.

A more objective assessment of the evidence suggests that the use of terror as an instrument of foreign policy might not be the exclusive domain of expansionist communists or mad mullahs. Even impeccably liberal democracies might engage in such action. In the 1980s, however, the firmly held belief was that the United States faced a deliberate and dedicated cadre of communists under orders from Moscow to undermine the West. Among the staunch proponents of this view were President Reagan and his Secretary of State, Alexander Haig. There can be little doubt that terrorist movements did receive assistance from the Eastern bloc in the 1980s. Members of the German Red Army Faction clearly found refuge and financial support in East Germany. In 1982, Congressional hearings revealed extensive Soviet-funded training facilities provided for liberation movements operating in Sub-Saharan Africa. However, the hearings failed to establish a definite link between the training facilities and Soviet bloc control over the liberation movements.

Generally speaking, financial support for a group may purchase influence but not control over its activities. The same holds true for relations between allies. The vast sums of money that the United States gives Israel translate into US government influence, not control, over Israeli policy. Similarly, in spite of all the aid given the mujahadeen in their fight against the Russians, the US government has precious little influence on the factious Afghan fighters.

For numerous reasons, a state might decide to sponsor terrorism as an instrument of foreign policy. Until the end of the Cold War, scholars widely maintained that the bipolar structure of the international system lent itself to the sponsorship of terrorism. According to the argument, the nuclear stalemate between the superpowers made direct conflict too costly to contemplate, but competition inevitable. Therefore, the superpowers sought indirect outlets for competition: arms races, proxy wars (as in Ethiopia), or sponsorship of terrorism (as in southern Africa). In light of the continuation of terrorism in the face of the transformation of the international power structure from a bipolar to a unipolar system, it is more difficult to argue that the international distribution of power determines the use of terror. Nevertheless, the attractions of sponsorship remain the same. The costs are low, and if the terrorists succeed, the benefits are high. However, if they fail, sponsors can easily and plausibly disavow the group's actions.

Seen in this light, it is easier to understand how US support for Chilean anti-Allende forces in the 1970s, the Nicaraguan Contras in the 1980s, or for anti-Castro forces throughout that period could be interpreted as the use of terror as an instrument of foreign policy—a more neutral concept than state-sponsored terrorism. The US government had many good reasons to undermine the regimes in Santiago, Managua, and Havana and certainly had the military prowess to do so. However, because overt action would have generated both an international and domestic uproar, the government sought to operate behind the scenes by helping local groups with the same goals. The US rationale was very similar to that offered by Eastern-bloc governments at the time, and it may explain the failure of communication between the right, which saw a Soviet-led, communist backed, terrorist conspiracy, and the left, which feared a US-led, antisocialist, terrorist conspiracy. Terrorism, then, can be sponsored both by strong states reluctant to demonstrate their strength openly and by weak states that believe that they have no other effective weapons in their arsenal.

Five Degrees of Separation

Important distinctions exist between different types of terrorist-sponsor relationships. These ties range from full state direction at one end of the spectrum to simple support at the other end. The case of Iran, the country widely and rightly viewed as the primary state sponsor of terrorism at present, illustrates several of these distinctions.

First, at one end of the continuum—where state control is complete—is the murder of dissidents. The State Department accuses Iran (and Iraq) of state-sponsored terrorism in their killing of dissidents overseas: either leaders of domestic opposition groups or, as in the case of Iran, former officials of the Shah's regime. These individuals are invariably killed by members of Iranian or Iraqi intelligence services operating abroad. Among the more celebrated Iranian cases are the 1991 murder of the former Prime Minister Shahpur Bakhtiar and his aide in Paris and the 1996 discovery in Belgium of a massive mortar in a ship's cargo of pickles. The ship in question belonged to a wholly-owned subsidiary of the Iranian intelligence service, and the mortar was believed to have been intended for a prominent Iranian dissident.

The second stage along the continuum of control is the recruitment and training of operatives specifically for an overseas mission. While accurate information about these cases is extremely difficult to obtain, a good example is the three-year-long German trial of an Iranian and four Lebanese charged with the 1992 murder of Kurdish dissidents in Berlin. The trial revealed the long arm of Iranian intelligence. The four accused were convicted while the prosecutors charged that supreme leader Khamenei and President Rafsanjani approved the operation. The judge indicted the Iranian Minister of Intelligence for the crime.

The murder of dissidents, while reprehensible, does not constitute terrorism per se. It represents a strategy of illegal state repression rather than state-sponsored terrorism. The action is highly discriminating and is carried out against an intended target by what amounts to an arm of the government. Thus, assassinations of dissidents remain quite distinct from the random violence associated with terrorism.

The third step along the continuum is reached when a government closely controls and directs the actions of a terrorist group. Complete control exists in only a few cases and generally involves the use of intelligence services. Nevertheless, some Middle Eastern terrorist movements, albeit not many, appear to have very little independence from their sponsors. Two such examples are the Saiqa Palestinian Group and the Popular Front for the Liberation of Palestine-General Command (PLFP-GC). Both organizations receive directions from their main sponsor, Syria. In the case of the PLFP-GC, its leader—Ahmad Jibril—is a former captain in the Syrian Army. Moreover, the movement has its headquarters in Damascus and is heavily dependent on Syria for financial and logistical support.

The fourth level of control is by far the most common. In this case, a government provides training, funds, and safe haven for an autonomous terrorist group. This relationship is common for most of the Palestinian groups which jealously guard their independence. They accept assistance from several sponsors, in part to avoid exclusive dependence on any one. Most groups, like Hamas, try to supplement their government funding—in this case from Iran—with support from Palestinian expatriates and private benefactors in places like Saudi Arabia. In some cases, groups even accept help from sworn enemies. For example, the Kurdistan Worker's Party (PKK) accepts support from both Iran and Iraq, as well as from Syria.

When one of these terrorist groups commits an atrocity, one of the sponsoring states is usually blamed. While the state may indeed be pleased by the action, it may not have had any prior-knowledge of it. Thus, the sponsoring state may be responsible for the action in a moral sense, by supporting the perpetrators, but it is not directly responsible.

In its years at the forefront of the Western alliance, the United States has reacted with frustration when its enemies have exaggerated its influence over its allies. The United States can only try to persuade its allies but cannot dictate to them. In the same fashion, the United States tends to exaggerate the influence of other states on the actions of the terrorists they sponsor. Certainly the states have the ability to hurt the movements by denying them support, but they are rarely in a position to dictate. In February 1996, for example, the Iranian vice president met with Hamas leaders in Damascus immediately after several bombings in Israel, and he praised their successful efforts. A week later, Hamas claimed responsibility for two more bombings. There is no reason to believe that Hamas was following explicit Iranian instructions. They did not need to. As both Iran and Hamas share a virulent antipathy to the State of Israel, one does not need to direct the operations of the other. At the final step on the continuum of state control, the actions of a terrorist movement merely serve the ends of a sponsoring state. The state then offers financial support because it identifies its interests with that of the group. The support of the Libyan leader, Muammar al-Qaddafi, for the Irish Republican Army (IRA) can be seen in this light. Qaddafi actually knew very little about the situation in Northern Ireland or about the campaign waged by the IRA. He nevertheless provided the organization with training facilities, financial support, and several ships full of weaponry, simply because he knew that they were operating against Britain. His goal was to punish Britain for its collaboration in the US bombing of Tripoli, and his support of the IRA was a means to that end. IRA acceptance of Qaddafi's support, however, in no way led them to alter their military strategy.

An undifferentiated view of state-sponsorship of terrorism—one which fails to appreciate these different types of relationships—is unlikely to facilitate an understanding of the motivations underlying trans-national terrorism. Hence, an effective counter terrorist strategy would be difficult to develop.

Exporting Revolution

Another aspect of state-sponsored terrorism differentiates Iran from other countries on the US government's list of state sponsors: Iran's efforts since the successful 1979 revolution to export its revolution overseas. Religion has long been a powerful trans-national force in international relations. It does not respect national boundaries and has generated centuries of jurisdictional disputes between secular and clerical leaderships. The Ayatollah

Khomeini, a Shiite Muslim cleric who led the Iranian revolution, provided a theological justification for fundamentalist terrorism. He argued that Islam was threatened with destruction and that Shiite believers were obliged to fight in its defense.

It is important to bear in mind, however, that Iranian-sponsored terrorism is not solely or even primarily directed against the West; rather, it is directed against surrounding Gulf states, particularly Bahrain, Kuwait, Saudi Arabia, and Iraq. The Western victims of Iranian-sponsored terrorism have often been incidental. They were either caught in the embassy at the onset of the revolution, were kidnapped by the Iranian-backed Hezbullah group in Lebanon, or were victims of Iranian-backed terror in Israel. The rhetoric denouncing the United States as "the Great Satan" notwithstanding, Iran has not, in fact, led a terrorist war against the West.

Iran's support for terrorism is closely linked to support for Shiite opposition groups in nearby Gulf states. In 1987, when a Kuwaiti Shiite bombed a Kuwaiti oil installation and a Bahraini engineer tried to sabotage Bahrain's oil refinery, Iran sanctioned both incidents. In the late 1980s, there was a wave of terrorist activity in Kuwait backed by Shiite terrorist groups, which in turn, were supported by Iran. At one point, a Kuwaiti airplane was hijacked in an effort to secure the release of seventeen members of an Iranian-backed terrorist group. This type of activity, of course, is precisely the kind to which the West has been exposed for years, but it is clearly a mistake to think that such hostility is directed solely against the West. In 1988, Iran adjusted its sights and began to focus on Saudi Arabia after the death of 257 Iranian pilgrims making the hajj. Iran publicly called for the overthrow of the Saudi ruling family. Shiite Muslims were recruited and trained by Iran, and they carried out a wave of attacks directed against Saudi officials and the Saudi airline. Harsh repression by the Saudi authorities could not eliminate the terrorist incidents.

The widely held view that Middle Eastern terrorism exclusively targets the West is misplaced. Iranian-backed groups have sought to export the Iranian revolution to surrounding states, while radical Islamic groups such as al-Gama'at al-Islamiyya and al-Jihad in Egypt have tried to overthrow the secular leadership of their own government.

Terrorist Networks

The relationships between states and terrorist movements do not correspond directly to the pure form of trans-nationalism because they include a state as part of the equation. These relationships do not correspond to trans-governmentalism either, as they are not connections between subgroups of governments. Rather, they reflect an under-theorized, hybrid type of trans-nationalism between a state and an autonomous movement. The traditional state-centric paradigm sufficed to explain the cases where a sponsoring government directly controls terrorist movements. However, the cases in which movements remain independent or quasi-independent of any particular state suggest yet another level of international interaction.

Terrorist movements demonstrate a purer form of trans-national interaction in the relationships they form with each other. Insofar as terrorist movements coalesce and form linkages to operate together and have an independent impact on state policy, they are indeed trans-national actors. Given the clandestine nature of most terrorist groups, it is difficult to find evidence to demonstrate the extent of these linkages. Nevertheless, the evidence that exists shows that connections between groups occur for a variety of reasons: a shared ideology, a shared enemy, or simply, shared training facilities.

The left-wing social revolutionary movements that operated in Europe in the 1970s and 1980s—the German Red Army Faction (RAF), the Italian Red Brigades, and the French Direct Action—had much in common. Their members came from a similar social strata—the disaffected children of privilege. These men and women were motivated by a desire to destroy the corruption of contemporary capitalism and to replace it with a new, but ill-defined order based on Marxist-Leninist principles. The European revolutionaries formed linkages based on ideological affinity, establishing anti-imperialist fronts facilitated by their geographic proximity.

Other less-likely groups formed trans-national links for the simple reason of a shared enemy, usually the United States. The cooperation between several Palestinian and European groups provide a fitting example. Palestinian groups offered financial support to groups like the Italian Red Brigades if they, in turn, would intensify their attacks on US and NATO targets. These linkages were driven less by ideological affinity and more by the imperatives of the age old political dictum, "the enemy of my enemy is my friend." Members of disparate terrorist groups often made initial contact during sessions in Middle Eastern or North African training camps. Shared operating procedures and training with particular weapons both facilitated the formation of personal contacts and the execution of future joint operations.

A simple examination of the personnel involved in several celebrated terrorist escapades unearths dramatic evidence of trans-national collaboration. Members of the German Red Army Faction and the Popular Front for the Liberation of Palestine have exhibited a particular adroitness at forming international terrorist teams. The RAF participated in the 1975 kidnapping of eleven OPEC oil ministers in Vienna. The following year, the group participated in the Palestinian hijacking of an Air France airliner to Entebbe, Uganda, and in 1977, collaborated again in a hijacking of a Lufthansa plane to Mogadishu. The Lod massacre of 1972 also demonstrated the extent of international connections. The attack in a Tel Aviv airport was executed by members of the Japanese Red Army which had earlier joined with the PFLP in a "Declaration of World War." Members of the JRA subsequently took refuge in North Korea.

Trans-national relations between terrorist movements are not confined to Europe and the Middle East. A 1993 explosion under an auto repair shop in Managua, Nicaragua, revealed what one diplomat at the scene deemed "a one stop shopping center for Latin terrorists." Aside from the extensive arsenal which included tons of explosives, hundreds of assault rifles, and tens of surface to air missiles, the cache revealed an extensive filing system documenting the collaboration of Argentinean, Basque, Canadian, Chilean, Nicaraguan, Salvadoran, and Uruguayan terrorists. Besides the treasure trove of hundreds of passports and identification papers, the files provided detailed documentation of observations on scores of wealthy Latin American businessmen, ten of whom had already been kidnapped. Those convicted in the kidnapping of the Brazilian supermarket chain owner Abilio Diniz included a multinational group of Argentinians, Canadians, Chileans, and a Brazilian.

Historically, shared support from Cuba served to forge international links between terrorist groups in Latin America. The Managua explosion demonstrated that groups also cooperated without Cuban support. Moreover, it is important to note that even with their massive arsenal and documentation, these groups are only known to have succeeded in kidnapping ten wealthy Latin Americans. Like most terrorists, they have not, in fact, posed a vital security threat to the countries in which they operate.

International links between terrorist movements take many forms. Some groups are directed by states, some are independent of states, some have state involvement. The transnational links between terrorist groups are so varied that any one power cannot possibly orchestrate the entire network even at a regional level, much less a global one. These findings have implications both for policy makers and for academics. For academics, insofar as many of these links reflect a hybrid form of interaction between trans-nationalism and trans-governmentalism, they suggest an under-theorized area of international interaction. For policy makers, the fear of the specter of state sponsored terrorism replacing the global Soviet threat to US interests is clearly misplaced. Policy makers as well as academics would do well to draw critical distinctions between the relationships of movements and those who assist them because the most effective counter-terrorist strategy will be one directed to the source of terrorism.

Political scientist **Louise Richardson** is the executive dean of the Radcliffe Institute for Advanced Study. Since 1989 she has taught at Harvard University on international relations, terrorist movements, foreign policy, and international security. Her current research focuses on decision making inside terrorist movements.

Chapter 3

The New Terrorism Model

The authors in this chapter examine the new model of terrorism.

Colonel Russell Howard presents a framework for understanding the new model of terrorism. This framework distinguishes between the old politically motivated terrorist and the new transnational religiously motivated terrorist. He argues that terrorism is more violent; groups operate globally; terrorism is better financed; groups are better trained; groups are more difficult to penetrate; and he points out that the potential use of weapons of mass destruction completely change the calculus of today's terrorists. The nexus of these six elements creates an enemy that is difficult to find, difficult to defeat, and very dangerous. In thinking about this more dangerous world, it is important to understand how terrorism has changed so that we can move to a better understanding of how to address the problem in a comprehensive manner. Howard's framework is the starting point for any such analysis.

John Arquilla, David Ronfeldt, and Michele Zanini examine changes in terrorism in the information age. The classic motivation and rationales will not change, but conduct and operational characteristics will. The authors explore—often in what they outline as a deliberately speculative manner—organizational changes in a new era that allow for less hierarchical structures and flatter networks of power with dense communications; they look at changes in strategy and technology and how terrorism is evolving in a direction they label *netwar*. The article covers implications for the U.S. military and a look at how recent developments in Middle Eastern terrorism can be seen as early signs of a move toward netwar-type terrorism.

Brent Ellis discusses the new terrorism and the implications of the changing environment for developing counterterrorism policy. This new religiously motivated terrorism increases the complexity of the set of actors creating a broader range of motivations, goals, and tactics. Ellis outlines not only the way in which terrorism has changed but discusses the implications of the changes in terms of policy responses. In the end, he looks at whether or not this is an insurmountable challenge. His conclusion is important. The threat is not insurmountable yet we must work to counter the rapid change of techniques and procedures used by the terrorists. At the same time, we must develop better tools for understanding and managing the threat.

Russell D. Howard, 2003

Understanding Al Qaeda's Application of the New Terrorism— The Key to Victory in the Current Campaign

Introduction

Bruce Hoffman, head of terrorist research at the Rand Corporation and arguably one of the world's leading terrorism experts, put it this way: "I don't mean to sound perverse, but there is maybe a certain nostalgia for the old style of terrorism where there wasn't the threat of loss of life on a massive scale.... It's a real commentary on how much the world has changed."[1]

In much the same way that many Cold War warriors miss the predictability and transparency of the U.S.-Soviet confrontation, many intelligence professionals, military operators, pundits, and academics miss the familiarity of the type of terrorism that was quite dangerous, but in the end was merely a nasty sideshow to the greater East-West conflict.[2] The commando-style terrorism waged by the likes of Andreas Baader and Ulrike Mainhof of the German extreme left Rote Armee Faction or by Abu Nidal of the Fatah National Council (who was killed in Baghdad last August) was ruthless. However, it was not nearly as deadly as the threat the world faces today.[3] Now the old, predominantly state-sponsored terrorism paradigm has been supplanted by a religiously and ethnically motivated terrorism that "neither relies on the support of sovereign states nor is constrained by the limits on violence that state sponsors observed themselves or placed on their proxies."[4]

This "new terrorism" has a much greater potential to cause harm to America, the West, and all secular countries, including those in the Muslim world. Led by al Qaeda and Osama bin Laden, it "is built around loosely linked cells that do not rely on a single leader or state sponsor." This new terrorism is transnational, borderless, and prosecuted by non-state actors, and it is very, very dangerous.[5]

The "old" and "new" terrorism are distinguishable in six different ways:

1. The "new terrorism" is more violent. Under the old paradigm, terrorists wanted attention, not mass casualties. Now they want both.
2. Unlike their Cold War counterparts, who were primarily sub-state actors trying to effect change in local politics, today's terrorists are transnational, non-state actors who operate globally and want to destroy the West and all Islamic secular state systems.

The views expressed in this paper are those of the authors and do not necessarily reflect the official policy or position of the United States Military Academy, the Department of the Army, the Department of Defense, or the U.S. government.

3. The "new terrorists" are much better financed than their predecessors, who relied mainly on crime or the largess of state sponsors to fund their activities. Today's terrorists have income streams from legal and illegal sources, and are not accountable to state sponsors—or anybody else.

4. Today's terrorists are better trained in the arts of war and the black arts than those in past decades. We know this from the materials captured in al Qaeda's training camps in Afghanistan and from very similar training materials of other Muslim extremist groups found in Europe and Central Asia.

5. This generation's terrorists, particularly the religious extremists, are more difficult to penetrate than terrorists of previous generations. The networked, cellular structure used by al Qaeda and its allies is especially difficult to penetrate, especially for a hierarchical security apparatus like that in the United States. While bribes and sex traps could help catch terrorists for prosecution and information in the old days, now it is difficult to "turn" religious extremists using the same methods. Today, the $25 million reward on Osama bin Laden has yet to be collected, and it is unclear how successful other methods have been in getting bin Laden's followers to talk.

6. Most insidious is the availability of weapons of mass destruction (WMD). Back in the 1980s, when I first became engaged in counterterrorism, we were concerned about small arms, explosives (particularly plastique), rocket-propelled grenades, and the occasional shoulder-fired anti-aircraft missile. Today, the concern is about nuclear, radiological, chemical, and biological weapons—all of which are potentially catastrophic, with massive killing potential.

This article discusses these six distinguishing characteristics and concludes with observation that the differences between the "old" and "new" terrorism must be understood and addressed if the United States and the West want to be victorious in the "campaign against terror." Osama bin Laden's al Qaeda is the case study for this work because his organization and followers epitomize the "new terrorism" and are the number-one threat to America's security.

More Violent

In the past, "terrorists wanted a lot of people watching, not a lot of people dead."[6] "Unlike the terrorists of the 1960s to the 1990s, who generally avoided high casualty attacks for fear of the negative publicity they would generate, al Qaeda is not in the least concerned by such matters."[7] Terrorists in past decades did not want large body counts because they wanted converts; they also wanted a seat at the table. Today's terrorists are not particularly concerned about converts, and rather than wanting a seat at the table, "they want to destroy the table and everyone sitting at it."[8] In fact, religious terrorists such as al Qaeda, in particular, want casualties—lots of them.[9]

In the past, civilians most often became victims of terrorists' operations because they either were captives of hostage-taking events, or because they happened to be in the wrong place at the wrong time. Terrorists took hostages for three reasons: attention for their cause, the release of imprisoned comrades, or ransom (profit). The odds were—96 percent of the time in the 1980s—that hostages would survive the event. Victims were generally casualties because they happened to be in the proximity of an explosion, ambush, or bank robbery.

However, the motive was to get attention or money, not cause the deaths of civilians. Today, however, mass casualties are a primary aspect of bin Laden's strategy:

> By causing mass casualties on a regular basis [bin Laden] could hope to persuade the Americans to keep clear of overseas conflicts. There was also a retributive element to the strategy... the militants of al-Qaeda and like-minded groups clearly wanted to punish the Americans for a whole range of policies, particularly for those it pursued in the Middle East, as well as for what they saw as its irreligious decadence.[10]

Despite successes against the al Qaeda by coalition military forces in Afghanistan and police agencies around the world, its strategy is persistent and pervasive, and some predict that the "frequency and reach of al-Qaeda's attacks will continue to increase, even though their lethality may decrease slightly."[11]

Truly Global Operations, Conducted by Transnational Non-State Actors

In the 1970s and 1980s terrorism was mostly local. The terrorists were sub-state actors intent on overturning a state's political and/or economic system. Today, there has been a shift from localized terrorist groups, supported by state sponsors, to loosely organized, global networks of terrorists. This shift parallels a change from primarily politically motivated terrorism to one that is more religiously motivated.[12]

Al Qaeda's global network consists of permanent or independently operating semi-permanent cells of trained militants that have been established in more than seventy-six countries.[13] In fact, since September 11, more than 3,300 al Qaeda operatives, hailing from 47 different countries have been arrested in 97 countries.[14]

There is also growing evidence that al Qaeda is now subcontracting work to like-minded terrorists. According to Jessica Stern:

> Bin Laden's organization has also nurtured ties and now works closely with a variety of other groups around the world, including Ansar al Islam, based mainly in Iraq and Europe; Jemaah Islamiah in Southeast Asia; Abus Sayyaf and the Moro Islamic Liberation Front in the Philippines; and many Pakistani jihadi groups.[15]

These affiliated or like-minded groups have the capacity to carry out attacks and inflict pain on the United States under al Qaeda's banner, says Bruce Hoffman. In fact, new revelations about the emerging al Qaeda network—the depth of its ranks and its ties to "franchise" terrorists in up to seventy countries—shows that the intent to attack America, the West, and secular states around the world has not gone away.[16]

Perhaps most troubling of all is recent evidence that al Qaeda, a Sunni organization, is now cooperating with Hezbollah, a Shi'a group considered by many to be the most sophisticated terrorist group in the world.[17] "Hezbollah, which enjoys backing from Syria and Iran, is based in southern Lebanon and in the lawless 'tri-border' region of South America, where Paraguay, Brazil, and Argentina meet."[18]

Al Qaeda's targeting is global, which is also different from the local, tactical focus of earlier terrorist groups. Now, not only are targets selected to cause casualties without limit, they are selected to undermine the global economy: "They might be called strategic acts of destruction, rather than the tactical terrorist acts of the past."[19] According to Air Marshall Sir Timothy Garden, "it may have been possible for the international community to live with occasional acts of local terrorism around the world; it is much more difficult to live with non-state actors who have a mission to destroy a large part of the global system."[20]

In summary, we have seen the emergence of terrorism that is not ideological in a political sense, but is inspired by religious extremists working in cells, small groups, and larger coalitions.[21] They do not answer completely to any government; they operate across national borders; and have access to funding and advanced technology.[22] Such groups are not bound by the same constraints or motivated by the same goals as nation-states. And, unlike state-sponsored groups, religious extremists such as al Qaeda are not susceptible to traditional diplomacy or military deterrence. There is no state with which to negotiate or to retaliate against.

Well-Financed Organization

Al Qaeda learned from some of the failings of previous terrorist groups such as the Baeder Meinhof, Red Brigades, and the Abu Nidal group, all of which were perennially under-capitalized. According to Bruce Hoffman, al Qaeda under Osama bin Laden "saw the need to be much more flexible and to maintain a steady supply of money, which is crucial to lubricate the wheels of terrorism."[23]

Estimates of Osama bin Laden's personal wealth range from $18 million to as high as $200 million but, "it is most commonly agreed that bin Laden inherited approximately $57 million at age sixteen."[24] Bin Laden has been able to leverage his millions into a global financial empire by investing in legitimate business, taking advantage of the globalizing financial system, abusing the Islamic banking (*hawala*) system, and coercing an entire network of Islamic philanthropic and charitable institutions. The total net worth of the al Qaeda financial empire is unclear—my estimate is that it is probably in the hundreds of millions. What is clear is that between September 11, 2001 and October 2002, more than 165 countries enacted blocking actions against terrorist assets and approximately $112 million of these assets have been frozen worldwide ($34 million in the U.S. and $78 million overseas).[25] Nevertheless, these successes have not forced al Qaeda to cease operations, which is indicative of their deep, well-lined pockets.

Osama bin Laden's entrepreneurial skills are legendary. During his five-year stint in Sudan, he cornered the market on gum arabic, the basic ingredient in fruit juices produced in the United States.[26] "He also started an Islamic Bank, built a tannery, created an export company, launched construction projects and developed agricultural schemes."[27] Other business ventures included a trading company in Kenya, and a ceramic plant, publishing outlet and appliance firm in Yemen.[28]

Al Qaeda's misuse of the ancient *hawala* underground banking system, which allows money transfers without actual money movement, is particularly instructive. Seemingly custom made for al Qaeda, the *hawala* is an ancient system that originated in South Asia and is still used worldwide to conduct legitimate business. It is also used for money laundering. The components of *hawala* that distinguish it from other parallel remittance systems are trust and the extensive use of connections, such as family relationships or regional

affiliations. Unlike traditional banking, *hawala* makes minimal use of any sort of negotiable instruments or documentation. Transfers of money take place based on communications between members of a network of *hawaladars*, or *hawala* dealers.[29] A recent Council on Foreign Relations study illustrates how the *hawala* system works:

> Customers in one city hand their local *hawaladar* some money. That individual then contacts his counterpart across the world, who in turn distributes money out of his own resources to the intended recipient. The volume of transactions flowing through the system in both directions is such that the two *hawaladars* rarely have to worry about settlement.[30]

Hawaladars charge their customers a nominal cash transaction fee for the service. They are willing to carry each other's debts for long periods of time because they are often related through familial, clan, or ethnic associations.[31]

Al Qaeda also uses other methods to move funds. Cash smuggling is one; moving assets in the form of precious metals and gemstones is another. The gold trade and the *hawala* are especially symbiotic, as they flourish in the same locales, and offer complementary services to those moving assets across borders. Al Qaeda also uses traditional smuggling routes and methods favored by international drug traffickers, arms dealers, and other organized criminal groups to move funds.[32]

Charities and philanthropic organizations have also been sources of al Qaeda funding. Since December 2001, the assets of more than a dozen Islamic charities worldwide have been frozen, three of them based in the United States."[33] For example, U.S. authorities have designated the U.S.-based Benevolence International Foundation (BIF) a terrorist financier with links to the al Qaeda network, and its assets have been frozen in the United States, Canada, and Bosnia. But the bin Laden network is not the only terrorist element skimming funds from U.S. based charities.[34] In fact, the U.S. Treasury Department acted on overwhelming evidence that the Holy Land Foundation for Relief and Development, the self-proclaimed largest Muslim charity in the United States, was an arm of the Hamas, a radical Islamic organization that operates in the West Bank and Gaza strip.[35]

Well-Trained Operatives

Formalized terrorist training during the Cold War was generally conducted by the states sponsoring terrorist groups. It is known, for instance, that the former Soviet Union ran terrorism training camps at Simferpol in the Crimea, Ostrova, Czechoslovakia, and Pankow, East Germany. Captured PLO terrorist Adnan Jaber has given a comprehensive account of his Soviet training:

> He did a six month course there during which Russian military and civilian instructors covered propaganda methods, political affairs, tactical and weapons training. Other such courses dealt with advanced explosives work, bomb making, and training in biological and chemical warfare.[36]

However, it would be incorrect to assume that most terrorists during the Cold War years went through such formal training. More than likely, many went into action without such instruction and simply learned by doing.[37]

Al Qaeda manuals and records captured in Afghanistan training camps portray a comprehensive training and education program that emphasizes paramilitary training, Islamic studies, and current politics. Common to all al Qaeda members and its associate groups are fourteen personality traits and qualifications that are required before one can become an Islamist military operative:

> Knowledge of Islam, ideological commitment, maturity, self-sacrifice, discipline, secrecy and concealment of information, good health, patience, unflappability, intelligence and insight, caution and prudence, truthfulness and wisdom, and the ability to observe and analyze, and the ability to act.[39]

Aspiring operatives are also taught forgery, assassination techniques, and the conducting of maritime or vehicle suicide attacks.[40]

An al Qaeda manual, *Military Studies in the Jihad Against the Tyrants*, which was seized in Manchester, England, at the home of a bin Laden follower, is a condensed version of thousands of pages of al Qaeda training materials seized in Afghanistan. An English translation of the 180-page Arabic document was placed into evidence during the recent Kenya and Tanzania bombing trials in New York City. The manual is extraordinarily comprehensive and instructs terrorist operatives on an array of terrorist techniques, including the Jihad (Holy War); military organization; financial precautions and forged documents; security measures in public transportation; special operations and weapons; guidelines for beating and killing hostages; how to assassinate with poisons, spoiled food and feces; methods of physical torture; and methods of psychological torture.[41]

Al Qaeda's training is very eclectic and comprehensive; its tacticians and trainers have taken much from the special operations forces of several nations, including the United States, United Kingdom, and Russia. Indeed, al Qaeda fighters are as well- or better-trained than those of many national armies (as was the case in Afghanistan). What is more startling is the al Qaeda's "intelligence" and "black operations" acumen. "Unlike the rag-tag terrorist groups of the Cold War period" says Rohan Gunaratna, "sophisticated terrorist groups of the post-Cold War period such as al Qaeda, have developed intelligence wings comparable with government intelligence agencies."[42]

Groups that Are Difficult to Penetrate

Another difference between old and new terrorism is that the latter has adopted a networked and less hierarchical form. "Both the anti-capitalist and national liberation terrorist groups of the 1970s and 1980s mostly had hierarchical forms and chains of command."[43] Presently, in response to improvements in counterterror capabilities and increased cooperation among governments, global terrorist groups such as al Qaeda have adopted networked structural models instead of hierarchical structures. Globalization and rapid advances in digital communication technology have also increased the viability of these networks, though they are not totally dependent on the latest information technology. "While information technology has made networks more effective, low-tech means such as couriers and landline telephones can enable networks in certain circumstances."[44]

Strict adherence to a flat, diffused, cellular, networked structure has allowed al Qaeda to maintain a high degree of secrecy and security. "These cells are independent of other local groups al Qaeda may be aligned with, and range in size from two to fifteen members."[45] Using code, targets are announced in the general media and individuals or independent cells are expected to use initiative, stealth, and flexibility to destroy them.

The network will obviously be more likely to achieve long-term effectiveness if its members share a unifying ideology, common goals, or mutual interests, as is the case with al Qaeda.[46] Networks are most effective when they distribute the responsibility for operations and provide redundancies for key functions. "Operating cells need not contact or coordinate with other cells except for those essential to a particular operation or function."[47] Avoiding unnecessary coordination or approval provides deniability to terrorist leaders and enhances the security of terrorist operations.

Weakened by the disruption of its finances and communications, its base destroyed and its leaders in flight, al Qaeda is still dangerous and very difficult to penetrate.[48] Though they may share a common militant Islamic ideology, they have become a loose and "ever-shifting alliance of like-minded groups."[49] Instead of large, well-orchestrated attacks like those of September 11, al Qaeda operations are now smaller and less ambitious. However, they remain extremely dangerous, and their "killer cells" seem to be both growing and spawning imitations around the world.[50]

Access to Weapons of Mass Destruction

The sixth way the "new terrorists" differ from terrorists of the past is the most worrisome: they are determined to obtain and use nuclear, radiological, chemical and biological weapons of mass destruction (WMD). In a single act, terrorists using a weapon of mass destruction could cause the deaths of thousands, even millions of people.[51] Acquiring WMD has been made easier thanks to Information Age technologies and the availability of suppliers,[52] and recent discoveries in Afghanistan have confirmed that al Qaeda and other terrorist groups are actively pursuing the capability to use biological agents against United States and its allies.[53] According to David Kaye, this should not be a surprise:

> Only a blind, deaf and dumb terrorist group could have survived the last five years and not been exposed at least to the possibility of the use of WMD, while the more discerning terrorists would have found some tactically brilliant possibilities already laid out on the public record.[54]

"We must be prepared for new types of attacks; anything could happen," says Koichi Oizumi, an international relations professor at Nihon University in Tokyo, the city where the Aum Shinrikyo used sarin nerve gas to kill 12 and injure 250 in the first major use of a chemical agent in a terrorist attack.[55]

Steven Miller, director of the International Security Program at Harvard's Kennedy School, says that policy-makers should be particularly concerned about terrorist access to nuclear weapons. According to him, "opportunities for well-organized and well-financed terrorists to infiltrate a Russian nuclear storage facility are greater than ever."[56] And he

cated the material as soon as it arrived."[58]

In the past, any state that allowed a terrorist group it sponsored to use WMD against the United States, knew it would be committing suicide. And fear of nuclear retaliation was enough for the sponsors to keep the lid on. Today, any terrorist group with a known base of operations, even if it does not have a state sponsor, would similarly risk annihilation for waging a WMD terrorist attack. But today's al Qaeda has no state sponsor and it is a loosely organized global network, all of which make retaliation much more problematic.

Conclusion

To recap, six key factors differentiate al Qaeda from the terrorist organizations of more recent generations. First, al Qaeda is more violent. It has been responsible for the most lethal terrorist attack in history and has achieved the highest rate of lethality per attack ever.[59]

Second, while earlier terrorist organizations had local aspirations, al Qaeda has global reach and strategic objectives. Its operators are transnational, non-state actors who hold allegiance to a cause, not a state. This is problematic because the traditional forms of state interaction—diplomatic, economic, and military—to solve differences prior to conflict are difficult to apply in a non-state actor context. When things get testy, with whom do you negotiate, who do you sanction, and whom do you threaten with force? And, if a transnational, non-state actor like bin Laden uses a weapon of mass destruction against you, whom do you nuke?

Third, al Qaeda is a wealthy, multinational organization with several income streams. It has investments and concealed accounts worldwide, many in the Western societies bin Laden most despises.[60] Osama bin Laden and his followers will use their wealth to continue to leverage (coerce) governments for access and safe haven, just as they have done in the Sudan and Afghanistan. They will also pay to subcontract and franchise the services of like-minded terrorist organizations, all for the purpose of killing Americans.

Fourth, as Rohan Gunaratna says, al Qaeda is not a ragtag outfit. Al Qaeda operatives are well trained in military, special operations, and intelligence functions. Notwithstanding the coalition's victory in Afghanistan, the allies learned what made the al Qaeda global terrorist network a daunting foe: "a relatively sophisticated, well-trained and financed organization that drew on ongoing grass-roots support and a fanatical willingness to fight to the death."[61]

Fifth, strict adherence to its networked, cellular structure makes penetrating al Qaeda extremely difficult. Composed of many cells whose members do not know one another, never meet in one place together, and use strict communication discipline, the al Qaeda model is more than a match for Western intelligence agencies that rely mainly on technical means of intelligence collection.[62] "America's new enemies can't be bought, bribed, or even blackmailed."[63] They want to kill Americans and will do so at any cost.

Sixth, and most worrisome, is al Qaeda's determination to acquire nuclear, radiological, chemical and biological weapons of mass destruction. The potential for acquiring these weapons is made easier because of globalization, information technology, and the availability of shady suppliers. Indeed, the "new terrorism" has a global reach today that it did not have before the information generation and globalization. It can ride the back of the Web, and use advanced communications to move immense financial flows from Sudan to the Philippines or from Australia to banks in Florida.[64] And for $28.50, any Internet surfer, can purchase *Bacteriological Warfare: A Major Threat to North America*, which teaches how to grow deadly bacteria. Shady suppliers come from many countries, particularly Russia, which cannot offer employment to many ex-Soviet scientists and weaponeers, who were the elites in the old Soviet Empire. In fact, there are many reports of some peddling plutonium across Eastern Europe and of Russian scientists who once worked in Soviet labs linked to germ warfare now selling their services in the Middle East for hefty fees.[65]

As envisioned by al Qaeda, the "perfect new warfare" day would combine multiple attacks against America, designed to produce the greatest number of casualties. For maximum effect, these attacks would take place nearly simultaneously and at multiple geographically separated locations, much like the attacks of September 11 in New York City, Washington D.C., and a field in Pennsylvania.[66]

One might say that America's war against the "new terrorism" is far colder than the Cold War ever was—"cold" as in the "cold-blooded murder" of September 11. At least with the Soviets, we always knew who was in charge and that we couldn't be attacked without his orders. In fact, the U.S. president had a direct line to the Soviet leaders and he could work through difficult moments with them—personally.[67] By contrast, on September 11, 2001 we lost thousands of people; we know Osama bin Laden ordered the killing, but have no direct line to him or anyone else in his leadership. We also know that he and his followers will continue to hit the United States, its allies, and secular Islamic states again and again, until he and his network are stopped.

It has been said that generals always make the mistake of preparing to fight the last war instead of the next one. This article has illustrated the changes in the terrorist threat from Cold-War decades so that today's generals and their civilian masters understand how to fight the current war, not the past, and in hopes that we will not have to fight a war like this ever again.

Notes

1. Quoted frequently from several sources, Dr. Hoffman has mentioned this to me personally on two occasions.
2. John Mearsheimer, "Why We Will Soon Miss the Cold War," *Atlantic Monthly*, August 1990. See also, Glenn Sacks, "Why I Miss the Cold War," Internet: www.glennsacks.com
3. Brian Murphy, "The Shape of Terrorism Changes," *Fayetteville Observer*, Aug. 21, 2002, p. 9A.
4. Steven Simon and Danier Benjamin, "America and the New Terrorism," *Survival*, vol. 42, no. 1, Spring 2000, p. 69.
5. Ibid.
6. Quote attributed to Brian Jenkins in 1974. See Jessica Stern, "Loose Nukes, Poisons, and Terrorism: The New Threats to International Security," June 19, 1996.
7. Rohan Gunaratna, *Inside Al Qaeda—Global Network of Terror* (New York: Columbia University Press), p. 91.
8. Quote attributed to James Woolsey, 1994.
9. Bruce Hoffman, *Inside Terrorism* (New York: Columbia University Press, 1998), p. 205.

12. Michael Whine, "The New Terrorism," Internet: www.ict.org.il/articles/articledet.cfm? articleid=427

13. Jerrold M. Post, "Killing in the Name of God: Osama Bin Laden and Al Qaeda," *Know Thy Enemy: Profiles of Adversary Leaders and Their Strategic Cultures,* ed. Barry R. Schneider and Jerrold M. Post (Maxwell Air Force Base: USAF Counterproliferation Center), p. 33.

14. Conversation with Dr. Rohan Gunaratna, November 15, 2002 in Garmisch, Germany.

15. Jessica Stern, "The Protean Enemy," *Foreign Affairs*, July–August, 2003, p. 33.

16. See Ann Tyson, "Al Qaeda Broken, but Dangerous," *Christian Science Monitor*, Jun. 24, 2002, Internet: http://www.csmonitor.com/2002/0624/p01s02-usgn.htm

17. Jessica Stern, "The Protean Enemy (Al Qaeda)," *Foreign Affairs*, July–August, 2003, p. 31

18. Ibid., p.32.

19. Ibid.

20. Timothy Garden, "Security and the War Against Terrorism," *Foreign and Security Policy by Tim Garden*. http://www.tgarden.demon.co.uk/writings/articles/2002/020320riia.html

21. Stephen A. Cambone, *A New Structure for National Security Policy Planning* (Washington DC: Government Printing Office), 1996, p. 43.

22. Gideon Rose, "It Could Happen Here—Facing the New Terrorism," *Foreign Affairs*, March–April, 1999, p. 1.

23. Brian Murphy.

24. Multiple conversations with John Dorschner. Also, see John Dorschner, "A Shadowy Empire of Hate Was Born of a War in Afghanistan," Knight Ridder Newspapers, September 24, 2001.

25. "CDI Primer: Terrorist Finances," Oct. 25, 2002. Internet: http://www.cdi.org/terrorism/finance_primer-pr.cfm

26. Robin Wright, *Sacred Rage* (New York: Simon & Schuster, 2001), p. 252.

27. Ibid.

28. Ibid.

29. Patrick M. Yost and Harjit Singh Sandhu, "The *Hawala* Alternative Remittance System and its Role in Money Laundering," Interpol General Secretariat, January 2002. Internet: http://www.interpol.int/Public/FinancialCrime/MoneyLaundering/hawala/default.asp

30. Maurice Greenberg, "Terrorist Financing," Council on Foreign Relations Report, 2002, p. 11.

31. Ibid.

32. Ibid.

33. Neil A. Lewis, "The Money Trail-Court Upholds Freeze on Assets of Muslim Group Based in U.S.," *New York Times*, June 21, 2003, p. A11.

34. "US Accuses Charity of Financing Terror," *BBC Online*, Nov. 20. 2002.

35. Neil A. Lewis.

36. Christopher Dobson and Ronald Payne, *The Terrorists, Their Weapons, Leaders and Tactics* (New York: Facts on File, 1982), p. 80.

37. Ibid.

38. Jerrold M. Post, "Killing in the Name of God: Osama Bin Laden and Al Qaeda," *Know Thy Enemy: Profiles of Adversary Leaders and Their Strategic Cultures*, ed. Barry R. Schneider and Jerrold M. Post (Maxwell Air Force Base: USAF Counterproliferation Center), p. 35.

39. Rohan Gunaratna, p. 73.

40. Ibid.

41. Abdullah Ali Al-Salama, *Military Espionage in Islam*, http://www.skfriends.com/bin-laden-terrorist-manual.htm

42. Rohan Gunaratna, *Inside Al Qaeda—Global Network of Terror* (New York: Columbia University Press, 2002), p. 76.

43. Michael Whine, "The New Terrorism," Internet: www.ict.org.il/articles/articledet.cfm? articleid=427

44. *A Military Guide to Terrorism in the Twenty-First Century*, Version 1.0, May 13, 2003, p. 40.
45. Ibid., p. 33.
46. John Arquilla and David Ronfeldt, *Networks and Netwars* (Santa Monica: RAND, 2001), p. 9.
47. *A Military Guide to Terrorism in the Twenty-First Century*, Version 1.0, May 13, 2003, p. 40.
48. "Al-Qaeda, An Ever-Shifting Web," *The Economist*, October 19–25, 2002, p. 26
49. Ibid.
50. Ibid.
51. Richard B. Myers, "Fighting Terrorism in an Information Age," U.S. Department of State, International Information Programs, Aug. 19, 2002, p. 2. Internet, http://usinfo.state.gov/regional/nea/sasia/text/0819info.htm
52. Ibid.
53. Judith Miller, "Lab Suggests Qaeda Planned to Build Arms, Officials Say," *New York Times*, September 14, 2002, p. 1.
54. David Kay, "WMD Terrorism: Hype or Reality," in James M. Smith and William C. Thomas, ed., *The Terrorism Threat and US Government Response: Operational and Organizational Factors* (US Air Force Academy: INSS Book Series, 2001), p. 12.
55. Murphy.
56. Doug Gavel, "Can Nuclear Weapons Be Put Beyond the Reach of Terrorists," *Kennedy School of Government Bulletin*, Autumn 2002, p. 43.
57. Ibid., p. 45.
58. Ibid., p. 48.
59. Bruce Newsome, "Executive Summary," *Mass-Casualty Terrorism: Second Quarterly Forecast by the University of Reading Terrorism Forecasting Group,* June 13, 2003, p. 3. Internet: http://www.rdg.ac.uk/GSEIS/University_of_Reading_Terrorism_Forecast_2003Q2.pdf
60. Robin Wright, p. 253.
61. Ann Tyson, "Al Qaeda, Resilient and Organized," *Christian Science Monitor*, Mar. 7, 2002, p. 1.
62. Rohan Gunaratna, p. 76.
63. Glenn Sacks, p. 1.
64. Paul Mann, "Modern Military Threats: Not All They Might Seem?" *Aviation Week & Space Technology*, April 22, 2002, p. 1. (Gordon Adams quote)
65. Robert Reich, "Russian Capitalism," *The American Prospect*, April 26, 2003, http://www.prospect.org/webfeatures/2001/04/reich-r-04-26.html
66. "A Military Assessment of the al Qaeda Training Tapes," June 28, 2003, Internet: http://www.strategypage.com/articles/tapes/5.asp
67. Glenn Sacks, "Why I Miss the Cold War," July 1, 2003, www.glennsacks.com.

Information-Age Terrorism

The rise of network forms of organization is a key consequence of the ongoing information revolution. Business organizations are being newly energized by networking, and many professional militaries are experimenting with flatter forms of organization. In this [selection], we explore the impact of networks on terrorist capabilities, and consider how this development may be associated with a move away from emphasis on traditional, episodic efforts at coercion to a new view of terror as a form of protracted warfare. Seen in this light, the recent bombings of U.S. embassies in East Africa, along with the retaliatory American missile strikes, may prove to be the opening shots of a war between a leading state and a terror network. We consider both the likely context and the conduct of such a war, and offer some insights that might inform policies aimed at defending against and countering terrorism.

A New Terrorism (With Old Roots)

The age-old phenomenon of terrorism continues to appeal to its perpetrators for three principal reasons. First, it appeals as a weapon of the weak—a shadowy way to wage war by attacking asymmetrically to harm and try to defeat an ostensibly superior force. This has had particular appeal to ethnonationalists, racist militias, religious fundamentalists, and other minorities who cannot match the military formations and firepower of their "oppressors"—the case, for example, with some radical Middle Eastern Islamist groups vis-à-vis Israel, and, until recently, the Provisional Irish Republican Army (PIRA) vis-à-vis Great Britain.

Second, terrorism has appealed as a way to assert identity and command attention—rather like proclaiming, "I bomb, therefore I am." Terrorism enables a perpetrator to publicize his identity, project it explosively, and touch the nerves of powerful distant leaders. This kind of attraction to violence transcends its instrumental utility. Mainstream revolutionary writings may view violence as a means of struggle, but terrorists often regard violence as an end in itself that generates identity or damages the enemy's identity.

Third, terrorism has sometimes appealed as a way to achieve a new future order by willfully wrecking the present. This is manifest in the religious fervor of some radical Islamists, but examples also lie among millenarian and apocalyptic groups, like Aum Shinrikyo in Japan, who aim to wreak havoc and rend a system asunder so that something new may emerge from the cracks. The substance of the future vision may be only vaguely defined, but its moral worth is clear and appealing to the terrorist.

In the first and second of these motivations or rationales, terrorism may involve retaliation and retribution for past wrongs, whereas the third is also about revelation and rebirth, the coming of a new age. The first is largely strategic; it has a practical tone, and the objectives may be limited and specific. In contrast, the third may engage a transcendental, unconstrained view of how to change the world through terrorism.

Such contrasts do not mean the three are necessarily at odds; blends often occur. Presumptions of weakness (the first rationale) and of willfulness (in the second and third) can lead to peculiar synergies. For example, Aum's members may have known it was weak in a conventional sense, but they believed that they had special knowledge, a unique leader, invincible willpower, and secret ways to strike out.

These classic motivations or rationales will endure in the information age. However, terrorism is not a fixed phenomenon; its perpetrators adapt it to suit their times and situations. What changes is the conduct of terrorism—the operational characteristics built around the motivations and rationales.

This [selection] addresses, often in a deliberately speculative manner, changes in organization, doctrine, strategy, and technology that, taken together, speak to the emergence of a "new terrorism" attuned to the information age. Our principal hypotheses are as follows:

- **Organization.** Terrorists will continue moving from hierarchical toward information-age network designs. Within groups, "great man" leaderships will give way to flatter decentralized designs. More effort will go into building arrays of transnationally internetted groups than into building stand-alone groups.
- **Doctrine and strategy.** Terrorists will likely gain new capabilities for lethal acts. Some terrorist groups are likely to move to a "war paradigm" that focuses on attacking U.S. military forces and assets. But where terrorists suppose that "information operations" may be as useful as traditional commando-style operations for achieving their goals, systemic *disruption* may become as much an objective as target *destruction*. Difficulties in coping with the new terrorism will mount if terrorists move beyond isolated acts toward a new approach to doctrine and strategy that emphasizes campaigns based on swarming.
- **Technology.** Terrorists are likely to increasingly use advanced information technologies for offensive and defensive purposes, as well as to support their organizational structures. Despite widespread speculation about terrorists using cyberspace warfare techniques to take "the Net" down, they may often have stronger reasons for wanting to keep it up (e.g., to spread their message and communicate with one another).

In short, terrorism is evolving in a direction we call *netwar*. Thus, after briefly reviewing terrorist trends, we outline the concept of netwar and its relevance for understanding information-age terrorism. In particular, we elaborate on the above points about organization, doctrine, and strategy, and briefly discuss how recent developments in the nature and behavior of Middle Eastern terrorist groups can be interpreted as early signs of a move toward netwar-type terrorism.

Given the prospect of a netwar-oriented shift in which some terrorists pursue a war paradigm, we then focus on the implications such a development may have for the U.S. military. We use these insights to consider defensive antiterrorist measures, as well as proactive counterterrorist strategies. We propose that a key to coping with information-age terrorism will be the creation of interorganizational networks within the U.S. military and government, partly on the grounds that it takes networks to fight networks.

Caucasus, for awhile in Central America, and seemingly forever in the Middle East, attest to the brutality that increasingly attends this kind of warfare. These are not conflicts between regular, professional armed forces dedicated to warrior creeds and Geneva Conventions. Instead, even where regular forces play roles, these conflicts often revolve around the strategies and tactics of thuggish paramilitary gangs and local warlords. Some leaders may have some professional training; but the foot soldiers are often people who, for one reason or another, get caught in a fray and learn on the job. Adolescents and children with high-powered weaponry are taking part in growing numbers. In many of these conflicts, savage acts are increasingly committed without anyone taking credit—it may not even be clear which side is responsible. The press releases of the protagonists sound high-minded and self-legitimizing, but the reality at the local level is often about clan rivalries and criminal ventures (e.g., looting, smuggling, or protection rackets).[1]

Thus, irregular warfare has become endemic and vicious around the world. A decade or so ago, terrorism was a rather distinct entry on the spectrum of conflict, with its own unique attributes. Today, it seems increasingly connected with these broader trends in irregular warfare, especially as waged by nonstate actors. As Martin Van Creveld warns:

> In today's world, the main threat to many states, including specifically the U.S., no longer comes from other states. Instead, it comes from small groups and other organizations which are not states. Either we make the necessary changes and face them today, or what is commonly known as the modern world will lose all sense of security and will dwell in perpetual fear.[2]

Meanwhile, for the past several years, terrorism experts have broadly concurred that this phenomenon will persist, if not get worse. General agreement that terrorism may worsen parses into different scenarios. For example, Walter Laqueur warns that religious motivations could lead to "superviolence," with millenarian visions of a coming apocalypse driving "postmodern" terrorism. Fred Iklé worries that increased violence may be used by terrorists to usher in a new totalitarian age based on Leninist ideals. Bruce Hoffman raises the prospect that religiously-motivated terrorists may escalate their violence in order to wreak sufficient havoc to undermine the world political system and replace it with a chaos that is particularly detrimental to the United States—a basically nihilist strategy.[3]

The preponderance of U.S. conventional power may continue to motivate some state and nonstate adversaries to opt for terror as an asymmetric response. Technological advances and underground trafficking may make weapons of mass destruction (WMD—nuclear, chemical, biological weapons) ever easier for terrorists to acquire.[4] Terrorists' shifts toward looser, less hierarchical organizational structures, and their growing use of advanced communications technologies for command, control, and coordination, may further empower small terrorist groups and individuals who want to mount operations from a distance.

There is also agreement about an emergence of two tiers of terror: one characterized by hard-core professionals, the other by amateur cut-outs.[5] The deniability gained by terrorists operating through willing amateurs, coupled with the increasing accessibility of ever more destructive weaponry, has also led many experts to concur that terrorists will be attracted to engaging in more lethal destruction, with increased targeting of information and communications infrastructures.[6]

Some specialists also suggest that "information" will become a key target—both the conduits of information infrastructures and the content of information, particularly the media.[7] While these target-sets may involve little lethal activity, they offer additional theaters of operations for terrorists. Laqueur in particular foresees that, "If the new terrorism directs its energies toward information warfare, its destructive power will be exponentially greater than any it wielded in the past—greater even than it would be with biological and chemical weapons."[8] New planning and scenario-building is needed to help think through how to defend against this form of terrorism.[9]

Such dire predictions have galvanized a variety of responses, which range from urging the creation of international control regimes over the tools of terror (such as WMD materials and advanced encryption capabilities), to the use of coercive diplomacy against state sponsors of terror. Increasingly, the liberal use of military force against terrorists has also been recommended. Caleb Carr in particular espoused this theme, sparking a heated debate.[10] Today, many leading works on combating terrorism blend notions of control mechanisms, international regimes, and the use of force.[11]

Against this background, experts have begun to recognize the growing role of networks—of networked organizational designs and related doctrines, strategies, and technologies—among the practitioners of terrorism. The growth of these networks is related to the spread of advanced information technologies that allow dispersed groups, and individuals, to conspire and coordinate across considerable distances. Recent U.S. efforts to investigate and attack the bin Laden network (named for the central influence of Osama bin Laden) attest to this. The rise of networks is likely to reshape terrorism in the information age, and lead to the adoption of netwar—a kind of information-age conflict that will be waged principally by nonstate actors. Our contribution… is to present the concept of netwar and show how terrorism is being affected by it.

The Advent of Netwar—Analytical Background[12]

The information revolution is altering the nature of conflict across the spectrum. Of the many reasons for this, we call attention to two in particular. First, the information revolution is favoring and strengthening network forms of organization, often giving them an advantage over hierarchical forms. The rise of networks means that power is migrating to nonstate actors, who are able to organize into sprawling multi-organizational networks (especially all-channel networks, in which every node is connected to every other node) more readily than can traditional, hierarchical, state actors. Nonstate-actor networks are thought to be more flexible and responsive than hierarchies in reacting to outside developments, and to be better than hierarchies at using information to improve decisionmaking.[13]

Second, as the information revolution deepens, conflicts will increasingly depend on information and communications matters. More than ever before, conflicts will revolve around "knowledge" and the use of "soft power."[14] Adversaries will emphasize "information operations" and "perception management"—that is, media-oriented measures that aim to attract rather than coerce, and that affect how secure a society, a military, or other actor

likely to be more diffuse, dispersed, multidimensional, and ambiguous than more traditional threats. Metaphorically, future conflicts may resemble the Oriental game of *Go* more
than the Western game of chess. The conflict spectrum will be molded from end to end by
these dynamics:

- *Cyberwar*—a concept that refers to information-oriented military warfare—is becoming an important entry at the military end of the spectrum, where the language
  has normally been about high-intensity conflicts (HICs).
- *Netwar* figures increasingly at the societal end of the spectrum, where the language
  has normally been about low-intensity conflict (LIC), operations other than war
  (OOTW), and nonmilitary modes of conflict and crime.[15]

Whereas cyberwar usually pits formal military forces against each other, netwar is
more likely to involve nonstate, paramilitary, and irregular forces—as in the case of terrorism. Both concepts are consistent with the views of analysts such as Van Creveld, who
believe that a "transformation of war" is under way.[16] Neither concept is just about technology; both refer to comprehensive approaches to conflict—comprehensive in that they
mix organizational, doctrinal, strategic, tactical, and technological innovations, for offense
and defense.

Definition of Netwar

To be more precise, netwar refers to an emerging mode of conflict and crime at societal
levels, involving measures short of traditional war, in which the protagonists use network
forms of organization and related doctrines, strategies, and technologies attuned to the information age. These protagonists are likely to consist of dispersed small groups who communicate, coordinate, and conduct their campaigns in an internetted manner, without a
precise central command. Thus, information-age netwar differs from modes of conflict and
crime in which the protagonists prefer formal, stand-alone, hierarchical organizations, doctrines, and strategies, as in past efforts, for example, to build centralized movements along
Marxist lines.

The term is meant to call attention to the prospect that network-based conflict and crime
will become major phenomena in the decades ahead. Various actors across the spectrum of
conflict and crime are already evolving in this direction. To give a string of examples, netwar
is about the Middle East's Hamas more than the Palestine Liberation Organization (PLO),
Mexico's Zapatistas more than Cuba's Fidelistas, and the American Christian Patriot movement more than the Ku Klux Klan. It is also about the Asian Triads more than the Sicilian
Mafia, and Chicago's Gangsta Disciples more than the Al Capone Gang.

This spectrum includes familiar adversaries who are modifying their structures and
strategies to take advantage of networked designs, such as transnational terrorist groups,
black-market proliferators of WMD, transnational crime syndicates, fundamentalist and
ethno-nationalist movements, intellectual property and high-sea pirates, and smugglers of
black-market goods or migrants. Some urban gangs, back-country militias, and militant

single-issue groups in the United States are also developing netwar-like attributes. In addition, there is a new generation of radicals and activists who are just beginning to create information-age ideologies, in which identities and loyalties may shift from the nation-state to the transnational level of global civil society. New kinds of actors, such as anarchistic and nihilistic leagues of computer-hacking "cyboteurs," may also partake of netwar.

Many—if not most—netwar actors will be nonstate. Some may be agents of a state, but others may try to turn states into *their* agents. Moreover, a netwar actor may be both subnational and transnational in scope. Odd hybrids and symbioses are likely. Furthermore, some actors (e.g., violent terrorist and criminal organizations) may threaten U.S. and other nations' interests, but other netwar actors (e.g., peaceful social activists) may not. Some may aim at destruction, others at disruption. Again, many variations are possible.

The full spectrum of netwar proponents may thus seem broad and odd at first glance. But there is an underlying pattern that cuts across all variations: the use of network forms of organization, doctrine, strategy, and technology attuned to the information age.

More About Organizational Design

The notion of an organizational structure qualitatively different from traditional hierarchical designs is not recent; for example, in the early 1960s Burns and Stalker referred to the organic form as "a network structure of control, authority, and communication," with "lateral rather than vertical direction of communication." In organic structure,[17]

> omniscience [is] no longer imputed to the head of the concern; knowledge about the technical or commercial nature of the here and now task may be located anywhere in the network; [with] this location becoming the ad hoc centre of control authority and communication.

In the business world, virtual or networked organizations are being heralded as effective alternatives to bureaucracies—as in the case of Eastman Chemical Company and the Shell-Sarnia Plant—because of their inherent flexibility, adaptiveness, and ability to capitalize on the talents of all members of the organization.[18]

What has long been emerging in the business world is now becoming apparent in the organizational structures of netwar actors. In an archetypal netwar, the protagonists are likely to amount to a set of diverse, dispersed "nodes" who share a set of ideas and interests and who are arrayed to act in a fully internetted "all-channel" manner. Networks come in basically three types (or topologies) (see Figure 1):[19]

- The *chain* network, as in a smuggling chain where people, goods, or information move along a line of separated contacts, and where end-to-end communication must travel through the intermediate nodes.
- The *star*, hub, or wheel network, as in a franchise or a cartel structure where a set of actors is tied to a central node or actor, and must go through that node to communicate and coordinate.
- The *all-channel network*, as in a collaborative network of militant small groups where every group is connected to every other.

well defined, or blurred and porous in relation to the outside environment. All such variations are possible.

Figure 1

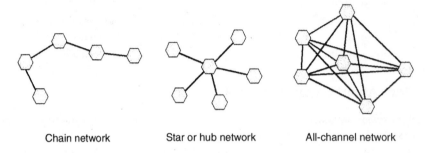

| Chain network | Star or hub network | All-channel network |

Each type may be suited to different conditions and purposes, and all three may be found among netwar-related adversaries—e.g., the chain in smuggling operations, the star at the core of terrorist and criminal syndicates, and the all-channel type among militant groups that are highly internetted and decentralized. There may also be hybrids. For example, a netwar actor may have an all-channel council at its core, but use stars and chains for tactical operations. There may also be hybrids of network and hierarchical forms of organization, and hierarchies may exist inside particular nodes in a network. Some actors may have a hierarchical organization overall, but use networks for tactical operations; other actors may have an all-channel network design, but use hierarchical teams for tactical operations. Again, many configurations are possible, and it may be difficult for an analyst to discern exactly what type of networking characterizes a particular actor.

Of the three network types, the all-channel has been the most difficult to organize and sustain historically, partly because it may require dense communications. However, it gives the network form the most potential for collaborative undertakings, and it is the type that is gaining strength from the information revolution. Pictorially, an all-channel netwar actor resembles a geodesic "Bucky ball" (named for Buckminster Fuller); it does not resemble a pyramid. The design is flat. Ideally, there is no single, central leadership, command, or headquarters—no precise heart or head that can be targeted. The network as a whole (but not necessarily each node) has little to no hierarchy, and there may be multiple leaders. Decision-making and operations are decentralized, allowing for local initiative and autonomy. Thus the design may sometimes appear acephalous (headless), and at other times polycephalous (Hydra-headed).[20]

The capacity of this design for effective performance over time may depend on the presence of shared principles, interests, and goals—at best, an overarching doctrine or ideology—that spans all nodes and to which the members wholeheartedly subscribe. Such a set of principles, shaped through mutual consultation and consensus-building, can enable them to be "all of one mind," even though they are dispersed and devoted to different tasks. It can provide a central ideational, strategic, and operational coherence that allows for tactical decentralization. It can set boundaries and provide guidelines for decisions and actions so that the members do not have to resort to a hierarchy—"they know what they have to do."[21]

The network design may depend on having an infrastructure for the dense communication of functional information. All nodes are not necessarily in constant communication, which may not make sense for a secretive, conspiratorial actor. But when communication is needed, the network's members must be able to disseminate information promptly and as broadly as desired within the network and to outside audiences.

In many respects, then, the archetypal netwar design corresponds to what earlier analysts called a "segmented, polycentric, ideologically integrated network" (SPIN):[22]

> By segmentary I mean that it is cellular, composed of many different groups.... By poly-centric I mean that it has many different leaders or centers of direction.... By networked I mean that the segments and the leaders are integrated into reticulated systems or networks through various structural, personal, and ideological ties. Networks are usually unbounded and expanding.... This acronym [SPIN] helps us picture this organization as a fluid, dynamic, expanding one, spinning out into mainstream society.

Caveats About the Role of Technology

To realize its potential, a fully interconnected network requires a capacity for constant, dense information and communications flows, more so than do other forms of organization (e.g., hierarchies). This capacity is afforded by the latest information and communications technologies—cellular telephones, fax machines, electronic mail (e-mail), World Wide Web (WWW) sites, and computer conferencing. Moreover, netwar agents are poised to benefit from future increases in the speed of communication, dramatic reductions in the costs of communication, increases in bandwidth, vastly expanded connectivity, and integration of communication with computing technologies.[23] Such technologies are highly advantageous for a netwar actor whose constituents are geographically dispersed.

However, caveats are in order. First, the new technologies, however enabling for organizational networking, may not be the only crucial technologies for a netwar actor. Old means of communications such as human couriers, and mixes of old and new systems, may suffice. Second, netwar is not simply a function of the Internet; it does not take place only in cyberspace or the infosphere. Some key battles may occur there, but a war's overall conduct and outcome will normally depend mostly on what happens in the real world. Even in information-age conflicts, what happens in the real world is generally more important than what happens in the virtual worlds of cyberspace or the infosphere.[24] Netwar is not Internet war.

Swarming, and the Blurring of Offense and Defense

This distinctive, often ad-hoc design has unusual strengths, for both offense and defense. On the offense, networks are known for being adaptable, flexible, and versatile vis-à-vis opportunities and challenges. This may be particularly the case where a set of actors can engage in *swarming*. Little analytic attention has been given to swarming, yet it may be a

idly and stealthily on a target, then dissever and redisperse, immediately ready to recombine for a new pulse. In other words, information-age attacks may come in "swarms" rather than the more traditional "waves."

In terms of defensive potential, well-constructed networks tend to be redundant and diverse, making them robust and resilient in the face of adversity. Where they have a capacity for interoperability and shun centralized command and control, network designs can be difficult to crack and defeat as a whole. In particular, they may defy counterleadership targeting—attackers can find and confront only portions of the network. Moreover, the deniability built into a network may allow it to simply absorb a number of attacks on distributed nodes, leading the attacker to believe the network has been harmed when, in fact, it remains viable, and is seeking new opportunities for tactical surprise.

The difficulties of dealing with netwar actors deepen when the lines between offense and defense are blurred, or blended. When *blurring* is the case, it may be difficult to distinguish between attacking and defending actions, particularly when an actor goes on the offense in the name of self-defense. The *blending* of offense and defense will often mix the strategic and tactical levels of operations. For example, guerrillas on the defensive strategically may go on the offense tactically; the war of the *mujahideen* in Afghanistan provides a modern example.

The blurring of offense and defense reflects another feature of netwar: it tends to defy and cut across standard boundaries, jurisdictions, and distinctions between state and society, public and private, war and peace, war and crime, civilian and military, police and military, and legal and illegal. A government has difficulty assigning responsibility to a single agency—military, police, or intelligence—to respond.

Thus, the spread of netwar adds to the challenges facing the nation-state in the information age. Nation-state ideals of sovereignty and authority are traditionally linked to a bureaucratic rationality in which issues and problems can be neatly divided, and specific offices can be charged with taking care of specific problems. In netwar, things are rarely so clear. A protagonist is likely to operate in the cracks and gray areas of society, striking where lines of authority crisscross and the operational paradigms of politicians, officials, soldiers, police officers, and related actors get fuzzy and clash.

Networks Versus Hierarchies: Challenges for Counternetwar

Against this background, we are led to a set of three policy-oriented propositions about the information revolution and its implications for netwar and counternetwar.[26]

Hierarchies have a difficult time fighting networks. There are examples across the conflict spectrum. Some of the best are found in the failings of governments to defeat transnational criminal cartels engaged in drug smuggling, as in Colombia. The persistence of religious revivalist movements, as in Algeria, in the face of unremitting state opposition, shows the robustness of the network form. The Zapatista movement in Mexico, with its legions of supporters and sympathizers among local and transnational nongovernmental organizations (NGOs), shows that social netwar can put a democratizing autocracy on the defensive and pressure it to continue adopting reforms.

It takes networks to fight networks. Governments that would defend against netwar may have to adopt organizational designs and strategies like those of their adversaries. This does not mean mirroring the adversary, but rather learning to draw on the same design principles of network forms in the information age. These principles depend to some extent upon technological innovation, but mainly on a willingness to innovate organizationally and doctrinally, and by building new mechanisms for interagency and multijurisdictional cooperation.

Whoever masters the network form first and best will gain major advantages. In these early decades of the information age, adversaries who have adopted networking (be they criminals, terrorists, or peaceful social activists) are enjoying an increase in their power relative to state agencies.

Counternetwar may thus require effective interagency approaches, which by their nature involve networked structures. The challenge will be to blend hierarchies and networks skillfully, while retaining enough core authority to encourage and enforce adherence to networked processes. By creating effective hybrids, governments may better confront the new threats and challenges emerging in the information age, whether generated by terrorists, militias, criminals, or other actors.[27] The U.S. Counterterrorist Center, based at the Central Intelligence Agency (CIA), is a good example of a promising effort to establish a functional interagency network,[28] although its success may depend increasingly on the strength of links with the military services and other institutions that fall outside the realm of the intelligence community.

Middle Eastern Terrorism and Netwar

Terrorism seems to be evolving in the direction of violent netwar. Islamic fundamentalist organizations like Hamas and the bin Laden network consist of groups organized in loosely interconnected, semi-independent cells that have no single commanding hierarchy.[29] Hamas exemplifies the shift away from a hierarchically oriented movement based on a "great leader" (like the PLO and Yasser Arafat).[30]

The netwar concept is consistent with patterns and trends in the Middle East, where the newer and more active terrorist groups appear to be adopting decentralized, flexible network structures. The rise of networked arrangements in terrorist organizations is part of a wider move away from formally organized, state-sponsored groups to privately financed, loose networks of individuals and subgroups that may have strategic guidance but enjoy tactical independence. Related to these shifts is the fact that terrorist groups are taking advantage of information technology to coordinate the activities of dispersed members. Such technology may be employed by terrorists not only to wage information warfare [IW], but also to support their own networked organizations.[31]

While a comprehensive empirical analysis of the relationship between (a) the structure of terrorist organizations and (b) group activity or strength is beyond the scope of this paper,[32] a cursory examination of such a relationship among Middle Eastern groups offers some evidence to support the claim that terrorists are preparing to wage netwar. The Middle East was selected for analysis mainly because terrorist groups based in this region have

Terrorist groups in the Middle East have diverse origins, ideologies, and organizational structures, but can be roughly categorized into traditional and new-generation groups. Traditional groups date back to the late 1960s and early 1970s, and the majority of these were (and some still are) formally or informally linked to the PLO. Typically, they are also relatively bureaucratic and maintain a nationalist or Marxist agenda. In contrast, most new-generation groups arose in the 1980s and 1990s, have more fluid organizational forms, and rely on Islam as a basis for their radical ideology.

The traditional, more-bureaucratic groups have survived to this day partly through support from states such as Syria, Libya, and Iran. The groups retain an ability to train and prepare for terrorist missions; however, their involvement in actual operations has been limited in recent years, partly because of successful counterterrorism campaigns by Israeli and Western agencies. In contrast, the newer and less hierarchical groups, such as Hamas, the Palestinian Islamic Jihad (PIJ), Hizbullah, Algeria's Armed Islamic Group (GIA), the Egyptian Islamic Group (IG), and Osama bin Laden's Arab Afghans, have become the most active organizations in and around the Middle East.

The traditional groups. Traditional terrorist groups in the Middle East include the Abu Nidal Organization (ANO), the Popular Front for the Liberation of Palestine (PFLP), and three PFLP-related splinters—the PFLP-General Command (PFLP-GC), the Palestine Liberation Front (PLF), and the Democratic Front for the Liberation of Palestine (DFLP).

The ANO was an integral part of the PLO until it became independent in 1974. It has a bureaucratic structure composed of various functional committees.[33] The activism it displayed in the 1970s and 1980s has lessened considerably, owing to a lessening of support from state sponsors and to effective counterterrorist campaigns by Israeli and Western intelligence services.[34] The very existence of the organization has recently been put into question, given uncertainty as to the whereabouts and fate of Abu Nidal, the leader of the group.[35]

The PFLP was founded in 1967 by George Habash as a PLO-affiliated organization. It has traditionally embraced a Marxist ideology, and remains an important PLO faction. However, in recent years it has suffered considerable losses from Israeli counterterrorist strikes.[36] The PFLP-General Command split from the PFLP in 1968, and in turn experienced a schism in the mid-1970s. This splinter group, which called itself the PLF, is composed of three subgroups, and has not been involved in high-profile acts since the 1985 hijacking of the Italian cruise ship *Achille Lauro*.[37] The PFLP was subjected to another split in 1969, which resulted in the Democratic Front for the Liberation of Palestine. The DFLP resembles a small army more than a terrorist group—its operatives are organized in battalions, backed by intelligence and special forces.[38] DFLP strikes have become less frequent since the 1970s, and since the late 1980s it has limited its attacks to Israeli targets near borders.[39]

What seems evident here is that this old generation of traditional, hierarchical, bureaucratic groups is on the wane. The reasons are varied, but the point remains—their way of waging terrorism is not likely to make a comeback, and is being superseded by a new way that is more attuned to the organizational, doctrinal, and technological imperatives of the information age.

The most active groups and their organization. The new generation of Middle Eastern groups has been active both in and outside the region in recent years. In Israel and the occupied territories, Hamas, and to a lesser extent the Palestinian Islamic Jihad, have shown their strength over the last four years with a series of suicide bombings that have killed more than one hundred people and injured several more.[40] Exploiting a strong presence in Lebanon, the Shi'ite Hizbullah organization has also staged a number of attacks against Israeli Defense Forces troops and Israeli cities in Galilee.[41]

The al-Gama'a al-Islamiya, or Islamic Group (IG), is the most active Islamic extremist group in Egypt. In November 1997 IG carried out an attack on Hatshepsut's Temple in Luxor, killing 58 tourists and 4 Egyptians. The Group has also claimed responsibility for the bombing of the Egyptian embassy in Islamabad, Pakistan, which left 16 dead and 60 injured.[42] In Algeria, the Armed Islamic Group (GIA) has been behind the most violent, lethal attacks in Algeria's protracted civil war. Approximately 70,000 Algerians have lost their lives since the domestic terrorist campaign began in 1992.[43]

Recently, the loosely organized group of Arab Afghans—radical Islamic fighters from several North African and Middle Eastern countries who forged ties while resisting the Soviet occupation of Afghanistan[44]—has come to the fore as an active terrorist outfit. One of the leaders and founders of the Arab Afghan movement, Osama bin Laden, a Saudi entrepreneur who bases his activities in Afghanistan,[45] is suspected of sending operatives to Yemen to bomb a hotel used by U.S. soldiers on their way to Somalia in 1992, plotting to assassinate President Clinton in the Philippines in 1994 and Egyptian President Hosni Mubarak in 1995, and of having a role in the Riyadh and Khobar blasts in Saudi Arabia that resulted in the deaths of 24 Americans in 1995 and 1996.[46] U.S. officials have pointed to bin Laden as the mastermind behind the U.S. embassy bombings in Kenya and Tanzania, which claimed the lives of more than 260 people, including 12 Americans.[47]

To varying degrees, these groups share the principles of the net-worked organization—relatively flat hierarchies, decentralization and delegation of decisionmaking authority, and loose lateral ties among dispersed groups and individuals.[48] For instance, Hamas is loosely structured, with some elements working openly through mosques and social service institutions to recruit members, raise funds, organize activities, and distribute propaganda. Palestinian security sources indicate that there are ten or more Hamas splinter groups and factions with no centralized operational leadership.[49] The Palestine Islamic Jihad is a series of loosely affiliated factions, rather than a cohesive group.[50] The pro-Iranian Hizbullah acts as an umbrella organization of radical Shiite groups, and in many respects is a hybrid of hierarchical and network arrangements; although the formal structure is highly bureaucratic, interactions among members are volatile and do not follow rigid lines of control.[51] According to the U.S. Department of State, Egypt's Islamic Group is a decentralized organization that operates without a single operational leader,[52] while the GIA is notorious for the lack of centralized authority.[53]

Unlike traditional terrorist organizations, Arab Afghans are part of a complex network of relatively autonomous groups that are financed from private sources forming "a kind of international terrorists' Internet."[54] The most notorious element of the network is Osama bin Laden, who uses his wealth and organizational skills to support and direct a multinational alliance of Islamic extremists. At the heart of this alliance is his own inner core group, known as Al-Qaeda ("The Base"), which sometimes conducts missions on its own, but more often in conjunction with other groups or elements in the alliance. The goal of the

he apparently does not play a direct command and control role over all operatives. Rather, he is a key figure in the coordination and support of several dispersed activities.[56] For instance, bin Laden founded the "World Islamic Front for Jihad Against Jews and Crusaders."[57] And yet most of the groups that participate in this front (including Egypt's Islamic Group) remain independent, although the organizational barriers between them are fluid.[58]

From a netwar perspective, an interesting feature of bin Laden's Arab Afghan movement is its ability to relocate operations swiftly from one geographic area to another in response to changing circumstances and needs. Arab Afghans have participated in operations conducted by Algeria's GIA and Egypt's IG. Reports in 1997 also indicated that Arab Afghans transferred training operations to Somalia, where they joined the Islamic Liberation Party (ILP).[59] The same reports suggest that the Arab Afghan movement has considered sending fighters to Sinkiang Uighur province in western China, to wage a holy war against the Chinese regime.[60] This group's ability to move and act quickly (and, to some extent, to swarm) once opportunities emerge hampers counterterrorist efforts to predict its actions and monitor its activities. The fact that Arab Afghan operatives were able to strike the U.S. embassies in Kenya and Tanzania substantiates the claim that members of this network have the mobility and speed to operate over considerable distances.

Although the organizational arrangements in these groups do not match all the basic features of the network ideal,[61] they stand in contrast to more traditional groups. Another feature that distinguishes the newer generation of terrorist groups is their adoption of information technology.

Middle Eastern Terrorist Groups and the Use of Information Technology

Information technology (IT) is an enabling factor for networked groups; terrorists aiming to wage netwar may adopt it not only as a weapon, but also to help coordinate and support their activities. Before exploring how Middle Eastern terrorist groups have embraced the new technology, we posit three hypotheses that relate the rise of IT to organization for netwar:

- The greater the degree of organizational networking in a terrorist group, the higher the likelihood that IT is used to support the network's decisionmaking.
- Recent advances in IT facilitate networked terrorist organizations because information flows are becoming quicker, cheaper, more secure, and more versatile.
- As terrorist groups learn to use IT for decisionmaking and other organizational purposes, they will be likely to use the same technology as an offensive weapon to destroy or disrupt.

Middle Eastern terrorist groups provide examples of information technology being used for a wide variety of purposes. As discussed below, there is some evidence to support the claim that the most active groups—and therefore the most decentralized groups—have embraced information technology to coordinate activities and disseminate propaganda and ideology.[62] At the same time, the technical assets and know-how gained by terrorist groups as they seek to form into multi-organizational networks can be used for offensive purposes—an Internet connection can be used for both coordination and disruption. The anecdotes provided here are consistent with the rise in the Middle East of what has been termed *techno-terrorism*, or the use by terrorists of satellite communications, e-mail, and the World Wide Web.[63]

Arab Afghans appear to have widely adopted information technology. According to reporters who visited bin Laden's headquarters in a remote mountainous area of Afghanistan, the terrorist financier has computers, communications equipment, and a large number of disks for data storage.[64] Egyptian "Afghan" computer experts are said to have helped devise a communication network that relies on the World Wide Web, e-mail, and electronic bulletin boards so that the extremists can exchange information without running a major risk of being intercepted by counterterrorism officials.[65]

Hamas is another major group that uses the Internet to share operational information. Hamas activists in the United States use chat rooms to plan operations and activities.[66] Operatives use e-mail to coordinate activities across Gaza, the West Bank, and Lebanon. Hamas has realized that information can be passed securely over the Internet because it is next to impossible for counterterrorism intelligence to monitor accurately the flow and content of Internet traffic. Israeli security officials have difficulty in tracing Hamas messages and decoding their content.[67]

During a recent counterterrorist operation, several GIA bases in Italy were uncovered, and each was found to include computers and diskettes with instructions for the construction of bombs.[68] It has been reported that the GIA uses floppy disks and computers to store and process instructions and other information for its members, who are dispersed in Algeria and Europe.[69] Furthermore, the Internet is used as a propaganda tool by Hizbullah, which manages three World Wide Web sites—one for the central press office (at www.hizbollah.org), another to describe its attacks on Israeli targets (at www.moqawama.org), and the last for news and information (at www.almanar. com.lb).[70]

The presence of Middle Eastern terrorist organizations on the Internet is suspected in the case of the Islamic Gateway, a World Wide Web site that contains information on a number of Islamic activist organizations based in the United Kingdom. British Islamic activists use the World Wide Web to broadcast their news and attract funding; they are also turning to the Internet as an organizational and communication tool.[71] While the vast majority of Islamic activist groups represented in the Islamic Gateway are legitimate, one group—the Global Jihad Fund—makes no secret of its militant goals.[72] The appeal of the Islamic Gateway for militant groups may be enhanced by a representative's claim, in an Internet Newsnet article in August 1996, that the Gateway's Internet Service Provider (ISP) can give "CIA-proof" protection against electronic surveillance.[73]

Summary Comment

This review of patterns and trends in the Middle East substantiates our speculations that the new terrorism is evolving in the direction of netwar, along the following lines:[74]

and the degree to which it adopts a networked structure.[75]

- Information technology is as likely to be used for organizational support as for offensive warfare.
- The likelihood that young recruits will be familiar with information technology implies that terrorist groups will be increasingly networked and more computer-friendly in the future than they are today.

Terrorist Doctrines—The Rise of a "War Paradigm"

The evolution of terrorism in the direction of netwar will create new difficulties for counterterrorism. The types of challenges, and their severity, will depend on the kinds of doctrines that terrorists develop and employ. Some doctrinal effects will occur at the operational level, as in the relative emphasis placed on disruptive information operations as distinct from destructive combat operations. However, at a deeper level, the direction in which terrorist netwar evolves will depend upon the choices terrorists make as to the overall doctrinal paradigms that shape their goals and strategies.

At least three terrorist paradigms are worth considering: terror as coercive diplomacy, terror as war, and terror as the harbinger of a "new world." These three engage, in varying ways, distinct rationales for terrorism—as a weapon of the weak, as a way to assert identity, and as a way to break through to a new world—discussed earlier in this [selection]. While there has been much debate about the overall success or failure of terrorism,[76] the paradigm under which a terrorist operates may have a great deal to do with the likelihood of success. Coercion, for example, implies distinctive threats or uses of force, whereas norms of "war" often imply maximizing destruction.

The Coercive-Diplomacy Paradigm

The first paradigm is that of coercive diplomacy. From its earliest days, terrorism has often sought to persuade others, by means of symbolic violence, either to do something, stop doing something, or undo what has been done. These are the basic forms of coercive diplomacy,[77] and they appear in terrorism as far back as the Jewish Sicarii Zealots who sought independence from Rome in the first century AD, up through the Palestinians' often violent acts in pursuit of their independence today.

The fact that terrorist coercion includes violent acts does not make it a form of war—the violence is exemplary, designed to encourage what Alexander George calls "forceful persuasion," or "coercive diplomacy as an alternative to war."[78] In this light, terrorism may be viewed as designed to achieve specific goals, and the level of violence is limited, or proportional, to the ends being pursued. Under this paradigm, terrorism was once thought to lack a "demand" for WMD, as such tools would provide means vastly disproportionate to the ends of terror. This view was first elucidated over twenty years ago by Brian Jenkins—though there was some dissent expressed by scholars such as Thomas Schelling—and continued to hold sway until a few years ago.[79]

The War Paradigm

Caleb Carr, surveying the history of the failures of coercive terrorism and the recent trends toward increasing destructiveness and deniability, has elucidated what we call a "war paradigm."[80] This paradigm, which builds on ideas first considered by Jenkins,[81] holds that terrorist acts arise when weaker parties cannot challenge an adversary directly and thus turn to asymmetric methods. A war paradigm implies taking a strategic, campaign-oriented view of violence that makes no specific call for concessions from, or other demands upon, the opponent. Instead, the strategic aim is to inflict damage, in the context of what the terrorists view as an ongoing war. In theory, this paradigm, unlike the coercive diplomacy one, does not seek a proportional relationship between the level of force employed and the aims sought. When the goal is to inflict damage generally, and the terrorist group has no desire or need to claim credit, there is an attenuation of the need for proportionality—the worse the damage, the better. Thus, the use of WMD can be far more easily contemplated than in a frame of reference governed by notions of coercive diplomacy.

A terrorist war paradigm may be undertaken by terrorists acting on their own behalf or in service to a nation-state. In the future, as the information age brings the further empowerment of nonstate and transnational actors, "stateless" versions of the terrorist war paradigm may spread. At the same time, however, states will remain important players in the war paradigm; they may cultivate their own terrorist-style commandos, or seek cut-outs and proxies from among nonstate terrorist groups.

Ambiguity regarding a sponsor's identity may prove a key element of the war paradigm. While the use of proxies provides an insulating layer between a state sponsor and its target, these proxies, if captured, may prove more susceptible to interrogation and investigative techniques designed to winkle out the identity of the sponsor. On the other hand, while home-grown commando-style terrorists may be less forthcoming with information if caught, their own identities, which may be hard to conceal, may provide undeniable evidence of state sponsorship. These risks for states who think about engaging in or supporting terrorism may provide yet more reason for the war paradigm to increasingly become the province of nonstate terrorists—or those with only the most tenuous linkages to particular states.

Exemplars of the war paradigm today are the wealthy Saudi jihadist, Osama bin Laden, and the Arab Afghans that he associates with. As previously mentioned, bin Laden has explicitly called for war-like terrorism against the United States, and especially against U.S. military forces stationed in Saudi Arabia. President Clinton's statement that American retaliation for the U.S. embassy bombings in East Africa represented the first shots in a protracted war on terrorism suggests that the notion of adopting a war paradigm to counter terror has gained currency.

The New-World Paradigm

A third terrorist paradigm aims at achieving the birth of what might be called a "new world." It may be driven by religious mania, a desire for totalitarian control, or an impulse toward ultimate chaos.[82] Aum Shinrikyo would be a recent example. The paradigm harks back to the dynamics of millennialist movements that arose in past epochs of social upheaval, when prophetae attracted adherents from the margins of other social movements and led small groups to pursue salvation by seeking a final, violent cataclysm.[83]

The Paradigms and Netwar

All three paradigms offer room for netwar. Moreover, all three paradigms allow the rise of "cybotage"—acts of disruption and destruction against information infrastructures by terrorists who learn the skills of cyberterror, as well as by disaffected individuals with technical skills who are drawn into the terrorist milieu. However, we note that terrorist netwar may also be a battle of ideas—and to wage this form of conflict some terrorists may want the Net *up*, not down.

Many experts argue that terrorism is moving toward ever more lethal, destructive acts. Our netwar perspective accepts this, but also holds that some terrorist netwars will stress disruption over destruction. Networked terrorists will no doubt continue to destroy things and kill people, but their principal strategy may move toward the nonlethal end of the spectrum, where command and control nodes and vulnerable information infrastructures provide rich sets of targets.

Indeed, terrorism has long been about "information"—from the fact that trainees for suicide bombings are kept from listening to international media, through the ways that terrorists seek to create disasters that will consume the front pages, to the related debates about countermeasures that would limit freedom of the press, increase public surveillance and intelligence gathering, and heighten security over information and communications systems. Terrorist tactics focus attention on the importance of information and communications for the functioning of democratic institutions; debates about how terrorist threats undermine democratic practices may revolve around freedom of information issues.

While netwar may be waged by terrorist groups operating with any of the three paradigms, the rise of networked groups whose objective is to wage war may be the one most relevant to and dangerous from the standpoint of the military. Indeed, if terrorists perceive themselves as warriors, they may be inclined to target enemy military assets or interests....

[Conclusion] Targeting Terrorists in the Information Age

The transition from hierarchical to networked terrorist groups is likely to be uneven and gradual. The netwar perspective suggests that, for the foreseeable future, various networked forms will emerge, coexisting with and influencing traditional organizations. Such organizational diversity implies the need for a counterterrorism strategy that recognizes the differences among organizational designs and seeks to target the weaknesses associated with each.

Counterleadership strategies or retaliation directed at state sponsors may be effective for groups led by a charismatic leader who enjoys the backing of sympathetic governments, but are likely to fail if used against an organization with multiple, dispersed leaders and private sources of funding. Networked organizations rely on information flows to function, and disruption of the flows cripples their ability to coordinate actions. It is no coincidence, for instance, that while the separation between Hamas political and military branches is well documented, this terrorist group jealously guards information on the connections and degree of coordination between the two.[84]

At the same time, the two-way nature of connectivity for information networks such as the Internet implies that the dangers posed by information warfare are often symmetric—the degree to which a terrorist organization uses information infrastructure for offensive purposes may determine its exposure to similar attacks by countering forces. While it is true that terrorist organizations will often enjoy the benefit of surprise, the IW tactics available to them can also be adopted by counterterrorists.

The key task for counterterrorism, then, is the identification of organizational and technological terrorist networks. Once such structures are identified, it may be possible to insert and disseminate false information, overload systems, misdirect message traffic, preclude access, and engage in other destructive and disruptive activities to hamper and prevent terrorist operations.

John Arquilla is a RAND Corporation consultant and an associate professor of defense analysis at the United States Naval Postgraduate School in Monterey, California.

David Ronfeldt is a senior social scientist at RAND whose research focuses on issues such as information revolution, netwar, and the rise of transnational networks of nongovernmental organizations.

Michele Zanini is a researcher at RAND. These experts are all contributors to the book *Countering the New Terrorism* (1999).

Notes

1. For an illuminating take on irregular warfare that emphasizes the challenges to the Red Cross, see Michael Ignatieff, "Unarmed Warriors," *The New Yorker*, March 24, 1997, pp. 56–71.
2. Martin Van Creveld, "In Wake of Terrorism, Modern Armies Prove to Be Dinosaurs of Defense," *New Perspectives Quarterly*, Vol. 13, No. 4, Fall 1996, p. 58.
3. See Walter Laqueur, "Postmodern Terrorism," *Foreign Affairs*, Vol. 75, No. 5, September/October 1996, pp. 24–36; Fred Iklé, "The Problem of the Next Lenin," *The National Interest*, Vol. 47, Spring 1997, pp. 9–19; Bruce Hoffman, *Responding to Terrorism Across the Technological Spectrum*, RAND, P-7874, 1994; Bruce Hoffman, *Inside Terrorism*, Columbia University Press, New York, 1998; Robert Kaplan, "The Coming Anarchy," *Atlantic Monthly*, February 1994, pp. 44–76.
4. See J. Kenneth Campbell, "Weapon of Mass Destruction Terrorism," Master's thesis, Naval Postgraduate School, Monterey, California, 1996.
5. Bruce Hoffman and Caleb Carr, "Terrorism: Who Is Fighting Whom?" *World Policy Journal*, Vol. 14, No. 1, Spring 1997, pp. 97–104.
6. For instance, Martin Shubik, "Terrorism, Technology, and the Socioeconomics of Death," *Comparative Strategy*, Vol. 16, No. 4, October–December 1997, pp. 399–414; as well as Hoffman, 1998.
7. See Matthew Littleton, "Information Age Terrorism," MA thesis, U.S. Naval Postgraduate School, 1995, and Brigitte Nacos, *Terrorism and the Media*, Columbia University Press, New York, 1994.

10. Caleb Carr, "Terrorism as Warfare," *World Policy Journal*, Vol. 13, No. 4, Winter 1996–1997, pp. 1–12. This theme was advocated early by Gayle Rivers, *The War Against the Terrorists: How to Fight and Win,* Stein and Day, New York, 1986. For more on the debate, see Hoffman and Carr, 1997.

11. See, for instance, Benjamin Netanyahu, *Winning the War Against Terrorism*, Simon and Schuster, New York, 1996, and John Kerry (Senator), *The New War*, Simon & Schuster, New York, 1997.

12. This analytical background is drawn from John Arquilla and David Ronfeldt, *The Advent of Netwar*, RAND, MR-678-OSD, 1996, and David Ronfeldt, John Arquilla, Graham Fuller, and Melissa Fuller, *The Zapatista "Social Netwar" in Mexico*, RAND, MR-994-A, forthcoming. Also see John Arquilla and David Ronfeldt (eds.), *In Athena's Camp: Preparing for Conflict in the Information Age*, RAND, MR-880-OSD/RC, 1997.

13. For background on this issue, see Charles Heckscher, "Defining the Post-Bureaucratic Type," in Charles Heckscher and Anne Donnelon (eds.), *The Post-Bureaucratic Organization*, Sage, Thousand Oaks, California, 1995, pp. 50–52.

14. The concept of soft power was introduced by Joseph S. Nye in *Bound to Lead: The Changing Nature of American Power*, Basic Books, New York, 1990, and further elaborated in Joseph S. Nye and William A. Owens, "America's Information Edge," *Foreign Affairs*, Vol. 75, No. 2, March/April 1996.

15. For more on information-age conflict, netwar, and cyberwar, see John Arquilla and David Ronfeldt, "Cyberwar is Coming!" *Comparative Strategy*, Vol. 12, No. 2, Summer 1993, pp. 141–165, and Arquilla and Ronfeldt, 1996 and 1997.

16. Martin Van Creveld, *The Transformation of War*, Free Press, New York, 1991.

17. T. Burns and G. M. Stalker, *The Management of Innovation*, Tavistock, London, 1961, p. 121.

18. See, for instance, Jessica Lipnack and Jeffrey Stamps, *The Age of the Network*, Wiley & Sons, New York, 1994, pp. 51–78, and Heckscher, "Defining the Post-Bureaucratic Type," p. 45.

19. Adapted from William M. Evan, "An Organization-Set Model of Interorganizational Relations," in Matthew Tuite, Roger Chisholm, and Michael Radnor (eds.), *Interorganizational Decisionmaking*, Aldine Publishing Company, Chicago, 1972.

20. The structure may also be cellular, although the presence of cells does not necessarily mean a network exists. A hierarchy can also be cellular, as is the case with some subversive organizations. A key difference between cells and nodes is that the former are designed to minimize information flows for security reasons (usually only the head of the cell reports to the leadership), while nodes in principle can easily establish connections with other parts of the network (so that communications and coordination can occur horizontally).

21. The quotation is from a doctrinal statement by Louis Beam about "leaderless resistance," which has strongly influenced right-wing white-power groups in the United States. See *The Seditionist*, Issue 12, February 1992.

22. See Luther P. Gerlach, "Protest Movements and the Construction of Risk," in B. B. Johnson and V. T. Covello (eds.), *The Social and Cultural Construction of Risk*, D. Reidel Publishing Co., Boston, Massachusetts, 1987, p. 115, based on Luther P. Gerlach and Virginia Hine, *People, Power, Change: Movements of Social Transformation*, The Bobbs-Merrill Co., New York, 1970. This SPIN concept, a precursor of the netwar concept, was proposed by Luther Gerlach and Virginia Hine in the 1960s to depict U.S. social movements. It anticipates many points about network forms of organization that are now coming into focus in the analysis not only of social movements but also some terrorist, criminal, ethno-nationalist, and fundamentalist organizations.

23. See Wolf V. Heydenbrand, "New Organizational Forms," *Work and Occupations*, No. 3, Vol. 16, August 1989, pp. 323–357.

24. See Paul Kneisel, "Netwar: The Battle Over Rec.Music.White-Power," *ANTIFA INFOBUL-LETIN*, Research Supplement, June 12, 1996, unpaginated ASCII text available on the Internet. Kneisel analyzes the largest vote ever taken about the creation of a new Usenet newsgroup—a vote to prevent the creation of a group that was ostensibly about white-power music. He concludes that "The *war* against contemporary fascism will be won in the 'real world' off the net; but *battles* against fascist netwar are fought and won on the Internet." His title is testimony to the spreading usage of the term netwar.

25. Swarm networks are discussed by Kevin Kelly, *Out of Control: The Rise of Neo-Biological Civilization*, A William Patrick Book, Addison-Wesley Publishing Company, New York, 1994. Also see Arquilla and Ronfeldt, 1997.

26. Also see Alexander Berger, "Organizational Innovation and Redesign in the Information Age: The Drug War, Netwar, and Other Low-End Conflict," Master's Thesis, Naval Postgraduate School, Monterey, California, 1998, for additional thinking and analysis about such propositions.

27. For elaboration, see Arquilla and Ronfeldt, 1997, Chapter 19.

28. Vernon Loeb, "Where the CIA Wages Its New World War," *Washington Post*, September 9, 1998. For a broader discussion of interagency cooperation in countering terrorism, see Ashton Carter, John Deutch, and Philip Zelikow, "Catastrophic Terrorism," *Foreign Affairs*, Vol. 77, No. 6, November/December 1998, pp. 80–94.

29. Analogously, right-wing militias and extremist groups in the United States also rely on a doctrine of "leaderless resistance" propounded by Aryan nationalist Louis Beam. See Beam, 1992; and Kenneth Stern, *A Force Upon the Plain: The American Militia Movement and the Politics of Hate*, Simon and Schuster, New York, 1996. Meanwhile, as part of a broader trend toward netwar, transnational criminal organizations (TCOs) have been shifting away from centralized "Dons" to more networked structures. See Phil Williams, "Transnational Criminal Organizations and International Security," *Survival*, Vol. 36, No. 1, Spring 1994, pp. 96–113; and Phil Williams, "The Nature of Drug-Trafficking Networks," *Current History*, April 1998, pp. 154–159. As noted earlier, social activist movements long ago began to evolve "segmented, polycephalous, integrated networks." For a discussion of a social netwar in which human-rights and other peaceful activist groups supported an insurgent group in Mexico, see David Ronfeldt and Armando Martinez, "A Comment on the Zapatista 'Netwar'," in John Arquilla and David Ronfeldt, 1997, pp. 369–391.

30. It is important to differentiate our notions of information-age networking from earlier ideas about terror as consisting of a network in which all nodes revolved around a Soviet core (Claire Sterling, *The Terror Network*, Holt, Rinehart & Winston, New York, 1981). This view has generally been regarded as unsupported by available evidence (see Cindy C. Combs, *Terrorism in the Twenty-First Century*, Prentice-Hall, New York, 1997, pp. 99–119). However, there were a few early studies that did give credit to the possibility of the rise of terror networks that were bound more by loose ties to general strategic goals than by Soviet control (see especially Thomas L. Friedman, "Loose-Linked Network of Terror: Separate Acts, Ideological Bonds," *Terrorism*, Vol. 8, No. 1, Winter 1985, pp. 36–49).

31. For good general background, see Michael Whine, "Islamist Organisations on the Internet," draft circulated on the Internet, April 1998 (*www.ict.org.il/articles*).

32. We assume that group activity is a proxy for group strength. Group activity can be measured more easily than group strength, and is expected to be significantly correlated with strength. The relationship may not be perfect, but it is deemed to be sufficiently strong for our purposes.

33. Office of the Coordinator for Counterterrorism, *Patterns of Global Terrorism*, 1996, U.S. Department of State, Publication 10433, April 1997.

34. Loeb, 1998; and John Murray and Richard H. Ward (eds.), *Extremist Groups*, Office of International Criminal Justice, University of Illinois, Chicago, 1996.

35. Youssef M. Ibrahim, "Egyptians Hold Terrorist Chief, Official Asserts," *New York Times*, August 26, 1998.

36. Murray and Ward, 1996.

37. *Patterns of Global Terrorism*, 1996, and Murray and Ward, 1996.

38. Murray and Ward, 1996.

bombers attacked a Jerusalem pedestrian mall, killing at least five persons (in addition to the suicide bombers), and injuring at least 181. The Palestinian Islamic Jihad has claimed responsibility (along with Hamas) for a bomb that killed 20 and injured 75 others in March 1996, and in 1995 it carried out five bombings that killed 29 persons and wounded 107. See *Patterns of Global Terrorism*, 1995, 1996, 1997.

41. See "Hizbullah," Israeli Foreign Ministry, April 11, 1996. Available on the Internet at *http://www.israel-mfa.gov.il.*

42. See *Patterns of Global Terrorism*, 1995, 1996, 1997.

43. *Patterns of Global Terrorism*, 1997.

44. "Arab Afghans Said to Launch Worldwide Terrorist War," *Paris al-Watan al-'Arabi*, FBIS-TOT-96-010-L, December 1, 1995, pp. 22–24.

45. William Gertz, "Saudi Financier Tied to Attacks," *Washington Times*, October 23, 1996.

46. Tim Weiner, "U.S. Sees bin Laden as Ringleader of Terrorist Network," *New York Times*, August 21, 1998; M. J. Zuckerman, "Bin Laden Indicted for Bid to Kill Clinton," *USA Today*, August 26, 1998.

47. Pamela Constable, "Bin Laden 'Is Our Guest, So We Must Protect Him'," *Washington Post*, August 21, 1998.

48. We distinguish between deliberate and factional decentralization. Factional decentralization—prevalent in older groups—occurs when subgroups separate themselves from the central leadership because of differences in tactics or approach. Deliberate or operational decentralization is what distinguishes netwar agents from others, since delegation of authority in this case occurs because of the distinct advantages this organizational arrangement brings, and not because of lack of consensus. We expect both influences on decentralization to continue, but newer groups will tend to decentralize authority even in the absence of political disagreements.

49. "Gaza Strip, West Bank: Dahlan on Relations with Israel, Terrorism," *Tel Aviv Yedi'ot Aharonot*, FBIS-TOT-97-022-L, February 28, 1997, p. 18.

50. The leader of the PIJ's most powerful faction, Fathi Shaqaqi, was assassinated in October 1995 in Malta, allegedly by the Israeli Mossad. Shaqaqi's killing followed the assassination of Hani Abed, another PIJ leader killed in 1994 in Gaza. Reports that the group has been considerably weakened as a result of Israeli counterleadership operations are balanced by the strength demonstrated by the PIJ in its recent terrorist activity. See "Islamic Group Vows Revenge for Slaying of Its Leader," *New York Times*, October 30, 1995, p. 9.

51. Magnus Ranstorp, "Hizbullah's Command Leadership: Its Structure, Decision-Making and Relationship with Iranian Clergy and Institutions," *Terrorism and Political Violence*, Vol. 6, No. 3, Autumn 1994, p. 304.

52. *Patterns of Global Terrorism*, 1996.

53. "Algeria: Infighting Among Proliferating 'Wings' of Armed Groups," *London al-Sharq al-Aswat*, FBIS-TOT-97-021-L, February 24, 1997, p. 4.

54. David B. Ottaway, "US Considers Slugging It Out With International Terrorism," *Washington Post*, October 17, 1996, p. 25.

55. "Saudi Arabia: Bin-Laden Calls for 'Guerrilla Warfare' Against US Forces," *Beirut Al-Diyar*, FBIS-NES-96-180, September 12, 1996.

56. It is important to avoid equating the bin Laden network solely with bin Laden. He represents a key node in the Arab Afghan terror network, but there should be no illusions about the likely effect on the network of actions taken to neutralize him. The network conducts many operations without his involvement, leadership, or financing—and will continue to be able to do so should he be killed or captured.

57. "Militants Say There Will Be More Attacks Against U.S.," *European Stars and Stripes*, August 20, 1998.

58. For instance, there have been reports of a recent inflow of Arab Afghans into Egypt's Islamic Group to reinforce the latter's operations. See Murray and Ward, 1996, and "The CIA on Bin Laden," *Foreign Report*, No. 2510, August 27, 1998, pp. 2–3.

59. This move was also influenced by the Taliban's decision to curb Arab Afghan activities in the territory under its control as a result of U.S. pressure. See "Arab Afghans Reportedly Transfer Operations to Somalia," *Cairo al-Arabi*, FBIS-TOT-97-073, March 10, 1997, p. 1.

60. "Afghanistan, China: Report on Bin-Laden Possibly Moving to China," *Paris al-Watan al-'Arabi*, FBIS-NES-97-102, May 23, 1997, pp. 19–20.

61. While it is possible to discern a general trend toward an organizational structure that displays several features of a network, we expect to observe substantial differences (and many hierarchy/network hybrids) in how organizations make their specific design choices. Different network designs depend on contingent factors, such as personalities, organizational history, operational requirements, and other influences such as state sponsorship and ideology.

62. Assessing the strength of the relationship between organizational structure and use of information technology is difficult to establish. Alternative explanations may exist as to why newer groups would embrace information technology, such as age of the group (one could speculate that newer terrorist groups have on average younger members, who are more familiar with computers), or the amount of funding (a richer group could afford more electronic gadgetry). While it is empirically impossible to refute these points, much in organization theory supports our hypothesis that there is a direct relationship between a higher need for information technology and the use of network structures.

63. "Saudi Arabia: French Analysis of Islamic Threat," *Paris al-Watan al-'Arabi*, FBIS-NES- 97-082, April 11, 1997, pp. 4–8.

64. "Afghanistan, Saudi Arabia: Editor's Journey to Meet Bin-Laden Described," *London al-Quds al-'Arabi*, FBIS-TOT-97-003-L, November 27, 1996, p. 4.

65. "Arab Afghans Said to Launch Worldwide Terrorist War," 1995.

66. "Israel: U.S. Hamas Activists Use Internet to Send Attack Threats," *Tel Aviv IDF Radio*, FBIS-TOT-97-001-L, 0500 GMT October 13, 1996.

67. "Israel: Hamas Using Internet to Relay Operational Messages," *Tel Aviv Ha'aretz*, FBIS-TOT-98-034, February 3, 1998, p. 1.

68. "Italy: Security Alters Following Algerian Extremists' Arrests," *Milan Il Giornale*, FBIS-TOT-97-002-L, November 12, 1996, p. 10.

69. "Italy, Vatican City: Daily Claims GIA 'Strategist' Based in Milan," *Milan Corriere della Sera*, FBIS-TOT-97-004-L, December 5, 1996, p. 9.

70. "Hizbullah TV Summary 18 February 1998," *Al-Manar Television World Wide Webcast*, FBIS-NES-98-050, February 19, 1998. Also see "Developments in Mideast Media: January–May 1998," Foreign Broadcast Information Service (FBIS), May 11, 1998.

71. "Islamists on Internet," FBIS Foreign Media Note-065EP96, September 9, 1996.

72. "Islamic Activism Online," FBIS Foreign Media Note-02JAN97, January 3, 1997.

73. The Muslim Parliament has recently added an Internet Relay Chat (IRC) link and a "Muslims only" List-Serve (automatic e-mail delivery service). See "Islamic Activism Online," FBIS Foreign Media Note-02JAN97, January 3, 1997.

74. Similar propositions may apply to varieties of netwar other than the new terrorism.

75. We make a qualification here. There appears to be a significant positive association between the degree to which a group is active and the degree to which a group is decentralized and networked. But we cannot be confident about the causality of this relationship or its direction (i.e., whether activity and strength affect networking, or vice-versa). A host of confounding factors may affect both the way groups decide to organize and their relative success at operations. For instance, the age of a group may be an important predictor of a group's success—newer groups are likely to be more popular; popular groups are more likely to enlist new operatives; and groups that have a large number of operatives are likely to be more active, regardless of organizational structure. Another important caveat is related to the fact that it is difficult to rank groups precisely in terms of the degree to which they are networked, because no terrorist organization is thought to represent either a hierarchical or network ideal-type. While the conceptual division between newer-generation and traditional groups is appropriate for our scope

Press, Boulder, 1994.

78. Alexander George, *Forceful Persuasion: Coercive Diplomacy as an Alternative to War*, United States Institute of Peace Press, Washington, DC, 1991.

79. Brian Jenkins, *The Potential for Nuclear Terrorism*, RAND, P-5876, 1977; Thomas Schelling, "Thinking about Nuclear Terrorism," *International Security*, Vol. 6, No. 4, Spring 1982, pp. 68–75; and Patrick Garrity and Steven Maaranen, *Nuclear Weapons in a Changing World*, Plenum Press, New York, 1992.

80. Carr, 1996.

81. Brian Jenkins, *International Terrorism: A New Kind of Warfare*, RAND, P-5261, 1974.

82. For a discussion of these motives, see Laqueur, 1996; Iklé, 1997; and Hoffman, 1998, respectively.

83. See, for instance, Michael Barkun, *Disaster and the Millennium*, Yale University Press, New Haven, 1974; and Norman Cohn, *The Pursuit of the Millennium: Revolutionary Messianism in Medieval and Reformation Europe and Its Bearing on Modern Totalitarian Movements*, Harper Torch Books, New York, 1961.

84. Bluma Zuckerbrot-Finkelstein, "A Guide to Hamas," *Internet Jewish Post*, available at *http://www.jewishpost.com/jewishpost/jp0203/jpn0303.htm*.

Brent Ellis, 2003

Countering Complexity: An Analytical Framework to Guide Counter-Terrorism Policy-Making

Abstract

The development of religiously motivated terrorism has increased the complexity of the terrorist phenomenon. We are currently faced with a wider range of actors with a broader set of motivations, strategies, tactics, organizational structures and goals than ever before. This increased complexity necessitates the development of analytical frameworks that can guide analysis of the terrorist phenomenon to assess terrorist threats and guide counter-terrorism policy-making. Such a framework is developed drawing upon analysis of religiously motivated terrorism in relation to three primary trends in contemporary international terrorism: first, the trend towards the increased lethality of terrorist attacks; second, the increasing threat of the use of weapons of mass destruction; and third, the trend towards decentralizing organization. In each case it is suggested that one can best understand these trends by placing each individual group along a spectrum characterizing either the group's motivation, use of technology or level of centralization. Moreover, this framework can be utilized as an organizational principle to allow a structured analysis of an individual group, the threat it represents and the counter-terrorism strategies to be utilized against it.

Introduction

Terrorism is a dynamic phenomenon. Its "motivations, tactics, strategy, logistics evolve (Canadian Security Intelligence Service 1999)." Since the end of the Cold War the nature of the rate and level of change within the subject of terrorism has been dramatic. Perhaps the greatest element of change within the subject of terrorism has been the changing nature of the actors themselves. Since the end of the Cold War analysts have observed the decline of left-wing ideological based terrorism, especially in Europe, and the persistence of many of the ethnic or nationalist groups (Wilkinson 1995, 2001; Laqueur 1996, 25; Laqueur 1999, 80). Furthermore, since the early 1980's, groups primarily motivated by religion have emerged.

The development of religiously motivated groups has had a significant impact upon the nature of contemporary international terrorism, and is a driving force behind many of the trends currently identified within the subject.[1] The increased lethality of terrorist attacks, the move towards a more decentralized structure and group organization, and the increasing threat of terrorist use of weapons of mass destruction are all linked to the development of religiously motivated terrorist groups.

109

weapons, the gun and bomb, to weapons of mass destruction. The overall result is that we face a much more complex phenomenon than ever before.

The implications of the complexity of contemporary terrorism are significant. This new complexity necessitates a reappraisal of our counter-terrorist strategies and indeed our wider understanding of the phenomenon in general. One area where research has the potential to contribute to counter-terrorism policy is through the creation of analytical frameworks that can guide analysis of the terrorist phenomenon in order to assess terrorist threats and guide counter-terrorism policy-making. This paper suggests such an analytical framework based upon the development of the new terrorism and the implications of religious terrorism in particular.

In order to develop the framework, the impact of the development of religiously motivated terrorism is assessed. Specifically, its relation to three primary trends in contemporary international terrorism are analyzed: first, the trend towards increased lethality of terrorist attacks; second, the increasing threat of the use of weapons of mass destruction; and third the trend towards decentralizing terrorist organization. In each case it is suggested that one can best understand these trends by placing each individual group along a spectrum characterizing either the group's motivation, use of technology or level of decentralization.[3] Such a framework can be utilized as an organizational principle to allow a greater and more structured analysis of an individual group, the threat it represents and the counter-terrorism strategies utilized against it.

The conclusion examines how "agent-based" forms of analysis have been suggested as a means of assessing the threat of terrorist use of weapons of mass destruction. This form of analysis is related to the suggested framework as it is premised upon an examination of terrorist motivations as a means of assessing terrorist threats. As such, agent-based models are examples of the form of thinking that can be developed through the utilization of the proposed framework. The final section of the paper also outlines the role and importance of further research in the area and suggests ways in which researchers can aid and assist policymakers in framing and developing counter-terrorism strategy.

Lethality and Changing Terrorist Motivation

One of the most frequently mentioned trends in contemporary terrorism is its rising lethality. Over the past decade there has been a dramatic rise in the number of terrorist incidents resulting in fatalities.[4] Indeed the number of fatalities resulting from terrorist attacks has increased even while the number of terrorist attacks has been on the decline (Wilkinson 2001, 50; Hoffman 1999, 7). While it is important to not read too much into these statistics that deal with only international terrorism and not with the overall phenomenon of terrorism in general, the trend towards increasing lethality of *international terrorism* is clearly apparent.

There have been many factors suggested to explain the rise in the lethality of terrorist attacks. Various commentators have pointed to the hardening of targets, the increased professionalism of terrorist actors, and the development of "spectacular attacks" among others, to explain the rising lethality of terrorist attacks. Yet, perhaps the most cited cause of the trend towards the increased lethality of terrorist incidents is the proliferation since the early 1980's of groups motivated by religion. The lethality of religious groups' operations is shown by the fact that Shia Islamic terrorist groups committed 8 percent of all international terrorist incidents from 1982 to 1989 but accounted for 30 percent of the deaths over that period. Thus, the proportion of fatalities to operations was much higher in operations launched by such groups (Hoffman 1999, 17). The lethality of religious terrorism is also reflected by the fact that in 1995 religious terrorist groups committed 25 percent of the recorded international terrorist incidents yet resulted in 58 percent of terrorist-related fatalities that year (Hoffman 1998b, 14).

Religious groups also tend to dominate high-casualty incidents and commit more "spectacular" attacks than secular groups. Examples of religious motivated spectaculars include the 1993 World Trade Centre attacks, the December 1994 hijacking of an Air France passenger jet by the Algerian GIA, the Tokyo nerve gas attack in 1995 by Aum Shinrikyo, the U.S. embassy bombings in August 1998, and of course the September 11 attacks of 2001.

It is clear that religious terrorist groups are more likely to use indiscriminate tactics producing mass casualties than traditional secular terrorists. The pattern is relatively apparent. Yet, what accounts for this difference between the traditional groups and the new religious terrorists? The answer lies in the nature, motivations and mindset of the newer groups (Hoffman 1998a). As a result of these factors, religious groups do not operate restrained by the traditional constraints which act to limit the level of traditional terrorist violence. Before the nature of the religiously motivated groups is analyzed these traditional constraints will be highlighted.

Traditional secular terrorist groups tend to be highly selective and discriminate in their operations. They possess a relatively narrow target set; that is they tend to target relatively few people. Traditional groups also tend to be conservative in their operations and in their goals overall (Hoffman 1998a, 197–198; Laqueur 1999, 33, 81). A number of disincentives act to constrain traditional groups' use of higher levels of violence. Increased levels of violence may affect the propaganda value of the attack, resulting in decreasing support for the terrorist group among their constituency or in the international community (Hoffman 1998a, 161; Tucker 2001, 7; Jenkins 1975); provoke an intense government crackdown threatening the continued operation of the group (Tucker 2001, 7; Jenkins 2001, 7; Hoffman 1998a, 162); or jeopardize group cohesion, perhaps leading to a splintering or dissolution of the group or increased cooperation of informants with security forces (Jenkins 2001, 7; Horgan and Taylor 1997, 23).

As suggested above the overall result of these constraints upon terrorist use of violence was that traditional groups tended to limit their use of violence. This led Jenkins to assert that terrorists operated on the principle of the minimum force necessary, stating that "They find it unnecessary to kill many as long as killing a few suffices for their purposes (1985, 6)." More recently Hoffman has asserted that being able to control their use of violence is a factor contributing to the success of terrorist campaigns. He concludes that "the more successful ethno-nationalist/separatist terrorist organization will be able to determine an effective level of violence that is at once 'tolerable' for the local populace, tacitly acceptable to international opinion and sufficiently modulated not to provoke massive

counting for this difference is the nature, motivation and mindset of the religious groups.

There are four main factors that differentiate the mindset and motives of the religious terrorist from those of the traditional secular terrorist. First, violence for the religious terrorist is not only a means to an end but an end in itself. Second, religious terrorists lack an external constituency. Third, religious terrorists tend to target a more broadly defined enemy group. Fourth, religious terrorists possess a fundamentally different world view and set of goals compared to traditional secular terrorists.

Traditional groups tend to operate within what has been called a coercive diplomacy framework. They utilize violence as a means to achieve certain ends. Hence their use of violence can be termed "instrumental (Arquilla, Ronfeldt and Zanini 1999, 68–69)." For religious terrorists, the use of violence not only has an instrumental purpose but violence also is an end in itself. It is viewed as "a sacred duty executed in direct response to some theological demand or imperative," and is often viewed as "a divine duty or sacramental act (Hoffman 1998a, 168, 88)." Thus, religion acts as a legitimizing force backing the use of higher levels of violence (Jeurgensmeyer 2002, 145; Ranstorp 2002, 127). This is reflected by the fact that many religious terrorist groups will only act if their attack is sanctioned by religious authorities (Hoffman 1998a, 94; Ranstorp 2002, 125).[5]

The replacement of the coercive diplomacy model has been noted by some analysts who suggest that some groups have adopted a "war paradigm", where the strategic aim is to inflict damage generally and conventional constraints, resulting in proportionality, are not present (Arquilla, Ronfeldt and Zanini 1999, 69–70). In such cases the instrumental use of violence gives way to a more "hostile" use of violence. It appears that religious groups would fit into this paradigm of motivation. Ranstorp notes how religious groups "perceive their struggle as all-out war against their enemies (2002, 126)." In other words, the religious terrorists perceive themselves as being engaged in a total war where ordinary morality does not apply.

The tendency of religious groups to perceive the conflict as a zero-sum game where no compromise is possible and as a battle between good and evil reinforces this perception of total war. As Jeurgensmeyer suggests, "If a battle of the spirit is thought to exist, then it is not ordinary morality but the rules of war that apply (2002, 145)." This factor is also reinforced by the common tendency for religious groups to perceive their struggle in defensive terms. In a defensive struggle even violent actions which normally would not be legitimate can be justified as being reactive in character and therefore perceived as a legitimate means of self-defence (Ranstorp 2002, 127). Thus the perception of religious groups that they are engaged in a total war and a defensive struggle reinforces and justifies the use of heightened levels of violence.

Religious terrorists do not seek to appeal to an external constituency, as do traditional secular terrorists. Hoffman describes them as being "at once activists and constituents engaged in what they regard as total war. They seek to appeal to no other constituency than themselves (1998a, 95)." This limits the need for religious terrorists to check their use of violence for fear of alienating either their own sympathizers or their external support

(Hoffman 1998a, 95). The result is "a sanctioning of almost limitless violence against a virtually open-ended category of targets: that is, anyone who is not a member of the terrorists' religion or religious sect (Hoffman 1998a, 95)." Indeed, some groups even aim their violence at the decimation of the majority of the population or even of mankind in general (Laqueur 1999, 81, 127–130). It is clear that this factor is interrelated with the total war mindset common to religious terrorists. The definition of large sections of the population as enemies reinforces the perception that the terrorists are involved in a battle of good versus evil. The propagation of dehumanizing and demonizing propaganda, which is facilitated by the terrorists acting within the war paradigm, also corrodes restrictions upon the indiscriminate use of violence. Such propaganda can be utilized to condone the use of higher levels of violence (Ranstorp 2002, 127).

A final factor, which influences religious terrorists' propensity to use more lethal tactics, is the fundamentally different world view and goals of religious terrorists. Religious terrorists tend to have a greater sense of alienation from the existing world system. Hoffman suggests "religious terrorists see themselves not as components of a system worth preserving but as 'outsiders', seeking fundamental changes in the existing order (1998a, 95)." He notes the relationship between this sense of alienation and increased lethality and states that the greater sense of alienation "enables the religious terrorist to contemplate far more destructive and deadly types of terrorist operations than secular terrorists (1998a, 95)." The greater sense of alienation possessed by religious terrorists is also reflected in the tendency of religious terrorists to have much more ill-defined, ambiguous and extreme goals than traditional secular terrorist groups. Laqueur summarizes this difference well:

> Traditional terrorism, whether of the separatist or the ideological (left or right) variety, had political and social aims…. Such terrorist groups aimed at forcing concessions, sometimes far-reaching concessions, from their antagonists. The new terrorism is different in character, aiming not at clearly defined political demands but at the destruction of society and the elimination of large sections of the population. In its most extreme form, this new terrorism intends to liquidate all satanic forces… as a precondition for the growth of another, better, and in any case different breed of human (1999, 81).

Thus religious terrorists may utilize more extreme forms of violence in the pursuit of more extreme goals, against a wider set of enemies than traditional secular terrorists, legitimized by religious sanction and the perception of their cause as a defensive struggle, in what amounts to a total war perceived in zero-sum terms where compromise is not an option.

However, Laqueur also implies that there is some amount of variation in the tendency of religious groups to pursue extreme levels of violence. It has been suggested that many of the religious terrorist groups also have political and social goals not unlike traditional secular terrorists. For example, religious terrorist groups may pursue the establishment of a state based on their religious beliefs. In such cases the constraints acting on traditional terrorist groups may have an effect (Tucker 2001, 7).

In such situations the restraining power of the traditional constraints will depend on the exact nature of the group, its perceptions, values, goals and world view. Thus, the same factors outlined above, that override the traditional restraints for religious terrorists have to be assessed in order to analyze and understand the constraints acting upon a particular

tential to use increased levels of violence and more indiscriminate tactics could then be illustrated according to its position along the spectrum. This potential would increase from left to right as one moves from the traditional secular groups on the left end of the spectrum to the various religiously motivated groups situated nearer the right end.[7]

Weapons of Mass Destruction

The debate surrounding the potential use of weapons of mass destruction by terrorists is not new; it dates back to the early 1970s (Jenkins 2002, 12). While some analysts believed that escalation to terrorist use of weapons of mass destruction was inevitable, the majority of terrorist groups did not seek to develop weapons of mass destruction capabilities. The same restraints which limit traditional terrorist groups' level of lethality dissuade terrorist use of weapons of mass destruction. Traditionally, fears of the loss of popular support, of provoking an intense government response, and threats to group cohesion tended to preclude the use of such weapons (Jenkins 2002, 13).

However, the rise of religious terrorism has forced a reappraisal of conventional wisdom surrounding the topic of terrorist WMD use. As Hoffman notes, "New adversaries, new motivations and new rationales have emerged in recent years to challenge at least some of the conventional wisdom on both terrorists and terrorism (1998a, 196)." Hoffman suggests that this trend is particularly relevant within the subject of weapons of mass destruction and notes that it has been religiously motivated terrorist groups that have pursued a weapons of mass destruction capability more vigorously over the past decades (1998a, 201).

Indeed the same willingness on the part of religious terrorist groups to engage in attacks of higher lethality has been interpreted as showing the potential for the use of weapons of mass destruction. An example of such thinking is the conclusion drawn by James K. Cambell in his study on weapons of mass destruction terrorism: "the 'qualitative rise' in terms of the casualties and damage produced by terrorist attacks provides an indication that terrorists may very well engage in more spectacular and sophisticated attacks that include the use of weapons of mass destruction (1997, 25)." The change in motivations and values that characterizes the different mindset of religious groups and permits the sanctioning of the use of indiscriminate tactics and higher levels of violence suggests that such groups may see utility in utilizing weapons of mass destruction.[8]

The increased probability of the use of weapons of mass destruction further complicates our understanding of terrorism generally and increases the range of threats that we now face. No longer are threats confined to conventional means. Attacks across the technological spectrum, from unsophisticated conventional threats to the high-end threat of weapons of mass destruction, must be defended against (Hoffman 1999, 28–31). Thus, building upon the analysis of terrorist motivation outlined above, a second spectrum reflecting the technological sophistication of the terrorist attacks is created. Moreover this second spectrum appears to have a connection to the first illustrating terrorist motivation.

Groups contemplating the use of weapons of mass destruction will have to measure the costs and benefits of using such weapons. It seems likely that religious groups possessing more traditional goals and aspirations will be less likely to utilize weapons of mass destruction. The traditional constraints precluding the use of such weapons would act more strongly upon them just as it is suggested the constraints precluding the use of more indiscriminate tactics have a greater effect on such groups. If this is the case, then the weapons of mass destruction threat is most acute among smaller cults that possess apocalyptic or millenarian type beliefs as argued by Merari (2000, 62–63).

It follows that, within the framework, the potential for a group to use weapons of mass destruction increases along the spectrum detailing terrorist motivation from left to right. Traditional terrorist groups, on the left side of the spectrum, are unlikely to use weapons of mass destruction and the groups that are most likely to utilize such weapons are the religious cults and sects on the far right of the spectrum. A significant implication of this line of reasoning is that the assessment of terrorist motivations is increasingly crucial to determining the level and indeed the character of the threat a particular group represents.

This analysis also indicates that the threat of the use of weapons of mass destruction is related to the number of groups positioned towards the right side of the motivations spectrum. If the number of such groups is small then the threat of WMD use would be relatively less compared to a scenario where the number of groups towards the right end of the spectrum was higher. It appears that this has been the case to this point as relatively few terrorist groups have attempted to develop a WMD capability. Yet, as Schmid notes, while the WMD threat may be widely regarded as being of low probability, the consequences of terrorist use of such weapons are grave (2000, 108). Thus, the danger of even a few terrorist groups possessing weapons of mass destruction could be greater that the threat of a larger number of terrorist groups utilizing conventional weapons and traditional terrorist tactics (Laqueur 1999, 155). As a result, the threat of terrorist use of WMD cannot be ignored.

Decentralizing Organization

A third trend that is noted in relation to the emergence of religious terrorist groups is the tendency towards less cohesive, more amorphous and decentralized organizational structures. The CSIS backgrounder notes that "terrorism today is complex and fluid, with reduced emphasis on a formalized group structure typical of terrorist insurgents in the past (2002)." RAND analysts have characterized this shift as a move towards a more "network" oriented structure by the new terrorist groups. They note how "experts have begun to recognize the growing role of networks—of networked organizational designs and related doctrines, strategies and technologies—among the practitioners of terrorism (Arquilla, Ronfeldt, and Zanini 1999, 45)." Such networked structures tend to comprise "loosely interconnected, semi-independent cells that have no single commanding hierarchy (Arquilla, Ronfeldt, and Zanini 1999, 56)." It is suggested that this development is related to the revolution in information technology and allows an increase in the transnationalization and geographic dispersion of terrorist groups (Arquilla, Ronfeldt, and Zanini 1999, 64–67).

Arquilla, Ronfeldt, and Zanini note that such networked and decentralized structures contrast markedly with the hierarchical and well-defined structure of traditional terrorist groups (1999, 56–63). An example of such a hierarchical structure is the organization of the Provisional IRA (PIRA). The group's organization is described as having "a cellular

is matched by an increase in the complexity of the forms of organization adopted by terrorist groups. This latter trend is complicated by the simple fact that no two terrorist groups are alike in structure. We do not see merely two categories of terrorist organization, hierarchical and decentralized. In reality the situation is much more vague and complex. Indeed Arquilla, Ronfeldt, and Zanini had to note this fact in their analysis. They qualify their analysis, noting the existence of a "general trend toward an organizational structure that displays several features of a network" and stating that they "expect to observe substantial differences in how organizations make their specific design choices. Different network designs depend on contingent factors, such as personalities, organizational history, operational requirements, and other influences such as state sponsorship and ideology (1999, 64 note 61)." They also note that they expect to see many "hierarchy/network hybrids" combining characteristics of hierarchical and networked structures in the organizational design of terrorist groups (1999, 64 note 61).

Thus contemporary international terrorism is characterized by a plethora of organizational structures ranging along a spectrum from highly centralized and authoritarian structures with centralized command and control to decentralized structures lacking such centralized control and decision-making.[9] Moreover, the newer terrorist groups that have developed in the past two decades tend to lie closer to the decentralized end of the spectrum.

The increased range in the organizational structure of terrorist groups has a number of implications for counter-terrorism strategy. First, operations conducted by decentralized groups, especially those utilizing "freelance" operatives unconnected to an existing terrorist group and without a previous track-record and organizational structure, are much tougher to prevent. Lacking information about the members of such elements, one is hard-pressed to identify them before they take action (Wilkinson 2001, 60; Hoffman 1999, 20–22; Tucker 2001, 11). It is also much tougher to determine the intentions and capabilities of such groups, making assessment of their overall threat a much tougher task (Hoffman 1999, 22). As one can imagine this makes the task facing those responsible for managing the terrorist threat much more difficult and complex.

Arquilla, Ronfeldt and Zanini note that networked forms of organization possess inherent defensive advantages which can make them tough to combat. In particular they argue that networked designs combining redundancy, interoperability, diversity and decentralized command and control are tougher to completely defeat than traditional hierarchical structures; such organizations are "redundant and diverse, making them robust and resilient in the face of adversity (1999, 54)." Assessing the impact of counter-terrorism operations against such actors is also more difficult due to the fact that only portions of the network may be identified and targeted, while other parts of the network remain unknown and viable in the face of such operations. In particular counter-leadership strikes would be less effective against decentralized actors lacking centralized command and control procedures. Actors with such decentralized structures are more flexible and better able to adapt to changed circumstances. Even if one node was removed by a military strike the overall effectiveness of the network would not be compromised (Arquilla, Ronfeldt, and Zanini 1999, 54).

While networked structures offer advantages to the defense they also have weaknesses. The adoption of a networked structure increases the level of communications necessary for the network to operate, and thus, decreases control over the management of such communications. Both the number of transmissions and the range of formats utilized may have to be increased. This may increase the potential for surveillance and intelligence gathering opportunities (Tucker 2001, 11; Arquilla, Ronfeldt, and Zanini 1999, 51–53). If the adoption of networked structures is related to the revolution of information technology, as the RAND analysts suggest, the increased use of information technology by networked terrorist may also increase their vulnerability to signals intelligence penetration (Arquilla, Ronfeldt, and Zanini 1999, 79–80). Indeed, terrorist reliance upon information technology may make them susceptible to information warfare attacks launched against them (Arquilla, Ronfeldt, and Zanini 1999, 80–81).

A second weakness of network structures is that the same decentralization, which increases some defensive aspects of the network, also limits command and control coordination within it. This may inhibit the network's ability to accomplish complex tasks (Tucker 2001, 10). As a result, the capabilities of terrorist organizations with a very decentralized structure may be limited to less sophisticated and coordinated means. Indeed, Brian Michael Jenkins has utilized this idea in his analysis of Al Qaeda; only if central decision-making is present are coordinated conventional attacks, multidimensional assaults calculated to magnify disruption, and weapon of mass destruction attacks possible. He suggests that in order to diminish the al Qaeda threat, strategy should focus on the elimination of the group's central decision-making element as a means to eliminate the possibility of the group utilizing such sophisticated modes of attack (2002, 11–12).

The efficacy of this proposed strategy is premised upon an analysis of al Qaeda's structure suggesting it would be affected by a counter-leadership strike. This reflects how analysis of the organizational structure of specific groups is a necessary first step in determining counter-terrorism policies to be used against them in an environment made extremely complex by a plethora of different organizational structures. As Arquilla, Ronfeldt and Zanini conclude, "Such organizational diversity implies the need for counter-terrorism strategy that recognizes the differences among organizational designs and seeks to target the weaknesses associated with each (1999, 80)."

Moreover, if a relationship exists between the level of decentralization of a terrorist organization and the level of sophistication of their attacks, the spectrum developed previously representing the technological sophistication of terrorist actors is related to that describing the structure of the organization. This suggests that both the motivation and organizational structure of any particular group will affect its ability to carry out sophisticated attacks including the use of weapons of mass destruction. Thus, not only will the organizational structure of the terrorist group have to be assessed, but the motivations and values of the group will have to be examined as well. These two factors become the main determinants of a terrorist group's willingness and ability to conduct sophisticated attacks. Only through such a coupled analysis can a truly accurate assessment of the threat a particular group represents be derived and the most suitable counter-terrorist policies determined.

clear terrorism should focus on the actors looking to acquire nuclear capabilities and not upon the containment (non-proliferation) of fissile materials. He suggests that the "primary threat of nuclear terrorism stems not from the availability of the materials but from the potential willingness of some groups to acquire them (2001, 39)." Thus, he argues that in order to fully understand the threat we must lower the level of analysis to assess the nuclear threat at the agent or group level, and develop an understanding of the motivations and actions of such groups. It is also suggested that this would allow a more efficient use of resources as analysis could be focused upon the groups that represent the primary threat (Badey 2001, 52–53). Such analysis is clearly within the realm of the framework presented in this paper. It supports the assertion that in order to fully understand, assess and counter the terrorist threat we must focus on an analysis of group structure and motivation. Not only does this form of analysis present a more detailed and accurate assessment of the threat, it may also prove to be more efficient in the use of counter-terrorism resources.

This example also reflects the wider need for more research necessary for the framework to be utilized successfully. Badey points to the need for further research upon non-state groups to facilitate a greater amount of knowledge surrounding the non-state actors who may seek to use weapons of mass destruction (2001, 42).[10] In order for groups to be classified accurately according to the framework each group will have to be assessed according to the various categories. This may require the development of analytical scales similar to that proposed by Arquilla, Ronfeldt and Zanini that could describe the "degree of religious motivation," "degree of sophistication" and "degree of networked structure (1999, 67)." Accurate classification would also be dependent upon the availability of accurate data to allow assessment. This would reinforce the need for intelligence gathering specifically and the development of information generally, both focused upon the terrorist threat.

The need for further research is increased by the fact that the framework can only guide counter-terrorism policymaking if counter-terrorism strategies are clearly developed and the criteria delimiting their successful implementation are known. Such knowledge can be divided into three categories: (1) conceptual models of each strategy—which would include not only the development of new strategies but reformulation of traditional strategies (eg. counter-leadership strikes, economic sanctions, information warfare, "root causes," etc.); (2) general knowledge of the conditions that favor the successful application of each strategy; and (3) actor specific models of the mind-sets, motivation, internal structure and politics, and behavioral style towards whom the strategies may be directed.[11] It appears that the first and third categories are most important in relation to counter-terrorism policy. It is doubtful that the second type of knowledge, that relating to general conditions that favor the application of specific strategies, would be of as much utility in shaping counter-terrorism policy due to the increased complexity and highly specific nature of the terrorist phenomenon today. Thus, the efforts of researchers would be well placed if they focused upon the development of conceptual models outlining counter-terrorism strategies and actor-specific models for their use.

The Current Task: An Insurmountable Challenge?

As a result of the evolution we have seen in terrorist motivations, organization, and tactics, characterized by the development of what is called the new terrorism, the level of complexity of the terrorist phenomenon has increased dramatically. We are now faced with a combination of new and traditional actors, a widened set of motivations and tactics, organizational structures and principles, as well as a wider range of threats along the technological spectrum, especially with the increased potential for the terrorist use of weapons of mass destruction.

Counter-terrorism now must deal with a wider range of threats simultaneously. In order to undertake this challenge, we need a "comprehensive understanding of terrorism in all of its dimensions (Hoffman 2001, 4)." This entails not only keeping up with trends and developments occurring within the wider subject of terrorism but developing an awareness and a conception of how these developments relate to specific actors. In order to facilitate this task, the creation of analytical frameworks is a critical first step. The framework presented in this analysis assesses terrorist groups according to the nature of their motivation, their level of organization and their level of technological sophistication. The first two factors, the nature of the group's motivation and its organizational structure, are the primary determinants of the third factor, the group's level of technological sophistication, which largely determines the nature and level of the threat posed by a particular terrorist group. This framework has the potential to be a powerful tool to facilitate the analysis of the terrorist threat and to guide counter-terrorism policy-making. Yet its development is only a first step. The potential for the framework to guide policy-making is largely dependent upon the development of knowledge surrounding specific counter-terrorism strategies and their implementation. Thus, more generally, the success of counter-terrorism will be largely dependent upon the development of our knowledge regarding terrorism, counter-terrorism strategies, and the application of such strategies. It is therefore clear that terrorism research has a crucial role to play in the management of the terrorist threat.

What are the prospects for success? Counter-terrorism may well be a major challenge of the twenty-first century, but countering the threat is not beyond our capability. Effort is required, as Hoffman makes clear: "Our search for solutions and new approaches must be continuous and unyielding, proportional to the threat posed by our adversaries in both innovation and determination (2001, 9)." Yet, in the past, new capabilities and strategies were developed to counter changes and developments in the terrorist threat as old capabilities became less effective (Tucker 2001, 9–10). The high rate of change within the terrorist phenomenon in the recent past may have increased the scope of the challenge, but the threat is not insurmountable.

A good comparison can be drawn to our experience with peace operations. The post-Cold War world saw the proliferation of new types of conflicts which proved to be unsuited to the application of conflict management mechanisms, in particular the application of what is now known as "traditional peacekeeping," that had been developed to deal with interstate conflict. The new post-Cold War context spurred the evolution of peacekeeping towards more robust and comprehensive mechanisms including peace-building, wider peacekeeping and peace enforcement. It was recognized that a more complex situation involving new and old threats co-existing simultaneously required a larger toolbox, composed of traditional strategies, but new tools as well, developed specifically to deal with new threats.

suggests that counter-terrorism too has the potential to evolve to meet the more complex threat now confronting it.

Indeed the increased level of interest in the study of terrorism in academic circles today (Gordon 2001), mirrors the increased level which surrounded conflict resolution and management throughout the past decade. If the study of terrorism follows conflict resolution and management and becomes more mainstream as an area of academic study, the amount of human capital contributed to the task of generating terrorism-related knowledge will only increase. With the rise of such knowledge our ability to confront the challenge of terrorism will only be strengthened. Thus, one could even suggest that the knowledge base needed to confront the terrorist threat is already increasing, indicating the considerable strength we possess to counter the terrorist threat and our overall prospects for success in its management.

Brent Ellis is a graduate of King's College, the University of Western Ontario and is currently completing an MA at the Norman Paterson School of International Affairs. His academic and research interests are broad and diverse, including Canadian defence and security policy, terrorism, conflict management, international law, political philosophy, the study of fascism, in particular its ideological roots, and military history. In addition, his article titled "Countering Complexity: An Analytical Framework to Guide Counter-Terrorism Policy-Making" received second place in the Canadian Defence and Foreign Affairs Institute Graduate Student Paper Competition.

Notes

1. It is important to clarify that a religious terrorist group is one that has "aims and motivations reflecting a predominant religious character or influence (Hoffman 1998, 90)." This criterion precludes groups such as the Provisional IRA, which is composed of Irish Catholics, from being included in the "religious" category as PIRA is motivated predominantly by a secular/nationalist goal and strategy.

2. The concept of the new terrorism is the subject of considerable debate. For descriptions of the new terrorism and its implications see, Hoffman (1998a, 1998b), Lesser et al. (1999), Laqueur (1999), Harmon (2000). For criticism of the concept see, Tucker (2001) and Merari (2000).

3. Thus, there is a spectrum for each trend: the group's motivation, secular/religious as classic types; the group's level of centralization, hierarchical/network oriented; and the group's level of technology, unsophisticated (low tech conventional weapons)/sophisticated WMD. In each case individual group would be placed along the spectrum according to its specific characteristics relating to the trait in question.

4. Bruce Hoffman notes that there has been an increase in the number of terrorist incidents resulting in one or more fatalities through the 1990's. From 1991 to 1995 the percentage of such incidents climbed from 14 percent, to 17.5 percent, to 24 percent in 1993, 27 percent in 1995 and leveled at 29 percent in 1995. Thus, the percentage increased each year from 1991 to 1995. While the percentage decreased in 1996 to 24 percent, it remained higher that the corresponding

average percentage for the two previous decades, 17 and 19 percent respectively (Hoffman 1999, 12–13).

5. Ranstorp (2002, 128) suggests many examples of this phenomenon including the first World Trade Centre bombing in 1993 and the assassination of Sadat, both sanctioned by a fatwa from Sheik Omar 'Abd al-Rahman, and the aborted Gush Emunim plot to blow up the Temple Mount which was not conducted because religious sanction was not given. The latter is more reflective of the importance of religious sanction as it proves that such sanction is a limiting factor.

6. For a review of these particular variants of religious terrorism refer to Laqueur (1999) and Hoffman (1998a). For the sake of organization one could place the traditional secular terrorist groups along the left end of the spectrum and the religious motivated groups towards the right end.

7. This would not indicate that terrorist groups would not use traditional tactics. Indeed, the overall incidence of "spectacular" attacks is quite small compared to the number of attacks overall. The vast majority of attacks can be considered within the scope of "traditional" tactics. Ranstorp indicates that religious terrorists commonly use such traditional tactics as assassination, kidnapping, and bombings and notes a tendency to choose symbolic targets (2002, 130–31).

8. This assertion, that there is a connection between the increased willingness of religious groups to engage in high lethality attacks and the use of weapons of mass destruction, is reinforced by the potential for religious beliefs to specifically legitimize the use of such weapons. Campbell notes that the belief that their cause is "sanctioned or mandated by God" or the potential for weapons of mass destruction to produce a "prophesied event" could legitimize the use of such weapons (1997, 29). It is also suggested that the more extreme goals of the new religious terrorists may sanction the use of weapons of mass destruction (Laqueur 1999, 81–82; Hoffman 1998a, 200–205).

9. Arquilla, Ronfeldt and Zanini (1999, 67) suggest the idea of a spectrum as an organizing tool and state that no terrorist organization can be considered a totally hierarchic or decentralized ideal type; groups would range along the spectrum, with "newer terrorist groups" approaching the decentralized end of the spectrum and traditional groups being closer to the hierarchical end of the spectrum. Yet no group would approach the limits of either end of the spectrum. They also suggest that in order to rank groups and place them along the spectrum in relation to other organizations would necessitate the creation of a an "analytical 'degree of networking' scale" to allow empirical research. Such a task would also necessitate a large amount of accurate data relating to the organizational structure of each group.

10. Schmid echoes this call for greater research in this area and suggests that analysis should focus upon "desperate actors" and the situations which may lead groups to use weapons of mass destruction (2000, 124). This analysis could also fit within the presented framework if it was based upon the premise that specific organizational structures and motivations are considered probable prerequisites for WMD use. Crelinstein (2000) also presents a favorable view of such an agent-based approach focused upon the assessment of terrorist motivations and goals, as well as their specific capabilities.

11. These categories are developed by Alexander L. George in an analysis of the potential contributions of academic scholars to foreign policy-making (1994). They appear also to be useful in discussing academic contributions to counter-terrorism policy-making which, in some instances, bridges the gap between foreign and domestic policy.

References

Arquilla, John, David Ronfeldt, and Michele Zanini. 1999. Networks, Netwar, and Information Age Terrorism. In *Countering the New Terrorism*, ed. Ian O. Lesser, Bruce Hoffman, John Arquilla, David Ronfeldt, and Michele Zanini, 39–84. Santa Monica: RAND.

Badey, Thomas J. 2001. Nuclear Terrorism: Actor-based Threat Assessment. *Intelligence and National Security 16*, no. 2: 39–54.

Crelinstein, Ronald J. 2000. Terrorism and Counter-terrorism in a Multi-Centric World. Challenges and Opportunities. In *The Future of Terrorism*. ed. Max Taylor and John Horgan, 170–196. London: Frank Cass.

CSIS. 1999. *Perspectives Report 2000/01:Trends in Terrorism*. http://www.csis~scrs.gc.ca/eng/miscdocs/200001_e.html.

CSIS. 2002. *Backgrounder Series No. 8: Counter Terrorism*. http://www.csis~scrs.gc.ca/eng/backgrnd/back8_e.html.

George, Alexander L. 1994. The Two Cultures of Academia and Policy-Making: Bridging the Gap. *Political Psychology 15*, no. 1: 143–172.

Gordon, Avishag. 2001. Terrorism and the Scholarly Communication System. *Terrorism and Political Violence 13*, no. 4: 116–124.

Harmon, Christopher C. 2000. *Terrorism Today*. London: Frank Cass.

Hoffman, Bruce. 1998. *Inside Terrorism*. New York: Columbia University Press.

_____. 1998. Old Madness New Methods. *Rand Review* (Winter): 12–17.

_____. 2001. Rethinking Terrorism in Light of a War on Terrorism. *Statement before the Subcommittee on Terrorism and Homeland Security House Permanent Select Committee on Intelligence.* U.S. House of Representatives. Santa Monica: RAND.

_____. 1999. Terrorism Trends and Prospects. In *Countering the New Terrorism*, ed. Ian O. Lesser, Bruce Hoffman, John Arquilla, David Ronfeldt, and Michele Zanini, 39–84. Santa Monica: RAND.

Horgan, John, and Max Taylor. 1997. The Provisional IRA: Command and Functional Structure. *Terrorism and Political Violence 9*, no. 3: 1–32.

Jenkins, Brian Michael. 2002. *Countering Al Qaeda*. Santa Monica: RAND.

_____. 1975. International Terrorism: A New Mode of Conflict. In *International Terrorism and World Security*. ed. David Carlton and Carlo Schaerf. London: Croom Helm.

_____. 1985. *The Likelihood of Nuclear Terrorism*. Santa Monica: RAND.

_____. 2001. Terrorism: Current and Long-Term Threats. *Statement of Brian Michael Jenkins Before the Senate Armed Services Subcommittee on Emerging Threats*. Santa Monica: RAND.

Jeurgensmeyer, Mark. 2002. The Logic of Religious Violence. In *Terrorism and Counterterrorism: Understanding The New Security Environment*. Readings & Interpretations. ed. Russel D. Howard and Reid L. Sawyer, 136–155. Guilford Conn: McGraw-Hill Companies.

Laqueur, Walter. 1996. Post-Modern Terrorism. *Foreign Affairs* (September/October): 24–36.

_____. 1999. *The New Terrorism*. New York: Oxford University Press.

Lesser, Ian O., Bruce Hoffman, John Arquilla, David Ronfeldt, and Michele Zanini. ed. 1999. *Countering the New Terrorism*. Santa Monica: RAND.

Merari, Ariel. 2000. Terrorism as a Strategy of Struggle: Past and Future. In *The Future of Terrorism*, ed.. Max Taylor and John Horgan, 52–65. London: Frank Cass.

Ranstorp, Magnus. 2002. Terrorism in the Name of Religion. In *Terrorism and Counterterrorism: Understanding The New Security Environment*. Readings & Interpretations, ed. Russel D. Howard and Reid L. Sawyer, 120–136. Guilford Conn.: McGraw-Hill Companies.

Schmid, Alex, P. 2000. Terrorism and the Use of Weapons of Mass Destruction. In *The Future of Terrorism*, ed. Max Taylor and John Horgan, 106–132. London: Frank Cass.

Tucker, David. 2001. What is New about the New Terrorism and How Dangerous is It? *Terrorism and Political Violence 13*, no. 3 (Autumn): 1–14.

Wilkinson, Paul. 1995. *CSIS Commentary No. 53: Terrorism Motivations and Causes*. http://www.cisis~scrs.gc.ca/end/comment/com53_e.html

_____. 2001. *Terrorism Versus Democracy: The Liberal State Response*. London: Frank Cass.

Chapter 4

Religion

The 1993 bombings of Manhattan's World Trade Center, Aum Shinrikyo's release of sarin nerve gas in the Tokyo underground, and the bombing of a U.S. Federal building in Oklahoma City were acts of terrorism carried out by players with vastly different origins, doctrines, and practices, writes Magnus Ranstorp. Yet Ranstorp recognizes one common thread among these terrorist acts: the perpetrators believed "their actions were divinely sanctioned, even mandated, by God."

Ranstorp charts the rise in terrorism for religious motives and reports that between the mid-1960s and mid-1990s there was a tripling in the number of fundamentalist movements of all religious affiliations. Nearly a quarter of all terrorist groups active in the world today are primarily motivated by religious concerns, yet these groups are also driven by practical political considerations—and it is difficult for observers to distinguish the political from the religious in the terrorist acts these groups commit. Ranstorp explores the motives, the "serious sense of crisis in their environment," which nearly all these groups experience and that fuels an escalation in their activities; the threats of secularization from foreign sources these groups identify and rail against; the hierarchy of power that emanates from a dynamic so-called spiritual leader; the role religious symbolism plays in selecting their targets; and the sense of hope and chance for vengeance these groups offer to followers who suffer under a history of grievances. Contrary to popular opinion, Ranstorp concludes, "Religious terrorism is anything but disorganized or random, but rather driven by an inner logic common among diverse groups and faiths who use political violence to further their sacred causes."

Mark Juergensmeyer looks at the complex relationship between religion and violence, particularly in the context of the militant Sikhs of India and the violence that seized the Punjab region in the 1980s. Juergensmeyer portrays the Sikhs as a group in crisis, "their separate identity within the Indian family is in danger.... Sikhs fear they could be reabsorbed into the amorphous cultural mass that is Hinduism and disappear as a distinct religious community," he writes. The author examines how the words and rhetoric of a charismatic militant leader, Jamail Singh Bhindranwale, can inspire a movement; and at how everyday, political issues can be mingled with a struggle for spiritual survival to create a cosmic struggle that validates violent means for religious and political ends.

Dolnik outlines an alternative approach to threat assessment by "defining specific motivational, behavioral and organizational characteristics that a terrorist group will need to satisfy" to conduct a mass-fatality attack using weapons of mass destruction. The identification of likely attributes of the "superterrorists" with regard to ideological, organizational, and behavioral traits is an important addition to the study of terrorism.

Magnus Ranstorp, 1996

Terrorism in the Name of Religion

Introduction

On 25 February 1994, the day of the second Muslim sabbath during Islam's holy month of Ramadan, a Zionist settler from the orthodox settlement of Qiryat Arba entered the crowded Ibrahim (Abraham's) Mosque, located in the biblical town of Hebron on the West Bank. He emptied three 30-shot magazines with his automatic Glilon assault-rifle into the congregation of 800 Palestinian Muslim worshippers, killing 29 and wounding 150, before being beaten to death. A longstanding follower of the radical Jewish fundamentalist group, the Kach movement,[1] Baruch Goldstein was motivated by a complex mixture of seemingly inseparable political and religious desiderata, fuelled by zealotry and a grave sense of betrayal as his prime minister was "leading the Jewish state out of its God-given patrimony and into mortal danger."[2] Both the location and the timing of the Hebron massacre were heavily infused with religious symbolism. Hebron was the site of the massacre of 69 Jews in 1929. Also, the fact that it occured during the Jewish festival of Purim symbolically cast Goldstein in the role of Mordechai in the Purim story, meting out awesome revenge against the enemies of the Jews.[3] Israeli Prime Minister Yithzak Rabin, speaking for the great mass of Israelis, expressed revulsion and profound sadness over the act committed by a "deranged fanatic." However, a large segment of militant and orthodox Jewish settlers in West Bank and Gaza settlements portrayed Goldstein as a righteous man and hailed him as a martyr.[4] During his funeral, these orthodox settlers also voiced religious fervor in uncompromising and militant terms directed not only against the Arabs, but also against the Israeli government, which they believed had betrayed the Jewish People and the Jewish state.

Israeli leaders and the Jewish community tried to deny or ignore the danger of Jewish extremism by dismissing Goldstein as belonging, at most, to "the fringe of a fringe"[5] within Israeli society. Sadly, any doubts of the mortal dangers of religious zealotry from within were abruptly silenced with the assassination of prime minister Yitzhak Rabin by a young Jewish student, Yigal Amir, who claimed he had acted on orders of God. He had been influenced by militant rabbis and their *halalic* rulings, which he interpreted to mean that the "pursuer's decree" was to be applied against Israel's leader.[6] Most Israelis may be astonished by the notion of a Jew killing another Jew, but Rabin was ultimately the victim of a broader force which has become one of the most vibrant, dangerous and pervasive trends in the post–Cold War world: religiously motivated terrorism.

Far afield from the traditionally violent Middle East, where religion and terrorism share a long history,[7] a surge of religious fanaticism has manifested itself in spectacular acts of terrorism across the globe. This wave of violence is unprecedented, not only in its scope and the selection of targets, but also in its lethality and indiscriminate character. Examples of these incidents abound: in an effort to hasten in the new millenium, the Japanese religious cult Aum Shinrikyo released sarin nerve gas on the Tokyo underground in June last

by God. Despite having vastly different origins, doctrines, institutions, and practices, these religious extremists are unified in their justification for employing sacred violence, whether in efforts to defend, extend or revenge their own communities, or for millenarian or messianic reasons.[11] This article seeks to explore these reasons for the contemporary rise in terrorism for religious motives and to identify the triggering mechanisms that bring about violence out of religious belief in both established and newly formed terrorist groups.

The Wider Trend of Religious Terrorism

Between the mid-1960s and the mid-1990s, the number of fundamentalist movements of all religious affiliations tripled worldwide. Simultaneously, as observed by Bruce Hoffman, there has been a virtual explosion of identifiable religious terrorist groups from none in 1968 to today's level, where nearly a quarter of all terrorist groups active throughout the world are predominantly motivated by religious concerns.[12] Unlike their secular counterparts, religious terrorists are, by their very nature, largely motivated by religion, but they are also driven by day-to-day practical political considerations within their context-specific environment. This makes it difficult for the general observer to separate and distinguish between the political and the religious sphere of these terrorist groups.

Nowhere is this more clear than in Muslim terrorist groups, as religion and politics cannot be separated in Islam. For example, Hizb'allah or Hamas operate within the framework of religious ideology, which they combine with practical and precise political action in Lebanon and Palestine. As such, these groups embrace simultaneously short-term objectives, such as the release of imprisoned members, and long-term objectives, such as continuing to resist Israeli occupation of their homelands and liberating all "believers." This is further complicated with the issue of state-sponsorship of terrorism: Religious terrorist groups become cheap and effective tools for specific states in the advancement of their foreign policy political agendas. They may also contain a nationalist-separatist agenda, in which the religious component is often entangled with a complex mixture of cultural, political, and linguistic factors. The proliferation of religious extremist movements has also been accompanied by a sharp increase in the total number of acts of terrorism since 1988, accounting for over half of the 64,319 recorded incidents between 1970 and July 1995.[13] This escalation by the religious terrorists is hardly surprising given the fact that most of today's active groups worldwide came into existence very recently. They appeared with a distinct and full-fledged organizational apparatus. They range from the Sikh Dal Khalsa and the Dashmesh organizations, formed in 1978 and 1982 respectively[14] and the foundation of the Shi'ite Hizb'allah movement in Lebanon in 1982; to the initial emergence of the militant Sunni organizations, known as Hamas and Islamic Jihad, in conjunction with the 1987 outbreak of the Palestinian Intifada as well as the establishment of the Aum Shinrikyo in the same year.

The growth of religious terrorism is also indicative of the transformation of contemporary terrorism into a method of warfare and the evolution of the tactics and techniques used by various groups, as a reaction to vast changes within the local, regional and global environment over the last three decades. These changes can be seen in numerous incidents, from the spate of hijackings by secular Palestinian terrorists and the mayhem of destruction caused by left- and right-wing domestic terrorists throughout Europe, to today's unprecedented global scope and level of religious extremism.

The evolution of today's religious terrorism neither has occurred in a vacuum nor represents a particularly new phenomenon. It has, however, been propelled to the forefront in the post–Cold war world, as it has been exacerbated by the explosion of ethnic-religious conflicts and the rapidly approaching new millenium.[15] The accelerated dissolution of traditional links of social and cultural cohesion within and between societies with the current globalization process, combined with the historical legacy and current conditions of political repression, economic inequality and social upheaval common among disparate religious extremist movements, have all lead to an increased sense of fragility, instability and unpredictability for the present and the future.[16] The current scale and scope of religious terrorism, unprecedented in militancy and activism, is indicative of this perception that their respective faiths and communities stand at a critical historical juncture: Not only do the terrorists feel the need to preserve their religious identity, they also see this time as an opportunity to fundamentally shape the future.[17] There are a number of overlapping factors that have contributed to the revival of religious terrorism in its modern and lethal form at the end of the millennium. At the same time, it is also possible to discern a number of features which are found in all religious terrorist groups across different regions and faiths. These features serve not only to define the cause and the enemy, but also fundamentally shape the means, methods and the timing of the use of the violence itself.

The Causes and the Enemies of Religious Terrorists

A survey of the major religious terrorist groups in existence worldwide in the 1990s would reveal that almost all experience a serious sense of crisis in their environment, which has led to an increase in the number of groups recently formed and caused an escalation in their activities. This crisis mentality in the religious terrorist's milieu is multifaceted, at once in the social, political, economic, cultural, psychological and spiritual sphere. At the same time, it has been greatly exacerbated by the political, economic and social tumult, resulting in a sense of spiritual fragmentation and radicalization of society experienced worldwide in the wake of the end of the Cold War and the extremist's "fear of the forced march toward 'one worldism.'"[18] Yet, this sense of crisis, as a perceived threat to their identity and survival, has been present to varying degrees throughout history. It has led to recurring phases of resurgence in most faiths. In these revivals, the believers use the religion in a variety of ways: they take refuge in the religion, which provides centuries-old ideals by which to determine goals; they find physical or psychological sanctuary against repression; or they may use it as a major instrument for activism or political action. Thus, religious terrorists perceive their actions as defensive and reactive in character and justify them in this way.[19] Islam's *jihad*, for example, is essentially a defensive doctrine, religiously sanctioned by leading Muslim theologians, and fought against perceived aggressors, tyrants, and "wayward Muslims." In its most violent form, it is justified as a means of last resort to prevent the extinction of the distinctive identity of the Islamic community against the forces of secularism and modernism. As outlined by Sheikh Fadlallah, the chief ideologue of

violence is also evident in the Sikh's fear of losing their distinct identity in the sea of Hindus and Muslims.[22] In the United States, the paranoid outlook of white supremacist movements is driven by a mixture of racism and anti-Semitism, as well as mistrust of government and all central authority.[23] This sense of persecution is also visible among the Shi'ites as an historically dominant theme for 13 centuries, manifest in the annual Ashura processions by the Lebanese Hizb'allah, commemorating the martyrdom of Imam Husayn. This event and mourning period have been used as justification and as a driving force behind its own practice of martyrdom through suicide attacks.[24]

Other than a few strictly millenarian or messianic groups (such as Aum Shinrikyo or some Christian white supremacist movements), almost all the contemporary terrorist groups with a distinct religious imperative are either offshoots or on the fringe of broader movements. As such, the militant extremists' decisions to organize, break away or remain on the fringe are, to a large extent, conditioned by the political context within which they operate. Their decisions are shaped by doctrinal differences, tactical and local issues, and the degree of threat that they perceive secularization poses to their cause. This threat of secularization may come either from within the movements themselves and the environment within which they come into contact, or from outside influences. If the threat is external, it may amplify their sense of marginality within, and acute alienation from, society. It may also fuel the need to compensate for personal sufferings through the radical transformation of the ruling order.[25] The internal threat of secularization is often manifest in a vociferous and virulent rejection of the corrupt political parties, the legitimacy of the regime, and also the lackluster and inhibited character of the existing religious establishment. Thus, religious terrorism serves as the only effective vehicle for violent political opposition.[26] As explained by Kach's leader, Baruch Marzel, "(w)e feel God gave us in the six-day war, with a miracle, this country. We are taking this present from God and tossing it away. They are breaking every holy thing in this country, the Government, in a very brutal way."[27] Similarly, as voiced by the late Palestinian Islamic Jihad's leader, Fathi al-Shaqaqi, with reference to the Gaza-Jericho agreement between the PLO [Palestine Liberation Organization] and Israel: "Arafat has sold his soul for the sake of his body and is trying to sell the Palestinian people's soul in return for their remaining alive politically."[28] The religious terrorist groups' perception of a threat of secularization from within the same society is also manifest in the symbolism used in the selection of their names, indicating that they have an absolute monopoly of the revealed truth by God. It is, therefore, not surprising that some of the most violent terrorist groups over the last decade have also adopted names accordingly: Hizb'allah (Party of God), Aum Shinrikyo (The Supreme Truth) and Jund al-Haqq (Soldiers of Truth). These names also endow them with religious legitimacy, historical authenticity, and justification for their actions in the eyes of their followers and potential new recruits. They also provide valuable insight into their unity of purpose, direction and degree of militancy, with names like Jundallah (Soldiers of God), Hamas (Zeal), Eyal (Jewish Fighting Organization) and Le Groupe Islamique du Armé (Armed Islamic Group, GIA) which promises unabated struggle and sacrifice.

The threat of secularization from foreign sources is also the catalyst for springing religious terrorists into action. Intrusion of secular values into the extremist's own environment and the visible presence of secular foreign interference provoke self-defensive aggressiveness and hostility against the sources of these evils. This is especially true against colonalism and neo-colonialism by western civilizations or against other militant religious faiths. These defensive sentiments are often combined with the visible emergence and presence of militant clerical leaders. Such leaders have more activist and militant ideologies than the mainstream movement from which they have emerged as either clandestine instruments or breakaway groups. It is often the case that these clerical ideologues and personalities act as a centrifugal force in attracting support, strengthening the organizational mechanisms and in redefining the methods and means through terrorism. At the same time, they provide theological justification, which enables their followers to pursue the sacred causes more effectively and rapidly. The so-called spiritual guides, who ultimately overlook most political and military activities while blessing acts of terrorism, can be found in almost all religious terrorist groups: Examples include Hizb'allah's Sheikh Fadlallah and Hamas' Sheikh Yassin, the militant Sikh leader Sant Bhindranwale and Aum Shinrikyo's leader, Shoko Ashara.

Most active terrorist groups with a religious imperative were actually propelled into existence in reaction to key events. These events either served as a catalyst or inspirational model for the organization or gravely escalated the perception of the threat of foreign secularization, or for messianic or millenarian groups, a heightened sense that time was running out. The latter is evident in the growth and increased activism of doomsday cults, awaiting the imminent apocalypse, whose self-prophetic visions about the future have triggered them to hasten the new millennium.[29] This messianic anticipation, for example, was clearly evident in the attack on the Grand Mosque of Mecca in 1979 (the Islamic year 1400) by armed Muslim militants from al-Ikhwan, who expected the return of their Madhi.[30] The formation of Lebanese Hizb'allah can be attributed to the context of the civil war environment and the inspiring example of Ayatollah Khomeini's Islamic revolution in Iran. However, it was Israel's invasion of Lebanon in 1982 and the subsequent foreign intrusion in the form of the western-led Multinational Forces (MNF) that served as a catalyst for Hizb'allah's actual organizational formation and which to this day has continued to fuel its militancy and religious ideology. Similarly, the 1984 desecration by the Indian army of the Golden Temple in Amritsar, Sikhism's holiest shrine, led not only to the assassination of Prime Minister Indira Gandhi in revenge, but also to a cycle of endless violence between the warring faiths, which hitherto has claimed over 20,000 lives.[31]

In many ways, religious terrorists embrace a total ideological vision of an all-out struggle to resist secularization from within as well as from without. They pursue this vision in totally uncompromising holy terms in literal battles between good and evil. Ironically, there is a great degree of similarity between the stands of the Jewish Kach and Islamic Hamas organizations: Both share a vision of a religious state between the Jordan River and the Mediterranean Sea; a xenophobia against everything alien or secular which must be removed from the entire land, and a vehement rejection of western culture. This distinction between the faithful and those standing outside the group is reinforced in the daily discourse of the clerics of these terrorist groups. The clerics' language and phraseology shapes the followers' reality, reinforcing the loyalty and social obligation of the members to the group and reminding them of the sacrifices already made, as well as the direction of the

desecration of Israeli and American flags by several Islamic groups across the Middle East. This collectiveness is also reinforced by the fact that any deviation or compromise amounts to treachery and a surrender of the principles of the religious faith is often punishable by death.

The sense of totality of the struggle for these religious warriors is one purely defined in dialectic and cosmic terms as believers against unbelievers, order against chaos, and justice against injustice, which is mirrored in the totality and uncompromising nature of their cause, whether that cause entails the establishment of Eretz Israel, an Islamic state based on *sharia* law or an independent Khalistan ("Land of the Pure"). As such, the religious terrorists perceive their struggle as all-out war against their enemies. This perception, in turn, is often used to justify the level and intensity of the violence. For example, this theme of war is continuously detectable in the writings and statements by the terrorists, as exemplified by Yigal Amir's justification for assassinating Rabin;[35] or by Article 8 of Hamas' manifesto justifying that *jihad* is its path and that "[d]eath for the sake of Allah is its most sublime belief."

This totality of the struggle naturally appeals to its acutely disenfranchized, oppressed, and alienated communities with the promises of change and the provision of constructive alternatives. Unlike their recent historical predecessors, like the fringe al-Jihad organization which assassinated the Egyptian President Anwar Sadat in 1981,[36] many of the existing religious terrorist cells are different in that they can often complement their violence with realistic alternatives to secular submission. This is especially true at the grassroots level, due to the penchant for organization inherent in religion and the backing of a vast network of resources and facilities.[37] This has meant that some religious terrorist groups are not solely relying on violence, but also have gradually built an impressive constituency through a strategy of "re-Islamization or re-Judaization from below."[38] The political dimension is complemented with terrorism in confrontation with the enemy or in defense of the sacred cause. This is a process which began in the early 1970s and culminated in the 1990s with a visible shift in strategy among groups, from relying on terrorism while re-Islamizing their environment to complementing terrorism with the use of the electoral process to advance their sacred causes.

Religious terrorism also offers its increasingly suffering and impatient constituents more hope and a greater chance of vengeance against the sources of their historical grievances than they would otherwise have. This is most effectively illustrated by the 1985 Sikh inflight bombing of an Air India airliner, causing 328 deaths, as well as by Hizb'allah's twin suicide-bombings of the U.S. Marine barracks and the French MNF headquarters in Beirut in 1983, killing 241 and 56 soldiers respectively. Violent acts give these groups a sense of power that is disproportionate to their size. The basis for this feeling of power is enhanced by a strategy of anonymity by the religious terrorist which confuses the enemy. In other words, the covernames are used according to where the religious terrorists have come from and where they are heading. Terrorists of the Muslim faith, particularly Shi'ite groups, employ a wide variety of covernames (in the Shi'ite case rooted in history with the notion of *taqiyyah*, or dissimulation) in efforts to protect their communities against repression or retaliation by the enemy after terrorist acts.[39] Yet, these covernames reveal significantly the currents or directions within movements in alignment with their struggles.[40] As such, the religious terrorists tend to "execute their terrorist acts for no audience but themselves."[41] Although the act of violence in and of itself is executed primarily for the terrorists own community as a sign of strength, it naturally embodies wider elements of fear in their actual or potential enemy targets. The perpetrators adeptly exploit this fear by invoking religious symbolism, such as the release of videotaped images of an endless pool of suicide bombers, ready to be dispatched against new targets.

While the religious extremists uniformly strike at the symbols of tyranny, they are relatively unconstrained in the lethality and the indiscriminate nature of violence used, as it is conducted and justified in defence of the faith and the community. Reflecting the dialectic nature of the struggle itself, various religious terrorist groups also refer to their alien or secular enemies in de-humanizing terms which may loosen the moral constraints for them in their employment of particularly destructive acts of terrorism.[42] As explained by an extremist rabbi in conjunction with the funeral of Baruch Goldstein: "There is a great difference in the punishment becoming a person who hurts a Jew and a person who hurts a gentile.... [t]he life of a Jew is worth much more than the lives of many gentiles." This moral self-purification points to the belief that the perpetrators view themselves as divinely "chosen people," who not only possess religious legitimacy and justification for their propensity for violence, but also often act out of the belief that the violence occurs in a divinely sanctioned juncture in history. For example, the Japanese cult leader Shoko Ashara and his followers believed the world would end in 1997 and launched a sarin nerve gas attack on Tokyo's subway system to hasten the new millennium.[43]

In fact, the lack of any moral constraints in the use of violence cannot only be attributed to the totality of the struggle itself but also to the preponderance of recruits of young, educated and newly-urbanized men (often with very radical, dogmatic, and intolerant worldviews), in contemporary religious terrorist organizations.[44] This increased militancy of a younger generation of religious terrorists can be explained by both the fragmentation of groups into rival splinter factions and also the killing or imprisonment of key founding leaders and ideologues.[45] Apart from removing the older generation of terrorist leadership, the experience of persecution and imprisonment has led to the radicalization of younger recruits into the organizations.[46] Also there seems to be an inverse relationship between size and militancy.[47] The Shi'ite terrorist groups are more prone to martyrdom than their Sunni counterparts, due to their different historical legacies and to the more powerful role of Shi'ite clergymen in directly interceding between man and God. However, some Sunni groups have recently broken the mold, as evident in the unprecedented series of 13 Hamas suicide-attacks inside Israel (which killed 136 people between 6 April 1994 and 4 March 1996) after the Hebron massacre and, to a lesser extent, the foiled plan by the GIA to explode its hijacked Air France plane over metropolitan Paris in December 1994. However, as explained by Sheikh Fadlallah: "There is no difference between dying with a gun in your hand or exploding yourself. In a situation of struggle or holy war you have to find the best means to achieve your goals."[48]

While the resort to martyrdom by certain groups can be explained by the heightened sense of threat to the groups and their causes within their own environment, it can also be explained by an increasing level of internationalization between groups both in terms of

as about national liberation."[49] As a significant example of a revolutionary cause within a Sunni context, as opposed to the more narrow Shi'ite example of the Iranian revolution, the Afghan conflict served as a training ground for their own struggles during the 1980s: Following the collapse of communism, these fighters returned to their respective countries to radicalize the Islamic struggle at home, resorting to increasing violence in the process, either within existing movements or as splinter groups.

Yet, the mechanisms of unleashing acts of religious terrorism, in terms of intensity, methods and timing, are tightly controlled by the apex of the clerical hierarchy and most often dependent on their blessing. This was clearly demonstrated in the 1984 Gush Emunim plot to blow up the Temple Mount (or Dome of the Rock), Islam's third holiest site, in part for messianic reasons (to cause a cataclysmic war between Jews and Muslims to hasten the coming of the Messiah) and in part to foil the return of Jewish sacred land to Arabs in return for peace under the Camp David accord. This act of terrorism never materialized due to the lack of rabbinical backing.[50] Similarly, the role of the spiritual leaders within Islamic terrorist organizations is equally pivotal, as displayed by the central role of Sheikh Omar 'Abd al-Rahman of the Egyptian al-Jama'a al-Islamiyya in issuing the directive, or *fatwa*, for both the 1981 assassination of Anwar Sadat and the 1993 bombing of New York's World Trade Center.[51] As such, in most cases the strictly hierarchical nature of religious terrorist groups with a highly disciplined structure and obedient cadres means not only that the main clerical leaders command full control over the political as well as military activities of the organization but also that the strategies of terrorism are unleashed in accordance with general political directives and agendas.[52]

Yet, the use and sanctioning of religious violence requires clearly defined enemies. The newly-formed religious terrorist groups today do not appear in a vacuum nor are their members naturally born into extremism. The identity of the enemy and the decision to use religious violence against them are dependent on, and shaped by, the heightened degree of the sense of crisis threatening their faiths and communities. This, in turn, is influenced by the historical legacy of political repression, economic inequality or social upheaval, and may be exacerbated by ethnic and military disputes. This sense of grievance is uniquely experienced between the faiths and the individual groups, as well as in alignment with the political strategies and tactics adopted to confront them according to local, regional and international contexts. Internally, this militancy may be directed against the corruption or injustices of the political system, or against other religious communities; externally, it may be focused against foreign influences, which represent a cultural, economic, or political threat to the respective religious communities. The West, particularly the United States as well as Israel, tends to be the favourite target of this militancy, especially by terrorists of the Muslim faith.[53]

Anti-western sentiments and intense hostility towards Israel for the Muslim terrorist is the result of the historical legacy of political oppression and socio-economic marginalization within the Arab world. These hostilities are combined with the discrediting of secular ideologies and the illegitimacy of current political and economic elites, especially after the 1967 defeat of the Arabs by Israel.[54] This sense of crisis has been exacerbated by the Arab-Israeli conflict which served to reinforce a Muslim inferiority complex due to the inability of either Arab regimes or secular Palestinians to defeat Israel. Simultaneously, the West is perceived to be practising neocolonialism through its Israeli surrogate and its unqualified support for existing "un-Islamic" and "illegitimate" regimes across the Arab world. As such, the Islamist movements and their respective armed "terrorist" wings have gradually propelled themselves to the forefront of politics as the true defender of the oppressed and dispossessed and as the only effective spearhead against Israel's continued existence in the heart of Muslim territory and against the West's presence and interference in the region. Apart from the obvious religious dimensions of the loss of Palestine to Zionism, Muslim militants draw heavily on the symbolism of the historical legacy of the Crusades, pitting Christendom against Islam, to explain their current condition of oppression and disinheritance, and to provide workable solutions and defences against the threat of western encirclement and secularization.[55] The Muslim terrorists rework these historic religious symbols to fit present-day conditions as a vehicle to inspire political action and revolutionary violence against its enemies.

While the identity of the enemy is deeply rooted in both distant and recent history, the turn towards, and the direction of, terrorism by militant Muslim movements against foreign enemies have been following distinct phases according to changes in the political and ideological context in the region. These phases are directly influenced by the Iranian revolution in 1979, the Muslim resistance struggle led by the Mujahadin against the Soviets in Afghanistan, the electoral victory of the Front Islamique du Salut (FIS) in Algeria (1990 to 1991), and the signing of the Israeli-Palestinian Declaration of Principles in September 1993. The Iranian revolution provided a revolutionary model of Islam and inspired Islamic movements to seriously challenge existing regimes at home. Additionally, the internationalization of Muslim terrorist violence against the West and Israel during the 1980s supported Iran's efforts to export the revolution abroad and was a cost-effective instrument to change the foreign policies of western states hostile towards the Islamic Republic.[56] The Lebanese Hizb'allah movement in particular, was very useful to the Iranian regime in achieving these ends. It also provided Iran with the opportunity to participate, both indirectly and militarily, in the Arab-Israeli conflict.[57] Additionally, Muslim fighters in Afghanistan during the 1980s forged important networks between various groups and individuals which accelerated the activism among Muslim groups on the homefront when these fighters returned home. The FIS electoral victory in Algeria demonstrated to Muslim terrorist groups that they could use the ballotbox rather than relying solely on bullets in efforts to come to power in various Arab states. The election's subsequent nullification by the Algerian military junta led to radicalization of the Islamists and their turn towards terrorism against the state itself and the French government for extending support.

Simultaneously, the gradual resolution of the Israeli-Palestinian conflict threatens the pan-Islamic goal of militant Islamic movements of liberating Jerusalem. This threat has led to accelerated co-ordination between Islamic terrorist groups in efforts to sabotage the peace process and an increased militancy and confrontation against the West, Israel, and supportive Arab regimes. At the same time, the political wings of these terrorist groups seek to continue and extend the process of re-Islamization of society from below. The confluence of these factors over the last two decades has accelerated the militancy of the Muslim terrorist while it clearly demonstrates that they are closely attuned to changes in the local,

In comparison to their secular counterparts, the religious terrorists have not been particularly inventive when it comes to using new types of weaponry in their arsenals, instead relying on the traditional bombs and bullets.[58] Yet the religious terrorists have demonstrated a great deal of ingenuity in terms of the tactics used in the selection of means, methods and timing of violence to cause maximum effect. They have utilized the notion of martyrdom and self-sacrifice through suicide bombings as a means of last resort against their conventionally more powerful enemies. The first time this tactic was employed by the Hizb'allah was against the American, French and later Israeli military contingents present in Lebanon in 1983. It was emulating the actions of the shock troops of the Iranian Revolutionary Guards in their war with Iraq. While the Hizb'allah clerics gradually encountered theological dilemmas in continuing the sanctioning of this method, as suicide is generally forbidden in Islam except for under exceptional circumstances, the Hamas movement felt compelled to adopt suicide bombings in 1994 as a means of last resort in order to sabotage the Israeli-Palestinian peace process.[59] They believed that its actual implemention on the ground would severely threaten Hamas' revolutionary existence. The tactic of suicide bombing was also used to take revenge against its "Zionist enemy" for the Hebron attack. While few terrorist groups adopt large-scale campaigns of suicide missions, the religious terrorist utilizes the traditional methods of assassination, kidnappings, hijackings, and bombings in a skillful combination in alignment with the current political context on the local, regional, and international level. Despite the growth and array of religious terrorist groups with diverse demands and grievances, they are all united not only in the level and intensity of violence used, but also in the role played by religious symbolism in selecting the targets and the timing of the violence itself.

Many of these terrorist groups are compelled to undertake operations with a distinct political agenda for organizational reasons to release imprisoned members or eliminating opponents. Nonetheless, the targets are almost always symbolic and carefully selected to cause maximum psychological trauma to the enemy and to boost the religious credentials of the terrorist group among their own followers. This is clearly evident from the selection by Muslim terrorists of western embassies, airlines, diplomats and tourists abroad as symbolically striking at the heart of their oppressors. This was evident in the selection of major New York City landmarks by Sheikh Rahman's followers or the multiple attacks by the Hizb'allah against U.S. diplomatic and military facilities.[60] In many instances, these groups have adopted a multi-pronged approach of using terrorism. For example, in Algeria the FIS has targeted foreign tourists, businessmen and diplomats, as well as Algerian officials and other Algerians who engage in un-Islamic behaviour (e.g unveiled women or any form of western culture). At the same time, it engages in the re-Islamization of society from below and simultaneously wages a war of attrition on French soil against symbolic civilian and official targets. In other cases, religious terrorists have used powerful symbolism to provoke deliberate reactions by the enemy, such as Dal Khalsa's severing of cows' heads outside two Hindu temples in Amritsar, which provoked massive disturbances between the

Sikhs and the Hindus in April 1982.[61] This type of symbolism is also seen in the 1969 arson attack on the al-Aqsa mosque in East Jerusalem by a Jewish extremist and the 1982 plan by Jewish fanatics to blow up Temple Mount in order to spark a cataclysmic war between Muslims and Jews.[62]

Finally, the timing of the violence by religious terrorists is carefully selected to coincide with their own theological requirements or to desecrate their enemies' religious holidays and sacred moments. For example, the 1995 bombing of the Alfred P. Murrah Federal Building in Oklahoma by white supremacists was reportedly scripted after *The Turner Diaries*, but also timed to "commemorate the second anniversary of FBI's assault on the Branch Davidian's Waco, Texas compound; [and] to mark the date 220 years before when the American revolution began at Lexington and Concord."[63] Similarly, the symbolism of the timing of religious violence was also evident in the Algerian GIA's decision to hijacking an Air France plane during Christmas after the killing of two Catholic priests, or the cycle of violence by Hamas' suicide bombings against Israel, occurring in February 1996, on the second commemoration of the Hebron massacre.

Conclusions

This article has sought to demonstrate that, contrary to popular belief, the nature and scope of religious terrorism is anything but disorganised or random but rather driven by an inner logic common among diverse groups and faiths who use political violence to further their sacred causes. The resort to terrorism by religious imperative is also not a new phenomenon, but rather deeply embedded in the history and evolution of the faiths. Religions have gradually served to define the causes and the enemies as well as the means, methods and timing of the violence itself. As such, the virtual explosion of religious terrorism in recent times is part and parcel of a gradual process of what can be likened to neo-colonial liberation struggles. This process has trapped religious faiths within meaningless geographical and political boundaries and constraints, and has been accelerated by grand shifts in the global political, economic, military and socio-cultural setting, compounded by difficult local indigenous conditions for the believers. The uncertainty and unpredictability in the present environment as the world searches for a new world order, amidst an increasingly complex global environment with ethnic and nationalist conflicts, provide many religious terrorist groups with the opportunity and the ammunition to shape history according to their divine duty, cause, and mandate while it indicates for others that the end of time itself is near. As such, it is imperative to move away from treating this new religious force in global politics as a monolithic entity but rather seek to understand the inner logic of these individual groups and the mechanisms that produce terrorism in order to undermine their breeding ground and strength, as they are here to stay. At present it is doubtful that the United States or any western government is adequately prepared to meet this challenge.

An internationally recognized expert on terrorism, **Magnus Ranstorp** is a lecturer in international relations at the University of St. Andrews (Scotland) and deputy director of the University's Centre for the Study of Terrorism and Political Violence, where he specialized in the behavior of militant Islamic movements in the Middle East and North Africa. Author of *Hizballah in Lebanon: The Politics of the*

1. The Kach movement was founded in 1971 by the ultra-orthodox American Rabbi Meir Kahane when he emigrated to Israel. The group calls for the establishment of a theocratic state in Eretz (Greater) Israel and the forced expulsion of Arabs. For a useful overview see Raphael Cohen-Almagor, "Vigilant Jewish Fundamentalism: From the JDL to Kach (or 'Shalom Jews, Shalom Dogs'), *Terrorism and Political Violence*, 4, No.1 (Spring 1992): pp.44–66; and Ehud Sprintzak, *The Ascendance of Israel's Radical Right* (New York: Oxford University Press, 1991).

2. "The Impossible Decision," *The Economist*, 11–17 November 1995, p.25.

3. For a discussion of Goldstein's decision to carry out the attack during Purim, see Sue Fiskhoff, "Gentle, Kind and Full of Religious Fervor," *Jerusalem Post*, 27 February 1994; and Chris Hedges and Joel Greenberg, "West Bank Massacre: Before Killing, a Final Prayer and a Final Taunt," *New York Times*, 28 February 1994, p. A1.

4. One of Goldstein's rabbinical mentors, Rabbi Dov Li'or, described him in compassionate terms as a man "who could no longer take the humiliation and the disgrace. Everything he did was in honor of Israel and for the glory of God," in *Yediot Aharanot*, 18 March 1994. Also see: Richard Z. Chesnoff, "It Is a Struggle for Survival," *U.S. News & World Report*, 14 March 1994.

5. Charles Krauthammer, "Deathly Double Standard," *Jerusalem Post*, 6 March 1994.

6. Prior to Rabin's assassination, Yigal Amir had tried two previous times. For a very useful biography of the assassin, see John Kifner, "A Son of Israel: Rabin's Assassin," *New York Times*, 19 November 1995; *idem.*, "Israelis Investigate Far Right; May Crack Down on Speech," *New York Times*, 8 November 1995. One of these traditional exemptions for killing is Din Rodef, or Law of the Pursuer. The rule was first set forth in the 12th century by the great Moses Maimonides, a Spanish Jewish scholar. Going beyond the principle of self-defense, it states that even a witness to the act of someone's trying to kill another is allowed to kill the potential assassin. For Yigal Amir's use of the principle as a defense for killing Rabin, see Raine Marcus, "Amir: I Wanted to Murder Rabin," *Jerusalem Post*, 16 March 1996.

7. As aptly observed by David C. Rapoport in his seminal work, the words "zealot," "assassin" and "thug" all derive from historic fanatic movements within, respectively, Judaism, Islam and Hinduism, respectively. See Bruce Hoffman, *"Holy Terror": The Implications of Terrorism Motivated by a Religious Imperative* (Santa Monica: RAND, 1993) pp. 1–2; and David C. Rapoport, "Fear and Trembling: Terrorism in Three Religious Traditions," *American Political Science Review*, 78, no. 3 (September 1984) pp. 668–72. For a useful historical overview, see David C. Rapoport, "Why Does Religious Messianism Produce Terror?" in *Contemporary Research on Terrorism*, ed. Paul Wilkinson and A.M. Stewart, (Aberdeen: Aberdeen University Press, 1987) pp. 72–88.

8. The attack on the Tokyo subway was the first recorded instance of a terrorist group committing mass murder with a weapon of mass destruction. The Aum Shinrikyou religious cult was established in 1987 by Shoko Ashara, a nearly blind acupuncturist and yoga master, and is composed of a synthesized mixture of Buddhist and Hindu theology. For a useful brief biographical sketch of Ashara, see James Walsh, "Shoko Asahara: The Making of a Messiah," *Time*, 3 April 1995. The sarin nerve gas attack on Tokyo's subway killed 8 and injured over 5,500. Also see Martin Wollacott, "The Whiff of Terror," *The Guardian*, 21 March 1995.

9. For a useful overview of al-Jama'a al-Islamiyya and its activities in Egypt, see Barry Rubin, *Islamic Fundamentalism in Egyptian Politics* (London: Macmillan 1990).

10. See Stephen Robinson, "The American Fundamentalist," *Daily Telegraph*, 24 April 1995.

11. For a very comprehensive discussion, see Mark Juergensmeyer, ed. "Violence and the Sacred in the Modern World," *Terrorism and Political Violence*, 3, no. 3 (Autumn 1991).

12. Bruce Hoffman (1993), p. 2. The year 1968 is widely recognized as the point of origin for modern international terrorism. It was the beginning of an explosion of hijackings from Cuba to the United States, as well as attacks against Israeli and Western airlines by various Palestinian

groups. Also see Barry James, "Religious Fanaticism Fuels Terrorism," *International Herald Tribune*, 31 October 1995, p. 3.

13. See Professor Yonah Alexander, "Algerian Terrorism: Some National, Regional and Global Perspectives," Prepared statement before the House Committee on International Relations, Subcommittee on Africa, *Federal News Service*, 11 October 1995. This figure should be compared with 8,339 acts of international terrorism during the period 1970 to 1994 with 3,105 incidents occurring after 1988, see RAND-St. Andrews, *Chronology of International Terrorism* (St. Andrews: Centre for the Study of Terrorism and Political Violence, University of St. Andrews, March 1996).

14. The Dashmesh (meaning "10th") organization was named after the Sikhs' last guru, Gobind Singh, who, in the eighteenth century, transformed the Sikh community into a warrior class by justifying force when necessary. Both the Dashmesh and the Sikh Dal Khalsa advocate the establishment of an independent Khalistan.

15. The emergence of ethnic-religious conflict over conventional inter-state warfare was illuminated by a 1994 report by the United Nations Development Programme in which only 3 out of a total of 82 conflicts worldwide were between states. See Roger Williamson, "The Contemporary Face of Conflict—Class, Colour, Culture and Confession," in *Jane's Intelligence Review Yearbook—The World in Conflict 94/95* (London: Jane's Information Group, 1995) pp. 8–10. Also see Julia Preston, "Boutros Ghali: 'Ethnic Conflict' Imperils Security," *Washington Post*, 9 November 1993, p. 13. Also see Hans Binnendijk & Patrick Clawson, eds., *Strategic Assessment 1995: U.S. Security Challenges in Transition* (Washington: National Defense University Press, 1995); and Martin Kramer, "Islam & the West (including Manhattan)," *Commentary* (October 1993) pp. 33–37.

16. For the wider debate of the religious resurgence, see Scott Thomas, "The Global Resurgence of Religion and the Study of World Politics," *Millenium*, 24, no. 2 (Summer 1995) and Peter Beyer, *Religion and Globalization* (London: Sage, 1994).

17. As observed: At a time when no one knows precisely what form the future may take, the strength of fundamentalism lies in its ability to promise radical change without having to specify its outlines—since God is claimed as its guarantor," in Mahmoud Hussein, "Behind the Veil of Fundamentalism," *UNESCO Courier*, December 1994, p. 25. Also as stated by an ideologue of Jewish extremist group, Kahane Chai: "We are accountable only to our Creator, to He who chose us for our mission in history," in Amir Taheri, "Comentary: The Ideology of Jewish Extremism," *Arab News*, 12 March 1994.

18. Robin Wright, "Global Upheaval Seen as Engine for Radical Groups," *Los Angeles Times*, 6 November 1995.

19. "Fundamentalism Unlimited," *The Economist*, 27 March 1993, p. 67; and Hussein, p. 25.

20. Muhammad Hussein Fadlallah, "To Avoid a World War of Terror," *Washington Post*, 4 June 1986. As reiterated by Sheikh Fadallah: "We are not preachers of violence. Jihad in Islam is a defensive movement against those who impose violence." Laura Marlowe, "A Fiery Cleric's Defense of Jihad," *Time*, 15 January 1996. For further elaboration on this by Sheikh Fadlallah, see *al-Majallah*, 1–7 October 1986.

21. This is often seen in the Sikh slogan: "The Panth [religion] is in danger." See Paul Wallace, "The Sikhs as a 'Minority' in a Sikh Majority State in India," *Asian Survey*, 26, no. 3 (March 1986) p. 363.

22. Laurent Belsie, "At a Sikh Temple, Opinions Reflect Conflicting Religious Traditions," *Christian Science Monitor*, 11 November 1984. For a detailed discussion of the use of violence, see Sohan Singh Sahota, *The Destiny of the Sikhs* (Chandigarh: Modern Publishers, 1970).

23. Bruce Hoffman, "American Right-Wing Terrorism," *Jane's Intelligence Review*, 7, no. 7 (July 1995) pp. 329–30.

24. See John Kifner, "Shiite Radicals: Rising Wrath Jars the Mideast," *New York Times*, 22 March 1987.

25. This theme is developed by David Rapoport, "Comparing Militant Fundamentalist Movements," in *Fundamentalism and the State*, ed. Martin E. Marty and R. Scott Appleby (Chicago: The University of Chicago Press, 1993).

part of] her," in Amos Oz, "Israel's Far Right Collaborates With Hamas in Thwarting Peace," *The Times*, 11 April 1995.

29. For a useful insight into the dynamics of cults, see Richardo Delgado, "Limits to Proselytizing," *Society* (March/April 1980) pp. 25–33; Margaret Thaler Singer, "Coming of the Cults," *Psychology Today* (January 1979) pp. 73–82.

30. See Robin Wright, "U.S. Struggles to Deal With Global Islamic Resurgence," *Los Angeles Times*, 26 January 1992.

31. For a useful overview, see Pranay Gupte, "The Punjab: Torn by Terror," *New York Times*, 9 August 1985; Vijah Singh, "Les Sikhs, une Secte Traditionnelle Saisié par la Terrorisme," *Liberation*, 1 November 1984.

32. For example, this uncompromising position is clearly evident by Hamas' own charter in Article 11: "The land of Palestine is an Islamic trust (*waqf*) to be maintained by succeeding generations of Muslims until the Day of Judgement. In this responsibility, or any part of it, no negligence will be tolerated, and no surrender." *Mithaq Harakat al-Muqawamah al-Islamiyah* (Hamas, 1988).

33. See Michael Kelly, "In Gaza, Peace Meets Pathology," *New York Times*, 29 November 1994, p. 56.

34. See Michael Parks, "Ready to Kill, Ready to Die, Hamas Zealots Thwart Peace," *Los Angeles Times*, 25 October 1994, p. A10. For interesting insight into mentality of suicide bombers, see Joel Greenberg, "Palestinian 'Martyrs,' All Too Willing," *New York Times*, 25 January 1995; and *Ma'ariv*, 30 December 1994, p. 8. For an example of this martyrology with an extensive list of Izzeldin al-Qassem martyrs since 1990, see *Filastin al'Muslimah*, November 1994, p. 14.

35. In a statement in Israeli court, Amir provided the justification: "When you kill in war, it is an act that is allowed," in Russell Watson, "Blame Time," *Newsweek*, 20 November 1995. As explained by Amir, "I did not commit the act to stop the peace process because there is no concept as the peace process, it is a process of war," *Mideast Mirror*, 6 November 1995.

36. For a useful overview of the incident, see Jihad B. Khazen, *The Sadat Assassination: Background and Implications* (Washington: Georgetown University's Center for Contemporary Arab Studies, 1981); and Dilip Hiro, "Faces of Fundamentalism," *The Middle East*, May 1988, pp. 11–12.

37. See Robert Fisk, "'Party of God' Develops Its Own Political Style," *Irish Times*, 9 February 1995.

38. For a very interesting discussion of this phenomenon, see Gilles Keppel, *The Revenge of God: The Resurgence of Islam, Christianity and Judaism in the Modern World* (London: Polity Press, 1995).

39. For a useful exposition of concealment in Shi'ism, refer to lecture by Prof. Etan Kohlberg, Hebrew University, delivered at the Tel Aviv University (Tel Aviv, Israel: 23 May 1993).

40. See Maskit Burgin, A. Merari, and A Kurz, eds., *Foreign Hostages in Lebanon*, JCSS Memorandum, no. 25, August 1988 (Tel Aviv: Tel Aviv University, 1988).

41. Bruce Hoffman (1993), p. 3.

42. See Bruce Hoffman, "'Holy Terror': The Implications of Terrorism Motivated by a Religious Imperative," in *The First International Workshop on Low Intensity Conflict*, ed. A. Woodcock et al. (Stockholm: Royal Society of Naval Sciences, 1995) p. 43.

43. See Andrew Pollack, "Cult's Prophesy of Disaster Draws Precautions in Tokyo," *New York Times*, 15 April 1995; and Andrew Brown, "Waiting for the End of the World," *The Independent*, 24 March 1995.

44. For example, a survey of imprisoned members of the Egyptian group al-Takfir wal-Hijra (Repentance and Holy Flight) revealed that the average member was in his 20s or early 30s, a university student or recent graduate; had better than average marks in school work; felt intensely about causes but was intolerant of conflicting opinions; and a willingness to employ violence

if necessary. See Ray Vicker, "Islam on the March," *Wall Street Journal*, 12 February 1980. For a similar profile of Sikh terrorists, see Carl H. Haeger, "Sikh Terrorism in the Struggle for Khalistan," *Terrorism*, 14 (1991) p. 227. Also see Hala Mustafa, "The Islamic Movements Under Mubarak," in *The Islamist Dilemma: The Political Role of Islamic Movements in the Contemporary Arab World*, ed. Laura Guazzone (Reading: Ithaca Press, 1995) p. 173.

45. For example, see Paul Wilkinson, "Hamas: An Assessment," *Jane's Intelligence Review* (July 1993) pp. 313–14; and Ziad Abu-Amr, *Islamic Fundamentalism in the West Bank and Gaza* (Indianapolis: Indiana University Press, 1994).

46. As demonstrated in the case of Egypt, "Jihad and other movements were born in [former Presidents] Nasser's and Sadat's prisons," see Robin Wright, "Holy Wars': The Ominous Side of Religion in Politics," *Christian Science Monitor*, 12 November 1987, p. 21. Also see Mustafa, p. 174.

47. Richard Hrair Dekmeijian, *Islam in Revolution: Fundamentalism in the Arab World* (Syracuse: Syracuse University Press, 1985) p. 61–62.

48. George Nader, *Middle East Insight* (June-July 1985).

49. See Anthony Davis, "Foreign Combatants in Afghanistan," *Jane's Intelligence Review* (July 1994) p. 327. Also see Raymond Whitaker, "Afghani Veterans Fan Out to Spread the Word—and Terror," *The Independent*, 16 April 1995.

50. For a detailed discussion of this plan, see Ehud Sprinzak, "Three Models of Religious Violence: The Case of Jewish Fundamentalism in Israel," in Marty and Appleby (1993), pp. 475–76. As stated by Sprinzak: "There has been no act by the Jewish underground which did not have a rabbinical backing." *Yediot Aharanot*, 18 March 1994.

51. See Youssef M. Ibrahim, "Muslim Edicts Take on New Force," *New York Times*, 12 February 1995; and Philip Jacobson, "Muhammad's Ally," *The Times Magazine*, 4 December 1993.

52. For example, see *Ma'ariv*, 28 February 1996; Ze'ev Chafets, "Israel's Quiet Anger," *New York Times*, 7 November 1995.

53. As revealed by Hizb'allah manifesto in 1985, "Imam Khomeini, the leader, has repeatedly stressed that America is the reason for all our catastrophes and the source of all malice. By fighting it, we are only exercising our legitimate right to defend our Islam and the dignity of our nation." See Hizb'allah's manifesto reprinted in Augustus Richard Norton, *Amal and the Shi'a: Struggle for the Soul of Lebanon* (Austin: University of Texas Press, 1987) pp. 167–87. See also Martin Kramer, "The Jihad Against the Jews," *Commentary* (October 1994) pp. 38–42.

54. For example, see David Wurmser, "The Rise and Fall of the Arab World," *Strategic Review* (Summer 1993) pp. 33–46.

55. See Fred Halliday, *Islam and the Myth of Confrontation* (London: I.B. Tauris, 1995).

56. For example see Alvin H. Bernstein, "Iran's Low-Intensity War Against the United States," *Orbis*, 30 (Spring 1986) pp. 149–67; and Sean K. Anderson, "Iran: Terrorism and Islamic Fundamentalism," in *Low-Intensity Conflict: Old Threats in a New World*, ed. Edwin G. Corr and Stephen Sloan (Oxford: Westview Press, 1992) pp. 173–95.

57. See Magnus Ranstorp, *Hizballah in Lebanon: The Politics of the Western Hostage-Crisis* (London: Macmillan, 1996).

58. See Bruce Hoffman (1993).

59. See Martin Kramer, "The Moral Logic of Hizbollah," in *Origins of Terrorism: Psychologies, Ideologies, Theologies, States of Mind*, ed. Walter Reich (Cambridge: Cambridge University Press, 1990) pp. 131–57.

60. See Robert M. Jenkins, "The Islamic Connection," *Security Management* (July 1993) pp. 25–30.

61. See Guy Arnold et al, eds., *Revolutionary & Dissident Movements: An International Guide* (Harlow: Longman Group, 1991) p. 141.

62. See Mir Zohair Husain, *Global Islamic Politics* (New York: Harper Collins, 1995) pp. 186–200.

63. Bruce Hoffman, "Intelligence and Terrorism: Emerging Threats and New Security Challenges in the Post–Cold War Era," *Intelligence and National Security*, 11, no. 3 (April 1996) p. 214. For a broader discussion of millenarian terrorism, see Michael Barkun, ed. *Millennialism and Violence* (London: Frank Cass, 1996).

When the struggle reaches the decisive phase may I die fighting in its midst.

—Jamail Singh Bhindranwale

In the mid-1970s, when militant young Sikhs first began to attack the Nirankaris—members of a small religious community perceived as being anti-Sikh—few observers could have predicted that that violence would escalate into the savagery that seized the Punjab in the 1980s. The Sikhs as a community were too well off economically, too well educated, it seemed, to be a party to random acts of terror. Yet it is true that militant encounters have often played a part in Sikh history, and in the mid-1960s a radical movement very much like that of the 1980s stormed through the Punjab. The charismatic leader at that time was Sant Fateh Singh, who went on a well-publicized fast and threatened to immolate himself on the roof of the Golden Temple's Akali Takht unless the government made concessions that would lead to the establishment of a Sikh-majority state. The Indian government, captained by Prime Minister Indira Gandhi, conceded, and the old Punjab state was carved in two to produce a Hindu-majority Haryana and a new Punjab. It was smaller than the previous one, and contained enough Sikh-dominated areas to give it a slim Sikh majority.

The violence of this decade, however, seems very different from what one saw in the 1960s.[1] For one thing, the attacks themselves have been more vicious. Often they have involved Sikhs and Hindus indiscriminately, and many innocent bystanders have been targeted along with politically active persons. The new Sikh leader, Jamail Singh Bhindranwale, was stranger—more intense and more strident—than Fateh Singh was, and the goals of Bhindranwale and his allies were more diffuse. Government officials who were trying to negotiate a settlement were never quite certain what their demands were. In fact there was no clear consensus among the activists themselves as to what they wanted, and the items on their lists of demands would shift from time to time. In 1984, shortly before she gave the command for the Indian Army to invade the Golden Temple, an exasperated Indira Gandhi itemized everything she had done to meet the Sikh demands and asked, 'What more can any government do?'[2]

It was a question that frustrated many observers outside the government as well, a good many moderate Sikhs among them. But frustration led to action, and those actions made things worse. The Indian army's brutal assault on the Golden Temple in June 1984, and the heartless massacre of Sikhs by Hindus in Delhi and elsewhere after the assassination of Mrs. Gandhi in November of that year caused the violence to escalate. Still, it is fair to say that quite a bit of bloodshed originated on the Sikh side of the ledger, and within the Sikh community anti-government violence achieved a religious respectability that begs to be explained.

The Rational Explanations

The explanations one hears most frequently place the blame for Sikh violence on political, economic and social factors, and each of these approaches is compelling. The political explanation, for instance, focuses on the weakness of the Sikh political party, the Akali Dal, and its inability to secure a consistent plurality in the Punjab legislature. This is no wonder, since the Sikhs command a bare 51 per cent majority of the post-1966 Punjab. Moreover, the Muslims, who comprised the Punjab's other non-Hindu religious community before 1948, were awarded a nation of their own at the time of India's independence, so it is understandable that many Sikhs would continue to long for greater political power, and even yearn for their own Pakistan.[3]

The economic explanation for Sikh unrest is largely a matter of seeing the achievements of the Sikhs in relation to what they feel their efforts should warrant, rather than to what others in India have received. Compared with almost every other region of India, the Punjab is fairly well-to-do. Yet Sikhs complain, with some justification, that for that very reason they have been deprived of their fair share: resources from the Punjab have been siphoned off to other parts of the nation.[4] Agricultural prices, for example, are held stable in India in part because the government maintains a ceiling on the prices that farmers in rich agricultural areas like the Punjab are permitted to exact. In addition some Sikhs claim that industrial growth has been hampered in the Punjab as the government has encouraged growth in other parts of India, and that the Punjab's agricultural lifeblood—water for irrigation from Punjabi rivers—has been diverted to farming areas in other states.

The social explanation for Sikh discontent is just as straightforward: the Sikhs are a minority community in India, and their separate identity within the Indian family is in danger. Since the religious ideas on which Sikhism is based grew out of the nexus of medieval Hinduism, Sikhs fear they could be reabsorbed into the amorphous cultural mass that is Hinduism and disappear as a distinct religious community.[5] The possibility is real: Sikhism almost vanished in the latter part of the nineteenth century. But in this century secularism is as much a threat as Hinduism, and like fundamentalist movements in many other parts of the world, Sikh traditionalists have seen the secular government as the perpetrator of a dangerous anti-religious ideology that threatens the existence of such traditional religious communities as their own. In the perception of some Sikhs, these two threats—the religious and the secular—have recently combined forces as the Hindu right has exercised increasing political power and Mrs Gandhi's Congress Party has allegedly pandered to its interests.[6]

There is nothing wrong with these political, economic and social explanations of Sikh unrest. Each is persuasive in its own sphere, and together they help us understand why the Sikhs as a community have been unhappy. But they do not help us understand the piety with which a few Sikhs have justified their bloody acts or the passion with which so many of them have condoned them—even the random acts of destruction associated with terrorism. Nor are they the sort of explanations one hears from Sikhs who are most closely involved in the struggle. The socioeconomic and political explanations usually come from observers outside the Sikh community or from those inside it who are least sympathetic to the militant protesters. The point of view of the activists is different. Their frame of reference is more grand: their explanations of the conflict and its causes achieve almost mythical dimensions. To understand this point of view we have to turn to their own words and see what they reveal about the radicals' perception of the world about them.

on one's point of view. During his lifetime he was called a *sant*, a holy man, and a few Sikhs have been bold enough to proclaim him the eleventh *guru*, and thus challenge the traditional Sikh belief that the line of ten gurus ended with Gobind Singh in the early eighteenth century.

Jamail Singh was born in 1947 at the village Rodey near the town of Moga. He was the youngest son in a poor family of farmers from the Jat caste, and when he was 18 years old his father handed him over for religious training to the head of a Sikh center known as the Damdani Taksal. The leader came from the village Bhindran and was therefore known as Bhindranwale, and after his death, when the mantle of leadership fell on young Jamail Singh, he assumed his mentor's name. The young leader took his duties seriously and gained a certain amount of fame as a preacher. He was a stern one at that: Jamail became famous for castigating the easy-living, easy-drinking customs of Sikh villagers, especially those who clipped their beards and adopted modern ways. He carried weapons, and on 13 April 1978, in a bloody confrontation in Amritsar with members of the renegade Nirankaris religious movement, he showed that he was not afraid to use them. This episode was followed by an attack from Nirankaris that killed a number of Bhindranwale's followers, and further counter-attacks ensued.[8] Thus began the bloody career of a man who was trained to live a calm and spiritual life of religious devotion.

Although he was initially at the fringes of Sikh leadership, during the late 1970s Bhindranwale began to be taken seriously within Akali circles because of his growing popularity among the masses.[9] He seemed to have been fixated on the Nirankaris: his fiery sermons condemned them as evil. He regarded them as a demonic force that endangered the very basis of the Sikh community, especially its commitment to the authority of the Sikh gurus. And in time he expanded his characterization of their demonic power to include those who protected them, including the secular government of Indira Gandhi.

Much of what Bhindranwale has to say in sermons of this period, however, might be heard in the sermons of methodist pastors in Iowa or in the homilies of clergies belonging to any religious tradition, anywhere on the globe. He calls for faith—faith in a time of trial—and for the spiritual discipline that accompanies it. In one sermon he rebukes the press and others who call him an extremist, and explains what sort of an extremist he is:

> One who takes the vows of faith and helps others take it; who reads the scriptures and helps others to do the same; who avoids liquor and drugs and helps others do likewise; who urges unity and cooperation; who preaches Hindu-Sikh unity and coexistence... who says: 'respect your scriptures, unite under the flag, stoutly support the community, and be attached to your Lord's throne and home'.[10]

Like many Protestant ministers, Bhindranwale prescribes piety as the answer to every need. 'You can't have courage without reading [the Sikh scriptures]', he admonishes his followers: 'Only the [scripture]-readers can suffer torture and be capable of feats of strength'.[11] He is especially harsh on backsliders in the faith. Those who cut their beards are targets of his wrath: 'Do you think you resemble the image of Guru Gobind Singh?' he asks them.[12] But then he reassures the bulk of his followers. Because of their persistence in the faith, he tells them, 'the Guru will give you strength', adding that 'righteousness is with you'.[13] They will need all the strength and courage they can get, Bhindranwale explains, because their faith is under attack.[14]

Lying only slightly beneath the surface of this language is the notion of a great struggle that Bhindranwale thinks is taking place. On the personal level it is the tension between faith and the lack of faith; on the cosmic level it is the battle between truth and evil. Often his rhetoric is vague about who the enemy really is. 'In order to destroy religion', Bhindranwale informs his congregation, 'on all sides and in many forms mean tactics have been initiated'.[15] But rather than wasting effort in explaining who these forces are and why they would want to destroy religion, Bhindranwale dwells instead on what should be the response: a willingness to fight and defend the faith—if necessary, to the end.

> Unless you are prepared to die, sacrificing your own life, you cannot be a free people....
> If you start thinking in terms of service to your community then you will be on the right path and you will readily sacrifice yourself. If you have faith in the Guru no power on earth can enslave you. The Sikh faith is to pray to God, take one's vows before the Guru Granth Sahib [scriptures] and then act careless of consequences to oneself.[16]

At other times Bhindranwale cites what appear to be specific attacks on Sikhism, but again the perpetrators are not sharply defined; they remain a vague, shadowy force of evil. 'The Guru Granth [scripture] has been buried in cowdung and thrown on the roadside', Bhindranwale informs his followers. 'That is your Father, your Guru, that they treat so.'[17] On another occasion he urges his followers to 'seek justice against those who have dishonored our sisters, drunk the blood of innocent persons, and insulted Satguru Granth Sahib'.[18] But the 'they' and the 'those' are not identified.

Occasionally, however, the enemy is more clearly specified: they are 'Hindus', 'the government', 'the press', the Prime Minister—whom he calls that 'lady born to a house of Brahmins'[19]—and perhaps most frequently Sikhs themselves who have fallen from the path. This somewhat rambling passage indicates these diverse enemies and the passionate hatred that Bhindranwale feels towards them:

> I cannot really understand how it is that, in the presence of Sikhs, Hindus are able to insult the [scriptures]. I don't know how these Sikhs were born to mothers and why they were not born to animals: to cats and to bitches.... Whoever insults the Guru Granth Sahib should be killed then and there.... Some youths complain that if they do such deeds then nobody harbours them. Well, no place is holier than this one [the Golden Temple].... I will take care of the man who comes to me after lynching the murderer of the Guru Granth Sahib; I'll fight for his case. What else do you want? That things have come to such a pass is in any event all your own weakness.... The man whose sister is molested and does nothing about it, whose Guru is insulted and who keeps on talking and doing nothing, has he got any right to be known as the son of the Guru? Just think for yourselves![20]

And in a similar vein:

> Talk is not enough against injustice. We have to act. Here you raise your swords but tomorrow you may wipe the dust from the sandals of sister Indira.... We have the right to be Sikhs.... The dearest thing to any Sikh should be the honor of the Guru.... Those

tles are simply the most recent chapters in a long ongoing war with the enemies of the faith. The foes of today are connected with those from the legendary past. Indira Gandhi, for instance, is implicitly compared with the Moghul emperors: 'The rulers [the Congress party leaders] should keep in mind that in the past many like them did try in vain to annihilate the Gurus.'[22] In other speeches, Bhindranwale frequently looks to the past for guidance in dealing with current situations. When Sikhs who had sided with government policies come to him for forgiveness, for instance, he refuses. 'I asked that man', explains Bhindranwale, 'had he ever read a page of our history? Was the man who tortured Guru Arjun pardoned?'[23]

Occasionally Bhindranwale refers to some of the specific political, economic and social demands made by more moderate Sikh leaders. He supports these demands, but they are not his primary concern. In fact, the targets of these demands are often characterized simply as 'injustices', illustrations of the fact that the Sikh community is abused and under attack.[24] Since the larger struggle is the more important matter, these specific difficulties are of no great concern to Bhindranwale; they change from time to time. And it is of no use to win on one or two points and fail on others. Compromise is impossible; only complete victory will signal that the tide has turned. For that reason Bhindranwale scolds the Akali leaders for seeking a compromise settlement of the political demands made by Sikh leaders at Anandpur Sahib in 1973. 'Either full implementation of the Anandpur Sahib resolution', Bhindranwale demands, 'or their heads'.[25]

In a sense, then, Bhindranwale feels that individual Sikh demands can never really be met, because the ultimate struggle of which they are a part is much greater than the contestation between political parties and factional points of view. It is a vast cosmic struggle, and only such an awesome encounter is capable of giving profound meaning to the motivations of those who fight for Sikh causes. Such people are not just fighting for water rights and political boundaries, they are fighting for truth itself.

Clearly the religious language of Sikh militants like Bhindranwale is the language of ultimate struggle. But two related matters are not so obvious: why is this language attached to the more mundane issues of human politics and economics? And why is it linked with violent acts?

A Pause for Definitions: Violence and Religion

Before we turn to these questions, however, it might be useful to pause for a moment for definitions. Since I want to look at issues having to do with the general relation between violence and religion, not merely those that affect the Sikhs, it might be useful if I describe what I mean by these terms.

I will restrict my use of the word violence to actions that are aimed at taking human life—that intend to, and do, kill. Moreover, I mean especially abnormal, illegal, shocking acts of destruction. All acts of killing are violent, of course, but warfare and capital punishment have an aura of normalcy and do not violate our sensibilities in the same way as actions that seem deliberately designed to elicit feelings of revulsion and anger from those who witness them.[26] By speaking of violence in this restricted way, I mean to highlight the characteristics that we usually associate with terrorist acts.

The term religion is more difficult to define. I have been impressed with the recent attempts of several sociologists to find a definition that is not specific to any cultural region or historical period, and is appropriate for thinking about the phenomenon in modern as well as traditional societies. Clifford Geertz, for instance, sees religion as the effort to integrate everyday reality into a pattern of coherence that takes shape on a deeper level.[27] Robert Bellah also thinks of religion as the attempt to reach beyond ordinary reality in the 'risk of faith' that allows people to act 'in the face of uncertainty and unpredictability'.[28] Peter Berger specifies that such faith is an affirmation of the sacred, which acts as a doorway to a different kind of reality.[29] Louis Dupré prefers to avoid the term 'sacred', but integrates elements of both Berger's and Bellah's definition in his description of religion as 'a commitment to the transcendent as to *another* reality'.[30]

What all of these definitions have in common is their emphasis on a certain kind of experience that people share with others in particular communities. It is an experience of another reality, or of a deeper stratum of the reality that we know in everyday life. As [Emile] Durkheim, whose thought is fundamental to each of these thinkers, was adamant in observing, religion has a more encompassing force than can be suggested by any dichotomization of the sacred and the profane. To Durkheim, the religious point of view includes both the notion that there is such a dichotomy, and that the sacred aspects of it will always, ultimately, reign supreme.[31] Summarizing Durkheim's and the others' definitions of religion, I think it might be described as the perception that there is a tension between reality as it appears and as it really is (or has been, or will be).

This definition helps us think of religion as the subjective experience of those who use religious language, and in fact it is easier with this definition to speak of religious language, or a religious way of looking at the world, than to speak of religion in a more reified sense.[32] When we talk of the various 'religions', then, we mean the communities that have a tradition of sharing a particular religious point of view, a world view in which there is an essential conflict between appearance and a deeper reality. There is the hint, in this definition, that the deeper reality holds a degree of permanence and order quite unobtainable by ordinary means, as religious people affirm. The conflict between the two is what religion is about: religious language contains images both of grave disorder and tranquil order, and often holds out the hope that despite appearances to the contrary, order eventually will triumph, and disorder will be contained.

Why Does Religion Need Violence?

There is nothing in this definition that requires religion to be violent, but it does lead one to expect religious language to make sense of violence and to incorporate it in some way into the world view it expresses. Violence, after all, shocks one's sense of order and has the potential for causing the ultimate disorder in any person's life: physical destruction and death. Since religious language is about the tension between order and disorder, it is frequently about violence.

The symbols and mythology of Sikhism, for instance, are full of violence. The most common visual symbol of Sikhism is the two-edged sword (*khanda*), supported by two scabbards and surrounded by a circle. Sikhs often interpret the two edges of this sword as

taken on a canonical character within Sikhism, and they more vividly capture the imagination than the devotional and theological sentiments of the scriptures themselves. The calendar art so prominent in most Sikh homes portrays a mystical Guru Nanak, of course, but alongside him there are pictures of Sikh military heroes and scenes from great battles. Bloody images also leap from brightly-colored oil paintings in the Sikh Museum housed in the Golden Temple. There are as many depictions of martyrs in their wretched final moments as of victors radiant in conquest.

Because the violence is so prominent in Sikh art and legend, and because many symbols of the faith are martial, one might think that Sikhs as a people are more violent than their counterparts in other areas of India. But if one leaves aside the unrest of the past several years, I do not think this can be demonstrated. It would be convenient to say that the prestige of violent symbols in the Sikh religion has increased Sikhs' propensity for violent action, or that the Sikh religion is violent because Sikhs as a people are violent, but I do not think either of these arguments can be made very convincingly.

The fact is that the symbols and mythology of most religious traditions are filled with violent images, and their histories leave trails of blood. One wonders that familiarity can prevent Christians from being repulsed by the violent images portrayed by hymns such as 'Onward Christian Soldiers', 'The Old Rugged Cross', 'Washed in the Blood of the Lamb', and 'There is a Fountain Flowing with Blood'. Or perhaps familiarity is not the issue at all. The central symbol of Christianity is an execution device—a cross—from which, at least in the Roman tradition, the dying body still hangs. From a non-Christian point of view, the most sacred of Christian rituals, the eucharist, looks like ritual cannabalism, where the devout eat the flesh and drink the blood of their departed leader. At a certain level, in fact, this interpretation is accurate; yet few would argue that the violent acts perpetrated by Christians over the centuries are the result of their being subjected to such messages.

The ubiquity of violent images in religion and the fact that some of the most ancient religious practices involve the sacrificial slaughter of animals have led to speculation about why religion and violence are so intimately bound together. Some of these speculators are among the best known modern theorists, Karl Marx, for instance, saw religious symbols as the expression of real social oppression, and religious wars as the result of tension among economic classes.[35] Sigmund Freud saw in religious rituals vestiges of a primal oedipal act that when ritually reenacted provide a symbolic resolution of feelings of sexual and physical aggression.[36] More recently, Rene Girard has revived the Freudian thesis but given it a social rather than psychological coloration. Girard sees the violent images of religion as a symbolic displacement of violence from one's own communal fellowship to a scapegoat foe.[37]

What these thinkers have in common is that they see religious violence as a symptom of and symbol for something else: social hostility, in the case of Marx; sexual and physical aggression, in the case of Freud; social competition, in the case of Girard. They may be right: religion and other cultural forms may have been generated out of basic personal and social needs. Yet it seems to me that even without these explanations the internal logic of religion requires that religious symbols and myths express violent meanings.

Religion deals with the ultimate tension between order and disorder, and disorder is inherently violent, so it is understandable that the chaotic, dangerous character of life is represented in religious images. Of course, the religious promise is that order conquers chaos; so it is also understandable that the violence religion portrays is in some way limited or tamed. In Christianity, for example, the very normalcy with which the blood-filled hymns are sung and the eucharist is eaten indicates their domestication. In ritual, violence is symbolically transferred. The blood of the eucharistic wine is ingested by the supplicant and becomes part of living tissue; it brings new life. In song a similarly calming transformation occurs. For, as Christian theology explains, in Christ violence has been corralled. Christ died in order for death to be defeated, and his blood is that of the sacrificial lamb who atones for our sins so that we will not have to undergo a punishment as gruesome as his.

In the Sikh tradition violent images are also domesticated. The symbol of the two-edged sword has become an emblem to be worn on lockets and proudly emblazened on shops and garden gates. It is at the forefront of the worship center in Sikh *gurudwaras* where it is treated as reverently as Christians treat their own emblem of destruction, the cross. And the gory wounds of the martyrs bleed on in calendar art. As I have suggested, Sikh theologians and writers are no more hesitant to allegorize the meaning of such symbols and stories than their Christian counterparts. They point toward the war between good and evil that rages in each person's soul.

The symbols of violence in religion, therefore, are symbols of a violence conquered, or at least put in place, by the larger framework of order that religious language provides. But one must ask how these symbolic presentations of violence are related to real violence. One might think that they should prevent violent acts by allowing violent feelings to be channelled into the harmless dramas of ritual, yet we know that the opposite is sometimes the case. The violence of religion can be savagely real.

Why Does Violence Need Religion?

A reason often given to explain why religious symbols are associated with acts of real violence is that religion is exploited by violent people. This explanation, making religion the pure and innocent victim of the darker forces of human nature, is undoubtedly too easy; yet it contains some truth. Religion in fact is sometimes exploited, and it is important to understand why people who are engaged in potentially violent struggles do at times turn to the language of religion. In the case of the Sikhs, this means asking why the sort of people who were exercised over the economic, political and social issues explored at the beginning of this article turned to preachers like Bhindranwale for leadership.

One answer is that by sacralizing these concerns the political activists gave them an aura of legitimacy that they did not previously possess. The problem with this answer is that most of the concerns we mentioned—the inadequacy of Sikh political representation, for instance, and the inequity of agricultural prices—were perfectly legitimate, and did not need the additional moral weight of religion to give them respectability. And in fact, the people who were primarily occupied with these issues—Sikh businessmen and political leaders—were not early supporters of Bhindranwale. Even when they became drawn into his campaign, their relation with him remained ambivalent at best.

We are religiously separate. But why do we have to emphasize this? It is only because we are losing our identity. Out of selfish interests our Sikh leaders who have only the success of their farms and their industries at heart have started saying that there is no difference between Sikh and Hindu. Hence the danger of assimilation has increased.[38]

When they say the Sikhs are not separate we'll demand separate identity—even if it demands sacrifice.[39]

Bhindranwale himself, interestingly, never came out in support of Khalistan. 'We are not in favor of Khalistan nor are we against it', he said, adding that 'we wish to live in India', but would settle for a separate state if the Sikhs did not receive what he regarded as their just respect.[40] Whatever his own reservations about the Khalistan issue, however, his appeal to sacrifice made his rhetoric attractive to the separatists. It also raised another, potentially more powerful aspect of the sacralization of political demands: the prospect that religion could give moral sanction to violence.

By identifying a temporal social struggle with the cosmic struggle of order and disorder, truth and evil, political actors are able to avail themselves of a way of thinking that justifies the use of violent means. Ordinarily only the state has the moral right to take life— for purposes either of military defense, police protection or punishment—and the codes of ethics established by religious traditions support this position. Virtually every religious tradition, including the Sikhs', applauds non-violence and proscribes the taking of human life.[41] The only exception to this rule is the one we have given: most ethical codes allow the state to kill for reasons of punishment and protection.[42]

Those who want moral sanction for their use of violence, and who do not have the approval of an officially recognized government, find it helpful to have access to a higher source: the meta-morality that religion provides. By elevating a temporal struggle to the level of the cosmic, they can bypass the usual moral restrictions on killing. If a battle of the spirit is thought to exist, then it is not ordinary morality but the rules of war that apply. It is interesting that the best-known incidents of religious violence throughout the contemporary world have occurred in places where there is difficulty in defining the character of a nation state. Palestine and Ireland are the most obvious examples, but the revolution in Iran also concerned itself with what the state should be like, and what elements of society should lead it. Religion provided the basis for a new national consensus and a new kind of leadership.

There are some aspects of social revolution in the Punjab situation as well. It is not the established leaders of the Akali party who have resorted to violence, but a second level of leadership—a younger, more marginal group for whom the use of violence is enormously empowering. The power that comes from the barrel of a gun, as Mao [Tse-tung] is said to have remarked, has a very direct effect. But there is a psychological dimension to this power that may be even more effective. As Frantz Fanon argued in the context of the Algerian revolution some years ago even a small display of violence can have immense symbolic power: the power to jolt the masses into an awareness of their potency.[43]

It can be debated whether or not the masses in the Punjab have been jolted into an awareness of their own capabilities, but the violent actions of the militants among them have certainly made the masses more aware of the militants' powers. They have attained a status of authority rivalling what police and other government officials possess. One of the problems in the Punjab today is the unwillingness of many villagers in the so-called terrorist zones around Batala and Taran Tarn to report terrorist activities to the authorities. The radical youth are even said to have established an alternative government.

By being dangerous the young Sikh radicals have gained a certain notoriety, and by clothing their actions in the moral garb of religion they have given their actions legitimacy. Because their actions are morally sanctioned by religion, they are fundamentally political actions: they break the state's monopoly on morally-sanctioned killing. By putting the right to kill in their own hands, the perpetrators of religious violence are also making a daring claim of political independence.

Even though Bhindranwale was not an outspoken supporter of Khalistan, he often spoke of the Sikhs' separate identity as that of a religious community with national characteristics. The term he used for religious community, *quam*, is an Urdu term that has overtones of nationhood. It is the term the Muslims used earlier in this century in defending their right to have a separate nation, and it is the term that Untouchables used in the Punjab in the 1920s when they attempted to be recognized as a separate social and political entity.[44] Another term that is important to Bhindranwale is *miri-piri*, the notion that spiritual and temporal power are linked.[45] It is this concept that is symbolically represented by the two-edged sword and that justified Sikh support for an independent political party. Young Sikh activists are buttressed in their own aspirations to leadership by the belief that acts that they conceive as being heroic and sacrificial—even those that involve taking the lives of others—have both spiritual and political significance. They are risking their lives for God and the Sikh community.

Not all of the Sikh community appreciates their efforts, however, and the speeches of Bhindranwale make clear that disagreements and rivalries within the community were one of his major concerns. Some of Bhindranwale's harshest words were reserved for Sikhs who he felt showed weakness and a tendency to make easy compromises. In one speech, after quoting a great martyr in Sikh history as having said, 'even if I have to give my head, may I never lose my love for the Sikh Faith', Bhindranwale railed against Sikh bureaucrats and modernized youth who could not make that sacrifice, and ended with a little joke:

> I am sorry to note that many people who hanker after a government position say instead, 'even if I lose my Faith, may I never lose my position'. And our younger generation has started saying this: 'even if I lose my Faith, may a beard never grow on my face'.... If you find the beard too heavy, pray to God saying... 'we do not like this Sikhism and manhood. Have mercy on us. Make us into women....'[46]

But most Sikhs in Bhindranwale's audience, including the youth, were not the sort who would be tempted to cut their hair; and few, especially in the villages where Bhindranwale had been popular, were in a position to 'hanker after a governmental position'. People, such as the Akali leaders whom Bhindranwale castigated for making compromises for the sake of personal gain, were no doubt objects of contempt in the villages long before Bhindranwale came along, and by singling them out, Bhindranwale identified familiar objects of

eventually opposed him, including the more moderate Akali leader, Sant Harchand Singh Longowal, regarded Bhindranwale as a prime obstacle to the very unity he preached. During the dark days immediately preceding Operation Bluestar in June 1984, the two set up rival camps in the Golden Temple and allegedly killed each other's lieutenants. It is no wonder that many of Bhindranwale's followers, convinced the Indian army had a collaborator inside the Golden Temple, were suspicious when Bhindranwale was murdered in the raid and Longowal was led off safely under arrest. No wonder also that many regarded Longowal's assassination a year later as revenge for Bhindranwale's.

While he was alive, Bhindranwale continued to preach unity, but it was clear that what he wanted was everyone else to unite around him. He and his supporters wished to give the impression that they were at the center, following the norm of Sikh belief and behavior, and that the community should therefore group around them. This message had a particular appeal to those who were socially marginal to the Sikh community, including lower-caste people and Sikhs who had taken up residence abroad. Some of the most fanatical of Bhindranwale's followers, including Beant Singh, the assassin of Indira Gandhi, came from the Untouchable castes (Beant Singh was from the lowest caste of Untouchables, the Sweepers), and a considerable amount of money and moral support for the Punjab militants came from Sikhs living in such faraway places as London, Houston, and Yuba City, California.

These groups gained from their identification with Bhindranwale a sense of belonging, and the large Sikh communities in England, Canada and America were especially sensitive to his message that the Sikhs needed to be strong, united and defensive of their tradition. Many of Bhindranwale's supporters in the Punjab, however, received a more tangible benefit from associating with his cause: politically active village youth and small-time clergy were able to gain support from many who were not politically mobilized before. In that sense Bhindranwale was fomenting something of a political revolution, and the constituency was not unlike the one the Ayatollah Khomeini was able to gather in Iran. In so far as Bhindranwale's message was taken as an endorsement of the killings that some of these fundamentalist youth committed, the instrument of religious violence gave power to those who had little power before.

When Does Cosmic Struggle Lead to Real Violence?

The pattern of religious violence of the Sikhs could be that of Irish Catholics, or Shi'ite Muslims in Palestine, or fundamentalist Christian bombers of abortion clinics in the United States. There are a great many communities in which the language of cosmic struggle justifies acts of violence. But those who are engaged in them, including the Sikhs, would be offended if we concluded from the above discussion that their actions were purely for social or political gain. They argue that they act out of religious conviction, and surely they are to some degree right. Destruction is a part of the logic of religion, and virtually every religious tradition carries with it images of chaos and terror. But symbolic violence does not lead in every instance to real bloodshed, and even the eagerness of political actors to exploit religious symbols is not in all cases sufficient to turn religion towards a violent end. Yet some forms of religion do seem to propel the faithful rather easily into militant confrontation: which ones, and why?

The current resurgence of religious violence around the world has given an urgency to attempts to answer these questions, and to identify which characteristics of religion are conducive to violence. The efforts of social scientists have been directed primarily to the social and political aspects of the problem, but at least a few of them have tried to trace the patterns in religion's own logic. David C. Rapoport, for instance, has identified several features of messianic movements that he believes lead to violence, most of which are characterized by a desire for an antinomian liberation from oppression.[48]

My own list of characteristics comes directly from our discussion of the religious language of cosmic struggle. It is informed by my understanding of what has happened in the Sikh tradition, but it seems to me that the following tenets of religious commitment are found whenever acts of religious violence occur.

1. The Cosmic Struggle Is Played Out in History

To begin with, it seems to me that if religion is to lead to violence it is essential for the devout to believe that the cosmic struggle is realizable in human terms. If the war between good and evil, order and chaos, is conceived as taking place in historical time, in a real geographical location, and among actual social contestants, it is more likely that those who are prone to violent acts will associate religion with their struggles. This may seem to be an obvious point, yet we have some evidence that it is not always true.

In the Hindu tradition, for instance, the mythical battles in the Mahabharata and Ramayana epics are as frequently used as metaphors for present-day struggles as are the actual battles in Sikh and Islamic history and in biblical Judaism and Christianity. Like members of these traditions, Hindus characterize their worldly foes by associating them with the enemies of the good in their legendary battles. The main difference between the Hindus and the others is that their enemies are mythical—that is, they seem mythical to us. To many pious Hindus, however, the stories in the epics are no less real than those recorded in the Bible or in the Sikh legends. A believing Hindu will be able to show you where the great war of the Mahabharata was actually fought, and where the gods actually lived. Moreover, the Hindu cycles of time allow for a cosmic destruction to take place in this world, at the end of the present dark age. So the Hindu tradition is not as devoid of images of divine intervention in worldly struggles as outsiders sometimes assume.[49]

The major tradition that appears to lack the notion that the cosmic struggle is played out on a social plane is Buddhism. But this is an exception that proves the rule, for it is a tradition that is characteristically devoid of religiously sanctioned violence. There are instances in Thai history that provide Buddhist justifications for warfare, but these are rare for the tradition as a whole. In general, Buddhism has no need for actual battles in which the pious can prove their mettle.

2. Believers Identify Personally With the Struggle

The Buddhist tradition does affirm that there is a spiritual conflict, however: it is the clash between the perception that this imperfect and illusory world is real and a higher consciousness that surmounts worldly perception altogether. And in a sense, the struggle takes place

This talk about the cosmic struggle as something inside the self would seem to be easily distinguishable from external violence, but in Sikh theology, including the rhetoric of Bhindranwale, they go hand in hand. 'The weakness is in us', Bhindranwale was fond of telling his followers. 'We are the sinners of this house of our Guru.'[51] Militant Shi'ite Muslims are similarly racked with a sense of personal responsibility for the moral decadence of the world, and once again their tendency toward internalization does not necessarily shield them from acts of external violence. The key to the connection, it seems to me, is that at the same time that the cosmic struggle is understood to impinge about the inner recesses of an individual person, it must be understood as occurring on a worldly, social plane. Neither of these notions is by itself sufficient to motivate a person to religious violence. If one believes that the cosmic struggle is largely a matter of large continuing social forces, one is not likely to become personally identified with the struggle; and if one is convinced that the struggle is solely interior there is not reason to look for it outside. But when the two ideas coexist, they are a volatile concoction.

Thus when Bhindranwale spoke about the warfare in the soul his listeners knew that however burdensome that conflict is, they need not bear it alone. They may band together with their comrades and continue the struggle in the external arena, where the foes are more vulnerable, and victories more tangible. And their own internal struggles impel them to become involved in the worldly conflict: their identification with the overall struggle makes them morally responsible, in part, for its outcome. 'We ourselves are ruining Sikhism', Bhindranwale once told his congregation.[52] On another occasion he told the story of how, when Guru Gobind Singh asked an army of 80,000 to sacrifice their heads for the faith, only five assented. Bhindranwale implied that the opportunity was still at hand to make the choice of whether they were to be one of the five or the 79,995.[53] He reminded them that even though the cosmic war was still being waged, and that the evil within them and outside them had not yet been purged, their choice could still make a difference.

Sikhism is not the only tradition in which this link is forged between the external and internal arenas of the cosmic struggle. Shi'ite Muslims bear a great weight of communal guilt for not having defended one of the founders of their tradition, Husain, when he was attacked and martyred by the vicious Yazid. During the Iranian revolution some of them relived that conflict by identifying specific foes—the Shah and President Jimmy Carter—as Yazids returned. There was no doubt that such people should be attacked. Radical Shi'ites in Iran were not about to compound their guilt and miss an historical opportunity of righting an ancient wrong.

The same sort of logic has propelled many Christians into a vicious anti-Semitism. It is a mark of good Christian piety for individuals to bear the responsibility for the crucifiction of Jesus: the theme of Christians taking part in the denial and betrayal of Jesus is the stuff of many a hymn and sermon. Some Christians believe that the foes to whom they allowed Jesus to be delivered were the Jews. Attacks on the present-day Jewish community, therefore, help to lighten their sense of culpability.

3. The Cosmic Struggle Continues in the Present

What makes these actions of Sikhs, Shi'ites and anti-Semitic Christians spiritually defensible is the conviction that the sacred struggle has not ended in some earlier period, but that it continues in some form today. It is a conviction that also excites the members of the Gush Emunim, a militant movement in present-day Israel, who have taken Israel's victory in the Six Day War as a sign that the age of messianic redemption has finally begun.[54]

Not all Israelis respond to this sign with the same enthusiasm, however, just as not all Christians or Shi'ite Muslims are convinced that the apocalyptic conflict prophesied by their tradition is really at hand. Many of the faithful assent to the notion that the struggle exists within, for what person of faith has not felt the internal tension between belief and disbelief, affirmation and denial, order and chaos? But they often have to be persuaded that the conflict currently rages on a social plane, especially if the social world seems orderly and benign.

Bhindranwale took this challenge as one of the primary tasks of his ministry. He said that one of his main missions was to alert his people that they were oppressed, even if they did not know it. He ended one of his sermons with this fervent plea: 'I implore all of you in this congregation. Go to the villages and make every child, every mother, every Singh realise we are slaves and we have to shake off this slavery in order to survive.'[55]

In Bhindranwale's mind the appearances of normal social order simply illustrated how successful the forces of evil had become in hiding their demonic agenda. His logic compelled him to believe that Punjabi society was racked in a great struggle, even if it showed no indication of it. Long before the Punjab was torn apart by its most recent round of violence, Bhindranwale claimed that an even fiercer form of violence reigned: the appearance of normal order was merely a demonic deception. Bhindranwale hated the veil of calm that seemed to cover his community and recognized that his own followers were often perplexed about what he said: 'Many of our brothers, fresh from the villages, ask, "Sant Ji, we don't know about enslavement." For that reason, I have to tell you why you are slaves.'[56]

The evidence that Bhindranwale gave for the oppression of Sikhs was largely limited to examples of police hostility that arose after the spiral of violence in the Punjab began to grow. Some of his allegations, such as the account he gave of the treatment meted out to followers who hijacked Indian airplanes, have a peculiar ring:

> If a Sikh protests in behalf of his Guru by hijacking a plane, he is put to death.... None of the Sikhs in these three hijackings attacked any passenger nor did they damage the planes. But the rule is that for a fellow with a turban, there is the bullet.... For a person who says 'Hare Krishna, Hare Krishna, Hare Rama', there is a government appointment. Sikh brothers, this is a sign of slavery.[57]

Those who attempted to combat Bhindranwale could not win against such logic. If they responded to Sikh violence they would be seen as oppressors. If they did not respond, the violence would escalate. And even if there was neither violence nor repression, the absence of the overt signs of conflict would be an indication to Bhindranwale of a demonical calm.

4. The Struggle Is at a Point of Crisis

On a number of occasions, in referring to the immediacy of the struggle, Bhindranwale seemed to indicate that the outcome was in doubt. His perception of the enormity of the evil

What is interesting about this apocalyptic rhetoric is its uncertainty. If the outcome were less in doubt there would be little reason for violent action. If one knew that the foe would win, there would be no reason to want to fight back. Weston LaBarre describes the terrible circumstances surrounding the advent of the Ghost Dance religion of the Plains Indians: knowing that they faced overwhelming odds and almost certain defeat, the tribe diverted their concerns from worldly conflict to spiritual conflict, and entertained the notion that a ritual dance would conjure up sufficient spiritual force to destroy the alien cavalry.[60]

LaBarre concludes that sheer desperation caused them to turn to religion and away from efforts to defend themselves. But by the same token, if they knew that the battle could be won without a struggle, there also would be little reason for engagement. The passive pacifism of what William James calles 'healthy-souled religion'—mainstream Protestant churches, for example, that regard social progress as inevitable—comes from just such optimism.[61] Other pacifist movements, however, have been directly engaged in conflict. Menno Simons, the Anabaptist for whom the Mennonite church is named, and Mohandas Gandhi are examples of pacifist leaders who at times narrowly skirted the edges of violence, propelled by a conviction that without human effort the outcome they desired could not be won. In that sense Gandhi and Bhindranwale were more alike than one might suspect. Both saw the world in terms of cosmic struggle, both regarded their cause as being poised on a delicate balance between oppression and opportunity, and both believed that human action could tip the scales. The issue that divided them, of course, was violence.

5. Acts of Violence Have a Cosmic Meaning

The human action in the Sikh case is certainly not pacifist, for Bhindranwale held that there would be 'no deliverance without weapons.'[62] He was careful, however, to let the world know that these weapons were not be used indiscriminately: 'It is a sin for a Sikh to keep weapons to hurt an innocent person, to rob anyone's home, to dishonor anyone or to oppress anyone. But there is no greater sin for a Sikh than keeping weapons and not using them to protect his faith.'[63] Contrariwise, there is no greater valor for a Sikh than to use weapons in defense of the faith. Bhindranwale himself was armed to the teeth, and although he never publically admitted to any of the killings that were pinned on him personally, Bhindranwale expressed his desire to 'die fighting', a wish that was fulfilled within months of being uttered.[64]

According to Bhindranwale, those who committed acts of religiously sanctioned violence were to be regarded as heroes and more. Although he usually referred to himself as a 'humble servant, and an 'uneducated fallible person',[65] Bhindranwale would occasionally identify himself with one of the legendary Sikh saints, Baba Deep Singh, who continued to battle with Moghul foes even after his head had been severed from his body. He carried it manfully under his arm.[66] In Bhindranwale's mind, he too seemed destined for martyrdom.

To many Sikhs today, that is precisely what Bhindranwale achieved. Whatever excesses he may have committed during his lifetime are excused, as one would excuse a lethal but heroic soldier in a glorious war. Even Beant Singh, the bodyguard of Indira Gandhi who turned on her, is held to be a saintly hero. Perhaps this has to be: if Indira was such a demonic foe, her assassin must be similarly exalted.

Even those who value the sense of order that religion provides sometimes cheer those who throw themselves into the arena of religious violence. Such people are, after all, struggling for good, and for that reason their actions are seen as ultimately producing order. But until such recognition of their mission can be achieved among the more conservative rank and file, such activists are forced, as prophets and agents of a higher order of truth, to engage in deeds that necessarily startle. Their purpose is to awaken good folk, mobilize their community, insult the evil forces, and perhaps even to demonstrate dramatically to God himself that there are those who are willing to fight and die on his side, and to deliver his judgement of death. The great promise of cosmic struggle is that order will prevail over chaos; the great irony is that many must die in order for certain visions of that victory to prevail and their awful dramas be brought to an end.

Mark Juergensmeyer is a professor at the University of California, Santa Barbara, and also serves as director of the Global & International Studies Program and chair of the Global Peace & Security Program. He was a Fulbright fellow (India), a senior researcher at the American Institute of Indian Studies (India), and a fellow at the Woodrow Wilson International Center for Scholars (Smithsonian Institution). He is the author of *The New Cold War? Religious Nationalism Confronts the Secular State* (1993) and *Terror in the Mind of God: The Global Rise of Religious Violence* (2001).

Notes

1. For general background on the Punjab crisis in the 1980s and a chronicle of events leading up to it, see Mark Tully and Satish Jacob, *Amritsar: Mrs Gandhi's Last Battle* (London: Cape, 1985), Amarjit Kaur, *et al., The Punjab Story* (New Delhi: Roli Books International, 1984), and Kuldip Nayar and Khushwant Singh, *Tragedy of Punjab: Operation Bluestar and After* (New Delhi: Vision Books, 1984).

2. Indira Gandhi, 'Don't Shed Blood, Shed Hatred', All India Radio, 2 June 1984, reprinted in V. D. Chopra, R. K. Mishra and Nirmal Singh, *Agony of Punjab* (New Delhi: Patriot Publishers, 1984), p. 189. Indian government officials seemed to be genuinely caught off-guard by the Sikh militancy. I remember once in the summer of 1984 when the Indian Consul General in San Francisco turned to me after we had been on a radio talk show and said, 'I haven't a clue; can you tell me why in the devil the Sikhs are behaving like this?'

3. The demand for a Khalistan—a Sikh state similar to Pakistan—was raised by a small number of Sikh militants, including a former cabinet minister of the Punjab, Jagjit Singh Chauhan, who set up a movement in exile in London. It was not, however, a significant or strongly supported demand among Sikhs in the Punjab until after Operation Bluestar in June 1984. The Indian government's account of Chauhan's movement is detailed in a report prepared by the Home Ministry, 'Sikh Agitation for Khalistan', reprinted in Nayar and Singh, *Tragedy of Punjab*, pp. 142–55.

4. The Anandpur Resolution supported by leaders of the Akali Dal focused primarily on economic issues. For an analysis of the Punjab crisis from an economic perspective, see Chopra, Mishra and Singh, *Agony of Punjab*.

which the Hindu and Sikh movements are a part, see Robert Eric Frykenberg, 'Revivalism and Fundamentalism: Some Critical Observations with Special Reference to Politics in South Asia', in James W. Bjorkman (ed.), *Fundamentalism, Revivalists and Violence in South Asia* (Riverdale, MD: Riverdale, 1986).

7. I am grateful to Professor Ranbir Singh Sandhu, Department of Civil Engineering, Ohio State University, for providing me with several hours of tape-recorded speeches of Sant Jamail Singh Bhindranwale. Professor Sandhu has translated some of these speeches, and I appreciate his sharing these translations with me. For this article I am relying primarily on the words of Bhindranwale. They are found in the following sources: 'Sant Jamail Bhindranwale's Address to the Sikh Congregation', a transcript of a sermon given in the Golden Temple in November 1983, translated by Ranbir Singh Sandhu, April 1985, and distributed by the Sikh Religious and Educational Trust, Columbus, Ohio; excerpts of Bhindranwale's speeches, translated into English, that appear in Joyce Pettigrew, 'In Search of a New Kingdom of Lahore', *Pacific Affairs*, Vol. 60, No. 1 (Spring 1987) (forthcoming), and interviews with Bhindranwale found in various issues of *India Today* and other publications.

8. The spiritual leader of the Nirankaris, Baba Gurbachan Singh, was assassinated at his home in Delhi on 24 May 1980. Bhindranwale was implicated in the murder, but was never brought to trial. Kuldip Nayar claims that Zail Singh, who became President of India, came to Bhindranwale's defense at that time (Nayar and Singh, *Tragedy of Punjab*, p. 37).

9. It is said that Bhindranwale was first brought into the political arena in 1977 by Mrs Gandhi's son, Sanjay, who hoped that Bhindranwale's popularity would undercut the political support of the Akali party (Nayar and Singh, *Tragedy of Punjab*, p. 31, and Tully, *Amritsar*, p. 57–61).

10. Bhindranwale, 'Address to the Sikh Congregation', pp. 10–11.

11. Bhindranwale, excerpt from a speech, in Pettigrew.

12. Ibid., p. 15.

13. Ibid.

14. Bhindranwale, 'Address to the Sikh Congregation', p. 1.

15. Ibid.

16. Bhindranwale, excerpt from a speech, in Pettigrew.

17. Ibid.

18. Bhindranwale, 'Address to the Sikh Congregation', p. 10.

19. Ibid., p. 2.

20. Bhindranwale, excerpt from a speech, in Pettigrew.

21. Ibid.

22. Ibid.

23. Ibid.

24. Bhindranwale, 'Address to the Sikh Congregation', pp. 1–5, and ibid., p. 14.

25. Bhindranwale, excerpt from a speech, in Pettigrew.

26. For an interesting discussion of the definition of violence and terror in political contexts see Thomas Perry Thornton, 'Terrorism as a Weapon of Political Agitation', in Harry Eckstein (ed.), *Internal War: Problems and Approaches* (New York: The Free Press, 1964); and David C. Rapoport, 'The Politics of Atrocity', in Y. Alexander and S. Finger (eds.), *Terrorism: Interdisciplinary Perspectives* (New York: John Jay, 1977).

27. Clifford Geertz defines religion as 'a system of symbols which acts to establish powerful, pervasive and long-lasting moods and motivations in men by formulating conceptions of a general order of existence and clothing these conceptions with such an aura of factuality that the moods and motivations seem uniquely realistic' ('Religion as a Cultural System', reprinted in William A. Lessa and Evon Z. Vogt, (eds.), *Reader in Comparative Religion: An Anthropological Approach* (New York: Harper & Row, 3rd ed., 1972), p. 168).

28. Robert Bellah, 'Transcendence in Contemporary Piety', in Donald R. Cutler, *The Religious Situation: 1969* (Boston: Beacon Press, 1969), p. 907.

29. Peter Berger, *The Heretical Imperative* (New York: Doubleday, 1980), p. 38. See also his *Sacred Canopy: Elements of a Sociological Theory of Religion* (Garden City, NY: Doubleday, 1967).

30. Louis Dupré, *Transcendent Selfhood: The Loss and Re-discovery of the Inner Life* (New York: Seabury Press, 1976), p. 26. For a discussion of Berger and Dupré's definitions, see Mary Douglas, 'The Effects of Modernization on Religious Change', *Daedalus*, Vol. III, No. 1 (Winter 1982), pp. 1–19.

31. Durkheim describes the dichotomy of sacred and profane in religion in the following way: 'In all the history of human thought there exists no other example of two categories of things so profoundly differentiated or so radically opposed to one another.... The sacred and the profane have always and everywhere been conceived by the human mind as two distinct classes, as two worlds between which there is nothing in common.... In different religions, this opposition has been conceived in different ways'. Emile Durkheim, *The Elementary Forms of the Religious Life*, trans. by Joseph Ward Swain (London: George Allen & Unwin, 1976) (originally published in 1915), pp. 38–9. Durkheim goes on to talk about the sacred things that religions encompass; but the first thing he says about the religious view is the perception that there is this dichotomy. From a theological perspective it seems to me that Paul Tillich is saying something of the same thing in arguing for the necessary connection between faith and doubt (see, for example, the first chapter of his *Dynamics of Faith*).

32. On this point I am in agreement with Wilfred Cantwell Smith who suggested some years ago that the noun 'religion' might well be banished from our vocabulary, and that we restrict ourselves to using the adjective 'religious' (*The Meaning and End of Religion: A New Approach to the Religious Traditions of Mankind* (New York: Macmillan, 1962), pp. 119–53).

33. For the significance of the two-edged sword symbol and its links with the Devi cult revered by people, such as Jats, who have traditionally inhabited the foothills of the Himalayas adjacent to the Punjab, see W. H. McLeod, *The Evolution of the Sikh Community* (Oxford: Clarendon Press, 1976), p. 13.

34. Ibid, pp. 15–17, 51–2. These five objects are known as the five K's, since the name for each of them in Punjabi begins with the letter 'k'. The other four are uncut hair, a wooden comb, a metal bangle and cotton breeches. See also W. Owen Cole and Piara Singh Sambhi, *The Sikhs: Their Religious Beliefs and Practices* (London: Routledge & Kegan Paul, 1978), p. 36.

35. Karl Marx, 'Contribution to the Critique of Hegel's Philosophy of Right', reprinted in Karl Marx and Friedrich Engels, *On Religion* (New York: Schocken Books), p. 42; see also Engels' class analysis of a religious revolt, 'The Peasant War in Germany' in the same volume, pp. 97–118.

36. Sigmund Freud, *Totem and Taboo*, trans. by James Strachey (New York: W. W. Norton, 1950).

37. Rene Girard, *Violence and the Sacred*, trans. by Patrick Gregory (Baltimore and London; Johns Hopkins University Press, 1977); see especially Chapters 7 and 8. What is not clear in this book is how symbolic violence leads to real acts of violence; this link is made in a subsequent study of Girard's, *Scapegoat*, trans. by Patrick Gregory (Baltimore and London: Johns Hopkins University Press, 1986).

38. Bhindranwale, excerpt from a speech, in Pettigrew.

39. Ibid.

40. Bhindranwale, 'Address to the Sikh Congregation', p. 9.

41. See my article, 'Nonviolence', in Mircea Eliade (ed.), *The Encyclopedia of Religion* (New York: Macmillan, 1987). For the ethic of non-violence in Sikhism see Cole and Sambhi, *The Sikhs*, p. 138. For Sikh ethical attitudes in general see Avtar Singh, *Ethics of the Sikhs* (Patiala, India: Punjabi University Press); and S. S. Kohli, *Sikh Ethics* (New Delhi: Munshiram Manoharlal, 1975).

42. An excellent anthology of statements of Christian theologians on the ethical justification for war is Albert Marrin (ed.), *War and the Christian Conscience: From Augustine to Martin Luther King, Jr.* (Chicago: Henry Regnery, 1971). On the development of the just war doctrine in Christianity, with its secular parallels, see James Turner Johnson, *Ideology, Reason, and the*

45. Joyce Pettigrew argues that the *miri-piri* concept 'gave legitimacy to the political action organized from within the Golden Temple' (Pettigrew, op. cit.). This 'political action' was the establishment of an armed camp of which Bhindranwale was the commander; it was to rout this camp that the Indian army entered the Golden Temple on 5 June 1984, in Operation Bluestar.

46. Bhindranwale, 'Address to the Sikh Congregation', p. 13.

47. Ibid., p. 8.

48. David C. Rapoport, 'Why does Messianism Produce Terror?' paper delivered at the 81st Annual Meeting of the American Political Science Association, New Orleans, 27 August–1 September 1985. Although I find Rapoport's conclusions helpful, and in many ways compatible with my own, his emphasis on messianic movements seems unnecessary. The notion of messianism is largely alien to the Asian religious traditions, and much of what he says about it could be said of religion in general. See also his 'Fear and Trembling: Terrorism in Three Religious Traditions', *American Political Science Review* 78:3 (Sept. 1984), pp. 658–77, which includes case studies of the Thugs, Assassins and Zealots and the essays in David C. Rapoport and Y. Alexander (eds.), *The Morality of Terrorism: Religious and Secular Justifications* (New York: Pergamon, 1982).

49. There are also examples in other cultures where mythic battles are thought to have had a historical effect. At a recent presentation at the Wilson Center, for instance, Professor Billie Jean Isbell described the influence of the notion of cosmic cycles of order and chaos in traditional Andean cosmology on the propensity for violence of the Sendero Luminoso tribal people of Peru ('The Faces and Voices of Terrorism', Politics and Religion Seminar, Wilson Center, 8 May 1986).

50. The term *jihad* is derived from the word for striving for something, and implies 'the struggle against one's bad inclinations' as well as what it has come to mean in the popular Western mind, holy war (Rudolph Peters. *Islam and Colonialism: The Doctrine of Jihad in Modern History*, The Hague: Mouton Publishers, 1979, p. 188).

51. Bhindranwale, 'Address to the Sikh Congregation', p. 7.

52. Bhindranwale, excerpt from a speech, in Pettigrew.

53. Bhindranwale, 'Address to the Sikh congregation', p. 13.

54. For an interesting analysis of the Gush Emunim, see Ehud Sprinzak's essay in this volume.

55. Bhindranwale, 'Address to the Sikh congregation', p. 8.

56. Ibid., p. 2.

57. Ibid., p. 3.

58. Bhindranwale, excerpt from a speech, in Pettigrew.

59. Ibid.

60. Weston LaBarre, *The Ghost Dance: Origins of Religion* (London: Allen & Unwin, 1972).

61. William James, *The Varieties of Religious Experience* (Cambridge, MA: Harvard University Press, 1985) (originally published in 1902), pp. 71–108.

62. Bhindranwale, 'Address to the Sikh Congregation', p. 10.

63. Ibid., p. 10.

64. Bhindranwale, excerpt from a speech, in Pettigrew.

65. Bhindranwale, 'Address to the Sikh Congregation', p. 14.

66. Bhindranwale, excerpt from a speech, in Pettigrew.

Adam Dolnik, 2003

All God's Poisons: Re-Evaluating the Threat of Religious Terrorism with Respect to Non-Conventional Weapons

Introduction

Over the course of the past several years, the possibility of the use of chemical, biological, radiological, and nuclear (CBRN) weapons by non-state actors has been a topic of extensive academic and public debate. Originally, the discussion concentrated primarily on capabilities, where the ease of acquisition of CBRN materials following the breakup of the Soviet Union, as well as more widespread availability of information needed for the production and weaponization of such agents, were the main sources of concern. More recently, the debate was brought to a more realistic level through the acknowledgment of technical hurdles associated with the successful delivery of CBRN agents, as well as the possible motivational constraints involved in the decision of terrorist groups to use such weapons. Another shift in the debate was represented by the claim that the rise of religious terrorism had eroded these constraints. According to this argument, religious terrorists whose operations have been observed to be responsible for the vast majority of all casualties in terrorist attacks worldwide are believed to be unconstrained by political considerations, as their only constituency is God. Further, the ability of religious terrorists to dehumanize their enemies indiscriminately is allegedly strengthened by the perceived divine sanction of their actions.[1] Based on this logic, the assertion that religious terrorist groups are more likely to use CBRN weapons than their secular counterparts has become one of the few widely accepted paradigms of terrorism studies. Unfortunately, this logical yet somewhat inaccurate conventional wisdom is often applied mechanically, without further inquiry into the nature of the given organization's belief system. As a result, many of today's simplified threat assessments are based solely on the frequency of the use of the word "God" in a given organization's statements, and consequently do not adequately reflect the CBRN threat level posed by the respective group.

This study will re-evaluate the above-stated conventional wisdom by providing alternative interpretation of the trends in terrorism and by putting to test several commonly cited assertions about the characteristics that allegedly set aside religious terrorism from other forms of the phenomenon. In addition this paper will attempt to outline an alternative approach to threat assessment by defining specific motivational, behavioral and organizational characteristics that a terrorist group will need to satisfy in order to perpetrate a successful mass-fatality CBRN attack in the future. Understanding the nature of this threat

statistics are pointed out, and alternative interpretations of commonly cited characteristics of "religious terrorists" are presented as well. The third part then focuses on identifying likely characteristics of potential "superterrorists" with respect to their ideological, organizational, and behavioral traits. This section also incorporates a threat assessment for the future based on patterns in terrorist innovation and compares the advantages and disadvantages of CBRN terrorism in light of conventional terrorist tactics. An overall evaluation of the threat of mass-casualty CBRN terrorism for the future is presented in the conclusion.

Part I

Traditional vs. "New" Terrorism

One of the two critical components of the contemporary debate about the likelihood of mass-casualty CBRN terrorism is the motivation to inflict indiscriminate mass casualties. But despite the fact that terrorism does typically involve killing and destruction, most terrorists practice a level of restraint on their activities. Traditionally, terrorists have not necessarily been interested in killing a lot of people, but rather in spreading fear among the general population by killing only the necessary few. In this respect, perhaps the best definition of terrorism is the ancient Chinese proverb "kill one, frighten ten thousand," or alternatively, renowned terrorism scholar Brian Jenkins' observation that "terrorists want a lot of people watching, not a lot of people dead."[2] Possibly for this particular reason, terrorists have traditionally not been interested in CBRN weapons because such weapons were deemed too large-scale to serve any purpose useful to the terrorists. Massive destruction is likely to be counterproductive for terrorists who typically strive to attract popular support in order to force a political change, such as creation of a homeland or implementation of social justice norms within the targeted state. Mass killing would likely hinder such support, rather than attract it. Moreover, a large-scale attack might also strengthen the affected government's resolve to track down and punish the terrorists, and may thus jeopardize the group's very existence.

While this traditional interpretation of terrorism has been the consensus for decades, many authors have observed that over the past 20 years, the phenomenon has experienced disturbing new trends. These indicate the rise of violent activities motivated by a religious imperative, as opposed to the still lethal but arguably more comprehensible motives of ethnic nationalism and revolutionary ideologies. Some authors have claimed that religious terrorists are not constrained by the traditional political concerns, such as popular image or the reaction of the constituency or the targeted state. Rather, since they base their justifications for using violence on the sanction of a supernatural authority whose will is absolute, the "new" terrorists are less rational, and therefore more prone to indiscriminate mass-casualty violence.[3]

Let us now look at more closely at this conventional argument as it has been developed by some of the most influential terrorism scholars.

The Conventional Argument

The conventional argument, which in many ways was pioneered by Bruce Hoffman, relies in many of its arguments on the trends in international terrorism. Over the last 20 years, the statistical data drawn from the RAND–St Andrews Chronology of International Terrorist Incidents demonstrates an alarming trend: a continual decrease in terrorist incidents, which is however accompanied by a larger number of overall casualties in those fewer incidents. This seems to confirm the hypothesis previously pronounced by various scholars that terrorist attacks are becoming increasingly lethal. Besides this overarching trend based on the average number of deaths per attack, the mode of individual terrorist incidents also seems to confirm this trend: while only 17 percent of terrorist attacks in the 1970s, and just 19 percent of attacks in the 1980s killed anyone, at least one fatality occurred in 29 percent of terrorist incidents in 1995.[4]

Another trend observed by Hoffman is the increasing proliferation of terrorist organizations motivated primarily by religion, which he documents by several striking statistics. For instance, Hoffman claims that "none of the eleven identifiable international terrorist groups in 1968 could be classified as religious: that is, having aims and motivations reflecting a predominant religious character or influence. Not until the 1980s did the first religious terrorist groups begin to emerge.... By 1995, 26 of the 56 active international terrorist organizations were religious in character."[5] The religions that are most commonly associated with the rise of religious terrorism are the Shi'ia branch of Islam in the 80s represented mainly by the Lebanese Amal and Hizballah, followed by the rise of Sunni violence in the 90s signified by the actions of the Palestinian Hamas and Palestinian Islamic Jihad (PIJ), al-Qaida, the Algerian Armed Islamic Group (GIA) and others; Jewish terrorism characterized by the activities of the Gush Emunim, Kach, Kahane Chai; Sikh terrorism most commonly associated with the Dal Khalsa, Babbar Khalsa and the Khalistan Commando Force; Christian terrorism of the various American militia movements, Christian paramilitary groups and anti-abortion activists; and various sects and cults, most notably the Japanese Aum Shinrikyo.[6]

The main contribution of Bruce Hoffman's work has been the linking of these two aforementioned trends into a directional causal relationship: Hoffman identified the rise of religious motivation among terrorist groups as the primary cause of the higher number of casualties per attack in the modern era:

> "Among the various factors that account for terrorism's increasing lethality (including the terrorist's perennial quest for attention; the increased prevalence of state sponsorship and the greater resources accorded by terrorists; developments in terrorist weaponry, which is getting smaller, more easy to conceal and more powerful; and the increasing sophistication of professional terrorism), the most significant is perhaps the dramatic proliferation of terrorist groups motivated by a religious imperative."[7]

Hoffman documents his assertion by statistical data for 1995, claiming that "although religious terrorists committed only 25 per cent of the recorded international terrorist incidents in 1995, they were responsible for 58 percent of the total number of fatalities recorded that year. Looking at the data from another perspective, those attacks that caused the greatest numbers of deaths in 1995 (8 or more fatalities) were all perpetrated by religious terrorists."[8] Hoffman also offers a concrete example in the record of terrorist acts by Shi'ia

of course, trigger the immediate question of why that seems to be the case. Hoffman offers a sound explanation:

> "The fact that for the religious terrorist violence inevitably assumes a transcendent purpose and therefore becomes a sacramental and divine duty arguably results in a significant loosening of the constraints on the commission of mass murder. Religion, moreover, functions as a legitimizing force, sanctioning if not encouraging wide scale violence against an almost open-ended category of opponents. Thus religious terrorist violence becomes almost an end in itself—a morally justified, divinely instigated expedient toward the attainment of the terrorists' ultimate ends. This is a direct reflection of the fact that the terrorists motivated by a religious imperative do not seek to appeal to any constituency but themselves and the changes they seek are not for any utilitarian purpose, but are only to benefit themselves. The religious terrorist, moreover, sees himself as an outsider from the society that he both abhors and rejects and this sense of alienation enables him to contemplate—and undertake—far more destructive and bloodier types of terrorist operations than his secular counterpart."[11]

Consequently, if we should expect a mass casualty CBRN terrorist attack in the future, it is the religious terrorist that is most likely to perpetrate such an act.

As one can see form the previous quote, an integral part of the conventional argument concerns the core characteristics of religious terrorists, which allegedly set them aside from their secular counterparts. Most authors confirm that drawing the line between religious and secular terrorists is challenging, as many secular organizations also have a strong religious component, and many religious terrorists in addition possess goals that are of a political nature. This distinction becomes even more blurred in the case of Islamic fundamentalism, as Islam draws no distinction between religion and politics.[12] Still, some terrorism scholars have attempted to define the core characteristics of religious terrorists, pointing mainly to the radically different value systems of religious terrorists, the different mechanisms of legitimization and justification, concepts of morality, mechanisms of victim dehumanization and an overall world view. According to Hoffman, for instance, the aims of "religious political" terrorists are defined as the attainment of the greatest possible benefits for themselves and for their co-religionists only, as opposed to the indiscriminately utilitarian goals of secular terrorists.[13] This allegedly further widens the gap between ends and means; "where the secular terrorist sees violence primarily as a means to an end, the religious terrorist tends to view violence as an end in itsself."[14] Another implication defined by Hoffman is that religious and secular terrorists also differ significantly in their constituencies:

> "Whereas secular terrorists attempt to appeal to a constituency variously composed of actual and potential sympathizers, members of communities they purport to "defend," of the aggrieved people they claim to speak for; religious terrorists are at once activists and constituents engaged in what they regard as a "total war." They execute their terrorist

acts for no audience but themselves. Thus, the restraints on violence that are imposed on secular terrorists by the desire to appeal to a tacitly supportive or uncommitted constituency are not relevant to the religious terrorists. Moreover, this absence of a constituency in the secular terrorist sense leads to a sanctioning of almost limitless violence against a virtually open-ended category of targets—that is, anyone who is not a member of the terrorist's religion or religious sect."[15]

Additional characteristics have been identified by Mark Jurgensmeyer, who characterizes religiously motivated struggles primarily as those involving images of divine warfare.[16] Such images represent what Jurgensmeyer calls a "cosmic struggle" which is played out in history as a war between good and evil, order and chaos.[17] Religious terrorists identify with such a struggle and project its images onto the present situation, which they seek to address. Such heavily mythologized conflict between the believers and their enemies then becomes absolute.

According to Jurgensmeyer, another distinct characteristic of religious terrorists is their dominant reliance on the concept of martyrdom. In the context of a cosmic war, he argues, martyrdom is not only regarded as a testimony of one's commitment, it is also a performance of the most fundamental religious act found in virtually every religious tradition in the world: the act of sacrifice.[18] The word has its roots in the Latin verb "*sacrificium*" which translates as "to make holy." The images of sacrifice thus transform destruction performed within the religious context into something positive, making killing not only permissible but even mandatory.[19]

Another interesting characteristic of religious terrorists defined by Jurgensmeyer is the intangibility of their goals. Terrorist acts are often "devices for symbolic empowerment in wars that cannot be won and for goals that cannot be achieved. The very absence of thought about what the activists would do if they were victorious is sufficient indication that they do not expect to be, and perhaps do not want to be."[20] This presumably makes the political calculus in their violent actions much less relevant, resulting in much more irrational acts of violence.

According to Jurgensmeyer, yet another core characteristic of religious terrorism is the absoluteness of the authority that is used to justify the acts of violence. Under normal circumstances, only the state has the recognized right to take life—for purposes either of military defense, police protection or punishment.[21] "Those who desire to attain moral sanction for their violent acts and who do not have the approval of an officially recognized government, find it helpful to have access to a higher source: the meta-morality that religion provides, which serves to break the state's monopoly on morally sanctioned killing."[22]

Part II

Let us now look at some of the difficulties with the conventional interpretation of the trends in terrorism, and the shortcomings in the definition of the characteristics of religious terrorists presented above.

Trends in Terrorism: The Problems of Statistics

The first major difficulty is the limited representativeness of the cited data. Even though various open source databases of terrorist incidents may seem to suggest that the number

common occurrence, however, the media starts paying significantly lesser attention to them. It is therefore not unfeasible, that once *individual* terrorist attacks have become deadlier and more spectacular, the world media gradually abandoned reporting the small scale attacks with explosive or incendiary devices that were so popular in the 60s and 70s. For this reason, it is quite possible that the frequency of such small scale terrorist attacks has not actually diminished but is only ignored by the media and consequently is no longer reflected in open source databases. This can then result in the perception of a decreasing terrorist activity and an increasing casualty-per-attack ratio. On the other hand, it is also possible that terrorists have in fact gradually abandoned small scale attacks due to the media's disinterest in reporting such events, and in that case the original hypothesis would be correct.

Another similar problem of the cited data is represented by the geographically uneven coverage of events by the international media—terrorist activity in countries of a greater international importance is simply reported on a much greater scale and in much greater detail than incidents in the internationally neglected parts of the world. Consider for instance the enormous differences in the media reporting of terrorist violence in Israel and Algeria. While detailed data on every single individual that was killed or injured in an act of terrorism in Israel is easily obtainable due to the heavy presence of news agencies in that country, the only obtainable data about the number of casualties in the Algerian conflict are guesstimates with a confidence interval in the range of tens of thousands. This is caused not only by the general perception of Algeria's international insignificance, but also by the fact that journalists are not welcomed in the country, neither by the terrorists nor by the government. The key implication of such a disproportion in reporting is that since terrorist violence in Algeria is of a much larger scale than it is in Israel, database records in terms of overall numbers of terrorist attacks and fatalities worldwide are very likely to be heavily skewed.

Yet another difficulty of a quantitative interpretation of the statistical data on terrorism is constituted by the practical obstacles in database maintenance faced by individual database managers. If for instance, the intensity of a certain terrorist campaign escalates profoundly at a given moment, it becomes nearly impossible to record every single incident. This is caused not only by the fact that the overall escalation of a given conflict results into a lesser media coverage of individual events, but also by the practical considerations involved in database maintenance, such as the number of resources and staff members available for data collection and entry. For this reason, most databases of terrorist incidents have incorporated all sorts of creative loopholes into their criteria, so that certain incidents can be omitted if the given armed conflict erupts into an uncontrollable and reciprocal clash between the terrorists and the their opponents. So when, for instance, the terrorist campaign of the Maoist rebels in Nepal escalated and turned into a civil war in 2002, most database managers chose to exclude the terrorist incidents perpetrated within this conflict from their collection. Similar examples can be given with regard to many other escalating conflicts, including the wars in Chechnya, Afghanistan, Colombia, etc. Another technique that has been used by some databases of terrorist incidents has been to collapse several attacks into a single database entry, which is a more honest approach, but which inevitably skews the statistics as well. Such, for instance, was the case of the multiple bombing campaigns perpetrated by Corsican separatists in the 1980s, which no existing open source database reported on individual basis, but rather compiled them together into single entries.

Yet another important aspect that one should bear in mind is the fact that the most of the statistics used to support the conventional argument presented above have originated in the RAND–St Andrews Chronology of International Terrorist Incidents, a database that is quite narrow in scope as it monitors only terrorist incidents that are *international* in nature, defined as "incidents in which terrorists go abroad to strike their targets, select domestic targets associated with a foreign state, or create an international incident by attacking airline passengers, personnel or equipment."[23] The main point to make here is that even though they usually attract much more media coverage, international terrorist incidents are significantly less frequent than domestic incidents. As a result, the commonly cited data that indicates the rise of religious terrorism is only applicable to international terrorism, a relatively small pool that is not necessarily representative of the trends in terrorism in general. So in the end, the correct interpretation of the statistics cited by Hoffman and others seems to document only an increasing *internationalization* of religious terrorism, and not necessarily a global *rise* of the phenomenon. And even though Hoffman's hypothesis is most likely correct, the cited data is limited only to a numerically less prevalent form of the terrorism phenomenon, and should be understood as such.

While I have brought into question the validity of the claims of decrease in the number of attacks over time and the rise of religion as a dominant motivation for terrorist activity, the hypothesis of ever-increasing number of fatalities seems rather convincing. And while this hypothesis is again supported on the basis of data which reflects only the trends in international terrorism, qualitative analysis of all terrorist attacks seems to provide additional support for this claim: while the deadliest incidents prior to the 1980s involved "only" dozens of fatalities, in the 80s and 90s the most lethal attacks were counted in the hundreds, and in the new millennium the plateau has reached into the thousands for the first time in history.

The Historical Record from Another Perspective

Let us now test the conventional hypothesis by looking at some additional qualitative data. The information presented in this section draws on multiple sources, mainly on the detailed chronologies of terrorist attacks compiled since 1968 by Edward F. Mickolus and his colleagues, the Weapons of Mass Destruction Terrorism and the Hydra databases compiled by the Monterey Institute of International Studies' Center for Nonproliferation Studies, and various other chronologies and listings available in the open source literature.

With regard to the hypothesis about religious terrorists being more lethal than their secular counterparts, perhaps the most surprising statistic will be the motivational distribution of perpetrators of the deadliest tactic that has historically been used by terrorists—the downing of civil airliners, either by detonating explosive devices on board, shooting them down with surface-to-air (SAM) missiles, rocket propelled grenades (RPG), or hijacking the planes and crashing them into buildings. Out of some 130 historical attacks or attempts to bring down airplanes in flight, *only 10* were perpetrated by organizations which can

that resulted in the death of more then 100 people, only 4 are attributable to organizations whose primary motivation is of a religious nature. Another interesting statistic concerns the use of suicide bombings, another widely destructive tactic: of the 30 single most deadly terrorist incidents carried out to date since 1990, 18 utilized suicide bombers.[24] Even though suicide bombings are in popular perception frequently associated with religious fanaticism, only one third of over 400 suicide bombings to date were perpetrated by organizations of a religious character. And finally, out of the 74 vehicular bombings that have killed 25 or more people, religious terrorists were again responsible for only one third of incidents.

As is apparent from these numbers, the deadliest forms of conventional terrorism have not been associated with an overarching presence of religious terrorists. Let us now take a closer look at the trends in non-conventional terrorism. Out of 90 Type I[25] uses of a CBRN agent recorded in the Monterey Institute's WMD Terrorism database,[26] only some 34 involved religious groups, with 12 attacks conducted by Aum Shinrikyo alone. With respect to fatalities resulting from these CBRN attacks, the numbers seem to confirm the hypothesis that religious groups are significantly more lethal than their secular counterparts: out of 1311 people listed in the database as killed in incidents involving CBRN, 1121 are associated with attacks perpetrated by religious groups. Upon taking a closer look however, we can see that this statistic is again not nearly as alarming as it may look: all of the 1121 fatalities occurred in the total of only five cases. The vast majority of the fatalities were the 778 members of the Movement for the Restoration of the Ten Commandments of God, which perished in the fire that consumed the cult shrine in Kanungu, Uganda, in March 2000. Later it was discovered that the majority of the people who died in what originally appeared to be a mass suicide were poisoned by an undisclosed substance.[27] Another 304 fatalities were attributed to the events of February 2000 in Kaduna, Nigeria, where the Hausa military youths violently attacked and killed Christian demonstrators who were protesting a government plan to implement the *sharia*. The victims were decapitated, mutilated, burned, and in some cases killed by arrows covered in poison.[28] The final 39 fatalities are people who died in a combination of several incidents perpetrated by Aum Shinrikyo in Japan: seven people were killed in the 1994 sarin attack near the mountain resort town of Matsumoto,[29] a total of 20 others were killed prior to 1994 in several assassinations of the cult's dissenters using VX nerve agent,[30] and 12 more people died in the notorious Tokyo subway sarin attack in 1995.

As we can see from this overview, the causes of the majority of the deaths in the first two instances are unknown, and it is therefore difficult to accept 1121 as the number of people killed by religious terrorists with CBRN. For this reason, it remains the case that none of the empirical data presented in this section seems to confirm the hypothesis that religious terrorists are significantly more lethal and therefore more susceptible to the use of CBRN weapons than their secular counterparts.

Linking Religious Motives and Escalation of Terrorist Violence

Let us now attempt to deconstruct the hypothesis regarding the casual relationship between the rise of religion as a primary motive for terrorists and the ever increasing deadliness of terrorist attacks, into individual components. Hoffman cites a number of reasons for why terrorism has become increasingly deadly, including the terrorists' constant quest for attention, the increased prevalence of state sponsorship, developments in terrorist weaponry, and the increasing sophistication of professional terrorism, but he considers proliferation of terrorist groups motivated by a religious imperative to be the single most important one.[31] Hoffman's list is quite comprehensive, but it should be emphasized that other important reasons exist as well. One is the terrorists' natural tendency to "out-do" their previous attacks, stimulated by the perception that if the present level of violence has thus far failed to succeed in forcing a radical change of the *status quo*, the campaign needs to intensified. Another reason is the fact that no matter how horrific a terrorist campaign might be, the intended audiences become desensitized to the current level of violence over time, forcing the terrorists to escalate in order to maintain or heighten the atmosphere of panic and fear among the general population, and to stay in the spotlight. An escalation in terrorist violence is also sometimes stimulated by the actions of other organizations, with which the given group competes for power or popularity. For instance, the decision of the secular Al Aksa Martyrs Brigades to engage in suicide bombings for the first time was clearly motivated by the growing power and popularity of the Hamas, a phenomenon that has often been attributed to the organization's use of suicide bombings as a tool for disrupting the peace process. Interestingly, following their first suicide bombing in January 2002, the Al Aksa Martyrs Brigades have begun to utilize this tactic with a greater frequency than any other Palestinian organization.

Another reason for the gradual escalation of overall terrorist violence over time has been the formation of new groups. Upon emergence, new violent organizations usually do not undergo the full process of radicalization, but rather pick up at the level of violence where other organizations active in the same struggle have left off. Alternatively, many existing organizations can give birth to new formations through the process of splintering, which usually results in the new entity being more radical and more violent than the core group. For instance, Ahmed Jibril's Popular Front for the Liberation of Palestine–General Command (PFLP-GC) resorted to several extraordinarily deadly bombings of commercial airliners in midcourse flight after its breakup with George Habash's Popular Front for the Liberation of Palestine (PFLP), in order to attain the image of a powerful new player in the Palestinian liberation movement.

The key point to make here is that the escalation of terrorist violence over time is a natural phenomenon, which occurs regardless of the transformation in ideological motives. Motivational factors, of course, do play a role, but they are not the main driving force behind the ever-escalating nature of terrorism—this function is generally fulfilled more significantly by the general dynamics that were defined by Hoffman and expanded upon here.

Terrorism and Religion

Earlier in this paper, the statistics that allegedly document the substitution of secular ideologies by divinely sanctioned violence have been questioned. One thing that remains true, however, is that over the last 20 years religious images have indeed become more prevalent

gies such as Marxism and purely secular nationalism.[32] The single most important factor for the rise of religion as a dominant motive has been the end of the Cold War, which signified the utter historical failure of communist ideologies, as well as the end of the bipolar world order. These events have not only diminished the attractiveness of ideological compliance with one of the two world power centers in order to attract state assistance, they also triggered immense fear of "one-worldism" symbolized by the emergence of the unipolar world order, which was perceived by radical members of various cultures as a threat to their identity and survival.[33] In the absence of alternatives among secular ideologies, many extremists shifted to religion as the main ideological foundation of their activities. This shift in ideological support mechanisms, however, does not necessarily mean that that the nature of core terrorist motivations and beliefs has changed, or that religion became the *primary* motivating factor for acts of violence. As previously noted by Walter Laqueur, terrorist belief systems may differ significantly based on history, culture or the influence of charismatic leaders. But the ideological content is only secondary to "burning passion," which serves as the primary driving force behind terrorist activity.[34] Or to use a psychologist's perspective:

> "Religion is first and foremost a fantasy system invented to merge with omnipotent forces that protect communities and individuals from death and predation, the terror of the unknown, and the viciousness of nature.... Religion may or may not teach violence, but what is responsible for the violence is the vengeful fantasy itself, which either utilizes, twists, or invents a divine sanction (religious precedent) to justify what is *psychologically* motivating the fantasy."[35]

In other words, religion did in the last 20 years become a more prominent factor as the supporting philosophical basis for many terrorist organizations, but the underlying motives in the belief systems of the majority of today's terrorists have *NOT* changed. Even the religious fanatic sees his violent activity as an essentially altruistic act of self-defense. It is still the perception of humiliation, victimization and injustice that drives the so-called "religious terrorist," rather than a perceived universal command from God. The use of holy rhetoric by most groups commonly labeled "religious" serves much more as a uniting and morale-boosting tool than as a universal justification for acts of unrestrained violence. That is not to say that for many terrorists, religion does not represent a tremendous legitimizing force and that it does not inspire the perception of enormous gratification and empowerment. But the terrorists are still primarily motivated by a grievance that is very real—even though just like most ordinary people, they also look for support of their arguments wherever they can. Religion then represents only one of the possible sources of support. At the same time Jurgensmeyer is probably correct when he claims that "those who are engaged in (acts of violence) would be offended if we concluded that their actions were purely for social and political gain. They argue that they act out of religious conviction, and surely they are to some degree right."[36] But this is not in any way contradictory to what has just been mentioned. Virtually *any* terrorist would be offended by the suggestion that he or she is motivated by political gain, as terrorists in general tend to see themselves and their actions as essentially altruistic, risking their lives for the benefit of future generations. The option of pointing to something greater then themselves not only gives the terrorists a legitimizing force but also provides support for their claims of altruism and self-sacrifice.

Now the key question arises: is it useful or even possible to make a distinction between religious and secular terrorists? Despite the problems of such a categorization, the answer is still yes, but is crucial to make this distinction at the level of *primary* rather than supporting motivations. In most cases, the perpetrators of terrorist violence will have multiple motives, and it will therefore be essential to identify the most dominant one. For example, Aum Shinrikyo's participation in elections does not make their primary motivation political, just as Hamas' constant praise of Allah does not make the primary motive a religious one. We should be careful to not fall into the trap of rhetorical nuances. In many cultures the word "God" figures very strongly in the language and in cultural and political traditions, which can sometimes be misleading. For instance, to an outsider phrases like "In God We Trust" printed on the American currency or the use of the popular slogan "God Bless America" by the American president could easily create the false impression that the United States is essentially a theocratic state. Another factor besides language that has the capacity to mislead us in terms of labeling a terrorist organization as religious is government propaganda. Virtually all states that are victims of a terrorist campaign insist on projecting their opponents as religious fanatics. This is quite understandable, as such labeling can have a de-legitimizing effect on the terrorists' cause—someone who sees himself as fighting on God's orders is popularly perceived as an irrational zealot, with whom no compromise is deemed possible. Rather, this "worshiper of evil" is seen as an exceptionally dangerous creature which uses claims of a just grievance only as a misleading cover, and who can only be stopped by merciless elimination. Israel and to a lesser extent Russia and India are examples of countries that have used such a strategy with some level of success. But while this strategy of promoting the opponent's image as one of an irrational religious fanatic may in some cases be politically successful, it caries the danger of failing to address the actual real-life grievances, which in turn can eventually result in increased support for the terrorists.

In conclusion, many factors contribute to the fact that today's distinctions between secular and religious terrorists are dubious at best. Let us now take a closer look at the some of the shortcomings in the definition of individual characteristics of religious terrorists as they have been defined by Hoffman and Jurgensmeyer.

Nature and Characteristics of Religious Terrorists

Jurgensmeyer in his book "Terror in the Mind of God" provides an excellent analysis of the characteristics of religious terrorists. The difficulty is, however, that nearly all of these characteristics apply to the vast majority of terrorist organizations regardless of the ideological foundations of their belief systems.[37] For instance, Jurgensmeyer describes in great detail the creation of martyrs and their role in religiously motivated violence. He also contends that by giving up their lives, martyrs not only demonstrate their commitment, but they also engage in sacrifice—the most fundamental form of religiosity.[38] But the key to emphasize here is that *all* violent campaigns find it useful to create and glorify martyrs. An act

spite of their military dominance are essentially weak.[39] The resulting perception among the group is that due to superior determination, their final victory is inevitable.[40]

Another allegedly distinct characteristic of religiously motivated struggles are the aforementioned images of divine warfare, which are equated to the present struggle and are consistently used to create a sense of historical purpose and urgency.[41] This, however, is again a characteristic that is psychologically natural to all ethnic, cultural, or national communities, and is consistently used by all violent movements. Jurgensmeyer's "cosmic struggles" in essence are what psychiatrist Vamik Volkan calls the "chosen traumas": "heavily mythologized historical sufferings that bring with them powerful experiences of loss and feelings of humiliation, vengeance and hatred that trigger a variety of unconscious defense mechanisms that attempt to reverse these experiences and feelings."[42] Such defense mechanisms serve as a powerful dehumanization tool for killing, regardless of ideological context—the new enemies of current conflicts are psychologically transformed into extensions of the old enemy from a historical event.[43] Whether they are the Crusades for the Muslims, the Holocaust for the Jews, the Black September for the Palestinians, the Battle of Karbala for the Shi'ias, the Bloody Sunday for Irish Catholics, the battles of Mahabharata and Ramayana for the Hindus, Operation Blue Star for the Sikhs, the Vietnam war or 9-11 for the Americans, the Wounded Knee Massacre for the Lakota Indians, deportation from Turkey for the Armenians, or the Battle of Stalingrad for the Russians, all of these events can become the mythological "chosen traumas" or "images of cosmic warfare," which will help to dehumanize the enemy in future conflicts. Religious groups are in this respect no different from secular entities.

As we can see from these examples, religious terrorists are essentially very similar to their secular counterparts: they are narrow-minded individuals who fail to see alternative perspectives on the issues on behalf of which they fight for. This is not only a natural, but also an absolutely necessary characteristic for any terrorist—one has to believe in the absolute nature of the cause in order to kill in its name. And while it is true that some organizations are more discriminate and restrained in their violent actions then others, *any* ideology used to support a terrorist campaign becomes in essence a religion—an absolute "perception that there is a tension between reality as it appears and as it really is (or has been or will be)" to use Jurgensmeyer's own definition.[44] Any terrorist is motivated by feelings of frustration and humiliation, any terrorist sees his use of violence as a defensive war, any terrorist fights in the name of the absolute good. As psychologist Ernest Becker has stated long ago, "the most violence perpetrated in history has been to *eradicate* evil."[45] In addition, any perpetrator of a terrorist act empathizes with his or her own victimization and protests against cruelty toward their own people, but at the same time demonstrates minimum empathy for those who he or she kills. Any perpetrator of such an act feels empowered by the execution of "just" violence in the name of a great cause. For all of the above stated reasons, Jurgensmeyer's characterizations are excellent descriptions of the characteristics of terrorists in general, but fail to provide a useful tool for identifying the dreaded religious terrorists.

In contrast, Hoffman's analysis of the distinct features of religious terrorists is much more specific, but in the end also suffers from different weakness—virtually none of the existing terrorist organizations of today fit Hoffman's description. For instance, the number of groups that execute their terrorist acts for "no audience but themselves or God" is rather limited. In fact, most of the existing religious terrorist organizations complement their violence with realistic alternatives to secular rule, by backing their "military" activities with social, medical, and other communal services. As a result, many religious terrorist organizations have over time developed impressive constituencies.[46] Thus, Hoffman's argument that "the restraints on violence that are imposed on secular terrorists by the desire to appeal to a tacitly supportive or uncommitted constituency are not relevant to the religious terrorists"[47] is hardly valid. Furthermore, religious organizations that "unlike secular terrorists who see violence as a means to an end, tend to view violence as an end in itself" are also quite scarce. Even though many terrorist groups today carry out acts of violence that are motivated by revenge, the altruistic component of such violence even when accompanied by religious rhetoric cannot be overemphasized. And while it is true that the goals of some religious terrorists tend to be less clearly defined and seem much less tangible, most organizations commonly labeled as religious nevertheless have a clear strategic calculation behind them and seek to benefit a specific group of people. Even Hoffmann more or less confirms this claim by stating that the aims of "religious political" terrorists are defined as "the attainment of the greatest possible benefits for themselves and for their co-religionists only, as opposed to the indiscriminately utilitarian goals of secular terrorists."[48] This observation again shows the complexity of defining the distinct features of religious terrorists. Are not all ethnically or nationalistically based secular organizations also restricted in their violent actions to the attainment of the greatest possible benefits to members of their own ethnic or national community only?[49] And does not, on the other hand, the religiously motivated Algerian Armed Islamic Group (GIA), indiscriminately kill their co-religionists in some of the most brutal ways imaginable?

As hopefully became apparent throughout the course of this paper, the commonly defined characteristics of the "new terrorists" as religious fanatics who do not seek to benefit a constituency and whose violent actions are not a means to an end but rather a self-serving end in itself, and who are therefore unrestrained in their violence and thus are more likely to perpetrate acts of mass destruction, do not apply to the absolute majority of today's terrorists. Implicitly, many of the organizations that are included in the statistics that show the rise of indiscriminate, divinely sanctioned violence do not belong into this narrowly defined category, rendering the alarmist interpretation of such statistics much less useful than generally believed. For the above-stated reasons, the unfortunate common practice of basing the assessment of future non-conventional terrorists solely on the frequency of the use of the word "God" in a given organization's statements does not adequately reflect the CBRN threat level posed by the respective group. Instead, a more productive approach may be to focus on the individual characteristics of potential mass-casualty terrorists in order to assess the threat. The final part of this paper will focus on identifying some of these characteristics, and will also incorporate an overall threat assessment with regards to the likelihood of a mass-fatality CBRN terrorist attack occurring in the near future.

possess the capability to acquire and deliver biological agents, as well as the motivation to kill thousands of people indiscriminately. Contrary to popular belief, however, only organizations possessing a rather unique combination of very specific characteristics are likely to satisfy the requirements for mass-casualty non-conventional terrorism.[50] Of greatest concern on the motivational level are cult-like groups that are completely isolated from the mainstream society and are driven by an apocalyptic ideology that could be described as destroying the world to save it. Religious and other cult-like organizations that share the worldview that our planet could use a radical makeover are not in short supply. Fortunately, most such organizations have yet to resort to outward violence. If such a turn of events were to occur, however, the potential ability of apocalyptic organizations to justify killing people as actually benefiting them by sending them to a better place than this world makes such groups particularly dangerous. As in most terrorist attacks, the use of violence in this scenario would again be perceived by the terrorists as altruistic, with the critical difference that the constituency in this case would be the victims themselves. In such cases, the victims would not necessarily be seen as an enemy whom one kills in hate or for symbolic value, but rather poor human beings that are going to be saved by being killed. Under such circumstances, killing thousands of people indiscriminately would be psychologically much easier than doing so as a part of a political strategy or revenge. For instance, the *Thuggees*, an Indian cult of Kali worshippers that according to some claims killed over a million people in acts of sacrificial violence between the 7th and mid-19th century,[51] displayed some of these motivational elements. According to David Rapoport, the *Thuggees* believed that if they do not shed blood, their victims will go to paradise, and allegedly for this reason, the cult used strangulation as its main operational method. And while many historians question even the sole existence of the *Thuggees* claiming that they were a myth that was developed by the British during their colonial rule of India, if this group actually existed and if the numbers are correct, the *Thuggees* are the deadliest terrorist group in history. With the possible exception of the Algerian GIA, their average killing rate of 1,200 people per year remains unchallenged to this day despite great advances in weapons technology.[52]

The *Thuggees* are just one example in history that demonstrates the dangers of "altruistic" desires of terrorist organizations to bring about the Armageddon. Aum Shinrikyo's Shoko Asahara, for instance, also advocated the moral acceptance of mercy killing and argued for the "right of the guru and of spiritually advanced practitioners to kill those who otherwise would fall into hells."[53] And while it would be difficult to claim that an act of mass-fatality CBRN terrorism will never occur in the absence of such an ideology, it is clear that similar belief systems should be a warning sign in this regard. Another key point to emphasize is that a terrorist group does not necessarily have to be religious in nature in order to reach an apocalyptic stage. Fundamentalist environmental or animal rights groups, as well as ethnic-based violent movements might under certain circumstances also reach this stage.

Another element also likely to be present among superterrorists is a strong sense of paranoia among the group's members. Not only will a paranoid worldview enhance the polarization of the terrorists' perception of the world into an "us versus them" mode, it will also consequently increase the ability to victimize the organization's non-members indiscriminately. The greater the presence of paranoia in the group's perception, the greater is also the sense of urgency among the group's members to unite into one cohesive unit and to eliminate dissenters. This is especially critical as the utility of mass-casualty violence tends to be a topic of disagreement among most terrorist groups, possibly creating undesirable schisms within the organization. If the given group can completely eliminate dissent, the restraining nature of a debate about the utility of using weapons of mass destruction will be lost.

Another important characteristic of future CBRN terrorists will be the expressive value attached to a particular mode of attack, in this case perhaps the desire to kill without shedding blood, or a divine fascination with poisons and plagues as God's tools. An example of this is the frequent reference to biblical plagues commonly used by various radical Christian groups, or the strange fascination of Shoko Asahara who wrote poems about sarin. Alternatively, environmentalist cults may interpret diseases as "natural" tools used by Mother Nature to eliminate the human race that has through technological advances and an inconsiderate use of natural resources caused a natural imbalance, which can only be restored by an elimination of the world's most destructive species.

Another important element likely to be present is the terrorists' self-perception of grandiosity and ideological uniqueness. And while it is true that most terrorist organizations believe in their exceptionality, which helps to explain why most armed struggles usually involve not one but several concurring terrorist organizations with virtually identical goals, few groups define their individuality based on such narrow distinctions as weapons selection. The most significant differences among terrorist groups with a common cause and enemy exist mainly in the realm of overall strategy of using violence as a part of the revolutionary process, leader personalities and ambitions, allegiance toward a particular state or non-state sponsor, the appropriateness in terms of intensity of individual acts of violence, legitimacy of targeting civilians, and other similar factors. Future superterrorists, however, are likely to attach extreme importance to the use of chemical or biological agents as a distinct feature of the group. If organizations that possess the above characteristic are in addition led by an uncontested charismatic leader who is violence-prone, and who has the ability to convince his followers that his instructions are direct orders from a supernatural authority, the deadly combination of motivational attributes needed to indiscriminately kill masses of people with biological weapons will likely be established.

Organization and Capability

At the organizational level, the group is likely to be structured as a very tight hierarchical formation or as a number of small independent cells, in order to prevent infiltration and obviation of their grandiose plans. Further, powerful mechanisms of social control such as heavy indoctrination, complete isolation and intimidation will probably be in place in order to prevent internal defections that could also jeopardize attack preparations. With respect to capabilities, a successful terrorist group will need significant financial, logistical and human resources, given the difficulty of weaponizing CBRN agents in a way that they can produce mass-fatalities. Very few groups possess such resources, even though the assistance of state sponsors has the potential of significantly altering this situation. Alternatively,

Another important attribute of future "superterrorists" is the desire and ability to innovate, both on technological and tactical level, in order to attain the ability to successfully attack with CBRN weapons. Most terrorist groups to date, however, have been rather conservative, usually innovating only when forced to do so by anti-terrorist countermeasures, such as barometric pressure chambers, metal detectors, x-rays, and vapor detectors at airports. As a result, most of the innovation that has taken place in terrorist campaigns took the form of advancing the methods of weapon concealment, as opposed to adopting new types of weaponry per se.[54] This is quite logical, considering that one of the terrorists' greatest fears is failure—an attack that fails wastes resources and leaves clues, but most importantly, it can have a negative effect on the outward image of the organization and on the self-esteem of the group's members. Most organizations will therefore stick to the methods that have proven to be successful in the past, unless such means become ineffective because of the defensive countermeasures put in place by the adversary, or unless some other factors create the perception of a need for a tactical or technological shift. Especially religious terrorists have not been particularly inventive when it comes to using new types of weaponry.[55]

On the tactical level, terrorist innovation has historically had a more or less cyclical, multiplying character, utilizing proven traditional tactics in a combined and synchronized fashion. An example of this phenomenon is the increasingly frequent use of secondary explosive devices, which are designed to target first responders or bystanders that gather around to watch the impact of the primary explosion. This method has proven to be very effective in reaching a high body count in many terrorist bombings.

Overall, the successful progression to CBRN weapons requires a much more significant level of innovation than the vast majority of terrorist groups have demonstrated so far. In order to undergo such a long and demanding process, an organization will have to possess a combination of several important attributes.[56] First, the decision to innovate requires a high level of technological awareness, something that most organizations that are completely isolated from the rest of the world may find difficult to maintain. Next, the group has to be open to new ideas, so that the organization's members are not afraid to put forward their proposals for adopting new methods. Most cult-like organizations that fulfill the motivational "superterrorist" characteristics identified earlier do not possess this attribute—their members are highly controlled, dissent is not tolerated, and individuality is suppressed. In order for such groups to pursue innovative means, it will be critical to have a leader who is fascinated with biological weapons or the process of innovation itself. Such an inclination on the part of the leader is likely going to be heavily reflected in the group's ideology as well. Highly innovative organizations will also have to demonstrate a positive attitude toward risk-taking, with respect to both the risk of failure and the physical risks associated with handling lethal CBRN agents.

Once the group makes the decision to innovate, other important factors influencing the successful adoption of new technology will emerge. Most importantly, it will be the nature of the technology and the difficulties associated with its acquisition and successful use. Agents that can be delivered via direct personal contact will be much easier to apply than pathogens or toxins that require aerosolization. Assistance of a state sponsor can be a valuable asset when attempting to adopt high-level technology, and organizations that have received such assistance have historically been significantly more deadly than the groups that receive no such support.[57] However, as mentioned above, states have traditionally stayed away from providing high-level technology to proxies, who can never be fully controlled and whose affection toward the sponsoring state may only be short-lived. Further, it is even less likely that any state, no matter how "rogue," would give lethal CBRN agents to an untested, highly volatile, and completely indiscriminate apocalyptic cult, whose ideological foundation does not even remotely resemble that of the state. Consequently, most organizations that satisfy the aforementioned motivational characteristics of potential mass-casualty bioterrorists cannot hope for state support and are left to their own abilities.

Besides financial or material resources, an organization will need personnel with the necessary expertise and the ample time to devote their full attention to acquiring and weaponizing CBRN agents. Organizations whose members are only part-time terrorists and hold daily jobs, or groups that are involved in reciprocal battles in the field, can hardly devote a significant number of their human resources to this type of activity. At the same time, groups that perpetrate terrorist operations infrequently and thus do have the time to devote to discovering new technologies are likely to have difficulties with learning to use such technology effectively, precisely because of the absence of experience resulting from the infrequent nature of their attacks.[58]

Conclusion

The trends in terrorism are ominous. The rising frequency of spectacular and highly lethal attacks along with the existence of global terrorist networks seems to confirm the hypothesis that the ever-escalating nature of terrorism is likely to yield a mass-casualty nonconventional terrorist incident at some point in the future. Advances in communications and weapons technologies, as well as the questionable security of the CBRN facilities in the former Soviet Union also seemingly provide the "new," more violent and reckless terrorists with the tools necessary to perpetrate such an attack.

However, the technological hurdles of perpetrating a mass-fatality CBRN incident are still significant and cannot be overlooked. Even Aum Shinrikyo, the infamous Japanese cult which possessed an estimated $1 billion in assets, some 20 university-trained microbiologists working in top-notch research facilities, and the freedom to conduct unlimited experiments, completely failed in all 10 attempts to attack with anthrax and botulinum toxin.[59] The conditions and resources that were available to Aum Shinrikyo are unparalleled by even the deadliest terrorist organizations today, including al-Qaida.

Moreover, most organizations do not start out directly with weapons of mass destruction; low to medium-level violence which will help the terrorists to get used to the idea of killing indiscriminately is likely to precede an escalation to mass-fatality attacks. It is therefore highly unlikely that organizations possessing both the motivational and the capability characteristics described in this chapter will be able to stay off the radar screen of intelligence agencies for long. At the same time, it should be noted that the low-level violent activity practiced by cult-like organizations may not be immediately obvious, as it is likely to

dition, the organizations that do manage to survive for a long enough period to be able to attain the capability to attack with biological weapons, over time usually develop support networks and constituencies, which by giving the given organization something at stake usually serve to create or reinforce rational strategic calculation among the group's leadership. This means that even organizations that rise to the spotlight by perpetrating exceptionally unrestrained high-fatality attacks are usually forced to adjust their strategies and to scale down the level of violence over time, in order to maintain the popular support that has, sometimes unwittingly, been accumulated. In the absence of such an adjustment, the given organization's credibility as an alternative to the existing world order will fade, lessening the chances of the group's long-term survival.[61]

On a final note, even the groups that do overcome all of the motivational constraints against indiscriminate mass-fatality violence have yet to exploit the full killing potential of their current conventional capabilities. If the desire is indeed to kill as many people as possible, why not just attack more often, at more locations, and on a greater scale with weapons that are available and have proven to be effective? Why invest a massive amount of precious resources into a new technology that only few if any know how to use and that could potentially end up killing the perpetrators themselves—all without any guarantee of success? Why risk a negative public reaction and a possibly devastating retaliation likely to be associated with the use of non-conventional weapons? Most of today's terrorist organizations have probably faced such questions at some point and have either decided that non-conventional weapons are not worth pursuing, or have made limited and unsuccessful attempts to explore this avenue. The groups that have decided or will in the future decide that such weapons are an attractive option are likely to possess a mix of unique and fortunately also quite rare characteristics. They are likely to be apocalyptic cults with violence-prone charismatic leaders who are fascinated with diseases and poisons and are not afraid to fail or the get killed in their attempts to pursue such technology. The greatest overall danger is posed by religious cults combining such apocalyptic visions with outward-oriented violence and suicidal tendencies. However, most suicide cults tend to direct their violence only inward, committing collective suicide without attacking others.[62] Apocalyptic cults that do kill non-members, on the other hand, surprisingly tend to be oriented toward survival.[63]

Also, the groups that are particularly dangerous with respect to their motivation to inflict mass casualties may be in a more difficult position to breach the technological hurdles of a biological weapons attack. Acquiring the necessary financial, logistical and human resources is challenging for isolated cults with an obscure ideology. In essence, the more extreme the organization, the less likely it is to attract mass support. For extremely radical groups, attracting state-level assistance and finding a safe haven in which they can conduct their research and low-level violent activities while remaining undetected by intelligence agencies may be particularly difficult. Moreover, the total suppression of individuality in such cults and their isolation from mainstream society does not provide for the organizational dynamics that would be favorable for successful adoption of new technology.

As a result, the same inverse relationship between the motivation to produce mass-fatalities and the ability to do so that was described by Post on the individual level seems to apply to organized formations as well.[64] For this reason, the likelihood of a successful mass-casualty "superterrorist" attack remains low. That being said, many conventional terrorist organizations must have inevitably noticed the enormous fear of chemical, biological and nuclear weapons among the general public, and some are certainly likely to attempt to exploit this fear to their advantage. Such attempts are likely to take the form of threats and expressed desire to use such weapons, attacks involving a small amount of crudely delivered chemical or pathogen, or the inclusion of some chemical, biological or radiological agent in a conventional bomb. Such attempts, however, should be understood as psychological operations that are aimed at creating disproportionate fear, but do not necessarily represent a terrifying shift to catastrophic terrorism.

Adam Dolnik is a research associate at the center for Nonproliferation Studies in Monterey, California. He is associated with the Weapons of Mass Destruction Terrorism Project in the Chemical and Biological Weapons Nonproliferation Program. He conducts research on terrorist motivations and justifications for the use of violence and other terrorist strategies. He has previously worked with the UN Terrorism Prevention Branch in Vienna, Austria.

Notes

1. Bruce Hoffman, *Inside Terrorism* (New York: Orion Publishing Co. 1998), p. 201.
2. Brian Michael Jenkins, "Will Terrorists Go Nuclear?" RAND Paper P-5541 (1975), p. 4.
3. Bruce Hoffman, *Inside Terrorism* (New York: Orion Publishing Co. 1998), p. 205.
4. Bruce Hoffman, *Inside Terrorism* (New York: Orion Publishing Co. 1998), p. 201.
5. Bruce Hoffman, *Inside Terrorism* (New York: Orion Publishing Co. 1998), p. 90–92.
6. Bruce Hoffman, "Holy Terror": The Implications of Terrorism Motivated by a Religious Imperative, RAND 1993, p. 5–6.
7. Bruce Hoffman, *Inside Terrorism* (New York: Orion Publishing Co. 1998), p. 201.
8. Bruce Hoffman, *Inside Terrorism* (New York: Orion Publishing Co. 1998), p. 201.
9. Bruce Hoffman, "Holy Terror": The Implications of Terrorism Motivated by a Religious Imperative, RAND 1993, p. 5.
10. Bruce Hoffman, "Holy Terror": The Implications of Terrorism Motivated by a Religious Imperative, RAND 1993, p. 5.
11. Bruce Hoffman, "Holy Terror": The Implications of Terrorism Motivated by a Religious Imperative, RAND 1993, p. 12.
12. Magnus Ranstorp, Terrorism in the Name of Religion. *Journal of International Affairs*, Summer 1996 Vol. 50, Num. 1.
13. Bruce Hoffman, "Holy Terror": The Implications of Terrorism Motivated by a Religious Imperative, RAND 1993, p. 3.
14. Bruce Hoffman, "Holy Terror": The Implications of Terrorism Motivated by a Religious Imperative, RAND 1993, p. 3.
15. Bruce Hoffman, "Holy Terror": The Implications of Terrorism Motivated by a Religious Imperative, RAND 1993, p. 3.
16. Mark Jurgensmeyer, *Terror in the Mind of God* (Los Angeles: University of California Press, 2000), p. 146.
17. Mark Jurgensmeyer, "The Logic of Religious Violence" in David C. Rapoport: *Inside Terrorist Organizations* (London: Frank Cass, 2001), p. 185–190.
18. Mark Jurgensmeyer, *Terror in the Mind of God* (Los Angeles: University of California Press, 2000), p. 167.

22. Mark Jurgensmeyer, "The Logic of Religious Violence" in David C. Rapoport: *Inside Terrorist Organizations* (London: Frank Cass, 2001), p. 183.
23. The database description can be found at www.mipt.org/randterrorismdb.asp.
24. Adam Dolnik, "Die and Let Die: Exploring Links between Suicide Terrorism and Terrorist Use of Chemical, Biological, Radiological, and Nuclear Weapons." *Studies in Conflict and Terrorism*, Vol. 26, No.1, pp. 17–35.
25. Incidents perpetrated by organizations or individuals motivated on ideological or religious grounds.
26. Further information about the database is available at: http://www.cns.miis.edu/dbinfo/about.htm#wmd.
27. Anna Borzello, "New Cult Graves Point to Murder," *Daily Mail and Guardian* (27 March 2000); Internet, available from http://www.mg.co.za/mg/news/, accessed on 5/22/00.
28. "Tears, Blood, as Kaduna Boils," *Post Express Wired* (29 February 2000); Internet, available from www.postexpresswired.com, accessed on 2/29/00.
29. "Asahara Ordered 1994 Sarin Attack, Aum Biologist Says," *Japan Economic Newswire* (14 January 1999).
30. "Aum 'Minister' Admits Using Toxic Chemical to Kill Cultists," *Asahi News Service* (27 June 1995).
31. Bruce Hoffman, *Inside Terrorism* (New York: Orion Publishing Co., 1998), p. 201.
32. Walter Laqueur, *The New Terrorism* (New York: Oxford University Press, 1999), p. 128.
33. Magnus Ranstorp, Terrorism in the Name of Religion. *Journal of International Affairs*, Summer 1996, Vol. 50, Num. 1. p. 18.
34. Walter Laqueur, *The New Terrorism* (New York: Oxford University Press, 1999), p. 230.
35. Jerry S. Piven, "On the Psychosis (Religion) of Terrorists," In Chris E. Stout, *Psychology of Terrorism*, Preager Publishers 2002, p. 121.
36. Mark Jurgensmeyer, "The Logic of Religious Violence" in David C. Rapoport: *Inside Terrorist Organizations* (London: Frank Cass, 2001), p. 185.
37. Further, the majority of the case studies used by Jurgensmeyer to demonstrate the logic of religious violence concern movements that cannot be accurately described as religious in nature.
38. Mark Jurgensmeyer, *Terror in the Mind of God* (Los Angeles: University of California Press, 2000), p. 167.
39. Reuven Paz, 'The Islamic Legitimacy of Suicide Terrorism,' *Countering Suicide Terrorism* (Herzliya: International Policy Institute for Counter-Terrorism, 2000), p. 93.
40. Adam Dolnik, "Die and Let Die: Exploring Links between Suicide Terrorism and Terrorist Use of Chemical, Biological, Radiological, and Nuclear Weapons." *Studies in Conflict and Terrorism*, Vol. 26, No.1, pp. 17–35.
41. Mark Jurgensmeyer, *Terror in the Mind of God* (Los Angeles: University of California Press, 2000), p. 146.
42. Vamik Volkan, *Blood Lines: From Ethnic Pride to Ethnic Terrorism* (New York: Farrar, Straus and Giroux, 1997), p. 82.
43. Vamik Volkan, *Blood Lines: From Ethnic Pride to Ethnic Terrorism* (New York: Farrar, Straus and Giroux, 1997), p. 46.
44. Mark Jurgensmeyer, "The Logic of Religious Violence" in David C. Rapoport: *Inside Terrorist Organizations* (London: Frank Cass, 2001), p. 178.
45. Cited in Jerry S. Piven, "On the Psychosis (Religion) of Terrorists," In Chris E. Stout, *Psychology of Terrorism*, Preager Publishers, 2002, p. 127.
46. Magnus Ranstorp, Terrorism in the Name of Religion. *Journal of International Affairs*, Summer 1996, Vol. 50, Num.1, p. 36.

47. Bruce Hoffman, "Holy Terror": The Implications of Terrorism Motivated by a Religious Imperative, RAND 1993, p. 3.

48. Bruce Hoffman, "Holy Terror": The Implications of Terrorism Motivated by a Religious Imperative, RAND 1993, p. 3.

49. Daniel Byman, The Logic of Ethnic Terrorism, *Studies in Conflict and Terrorism,* Vol.21, Number 2, 1998, p. 151.

50. Stern, Jessica: *Ultimate Terrorists* (London: Harvard University Press 1999), p. 70.

51. Bruce Hoffman, *Inside Terrorism* (New York: Orion Publishing Co. 1998), p. 89.

52. Even though the exact numbers are unknown, only the Groupe Islamique Arme (GIA) of Algeria can challenge the *Thuggees* in terms of killing intensity. Interestingly, the GIA also relies on very primitive weapons in its campaign.

53. Mark Jurgensmeyer, *Terror in the Mind of God* (Los Angeles: University of California Press, 2000), p. 114.

54. Hoffman, Bruce, "Terrorist Targeting: Tactics, Trends, and Potentialities," in Paul Wilkinson ed. *Technology and Terrorism* (Frank Cass: London, 1993), p. 12.

55. Magnus Ranstorp, Terrorism in the Name of Religion. *Journal of International Affairs*, Summer 1996, Vol. 50, Num. 1.

56. Jackson, Brian: "Technology Acquisition by Terrorist Groups: Threat Assessment Informed by Lessons from Private Sector Technology Adoption," Studies in *Conflict & Terrorism*: 24 (2001), p. 189–213.

57. According to some experts, organizations that enjoy the support of a state sponsor have been on average eight times more deadly than groups that receive no such support. (Bruce Hoffman, quoted in Brian Jackson, "Technology Acquisition by Terrorist Groups: Threat Assessment Informed by Lessons from Private Sector Technology Adoption," *Studies in Conflict & Terrorism*: 24, 2001, p. 199.)

58. Jackson, Brian: "Technology Acquisition by Terrorist Groups: Threat Assessment Informed by Lessons from Private Sector Technology Adoption," Studies in *Conflict & Terrorism*: 24 (2001), p. 189–213.

59. Center for Nonproliferation Studies: *Chronology of Aum Shinrikyo's CBW Activities* (March 2001), Internet, available at http://cns.miis.edu/pubs/reports/aum_chrn.htm. (Accessed on 12/12/02)

60. Rapoport quoted in Hoffman, Bruce: *Inside Terrorism* (New York: Orion Publishing Co. 1998), p. 89.

61. The Lebanese Hizballah is a good example of such a transformation.

62. For example 914 members of the People's Temple committed mass suicide in 1978 in Jonestown, Guyana; 39 members of Heaven's Gate committed a similar act in 1997 in Rancho Santa Fe, California.

63. The author is aware of two exceptions: the Zealots who committed mass suicide in the 1st century BC, and the Concerned Christians, a Colorado cult that allegedly planed to perpetrate attacks in Israel in 1999 and whose members reportedly also had plans to commit mass suicide.

64. Post has argued that individuals who want to kill a lot of people indiscriminately are likely to suffer from significant psychological idiosyncrasies. For individuals suffering from such idiosyncrasies it is nearly impossible to function in groups. But one does need to operate in groups in order to be successful in producing a grandiose mass-casualty attack. (Jerrold Post, "Psychological and Motivational Factors in Terrorist Decision-Making: Implications for CBW Terrorism," in Jonathan Tucker ed. *Toxic Terror* (London: MIT Press, 2000), 271–289.

Weapons of Mass Destruction

The threat of weapons of mass destruction (WMD) is a complex issue—not just in the discussion of how to detect, deter, and defend against their use, but also in the complicated differences between the devices, technology, and processes needed to obtain and use these weapons. The authors in this chapter look at the likelihood of terrorists and nonstate actors making use of these weapons, and the issues surrounding biological security and the use of chemical weapons.

Nuclear, chemical, and biological weapons are inherently terrorizing—causing moral dread and panic, says Jessica Stern. But despite their appeal, terrorist groups have seldom used them. Stern surveys the likelihood of groups using these agents—including the varying ease or difficulty involved in obtaining the raw materials and having the technical means to disseminate them—and details two successful acts of this type of terrorism: Aum Shinrikyo's attack on the Tokyo subway, and the Rajneesh cult's 1984 act of poisoning salad bars in Oregon with *Salmonella typhimurium*. In the case of Aum Shinrikyo, the author details the massive and long-term organization behind the act: in a November 1995 hearing, the staff of Senator Sam Nunn testified that at the time of the Tokyo attacks, the group had some 50,000 members and assets worth $1.4 billion. However, despite the lack of success by groups attempting to use WMD for terrorist purposes, Stern concludes with a word of caution. Although Aum Shinrikyo's large-scale attacks with biological agents are believed to have failed, Stern warns, "were terrorists to master these technologies they would have the potential to kill not just hundreds but hundreds of thousands of people."

When analysts and policymakers refer to WMD, they group nuclear, biological, chemical, and radiological weapons together, "as if the latter were merely variants on the same type of device," says Christopher F. Chyba. But these weapons "differ greatly in their ease of production, in the challenges they pose for deterrence, and in the effectiveness of defensive measures against them," contends the author. Biological weapons differ from nuclear and chemical, and the United States needs a biological security strategy—both domestic and international—to guard against these unique threats. Chyba details the approaches and the complexities involved in biological security. In some cases, there will be a synergy between guarding against biological weapons and natural disease outbreak; in some cases, there will not be a dual-purpose benefit, such as when it is necessary to stockpile an antibiotic supply to guard against a disease that does not occur naturally. Chyba also points to the importance of a strategy that addresses the potential international threat. In the end, says Chyba, it will be vital for scientists to communicate the complexity of the problem to policy makers, and for policy makers to incorporate scientific advice into their decision making.

According to Richard Pilch, most analysis of the bioterrorist threat predates September 11, 2001, and does not offer a comprehensive analysis of the current threat in the United States. Pilch brings the analysis of the threat up to date through an uncomplicated model (THREAT = Vulnerability x Capability x Intent), which offers the possibility for a very nuanced analysis of the threat. He gives special consideration to the capability aspect of the threat, often times the most exaggerated element, and reviews the major technical hurdles involved in the acquisition, production, and dissemination of a biological agent. Pilch presents the reader with an oft-discussed scenario involving the aerial dissemination of anthrax using a crop duster as an example. His conclusion is that while the threat for any given individual is small, the government must consider the worst-case scenario.

Humans, regrettably, have used available technologies for destructive as well as for beneficial purposes throughout history.

—Journal of the American Medical Association, 1997

Nuclear, chemical, and biological agents, as we have seen, are inherently terrorizing. They evoke moral dread and visceral revulsion out of proportion to their lethality. The government of a country attacked with such weapons would have difficulty controlling panic. Because chemical and biological weapons are silent killers, an attack could occur at any time without warning. The first sign of a biological attack might be "hundreds or thousands of ill or dying patients," a U.S. government scientist warns.[1]

Despite the evident appeal of such weapons as instruments of terror, terrorists have seldom used them. Terrorists have never detonated a nuclear device. They have used chemical agents rarely—most often to poison foods—and biological and radiological agents more rarely still. Except for the chemical attacks carried out by the Aum Shinrikiyo cult in Japan in 1994 and 1995, there have been no cases of large-scale, open-air dissemination. What has held terrorists back? The answer involves both technical constraints, which I discuss [here], and motivational or organizational constraints.... The technical hurdles would be considerable: acquiring the agent or weapon would present one set of difficulties; disseminating or exploding it would present another.

Chemical and Biological Agents

Terrorists might be able to acquire chemical or biological (CB) agents from governments favorable to their cause. CB agents are proliferating. In 1997 Secretary of Defense William Cohen estimated the number of countries with "mature chemical and biological weapons programs" at "about thirty," and the CIA claimed that around twenty nations had developed these weapons.[2] Iran, Iraq, Libya, North Korea, and Syria—all listed by the State Department as supporters of terrorism—are believed to possess chemical weapons and at least some biological weapons. Iraq's CB programs are quite extensive. The small quantities of CB agents required for an attack would make it very difficult to track the flow of the weapons or their component chemicals to terrorist groups.

Terrorists also might be able to steal CB agents from national stockpiles. In Albania in 1997, according to an Albanian military official, antigovernment bandits stole chemical weapons and radioactive materials from four army depots. The stolen materials, the official warned, posed serious health hazards.[3]

Russia's security for chemical weapons is particularly problematic. The storage sites for chemical weapons were revealed in the newspaper *Rossiyskaya Gazeta* in January 1994, and in 1995 the army chief of staff, General Kolesnikov, expressed concern that publication of the locations increased the risk of theft. Kolesnikov also warned that the increases in crime in Russia are worsening the risk of "chemical weapons attacks."[4]

Because chemical and biological agents are relatively easy to produce, a single person with the right expertise could design an entire weapons program. Thus terrorists might acquire CB weapons by taking advantage of the "brain drain"—the prospect that weapons scientists will sell their expertise to the highest bidder. "Because of the deteriorating condition of the military-industrial complex in the former Soviet Union, many specialists in the field of chemical weaponry do not have enough sources of income to support their families and are ready to go anywhere to earn money," Vil Mirzayanov, a Russian chemical weapons scientist, said in 1995. Russian physicists are reportedly providing consulting services to missile and nuclear energy programs in Iran and Pakistan. One physicist reportedly claimed his conscience did not trouble him at all, since, with so many defense specialists now out of work, "If I had not agreed, they would have just found someone else." And Russia is by no means the only country where disaffected or underemployed weapons scientists can be found. Libya has reportedly tried to hire scientists formerly employed in developing biological agents for South Africa.[5]

Terrorist groups that include—or hire—trained chemists would have no difficulty producing chemical agents. A report by the U.S. Office of Technology Assessment claims that "the level of technological sophistication required... may be lower than was the case for some of the sophisticated bombs that have been used against civilian aircraft."[6] Many of the components of these agents are widely sold for industrial purposes. For example, thiodiglycol, an immediate precursor to mustard agent, is used to make ink for ballpoint pens. All that is required to produce mustard from this material is a simple acid that also is easy to obtain.

Pathogens that could be used as crude biological weapons—such as the common food poisons salmonella, shigella, and staphylococcus—are readily available at clinical microbiology laboratories. Terrorists could also produce more deadly agents. Knowledge of microbiology, and of its potential applications to weapons, is increasingly widespread. Kathleen Bailey, after interviewing professors, graduate students, and pharmaceutical manufacturers, concluded that several biologists with only $10,000 worth of equipment could produce a significant quantity of biological agent. The requisite equipment would fit in a small room, she claims, and "the glassware, centrifuges, growth media, etc., can all be manufactured by virtually any country."[7]

Detailed information about how to set up a chemistry laboratory and how to order chemicals without arousing suspicion is published in manuals on poisoning. One manual instructs readers how to disseminate chlorine (a poisonous gas widely used in industry, which was used as a weapon during World War I) in a crowd. In 1982, the year of the first widely reported incident of tampering with pharmaceuticals, the Tylenol case, only a few poisoning manuals were available, and they were relatively hard to find. Today, how-to manuals on producing chemical and biological agents are advertised in paramilitary journals sold in magazine shops all over the United States, as well as on the Internet.[8] Although criminals are known to have used such manuals in plotting crimes, publishers maintain that publication of murder manuals is protected by the First Amendment.[9]

One of these manuals, *Bacteriological Warfare: A Major Threat to North America*, is described on the Internet as a book for helping readers survive a biological weapons attack. But in fact it also describes the reproduction and growth of biological agents and the question of how to use them against their targeted populations. Chemical agents are relatively easy to disseminate in enclosed spaces, and they are significantly easier than biological agents to spread over large areas. Key differences for the purposes of dissemination are that chemical agents are volatile (that is, some of the agent will spontaneously form a poisonous gas), while biological agents are not; and most biological agents are susceptible to humidity, desiccation, oxidation, air pollution, heat and shock (such as from explosions), and ultraviolet light, while chemical agents are not. (Anthrax in spore form is less susceptible to these insults than other biological agents.)

The most likely way to spread chemical agents in air would be to disseminate them in enclosed areas. If a suitcase full of nerve agent were opened into the air intake ducts of a building, many of the people inside would probably die. Even less of the agent would be needed to poison passengers on an airplane. Dissemination in open areas would be considerably more difficult. For example, a specially equipped car might be used to spread chemical agent in city streets. Some terrorists might have access to planes or helicopters fitted with crop sprayers, or even (probably only for state-sponsored groups) bombs or missiles.

As for biological agents, the U.S. Army has conducted tests of their dissemination in populated areas using nonlethal microorganisms to simulate biological agents. Six of these tests were conducted in San Francisco in 1950. A ship used an aerosol spray device to release two simulant agents (*Bacillus globigii* and *Serratia marcescens*) at various distances from shore. Air samples were taken at forty-three locations around the Bay Area. The Army's analysts concluded that it was feasible to attack a seaport city by disseminating biological agents from a ship offshore, and that success or failure would largely depend on the meteorological conditions at the time of the attack.[10]

The Army also conducted a test on the New York City subway in June 1966, employing another simulant (*Bacillus subtilis variant niger*). Technicians dropped light bulbs filled with bacteria into the system, either through ventilating grates or onto the roadbeds as the trains entered or left the station. The bulbs broke, releasing the bacteria. Aerosol clouds were momentarily visible after the bulbs were broken, but were ignored by most passengers, some of whom merely brushed off their clothes. Army scientists concluded that a large portion of the working population in downtown New York City would be exposed to disease if pathogenic agents were disseminated in several subway lines during rush hour.[11] New York City authorities were not informed of the test until 1980, when the Army's findings were made available to the general public. The results of this test in particular are quite frightening, but this scenario would require drying and milling or coating of the agent, tasks that might be beyond the capability of terrorist groups.

The Army also tested anti-animal and anti-crop agents, presumably spread with a crop duster. Nonbiological simulants were used in the anti-animal tests, but live agents, including wheat rust and rice blast, were used against crops. The tests were carried out until 1968, principally in Minnesota and Florida.[12]

The three ways of disseminating CB agents tested by the Army—from ships near seaports, on the subway, and with crop dusters—illustrate the kinds of low-technology attacks some terrorists might like to carry out. But it is not clear that they would be able to do so. Agents that kill humans or livestock must be disseminated in the form of aerosols that are respirable: that is, that can be taken into the body through the lungs. To be respirable, particles must be between one and five microns in diameter. Experts disagree about whether terrorists would be able to create such aerosols. Some claim that any college-trained molecular biologist is capable of killing hundreds of thousands of people in a single attack. Others cite Iraq as evidence that even governments have trouble overcoming the technical difficulties of dissemination, implying that terrorists without state sponsors would certainly fail. The Aum Shinrikiyo attacks in Japan lend credence to the latter view, but the truth is probably somewhere between these two viewpoints.[13] Terrorists might not be able to maximize efficiency in designing and building their weapons, but if they used massive amounts of agent it would hardly matter that less than one percent of the agent was effective. It would hardly matter to the victims, at any rate.

Biological agents can be disseminated in liquid or powder form. While producing liquid agent is relatively easy, disseminating it as an infectious aerosol is not. Dry powders can be disseminated far more easily. High-quality powders are complicated to make, however, involving skilled personnel and sophisticated equipment. Milling these powders, according to a U.S. government scientist, "would require a level of sophistication possessed [only] by some state sponsors of terrorism"; this implies that terrorists without state sponsors would have a difficult time indeed.[14]

Terrorists without state sponsors would be unlikely to master the technology required for dispersing liquid agents over broad areas unless they were able to hire skilled scientists trained in government biological weapons programs. But if terrorists used large quantities of liquid agent, then even an off-the-shelf sprayer could pose a significant threat—not to an entire city, but to, for example, passengers on a train.

Besides releasing CB agents into the air, terrorists might try contaminating a water supply or tampering with pharmaceuticals or foods. If the aim was to damage the target country's economy or to injure a particular company, the terrorists would only have to poison a fraction of the target foods in order to create fear. In the United States, cola, milk, and baby food could be particularly vulnerable targets.

Water supplies require collection, treatment, storage, and distribution. The two common sources from which drinking water is collected are ground water (wells) and surface water (rivers and lakes). Wells are more commonly used in rural areas for individual homes, and surface water is more common in big cities. Well systems make easy targets, but they tend to be small. Most surface water systems in the United States are so large that any contamination would probably be diluted too quickly to be harmful. This may not be the case in other countries.

Treatment plants are not very vulnerable, according to an Army study, because an attack would be detected before the contaminated water was widely distributed. But a case of contaminated water in Washington, D.C., in 1994 (not caused by terrorists) suggests that this is not necessarily true. Authorities did not detect high levels of cryptosporidium growing in Washington's water supplies until after the water had been distributed. Residents were instructed to drink only bottled water until authorities could purify the water. A similar outbreak in Milwaukee killed some 100 people. Chemical agents can also be removed from water, although some agents require more elaborate procedures than others.[15]

water quality is monitored less often. Attacking distribution networks would require significantly lower quantities of contaminants than attacking an entire reservoir, but the number of people put at risk would decrease commensurately. Distribution networks might be vulnerable, however, to terrorists whose goal was to attack a particular symbolic target or a building of strategic importance.[17]

Radiological Weapons

Detonation of a nuclear device is the least likely form of terrorism involving weapons of mass destruction. But technical challenges would not prevent less dramatic uses of radiological materials, which, although unlikely to kill or injure many people, could impose heavy financial and psychological costs on the targeted government.

Radioactive isotopes can be found at a number of diverse facilities, including hospitals and industrial plants, and in waste from nuclear power plants. While industrial isotopes are found in higher quantities in industrialized countries, nuclear waste is found all over the world. Unlike chemical, biological, or nuclear weapons, radiological weapons (now generally called radiation-dispersal devices or RDDs) are not banned by any international treaty.

The U.S. Department of Energy maintains a database of cases of smuggling of nuclear materials reported in the press, including not only fissile materials but also nonfissile radioisotopes. Most thefts of nuclear materials have occurred in the former Soviet Union, and most have involved nonfissile radioisotopes. But other countries are by no means immune to loss or theft. The U.S. General Accounting Office estimates that, between 1955 and 1977, unaccounted-for special nuclear (that is, fissile) materials totaled in the thousands of kilograms.[18] These losses are almost certainly attributable to accounting errors, but they indicate a distressing lack of care.

Terrorists who obtained radiological materials would next face the technical hurdles of turning them into RDDs. In experiments conducted in the 1940s and 1950s, the U.S. military found that disseminating gamma-emitting radiological agents in air involved enormous difficulties because of the heat generated by the material and the problem of dissipation.[19] Gamma emitters require heavy shielding, and some have to be used immediately because of radioactive decay. The military contemplated dispersing the substances using artillery shells, mortar shells, aircraft, and "fission aerial bombs or fission projectiles." The effects would be highly dependent on weather conditions and terrain. Cities would be very costly to attack. Stafford Warren found that "something approaching 100 times greater concentration" would be required for built-up areas because structures would absorb a large portion of the radiation.[20]

The U.S. government concluded after years of study that RDDs were not militarily useful. Iraq, too, apparently renounced them as impractical. But radiological weapons might meet some terrorists' objectives, especially if the terrorists were more interested in imposing financial costs or creating panic than in killing. Even if the terrorists used a crude dissemination device or a quantity of radioactive material too small to present a serious threat to health, fear of radiation could cause panic. When the United States was considering producing RDDs in the 1940s and 1950s, the demoralizing of personnel was explicitly mentioned as one of the "specific uses" of radiological warfare.[21]

The costs imposed on a targeted facility or government would be immense. In 1966 an American B-52 bomber collided with another plane over Spain. The conventional explosives in two of the B-52's hydrogen bombs detonated and dispersed plutonium over several hundred acres. Workers had to plow up 285 acres and remove soil from 5.5 acres, which was shipped back to the United States. The cost of the cleanup, including finding and recovering the bombs, was $100 million (in 1966 dollars), including $10 million for recovery of a bomb that fell into the sea.[22]

A relatively easy way for terrorists to disperse radioisotopes (or chemical or biological agents) would be through the ventilation system of a building. Terrorists might also use sprayers or blowers to disseminate fine powder, or release the powder from the top of a tall building. The U.S. military also considered placing radioactive material in enemy water supplies, which might work for small-scale operations but would not be very effective where water is kept in large reservoirs.[23]

After police seized a series of small nuclear caches in Germany in the spring and summer of 1994, numerous stories in the press warned that terrorists could use stolen plutonium to poison water supplies. It is possible to make soluble plutonium compounds, but in fact metallic plutonium sinks. Moreover, plutonium is more readily absorbed by the lungs than by the gastrointestinal tract, so it is an inefficient agent for poisoning water or food.

Nuclear facilities such as power plants may be attractive targets for terrorists. People who live near these facilities are highly sensitized to the health risks of radiation. The regulatory procedures that have been devised to deal with reactor accidents are more rigorous than required for public safety but not rigorous enough to reassure the public. For example, if a radiation level five times higher than background were detected outside Rocky Flats in Colorado, officials would be required to evacuate the city even though scientists consider this level harmless.[24] A terrorist whose objective was to create panic and wreak havoc (rather than to kill people) could take advantage of these tight regulations: a relatively small amount of radioactive material disseminated near Rocky Flats would be enough to force the city to evacuate—with significant economic and psychological repercussions for residents.

Power reactors are also vulnerable to sabotage. Spent fuel rods contain cesium-137 and other gamma-emitting isotopes. Sabotage would probably require the complicity of plant employees, but terrorists might also be able to damage a reactor or a tank holding radioactive waste by placing explosives outside the fence or attacking the plant by plane.[25] An explosion would be significantly more dangerous than a fire. Antinuclear terrorists in Germany have already tried to sabotage the transport of spent fuel rods, although there is no evidence that they were trying to steal the rods.[26]

Nuclear Weapons

Only the most sophisticated terrorist groups would be likely to consider manufacturing their own nuclear weapons. For these groups, the binding constraint would probably be the acquisition of fissile materials, which are much more highly protected than nonfissile radioactive isotopes. A spate of thefts of nuclear materials in the former Soviet Union makes it clear that the current system for protecting fissile materials is inadequate.

guards had quit "in disgust" a month earlier, claiming that he could no longer ensure the safety of Denver's citizens. He also warned that an antigovernment group called the Montana Militia had tried to recruit members from among the plant's guards. Although the recruitment attempts were reportedly unsuccessful, they suggest that antigovernment groups may be interested in nuclear or radiological terrorism. A government inquiry also revealed security lapses at other U.S. nuclear sites.[27]

In the unlikely, but not impossible, event that terrorists managed to buy or steal a sufficient quantity of fissile material, a key question is whether they could make a detonatable nuclear device, with or without state sponsorship. A group of designers of nuclear weapons was commissioned in 1987 to consider this possibility. The group concluded that building a crude nuclear device was "within reach of terrorists having sufficient resources to recruit a team of three or four technically qualified specialists," with expertise in "several quite distinct areas [including] the physical, chemical and metallurgical properties of the various materials to be used... technology concerning high explosives... electric circuitry; and others."[28] Terrorists might even be able to detonate plutonium oxide powder without actually making a bomb, the designers said, although such an operation would be extremely dangerous and would require "tens of kilograms" of material. The new availability of nuclear material on the black market is therefore particularly troubling.

South Africa's secret nuclear program, closed down in 1989 and revealed to the world by President de Klerk in 1993, provides some insight into how a sophisticated terrorist group could build a nuclear bomb if it had access to fissile materials. The South African experience makes clear that "virtually anybody can make a bomb," according to Ambassador Thomas Graham: "The number of people required is relatively small, and a wealthy backer of a terrorist organization could provide the funds. We're talking about millions—not billions—of dollars, and hundreds—not thousands—of people (including support staff)."[29]

While enriching the uranium required a large infrastructure and technical expertise, South African officials demonstrated the ease of making nuclear weapons once the highly enriched uranium (HEU) is in hand. Most of the equipment required to make the bombs was easy to procure covertly. By the time de Klerk canceled the program, South Africa had acquired a secret plant for enriching uranium for bombs; a stockpile of weapons-grade uranium; and six gun-assembly fission weapons (the kind of weapon the United States used against Hiroshima).[30]

Waldo Stumpf, the head of South Africa's Nuclear Energy Corporation, estimated in 1994 that the entire project, including enriching the uranium, cost $200 million. "The nuclear deterrent programme was considered to be a far more cost-effective alternative to the development of, for example, a fighter aircraft capability," Stumpf said. It cost "less than 5 percent of the defense budget at the time."[31] Costs would have been significantly lower had South Africa been able to purchase the HEU. Thus, if a terrorist group had access to HEU, the cost of producing the bomb could be significantly less than $200 million.

Whenever possible, the South African technicians used simple machines not controlled for export. For example, they used a two-axis machine tool (designed for making two-dimensional shapes) to create the three-dimensional shape necessary for the gun-assembly device.[32]

In the early 1980s the project employed about 100 people, more than half of them in administrative support and security; 40 people worked in the weapons program, David Albright reports, but only 20 were actually building the weapons. By 1989, when the program ended, the workforce had risen to 300, half of whom worked in the weapons program.[33]

The number of people actually involved in making the weapons is shockingly small, but it is significantly more than the "three or four technically qualified specialists" envisioned by the group of nuclear weapons designers. Nonetheless, South Africa's experience shows that some terrorist groups (for example Hezbollah) have sufficient financial resources, although they apparently lack the requisite expertise and/or the requisite fissile material.

Instead of building their own weapon, terrorists (or a terrorist-supporting regime) might try to steal or buy a nuclear warhead. Stealing a warhead would require overcoming security at a site where weapons are stored or deployed, taking possession of the bomb, and bypassing any locks intended to prevent unauthorized detonation of the weapon. This would clearly be easier if the terrorists were able to obtain the assistance of insiders (whether through persuasion, coercion, or bribery). Reports occasionally surface about former Soviet soldiers who are willing to sell warheads, and about terrorists' alleged interest in purchasing them, but no instance of an actual sale has been confirmed.[34]

Russia's approximately 6,000 long-range strategic weapons are protected by locks, making it impossible—at least in principle—to launch them without high-level authority. But thousands of shorter-range tactical weapons have less sophisticated protections or no locks at all. These short-range weapons would be both easier to steal and easier to detonate.

A leaked CIA report warns of the potential in Russia for "conspiracies within nuclear armed units." The report attributes the increased risk of conspiracy to deteriorating living conditions and morale, "even among elite nuclear submariners, nuclear warhead handlers, and the Strategic Rocket Forces." Submarines are a particular source of concern: Russian naval officers know a lot more about nuclear weapons than their ground force counterparts, since they must be able to operate autonomously at sea.[35]

General Aleksandr Lebed, a former head of President Yeltsin's Security Council, has claimed that most of the atomic demolition munitions or "suitcase bombs" in the former Soviet arsenal are unaccounted for. It is not possible at this point to confirm or deny Lebed's claim, but these bombs, if they exist, would be perfect terrorist devices because they would be small enough to be carried by one man.[36]

The Case of Aum Shinrikiyo

The most successful and most publicized terrorist use of weapons of mass destruction to date was the case of the Japanese cult called Aum Shinrikiyo. In our attempt to understand modern terrorism it is worth taking a detailed look at this cult and its leader.[37]

Shoko Asahara, whose original name was Chizuo Matsumoto, was born on the southern Japanese island of Kyushu. His father wove straw floor mats (tatami) for a living, and was barely able to feed his family. The family of six lived in a small shack with a dirt floor. Asahara was blind in his left eye and only half-sighted in his right. Sighted children taunted him, and he in turn taunted those whose vision was worse than his own. At the boarding school for blind children that he attended, he tortured and tricked his classmates

hotels, charging them thousands of dollars to "cure" their rheumatism with tonics made of ingredients such as dried orange peel and alcohol. Eventually he was arrested for fraud, but the court-imposed fine of about $1,000 was a tiny fraction of his profits.

In 1984 Asahara formed a company called Aum Inc., which produced health drinks and ran yoga schools. Like many Japanese people in the 1980s, Asahara developed an interest in spirituality. He traveled to India, where he perfected his meditation technique, learning, he claimed, to levitate. He also claimed he could pass through solid walls, intuit people's thoughts, and chart people's past lives.

In 1986 a Japanese New Age journal, *Twilight Zone*, ran pictures of Asahara apparently suspended in midair in the lotus position. Attendance at his yoga schools rose, and with the profits Asahara was able to open schools throughout Japan. Soon afterward he claimed he heard a message from God while meditating, telling him that he had been chosen to lead God's army. At about the same time he met a radical historian who predicted that Armageddon would come by the year 2000. Only a small group would survive, the historian told Asahara, and the leader of that group would emerge in Japan. Asahara immediately cast himself as that leader. He began planning for Armageddon and his leadership role, and changed the name of his company to Aum Shinrikiyo (Aum Supreme Truth).

Asahara chose Shiva the Destroyer as the principal deity for Aum Supreme Truth, though he also emphasized the Judeo-Christian notion of Armageddon. At a seminar in 1987 he made his first prediction: nuclear war would break out between 1999 and 2003. There were fewer than fifteen years to prepare, he warned. Nuclear war could be averted, but only if Aum opened a branch in every country on earth. Those who were spiritually enlightened would survive even a nuclear holocaust.

Asahara found new ways to expand his revenues. He encouraged his students to cut off all ties with the outside world and to hand over all their assets as a way to foster their spiritual development. Asahara sold clippings from his beard for $375 a half-inch and his dirty bath-water (called Miracle Pond) for $800 a quart. He also opened a compound near Mount Fuji, which eventually included a very expensive (and hazardous) hospital, as well as laboratories for research on weapons of mass destruction [WMD].

Many of those attracted to Asahara's promise of spiritual enlightenment were scientists, physicians, and engineers from Japan's top schools. One was Seiichi Endo, who had been trained at Kyoto University and was working at the university's viral research center. Another was Hideo Murai, a brilliant astrophysicist who became Asahara's "engineer of the apocalypse." According to David Kaplan and Andrew Marshall, who have studied Aum Shinrikiyo, "The high-tech children of postindustrial Japan were fascinated by Aum's dramatic claims to supernatural power, its warnings of an apocalyptic future, its esoteric spiritualism."[38]

Asahara was able to attract Russian scientists and engineers to the cause. Russia was like a supermarket for Asahara. He bought weapons and training, and he recruited among Russia's scientific elite, who were now unemployed or unpaid and seeking new missions. During the early 1990s Russia's Minister of Defense Grachev reportedly paved the way for three groups of Aum Shinrikyo cult members to spend three days with military units in the Taman and Kantemirov divisions, where, for a fee, they were trained to use military equipment. The cult reportedly also received substantial assistance from Oleg Lobov, who was then the head of President Yeltsin's Security Council. The Russian Prosecutor General's office is investigating allegations by a Japanese cult member that Lobov provided assistance to the poison gas program.[39]

Asahara became obsessed with WMD, in part because he was convinced that the CIA planned to use such weapons against Japan. Moreover, he believed his group would need every available weapon to survive Armageddon. He put his scientists to work on developing WMD. He also sent a deputy on several trips to Russia to purchase weapons and scientific assistance.

Soon these efforts began to pay off. Asahara directed a series of attacks using biological agents. Cult members have confessed to carrying out nine such attacks, including at the Japanese Diet, at the Imperial Palace, elsewhere in Tokyo, and at two American naval bases: Yokosuka and Yokohama. In April 1990 members reportedly drove through the city of Tokyo with a convoy of three trucks outfitted to spray botulinum toxin. The convoy drove by the American naval bases, where they attempted to spread the poison, and to Narita airport. No botulinum was reported detected, however, during any of these attacks, and no one was reported ill. Next the cult tried spreading anthrax. In July 1993 members tried to disseminate anthrax at several sites, including near the Imperial Palace and near the Diet. They again fitted a truck with a special sprayer and drove it around the city. These attacks also failed.[40]

The cult tried spreading anthrax from the roof of its headquarters building. Members put a steam generator on the roof and poured anthrax spores into it, then turned on a sprayer and fan and waited to see the results. Small birds died, and the generator emitted a putrid smell that permeated the neighborhood. It smelled like burning flesh, one resident told the press. When inspectors went to the Aum building to ask questions, they were told that the smell was from a mix of soybean oil and perfume—Chanel No. 5—which the cult was burning to purify the building.[41]

The group was more successful with chemical weapons. In June 1994 residents of Matsumoto, a mountain resort a hundred miles west of Tokyo, noticed a strange fog hugging the earth. Soon thereafter some residents experienced nausea, vomiting, pain in their eyes, and difficulty breathing. By the next morning 7 people had died and 200 were ill. A total of 600 eventually became ill. Dogs lay dead in the streets, and dead fish floated in a nearby pond. Doctors investigating the incident noted that victims had markedly reduced levels of acetylocholinesterase (an enzyme necessary for proper functioning of the nervous system), a sign that they had been exposed to toxic organophosphate-based insecticides or nerve agents. But even after traces of sarin, a nerve agent, were found in the pond, authorities did not suspect terrorism. No terrorist group had claimed responsibility, and the idea that terrorists could be responsible for such a heinous crime seemed too far-fetched to be believed. In fact, as subsequently became known, Aum Shinrikyo had carried out the attack. Asahara's intention was to poison three judges living in the area. The judges survived the attack when the wind changed direction, but the poison spread over the town.[42]

Nine months later, on March 20, 1995, the cult used sarin again, this time in a deadly incident that attracted media attention. By this time the police were closing in on the group, and its scientists had to work fast. The terrorists placed hastily made sarin-filled polyethylene pouches on five Tokyo subway cars, and then punctured the pouches with sharpened

plastic bags, one containing sodium cyanide and the other sulfuric acid, in Tokyo's Shinjuku train station with the intention of disseminating cyanide gas. And on July 4, 1995, similar improvised chemical devices were found in restrooms in four stations.[43]

The Aum Shinrikiyo cult intended to kill many thousands of people. The 1995 poison-gas attack in the Tokyo subway was carried out in haste and did not represent the cult's full potential. The group had built up a large production capacity for chemical weapons and was working on plans for disseminating chemical and biological agents over some major Japanese city. Cult members had hidden a bottle containing an ounce of VX—reportedly enough to kill about 15,000 people—which was recovered by the Tokyo police in September 1996. They had amassed hundreds of tons of chemicals used in the production of sarin—reportedly to make enough sarin to kill millions. They had bought a Russian Mi-17 combat helicopter and two remotely piloted vehicles to disseminate the agent over populated areas. Police found a large amount of *Clostridium botulinum*, together with 160 barrels of growth media (required for growing the bacteria). The cult was reportedly cooperating with North Korea, with former Soviet Mafia groups, and indirectly with Iran, in smuggling nuclear materials and conventional munitions out of Russia through Ukraine.[44] Members reportedly visited Zaire on the pretext of providing medical assistance to victims of the Ebola virus, with the actual objective of acquiring a sample of the virus to culture as a warfare agent. The group was also actively trying to purchase Russian nuclear warheads, according to the CIA, and may have been plotting a chemical attack in the United States.[45]

In November 1995 Senator Sam Nunn held a hearing on Aum Shinrikiyo. The senator's staff testified that at the time of the Tokyo attack Aum Shinrikiyo had some 50,000 members, 30,000 of whom were Russians. It had assets worth $1.4 billion and offices in Bonn, Sri Lanka, New York, and Moscow as well as in several Japanese cities. U.S. officials admitted that, despite the alarming range of Aum Shinrikiyo's activities, it was not on the "radar screen" of the U.S. intelligence community.[46]

Other Cases

Before the Aum Shinrikiyo incidents, other terrorists had attempted or threatened to use chemical, biological, or radiological agents, but usually on a scale so small that the media hardly noticed. Most of the incidents involved threats that were never carried out, although some of the threats were very costly to the targeted companies or governments. In the rare cases when these agents have been used, they have been used more as weapons of mass impact than as weapons of mass destruction: few people have been killed.

A common use of these agents is to commit economic sabotage either against specific companies or against entire industries. For example, the Animal Liberation Front (ALF) claimed to have spiked Mars chocolate bars with rat poison to protest research on tooth decay conducted on live monkeys. No poison was found, but Mars reported losses of $4.5 million. British police later charged four members of the ALF with injecting toxic mercury into turkeys sold in supermarkets as a protest against their slaughter during the Christmas season. The same group was suspected of poisoning eggs in British supermarkets in 1989. The eggs were punctured and marked with a skull and crossbones. An attached message signed "ALF" warned that the eggs had been poisoned. While the product-tampering crimes committed in the United States in the late 1980s were not committed by terrorists, the costs imposed on industry demonstrate the potential effectiveness of economic terrorism. In 1986 alone, U.S. pharmaceutical manufacturers destroyed over $1 billion worth of pharmaceuticals because of tampering or threats of tampering and spent another $1 billion making their products more resistant to tampering.[47]

Chemical and radiological agents have also been used to meet more traditional terrorist objectives: to attack symbolic targets, to assassinate individuals, or to commit small-scale acts of random violence. Several groups have planned to attack water supplies, although no known attack has been successful. In 1972, a U.S. neo-Nazi group, the Order of the Rising Sun, was found in possession of a large quantity of typhoid bacillus, which it reportedly intended to use to poison water supplies in several midwestern cities. Another incident involved a plot by several right-wing extremist groups to overthrow the U.S. government. One of the groups, The Covenant, the Sword, and the Arm of the Lord, had stockpiled some thirty gallons of cyanide for the purpose of polluting municipal water supplies. The group was apprehended before the plot could be carried out.[48]

While the terrorists involved in these two incidents were plotting alarmingly destructive attacks, it is unlikely that either of the planned attacks would have succeeded. The chlorine in U.S. reservoirs would have killed the typhoid bacillus, and dilution would have rendered the cyanide harmless. Attacking a small, unprotected water supply could be more effective. Ramzi Youssef, the convicted mastermind of the bombing of the World Trade Center [1993], reportedly threatened in a letter to poison water supplies in the Philippines. The letter was found on his person at the time of his arrest. In it he claimed to be able to produce chemical agents for use against "vital institutions and residential populations and the sources of drinking water."[49]

A few attacks have involved radioactive isotopes. In 1995 Shamil Basayev, the leader of the Chechen group that had earlier taken more than 1,000 hospital patients hostage, buried a packet of radioactive cesium in Izmailovski Park in Moscow to demonstrate his capabilities.[50] Izmailovski Park is a popular recreation spot for both Russians and tourists. Had Basayev actually disseminated radioactive cesium, he would have imposed heavy costs on the Russian government. In a bizarre case on Long Island in 1996, three people became convinced that county officials were covering up the crash landing of space aliens in their county. They acquired five canisters of radioactive radium, with which they planned to assassinate county officials by poisoning the officials' toothpaste, air conditioning, and automobiles. Their ultimate objective was to seize control of the county government, but members were apprehended before they were able to poison anyone, much less achieve their ambitious agenda.[51]

The single U.S. case involving the actual use of biological agents occurred in September 1984, when members of the Rajneeshee cult in Oregon poisoned salad bars with *Salmonella typhimurium*. The cult had established a commune on a large ranch, part of which was incorporated as the city of Rajneeshpuram. Local residents objected to the commune and challenged the city's charter in the courts. The cult sought to ensure the victory of its own candidate in the November 1984 elections for county commissioner. Members considered various ideas for accomplishing this goal, including vote fraud, and decided to

until a year later, during investigations of cult members for other, unrelated crimes.

These cases are instructive. First, no terrorist group has acquired a nuclear weapon, although Aum Shinrikiyo attempted to do so. Second, the most destructive biological attack involved a crude food poison, rather than air dissemination of a deadly agent. While such poisons are somewhat easier to procure than deadlier agents, the ability of a terrorist group to contaminate a salad bar is alarming, as is the health authorities' difficulty in determining the cause of the outbreak of illness. This case raises the question of whether other outbreaks of disease, assumed to have resulted from natural causes, may actually have been caused by deliberate sabotage or terrorism.

The most destructive incident, Aum Shinrikiyo's attack on the Tokyo subway, involved disseminating a chemical agent in an enclosed space. This method and the contamination of food are probably the easiest ways to use weapons of mass destruction, and are likely to remain the most common forms of terrorism involving these weapons.

All of Aum Shinrikiyo's large-scale attacks with biological agents are believed to have failed. Very little is known about why they were unsuccessful. There are many strains of *Clostridium botulinum* and *Bacillus anthracis*. Experts now believe the cult may have grown weak strains of the microbes, possibly, in the case of the anthrax, a relatively harmless vaccine strain. The cult also had difficulty aerosolizing the agent in respirable particle size. Sprayers used to create anthrax mists became clogged, for example, a problem that other terrorists would be likely to confront as well.[53] Were terrorists to master these technologies they would have the potential to kill not just hundreds but hundreds of thousands of people.

Jessica Stern is a faculty affiliate of the Belfer Center for Science and International Affairs and a lecturer in public policy at the Kennedy School. She served formerly as the director for Russian, Ukrainian, and Eurasian Affairs at the National Security Council, responsible for national-security policy toward Russia and the former Soviet states and for policies to reduce the threat of nuclear smuggling and terrorism. She is the author of *The Ultimate Terrorists* (1999) as well as many articles on terrorism and weapons of mass destruction.

Notes

1. Prepared statement of Edward Eitzen, U.S. Congress, Senate, Committee on Governmental Affairs, Permanent Subcommittee on Investigations, *Hearings on Global Proliferation of Weapons of Mass Destruction*, 104th Cong., 1st sess., pt. 1, Oct. 31, 1995, 112. More likely, doctors would observe large numbers of cases that resembled the flu. By the time doctors realized their patients had been victims of an attack, it would be too late to save their lives.
2. Cohen, speech to the Conference on Terrorism, Weapons of Mass Destruction, and U.S. Strategy, University of Georgia, April 28, 1997. Prepared statement of George Tenet, U.S. Congress, Senate, Select Committee on Intelligence, *Hearing on Current and Projected National Security Threats to the United States*, 105th Cong., 1st sess., Feb. 5, 1997.
3. "Albania: Army Officer Urges Return of Looted Chemical Weapons," FBIS-EEU-97-096, transcribed text, April 6, 1997. Source: Paris AFP in English 1740 GMT April 6, 1997.

4. Agence France Presse, "Russian Security Inadequate for Chemical Weapons Storage," Aug. 2, 1995.
5. Prepared statement of Vil Mirzayanov, U.S. Senate, *Hearings on Global Proliferation of WMD*, Nov. 1, 1995. A. Cooperman and K. Belianinov, "Moonlighting by Modem in Russia," *U.S. News and World Report*, April 17, 1995. James Adams, "Gadaffi Lures South Africa's Top Germ Warfare Scientists," *Sunday Times*, Feb. 26, 1995.
6. Office of Technology Assessment, *Technology against Terrorism: The Federal Effort* (Washington: GPO, 1991), 51–52.
7. Raymond Zilinskas, "Terrorists and BW: Inevitable Alliance?" *Perspectives in Biology and Medicine* 34 (Autumn 1990). Eitzen, prepared statement. Interview with Dr. Kathleen Bailey, Dec. 1995.
8. It is quite easy to purchase these manuals. I called one such publishing house and told the operator I wanted to buy manuals with instructions on how to poison people. She asked whether I was interested in bombs or silencers as well. I told her no, I only wanted to poison people. She asked for my credit card number and mailing address, and that was the end of our conversation.
9. The most prominent example is a case in which a killer followed instructions provided in a manual entitled *Hit Man*. See *Rice v. Paladin Enterprises, Inc.*, 940 F. Supp. 836 (D. Md. 1996), appeal docketed, no. 96-2412 (4th circuit).
10. Leonard A. Cole, *Clouds of Secrecy: The Army's Germ Warfare Tests over Populated Areas* (Totowa, N.J.: Rowman and Littlefield, 1988), 163. The Army carried out the tests in the belief that the simulants were harmless to human health, but a few people were adversely affected and one hospital patient died. The Army ended such simulated attacks against human beings in the 1960s.
11. Ibid., 68. *U.S. Army Activities in the United States Biological Warfare Programs*, 1942–1977 (Washington: Department of the Army, 1977), vol. 1, 6–3; vol. 2, IV-E-1-1.
12. *U.S. Army Activities in Biological Warfare Programs*, vol. 2, IV-E-5-1-5A-1.
13. See Ron Purver, "Chemical and Biological Terrorism: The Threat According to the Open Literature," Canadian Security Intelligence Service, June 1995.
14. William Patrick, "Biological Terrorism and Aerosol Dissemination," *Politics and the Life Sciences*, Sept. 1996, 209; and interviews at Fort Detrick. Eitzen, prepared statement, 112.
15. Stephen C. Reynolds, "The Terrorist Threat to Domestic Water Supplies" (U.S. Army Corps of Engineers, Aug. 1987), unclassified/limited distribution. Seymour S. Block, *Disinfection, Sterilization, and Preservation* (Philadelphia: Lea and Febiger, 1991). U.S. Army Environmental Hygiene Agency, Aberdeen Proving Ground, "Position Paper: Threat of Chemical Agents in Field Drinking Water," March 1982. Cryptosporidium lives in human and animal intestines and is secreted in feces. It can be found in most surface water, particularly after heavy rains. It is often difficult to identify and is not always killed by routine chlorination.
16. B. J. Berkowitz et al., "Superviolence: The Civil Threat of Mass Destruction Weapons" (Washington: Advanced Concept Research, 1972). Zilinskas, "Terrorists and BW."
17. Reynolds, "Terrorist Threat to Water Supplies."
18. General Accounting Office, "Commercial Nuclear Fuel Facilities Need Better Security," May 2, 1977, ii, cited in J. K. Campbell, "The Threat of Non-State Proliferation" (manuscript, Defense Intelligence Agency).
19. Letter from V. Bush to General Groves, Nov. 15, 1943, Bush-Conant Files, RG 227, folder 157, National Archives.
20. "Military Use of Radio-Active Materials and Organization for Defense," S-1 files, and "Report of the Subcommittee of the S-1 Committee on the Use of Radioactive Material as a Military Weapon," 7, in Bush-Conant Files, RG 227, folder 157, National Archives. "Fission aerial bombs or fission projectiles" may refer to atomic weapons wrapped in cobalt or another gamma emitter or, more likely, a conventional bomb containing radioactive material.
21. "Military Use of Radio-Active Materials," Bush-Conant Files.
22. Information provided by Doug Stephens, Lawrence Livermore National Laboratory. W. M. Place, F. C. Cobb, and C. G. Defferding, "Palomares Summary Report," Field Command, Defense Nuclear Agency, Technology and Analysis Directorate, Kirtland Air Force Base (Jan. 1975). Randy Maydew, "Find the Missing H-Bomb," *Air Combat*, Nov.-Dec. 1996.
23. "Military Use of Radio-Active Materials," Bush-Conant Files.
24. David Albright, personal communication, Sept. 24, 1996.

April 20, 1984, enclosure E, 3. In 1994 the Nuclear Regulatory Commission demanded security upgrades at commercial reactors that would make a truck bomb attack more difficult.

26. Germany's federal counter-sabotage agency, the BFV, determined that escalating violence accompanying the transport of spent fuel was the "work of terrorists" who might have contacts with the Red Army Faction. "State, GNS Differ over Strategy to Defy Saboteurs at Gorleben," *Nuclear Fuel*, Jan. 13, 1997, 11.

27. Rocky Flats held 11.9 metric tons of weapons-grade plutonium as of Sept. 1994 and 2.8 metric tons of HEU as of Feb. 1996. U.S. Department of Energy, "Storage and Disposition of Weapons-Usable Fissile Materials Final Programmatic Environmental Impact Statement, Summary," DOE/EIS-0229, Dec. 1996, S-5. Jim Carrier, "Flats Security Lax, Ex-Officials Warn," *Denver Post*, May 20, 1997. James Brooke, "Plutonium Stockpile Fosters Fears of a Disaster Waiting to Happen," *New York Times*, Dec. 11, 1996. John J. Fialka, "Energy Department Report Faults Security at Weapons Plants," *Wall Street Journal*, June 16, 1997.

28. Paul Leventhal and Yonah Alexander, *Preventing Nuclear Terrorism* (Lexington, Mass.: Lexington Books, 1987), 9, 58.

29. Interview with Ambassador Thomas Graham, Nov. 25, 1996.

30. David Albright, "South Africa's Secret Nuclear Weapons," ISIS Report (Institute for Science and International Security), May 1994. Graham interview, Waldo Stumpf, "South Africa's Nuclear Weapons Programme," in Kathleen C. Bailey, *Weapons of Mass Destruction: Costs Versus Benefits* (New Delhi: Manohar, 1994), 71. Albright claims there were seven weapons, but Stumpf says only six were completed.

31. Stumpf, "South Africa's Nuclear Weapons Programme," 75, 76. Cost figures assume 1994 exchange rates (presumable in 1994 dollars).

32. Albright, "South Africa's Secret Nuclear Weapons."

33. Ibid. I was able to confirm in general terms these approximate figures in interviews with U.S. government officials who had interviewed South African nuclear specialists.

34. William Arkin of Greenpeace says he came close to buying a nuclear warhead from a Russian soldier working at a storage site in East Germany in the early 1990s. The soldier told Arkin he had found a way to gain access to the warheads during the transition between shifts. "The orientation of security," Arkin explains, "was very heavily weighted toward defending against a NATO attack. It was not heavily weighted toward protesters, or public intervention, or terrorists." Quoted in William Burrows and Robert Windrem, *Critical Mass* (New York: Simon and Schuster, 1994), 249. The CIA has noted Aum Shinrikiyo's apparent interest in buying nuclear warheads from Russia: Statement for the record by John Deutch, U.S. Senate, *Hearings on Global Proliferation of WMD*, pt. 2, S.Hrg 104–422, 104th Cong., 2nd sess., March 20, 1996, 7. And Rensslaear Lee cites a 1991 letter reportedly faxed to the Russian nuclear weapons laboratory Arzamas-16, allegedly from Islamic Jihad, offering to buy a nuclear warhead. The director of Arzamas reportedly also told Lee that Iraqi agents had offered $2 billion for a warhead in 1993. Interview with Lee, Nov. 12, 1996. I have found no other reports of this letter.

35. Bill Gertz, "Russian Renegades Pose Nuke Danger," *Washington Times*, Oct. 22, 1996. Interview with an expert on Russian nuclear weapons, Oct. 16, 1996.

36. Unclassified cable, Moscow 13851, TOR: 0316032, June 1997.

37. This section is based on David E. Kaplan and Andrew Marshall, *The Cult at the End of the World* (New York: Crown, 1996).

38. Ibid., 28.

39. "Prosecutors Investigate Lobov's Links to Religious Sect," FBIS-SOV-97144, May 24, 1997; "Lobov Faces Questions over Investigation of Japanese Sect," FBIS-SV-97-084, April 25, 1997; both trans. from Moscow Interfax.

40. CIA, "The Chemical, Biological and Radiological Terrorist Threat from Non-State Actors," paper presented to Aspen Strategy group conference "The Proliferation Threat of Weapons of Mass Destruction and U.S. Security Interest," Aspen, Colo., Aug. 1996. William Broad, "How Japan Germ Terror Alerted World," *New York Times*, May 26, 1998.

41. Ibid. Another biological attack also failed: on March 15, 1995, cult members planned to release botulinal toxin at Kasumigaseki station, but a member struck by a guilty conscience neglected to arm the devices.

42. John F. Quinn, "Terrorism Comes to Tokyo: The Aum Shinri Kyo Incident," paper presented to the Association of Former Intelligence Officers, 1996 Annual Convention, Falls Church, Va., Oct. 1996. Authorities assumed the sarin had formed spontaneously from pesticide residues. Leonard Cole, *The Eleventh Plague* (New York: Freeman, 1996), citing *Mainichi Daily News*, June 30, July 2, July 9, and July 16, 1994.

43. See Jonathan B. Tucker, "Chemical/Biological Terrorism: Coping with a New Threat," *Politics and the Life Sciences* 15 (Sept. 1996). Ron Purver, "The Threat of Chemical/Biological Terrorism" *Commentary* 60 (Aug. 1995). Kaplan and Marshall, *Cult at the End of the World.* Interviews with John Sopko Quinn, "Terrorism Comes to Tokyo." CIA, "Chemical, Biological and Radiological Threat."

44. "Tokyo Police Find Bottle of a Cult's Deadly Gas," Associated Press, *New York Times*, Dec. 12, 1996, 15. Nicholas D. Kristof, "Tokyo Syspect in Gas Attack Erupts in Court," *New York Times*, Nov. 8, 1996, 14. Cole, *Eleventh Plague*, 155. Ed Evanhoe says that after Asahara was arrested North Korea may have moved its nuclear smuggling base of operations to Tumen, China, making use of a North Korean organized-crime ring to smuggle nuclear-related equipment as well as nuclear materials. Email from Evanhoe, Nov. 5, 1996.

45. Staff Report, U.S. Senate, *Hearings on Global Proliferation of WMD*, Nov. 1, 1995. Statement for the Record by John Deutch, 7. Nicholas D. Kristof, "Japanese Cult Said to Have Planned Nerve-Gas Attacks in U.S.," *New York Times*, March 23, 1997.

46. Staff Report, U.S. Senate, *Hearings on Global Proliferation of WMD*, Nov. 1, 1995.

47. Joseph Pilat, "World Watch: Striking Back at Urban Terrorism," *NBC Defense and Technology International* (June 1986), 18. "Animal Rights Activists Attack Scientists' Homes," Associated Press, *Los Angeles Times*, March 13, 1985. Rand database. *Product Tampering and the Threat to Tamper* (Los Angeles: Foundation for American Communications, undated), 3.

48. James Campbell, "Weapons of Mass Destruction and Terrorism: Proliferation by Non-State Actors" (Master's thesis, Naval Postgraduate School, 1996). Rand database. *Arkansas Gazette*, April 27, 1987, cited in Bruce Hoffman. " 'Holy Terror': The Implications of Terrorism Motivated by Religious Imperative," Rand Paper P-7834, 1993.

49. "New Charges Filed against Alleged Leader of Bombing," *Washington Post*, Oct. 7, 1995, 14.

50. Cesium-137, a radioisotope used in the treatment of cancer, is a waste product of nuclear reactors. It has a relatively long half-life, and areas contaminated with it require extensive cleanup. It can be absorbed into the food chain and is carcinogenic. Mark Hibbs, "Chechen Separatists Take Credit for Moscow Cesium-137." *Nuclear Fuel* 20, no. 25 (Dec. 4, 1995), 5.

51. John McQuiston, "Plot against L.I. Leaders Is Tied to Fear of UFO's" *New York Times*, June 22, 1996. "Two Charged in Plot to Poison Long Island GOP Officials; Radium, Weapons Cache Found in House," *Washington Post*, June 14, 1996. Larry Sutton, "Bail Denied in Radium Plot," *New York Daily News*, June 25, 1996.

52. Prepared Statement of John O'Neill, U.S. Senate, *Hearings on Global Proliferation of WMD*, Nov. 1, 1995, 241. Thomas J. Torok et al., "A Large Community Outbreak of Salmonellosis Caused by International Contamination of Restaurant Salad Bars," *JAMA* 278, no. 5 (Aug. 6, 1987); Seth Carus, "The Rajneesh in Oregon," paper presented at a workshop on Patterns of Behavior Associated with Chemical and Biological Terrorism, Monterey Institute, Washington, June 1998. The Rajneeshees' true motivations are not clear. If their goal was exclusively to make their victims ill, rather than to affect a target audience (by, for example, frightening the local residents), this incident may not, strictly speaking, fit the definition of terrorism used in this book.

53. Broad, "How Japan Germ Terror Alerted World."

Misplaced Analogies

The anthrax attacks on the United States in the autumn of 2001, and the fear and confusion that followed, made clear that the country lacks a comprehensive strategy for biological security—the protection of people and agriculture against disease threats, whether from biological weapons or natural outbreaks. Too often, thinking about biological security has been distorted by misplaced analogies to nuclear or chemical weapons. An effective strategy must leave these analogies largely behind and address the special challenges posed by biological threats.

A strategy for biological security must confront drug-resistant and emerging diseases—more than 30 of which have entered the human population over the past quarter-century. There is no good analogue to this naturally occurring threat in the realm of nuclear or chemical weapons. Moreover, diseases may be targeted against livestock or crops as well as against human populations. And outbreaks of deadly, contagious, and long-incubating diseases such as smallpox have to be detected and stopped rapidly wherever in the world they occur. Fortunately, once formulated, a sound strategy for biological security will help sustain itself because many of its core provisions will benefit public health even apart from acts of bioterror.

In fact, many of the tools used to address natural disease threats will be needed to respond to an intentional attack. The U.S. response to the anthrax attacks has emphasized the importance of improving domestic defenses. These measures include stockpiling vaccines and antibiotics, as well as improving local and national disease surveillance and other public health tools. To be effective these domestic measures must be sustained for decades and keep pace with the biotechnology revolution. International steps—such as improving surveillance for and response to outbreaks of infectious diseases and securing pathogen stocks worldwide—are also crucial to an effective strategy. Yet most of these international measures have been ignored so far in the current focus on immediate domestic needs.

Part of the problem is the very vocabulary we use. Analysts and policymakers refer casually to "WMD" (weapons of mass destruction) or "NBCR" (nuclear/biological/chemical/radiological) weapons, as if the latter were merely variants on the same type of device. In fact, these weapons differ greatly in their ease of production, in the challenges they pose for deterrence, and in the effectiveness of defensive measures against them. The post–September 11 focus on WMD and whether they are in the hands of enemy states or groups risks overlooking these complexities. Put simply, biological weapons differ from nuclear or chemical weapons, and any biological security strategy should begin by paying attention to these differences.

The WMD Continuum

Imagine a line that begins with nuclear weapons at one extreme, continues through chemical, radiological, and biological weapons, and terminates with cyber-weapons (designed to attack computers or critical infrastructure) at the far end. As one moves along this continuum through the different so-called weapons of mass destruction (to which "cyber-weapons" have been added here for purposes of illustration), the difficulties facing nonproliferation become increasingly apparent. At the nuclear extreme, nonproliferation is comparatively robust, whereas at the cyber end it is enormously difficult.

Nuclear nonproliferation policy seeks to limit the number of nations that have nuclear weapons and keep such weapons out of the hands of subnational groups altogether. Any effective approach must guarantee warhead security and prevent the diversion of nuclear material from civilian programs to military or terrorist uses. Article III of the nuclear Nonproliferation Treaty (NPT) provides the legal basis for a near-global verification regime to detect the diversion of fissile material—verification carried out by the UN's International Atomic Energy Agency (IAEA). The agency uses inspections, audits of nuclear material and records, and surveillance cameras and instrumentation to monitor more than 1,000 facilities worldwide.

The IAEA's verification efforts have worked in part because the facilities needed to produce uranium or plutonium for weapons are big and hard to hide. Of course, inspections are not foolproof. Iraq, for example, made significant progress in enrichment of indigenous uranium despite being a party to the NPT and subject to IAEA inspections. This experience led the IAEA to propose strengthened safeguards to include the right to inspections on short notice of undeclared, suspect locations. Yet there have also been important successes. In 1992, IAEA inspectors in North Korea found discrepancies indicating that a plutonium reprocessing plant at Yongbyon had been used more often than the government had declared. In the face of new challenges, the NPT verification regime must evolve rapidly enough to continue playing an important nonproliferation role.

The United States and the nearly 40 other nations of the Nuclear Suppliers Group further pursue nonproliferation by adhering to consensual guidelines restricting nuclear and nuclear-related "dual-use" exports—i.e., material that can serve both civilian and military purposes. These guidelines are intended to supplement the NPT by controlling the transfer of listed items without hindering the legitimate international nuclear cooperation called for by Article IV of the NPT. Through the Cooperative Threat Reduction (CTR) program with the Soviet Union's successor states, the United States has also acted to impede the theft or sale of nuclear material as well as the movement of nuclear scientists from the former Soviet Union to what the Clinton administration first called "rogue states" and later termed "states of concern." Of course, in addition to these multilateral and bilateral measures, diplomatic pressure and security guarantees have also played their roles, and intelligence has been vital throughout.

For all its difficulties, nuclear nonproliferation has been reasonably successful in part because the production of weapons-grade plutonium or uranium is difficult (requiring reactors or enrichment plants, respectively), and this imposes conspicuous bottleneck on any would-be weapons programs. Few of the necessary facilities exist and they can be monitored if declared, or risk discovery by intelligence-gathering if not. (Of course, intelligence findings do not guarantee an end to proliferation concerns, as Iran's case shows.) Because the theft of

can be launched from almost any of the more than 100 million computers worldwide that have access to the Internet. Applying standard nonproliferation techniques to these computers would therefore ultimately require unannounced inspections or the monitoring of hundreds of millions of residences and businesses. Cyber-security may benefit from certain nonproliferation measures, but it renders traditional inspection approaches absurd. Moreover, automated monitoring of the source and content of electronic messages to identify illicit activities would face its own enormous obstacles.

Falling between the nuclear and cyber extremes of the WMD continuum are chemical, radiological, and biological weapons. Maintaining an international verification regime for chemical weapons is harder than for nuclear weapons because of the larger number of relevant facilities and dual-use materials. The Organization for the Prohibition of Chemical Weapons, established under the Chemical Weapons Convention (CWC), must contend with an entire industrial sector and more than 6,000 inspectable facilities. Nevertheless, under the CWC, governments have declared chemical weapons stocks and opened them to international verification, three of the four declared possessor states have begun destroying their stocks, and inspectors have examined hundreds of dual-use chemical plants. The declaration of 70,000 metric tons of chemical agents by the United States, Russia, India, and South Korea, along with additional states' declarations of chemical weapons production facilities, old chemical weapons, and abandoned chemical weapons, constitute a valuable achievement. The verified elimination of chemical stockpiles and the destruction or conversion of production facilities will be a clear gain for international security—especially once Russia begins destroying its 40,000 metric tons of chemical weapons, some of which currently remains vulnerable to theft. These achievements are valuable regardless of the disturbing absence of Iraq, North Korea, and other states of concern from the CWC regime. The regime is further supplemented by the Australia Group of 33 nations that, like the Nuclear Suppliers Group, establishes consensual national guidelines restricting the export of chemicals and technology that can be used to make weapons.

Biological weapons also fall between the nuclear and cyber ends of the WMD continuum but are even harder to control than chemical weapons. True, the Biological and Toxin Weapons Convention (BWC) established a norm against the production and stockpiling of biological weapons, and the 1925 Geneva Protocol forbids their use. The Australia Group also works to impede the transfer of biological agents and technology where possible through national export controls. Nevertheless, any biological nonproliferation regime will necessarily be less robust than its nuclear counterpart, because much of the relevant material, technology, and knowledge is already far more widely distributed and will become more so in the coming decades.

Scientists can acquire potentially deadly biological agents in the course of legitimate research: for instance, U.S. and British government institutes previously distributed the Ames anthrax strain used in the autumn 2001 attacks to a dozen or so laboratories. Naturally occurring disease outbreaks are another source of lethal organisms: the Ames strain is common in eastern Texas, for example. Indeed, natural outbreaks are the ultimate origin of the agents historically used in nations' biological weapons programs. Moreover, the fermenters required to produce these biological agents in large quantities are widely used in the pharmaceutical, biotechnology, and even beer industries.

Weaponizing these diseases—going from the organism to a preparation that is particularly suitable for distribution as a powder or liquid aerosol—has proved difficult for terrorists. The Japanese group Aum Shinrikyo failed to weaponize anthrax despite devoting substantial financial and scientific resources to the task. But the group's repeated, unsuccessful attempts to spray liquid anthrax aerosol throughout downtown Tokyo in 1993 demonstrated that attacks designed to cause massive urban casualties were no longer in the realm of the fantastic. Then, last autumn's attacks in the United States, when professional-grade anthrax powder was sent through the mail, made clear that an individual or group has now either successfully crossed the weaponization threshold or succeeded in acquiring such material from a national weapons program.

Genetic modification of biological agents (to make them resistant to vaccines or antimicrobial drugs, for instance) probably remains beyond the capabilities of terrorist groups for the time being—although the illicit Soviet program did carry out such work and scientists have in effect done the same in research contexts. This sort of biotechnical know-how is spreading quickly.

Blocking Biology

The challenges posed by biological nonproliferation—the dual-use character of materials and equipment, the small amounts of agents initially needed and their availability from natural outbreaks, and the dynamic nature of biotechnology—guarantee that an effective strategy for biological security will look very different from the corresponding techniques used to curtail the spread of nuclear or chemical weapons. Biological security requires a different mix of nonproliferation, deterrence, and defense.

The BWC provides the legal basis for preventing the spread of biological weapons. However, the Bush administration in July 2001 rejected the draft compliance protocol to the BWC, arguing that it could jeopardize U.S. companies' proprietary information, did not provide sufficient protection for U.S. biodefense programs, and would not improve verification capabilities. By thus abandoning six years of negotiations, the United States is now not in a strong political position to pursue multilateral nonproliferation initiatives. Nevertheless, Washington should act to improve international control of dangerous pathogens, either within the BWC framework (perhaps by supporting the proposal of a like-minded ally) or in a new forum. Within the United States, the shipment of deadly diseases has been monitored since 1997. A national inventory and consolidation of facilities with dangerous strains and development of a gene library are the obvious next steps. Had these been in place in October 2001, the anthrax investigation could have proceeded more quickly.

Hundreds of culture collections containing dangerous organisms also exist around the world. Although terrorists can acquire pathogens from natural disease outbreaks, existing collections offer the easiest sources. The United States should therefore work with other nations to put into place international standards for the secure storage and transport of biological stocks that could be used for weapons. If it is no longer politically feasible for the United States to pursue such an objective within the BWC framework after having rejected the draft compliance protocol, it should consider, as Michael Barletta, Amy Sands, and Jonathan

United States with details of the biological weapons programs in Ukraine, Kazakhstan, and Uzbekistan, as well as Russia's Biopreparat program. But other key Russian facilities under the ministries of defense and health have remained closed to outsiders. Spending for the biological component of CTR has now been increased from three percent to ten percent of the total CTR budget; at a minimum Washington should maintain this level of commitment. The Bush administration should also approach the Russian government at a high level so that the United States can inventory, consolidate, secure, and ultimately acquire samples or gene sequences of Russian bioweapons strains and conduct scientific exchanges with those Russian bioweapons facilities that remain closed. A similar bilateral agreement with Uzbekistan in summer 2001 gave the United States access to Vozrozhdeniye Island in the Aral Sea, where Americans will help dismantle Soviet-era bioweapons facilities and clean up remaining live agents, including those that resulted from open-air testing.

Unstoppable?

Deterrence through the threat of retaliation has been the central strategy for preventing the use of weapons of mass destruction against the United States or its allies. And deterrence may remain effective against a state's use of biological weapons. But biological terrorism by subnational groups poses special challenges in this regard. Deterring any form of terrorism is difficult, since some terrorist groups may be unconcerned about retaliation or may hope to remain unidentified. But the biological case is especially problematic. Because some diseases incubate without symptoms for days or even weeks, tracing an attack back to its perpetrators can prove difficult. Terrorists might even hope that their attack would go unrecognized as such. For instance, when followers of the Bhagwan Shree Rajneesh infected 750 Oregonians with salmonella in 1984, it was more than a year before authorities determined that the infection had been intentionally spread.

The summer 1999 outbreak of the West Nile Virus in New York illustrates how difficult it can be in some circumstances to distinguish an intentional attack from a natural outbreak. Before the disease killed seven people in the New York City area, West Nile had never before occurred in the western hemisphere. Due to bird migration, the virus has now spread to 27 states. Although the outbreak was apparently "natural" in origin, perhaps caused by an infected traveler or mosquito transported from the Middle East, it is remarkable that in April 1999, only a few months before the outbreak, an Iraqi defector had claimed that Saddam Hussein planned to weaponize the virus.

The United States should do what it can to increase the likelihood that an attack will be attributable. An essential resource is a DNA library of as many strains of relevant biological agents as can be assembled. DNA "fingerprinting" of the agent causing an outbreak is an important forensic tool, but it is most useful if the fingerprints are already on file. (DNA fingerprinting does not identify the perpetrator, however—only the weapon used. In this sense it is more like ballistics testing than human fingerprinting.) The United States needs a DNA library not only of natural and weaponized strains within U.S. collections but also of those located in inventories around the world. Again, cooperation with the states of the former Soviet Union is important.

In addition to the difficulties of attribution, some terrorist groups may also believe themselves to be invulnerable to retaliation, may be unconcerned by it, or may even intend to provoke it. Such groups are obviously poor candidates for deterrence through the threat of retaliation. However, deterrence by denial—deterring enemies by convincing them that biological defenses are credible and that therefore an attack would be unlikely to succeed— may be a more useful tool for biological security than it was for nuclear weapons. Of course, warning and prevention are preferable to coping with the consequences of an attack, so intelligence remains vital. But as the anthrax mail attacks made clear, biological terrorism can occur with little or no warning.

Defense Without Borders

The intrinsic challenges of stopping the spread of biological weapons, and the difficulties posed for deterrence suggest that biological security strategy should lean more heavily toward defense than has been true of nuclear or chemical security strategy. Building biological defenses will of course require appropriate steps by the Defense and Justice Departments. But just as important, and for too long overlooked, biological security means improvements in domestic and international public health.

Prior to September 11, 2001, a number of analysts had in fact argued just this point: that a robust defense against bioterrorism must be based on improved public health. Because disease incubation times for some agents can be as long as weeks, the first responders to a biological attack are likely to be health care workers rather than fire, police, or military personnel. Public health surveillance for signs of unusual disease is therefore critical. Improvements in "sensitivity" and "connectivity" are required. Sensitivity means the recognition by health care workers that an illness is out of the ordinary; connectivity is the reporting of this recognition to local, state, and national authorities, and consequent timely help with diagnosis and treatment. The anthrax mail attacks tragically confirmed the importance of disease surveillance, since the speed with which doctors recognized the signs of anthrax infection determined whether patients were treated immediately or sent home, only to return later to die.

In 1999, the U.S. government initiated the Biological Preparedness and Response Program (BPRP) within the Centers for Disease Control and Prevention. This program put in place many of the crucial steps required for a domestic public health defense against bioterrorism. The BPRP created the National Pharmaceutical Stockpile (NPS) of antibiotics and other drugs that could be rapidly deployed to counter domestic outbreaks. The BPRP also funded pilot projects to bolster disease surveillance, improved capacity at the state and local levels, and sponsored research. In fiscal year 2000, the BPRP budget stood at $155 million, an amount that some experts viewed as only one-tenth the funding needed for the tasks required. But at the time, there was legitimate disagreement—indeed, there still is— over the right balance between spending to prepare for rare but potentially disastrous events such as bioterrorism, and spending to counter naturally occurring infectious diseases that are already killing many individuals every day.

Nonetheless, the October 2001 anthrax crisis would have seemed far more dire had the NPS not existed, and the understandable public tendency to begin self-medicating with

logical security strategy must cast its net far wider than traditional national security issues.

Fortunately, many of the steps that are needed to prepare for bioterrorism will also improve recognition of and responses to natural disease outbreaks. Spending on biological defenses therefore represents a win-win situation in which society benefits even if no further bioterrorist attacks take place. The West Nile outbreak again provides an example: had better communication between veterinarians and public health officials existed in early summer 1999, when crows began to die in New York City, the outbreak could have been recognized months earlier.

After the anthrax mail attacks, attitudes toward domestic public health spending to prepare for bioterrorism rapidly changed. In a discussion of how much annual spending would be required to improve preparedness, a member of Congress remarked last autumn, "One or two billion dollars? That kind of money is easier done than said right now." Indeed, the 2002 emergency supplemental appropriations bill and a separate bioterrorism bill include billions of dollars in new spending for biological defense. These bills include steps to expand the pharmaceutical stockpile, increase stores of the smallpox vaccine, strengthen state and local preparedness, and improve food safety. Domestically, the right steps are being funded. The challenge will be to sustain this commitment as the psychological distance from September 11 grows.

Admittedly, not all measures taken against bioterrorism have dual uses. The NPS antibiotic supply is unlikely to be needed to counter natural outbreaks, and storing the smallpox vaccine prepares for a disease that no longer exists in the natural world. Because antibiotics have a finite shelf life, making the expanded NPS financially sustainable may require the government to create incentives for research into extending antibiotic shelf life (something that market forces themselves may not encourage) and ensuring sufficient extra production capacity in the event of a crisis.

Other forms of research must also continue. Standard antibiotics are effective against all the bacteria that are commonly listed as biological agents, but the Soviet bioweapons program produced strains of anthrax resistant to some antibiotics, and such bioengineering will become more widely available. Vaccines are available for some viral agents, such as smallpox, but there are no effective drugs for others, such as many of the viral hemorrhagic fevers (e.g., Ebola or Marburg, which the Soviets reportedly weaponized). For the foreseeable future, therefore, we are locked into a kind of biological defensive arms race in which researchers will need to develop different or more broadly effective antimicrobial drugs and vaccines against possible new threats.

An effective defense against bioterror also requires the means to distribute vaccines and antimicrobial drugs effectively, perhaps amid the extremely challenging circumstances of public panic. The effects of public fear should not be underestimated, and the lessons from real or potential mass casualty situations involving invisible, lingering threats are sobering. Aum Shinrikyo's 1995 sarin nerve gas attack in the Tokyo subway system injured hundreds of Japanese citizens, but 5,000 sought help at hospital emergency rooms. Similarly, when the governor of Pennsylvania in 1979 suggested the evacuation of pregnant women and preschool children living within a five-mile radius of the Three Mile Island nuclear power plant—in effect recommending that a few thousand people leave the area—between one and two hundred thousand fled. Responses to these sorts of reactions should be planned before crises occur.

Beyond the Water's Edge

The U.S. government's response to last fall's bioterrorist attacks rightly highlighted the importance of domestic public health measures but showed little appreciation for the fact that no response can succeed if it stops at the nation's borders. International measures are crucial to a successful strategy for reasons as simple as arithmetic. Many diseases, such as plague and smallpox, have lengthy incubation times (an average of 2 to 3 days and 12 days, respectively). But the flight time between virtually any two cities in the world is now less than 36 hours. Carriers of smallpox, whether terrorists or unwitting victims, could transport the disease around the world before they ever showed signs of illness. Some 140 million people enter the United States by air every year. Although improvements to border protection are important, neither the United States nor other nations can hope to protect themselves exclusively by guarding their frontiers. For both humanitarian and national security reasons, outbreaks of emerging infectious diseases need to be addressed overseas as well as domestically. When possible they should be prevented, but if that does not happen, such outbreaks need to be detected, diagnosed, and controlled as quickly as possible.

Any outbreak of a highly contagious, lethal, and long-incubating disease such as smallpox poses a grave international threat. In 1972, a single religious pilgrim returned to Yugoslavia from Mecca via several days in Iraq, where he had contracted smallpox. Smallpox had spread to Iraq from Iran, where a family had introduced it after acquiring it while traveling through Afghanistan. The disease in Yugoslavia went undiagnosed while the original infected individual spread the disease to others, one of whom traveled 100 miles by bus. To contain the resulting outbreak, Tito's government vaccinated 18 million people and quarantined some 10,000 in commandeered hotels and apartment buildings ringed with troops and barbed wire. By comparison, on September 11, 2001, the United States had fewer than 15 million doses of smallpox vaccine available to a larger and far more mobile society. Epidemiological models indicate that quarantine can to some extent be traded off against vaccination to control an outbreak. But better preparation with appropriate vaccines or drugs will diminish the curtailment of civil liberties that would otherwise be needed to control contagious outbreaks.

These lessons are not limited to bioterrorist outbreaks. AIDS is a naturally occurring disease that recently emerged in the human population. It has since killed more than 450,000 Americans and 22 million people worldwide. The importance of recognizing such new contagious illnesses early, rather than after they have spread across the globe, is terribly clear. The United States must act to prevent disease outbreaks, detect those (whether natural, artificial, or ambiguous) that do occur, and ensure an effective response. The six laboratories that the Defense Department has overseas to perform research on infectious diseases are an important resource that should be further strengthened, but a broader international response is also required.

Rapid detection of outbreaks requires improvements in international disease surveillance, for which the chronically underfunded World Health Organization (WHO) is central.

ever possible on existing facilities. With its vast new spending on bioterrorism defense, the United States should allocate resources to fund these and other such serious, sustainable improvements in global public health. Whether the next threat is smallpox or a new AIDS-like epidemic disease, improving global infectious disease surveillance and response will be good for both humanitarian reasons and national security.

The United States is also creating a smallpox vaccine stockpile sufficient for all Americans. Although one recent epidemiological simulation suggests that a stockpile of 40 million doses would be sufficient to control likely outbreaks, it is difficult to predict whether a real attack would be as limited as that simulation assumes. Moreover, it should be clear from the public response to last autumn's anthrax scare that no White House will want to find itself in a position of having to explain to the American people why only some are eligible to receive vaccinations after an attack. The American people—like most people throughout the world—have for decades not been routinely vaccinated against smallpox, and the vaccine's effectiveness attenuates after ten years. The global population is now more vulnerable to smallpox than any large population has been since the illness devastated Native Americans after European explorers brought it to the Americas.

But even a stockpile for all U.S. citizens is insufficient. In the event of a smallpox outbreak overseas—whether in a NATO ally or in the developing world—humanitarian concern, international opinion, and its own self-interest will pressure the United States to shut down the outbreak and limit its spread. The WHO smallpox vaccine stockpile stands at half a million doses. The United States must either augment its national stockpile so that it can respond internationally without jeopardizing its own citizens or work with the WHO to increase international supplies. Of course, the United States should encourage other nations to do the same, but it should not allow others' inaction to prevent it from acting in its own security interest to improve global public health.

Speaking Truth in Power

An effective strategy for biological security will encompass nonproliferation, deterrence, and defense, but the required mix of these components will be very different from those in strategies for nuclear or even chemical weapons. Perhaps most strikingly, effective biological security demands that the United States act to improve global disease surveillance and response capacity—an element of "defense" that has no good nuclear or chemical analogue. Biological security also requires ongoing research to counter emerging potential threats driven by biotechnology. It is as much about public health, science, and technology as it is about military strategy.

These needs emphasize the vital role that scientific advice will continue to play in national security. Yet the U.S. government is not well equipped to harness such advice. Congress eliminated its Office of Technology Assessment in 1995, and the president's science adviser has played a diminishing White House role over the past few decades. The Office of Science and Technology Policy [OSTP], which is directed by the science adviser, is inherently weak bureaucratically. Few national security decisions naturally flow through it. As a result, the OSTP is only as strong in this arena as is the relationship between the science adviser and the president.

And too often, that relationship is weak. Both sides are to blame: too few scientists are good communicators and effective bureaucrats, and too few presidents recognize science as a priority. Nor does every policymaker appreciate that scientific integrity will at times require an unpopular answer. But as with intelligence, bending technical analysis to a particular policy risks producing deception rather than information.

The scientific and technical challenges of the coming decades will grow only more grave and incessant. Scientific complexity will be increasingly important for policymakers to understand and to communicate competently to the public. Policymakers must better incorporate scientific advice into their decision-making, or they risk falling prey to more, and more dangerous, misplaced analogies.

Christopher F. Chyba is an associate professor and codirector of Stanford University's Center for International Security and Cooperation (CISAC). He holds the endowed Carl Sagan Chair for Study of Life in the Universe at the SETI Institute (Mountain View, Calif.). Chyba served on the staff of the National Security Council in the Clinton administration.

Only a year ago, the United States was still reeling from the effects of September 11th and the subsequent distribution of "anthrax letters" through the mail.[1] Yet assessments of the bioterrorist threat generally predate these landmark events and do not offer a comprehensive analysis of the current threat level in the United States. Thus, an updated assessment of the current bioterrorist threat is presented, using the following formula for analysis: THREAT = Vulnerability × Capability × Intent. Special consideration is given to the capability aspect of the threat, with review of the major technical hurdles involved in the acquisition, production, and delivery of a prospective biological warfare agent. A scenario addressing the use of a crop-duster for the aerosol dissemination of Bacillus anthracis *spores is provided as an example. The author concludes that while the bioterrorist threat for any given individual is very small, from a policy-making standpoint a worst-case scenario must be considered. Most likely, both "high probability, low impact" and "low probability, high impact" biological attacks will be attempted over the next decade. Because vulnerabilities are established and intent and organizational capability have both been demonstrated, whether a terrorist group or individual can overcome the technical hurdles outlined may ultimately determine whether such an attack is successful.*

Introduction

Shortly after last fall's September 11th attack, a series of stories surfaced that Mohammed Atta, the leader of the attack and presumably the pilot of American Airlines flight 11—the Boeing 767 that struck the north tower of the World Trade Center—had demonstrated a persistent interest in crop-dusters over the previous year.[2] This information came prior to the subsequent anthrax mail attacks, but the fear persisted that Atta's terrorist group had somehow acquired a biological warfare (BW) agent and had been seeking a means to deliver it over an unsuspecting population.

Arguably the most curious evidence of Atta's interest was provided by Ms. Johnell Bryant, a U.S. Department of Agriculture (USDA) loan officer from Florida City, Florida, who saw Atta's picture on television after the attack and recognized him from an encounter she'd had in early 2000, some months before Atta and another member of his group began

---

*The author would like to thank Dr. Raymond A. Zilinskas for his extensive support and guidance throughout the writing of this paper.

taking flying lessons in the nearby town of Venice.[3] According to Bryant's account, Atta had come to her office requesting a $650,000 loan to "finance a twin-engine six passenger aircraft."[4] He had claimed to be an engineer and said he "wanted to [remove the seats and] build a chemical tank that would fit inside the aircraft and take up every available square inch [inside] except for where the pilot would be sitting," essentially converting a passenger plane into a modified crop-duster.

Bryant denied Atta the loan, but not because of his unusual request. Instead, she rejected him because he was not a U.S. citizen, at which point he asked her, in her words, "What would prevent him from going behind [her] desk and cutting [her] throat and making off with the millions of dollars in [the] safe?"

At this point during the encounter, Atta apparently noticed an enlarged aerial photograph of Washington, DC, hanging on Bryant's wall. The single photograph contained numerous targets of symbolic, political, and military significance, namely the structures on Independence Mall—the White House, Capitol Building, Washington Monument, and Lincoln Memorial—and the Pentagon. Atta was very interested in this photograph and offered twice to pay cash for it on the spot, but Bryant informed him that it was not for sale. He then asked her, again in her words, "How would America like it if another country destroyed that city and some of the monuments in it like the cities in his country [have] been destroyed?"

Atta was a citizen of Saudi Arabia but was Egyptian by birth. Thus, when he said "my country," perhaps he was referring to a pan-Arab entity and was hinting at the possibility of retribution for U.S. bombing in Iraq. Alternatively, he may have been referring to the November 17, 1997, terrorist attack at the Hatshepsut Temple in the Valley of the Kings near Luxor, Egypt, in which members of al-Gama'a al-Islamiyya ("the Islamic Group") shot and killed 58 foreign tourists and four Egyptians and wounded 26 others, and was suggesting that the same fate could befall similar American monuments. Al-Gama'a is among the three major Egyptian-led terrorist groups, and one of its leaders, Sheikh Omar Abdel Rahman, is currently imprisoned in the U.S. serving a life sentence for his role in the first World Trade Center bombing in 1993.

The world now knows that Atta was a part of the loose network of terrorist cells of al-Qa'ida. Apart from their Islamic fundamentalist ideology—and presumably a love for Usama bin Ladin, whom Atta had claimed "would someday be known as the world's greatest leader," according to Bryant—a common element among al-Qa'ida operatives is their training. In the al-Qa'ida training manual there is no mention of crop-dusters, nor is there discussion of chemical or biological attacks.[5] However, the extraction process of the toxins ricin and abrin for assassination purposes is described in some detail, as is the production of botulinum toxin (although never named specifically, the preparation and effects of botulinum toxin are covered in a segment entitled "Poisoning from Eating Spoiled Food"). Toxins are chemicals of biological origin, and ricin in particular, which is derived from castor beans of the abundant *Ricinus communis* plant widely used in the production of castor oil, is relatively easy to acquire.[6] Approximately one million tons of castor beans are processed for this purpose each year, yielding a waste product that is 5 percent ricin by weight.[7]

According to a series of August 2002 news reports, the Kurdish group Ansar al-Islam, which has known ties to al-Qa'ida, tested ricin on animals and possibly even a man in Northern Iraq.[8] Ricin acts on a cellular level with lethal effect such that in mouse assays,

Despite the absence of explicitly relevant information in the training manual, a number of clues exist that suggest a push by al-Qa'ida in the crop-duster direction. First, it has been learned that Atta had visited Belle Glade Municipal Airport in South Florida, which at the time was home to 8 crop-dusters, at least twice to ask questions about the aircraft,[10] mainly how to start them, how far they could fly, and what load they carried in terms of both fuel and pesticide.[11] Other groups of "Middle Eastern" men had reportedly come and gone frequently during the months preceding the September 11 attack as well, asking similar questions, attempting to take photographs and video of the cockpit (and exterior), and asking to sit in the plane. These groups, which usually consisted of 2 to 3 men, had visited the airport nearly every weekend for six or eight weeks prior to September 11th, including the weekend before the attack.[12]

Second, a search of the residence of Zacarias Moussaoui, who most security analysts believe would have been the 20th hijacker, led to the discovery of operational manuals for crop-dusting equipment.[13] Moussaoui was arrested on immigration charges on August 17, 2001, approximately three weeks before the September 11th attack, after drawing suspicion from a flight school instructor (Moussaoui had asked the instructor how to steer a commercial jetliner in mid-air but stated that he didn't need to know how to take off or land).[14] Apparently, the search also revealed that Moussaoui had downloaded information on aerosol dispersal from the Internet.

Third, Essam al-Ridi, an Egyptian-born citizen of the United States who testified as a federal witness in the trial of four men accused in the 1998 U.S. Embassy bombings in Kenya and Tanzania, has claimed that Bin Ladin himself once asked him to look into starting a crop-dusting business.[15]

Fourth, al-Qa'ida operative Ahmad Rassam, arrested in 2001 for plotting to bomb Los Angeles International Airport, testified that Bin Ladin has displayed a personal interest in dispersing biological agents from low-flying aircraft.[16]

Fifth, Abdul Hakin Murad—currently serving life in prison for his involvement in a plot to bomb 12 U.S. jetliners[17] planned by Ramzi Yousef, the man behind the first World Trade Center bombing in 1993 and who has established links with al-Qa'ida—has described plots involving the use of crop-dusters to distribute biological and chemical weapons over U.S. cities.[18]

And sixth, Johnell Bryant, the USDA loan officer, has passed a polygraph, which lends substantial credibility to her account.[19]

When compiled, this information led to a Federal Bureau of Investigation (FBI) warning about the possibility of crop-duster use by terrorists and the grounding of the approximately 5,000 crop-dusters in the U.S. on at least two separate occasions, and also raised the question of how great the threat really was, and still is, with this type of aircraft and with biological agents in general.[20]

Threat Assessment Defined

The formula for a threat assessment is Threat = Vulnerability × Capability × Intent, with threat being the probability that an adversary will inflict injury or damage. Vulnerability is the extent to which a potential target is open to attack. Capability is whether a given adversary has the technical and also the organizational ability to carry out an attack. With respect to biological weapons, the technical aspect of this component of the threat assessment consists of three major hurdles upon BW agent selection: acquisition of a pathogenic strain, production, and effective delivery. Intent is whether an adversary would actually be likely to carry out an attack. Generally speaking, this component of the assessment requires that a distinction be made between desired acquisition for deterrence, prestige, or other motivations unrelated to imminent use, and desired use in place of or in conjunction with conventional weapons or other weapons of mass destruction (WMD), namely chemical weapons (CW) and radiological and nuclear weapons.[21]

In comparison, a risk assessment follows the formula Risk = Hazard × Exposure, where risk is the magnitude and likelihood of adverse effect, hazard is the harm the agent will cause, and exposure is what population will be exposed to the agent, at what concentration, and for how long. Studies have been done that show that the risk of bioterrorism cannot be accurately assessed due to the imprecision inherent to such an undertaking.[22] Thus, using the above crop-duster scenario as a guide, the author will instead analyze the three dimensions of the threat assessment, paying specific attention to any recent changes that have taken place within each, in order to determine the current level of the bioterrorist threat in the United States.[23]

First, the vulnerability of the U.S. as a nation will be established in general terms. A discussion of capabilities will follow, addressing the following points: what agents warrant the most concern and why; who is in possession of or has access to seed cultures of pathogenic strains; and who can mass-produce and deliver them, and in what situations. Finally, the author will examine terrorist motivations in an attempt to elucidate who would actually use these agents if they could. The author will conclude with recommendations for addressing the current threat, as determined by the threat assessment.

I. Vulnerability

Vulnerability studies are most effective when addressing specific targets, for example the New York City subway system or the Capitol building, as opposed to the United States as a whole. In nonspecific terms, however, it can be stated with some certainty that this nation is in fact vulnerable on a number of levels.[24]

With open borders to goods and people and unregulated interstate movement, the transport of key personnel, equipment and pathogens is possible both into and within the country, despite the concerted efforts of officials and others in the wake of September 11th to tighten physical security along our borders and nationwide. Add to this the fact that the U.S. public health system has essentially been a victim of its own successes. For example, advances in infectious disease management, particularly heralded by the advent of new and improved antibiotics, led to the steadily improving general health of civilians of the middle and upper socioeconomic strata over the past few decades. Neglect in the form of budget cuts followed, leaving the nation largely unguarded against both emerging natural biological

those diseases most likely to be encountered in such an attack and at present have not been extensively trained to overcome this shortfall. And critical targeting information, for example the schematics of symbolic structures in the US, is available both in the open literature and over the Internet, making a potential terrorist's task that much easier.[25]

The hypothetical crop-duster scenario serves to illustrate these points. At that time, Washington DC would have been essentially defenseless against such a threat. While flight restrictions did exist over the metropolitan area (more on this later), crop-dusters are designed to fly low to the ground, below radar coverage of the Federal Aviation Administration (FAA).[26] Thus, it would have been feasible for an aircraft to take off from a remote location and proceed below radar coverage to the target area regardless of any restrictions, or even if radar identification had been made as it was on September 11th. Also, aerial photographs and maps, along with meteorological information vital for the delivery of a BW agent, were (and still are) commonly available in the public domain. And the civilian population was vulnerable: front-line physicians weren't aware of the presenting symptoms caused by the classical biological agents that would most likely be used in an attack, procedures for the rapid mobilization of national pharmaceutical stockpiles were untested, and the public wasn't psychologically ready.

The psychological component of bioterrorism is not to be underestimated because in any attack, biological or otherwise, mass hysteria has the potential to do far more damage than the agent itself. As just one example of this, the emergency department of Tel Aviv's Bellinson Medical Center reported that in 1991, during a stretch of a little over a month in which 39 modified Iraqi SCUD missiles reached Israeli terrain and 23 missile alerts were issued in Tel Aviv, the vast majority of patients who presented to the emergency department suffered from either acute psychological (anxiety) reaction or false atropine injection.[27] Appropriately, the ability to generate public panic has been specified by the Strategic Planning Workgroup of the Centers for Disease Control and Prevention (CDC) as one necessary criterion in order for a prospective agent to be considered a "high priority" threat to national security, as delineated by the workgroup's Category A listing of critical biological agents.[28]

In sum, the recently-released National Strategy for Homeland Security perhaps best states the inherent vulnerability of the US: "[o]ne fact dominates all homeland security threat assessments: terrorists are strategic actors. They choose their targets deliberately based on the weaknesses they observe in our defenses and our preparedness.... Our society presents an almost infinite array of potential targets that can be attacked through a variety of methods."[29]

II. Capability

Conceding that the United States is in fact vulnerable as a nation, the next question is whether a terrorist organization possesses the technical and organizational ability to conduct an attack. In order to attain a technical capability, four steps must be taken: an appropriate agent must be selected, a pathogenic strain of that agent must be acquired, the strain must be used to produce a sufficient amount of the agent in question, and the agent must be effectively delivered.

In terms of the hypothetical crop-duster scenario, before addressing these four points it first must be established that the interest expressed by Atta's group had in fact been with the dissemination of a BW agent in mind. It is important to point out that quite possibly Atta had been considering the crop-duster for something other than the dispersal of a BW agent.

The delivery of a CW agent may have been intended, for example the nerve agent sarin, which killed 12, injured over 1000, and led to the flooding of hospitals and emergency departments (again illustrating the significance of mass hysteria) in the 1995 Tokyo subway attack carried out by the doomsday cult Aum Shinrikyo ("Supreme Truth").[30] A 300-gallon crop-duster hopper tank, the smallest size available, would still be large enough to hold more than a ton of sarin, which according to Pentagon calculations is enough to kill 10,000 people.[31] In 1952, the U.S. BW program compared the effects of sarin with botulinum toxin, an apparent staple of today's suspected BW programs (as discussed below), and found that while botulinum toxin was more toxic upon inhalation, sarin was the more efficient agent in terms of its ability to both withstand the physical stressors of dispersal and create a lethal effect with minimal exposure.[32] Chemical agents are generally easier to produce than biological agents, and precursors for classical CW agents like hydrogen cyanide, which could be used for crude reparations such as those demonstrated in the al-Qa'ida videos discovered during the summer of 2002, are widely available.[33] When so-called toxic warfare is considered, which encompasses the use as a weapon of readily and legally accessible industrial chemicals and waste, this availability increases exponentially.[34] Chemical agents have the drawback of being highly susceptible to the effects of the wind, however, and the universal drawbacks to crop-duster use discussed below apply as well.

Another possibility is that Atta had planned to use the plane as a gasoline bomb, much like the airliners in the September 11th attack (airliners use a kerosene-based jet fuel, but the effect witnessed on 9/11 is essentially analogous to what would be expected with the same amount of gasoline). An Air Tractor 502–A, the prototypical aerial applicator worldwide, holds about 1,900 liters of liquid agent for dispersal and 800 liters of fuel.[35] Thus, if the hopper tank were filled with fuel as well, that plus the fuel in the tank would create a devastating explosion upon impact.[36] This possibility is particularly noteworthy because in light of 9/11 there was, at least prior to the anthrax letters, some renewed doubt as to whether terrorists were preparing to "cross the threshold" to WMD or whether the trend toward the use of conventional weapons—in line with what had previously been the most costly terrorist attack on U.S. soil in terms of human life, the Oklahoma City Bombing of 1995—would continue.

But assuming that the intention had been to employ a biological agent, a post-September 11th report by Dr. Christos Tsonas, an ER physician at Holy Cross Hospital in Fort Lauderdale, Florida, might offer a clue as to what agent Atta's group had intended to use.[37] Tsonas had seen two men in June, about three months before the attack, both of whom had identified themselves as pilots. One of these men presented with a lesion on his leg which he claimed had appeared after bumping into a suitcase two months earlier. The affected area, a well-demarcated dark lesion just less than an inch wide with raised red borders, did not appear to be a bruise, however.

The physician removed the dry scab, cleaned the wound, prescribed the antibiotic Keflex, and discharged the patient. At the time, he had viewed the bump explanation with

all term for the inflammation of connective tissue, often of bacteriological origin.

After 9/11, the prescribed antibiotic was found among the personal belongings of hijacker Ahmed Alhaznawi of United Airlines Flight 93, which crashed in Pennsylvania. The man with him that day in the ER is believed to have been hijacker Ziad al-Jarrah, the suspected pilot of Flight 93. Apparently, the hijackers were well-dressed and had used their own names during their visit to the ER.

FBI officials showed Tsonas pictures of these two men, and he made positive identification. The FBI then gave Tsonas a copy of his own chart, and upon reviewing the case he offered that the lesion had been consistent with cutaneous anthrax. This was after the anthrax mail attacks had begun, the first letter of which had been to American Media Corporation in nearby Boca Raton, and Tsonas had been studying up on the disease. A subsequent review by experts from the Johns Hopkins Center for Civilian Biodefense Strategies verified Tsonas' impression, concluding that a diagnosis of cutaneous anthrax was "the most probable and coherent interpretation of the data available."[38]

In a separate report, a Delray Beach, Florida pharmacist claimed that Atta and another hijacker, Marwan al-Shehhi, had asked him for something to treat infections on Atta's hands.[39] Other circumstantial links between the hijackers and the anthrax mail attacks exist as well, including the close proximity of American Media to the hijackers' places of residence and the fact that Atta had rented his apartment from a woman whose husband was employed by the company. Anthrax, the disease resulting from *Bacillus anthracis* infection, occurs in three forms: cutaneous, gastrointestinal, and inhalational. While the major concern from a BW standpoint is the inhalational form of the disease, skin infections might offer a clue that the agent had been handled.

Ultimately, the FBI searched the cars, apartments and possessions of all of the known hijackers with negative results.[40] If some of the hijackers had been exposed to anthrax, it seems likely that the FBI would have found something; it also seems likely that any data points discussed here are an entirely separate debate from the anthrax letters. Regardless, these interesting coincidences—and more importantly the mail attacks themselves—offer a direction in terms of what might be the BW agent of choice in the terrorism sphere.

Agent Selection

The world seems on the surface to be filled with potential BW agents, but the truth is that many can be ruled out based on (1) access, and (2) infectiousness and pathogenicity.[41] The NATO Handbook on the Medical Aspects of NBC Defensive Operations lists 39 potential BW agents, but of these only a small number can be cultivated and dispersed effectively.[42] Thus, accessible and dangerous agents can be further limited to those that can be effectively produced and delivered. Other considerations include hardiness (environmental stability), resistance (e.g., to host immune defenses), senescence (aging characteristics), viability by aerosol, whether the agent is susceptible to current detection methods, availability of prophylactic and therapeutic measures, and contagiousness (the ability to spread from human to human, which may be seen as a desirable or undesirable trait).

In 1994, a Russian panel of BW experts listed in ranking order 11 agents "very likely to be used" in an attack based on the stringent evaluation of 10 criteria for efficient and effective BW use (see Figure 1.).[43] This list may also effectively represent what is available on the international market as a result of the Soviet Union's collapse, because most of the agents listed are known to have been weaponized, or suitably developed for use in a weapons system, by the former Soviet Union, with typhus and influenza being the only exceptions (typhus, however, is known to have been researched by the Soviets).[44]

Figure 1.

Agents most likely to be used in a BW attack according to the Criterion Rating

1. Variola major (smallpox)
2. *Bacillus anthracis* (anthrax)
3. *Yersinia pestis* (plague)
4. Botulinum toxin (botulism)
5. *Francisella tularensis* (tularemia)
6. *Burkholderia mallei* (glanders)
7. *Rickettsia typhi* (typhus)
8. *Coxiella burnetii* (Q fever)
9. Venezuelan Equine Encephalitis (VEE)
10. Marburg virus
11. Influenza virus

More recently in the year 2000, the Centers for Disease Control and Prevention's (CDC) Strategic Planning Workgroup devised a list of three categories of critical biological agents based in part on intelligence on the credibility of the threat each one poses, as determined by its toxicity, ease of production and delivery, and transmissibility, as well as the potential public health impact of its use.[45] This last consideration includes the effects of social disruption and panic, emphasizing yet again the mass hysteria effect discussed above. Threat Categories are denoted as A, B, and C, with Category "A" Agents deemed to be the greatest threat (see Figure 2.).

Figure 2.

Category "A" agents as listed by the CDC

1. Variola major
2. *Bacillus anthracis*
3. *Yersinia pestis*
4. Botulinum toxin
5. *Francisella tularensis*
6. Filoviruses and Arenaviruses

as Bolivian and Argentinean hemorrhagic fevers and Lassa fever.[47]

Of the seven state sponsors of terrorism, as designated by the U.S. State Department, at least five are suspected of having active BW programs: Iran, Iraq, Libya, North Korea, and Syria.[48] It has also been suggested that Cuba and Sudan, which round out the State Department's list, possess at least some capability in this area.[49] So-called failed states such as Afghanistan and Chechnya are also important to consider in the context of terrorism sponsorship as well as BW development, as experiences in these locations have shown. Discussion here will be limited to the five designated state sponsors listed above, however, with the goal being to gain some insight into what agents might be available through what state programs and to what terrorist groups.

For the record, it must first be stated that there is no evidence to date that any state has supplied BW capabilities to a terrorist organization. Regardless, it seems wise to prepare for this eventuality, and a superficial analysis of the biological agents thought to have been developed by these states of concern therefore appears to be in order.[50] It is believed that Iran has produced anthrax and botulinum toxin, as well as foot and mouth disease (a potentially devastating anti-livestock agent) and trichothecene mycotoxins (produced by fungi mainly of the *Fusarium* sp. and implicated in the alleged "yellow rain" attacks in Southeast Asia during the 1970s and early 1980s).[51] Following the Gulf War, it was revealed that Iraq had weaponized anthrax and botulinum toxin, along with ricin, aflatoxin (a hepatotoxic carcinogen produced by fungi of the genus *Aspergillus*), and wheat cover smut (an anti-plant agent).[52] Iraq had also researched camelpox and possibly plague—both of which will be discussed below—brucellosis, enterovirus 70 (a.k.a. hemorrhagic conjunctivitis), rotavirus, *Clostridium perfringens*, and trichothecene mycotoxins.[53] The current state of Iraq's BW program is unknown. Also unknown is what agents have been developed by Libya.[54] North Korea is thought to have worked with smallpox, anthrax, plague, and botulinum toxin, as well as typhus (number seven of the Russian expert list), yellow fever, typhoid, cholera, and tuberculosis.[55] And Syria is believed to have developed anthrax, botulinum toxin, and ricin.[56] A trend emerges from the above outline, namely that anthrax appears to be a primary component of every BW program, as does botulinum toxin.

Focusing on Iraq's list—derived from both the fourth Full, Final, and Complete Disclosure of the Iraqi National Biological Program compiled through 1996 for the United Nation's Special Committee (UNSCOM) as part of UN Security Council Resolution 687, the conditional cease-fire agreement that effectively ended the Gulf War, as well as from other governmental and nongovernmental evaluations—four agents that topped both the Russian expert list and the CDC list are prominent in this compendium as well: *Bacillus anthracis*, botulinum toxin, camelpox virus, and *Yersinia pestis*, the causative agent of bubonic and pneumonic plague.[57] Three of the four are classical BW agents, but why camelpox?

In terms of estimating the potential threat of Iraq's BW program, the camelpox virus has to be seen as representing smallpox, or Variola major. Both camelpox and smallpox are orthopoxviruses, a family of 11 closely-related DNA viruses. The central region of the orthopox family's genome is usually conserved from species to species because it houses genes essential for replication, while the outer ends, which contain variable instructions for host targeting, infectiousness, and resistance, tend to vary. The outer regions of the camelpox and smallpox virus genomes, however, are remarkably similar.[58] This close resemblance suggests to some that the Iraqis may have intended to develop an "ethnic weapon" from camelpox as a result of the selective pressures of mass production or even genetic engineering that in theory would affect populations not routinely exposed to camels more than the populations of Iraq, where the disease is endemic and where inhabitants presumably have developed or could easily develop antibodies to the virus. Others theorize that camelpox could be used to fill the evolutionary niche vacated by smallpox.[59] The main theory, however, is that in light of this close resemblance camelpox was used as a simulant for smallpox, offering the Iraqis a model for everything from the formulation, production, and delivery of the virus to the manipulation of its genome.

There are multiple points corroborating this final idea, all of which are circumstantial.[60] In 1994, UNSCOM inspectors discovered a large freeze-dryer, used to make biological products stable over long periods of time (and also to convert wet agents to dry form, a process discussed in some detail below), labeled with the Arabic word for "smallpox." The discovery was made at the maintenance shop of the State Establishment for Medical Appliances on the outskirts of Baghdad. Iraqi officials ensured the inspectors that the freeze-dryer was used for lyophilization of vaccinia, the smallpox vaccine virus, and not smallpox itself, an explanation which was accepted at the time but later called into question when after close to 4 years of steadfast denial Iraq finally admitted to the existence of an extensive BW program. That same year, the Defense Intelligence Agency reported that according to an unidentified scientist of the former Soviet BW program, Russia had provided both Iraq and North Korea with smallpox technology in the early 1990s. In the wake of Iraq's disclosure, the state relinquished a number of documents related to BW, among which were at least 3 papers on smallpox. Later, another document was recovered listing smallpox as one of the diseases against which Iraqi troops were being vaccinated in 1997. This information correlated with a 1991 report issued by the Armed Forces Medical Intelligence Center that the bloodwork of 8 out of 69 Iraqi enemy prisoners of war (EPWs) had revealed neutralizing antibodies against smallpox, indicating that they may have been vaccinated against the disease (these same blood samples had revealed protective antibodies against anthrax as well). This information, along with whatever intelligence had been amassed in the classified realm, led the CIA in 1998 to inform White House officials that Iraq had most likely been in possession of the smallpox virus, and that stockpiles of this agent had probably been effectively hidden from UNSCOM inspectors throughout the nineties.

If, for argument's sake, camelpox is taken to represent smallpox in the Iraqi arsenal, the core list of biological agents becomes *B. anthracis*, Variola major, botulinum toxin, and *Y. pestis*. It should be noted that this list reflects North Korea's suspected arsenal as well. Although any one of a number of agents could potentially be used for illicit purposes, the agents on the Russian expert list, narrowed down first to the CDC list and then further to these four agents, appear to be the most serious threats as far as impact is concerned. These are low probability but high impact threats, and because of the potentially devastating effects of their use, as well as limited time and resources, these threats presently warrant the focus of U.S. preparatory efforts despite the fact that other agents may still be used in lower impact scenarios, as discussed below.[61]

characteristics in terms of effective dissemination.[63] An inhaled dose of 5 to 10 thousand spores is usually enough to cause infection, though the anthrax letter attacks suggest that this number may be much lower with respect to elderly or immunocompromised victims. There are approximately 5×10^{10} spores per gram in a dry, weapons-grade formulation of this agent. Therefore, one gram of weaponized spores is theoretically capable of generating 5×10^6 casualties if evenly dispersed over a densely populated city. In reality, a substantial portion of the payload would not reach the target population, but even if only 1 in 10,000 spores were to do so, an efficiency rate of 0.01%, given appropriate atmospheric conditions the release of one kilogram of anthrax spores over a large population could theoretically cause 500,000 casualties. Mortality for untreated inhalational anthrax is estimated to be about 80 percent, though it must be noted that the anthrax letters led to a mortality rate that was only half of that number,[64] presumably due to heightened awareness and rapid diagnosis and treatment of the disease following identification of the index case.

The smallpox virus would be very difficult for terrorists to acquire, but due to its contagiousness, disfiguring nature and estimated 30 percent lethality among unvaccinated individuals it has become the representative nightmare scenario as far as biological weapons are concerned. Unlike anthrax, Y. pestis and the other bacterial agents considered potential BW threats don't produce spores and thus require adequate formulation to prevent rapid die-off upon release, even under favorable meteorological conditions.[65] The pre-1969 U.S. biological weapons program demonstrated that effectively producing and dispensing Y. pestis is extremely challenging.[66] Similarly, scientists of the U.S. program learned that botulinum toxin is a very difficult substance to implement in any type of large-scale battlefield scenario because, like most toxins, its protein nature hinders stabilization and effective dissemination via aerosol. However, it is important to note that botulinum toxin, the most toxic substance known to science and more than 100 times more toxic than the nerve agent VX, was the agent of choice in Iraq's arsenal: as far as is known, the Iraqis deployed far more SCUD missiles and artillery shells armed with botulinum toxin than with any other agent, including anthrax spores.[67]

The other end of the spectrum, the "high probability, low impact" agents, generally consists of food- and waterborne pathogens such as Salmonella, Shigella, and Vibrio species, Listeria monocytogenes, and Bacillus cereus. The toxin SEB (staphylococcal enterotoxin B) might be added to this group for simplification. These agents are for the most part easy to acquire, particularly because they are often available in unprotected hospital labs. They are also cheap and easy to produce and use, and such use would conceivably equate to a public reaction equivalent to the anthrax letter attacks despite their generally non-lethal quality. There is a historical precedent for the illicit use of this type of agent. In 1984, the religious cult the Rajneeshees used a crude preparation of Salmonella typhimurium to contaminate a number of restaurant salad bars in the Dalles, Oregon, with the ultimate goal of swaying a local election.[68] This was the first known bioterrorist attack in the United States, and resulted in 751 illnesses but no deaths.[69] A similar agent, Shigella dysenteriae type 2, was used in 1996 to contaminate a number of muffins that were then placed in the employees' cafeteria of St. Paul Medical Center in Dallas, Texas. Hospital workers subsequently received an email saying to help themselves to the muffins, which many did, resulting in 12 illnesses and 4 hospitalizations.[70] 2 years later, Diane Thompson, a former employee of the hospital's laboratory, admitted to stealing and using a stock culture of *Shigella* for this and was sentenced to 20 years in prison.

A comparison of these 2 cases manifests the need to distinguish between *bioterrorism* and *biocriminality*. For the purposes of this assessment, bioterrorism will be defined as "the use of pathogens or toxins against human, animal, or plant populations by a terrorist group to achieve political, social, or religious aims."[71] The Rajneeshee incident is a good example.[72] Biocriminality, as was seen in the Diane Thompson case, will be defined as "the use of pathogens or toxins by an individual or group to attack human, animal, or plant populations for reasons of greed, blackmail, revenge, or other apolitical objectives."[73] It should be noted that it is often challenging to make this distinction.

The high probability, low impact agents serve as a reminder that the deadliest weapons are not necessarily the ones most likely to be used. What is the desired effect? What agents have been successfully used in the past to generate this effect? And what agents are the most accessible?

Acquisition

Agent acquisition is the first step toward establishing a capability, and as such presents a significant technical hurdle that must be overcome in order for an attack to be possible. While many potential sources for pathogens and toxins exist, some knowledge of and familiarity with a given agent is generally required in order to successfully procure it. Some locations where prospective BW agents may be available are (1) the environment, including soil, buried animals, and infected animals and humans; (2) U.S. culture collections, for example the American Type Culture Collection (ATCC); (3) foreign culture collections; (4) BW facilities of the former Soviet Union; (5) incubators and private culture collections housed in hospital microbiology laboratories, commercial medical laboratories, and academic laboratories; (6) military laboratories; and (7) vendors (see Figure 3.).

Figure 3.

Examples of BW agent acquisition by terrorist groups[74]

Rajneeshees: purchased "bactrol disks," used in quality control and which contain *S. tphimurium*, from a medical supply company through a legitimate medical laboratory

Aum Shinrikyo: obtained *C. botulinum* spores from soil, *B. anthracis* from a Japanese lab, and attempted to secure Ebola from victims of an outbreak in Zaire

Acquiring pathogens from the environment is a possibility, but attempts to do so would likely be ineffective unless the perpetrator possessed a firm understanding of certain epidemiological and microbiological techniques. Techniques described in the open literature could be employed to recover *B. anthracis* spores, for example, from the soil, where they exist in nature.[75] The monitoring of online surveillance sites such as ProMED for evidence of animal and human outbreaks could offer some direction to the search, as the soil

Buried animals are another potential source of pathogens in the environment. In most industrialized countries, however, animals that succumb to anthrax, for example, are incinerated.[79] In other countries, if the number of dead animals overruns the capacity for incineration these cadavers may be buried in mass graves, but the locations of these graves are for the most part unpublicized such that only a few local inhabitants and officials know exactly where they might be found.[80] Presumably, an outsider asking questions about or digging in the vicinity of one of these graves would raise some suspicion, but if by chance he or she were able to dig up the site without being discovered the probability of collecting a sample containing viable organisms would still be quite low, because most pathogens are germinating cells and thus die soon after the host itself dies.[81] Even anthrax spores would be difficult to recover because the vegetative cells that cause death would be rapidly killed by resultant putrefaction and acidification, in most cases before spores could be formed.[82]

Briefly, it can be added that some perpetrators might travel to hot areas and pose as health care workers in order to gain access to certain agents. The precedent for this is what is believed to have been an unsuccessful attempt by members of Aum Shinrikyo to acquire Ebola virus from the blood of victims in Africa.[83]

The American Type Culture Collection (ATCC) and other U.S. culture collections contain seed stocks of a number of dangerous agents. In the mid-1980s, the Iraqi government purchased multiple strains from the ATCC which were subsequently developed into BW, an exchange which ultimately led to increased restrictions on the selling of pathogens from these collections. Then in 1996, trained microbiologist and anti-government Christian Patriot Larry Wayne Harris acquired three vials of freeze-dried *Y. pestis* from the ATCC as well, resulting in new legislation enacted by the U.S. Congress that made the transfer of certain pathogens across state borders without CDC clearance a criminal offense.[84] These two steps have made it more difficult, but not impossible, to attain pathogens from U.S. culture collections without proper credentials. Further, even if the system were to be subverted from within, for example by an employee of one of the organizations listed with the CDC, this action would now leave a substantial paper trail that would presumably lead to the rapid identification of the perpetrator (and that might therefore serve as a deterrent to acquisition in this fashion as well). The major weakness of the present system is that it does not regulate secondary shipment, such that if someone were to request a subculture from a colleague or acquaintance the transfer would probably go unnoticed.

In addition to the U.S. collections, there are approximately 1200 culture collections throughout the world, for example the Persian Culture Collection in Tehran, Iran. Very little open source information is available on the security of these facilities or the precautions they take to screen purchasers (if in fact they take any precautions at all).

Facilities of the former Soviet Union such as those that were once a part of Biopreparat, a network of approximately 50 pharmaceutical complexes secretly engaged in the development and production of biological weapons during the Cold War, may still house a number of already weaponized biological agents. The majority of these facilities have poor security, and most scientists working at them are poorly paid. Thus, a terrorist group might try to break in and steal certain cultures or attempt to bribe a scientist already on the inside to commit the act on its behalf. In April 1999, Agence France Presse reported that the terrorist group Islamic Jihad had obtained biological and chemical weapons from one of these facilities, and although this report has never been verified it serves to illustrate the potential for such acquisition.[85] More recently, a man was arrested in November 2002 after entering the Scientific Center of Quarantine and Zoonotic Infections, a former Soviet BW research facility in Almaty, Kazakhstan; allegedly, the man intended to steal vials and cultures of pathogens from the Center.[86]

Hospital microbiology laboratories are often unlocked and unguarded, as are the incubators inside these laboratories. Lab request forms identify each sample that passes through the laboratory in terms of its source, the organism recovered, and the antibiotic sensitivities of that organism, offering a potential roadmap to those in search of more dangerous or resistant pathogens. Further, most clinical microbiologists maintain private culture collections in unlocked cupboards or freezers. Hospital labs are not only accessible to staff, such as Diane Thompson of the *Shigella* incident, but ostensibly to outsiders as well, especially if the outsiders are disguised as hospital staff and act familiar with the setting. Academic laboratories at university hospitals are particularly noteworthy because their research is often highlighted on university websites and brochures, such that a terrorist group could potentially locate a specific pathogen based on knowledge of a given facility's work. However, the majority of these labs are protected by coded entry systems. While outsider access is generally limited by tight physical security, commercial clinical laboratories or reference laboratories containing a wide array of pathogens could potentially be targeted from within. As a final point, facilities within the pharmaceutical industry—for example Allergan, which is known to work with and produce botulinum toxin—could theoretically be targeted as well.

Military laboratories are generally considered in the context of state sponsorship, i.e., a state allowing a terrorist organization access to the pathogens in its lab. In addition, military laboratories in the U.S. might be considered potential sources of BW agents. For example, multiple specimens of anthrax spores, Ebola virus and other pathogens have over the past decade been reported missing from the U.S. Army Medical Research Institute of Infectious Diseases (USAMRIID), which took over facilities at Fort Detrick after the U.S. offensive BW program was abandoned under President Richard Nixon, a fact that suggests at least some level of vulnerability at this type of site.[87]

Vendor sources of potential BW agents can be legitimate, for example agricultural or chemical supply companies, or what would generally be considered illegitimate (albeit legal in many cases). As an example of the latter, in 1994 and 1995 four members of the anti-government group the Minnesota Patriots Council were convicted under the United States' 1989 Biological Weapons Anti-Terrorism Act for conspiring to kill law enforcement officials using ricin.[88] Years previously, these men had responded to a March 1991 advertisement in the right-wing *CBA Bulletin* for a "Silent Tool of Justice... Castor Beans... Silent Death... Including instructions for extracting the deadly poison 'Ricin' from Castor Beans."[89] Such extraction, which requires chemicals generally available in the average grocery store, was achieved by these individuals despite a lack of education and expertise: FBI analysis of the group's recovered stockpile revealed 0.7 grams of powdered ricin of 5 percent strength, estimated by USAMRIID to theoretically contain 129 lethal doses if evenly and effectively distributed.[90]

operative in Prague have gone unconfirmed by the CIA, FBI, and British Intelligence,[91] and reports of training links between Iraq and al-Qa'ida—mainly from a defector who served in Saddam Hussein's Fedayeen, one of Iraq's most brutal militias—are uniformly devoid of information pertaining to the transfer of agents or other sensitive materials.[92] As for al-Qa'ida itself, there is evidence of what had been a limited infrastructure for the development of BW agents in Afghanistan prior to U.S. military operations in the region.[93] In March 2002, it was learned that U.S. troops had discovered a laboratory under construction in southern Afghanistan intended for the production of *B. anthracis* and other deadly agents, a conclusion deduced from documents and equipment found at the site (although no traces of any agents themselves were found).[94] That same month, it was reported that trace amounts of both anthrax spores and ricin were found at 5 or 6 of the approximately 110 sites searched throughout Afghanistan, but that the amounts recovered were so small that they may have existed naturally in the environment and regardless were not significant enough to make any accurate determinations.[95] As a final point, it should be noted that outside Afghanistan, for example among the individual terrorist cells, the extent of al-Qa'ida's capability is unknown.[96]

Production

Assuming Atta's group were somehow able to acquire a *B. anthracis* seed stock, the next question is whether it could have successfully produced a substantial amount of spores.[97]

The initial consideration is acquiring the expertise, whether from imported, hired, or homegrown scientists, to carry out such a task. The major concern with respect to imported or hired scientific expertise, dubbed "brain drain," is the former Soviet BW program once again, which employed approximately 65,000 scientists.[98] For example, a December 1998 report by the *New York Times* stated that Iran had recruited at least five Russian BW experts by offering them $5000 a month for their services (versus their regular salary of $100 a month).[99] South Africa's apartheid-era BW program, Project Coast, also trained a number of scientists and therefore must be considered a potential source of brain drain as well. It has been reported for example that Wouter Basson, the program's alleged ringleader, made 5 trips to Libya for unknown reasons after Coast was dissolved in the 1990s.[100] While these examples illustrate the potential transfer of knowledge to states and not necessarily terrorist organizations, the concept is the same.

It should be remembered that these scientists might be pursued simply as consultants. For example, it has been reported that on at least one occasion during a trip to Russia, Aum Shinrikyo chief engineer Kyohide Hayakawa attempted to contact former Biopreparat deputy Anatony Vorobyov in order to learn the technological secrets of the former Soviet BW program.[101] Theoretically, this approach could also be carried out over the Internet, enabling a given terrorist group to benefit from a scientist's technical know-how without physically recruiting him or her, but there is no evidence for or against such distant collaboration at present. Information on how to grow many of the bacterial and viral pathogens on the CDC list—as well as information on aerosolized microbes, dispersal systems, and so on—is widely available in the public domain.[102] And over the past few decades, the number of trained microbiologists has been steadily increasing worldwide, making this information particularly useful to an ever growing number of individuals able and possibly willing to misuse it.

The equipment required to produce biological weapons is widely available on the open market because of its dual-use nature, meaning that the same materials and thus knowledge required for the peaceful development and production of commercial products like food additives, pesticides, pharmaceuticals, and vaccines can be diverted toward the production of biological weapons with relative ease. For example, the large-scale production of the biopesticide *Bacillus thuringiensis* reflects in striking detail the manufacture of *Bacillus anthracis* as a weapon in terms of both equipment and methodology. Dual-use equipment is notoriously difficult to identify and track, and such varied techniques as those used to produce live vaccines, single-celled protein, and even beer can be applied to BW production.

Equipment doesn't necessarily have to be acquired in order to produce BW, however, as illustrated by the late 1971 and 1972 group RISE (an acronym for the Reconstruction—the meaning of the "I" remains uncertain—of Society Extermination).[103] Formed by teenagers Allen Schwandner and Steven Pera (along with five other friends), RISE apparently sought, at least initially, to wipe out all of mankind with the exception of its own members and a few friends.[104] Pera, a laboratory assistant in a Chicago hospital at the time, used the hospital's equipment to successfully grow small amounts of *C. botulinum*, *Neisseria meningitidis*, *Salmonella typhi*, *Shigella sonnei*, and *Corynebacterium diphtheriae* for this purpose (note the prominence of high probability, low impact agents in Pera's collection).[105] The group was discovered shortly thereafter, before any further preparations could be made and before any specific attack was planned.

The primary concern in terms of production is the successful manufacture of an aerosolizable agent that can be delivered in 1 to 5 micron size particles.[106] This is the desired range because particles of this size are readily absorbed in the lungs upon inhalation, but it should be added that larger particles up to 20 microns in size may embed in the upper respiratory tract with significant effect as well. Because biological weapons are not volatile like chemical weapons, the endpoint of production is either a wet or dry agent. As a rule, the preparation of a dry agent, like the anthrax spores used in the mail attacks, requires more elaborate equipment than that of a wet agent.

Some viruses are sufficiently hardy to be used in either wet or dry preparations, especially smallpox, but again the acquisition of a seed stock is a nearly insurmountable obstacle to acquiring a capability with this particular agent. Bacteria are generally easier to produce than viruses because viruses are most often grown in either fertilized eggs or cell culture in order to provide the host machinery they require for replication.[107] At least one alternative to these technically demanding production techniques does exist, however, that is far more basic and would allow for the propagation of a virus with very little technical expertise.

As far as bacterial production is concerned, if a virulent strain of *B. anthracis* were acquired, it could probably then be cultured and propagated fairly easily in a home laboratory because it grows well in commonly available nutrient media at an achievable temperature. Although it is technically more demanding to convert these germinating cells to

room temperature or 6 weeks at 4 degrees Celsius, while *B. anthracis* might survive a month.[108]

A large financial investment is not required to accomplish such a task. A 2-liter batch fermenter costs approximately $1400, while a 2-liter continuous fermenter, which yields almost ten times as much product per volume of culture as a batch fermenter, can currently be purchased on the open market for approximately $5500.[109] For less than $10,000 then, a scientist or group could in fact establish an effective production capability. In order to gain insight into the feasibility of such efforts, in the late 1990s the CIA built a much larger capacity fermenter for approximately $1 million with parts purchased from hardware stores and other suppliers in the public domain.[110] Due to the lack of signatures associated with BW development, this project remained hidden from both the media and the public until the CIA chose to disclose it, illustrating the ease with which a group might keep such an endeavor secret.

The major technical hurdle to aerosol delivery of a basic wet preparation is overcoming the rapid clogging of disseminating nozzles upon initiation of dispersal. Further, the bulk of agent successfully extruded before clogging forms heavy particles that fall innocuously to the ground. Regardless, this approach can in theory generate mass casualties. It should be added that a very low tech approach precluding the need for a fermenter also exists that might offer a terrorist a proportionally lower chance of success, but a chance nonetheless.

The initial wet preparation can be taken a step further in two separate ways. It can either be suspended in a "formulation" of adjuvants, preservatives, and other chemicals, or dried and then milled to attain the proper-sized particles. Either of these processes demands much more technical ability but yields a far better agent in terms of ease of dissemination and overall effect. The resulting agent can also be stored for much longer periods of time in either case. Dry agents can be taken an additional step further and specially formulated as well, as was the case in the anthrax letters, to prevent clumping due to electrostatic forces. This clumping results in large particles that are either blocked by the mucociliary response of the respiratory tract or fall harmlessly to the ground.

After the Gulf War, it was learned that the Iraqi program, which had been operating for at least 5 years and was very well-funded, had only deployed BW arms in wet formulations despite the possession of dryers and grinders.[111] This effectively illustrates the extent of the leap in going from wet to dry. It must be recognized, however, that years of trial-and-error time toward accomplishing this feat have since passed, and in that time an abundance of information has emerged in the public domain that would prove useful in such an undertaking. Moreover, it has now been demonstrated to the world that this technical hurdle can be overcome.

The anthrax letters of 2001 proved that the technical demands of dry preparation, formulation, and aerosol dissemination can be met, conceivably outside the construct of a state-level program. Regardless of who or what group was responsible, these technical hurdles appear to be eroding. In addition, the letters demonstrated the extensive impact that even a limited threat can have: at the outset of the research process for this writing, the price tag on 23 CDC-confirmed cases and 5 deaths was approximately $6 billion. This profound impact may lead to what's known as a demonstrator effect, i.e., an increased prevalence of copycat letters. Such has indeed been the case, as illustrated by the increased number of hoaxes witnessed in the wake of the mail attacks: while over 400 anthrax threats were documented from March of 1998 to September 11, 2001, more than 1500 threats or hoaxes were recorded from September 11th through mid-2002.[112] While these hoaxes were in many cases handled routinely or even dismissed altogether prior to the events of last fall, such a lax response is no longer possible. Thus, hoaxes now categorically serve as a significant drain on public health resources, an effect compounded by the economic and psychological consequences of these false alarms. Perhaps more importantly, the demonstrator effect is not necessarily limited to hoaxes. Determined individuals or groups who have witnessed the success of the letters could conceivably be motivated to redouble their efforts with the newfound confidence that what was once though nearly impossible can in fact be done.

Delivery

Mode of delivery is generally based on whether the agent is contagious, like the smallpox virus or *Y. pestis*, or noncontagious, like *B. anthracis* or botulinum toxin. As a general rule, contagious agents require a comparatively low tech delivery system that begins with the deliberate infection of a small group or individual, whether that group or individual is unaware of it or is knowingly infected as a so-called smallpox "suicide bomber" would presumably be. This group or individual then serves as a delivery device, spreading the disease by secondary transmission. Such an approach eliminates the need for mass production of the contagious agent (only a small amount is needed to initiate the chain of events potentially leading to an epidemic), specific formulation, or the design of an effective dissemination device. It should be noted, however, that the use of more sophisticated delivery methods for contagious agents cannot be ruled out, as suggested by both the aerosol testing of smallpox and the deployment of ICBMs containing smallpox as [their] payload by the former Soviet Union. Other possible means for spreading a contagious agent, such as the exploitation of zoonotic transmission or the contamination of illicit drugs, exist as well.

The threat of a smallpox suicide bomber has been the focal point of numerous media reports over the past year. A focused assessment has yet to be presented, however, to offer the public some perspective on the potential for success with this type of attack. Without vaccination the human body is susceptible to smallpox, indicating an underlying vulnerability of the U.S. and world population to this virus. However, even if intent—in other words whether what is known about conventional suicide bombers would translate to this type of event—is conceded, there is still a capability issue that must be addressed in order to gain an accurate understanding of this threat.[113] Indeed, if the agent were somehow to be acquired, initiating an epidemic would nevertheless be more complicated than simply injecting it, waiting for a rash, and going to a public place. This is similar to variolation, the immunization technique employed against smallpox before Dr. Edward Jenner developed his breakthrough vaccine from cowpox in 1796 (this cowpox vaccine is the predecessor to the vaccinia vaccine used today).[114] Although a potential suicide bomber might develop fulminating smallpox from such an injection, he or she would be more likely to develop a

half of Arnold's men.[116] Regardless, the overall likelihood of success with this type of attack is believed to be quite low, especially when the difficulty of acquisition is taken into account.

Non-contagious agents can be delivered using methods ranging from injection to the contamination of food or water to airborne dissemination. Delivery via injection was seen in the 1978 assassination of Bulgarian dissident Georgii Markov with a steel pellet filled with ricin. The pellet was covertly delivered by a Bulgarian secret service agent through the tip of a pneumatic umbrella as Markov was waiting for a bus on Waterloo Bridge in London. A fragmentary bomb with laced shrapnel offers an alternative means for this type of delivery. Such bombs were developed, for example, by scientists of Japan's World War II era BW program "Unit 731," using *Clostridium perfringens*, the causative agent of gas gangrene. More recently, penetrating bone fragments from a suicide bomber in Israel infected a victim with hepatitis B.[117] Although it is highly unlikely that this transmission was deliberate, the event shows that explosive dissemination of an infectious agent in this way is in fact possible.

Contamination of a targeted water supply is very challenging in a number of respects. A given water supply can in the simplest terms be divided into two systems, the pretreatment system and the post-treatment system. The pretreatment portion is almost always a closed system that carries water from its source (for example, a reservoir, Lake Michigan, or the Potomac River) through multiple filters designed to remove particles as small as 0.03 microns in size to a treatment plant, where it is then chlorinated and often treated with ozone as well.[118] The vulnerability comes in the post-treatment area, where contamination can occur via access to storage towers or reservoirs or alternatively via back pressure, in which a vacuum pump is used at a remote faucet or water fountain to force an agent back into the water supply.[119] There remains a very large dilutional effect as well as residual chlorination in the post-treatment system, however, likely minimizing the chance of success with this type of attack.[120] Food and beverage industries are also minimally vulnerable: a terrorist operative covertly placed inside a production or distribution facility could conceivably mount a successful attack from within that with the aid of a given company's own distribution system would then reach a wide target population.

Except for a few very rare exceptions, aerosolized biological agents have to be inhaled to be effective, unlike classical chemical weapons like mustard gas and nerve agents (sarin and VX, for example) that can be absorbed through the skin.[121] Thus, the aerosol dissemination of a BW agent almost always targets the human respiratory system, necessitating (as stated previously) the distribution of proper-sized particles in order for successful absorption and effect. Three general approaches exist for this type of delivery: point source, multiple point source and line source delivery.

Point source delivery traditionally employs a munition—for example an artillery shell, bomb, or rocket (but possibly something as simple as a glass flask containing a biological agent that could be smashed to create a dispersive effect)—that delivers its payload as a stationary source. Impact or detonation causes a burster charge within the munition to explode and the payload to be released. The wind then directs the payload's spread over (or away from) a target population. Point source delivery is considered highly inefficient because approximately 95 to 99 percent of the agent is destroyed in the blast, and much of what survives is driven into the ground or broken down into very small particles that either disperse too widely or are inhaled and exhaled right back out again.

Other theoretically more efficient methods for point source attacks do exist, however, that are considered to be more likely to be seen in a terrorism scenario. An example is the attack of a building's air handling system in which the nozzle of a spraying device is placed into the air intake duct and flow initiated, allowing fans within the air handling system to circulate the agent throughout the building. It should be emphasized that some question remains as to whether the filtration devices inside these systems might offer some protection in the event of an attack, as well as whether anthrax spores in particular might stick to the walls inside the system. Of note, the anthrax letters served as munitions for point source dispersal, and when delivered simultaneously for multiple point source dispersal as well (see below).

Aum Shinrikyo carried out several unsuccessful biological attacks using the point source approach.[122] On two separate occasions, cult members used a sprayer system to release wet anthrax into a giant fan situated atop an eight story building. Apparently, the attempts were made with an avirulent strain of the pathogen used in animal prophylaxis against anthrax and were therefore ineffective.[123]

Multiple point source dispersal is fairly self-explanatory. The classic example is what would be seen in a bombardment. Another approach is the implementation of multiple dispersal devices coordinated by timing mechanisms, a technique also employed by Aum in an unsuccessful attempt to deliver botulinum toxin among a localized target population.[124] Cult members positioned three briefcases equipped with small tanks, vents, and battery-powered fans in a Tokyo subway station, but upon activation the released contents had no effect because an Aum member had sabotaged the operation by filling the tanks with water. Regardless, it appears that Aum was never able to acquire a toxigenic strain of *C. botulinum*, suggesting that even if the operator had loaded what he or she believed to be botulinum toxin into the tanks the attack would nevertheless have been ineffective. It is widely held that this failed attack directly led to the group's decision to use sarin (and to deliver it in a relatively unsophisticated way) in the successful Tokyo subway attack, which took place only five days later.

Line source distribution removes the static element of the dispersal system, such that a moving delivery device releases a flow of agent over an extended period of time. Aum attempted this type of dispersal on multiple occasions as well, again unsuccessfully.[125] As just one example, cult members drove a truck equipped with a custom-made spraying device around the Imperial Palace and Tokyo Tower, intent on distributing a wet anthrax solution. They again used a non-pathogenic strain for this, however, and in any event the nozzle on the truck had apparently clogged prior to the operation and was thus nonfunctional at the time of intended release.

In general, Aum's biological effort can be summarized by its unsuccessful nature. Although a relatively sophisticated operation powered by physicians and scientists with substantial finances and equipment at their fingertips, the program's advance was persistently stalled by the inability of its members to overcome two specific hurdles: acquisition of a pathogenic strain and effective delivery.[126] This experience provides support for the notion

portant to remember that the bulk of Aum's biological pursuits occurred approximately 10 years ago. Since that time, the availability of mass casualty agents has increased, as has the number of microbiologists capable of producing such agents; access to Soviet agents and expertise has improved, as has that to the scientists of current and deceased state level programs such as the Iraqi program and Project Coast; information has become more readily available as a result of the Internet; technical hurdles have been steadily eroding, as demonstrated by the anthrax letters; genetic engineering has gained prominence, and so on. And perhaps most importantly, it must be remembered that Aum unequivocally demonstrated that groups do exist that are willing to use these agents, as discussed below.

The classic line source dispersal device is a crop-duster, ideally flown crosswind upwind of a target such that the stream of released agent is carried over the target area.[127] The spraying mechanism of a crop-duster, like that of other agriculture and painting equipment, consists of a hopper tank, a source of compressed air, one or multiple feeding tubes from the hopper tank, and nozzles for expulsion.[128] The compressed air propels material from the hopper tank through the tube or tubes and out the nozzles, which break up the dispersed agent unevenly to produce a wide range of particle sizes. Some of these are 1 to 5 microns, and are thus readily absorbed in the lungs. Most, however, are either too large and fall to the ground or get trapped by mucociliary defenses of the upper respiratory system, or too small and float away or get breathed in and out. The average particle size produced by a crop-duster is approximately 100 microns (a size that causes the particles to descend to the ground, as intended).

Special nozzles with small orifices can be attached to deliver a more uniform size in the desired range. Pressure must be increased accordingly to adequately force the material through these smaller outputs, but as far as crop-dusters are concerned this does not present an insurmountable challenge: most crop-dusters are capable of delivering 40 pounds-per-square-inch of pressure already, which can be enough to overcome wall tension without alteration. Nozzle adjustment, on the other hand, demands a great leap in terms of technical capability, and effectively eliminates the possibility of a "grab-and-go" scenario in which a crop-duster is commandeered at an airfield and used immediately without modification. Regarding the hypothetical crop-duster scenario, this discussion might offer some insight into why Atta had perhaps planned to build the dispersal system himself: if his intention had been to dispense a biological agent, he conceivably could have been aware of the need to incorporate a proper nozzle size.

Even if a group or individual were to successfully modify the aircraft, because a given biological preparation contains protein it would clog the altered nozzles fairly quickly upon initiation of dispersal. This is particularly true if a wet agent were used, as was the case in the Aum Shinrikyo attack described above. In addition, the propulsion of a given preparation through any type of sprayer creates a shearing effect that can kill 95 percent or more of the agent. Because crop-duster hopper tanks hold from approximately 1100 to 3000 liters of solution, however, the five percent that does survive might still be enough to have a devastating effect if a substantial amount of the total potential payload is released before the nozzles clog.

The challenges inherent to any type of wet aerosol delivery are significant but not insurmountable, as illustrated by the fact that both the former U.S. and former Soviet Union's BW programs were able to develop reliable methods for wet agent dispersal. Further, UNSCOM inspections revealed that sprayers and holding tanks had been installed on a number of Iraqi military aircraft and land vehicles. It was subsequently learned that in 1990, the Iraqis had modified a Mig-21 so that it could be a remotely piloted, equipped it with a 2200 liter belly tank from a Mirage F1 fighter plane, put in a spray mechanism, and field tested it with the anthrax simulant *Bacillus subtilis var. niger* (BG) in January 1991.[129] Although the results of the test are unknown, the delivery system nevertheless represents a significant advance in Iraq's technical capability. Of course, these accomplishments were fueled by the virtually limitless funding of dedicated state BW programs, and therefore do not reflect the capabilities of most if not all terrorist organizations at this time.

With respect to the use of a crop-duster as a dissemination device, handling the plane itself is considered the final hurdle to acquiring technical capability. Loading the hopper tank is challenging; taking off requires considerable skill on the part of the pilot; and once airborne, the plane is very difficult to fly, especially with a full load at a low altitude. This might explain why Atta had planned to modify a twin-engine passenger plane instead.

The Hypothetical Attack

Hurdles aside, the potential for the equipment and know-how to fall into the wrong hands is real. Thus, it may prove useful to contemplate what might have happened had Atta's group overcome the technical barriers of acquisition, production and formulation, as well as the barriers to crop-duster use, and carried out an attack on the Washington, DC area.

In a 1950 U.S. Army simulation, BG was dispersed and its spread monitored to assess the potential impact of a comparable release of anthrax spores.[130] Of note, the test employed off-the-shelf technology that has improved tremendously in the last half-century. Despite this limitation, a 2-mile dissemination line yielded a highly infectious area approximately 6 miles in length, with simulant traveling a maximum distance of 23 miles. In all, the release covered approximately 100 square miles, with an infectious area large enough to cover the entire metropolitan DC area.

The simulation began at 5 PM and lasted only 29 minutes. Test conditions included a relative humidity of 100 percent and a 5 mile-per-hour (mph) wind. The agent was released from the deck of a boat, so no data was generated supporting a certain altitude as the most effective for the release of BG (data which would be useful in the crop-duster scenario). However, field tests have shown that 1 to 5 micron particles sprayed by aircraft traveling at an altitude of over a few hundred meters quickly dissipate and thus have virtually no effect, demonstrating the need for a low altitude release in order to achieve the goal of the mission. As mentioned, flying at a low altitude also helps avoid radar detection.

Two atmospheric conditions are desirable in the planning of a biological attack: a 3 to 6 mph wind is considered optimal, as is the presence of an inversion layer, which occurs when a relatively low-lying blanket of warmer air holds a layer of cool air in place below it. This cool air in turn holds the aerosol cloud close to the ground and thus the target population. Inversion layers usually occur a few hours before sunrise, at a time when there is no ultraviolet (UV) light from the sun. UV light kills most pathogens, and also causes atmospheric turbulence that can break up an aerosol cloud. For all of these reasons, the

be noted that the simulation, although it had the right wind, did not take place in the presence of an inversion layer or in the absence of sunlight and was still very effective. It is also important to note that *B. anthracis* spores remain stable for several hours in an atmosphere devoid of sunlight, and a considerable amount of time when exposed to UV light as well.

As a basic rule, the higher the temperature and the lower the relative humidity, the faster the desiccation (i.e., dehydration) of an aerosolized agent. Therefore, the 100 percent humidity at the time of the simulation may have allowed for improved dispersal, although it must be conceded that anthrax spores are by nature resistant to desiccation (which, as mentioned, is one of the reasons why they make such a good weapon). Other factors like pollution fall outside the scope of this discussion, but it should be remembered that such less obvious considerations play a role as well.

Had Atta known what time of day was best to go, with what humidity and what wind, he could have monitored the National Weather Service or other sites and waited for the desirable conditions to be present.[131] A 1993 Office of Technology Assessment (OTA) study estimated that the release of 100 kilograms of anthrax spores upwind of the Washington, DC area in such conditions could result in between 130,000 and 3 million deaths, a lethality matching or exceeding that of a hydrogen bomb.[132] Although HEPA (High Efficiency Particulate Air) filters—which advertise a 99.97 percent filtration rate of particles 0.3 microns in size (indicating even better filtration of particles both larger and smaller than 0.3 microns)—and other barriers would limit the impact of this release inside certain buildings, most interior areas would be vulnerable to penetration of the spores via open windows or air intake ducts, meaning that those individuals outside in the hours following the attack would not be the only ones at risk of infection.[133]

The repercussions of such an attack, if successful, would ultimately be profound. Thus, this hypothetical scenario serves as an effective illustration of the inverse relationship between probability and impact, a relationship characteristic of those biological threats most commonly feared by security analysts and civilians alike.

Organizational Capability

While it will only receive very brief mention here, organizational capability is in fact a critical component of every step in the capability progression, from acquisition to production to delivery. Essentially, this is the ability of a group to avoid being penetrated by informers or being discovered in any way. Both Aum Shinrikyo and the Rajneeshees possessed this capability, and thus their attacks were not discovered until long after they had actually taken place. Given Atta's behavior in the USDA office, it might seem that his group would not have had the organizational capability to elude discovery prior to any kind of attack, but on September 11th that certainly was not the case… which leads to intent.

III. Intent

Even if the technical and organizational capability is there, in order for a threat to be considered real there must be intent. Who might actually want biological weapons and why, and who would use them if they could? To address this complex question, it proves useful to first consider four broad categories—among which significant crossover exists—of terrorists or criminals who might try to acquire a BW capability: state-sponsored terrorist groups; large terrorist or criminal groups; small terrorist or criminal groups; and the lone operator.

State-sponsored terrorist groups such the Palestinian groups HAMAS and Islamic Jihad top the list because these groups potentially have access to state BW programs and their agents. Representatives of these groups have at times publicly expressed an interest in BW. For example, Nassar Asad Al-Tamimi, a leader of Palestinian Islamic Jihad, stated in April 1998 that "Jihad has at last discovered how to win the holy war—lethal germs."[134] It is difficult to assess whether agent possession in such a case would serve only as a deterrent or whether use would follow. Because most state-sponsored groups are in some way political entities enmeshed in their respective societies, many analysts believe that such use would be counterproductive to the perpetrator's cause.

The second category consists of large terrorist or criminal groups with substantial resources, namely major drug cartels (or gangs) such as those in Afghanistan and Colombia, large independent terrorist groups like al-Qa'ida or the IRA and religious cults like Aum Shinrikyo, and multinational corporations. Drug cartels already possess well-equipped and well-staffed chemical laboratories that could be redirected to produce biological agents with relative ease, the likelihood of which will assuredly increase should the United Nations Drug Control Program (UNDCP) ever choose to use those fungal agents it has specifically developed to kill opium poppies (certain strains of *Pleospora papaveracea*, for example) on the crops of these cartels.[135] Large terrorist groups and religious cults have access to the funding and manpower necessary to establish a BW capability.[136] And multinational corporations, although not perceived as a present threat, do possess extensive dual-use equipment along with educated scientists and staff that could conceivably be misappropriated to produce BW if a pathogenic strain were acquired. Possible goals in this case might be to eliminate a particular competitor or to increase demand for one of its own products. No such action has ever been reported.

If smaller groups such as domestic militias or criminal organizations were to pursue a BW capability, they would presumably be limited in a number of respects. Expertise and equipment would most likely be of local origin and agents locally acquired, for example from unprotected hospital laboratories. Thus, the predominant threat with respect to these groups is a high probability, low impact threat, as demonstrated by the Rajneeshee attack of 1984. The Minnesota Patriots Council did manage to acquire a lethal agent in ricin, but this does not necessary reflect a large potential for lethal capability among these smaller groups, as ricin in particular is an unusual entity in that castor beans are easy to obtain and the subsequent extraction process is very straightforward. Upon acquisition of a BW capability, potential targets for these agents include the federal or state government and specific nations, races, or populations.

The final category is the lone operator, which essentially represents the disgruntled scientist and which some security analysts still believe to be the greatest domestic threat in

demonstrator effect described above, indirectly providing terrorist organizations with knowledge or ideas beneficial to their own pursuits. For example, had a terrorist group learned that Larry Wayne Harris successfully acquired *Y. pestis* from the ATCC before more stringent regulations were enacted, it could have tried the same approach.[138]

Over the past few decades, the potential for establishing a BW capability has been steadily increasing. Knowledge has become more available, and agents more accessible. Yet for a substantial portion of that time, terrorist motivations to acquire such a capability remained relatively low. In the year 1995, however, certain events led many security analysts to doubt whether the trend would continue: the Oklahoma City Bombing, Aum Shinrikyo's Tokyo subway attack, the disclosure of South Africa's former BW program Project Coast, and verification by the Iraqi government that it had built an extensive BW program of its own (this all only a short time after the dissolution of the Soviet Union and the containment problems that followed). These isolated incidents were essentially viewed by the international community as pieces of the same puzzle, and the term "new terrorism" was born.

The term has since been transformed to represent the present phase of a dynamic threat. Loosely-linked transnational terrorist networks motivated primarily by religious ideologies have replaced the more "traditional" terrorists motivated primarily by politics, and these new organizations do not appear to be bound by the same constraints as their predecessors. New terrorism, as it is now commonly understood, is therefore considered to be much more in line with the intent to pursue and actually use a biological weapon.

Historically, eight characteristics have suggested a propensity for such intent (see Figure 4.). Do these qualities and motivational factors translate to the so-called new terrorist? Evidence appears to be mounting that the answer will be yes. Al-Qa'ida, for example, has demonstrated each of these attributes. More data is warranted, however, before this can be stated with any degree of conviction.

Figure 4.

Attributes associated with CW and BW terrorism in the past[139]

1. Paranoia and grandiosity
2. Lack of political constituency
3. Closed cult or splinter group (or loner)
4. Charismatic, violence-prone leader
5. Apocalyptic ideology
6. Escalatory pattern of violence[140]
7. Technical and tactical innovation
8. Fascination with poisons or plagues

In the final analysis, the willingness of Mohammad Atta and his group to indiscriminately inflict mass casualties, coupled with the organizational and technical ability to do so, suggests to some an escalating trend toward the inevitable use of WMD. Others in the security community question this interpretation, citing the need for a better understanding of a given group's individual goals before such a determination can be made. While it is of course possible to have a best guess with respect to this issue, there is always some underlying level of uncertainty. Thus, from a policy-making standpoint intent must be assumed.

Conclusion: Threat = Capability?

From the above threat assessment, a number of important conclusions can be drawn. First, open societies, the U.S. in particular, are inherently vulnerable to a biological attack. Second, there has been a sharp increase in threats and hoaxes in the past year plus, largely as a result of the anthrax letters. Third, the organizational capability necessary to carry out a biological attack has been demonstrated, both by the anthrax mail attacks and the coordinated attacks of September 11th. Fourth, because intent cannot be uniformly determined with a high degree of accuracy (despite the delivery of the anthrax letters last fall), this intent must be assumed by policymakers tasked with establishing an appropriate level of preparedness and adequate response capability. Fifth, while high probability, low impact threats offer the greatest likelihood of success, in view of limited resources and a pressing timeline it is prudent at this juncture to direct preparedness efforts toward the management of the "low probability, high impact" threats such as anthrax and smallpox, the effective delivery of which could not only devastate a population and trigger large-scale economic fallout but also scar the collective consciousness of humanity for untold generations to come.[141] And finally, these conclusions suggest that whether an individual or group can overcome the technical hurdles of acquisition, production, and delivery will determine whether an attack is ultimately carried out, and if so whether that attack will be successful.

But that doesn't mean that the world is helpless. The potential threat can be addressed, and defensive measures can be taken. These measures exist on three levels: immediate steps, middle range goals that are feasible with effort, and long term goals that require substantial attention. Essentially, these three levels reflect the three components of the threat assessment.

Immediate measures tend to address vulnerabilities. A primary objective in this respect is the enhancement of physical security around potential targets. Another is the improved surveillance, detection and reporting of infectious diseases in the public health sector, a critical task in that it improves the ability of a nation such as the U.S. and the international community at large to identify and manage not only deliberate outbreaks orchestrated by terrorists or states but also the natural outbreaks of emerging and re-emerging diseases. In terms of worldwide impact, natural disease remains the much greater threat when all is said and done, and this type of "dual-use" preparedness and response capability would therefore be highly beneficial to humanity regardless of what malign human intention does or does not lie in wait in the coming years. Public health infrastructure, including finances and resources, must also be augmented to allow for this rapid recognition and response, and front-line physicians must be educated on the classical presentations of the major biological threat agents. Furthermore, measures for effective consequence management must be established, such as the stockpiling of antibiotics and vaccines and the

arranged. Fortunately, involved parties across the U.S. and around the world are already taking steps to ensure that the majority of these immediate objectives have been met.

In addition to vulnerabilities, middle range goals often address capabilities as well. Of particular importance are the securing of Soviet stockpiles and containment of the "brain drain" phenomenon, for example by providing knowledgeable scientists with constructive research alternatives to those opportunities available within the BW sphere (and often involving terrorist groups or states of proliferation concern). The establishment of an effective intelligence network is another key to curtailing the efforts of both states and terrorist organizations to acquire a BW capability. Building upon earlier objectives, diagnostic methods and materials should be improved to augment existing approaches to the rapid analysis and identification of biological agents, and an increased number of Biosafety Level 4 (BL4) facilities should be made available to perform such work. The scientific community must assume a leadership role in addressing the concern of important and legitimate but potentially dual-use research, and further in limiting access to potential pathogens by providing guidelines for safe storage, shipping, and use of these agents. And international control regimes such as the Biological Weapons Convention (BWC) must be implemented to hinder the production, stockpiling, and use of biological weapons and to further inhibit the proliferation of these weapons to terrorists and non-state actors not bound by the Convention.

Long term objectives mainly involve research. For example, further improvements not only upon existent treatment modalities (e.g., the development of vaccines with improved efficacy and reduced side effects) but also upon detection and identification techniques would serve to greatly improve consequence management in the future. Research is also necessary to better understand the probable threat agents in terms of their fundamental pathogenic mechanisms, as well as the human immune response to these mechanisms. And the investigation of environmental safety and decontamination measures would certainly prove beneficial in the long run. But the notion of intent should be addressed as well, with the goal of generating a mutual understanding of conflicting belief systems and ideologies that might provide new means to conflict resolution in the future.

In closing, the crop-duster scenario serves to illustrate how at least one of the above recommendations might be—and in fact has been—implemented. The initial hope of course is that civilians are now aware of this type of threat, and that this awareness will promote the active reporting of suspicious activities with respect to these aircraft, whether witnessed in and around airfields, observed in pilot training classes, or even acknowledged in chat rooms on the Internet. But should this fail, the FAA currently maintains what is essentially a no fly zone 15 nautical miles in diameter over metropolitan Washington, DC.[142] Regardless of whether this is being enforced to prevent a biological attack or simply another suicide hijacking, it is worth noting that the border of the restricted area is just far enough removed to prevent the effective aerosol dispersal of a given agent over the heart of the city.

Richard F. Pilch serves as scientist-in-residence at the Center for Nonproliferation Studies (Monterey, California). Dr. Pilch, M.D., is working on a joint program to clarify the role of toxins in international law. He also maintains interests in the medical and healthcare aspects of chemical, biological, and radiological threats, and in the monitoring of biotechnological advances for possible offensive or defensive application in a weapons of mass destruction context.

Notes

1. The term "anthrax letters" is technically inaccurate but is nevertheless commonly used to describe the fall 2001 letters containing *Bacillus anthracis* spores. The term will be used as such throughout this paper for the sake of simplicity.
2. While the term "crop-duster" is commonly used by the lay public, "aerial applicator" is the proper name for these aircraft in the agricultural industry. For the sake of simplicity, however, the lay term will be used in this analysis.
3. "USDA official: Atta tried to get loan to buy airplane," Associated Press, June 8, 2002; "Testimony Huffman Aviation by CEO President Rudi Dekkers," March 19, 2002, www.house.gov/judiciary/dekkers031902.htm. As uncovered and widely reported in the aftermath of 9/11, Atta's cell had largely operated out of South Florida, in locations ranging from Vero Beach to Coral Springs, etc. See, for example: "Evidence trails lead to Florida," *BBC News Online*, September 13, 2001.
4. Twin-engine aircraft can generally be divided into two categories, props and jets. An example of a twin-engine, six passenger prop plane is the Beechcraft 300. Examples of twin-engine civilian jets include the Learjet 20/30/55; Cessna Citation 500, 550, and 560; Hawkers 700 and 800; and Raytheon Premier. Captain Lansing R. Pilch, United States Air Force, personal communication with author, August 2002.
5. *Al-Qa'ida Training Manual*, available online at www.fas.org/irp/world/para/manualpart1.html.
6. Because toxins are chemicals of biological origin, many analysts believe that they should only be considered in the context of chemical weapons (CW), despite the fact that toxin production resembles BW production much more closely than CW production. As a further illustration of this gray area, toxins fall under the purview of both the Biological and Toxins Weapons Convention (BWC) and Chemical Weapons Convention (CWC). For the purposes of this paper, toxins will considered BW agents and thus included in the discussion of the bioterrorist threat.
7. See, for example, www.hort.purdue.edu/newcrop/proceedings1996/v3-342.html.
8. David S. Cloud, "Kurdish Militants Conducted Tests With Deadly Toxin Ricin," *Wall Street Journal*, August 20, 2002; John McWethy, "Bush Cancels Iraqi Strike," *ABCNews.com*, August 20, 2002.
9. Franz, D. and Jaax, N., "Ricin Toxin," in Zajtchuk, R. ed., *Textbook of Military Medicine: Medical Aspects of Chemical and Biological Warfare* (Office of the Surgeon General, Department of the Army, United States of America), p. 633.
10. Once in a green van with two men and once alone in a Cessna.
11. See, for example, Brinkley-Rogers, P., et al., "FAA Grounding Order Raises Bioterrorism Suspicions," *Pittsburg Post-Gazette*, September 24, 2001; Blum, J. and Eggen, D., "Crop-Dusters Thought to Interest Suspects," *Washington Post*, September 24, 2001.
12. Brinkley-Rogers et al., "FAA Grounding Order Raises Bioterrorism Suspicions," September 24, 2001.
13. The most complete article on Moussaoui to date is Downey, S., "Who is Zacarius Moussaoui?" *MSNBCNews.com*, December 26, 2002. See also Calabresi, M. and Donnelly, S., "Cropduster Manual Discovered," *Time.com*, September 22, 2001.
14. Initially, FBI headquarters determined that there wasn't enough evidence… to search Moussaoui's residence. After September 11th, however, a complete search was authorized that revealed, in addition to the findings described, a German phone number linked to al-Qa'ida.

ers (forthcoming in March 2003).

19. "USDA official: Atta tried to get loan to buy airplane," June 8, 2002.

20. Transcript, *ABC World News Tonight*, ABC TV, September 24, 2001. The number of crop-dusters in the U.S. has alternatively been reported as 4000; see Blum and Eggen, "Crop-Dusters Thought to Interest Suspects," September 24, 2001.

21. WMD is a categorical term used to describe the large-scale use of CBRN—chemical, biological, radiological, and nuclear—weapons. Technically, chemical and biological weapons are classified separately as mass casualty weapons (MCW) because they do not cause the physical damage implied by the term "destruction," but for the purposes of this paper WMD will be the representative acronym for the full range of CBRN weapons.

22. Homsy, R. and Zilinskas, R., Draft Report on the "Bioterrorist Threat Assessment and Risk Management Workshop," held at the Monterey Institute of International Studies, November 12–13, 2001.

23. It is important to point out that agricultural bioterrorism, which includes the targeting of both crops and livestock, is an integral component of the bioterrorist threat, as is the use of anti-machinery agents and even the dispersal of persistent agents such as anthrax spores as tactical or strategic environmental contaminants, for example to disable a specific highway or airport. For the purposes of this discussion, however, only bioterrorism against living, human targets will be considered.

24. The following review of U.S. vulnerabilities draws extensively from Pate, J., "Anthrax and Mass-Casualty Terrorism: What Is the Bioterrorist Threat After September 11?" *U.S. Foreign Policy Agenda*, November 14, 2001.

25. See, for example, the "Architecture, Design, and Engineering Drawings" available from the Prints and Photographs Online Catalog at http://memory.loc.gov/pp/pphome.html.

26. Class G airspace is uncontrolled airspace from ground level to 700 feet. Planes traveling in this airspace are essentially free from scrutiny. However, should a plane enter restricted airspace, for example around an airport (class B, C, and D), it would be monitored. Thus, for an operation to remain covert a plane would have to take off from a remote location, for example a field or private air strip, and avoid all classes of controlled airspace (anything other than class G). Captain Lansing R. Pilch, United States Air Force, personal communication with author, December 2002.

27. Information on all patients who presented with injuries or complaints directly related to the attacks within an eight hour period of each nationwide alert was collected, with the following results: a total of 103 patients presented with symptoms, 70 of whom suffered from acute psychological reaction, 19 from false atropine injection, 9 from physical injuries resulting from the explosion, 4 from (mild) smoke inhalation, and 1 from myocardial infarction. Rotenberg Z. et al., "Israeli ED experience during the Gulf War," *American Journal of Emergency Medicine*, 1994; 12:188–189.

28. Rotz, L., et al., "Public Health Assessment of Potential Biological Terrorism Agents," *Emerging Infectious Diseases*, Vol. 8, No. 2, February 2002.

29. *National Strategy for Homeland Security*, Office of Homeland Security, July 2002, pg. 7.

30. "Chronology of Aum Shinrikyo's CBW Activities," Monterey Institute of International Studies, 2001; available online at: http://cns.miis.edu/pubs/reports/aum_chrn.htm.

31. A discussion of crop-duster components can be found below. Generally speaking, the hopper tank is the compartment that holds the pesticide or agent for dispersal. Its capacity ranges from 300 to 800 gallons (1,100 plus to 3,000 plus liters). For a discussion of crop-duster dispersal of chemical (and biological) weapons, see the Henry L. Stimson Center webpage: http://www.stimson.org/cbw/?sn=CB2001121259.

32. "Military Utility of Agent X," CMLWG-ORG/TS-006 (19 Feb 52).

33. Miller, J., "Qaeda Videos Seem to Show Chemical Tests," *New York Times*, August 19, 2002.

34. Karasik, T., "Toxic Warfare," *RAND*, 2002; available online at: http://www.rand.org/publications/MR/MR1572/MR1572.pdf.
35. See, for example, http://www.airtractor.com/models/502/AT502B.html. The standard hopper tank for this make and model crop-duster is 500 gallons, while its standard fuel tank is 216 gallons.
36. On a per weight basis, gasoline mixed with air produces 15 times the energy of TNT (based on a conversion rate of 1 gram of gasoline plus air = 10 kilocalories, versus one gram of TNT = 0.65 kilocalories). TNT isn't used so much because of its energy as it is for the power that accompanies the rapid delivery of this energy, which amounts to a significant destructive force. Muller, R., "Cropduster Terrorism," *Technology Review*, March 11, 2002.
37. Broad, W. and Johnston, D., "Report Linking Anthrax and Hijackers Is Investigated," *New York Times*, March 23, 2002.
38. *Ibid.*
39. See, for example, Brennan, P., "FBI Rejects Link Between Anthrax, 9/11 Terrorists," *NewsMax.com*, August 16, 2002.
40. Broad and Johnston, "Report Linking Anthrax and Hijackers Is Investigated," March 23, 2002.
41. Infectiousness for a microbe or virus is often described in terms of its ID50, or the amount of agent required to cause infection in fifty percent of those exposed. The lower the number, the more infectious the agent. "Pathogenicity" then describes the ability to cause disease once infection has occurred. For toxins, the term ED5O is used rather than 1D50 (effective dose as opposed to infectious dose, because toxins do not cause infection), and "toxicity" rather than pathogenicity.
42. *NATO Handbook on the Medical Aspects of NBC Defensive Operations* (Washington, D.C.: Departments of the Army, the Navy, and the Air Force, 1996).
43. Vorobjev, A., "'Criterion Rating' as a measure of probable use of Bioagents as Biological Weapons," presented to the Working Group on Biological Weapons Control of the Committee on International Security and Arms Control, National Academy of Sciences, Washington DC, 1994. The criteria used were as follows: 1. Human sensitivity to microbe; 2. ID50 by aerosol; 3. Contagiousness (Index); 4. Possible routes of infectivity (aerosol, oral, parenteral); 5. Stability in environment; 6. Character of disease (severity, lethality, duration); 7. Feasibility of mass production (cultivation, physical-chemical forms, stability on storage. aerosolization); 8. Feasibility of rapid diagnosis; 9. Available prophylaxis; 10. Available treatment. Those agents rated with a score greater than or equal to 15 were considered "very likely to be used."
44. "Chemical and Biological Weapons: Possessions and Programs Past and Present," published online by the Monterey Institute of International Studies, http://cns.miis.edu/research/cbw/possess.htm.
45. The following characteristics were taken into account when classifying agents: "(1) public health impact based on illness and death; (2) delivery potential to large populations based on stability of the agent, ability to mass produce and distribute a virulent agent, and potential for person-to-person transmission of the agent; (3) public perception as related to public fear and potential civil disruption; and (4) special public health preparedness needs based on stockpile requirements, enhanced surveillance, or diagnostic needs." Rotz, L., et al., "Public Health Assessment of Potential Biological Terrorism Agents," February 2002.
46. "Chemical and Biological Weapons: Possessions and Programs Past and Present," http://cns.miis.edu/research/cbw/possess.htm.
47. *Ibid.* Argentinean hemorrhagic fever is also known as Junin.
48. *Patterns of Global Terrorism—2000*, Office of the Coordinator for Counterterrorism, U.S. Department of State, April 30, 2001; Committee on Armed Services, House of Representatives, "Special Inquiry into the Chemical and Biological Threat," Countering the Chemical and Biological Weapons Threat in the Post-Soviet World (Washington, D.C.: U.S. Government Printing Office, 23 Feb 1993), Report to the Congress, as cited in Zajtchuk, R. ed., *Textbook of Military Medicine: Medical Aspects of Chemical and Biological Warfare*, pg. 456.
49. Most often cited in this respect is Cuba's well-developed pharmaceutical industry and thus abundance of dual-use equipment, and reports that Usama bin Ladin had expressed an interest in developing BW agents in Sudan. See, for example, Hays, D., "Don't Trust Castro—Verify,"

51. See, for example, Carus, W., "Iran and Weapons of Mass Destruction," December 2000.

52. Zilinskas, R., "Iraq's Biological Weapons: Past as Future?" *Journal of the American Medical Association*, Vol. 278, No. 5, August 6, 1997.

53. *Ibid.*

54. See, for example, http://www.nti.org/e_research/el_libya_1.html.

55. North Korea Advisory Group, Report to the Speaker, U.S. House of Representatives, November 1999.

56. See, for example, http://www.nti.org/e_research/e1_syria_1.html.

57. Sources including *Y. pestis* in the list of pathogens developed by Iran are limited. See, for example, Bowman, S., "Iraqi Chemical and Biological Weapons," Congressional Research Service, Library of Congress, February 17, 1998.

58. Gubser, C. and Smith, G.L., "The Sequence of Camelpox Virus Shows It Is Most Closely Related to Variola Virus, the Cause of Smallpox," *Journal of General Virology*. 83, 855–872 (2002).

59. As an example, Lev Sandakhchiev, head of Russia's Vector Laboratory (State Research Center for Virology and Biotechnology), has voiced this opinion in the past.

60. For information on circumstantial links between Iraq with the smallpox virus, see Milloy, S., "Small Pox Threat Exaggerated, Part II," *Foxnews.com*, October 10, 2002; Broad, W., "White House Debate on Smallpox Slows Plan for Wide Vaccination," *New York Times*, October 13, 2002; Gellman, B., "4 Nations Thought to Possess Smallpox," *Washingtonpost.com*, November 5, 2002.

61. Henderson, D.A., "The Looming Threat of Bioterrorism," *Science*, Vol. 283, pp. 1279–1282, 1999.

62. Inglesby, T., et al., "Anthrax as a Biological Weapon," *Journal of the American Medical Association*, Vol. 281, No. 18, May 12, 1999.

63. Acquisition, production, and dissemination will be discussed in detail below.

64. Only 5 of the 11 inhalational anthrax cases following exposure to the anthrax-laden letters resulted in death, a mortality rate of 45%.

65. The concept of formulation is discussed in detail below, as are the effects of various meteorological factors on a BW attack.

66. Zilinskas, R. and Carus, W., "Possible Terrorist Use of Modern Biotechnology Techniques," *Chemical and Biological Defense Information Analysis Center*, April 2002.

67. Zilinskas, "Iraq's Biological Weapons: Past as Future?" August 6, 1997. The deployed missiles were modified SCUDs called al-Husseins, which had been adjusted in order to double their range.

68. Specifically, cult members contaminated coffee creamers and salad dressing containers at multiple restaurants in the area.

69. See Carus. W., "The Rajneeshees (1984)," in Tucker, J. ed., *Toxic Terror: Assessing Terrorist Use of Chemical and Biological Weapons* (Cambridge: MIT Press, 2000), pp. 115–137.

70. Zilinskas and Carus, "Possible Terrorist Use of Modern Biotechnology Techniques," April 2002.

71. *Ibid.*

72. However, it should be noted that according to some definitions the Rajneeshee incident does not qualify as terrorism per se. For example, Hoffman's definition of terrorism as "the deliberate creation and exploitation of fear through violence or the threat of violence in the pursuit of change" touches upon the notion that terrorism "is meant to instill fear within, and thereby intimidate, a wider 'target audience.'" Hoffman, B. *Inside Terrorism* (New York, Columbia University Press, 1998), pp. 43–44. The Rajneeshees never intended to affect anyone other than

those individuals directly exposed to the agent, and thus did not desire what Hoffman describes as "far-reaching psychological effects beyond the immediate victims." *Ibid.*, pg. 44.

73. Zilinskas and Carus, "Possible Terrorist Use of Modern Biotechnology Techniques," April 2002.

74. Carus, "The Rajneeshees (1984)," pp. 115–137, and Kaplan, D., "Aum Shinrikyo (1995)," pp. 207–226, both in Tucker, ed., *Toxic Terror: Assessing Terrorist Use of Chemical and Biological Weapons* (2000).

75. Zilinskas and Carus, "Possible Terrorist Use of Modern Biotechnology Techniques," April 2002.

76. See http://www.promedmail.org/pls/askus/f?p=2400:1000.

77. Zilinskas and Carus, "Possible Terrorist Use of Modern Biotechnology Techniques," April 2002.

78. *Ibid.*

79. *Ibid.* Examples of countries that incinerate infected animals in this manner are Australia, Canada, and the US.

80. *Ibid.*

81. *Ibid.*

82. *Ibid.*

83. "Chronology of Aum Shinrikyo's CBW Activities;" http://cns.miis.edu/pubs/reports/aum_chrn.htm.

84. Stern, J., "Larry Wayne Harris (1998)," in Tucker, ed., *Toxic Terror: Assessing Terrorist Use of Chemical and Biological Weapons* (2000), pp. 227–246.

85. Zilinskas and Carus, "Possible Terrorist Use of Modern Biotechnology Techniques," April 2002.

86. See, for example, "Concern over Kazakhstan bio-theft bid," *CNN.com*, November 6, 2002.

87. "Report: Specimens disappeared from Army lab," T*he Hartford Courant*, January 21, 2002.

88. Tucker, J. and Pate, J., "The Minnesota Patriots Council (1991)," in Tucker, ed., *Toxic Terror: Assessing Terrorist Use of Chemical and Biological Weapons* (2000), pp. 159–183.

89. *Ibid.*

90. *Ibid.* Another example of vendor acquisition is the purchase of "virus kits" over the Internet. These kits, such as the UK company Sigma-Genosys's Ebola kit, contain DNA strands and the genetic sequence of the virus in question so that the consumer can conceivably assemble the virus himself. Walsh, G. and Robbins, T., "UK Company Offers Ebola Virus 'Kit' for Sale Over Internet," *London Sunday Times*, August 4, 2002.

91. See, for example. Evans, M., "Whitehall Dossier Says Saddam Plans Biological Weapons for Palestinians," *London Sunday Times*, August 3, 2002.

92. This defector alleges that Iraq's military intelligence organization, Unit 999, offered six month training sessions to outsiders, such as members of Mojahedin-e Khalq (an Iranian opposition movement), the Kurdistan Workers Party (PKK, a group of Kurdish rebels based in Turkey), and al-Qa'ida. He claims to have met al-Qa'ida members at Salman Pak, a large BW and military facility southeast of Baghdad where three months of this training was performed. According to the defector, training was specifically directed toward U.S. targets and included such concepts as how to attack a water supply and how to target a building's ventilation system. "Iraq: Defectors Describe Camp Where Weapons Were Made," *Global Security Newswire*, November 8, 2001; Roberts, G., "Militia Defector Claims Baghdad Trained Al-Qaeda Fighters in Chemical Warfare," *London Sunday Times*, July 14, 2002.

93. Johnston, D. and Risen, J., "U.S. Concludes Al Qaeda Lacked a Chemical or Biological Stockpile," *New York Times,* March 20, 2002.

94. Gordon, M., "U.S. Says It Found Qaeda Lab Being Built to Produce Anthrax," *New York Times*, March 23, 2002; Zakaria, T., "US: Al Qaeda Tried for Bio Weapons in Afghanistan," *Yahoo! News*, July 17, 2002; Miller, J., "Lab Suggests Qaeda Planned to Build Arms, Officials Say," *New York Times*, September 14, 2002.

95. Air Force General Richard Meyers, Chairman of the Joint Chiefs of Staff, quoted March 25, 2002. See Weisman, J., "Possible Anthrax Lab Unearthed," *USA Today*, March 26, 2002;

coalition intelligence agency reported that enough equipment to establish 5 new laboratories capable of producing biological or chemical weapons was purchased by unidentified parties in 1999 and shipped from the Ukraine to Afghanistan; the same intelligence agency reported that in 2002 the Wafa Humanitarian Organization, the assets of which were frozen by the U.S. after it was identified as having terrorist links in the wake of 9/11, purchased roughly the same amount of similar equipment that was then shipped from the United Arab Emirates to Afghanistan, bringing the total to 6 possible labs altogether; A new CD-ROM version of al-Qa'ida's Encyclopedia of Afghan Resistance reportedly contains substantial, technically accurate descriptions of BW production and delivery (although apparently no information related to anthrax in this respect); And on July 10, 2002, U.S. forces detained a suspected BW smuggler in the Afghan village of Hesarak. Testing of the materials in his possession revealed trace amounts of ricin, but testing in the U.S. did not confirm this result. See, for example, Boettcher, M., "Evidence suggests al Qaeda pursuit of biological, chemical weapons," *CNN.com*, November 14, 2001; "Al-Qaeda: U.S. Forces Suspect, But Clear Detainee of CW Possession," *Global Security Newswire*, July 19, 2002.

97. It should be noted that a deliverable amount of agent, as opposed to just a seed culture, could conceivably be provided by a state sponsor, thus eliminating the need for an extensive production capability. In addition, contagious agents such as smallpox do not necessarily require any additional production measures upon acquisition of a pathogenic strain, as discussed in the analysis of delivery mechanisms below. It should be noted that the handling of contagious agents, whether bacteria or viruses, requires a high level of expertise because of demanding isolation techniques.

98. Tucker, J. and Vogel, K., "Preventing the Proliferation of Chemical and Biological Weapons Materials and Know-How," *Nonproliferation Review*, Spring 2000, pp. 88–96.

99. *Ibid.*

100. See, for example, " 'Dr. Death' and His Accomplice," *CBSNews.com*, November 4, 2002.

101. Zilinskas. and Carus, "Possible Terrorist Use of Modern Biotechnology Techniques," April 2002.

102. In addition, certain manuals sold at gun shows across the U.S. and books available at popular retail and online shopping venues describe BW production in thorough, although not always technically accurate, detail. Zilinskas, R., "Open publication as sources of biological and chemical terrorism: Defining the problem and applying remedies," in *Implications of 9/11 on National Security and the Path Forward to Peace*, Conference Proceedings of the Twelfth Annual Arms Control Conference, held April 18–20, 2002 (Albuquerque: Sandia National Laboratories), pp. 144–160.

103. Carus, W., "R.I.S.E. (1972)," in Tucker, ed., T*oxic Terror: Assessing Terrorist Use of Chemical and Biological Weapons* (2000), pp. 55–70.

104. *Ibid.*

105. *Ibid.*

106. As will be discussed, injected or ingested agents need not fit these criteria.

107. Viruses are also generally considered to be more hazardous than bacteria because while bacterial infections can often be treated with antibiotics (especially when identified in a timely fashion), most viral diseases have no specific treatment.

108. Zilinskas and Carus, "Possible Terrorist Use of Modern Biotechnology Techniques," April 2002.

109. *Ibid.* The continuous fermenter achieves its higher yield due to both a shorter turnaround time and the indefinite maintenance of the cultured agent in a phase of exponential growth. U.S. Congress, Office of Technology Assessment, *Technologies Underlying Weapons of Mass Destruction, OTA-BP-ISC-115* (Washington, DC: U.S. Government Printing Office, December 1993), pg. 88.

110. Miller, J., et al., "U.S. Germ Warfare Research Pushes Treaty Limits," *New York Times*, September 4, 2001.

111. Zilinskas, R., "Iraq's Biological Weapons: Past as Future?" August 6, 1997.

112. Snyder, L. and Pate, J., "Tracking Anthrax Hoaxes and Attacks," published online by the Monterey Institute of International Studies, May 20, 2002; http://cns.miis.edu/pubs/week/020520.htm.

113. For example, a key component of the suicide bombing tactic is the promise of a quick and honorable death. Dolnik, A., "Die and Let Die: Exploring Links between Suicide Terrorism and Terrorist Use of Chemical, Biological, Radiological, and Nuclear Weapons," *Studies in Conflict and Terrorism* (forthcoming in March 2003).

114. The process of variolation, which consisted of inoculating unexposed individuals—through incisions in their skin—with scabs or pus from mildly infected smallpox patients, began sometime before 1000 B.C. This transdermal approach effectively reduced the fatality rate of subsequent infections from 30 percent to approximately 1 percent. Tucker, J., *Scourge: The Once and Future Threat of Smallpox* (New York: Atlantic Monthly Press, 2001), pg. 15.

115. It should be noted, however, that if the virus were successfully injected intravenously rather than simply into the skin these expectations would conceivably differ.

116. Tucker, J., *Scourge: The Once and Future Threat of Smallpox* (New York: Atlantic Monthly Press, 2001), pg. 21.

117. Braverman, I., et al., "A Novel Mode of Infection with Hepatitis B: Penetrating Bone Fragments Due to the Explosion of a Suicide Bomber," *Israeli Medical Association Journal*, Vol. 4: 528–529. July 2002.

118. Zilinskas and Carus, "Possible Terrorist Use of Modern Biotechnology Techniques," April 2002.

119. *Ibid.* Hearings Before the Select Committee to Study Governmental Operations With Respect to Intelligence Activities of the United States Senate, *Unauthorized Storage of Toxic Agents* (Washington, DC: U.S. Government Printing Office, 1976), pg. 113.

120. Other methods of attacking a water supply exist as well, for example disabling water treatment mechanisms by interrupting the flow of disinfectants and thus allowing nature to take over and contaminate the supply. *Ibid.*; Croddy, E., *Chemical and Biological Warfare: A Comprehensive Survey for the Concerned Citizen* (New York: Copernicus Books, 2001), pg. 81.

121. Agents with skin effects include the trichothecene mycotoxins, along with a limited number of other toxins not generally considered in the context of BW. It is important to keep in mind, however, that anthrax spores can cause cutaneous infection as well.

122. "Chronology of Aum Shinrikyo's CBW Activities"; http://cns.miis.edu/pubs/reports/aum_chrn.htm.

123. Keim, P., et al., "Molecular Investigation of the Aum Shinrikyo anthrax release in Kameido, Japan," *Journal of Clinical Microbiology*, 39 (12), December 2001, pp. 4566–7.

124. "Chronology of Aum Shinrikyo's CBW Activities;" http://cns.miis.edu/pubs/reports/au_chrn.htm.

125. *Ibid.*

126. The group apparently had some difficulty with production as well. For example, a number of cult members, including leader Shoko Asahara himself, reportedly fell ill after attempting to prepare *Coxiella burnetii*, the causative agent of the incapacitating illness Q fever. Kaplan, "Aum Shinrikyo (1995)," in Tucker, ed., *Toxic Terror: Assessing Terrorist Use of Chemical and Biological Weapons* (2000), pg 7.

127. The goal with this approach, and generally with the use of any type of spray device, is to generate an aerosol cloud of the necessary particle size range of 1 to 5 microns in a high enough concentration to cover a broad area.

128. Zilinskas and Carus, "Possible Terrorist Use of Modern Biotechnology Techniques," April 2002.

129. Zilinskas, R., "Iraq's Biological Weapons: Past as Future?" August 6, 1997. The system was tested with water on three other occasions around that time, twice in December 1990 and once in January 1991. Director of Central Intelligence, *Iraq's Weapons of Mass Destruction*

speed, cloud cover, and temperature every three hours in accordance with World Meteorological Organization guidelines.

132. U.S. Congress, Office of Technology Assessment, *Proliferation of Weapons of Mass Destruction, OTA-ISC-559* (Washington, DC: U.S. Government Printing Office, 1993), pp. 53–55, as cited in Inglesby et al., "Anthrax as a Biological Weapon," May 12, 1999.

133. HEPA filtration data drawn from "Holmes HEPA Air Purifier Owner's Guide," info hot-line: 1-800-5-Holmes; see also, www.totalaircare.co.nz/abouthep.htm.

134. Carus, W., "Bioterrorism and Biocrimes: The Illicit Use of Biological Agents in the 20th Century," Center for Counterproliferation Research, National Defense University, August 1998. Similarly, al-Qa'ida spokesman Suleiman Abu Gheith, on June 12, 2002, stated, "We have the right to kill four million Americans—two million of them children—and to exile twice as many and wound and cripple hundreds of thousands. Furthermore, it is our right to fight them with chemical and biological weapons."

135. Stone, R., "Experts Call Fungus Threat Poppycock," *Science*, 290:246, 2000.

136. Cameron, G., "Multi-track Microproliferation: Lessons from Aum Shinrikyo and Al Qaida," *Studies in Conflict and Terrorism*, 22:277–309, 1999.

137. At least prior to 9/11, government officials had expressed this belief as well. For example, FBI and Department of Justice (DOJ) officials quoted in a 1998 article stated that lone operators are "considered the most dangerous domestic terrorists." Suro, R., "Terrorism's New Profile: the Lone Wolf," *Washington Post*, July 22, 1998.

138. Zilinskas and Carus, "Possible Terrorist Use of Modern Biotechnology Techniques," April 2002.

139. Tucker, ed., *Toxic Terror: Assessing Terrorist Use of Chemical and Biological Weapons* (2000), pp. 255–266.

140. A notable exception is the Rajneeshees, whose attack with *S. typhimurium* was the group's first move toward "violence" of any kind.

141. Henderson, "Looming Threat of Bioterrorism," 1999.

142. 15 nautical miles translates to 17.262 miles (1 nautical mile equals 1.1508 miles), giving the restricted area a radius of 8.631 miles.

Chapter 6

The Threat of Other Forms of Terrorism

In this chapter, authors explore other threats: ways in which terrorist groups could expand their power and their powers of destruction. A criminal-terrorist connection—where terrorist groups look to crime as a way to generate more operational funds—cyberterrorism, and suicide terrorism are potentially three such areas.

According to Barry R. McCaffrey and John A. Basso, the September 11 attacks demonstrated the power produced by the collision of three explosive trends: the United States as a sole superpower in the post–cold war era, and the one clear oppressor left to blame for the woes of underdeveloped peoples; a funding vacuum left after the end of the cold war, which led insurgent and terrorist organizations to turn to criminal activity to gain funds; and terrorists' perceived need for massive loss of life, to gain the attention of the media and the world. "Money is a natural centrifugal force," say McCaffrey and Basso in their exploration of this second trend. "Terrorists are necessarily pulled toward it. Criminals have always sought it. Money, and the means of gaining it, brings these two very different lethal organizations together. This magnetic attraction was born of post–cold war conditions."

Suicide bombers have been termed "the ultimate smart bomb." The foremost authority on the issue, Bruce Hoffman, provides a rare insight into this very dangerous and potentially imminent threat to the United States. In the past year, the world has seen these tactics used in Israel, Saudi Arabia, Indonesia, and Colombia to name but a few. The threat of suicide bombers is front and center for individuals at all levels of government—from city police and fire departments to the Department of Homeland Security. Ultimately "suicide terrorism is embraced as a psychological weapon designed to induce paralysis in one's opponent," explains Hoffman. One question often asked is when will such a threat come to the United States or other Western democracies. Hoffman's answer is that the United States has already experienced such events and not just the attacks of September 11, 2001. Through examination of Palestinian suicide bombers, Hoffman offers the reader insight as to what other countries might be able to expect and the challenges faced in defending against such attacks.

cyberterrorism. As with many other elements of globalization, the Internet and the interconnectedness that are so essential to our daily lives and commerce also present a vulnerability that can be exploited by terrorist organizations. The potential for this type of attack will only increase as organizations gain in technical capability and savvy.

However, as Madeleine Gruen explains, the Internet is not only a vulnerable point of attack for the terrorists, but it provides all types of extremists with a platform for recruiting that is being employed across a wide spectrum of groups. Not only are groups employing the Internet in new ways, they are using visual graphics and other tools to specifically target youth. These two articles present a very different picture of the Internet and its potential.

In perhaps the most frightening essay in this volume, John Ellis presents the future of biological warfare—genomic terrorism. Ellis describes genetically altered weapons that are engineered to strike, selectively killing one race and not another. While to many this may sound like science fiction, the future is already upon us. Today much of the food we eat is genetically modified and the Soviet Union, before its demise, developed a vaccine-resistant form of smallpox. This type of genetic engineering when combined with the complete sequencing of the human genome creates a power that, as Ellis terms it, is unprecedented. Genomics, he argues, will change the global economy. Not only do the world economies benefit from improved flows of capital, information, and travel, so too do terrorists who seek to take advantage of these structures. Genomics is no different yet all that much more powerful. Ellis points out that terrorists will not be the only consumers of this new information, but that drug cartels will profit from genomic research in building a more powerful version of ecstasy. The questions raised by this essay are important and timely and force the reader to ask difficult questions of the future.

Barry R. McCaffrey, General, USA (Retired)
John A. Basso, Major, USA, 2003

Narcotics, Terrorism, and International Crime: The Convergence Phenomenon

Introduction

The recent acceleration of America's unipolar role, when linked to greater interaction between terrorist organizations and transnational criminal organizations (TCOs), increases the possibility of another attack against the United States and the likelihood that terrorist groups will be able to gain the resources necessary for even more devastating attacks. Future terrorist mega-events may well include the use of chemical, biological, radiological, and nuclear (CBRN) material. It is the American government's role to defuse this terrorist explosion before it goes off. The wire that needs to be snipped can be found in the link between terrorist and criminal organizations.

Significance

The introduction of CBRN material to the terrorist-criminal equation underscores why it is so important to comprehend the links between terrorist organizations and transnational criminal organizations (TCOs). If scholars are correct in the conclusion that criminal organizations are increasingly linked to each other and form a global criminal network, then a terrorist who taps into this network will gain extraordinary reach.[1] For instance, a terrorist group may acquire the capability to access not only drug production revenue in Latin America, but also highly enriched uranium (HEU) or plutonium through the Russian Mafia. Additionally, tapping into this network facilitates contact with other terrorist organizations, each of which may provide other valuable services, such as a transportation network. Understanding the convergence of terrorist organizations and TCOs will be one of the keys to the future security of American citizens. To help advance this knowledge we elaborate on three emerging environmental trends that set the conditions for 9/11, and we identify the conditions that foster connections between terrorist organizations and criminal organizations. We then use representative examples to show how these connections are made and,

The views expressed in this paper are those of the authors and do not necessarily reflect the official policy or position of the United States Military Academy, the Department of the Army, the Department of Defense, or the U.S. government.

The United States as Target

History has shown that a clear way to gain the support of a constituency is to blame its problems on someone other than itself. In the post–Cold War era, the United States, as the only remaining superpower, became the natural target for blame. Osama bin Laden made that clear in a 1997 interview with CNN's Peter Arnett: "The collapse of the Soviet Union made the U.S. more haughty and arrogant and it has started to look at itself as a master of this world and established what it calls the New World Order."[2] Additionally, as Yossef Bodansky (director of the Congressional Task Force on Terrorism and Unconventional Warfare) reported, bin Laden places the blame for the Saudi financial crisis, increased Saudi taxes, and the deteriorating Saudi education system on the United States.[3]

CIA counterterrorism expert Paul Pillar points out that the proportion of attacks on U.S. interests have risen from 31 percent in the 1980s to 37 percent in the 1990s.[4] The role of America as a primary target will continue based on widespread perceptions of the United States as carrying out unilateral policy and maintaining close ties to Israel, as well as the consistent global poverty coupled with self-evident U.S. massive material wealth. Additionally, those terrorist groups that do not wish to attack the United States directly, such as the IRA, may well try to influence their target by gaining U.S. support. Even attacks not carried out directly against American citizens seek to influence U.S. policy.

Changes to Funding Sources

Money is a natural centrifugal force. Terrorists are necessarily pulled toward it. Criminals have always sought it. Money, and the means of gaining it, brings these two very different lethal organizations together. This magnetic attraction was born of post–Cold War conditions. Money has always been a concern for insurgent groups. War requires weapons. However, since the end of Cold War superpower state sponsorship, ideological insurgents have had to look for alternative ways to raise funds. And these insurgents have had to often turn to terrorism because the states they rebel against have become too strong militarily to allow any reasonable chance at success in conventional civil war. Even some of the modern extremist terrorist groups that never benefited from Cold War funding have moved toward criminal-based funding. The ability to use the chaos wrought by terrorism and insurgency to produce coca or opium and then move narcotics through the soft borders created by the collapse of the USSR is tempting. Likewise, kidnapping of foreign company employees and extortion have grown in prevalence. These groups are drawn together because of their complimentary capabilities. Terrorists can create chaotic circumstances that allow for illicit activities. Criminal organizations have preestablished networks to move and sell narcotics and launder money. The result is that some terrorists and criminal organizations converge and become partners working together to gain revenue. Additionally, some terrorist organizations transform themselves to be able to conduct criminal activities in-house so that they can generate their own revenue. In either case, these terrorist groups become part of a network of criminal organizations, which are considered to be possible sources for CBRN material.

Increased Scope of Attacks

Terrorist organizations now perceive the need for massive loss of life to capture global attention. This perception evolved as 24-hour news media bombarded consumers with an enormous number of stories each week. Insurgents and terrorists learned quickly: To be heard, be loud. Just how loud has evolved over the last 30 years. Black September surprised the world with their 1972 attack on the Israeli Olympic team. Twelve innocent people died. Islamic Jihad stunned the world in 1983 with their attack on the Marine barracks in Beirut. 241 U.S. Marines died. Aum Shinrikyo raised world terror to new levels with their 1995 Tokyo subway attack; 12 Japanese died and over 3,000 were hospitalized from exposure to sarin gas. Al-Qaeda's staggering 1998 East Africa U.S. embassy bombings killed 264 and wounded over 5,000 people. The magnitude of the 9/11 attack was not an aberration. While there are some exceptions, generally terrorists are trying to increase the scope of their carnage in each successive campaign of attacks.[5] This observation holds true not just for extremist terrorist groups but also for ethno-nationalist groups.[6] Terrorists believe that gaining international attention is vital to their cause. In the mind of a terrorist, to get the world's attention—to win—dramatic bloodshed is necessary.[7] Massive bloodshed, though, is not easy to achieve. As the world wakes up to the threat of terrorism, it will be even more difficult to successfully plan, resource, and execute dramatically successful attacks. Success will require flexibility, particularly in acquiring resources for these terrorist operations. Both single spectacular attacks and sustained operations may require large amounts of cash. Shoestring budgets are unlikely to suffice. And, as the previous section outlined, the financial tactics of terrorist groups like Abu Sayyaf, the FARC, and al-Qaeda have evolved as rapidly as the scope of attacks seen in Munich, Beirut, and Tokyo. It has been widely reported that each of these groups has to some degree pursued criminal activities to fund its ultimate goals. In order to craft effective counterterrorism strategy, we must understand how and why terrorist groups collaborate with criminal organizations.

Hypothesis

Previous Work

Some very impressive scholarly work has been done outlining the factors that influence insurgent group behavior.[8] Insurgent groups differ from terrorist groups. Specifically, we define terrorist groups as those who have crossed a line and chosen to target innocent civilians for psychological impact. Once this line is crossed, they are more willing to expand their range of funding sources and the nature of their attacks. The new breed of extremist terror groups significantly differ in their aims from ethno-nationalist groups and in their use of terror as not just an isolated tactic, but as an all-encompassing strategy to gain the change they seek.[9] Nonetheless, there are enough similarities between typical rebel groups and terrorists to warrant an analysis of the burgeoning literature on the incidence of civil war. Paul Collier, director of the Development Research Group of the World Bank, has examined civil wars since 1965 to determine if evidence exists to support the popular perception that

Terrorism scholar Chris Dishman superbly extends this type of analysis to the relationship between terrorist groups and organized crime.[11] Based on his conclusion that the costs of collaboration outweigh the benefits, Dishman finds that cooperation between the two groups may occur, but it will be short-lived. He further argues that terrorist organizations and criminal organizations will continue to shy away from collaborative arrangements, because their aims and motivations are different than those of their potential collaborators. In general, he believes that these different groups will instead choose to remain on an authentic political or criminal course.[12] Dishman supports this hypothesis by using case studies to outline out how terrorist groups and organized crime have used violence in the past. The terrorist and criminal groups he studies draw and maintain a clear distinction between violence used to advance profit aims and violence used for political reasons. He demonstrates, however, that criminal motives and the lure of profit will transform the aims of some terrorist leaders. This transformation toward profit-making blurs the distinction between violence used to advance political aims and that used to increase revenue. In particular, Dishman warns, "Terrorists and guerrilla groups who view their cause as futile, might turn their formidable assets towards crime—all the while under a bogus political banner." While Dishman's work is excellent, some might suggest that it is far too general and relies too heavily on cases that existed in a world that did not have such open borders and information technologies for coordinating activities on a global basis. By failing to distinguish between insurgent groups and terrorists or between different types of terrorist groups, and by failing to recognize that historical cases miss the complexity of the modern relationship between organized crime and terrorists, we believe that Dishman has missed the meaningful convergence relationships between these dangerous organizations. Instead, Dishman believes that terrorist organizations simply undergo transformation, a conclusion that some experts believe is incorrect.

Typology and Hypothesis

To understand why the terrorist groups most likely to strike the United States are likely to converge into partnerships with criminal organizations, we must analyze their motivations. As the United States prosecutes a broad war on terror, we must sort out which terrorist groups will transform themselves to take on the capabilities of a profit-driven criminal group, and which terrorists groups will remain true to their ideological cause. The vital first step in crafting policy options to defeat these groups will be understanding their vulnerabilities. Three general outcomes exist for terrorist organizations in their dealings with criminal organizations. Terrorist organizations may converge, meaning form a partnership with criminal organizations; terrorist groups may transform themselves into quasi-criminal organizations; or they may maintain themselves as pure terrorist organizations.

Terrorist groups will approach the decision of what type of partnership to pursue based on two independent variables. First, terrorist groups must identify whether they

Figure 1

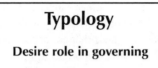

Typology

Desire role in governing

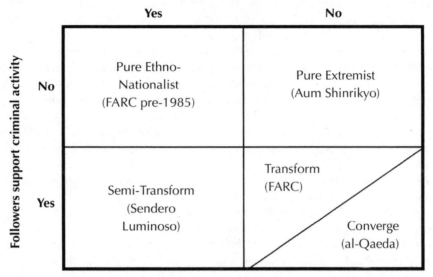

intend to seek a future legitimate governance role. While terrorist actions will always have some political aspect to them (or they would not meet RAND terrorism expert Bruce Hoffman's regularly cited definition of terrorism), the political action may have little to do with gaining a governing role in a state.[13] In fact, we suggest that a sea change in terrorism has taken place. Many new groups are extremist in nature instead of ethno-nationalist and will generally not seek a role in state governance. Second, all terrorist groups must determine whether their followers will continue to support them if they pursue criminal activities to gain revenue or resources for future terror attacks. Wesleyan professor and terrorism expert Martha Crenshaw has outlined the rational calculations terrorists make in deciding whether to act. We believe they make this same calculation regarding funding. Terrorists must determine if their actions will cause a loss of popular support from their followers.[14] If so, their ability to interact with criminal organizations is constrained. These two variables, desire to govern and support for criminal activity, interact to determine in large part which path terrorist groups take regarding cooperation with criminal organizations.

Clear logic underlies each part of the typology. For instance, Sendero Luminoso (The Shining Path) participated in criminal activities that its followers supported, but only in an effort to fund Abimael Guzman's bizarre Maoist vision. Sendero never lost its desire to govern. On the other hand, we would suggest that the FARC, after determining that it could not play an active role in the Colombian state, fully transformed itself and turned its focus almost exclusively to profit via criminal activity. In doing so, the FARC lost all but the most determined of its ideological followers. While these two cases briefly

not seek an active role in governing a state. Moreover, the ideal they seek to achieve so overshadows the distortions to that ideal that their followers see criminal activity as a minor irritant. For example, Shoko Asahara's followers in the millenarian cult Aum Shinrikyo have been accurately described as extremely well educated. Yet, as Walter Laqueur of the Center for Strategic and International Studies perceptively points out, these same followers not only supported the smuggling of weapons from Russia, they also managed to make the cruel and bizarre mental leap that releasing sarin gas on innocent Japanese citizens in the Tokyo subway would aid in preventing an American WMD attack on Japan.[15]

These groups always believe that the ends justify the means. Osama bin Laden implicitly made this point in a 1998 interview with ABC News, during which he altered his previous sentiment that only U.S. military personnel and facilities were targets of his terror campaign and added American civilians to his target list. As experts have pointed out, this escalation was made, "despite the fact that the Koran itself is explicit about the protections offered to civilians."[16] We suggest that the ramifications are clear. If the ends justify any means for some terrorist organizations, then collaboration with criminal organizations will be likely. This partnership is particularly probable if those criminal organizations can provide both revenue and a capability that the terrorist organization does not possess. As our typology indicates in the lower right corner of the box in figure 1, in the future we can expect to see convergence between criminal groups and so-called extremist terrorist groups like al-Qaeda. Extremist groups generally have no genuine desire to govern and their followers are not averse to these groups' criminal connections.

Given al-Qaeda's alleged business structure, which Peter Bergen expertly outlines in *Holy War, Inc.*, this focus on capabilities should not surprise us. Seeking out a partner to gain a capability that you lack has long been the model in the business world, and now we are seeing terrorist groups sophisticated enough to organize as businesses. The frightening part of these capability-based partnerships is that some criminal organizations may have more to exchange than a narcotics distribution network and the cash to fund terrorist operations and training. Some of these TCOs, particularly those that operate in the former Soviet Union and in Pakistan, may also have the capability to acquire CBRN material. Some observers have questioned whether these criminal groups would have the motivation to pursue such transactions, particularly given the assumption that collaboration with terrorists would naturally lead to greater law enforcement attention.

Observers who make this case about criminal organizations are trapped in the same thinking that led to faulty logic regarding whether terrorists would converge with TCOs. We believe that transnational criminal organizations are businesses. Just as businesses seek partners to gain the capabilities they lack, so too will TCOs seek partners. As we have already seen in Colombia, Afghanistan, and Burma, terrorist groups will bring narcotics production and some distribution capacity to the bargaining table. Terrorist groups are particularly well suited to the task of narcotics production since the chaotic environment they create will lead to lawlessness and the ability to conduct illicit business. Effective monopolies create barriers to entry by other firms through legal restrictions, like patents and copyrights, or through exorbitant start-up costs as seen in the jumbo-jet industry. Terrorist groups involved in drug production gain a monopoly on the control of land for the growing of coca or opium. They maintain a barrier to entry through violence. The behavior and values of both the criminal organizations and their terrorist partners becomes congruent.

A second potential argument that might cause criminal organizations to avoid partnering with terrorist groups is the question of scope of violence. Terrorists, even those seeking a legitimate role in a state, are willing to cross lines that many citizens see as sacrosanct. They will carry out kidnapping and murder for instance, and see these terrible acts as legitimate in order to further their cause. Criminal organizations, or at the very least some of their operatives, will also not be queasy about the mass casualty situations that they would create through the sale of CBRN material to terrorists. Crossing this criminal line would not be difficult since both parties will likely feel that the target—the United States—deserves what it gets. It is no secret that some of the poorly paid Russian, Pakistani, North Korean, or Iranian military who may have access to CBRN material maintain strong feelings of animosity toward America.[17] Valentin Tikhonov frighteningly points out in a Carnegie Endowment for International Peace report that given the lack of accountability of tactical nuclear weapons, not to mention weapons grade nuclear material, as well as biological, chemical, and radiological material, the ability of soldiers and scientists to covertly sell this material seems unquestioned.[18] Both sides of the marriage—extremist terrorist organizations and transnational criminal organizations—will see benefits in converging into such a lethal partnership. Arguments that this relationship will be short-lived are moot. It only takes one such criminal-terrorist partnership to realize our greatest fear: terrorists armed with nuclear, chemical, or biological weapons.

Case Studies—Testing the Hypothesis

To flesh out this argument more thoroughly, we believe it is beneficial to examine representative cases of transformed and converged terrorist groups and to outline the evolution of a criminal organization, in order to see characteristics evident in each case. We do not illustrate a pure terrorist group case; each of the groups we examine began as a pure case and eventually changed with its environment. It is useful to see which independent variables mutated over time leading these groups from a pure state to a transformed or converged state. Our purpose is to gain predictive capability for future instances and devise strategies to attack the exposed flank of terrorist organizations. We realize that our examination is only an initial overview and that it ultimately deserves more detailed case study analysis. However, it is clear that the differences in the cases we cite hinge to a certain extent on whether terrorists use terror, as a tactic, as has been prevalent with traditional ethno-nationalist terrorist groups, or if they use terror as a fundamental strategy, as we have witnessed in contemporary terrorist organizations. Additionally, we should note that a comprehensive study should examine a number of factors that help steer a terrorist group's decision on whether to partner with criminal organizations. A vital element included in these factors is having the geography that supports criminal trafficking.

inal activity has dramatically strengthened the fighting capacity of Colombia's terrorist groups. They have been ultimately transformed into terrorist organizations that use massive violence against the state to cement their capacity to maintain narcotics profits. This dramatic change from a Marxist revolutionary political organization to a transformed terrorist organization occurred as a response to political failure. Colombia's main rebel group, the Revolutionary Armed Forces of Colombia (FARC), failed in its attempt to gain a voice in Colombian governance via politics.

The FARC attempted to enter mainstream Colombian politics in the mid-1980s by establishing the Patriotic Union party. Threatened by its electoral successes, large landowners used paramilitary units, often with the support of Colombia's armed forces, to carry out a methodical campaign of murder against Patriotic Union officials.[20] These paramilitary units later combined to form the United Self-Defense Forces of Colombia (AUC). The introduction of this other armed force, the paramilitary AUC, now estimated at 4,000 to 5,000 strong, marked a critical intensification in Colombian violence. The FARC responded to this threat by increasing its military capacity. However, it had to seek alternate funding sources, primarily narcotics, to gain this increased capability for violence. While the AUC's use of assassinations hurt the FARC's political ambitions, ultimately, it was its immersion in narcotics activities that eliminated all of the FARC's political legitimacy. Additionally, the FARC's great success in gaining drug money—the State Department's 2002 International Narcotics Control Strategy Report (INCSR) says that Colombia's rebel groups now control much of the country's narcotics production and distribution capacity—has in the eyes of many observers completely transformed it from its Marxist past.[21] With around $500 million in profits from processing and shipping cocaine, "FARC rebels are so involved in the drug business that [a senior Colombian military leader] bluntly calls them 'a cartel'."[22] In other words, the FARC no longer appears to seek any significant role in the governance of Colombia, and it has a group of followers who will ruthlessly support all types of criminal activity from narcotics and kidnapping to outright extortion of the oil and gas industry. These narco-insurgents who fight under the guise of political grievance will back any criminal actions by the leaders of the FARC. They recognize that these terrorist attacks maintain the chaotic environment that creates the conditions for continued narcotics profits.

PKK—Ethno-Nationalist Converged

Abdullah Ocalan formed the Kurdistan Workers Party (PKK) in 1978. The PKK professed Marxist ideology at its inception; however, by the 1990s it advocated nationalism over communism. To that nationalist end, the PKK began including Islam in its literature in 1989. In 1984 the PKK made its critical strategic change—the adoption of violent terrorist tactics. Between 1984 and 1994, 128 teachers were killed as the PKK attacked the educational institutions that it saw as representative of the Turkish state. As the PKK enlarged its campaign of violence from May 1993 to October 1994, 1,600 total deaths were attributed to the group. In response to this increased violence, the Turkish military was given free rein to defeat the terrorists, and by the spring of 1994, the PKK's impact in Turkey had dramatically decreased.[23] However, the PKK's level of involvement in criminal activity to generate the resources needed to continue its war against Turkey did not diminish.

The U.S. State Department indicated in 1992 that the PKK was involved in the acquisition, importation, and distribution of drugs in Europe. Presumably this move toward illicit activities was driven by the need for funds required to support its desperate struggle against Turkey's escalated anti-terror offense. Yet, after the Turkish Armed Forces stunningly defeated the PKK, by 1994 few Turkish Kurds supported the terrorists' violent tactics. However, they continued to pursue drug trafficking, even reportedly partnering with the Medellin cartel by 1995. Interestingly, although the PKK did not gain internal legitimacy from its own followers, it did gain external recognition. The wife of French president Mitterand even penned a letter of support to "President Ocalan" in 1998.[24] Nonetheless, when Ocalan was captured in Nairobi, Kenya, in 1999, the final end of the PKK seemed near. It is curious to note that some elements of the PKK have maintained a discourse that indicates that even now they want some role in governance. Indeed, by February of 2002, the PKK was again threatening to resume its war as the defenders of Kurd cultural autonomy.[25] Regardless of the outcome of its continued political signals, the PKK seems to have effectively converged with criminal organizations. A political group that began as a pure ethno-nationalist terrorist group now has all of the characteristics of a partner of criminal organizations. The 1998 State Department INCSR alleges that the PKK used narcotics trafficking to finance its terror operations. However, the capture of Ocalan and the inevitable drop in funding from Kurds living abroad makes it more likely that the PKK is now using terrorism to support its bottom line.

Al-Qaeda—Extremist Converged

Afghanistan under Taliban rule became the world's leading opium and processed heroin producer. Despite Mullah Omar's ban on poppy cultivation as a first grudging response to world pressure in July 2000, trafficking of Afghan heroin continued through the use of massive stockpiles. It seems almost certain that al-Qaeda used their controlling link to the Taliban to profit from narcotics trafficking.[26] In 1998, before the Taliban's prohibition on production, the Italian government had established a link between the financing of Islamic fundamentalist groups and drug trafficking.[27] This conclusion certainly matches logic: The Taliban was said to have levied a 20 percent tax on drug runners, and it is clear that Taliban ties to al-Qaeda were very close and indeed had elements of a subordinate relationship. Moreover, after bin Laden's international bank accounts were frozen, it was clear that he would have had little problem justifying the use of drug money to finance his operations.[28] Bin Laden's closest followers also would have had few problems with this financing method, particularly when the narcotics were being trafficked to Westerners. In fact, fatwas from extremist Islamic leaders allow these highly irregular, seemingly un-Islamic actions because they add to the destruction of Western society.

Finally, there is evidence that bin Laden has spent in excess of $3 million dollars trying to purchase a nuclear device from the former Soviet Union. Given his close relationship with the Chechens, it seems likely that the Chechen Mafia facilitated these efforts. It is also probable that he would have approached the Russian Mafia, as evidence indicates that they have the capacity to acquire CBRN material.[29]

less visible criminal networks.[30] Russian organized crime reportedly consists of some 110 transnational criminal groups allegedly operating in 40 different countries. The 70,000 members of this extended crime family are believed to control an estimated 50 percent of the Russian economy. There is some evidence of formal agreements linking the Russian Mafia to Colombian narcotics traffickers.[31] There is very little evidence linking the Russian Mafia to terrorist groups. Nonetheless, given the global nature of its business, and the active role the Russian Mafia takes in narcotics trafficking across the porous borders of the former Soviet Union, it seems likely that connections have been made with terrorist groups who participate in narcotics trafficking. As the State Department reports, heroin in Russia is primarily imported by Afghans, Tajiks, and other Central Asians across the southern border with Kazakstan, and then distributed by Russian criminal organizations.

In other words, nationality matters little. Capabilities determine business partnerships. For example, circumstantial evidence exists that links the Russian Mafia to terrorists in an arms-for-cash (or narcotics) transaction. Between 1992 and 1994, the Russian Army lost 14,400 assault rifles and machine guns and 17 shoulder-fired anti-tank weapons.[32] There is little doubt that a profit-driven organization like the Russian Mafia would be willing to take the next step and trade CBRN material for revenue. This transaction is particularly likely in a financial environment in which deregulation has made the control and monitoring of payments virtually impossible. Evidence suggests that $300 to $500 billion of crime proceeds are transferred undetected through the world's financial markets each year.[33] The threat of a nuclear armed al-Qaeda is monumental, and it is unquestionably worth asking: Will a profit-driven organization that will have eventually squeezed every possible corrupt dime out of the Russian state apparatus then turn to an even more profitable transaction if its chances of being caught are minimal?

Conclusion and Recommendations

Case Findings

We believe there is a broad trend that suggests terrorist groups transformed themselves or converged with criminal organizations when they saw diminished chances of defeating government forces or when their funding apparatus collapsed. From the perspective of criminal organizations, there are clear costs to collaboration: The discovery of a criminal-terrorist link would bring unwanted response from national and international law enforcement agencies. But, if it is possible to conceal the link to terrorist organizations, these partnerships could prove to be very valuable. We also suggest that the increasing technical ease of laundering funds in the information age global economy makes discovery unlikely for sophisticated money launderers. In the specific case of al-Qaeda, effective law enforcement against illegal contributions via the money laundering rules put in place post-9/11 might produce the unintended consequence of pushing al-Qaeda away from Saudi contributors and toward more extensive partnerships with criminal organizations.[34] If we do not see this reaction by al-Qaeda, we could certainly see the same outcome by other terrorist organizations that will follow bin Laden's operational lead. As Harvard terrorism expert Jessica Stern points out, terrorists tend to copy each other.[35] This type of convergence from a group with the capabilities of al-Qaeda signals the dangers of the fourth trend—the emergence of CBRN weapons. The possession of CBRN weapons combined with the other three trends would return us to the horror we first saw at the birth of nuclear weapons in 1945. Our current policy must identify effective and rational strategic alternatives for our long-term campaign against terror.

Recommendations

Many would argue that the past 15 years have been marked by a lack of adequate leadership and sensible policy judgments by our democracy's political, economic, media, and military elites in the struggle against global terror. Our leadership was collectively incompetent in the face of growing mountains of evidence indicating that our nation was increasingly at risk of catastrophic losses from terrorist attacks on our citizens, our armed forces, and our economic and political interests. The United States did make multiple calls on the global community to create a new international consensus. Still, we never defined the reward and punishment coefficients that would apply to coerce positive responses in the international community.[36] These failures are not excusable. However, our mind-numbing inactivity occurred during an era when terrorism was not at the forefront of the collective American conscience. To persist in our previous mistakes would be criminal given the clear evidence of convergence between criminal organizations and terrorist groups and the potentially deadly CBRN threat that goes along with this partnership. The global community must use the information gathered through the analysis of this convergence trend to forestall or prevent future attacks by applying the information to the four critical areas outlined below.

1. **Common Conceptual Framework:** Our counterterrorism effort lacks a conceptual framework and the leadership necessary to effectively combat this global problem.[37] We cannot hope to tackle this problem piecemeal. Instead, we must construct a broad strategy that examines our intelligence requirements, includes our foreign policy actions writ large, and imaginatively considers the vulnerabilities and weaknesses of terrorist groups. We must analyze each of the specific weapons we hold for severing the bond between terrorists and criminal organizations—and between separate terrorist groups—in a growing global network. Identifying whether terrorist groups will remain pure, transform themselves, or converge with criminal organizations is a critical part of pinpointing those weaknesses.

2. **Intelligence:** The different relationships that convergence and transformation breed denote distinct weaknesses inherent in terrorist groups. With these weaknesses in mind, convergence and transformation trends point our intelligence community toward making three necessary structural changes. First, the Central Intelligence Agency and the Defense Intelligence Agency need to embark on a 10-year crash program to rebuild a global human intelligence capability adequate to warn the United States and our allies of the new national security nexus of threats posed by terrorism, drugs, and international criminal organizations. Additionally, these agencies must pursue an ethnically diverse group of intelligence operatives. America is the melting pot, and

America's intelligence community must allocate assets not only to intelligence collection but also, more critically, to intelligence analysis. We are suffering from information overload. We need sophisticated analysts to digest this raw data and find the operationally useful insights. The convergence and transformation trends are an excellent place to begin this analysis. These trends underscore the need to bridge the gap between the CIA and the FBI and our other intelligence bodies. Lastly, the United States must lead the way in creating international mechanisms to coordinate and link national law enforcement and intelligence capabilities in close partnership with global finance and treasury officials.[38]

3. **Legitimacy:** Al-Qaeda and other terrorist groups expose themselves to counterattack by partnering with criminal organizations, particularly when they use narcotics trafficking as a revenue source. Al-Qaeda has survived this weakness because it had a higher calling—a Jihad against the West—on which to focus its constituents. To take advantage of this vulnerability, the international community needs to fashion a Jihad against narcotics trafficking that includes antidrug education by Muslim clerics in the Muslim world. This psyops strategy—linking al-Qaeda to the very narcotics that have been ruled as unholy by Islamic clerics—could potentially weaken some of al-Qaeda's legitimacy with the young men who in their most impressionable years are shaped by extremist education. Perceived religious legitimacy acts as a catalyst for the young people who choose to martyr themselves for this cause. Any step taken to reduce it is worthwhile.

   The difference between a converged terrorist group that still has legitimacy with a broad array of followers and a transformed terrorist group that no longer has broad legitimacy helps define primary steps against these distinct terrorist organizations. For example, al-Qaeda has a legitimacy anchored by anti-Western feelings, so we must also be careful with our military operations in the Arab world. Each person who dies as part of a Western military campaign may add to al-Qaeda's legitimacy and add to the creation of other martyrs, whereas attacking al-Qaeda's legitimacy would weaken the group without the negative side effects. On the other hand, a strategy attacking the legitimacy of the FARC would not significantly affect its followers. A transformed terrorist organization like the FARC, which has substituted the power of criminal gain for ideological purity, has followers that are unaffected by the obvious criminal nature of the group. In the case of these transformed groups, we need to focus our campaign on crippling them by attacking their means of producing terror, including their narcotics revenue source and the narco-insurgents who defend their drug production facilities.[39] These attacks will not add to the FARC's supporters as they might if carried out against al-Qaeda.

4. **Tailored Response:** The United States should also develop new operational response packages created from all the tools of international power including diplomacy, economic aid, and preemptive offensive action. There are enough similarities between the types of terrorist organizations, represented on one hand by al-Qaeda and

on the other by the FARC, to guide the analysis that will allow us to defeat them. Determining whether we expect these terrorist groups to stay pure, to transform themselves to gain criminal capabilities, or to partner with criminal organizations is a good place to start in crafting our mix of responses.

a. **Aid:** The United States must develop the political will to devote significant levels of foreign aid—on the order of $5 billion per year—as a central element of our foreign policy.[40] We cannot continue to prosecute the war on terror as an independent part of our foreign policy, which relies primarily on military action. Counterterrorism operations must be broad in scope. Directed U.S. economic aid can help a fledgling democracy strengthen its institutions of government. Directed aid can also help reduce gross extremes in income disparity and poverty, and aid can create educational opportunities by providing alternative schools to compete with fanatical madrassas.

b. **Preemptive Offensive Action:** Understanding the differences between terrorist and criminal groups that have remained pure, transformed, or converged will help identify the constraints on preemptive offensive action. We must consider the long-term impact of offensive action based on the strength of each of these groups' followings. We must not be paralyzed by the notion of preemption and direct offensive action against the terrorists and their supporters. Terrorist groups that maintain devoted followers can still be aggressively attacked if we more effectively share our proof of terrorist involvement with Arab media outlets and international organizations. And our actions and information-sharing would be less constrained when dealing with those terrorist groups that have completely transformed to criminal organizations. In most cases, these criminal-terrorist groups simply seek to make a profit. They use terrorism to maintain a chaotic state that allows for illicit activity. These groups have few supporters outside of their organization. It is not normally necessary to constrain our actions based on the unintended production of more terrorists. As an example, the United States may consider expanding its Plan Colombia campaign to directly include the FARC. We may also develop a far more aggressive campaign against the Abu Sayyaf Group, which, because of its ties with the Philippines Triad and with Cebu-based smugglers, has lost legitimacy in the eyes of traditional Moro leaders.[41]

In addition to U.S. targeting of terrorists, we must focus on transnational criminal organizations and place them at risk if we have proof that they are linked with terrorists. Foreign nations, even those whose economic, military, and political capabilities we value or fear, must also recognize that we will punish them for any support of terror organizations or the criminal groups partnered with them.[42] We must also be willing to reward those who cooperate. A global campaign requires carrots and sticks. The United States finds itself in the unique position to be able to effectively use both. Our recommendations, which are focused on unraveling the next terrorist plot—not the last one—will sharpen the effectiveness of our counterterrorist policy.

also a national security and terrorism analyst for NBC News.

John A. Basso is a Major in the U.S. Army and an instructor in economics at the U.S. Military Academy, West Point.

Endnotes

1. Alison Jamieson, "Transnational Organized Crime: A European Perspective," in *Studies in Conflict & Terrorism*, Vol. 24, 2001, p. 379.
2. Peter Bergen, *Holy War, Inc.: Inside the Secret World of Osama Bin Laden*, New York: Free Press, 2001, p. 20.
3. Yossef Bodansky, *Bin Laden: The Man Who Declared War on America*, New York: Random House, 2001, pp. 190–191.
4. Paul R. Pillar, *Terrorism and U.S. Foreign Policy*, Washington, D.C.: Brookings Institution Press, 2001, pp. 57, 233.
5. Jessica Stern, *The Ultimate Terrorists*, Cambridge: Harvard University Press, 1999, p. 6. Stern points out that 4,798 deaths were attributed to terrorists in the 1970s, whereas between 1990 and 1996, 51,797 deaths were attributed to terrorists.
6. The FARC admit to firing a homemade mortar on 1 May 2002 that killed 117 Colombians seeking protection in a church in the northwest Colombian village of Bojaya. Palestinian suicide bombers have killed over 400 Israelis in the last 18 months of the second intifada.
7. Stern, p. 35.
8. Among the excellent pieces on insurgent groups and civil wars are: I. William Zartman, "The Unfinished Agenda," in Roy Licklider, ed., *Stopping the Killing: How Civil Wars End*, (NYU, 1993) pp. 20–34. Michael E. Brown, ed., *The International Dimensions of Internal Conflict*, (MIT, 1996). Robert Harrison Wagner, "The Causes of Peace," in Roy Licklider, ed., *Stopping the Killing: How Civil Wars End*, (NYU, 1993) pp. 235–268. Mats Berdal and David Malone, eds., *Greed and Grievance: Economic Agendas in Civil Wars*, Boulder: Lynn Rienner, 2000.
9. Presentation by Bruce Hoffman, West Point, N.Y., 16 April 2002.
10. Paul Collier, "Doing Well Out of War: An Economic Perspective," in *Greed and Grievance: Economic Agendas in Civil Wars*, Boulder: Lynn Rienner, 2000, p. 96.
11. Chris Dishman, "Terrorism, Crime, and Transformation," in *Studies in Conflict and Terrorism*, Jan. 2001, Vol. 24, pp. 43–59.
12. Ibid, p. 44.
13. Bruce Hoffman, *Inside Terrorism*, New York: Columbia University Press, 1998, p. 43. Hoffman's definition of terrorism: it is political in aims and motives; it is violent or threatens; it is designed to have far-reaching psychological repercussions; it is conducted by an organization or cell and perpetrated by a nonstate entity or subnational group.
14. Martha Crenshaw, "The Logic of Terrorism: Terrorist Behavior as a Product of Strategic Choice," in Walter Reich, ed., *Origins of Terrorism*, Washington, D.C.: Woodrow Wilson Center Press, 1990, p. 17.
15. Walter Laqueur, *The New Terrorism: Fanaticism and the Arms of Mass Destruction*, Oxford: Oxford University Press, 1999, p. 242.
16. Bergen, p. 20.
17. Bill Keller lays out this argument for both Pakistan and Russia in, "Nuclear Nightmare," in the *New York Times Magazine*, 26 May 2002.

18. Valentin Tikhonov, *Russia's Nuclear and Missile Complex: The Human Factor in Proliferation*, Washington, D.C.: Carnegie Endowment for International Peace, 2001.

19. Most date the guerrilla groups back to *la violencia*'s start in 1948. Some, however, date the rebellion's beginning to 1965, the year *la violencia* ended.

20. Michael Shifter, "Colombia on the Brink; There Goes the Neighborhood," *Foreign Affairs*, July-August 1999, p.2.

21. State Department, *2002 Colombia INCSR*.

22. Linda Robinson, "In for a Dime, In for a Dollar?," *U.S. News and World Report*, 4 October 1999, p.32.

23. Cindy Jebb, *The Fight for Legitimacy: Liberal Democracy versus Terrorism*," The Center for Naval Warfare Studies, June 2001, Newport: U.S. Naval War College, pp. 80–81.

24. Ibid, p. 90.

25. "Europe: A Turn for the Worse; Turkey and its Kurds," The Economist, 2 Feb. 2002.

26. State Department, *2002 Afghanistan INCSR*.

27. Jamieson, p. 383.

28. Ibid.

29. Bodansky, p. 328.

30. Jamieson, p. 378.

31. Ibid.

32. Chris Smith, "Light Weapons—The Forgotten Dimension of the International Arms Trade," in *Brassey's Defence Yearbook*, 1994 (London: Centre for Defence Studies). The authors thank Cadet Adam Scher, U.S. Military Academy, Class of 2004, for his research assistance on the Russian Mafia.

33. Jamieson, p. 379.

34. "Terrorist Finance: Follow the Money," in *The Economist*, 1 June 2002, p. 67.

35. Stern, p. 74.

36. Some of these comments previously printed in the October 2001 issue of *Armed Forces Journal International*. Reprinted with the editor's permission from "Challenges to U.S. National Security—Dealing with Madness," by General Barry R. McCaffrey, USA (Ret).

37. Ibid.

38. Elements of this recommendation previously printed in February 2002 issue of *Armed Forces Journal International*. Reprinted with the editor's permission from "Challenges to U.S. National Security—Afghanistan: Denying a Sanctuary to Terror," by General Barry R. McCaffrey, USA (Ret).

39. The State Department's *2002 Colombia INCSR* reports that JTFS UH-1N helicopters "were struck 50 times by small arms fire from narcoterrorists attempting to disrupt counternarcotics operations."

40. Elements of this recommendation previously printed in February 2002 issue of *Armed Forces Journal International*. Reprinted with the editor's permission from "Challenges to U.S. National Security—Afghanistan: Denying a Sanctuary to Terror," by General Barry R. McCaffrey, USA (Ret).

41. Military sources in the Philippines confirm open source documents like "Abu Sayyaf Financiers and Couriers Nabbed," in the *Philippine Daily Inquirer*, 3 July 2001, that indicate clear evidence of ties between Abu Sayyaf and criminal organizations and the ramifications of these ties on ASG legitimacy.

42. McCaffrey, "Afghanistan: Denying a Sanctuary to Terror."

The Logic of Suicide Terrorism

First you feel nervous about riding the bus. Then you wonder about going to a mall. Then you think twice about sitting for long at your favorite café. Then nowhere seems safe. Terrorist groups have a strategy—to shrink to nothing the areas in which people move freely—and suicide bombers, inexpensive and reliably lethal, are their latest weapons. Israel has learned to recognize and disrupt the steps on the path to suicide attacks. We must learn too.

Nearly everywhere in the world it is taken for granted that one can simply push open the door to a restaurant, café, or bar, sit down, and order a meal or a drink. In Israel the process of entering such a place is more complicated. One often encounters an armed guard who, in addition to asking prospective patrons whether they themselves are armed, may quickly pat them down, feeling for the telltale bulge of a belt or a vest containing explosives. Establishments that cannot afford a guard or are unwilling to pass on the cost of one to customers simply keep their doors locked, responding to knocks with a quick glance through the glass and an instant judgment as to whether this or that person can safely be admitted. What would have been unimaginable a year ago is now not only routine but reassuring. It has become the price of a redefined normality.

In the United States in the twenty months since 9/11 we, too, have had to become accustomed to an array of new, often previously inconceivable security measures—in airports and other transportation hubs, hotels and office buildings, sports stadiums and concert halls. Although some are more noticeable and perhaps more inconvenient than others, the fact remains that they have redefined our own sense of normality. They are accepted because we feel more vulnerable than before. With every new threat to international security we become more willing to live with stringent precautions and reflexive, almost unconscious wariness. With every new threat, that is, our everyday life becomes more like Israel's.

The situation in Israel, where last year's intensified suicide-bombing campaign changed the national mood and people's personal politics, is not analogous to that in the United States today. But the organization and the operations of the suicide bombers are neither limited to Israel and its conflict with the Palestinians nor unique to its geostrategic position. The fundamental characteristics of suicide bombing, and its strong attraction for the terrorist organizations behind it, are universal: Suicide bombings are inexpensive and effective. They are less complicated and compromising than other kinds of terrorist operations. They guarantee media coverage. The suicide terrorist is the ultimate smart bomb. Perhaps most important, coldly efficient bombings tear at the fabric of trust that holds societies together. All these reasons doubtless account for the spread of suicide terrorism from

260

the Middle East to Sri Lanka and Turkey, Argentina and Chechnya, Russia and Algeria—and to the United States.

To understand the power that suicide terrorism can have over a populace—and what a populace can do to counter it—one naturally goes to the society that has been most deeply affected. As a researcher who has studied the strategies of terrorism for more than twenty-five years, I recently visited Israel to review the steps the military, the police, and the intelligence and security services have taken against a threat more pervasive and personal than ever before.

I was looking at x-rays with Dr. Shmuel Shapira in his office at Jerusalem's Hadassah Hospital. "This is not a place to have a wristwatch," he said as he described the injuries of a young girl who'd been on her way to school one morning last November when a suicide terrorist detonated a bomb on her bus. Eleven of her fellow passengers were killed, and more than fifty others wounded. The blast was so powerful that the hands and case of the bomber's wristwatch had turned into lethal projectiles, lodging in the girl's neck and ripping a major artery. The presence of such foreign objects in the bodies of his patients no longer surprises Shapira. "We have cases with a nail in the neck, or nuts and bolts in the thigh..., a ball bearing in the skull," he said.

Such are the weapons of war in Israel today: nuts and bolts, screws and ball bearings, any metal shards or odd bits of broken machinery that can be packed together with homemade explosive and then strapped to the body of a terrorist dispatched to any place where people gather—bus, train, restaurant, café, supermarket, shopping mall, street corner, promenade. These attacks probably cost no more than $150 to mount, and they need no escape plan—often the most difficult aspect of a terrorist operation. And they are reliably deadly. According to data from the Rand Corporation's chronology of international terrorism incidents, suicide attacks on average kill four times as many people as other terrorist acts. Perhaps it is not surprising, then, that this means of terror has become increasingly popular. The tactic first emerged in Lebanon, in 1983; a decade later it came to Israel, and it has been a regular security problem ever since. Fully two thirds of all such incidents in Israel have occurred in the past two and a half years—that is, since the start of the second intifada, in September of 2000. Indeed, suicide bombers are responsible for almost half of the approximately 750 deaths in terrorist attacks since then.

Last December, I walked through Jerusalem with two police officers, one of them a senior operational commander, who were showing me the sites of suicide bombings in recent years. They described the first major suicide-terrorist attack in the city, which occurred in February of 1996, early on a Sunday morning—the beginning of the Israeli work week. The driver of the No. 18 Egged bus was hurrying across a busy intersection at Sarei Yisrael Street as a yellow light turned red. The bus was about halfway through when an explosion transformed it into an inferno of twisted metal, pulverized glass, and burning flesh. A traffic camera designed to catch drivers running stop lights captured the scene on film. Twenty-five people were killed, including two U.S. citizens, and eighty were wounded.

The early years of suicide terrorism were a simpler time, the officers explained. Suicide bombers were—at least in theory—easier to spot then. They tended to carry their bombs in nylon backpacks or duffel bags rather than in belts or vests concealed beneath their clothing, as they do now. They were also typically male, aged seventeen to twenty-

and some of them have children. Some of them, too, are women, and word has it that even children are being trained for martyrdom. "There is no clear profile anymore—not for terrorists and especially not for suicide bombers," an exasperated senior officer in the Israel Defense Forces told me last year. Sometimes the bombers disguise themselves: male *shaheed* (Arabic for "martyrs") have worn green IDF fatigues; have dressed as *haredim* (ultra-Orthodox Jews), complete with yarmulkes and tzitzit, the fringes that devout Jews display as part of their everyday clothing; or have donned long-haired wigs in an effort to look like hip Israelis rather than threatening Arabs. A few women have tried to camouflage bombs by strapping them to their stomachs to fake pregnancy. And contrary to popular belief, the bombers are not drawn exclusively from the ranks of the poor but have included two sons of millionaires. (Most of the September 11 terrorists came from comfortable middle- to upper-middle-class families and were well educated.) The Israeli journalist Ronni Shaked, an expert on the Palestinian terrorist group Hamas, who writes for *Yedioth Ahronoth*, an Israeli daily, has debunked the myth that it is only people with no means of improving their lot in life who turn to suicide terrorism. "All leaders of Hamas," he told me, "are university graduates, some with master's degrees. This is a movement not of poor, miserable people but of highly educated people who are using [the image of] poverty to make the movement more powerful."

Buses remain among the bombers' preferred targets. Winter and summer are the better seasons for bombing buses in Jerusalem, because the closed windows (for heat or air-conditioning) intensify the force of the blast, maximizing the bombs' killing potential. As a hail of shrapnel pierces flesh and breaks bones, the shock wave tears lungs and crushes other internal organs. When the bus's fuel tank explodes, a fireball causes burns, and smoke inhalation causes respiratory damage. All this is a significant return on a relatively modest investment. Two or three kilograms of explosive on a bus can kill as many people as twenty to thirty kilograms left on a street or in a mall or a restaurant. But as security on buses has improved, and passengers have become more alert, the bombers have been forced to seek other targets.

The terrorists are lethally flexible and inventive. A person wearing a bomb is far more dangerous and far more difficult to defend against than a timed device left to explode in a marketplace. This human weapons system can effect last-minute changes based on the ease of approach, the paucity or density of people, and the security measures in evidence. On a Thursday afternoon in March of last year a reportedly smiling, self-satisfied bomber strolled down King George Street, in the heart of Jerusalem, looking for just the right target. He found it in a crowd of shoppers gathered in front of the trendy Aroma Café, near the corner of Agrippas Street. In a fusillade of nails and other bits of metal two victims were killed and fifty-six wounded. Similarly, in April of last year a female suicide bomber tried to enter the Mahane Yehuda open-air market—the fourth woman to make such an attempt in four months—but was deterred by a strong police presence. So she simply walked up to a bus stop packed with shoppers hurrying home before the Sabbath and detonated her explosives, killing six and wounding seventy-three.

Suicide bombing initially seemed the desperate act of lone individuals, but it is not undertaken alone. Invariably, a terrorist organization such as Hamas (the Islamic Resistance Movement), the Palestine Islamic Jihad (PIJ), or the al Aqsa Martyrs Brigade has recruited the bomber, conducted reconnaissance, prepared the explosive device, and identified a target—explaining that if it turns out to be guarded or protected, any crowded place nearby will do. "We hardly ever find that the suicide bomber came by himself," a police officer explained to me. "There is always a handler." In fact, in some cases a handler has used a cell phone or other device to trigger the blast from a distance. A policeman told me, "There was one event where a suicide bomber had been told all he had to do was to carry the bomb and plant explosives in a certain place. But the bomb was remote-control detonated."

The organizations behind the Palestinians' suicide terrorism have numerous components. Quartermasters obtain the explosives and the other materials (nuts, bolts, nails, and the like) that are combined to make a bomb. Now that bomb-making methods have been so widely disseminated throughout the West Bank and Gaza, a merely competent technician, rather than the skilled engineer once required, can build a bomb. Explosive material is packed into pockets sewn into a canvas or denim belt or vest and hooked up to a detonator—usually involving a simple hand-operated plunger.

Before the operation is to be launched, "minders" sequester the bomber in a safe house, isolating him or her from family and friends—from all contact with the outside world—during the final preparations for martyrdom. A film crew makes a martyrdom video, as much to help ensure that the bomber can't back out as for propaganda and recruitment purposes. Reconnaissance teams have already either scouted the target or received detailed information about it, which they pass on to the bomber's handlers. The job of the handlers, who are highly skilled at avoiding Israeli army checkpoints or police patrols, is to deliver the bomber as close to the target as possible.

I talked to a senior police-operations commander in his office at the Russian Compound, the nerve center of law enforcement for Jerusalem since the time when first the Turks and then the British ruled this part of the world. It was easy to imagine, amid the graceful arches and the traditional Jerusalem stone, an era when Jerusalem's law-enforcement officers wore tarbooshes and pressed blue tunics with Sam Browne belts rather than the bland polyester uniforms and blue baseball-style caps of today. Although policing this multi-faith, historically beleaguered city has doubtless always involved difficult challenges, none can compare with the current situation. "This year there were very many events," my host explained, using the bland generic noun that signifies terrorist attacks or attempted attacks. "In previous years we considered ten events as normal; now we are already at forty-three." He sighed. There were still three weeks to go before the end of the year. Nineteen of these events had been suicide bombings. In the calculus of terrorism, it doesn't get much better. "How easy it has become for a person to wake up in the morning and go off and commit suicide," he observed. Once there were only "bags on buses, not vests or belts" to contend with, the policeman said. "Everything is open now. The purpose is to prove that the police can do whatever they want but it won't help."

This, of course, is the age-old strategy of terrorists everywhere—to undermine public confidence in the ability of the authorities to protect and defend citizens, thereby creating

four months of last year illustrated this careful strategy, beginning at bus stops and malls and moving into more private realms, such as corner supermarkets and local coffee bars. In March, for example, no one paid much attention to a young man dressed like an ultra-Orthodox Jew who was standing near some parked cars as guests left a bar mitzvah celebration at a social hall in the ultra-Orthodox Jerusalem neighborhood of Beit Yisrael. Then he blew himself up, killing nine people, eight of them children, and wounding fifty-nine. The tight-knit religious community had felt that it was protected by God, pointing to the miraculous lack of injury a year before when a booby-trapped car blew up in front of the same hall. Using a strategy al Qaeda has made familiar, the terrorists revisited the site.

Less than a month after the Beit Yisrael attack the suicide bombers and their leaders drove home the point that Israelis cannot feel safe anywhere by going to the one large Israeli city that had felt immune from the suspicion and antipathy prevalent elsewhere—Haifa, with its successful mixture of Jews, Christian and Muslim Arabs, and followers of the Bahai faith. The University of Haifa has long had the highest proportion of Arab students of any Israeli university. The nearby Matza restaurant, owned by Jews but run by an Israeli Arab family from Galilee, seemed to embody the unusually cordial relations that exist among the city's diverse communities. Matza was popular with Jews and Arabs alike, and the presence of its Arab staff and patrons provided a feeling of safety from attack. That feeling was shattered at two-thirty on a quiet Sunday afternoon, when a suicide bomber killed fifteen people and wounded nearly fifty.

As we had tea late one afternoon in the regal though almost preternaturally quiet surroundings of Jerusalem's King David Hotel, Benny Morris, a professor of history at Ben Gurion University, explained, "The Palestinians say they have found a strategic weapon, and suicide bombing is it. This hotel is empty. The streets are empty. They have effectively terrorized Israeli society. My wife won't use a bus anymore, only a taxi." It is undeniable that daily life in Jerusalem, and throughout Israel, has changed as a result of last year's wave of suicide bombings. Even the police have been affected. "I'm worried," one officer told me in an aside—whether in confidence or in embarrassment, I couldn't tell—as we walked past Zion Square, near where some bombs had exploded. "I tell you this as a police officer. I don't come to Jerusalem with my children anymore. I'd give back the settlements. I'd give over my bank account to live in peace."

By any measure 2002 was an astonishing year for Israel in terms of suicide bombings. An average of five attacks a month were made, nearly double the number during the first fifteen months of the second intifada—and that number was itself more than ten times the monthly average since 1993. Indeed, according to a database maintained by the National Security Studies Center, at Haifa University, there were nearly as many suicide attacks in Israel last year (fifty-nine) as there had been in the previous eight years combined (sixty-two). In Jerusalem alone there were nine suicide attacks during the first four months of 2002, killing thirty-three and injuring 464. "It was horrendous," a young professional woman living in the city told me. "No one went out for coffee. No one went out to restaurants. We went as a group of people to one another's houses only."

Again, terrorism is meant to produce psychological effects that reach far beyond the immediate victims of the attack. "The Scuds of Saddam [in 1991] never caused as much psychological damage as the suicide bombers have," says Ami Pedahzur, a professor of political science at Haifa University and an expert on political extremism and violence who manages the National Security Studies Center's terrorism database. As the French philosopher Gaston Bouthoul argued three decades ago in a theoretical treatise on the subject, the "anonymous, unidentifiable threat creates huge anxiety, and the terrorist tries to spread fear by contagion, to immobilise and subjugate those living under this threat." This is precisely what the Palestinian terrorist groups are trying to achieve. "The Israelis... will fall to their knees," Sheikh Ahmad Yassin, the spiritual leader of Hamas, said in 2001. "You can sense the fear in Israel already; they are worried about where and when the next attacks will come. Ultimately, Hamas will win." The strategy of suicide terrorists is to make people paranoid and xenophobic, fearful of venturing beyond their homes even to a convenience store. Terrorists hope to compel the enemy society's acquiescence, if not outright surrender, to their demands. This is what al Qaeda hoped to achieve on 9/11 in one stunning blow—and what the Palestinians seek as well, on a more sustained, if piecemeal, basis.

After decades of struggle the Palestinians are convinced that they have finally discovered Israel's Achilles' heel. Ismail Haniya, another Hamas leader, was quoted in March of last year in *The Washington Post* as saying that Jews "love life more than any other people, and they prefer not to die." In contrast, suicide terrorists are often said to have gone to their deaths smiling. An Israeli policeman told me, "A suicide bomber goes on a bus and finds himself face-to-face with victims and he smiles and he activates the bomb—but we learned that only by asking people afterwards who survived." This is what is known in the Shia Islamic tradition as the *bassamat al-farah*, or "smile of joy"—prompted by one's impending martyrdom. It is just as prevalent among Sunni terrorists. (Indeed, the last will and testament of Mohammed Atta, the ringleader of the September 11 hijackers, and his "primer" for martyrs, *The Sky Smiles, My Young Son*, clearly evidence a belief in the joy of death.)

This perceived weakness of an ostensibly powerful society has given rise to what is known in the Middle East as the "spider-web theory," which originated within Hizbollah, the Lebanese Shia organization, following a struggle that ultimately compelled the Israel Defense Forces to withdraw from southern Lebanon in May of 2000. The term is said to have been coined by Hizbollah's secretary general, Sheikh Hassan Nasrallah, who described Israel as a still formidable military power whose civil society had become materialistic and lazy, its citizens self-satisfied, comfortable, and pampered to the point where they had gone soft. IDF Chief of Staff Moshe "Boogie" Ya'alon paraphrased Nasrallah for the Israeli public in an interview published in the newspaper *Ha'aretz* last August.

> The Israeli army is strong, Israel has technological superiority and is said to have strategic capabilities, but its citizens are unwilling any longer to sacrifice lives in order to defend their national interests and national goals. Therefore, Israel is a spider-web society: it looks strong from the outside, but touch it and it will fall apart.

Al Qaeda, of course, has made a similar assessment of America's vulnerability.

United States is roughly forty-seven times that of Israel, meaning that the American equivalent of the March figure would have exceeded 5,000—another 9/11, but with more than 2,000 additional deaths. After April of 2002, however, a period of relative quiet settled over Israel. The number of suicide attacks, according to the National Security Studies Center, declined from sixteen in March to six in April, six in May, five in June, and six in July before falling still further to two in August and similarly small numbers for the remainder of the year. "We wouldn't want it to be perceived [by the Israeli population] that we have no military answers," a senior IDF planner told me. The military answer was Operation Defensive Shield, which began in March and involved both the IDF's huge deployment of personnel to the West Bank and its continuing presence in all the major Palestinian population centers that Israel regards as wellsprings of the suicide campaign. This presence has involved aggressive military operations to pre-empt suicide bombing, along with curfews and other restrictions on the movement of residents.

The success of the IDF's strategy is utterly dependent on regularly acquiring intelligence and rapidly disseminating it to operational units that can take appropriate action. Thus the IDF must continue to occupy the West Bank's major population centers, so that Israeli intelligence agents can stay in close—and relatively safe—proximity to their information sources, and troops can act immediately either to round up suspects or to rescue the agent should an operation go awry. "Military pressure facilitates arrests, because you're there," one knowledgeable observer explained to me. "Not only do you know the area, but you have [covert] spotters deployed, and the whole area is under curfew anyway, so it is difficult for terrorists to move about and hide without being noticed, and more difficult for them to get out. The IDF presence facilitates intelligence gathering, and the troops can also conduct massive sweeps, house to house and block to block, pick up people, and interrogate them."

The IDF units in West Bank cities and towns can amass detailed knowledge of a community, identifying terrorists and their sympathizers, tracking their movements and daily routines, and observing the people with whom they associate. Agents from Shabak, Israel's General Security Service (also known as the Shin Bet), work alongside these units, participating in operations and often assigning missions. "The moment someone from Shabak comes with us, everything changes," a young soldier in an elite reconnaissance unit told me over coffee and cake in his mother's apartment. "The Shabak guy talks in Arabic to [the suspect] without an accent, or appears as an Arab guy himself. Shabak already knows everything about them, and that is such a shock to them. So they are afraid, and they will tell Shabak everything." The success of Defensive Shield and the subsequent Operation Determined Way depends on this synchronization of intelligence and operations. A junior officer well acquainted with this environment says, "Whoever has better intelligence is the winner."

The strategy—at least in the short run—is working. The dramatic decline in the number of suicide operations since last spring is proof enough. "Tactically, we are doing everything we can," a senior officer involved in the framing of this policy told me, "and we have managed to prevent eighty percent of all attempts." Another officer said, "We are now bringing the war to them. We do it so that we fight the war in *their* homes rather than in *our* homes. We try to make certain that we fight on their ground, where we can have the maximum advantage." The goal of the IDF, though, is not simply to fight in a manner that plays to its strength; the goal is to actively shrink the time and space in which the suicide bombers and their operational commanders, logisticians, and handlers function—to stop them before they can cross the Green Line, by threatening their personal safety and putting them on the defensive.

Citizens in Israel, as in America, have a fundamental expectation that their government and its military and security forces will protect and defend them. Soldiers are expected to die, if necessary, in order to discharge this responsibility. As one senior IDF commander put it, "It is better for the IDF to bear the brunt of these attacks than Israeli civilians. The IDF is better prepared, protected, educated." Thus security in Israel means to the IDF an almost indefinite deployment in the West Bank—a state of ongoing low-level war. For Palestinian civilians it means no respite from roadblocks and identity checks, cordon-and-search operations, lightning snatch-and-grabs, bombing raids, helicopter strikes, ground attacks, and other countermeasures that have turned densely populated civilian areas into war zones.

Many Israelis do not relish involvement in this protracted war of attrition, but even more of them accept that there is no alternative. "Israel's ability to stand fast indefinitely is a tremendous advantage," says Dan Schueftan, an Israeli strategist and military thinker who teaches at Haifa University, "since the suicide bombers believe that time is on their side. It imposes a strain on the army, yes, but this is what the army is for." Indeed, no Israeli with whom I spoke on this visit doubted that the IDF's continued heavy presence in the West Bank was directly responsible for the drop in the number of suicide bombings. And I encountered very few who favored withdrawing the IDF from the West Bank. This view cut across ideological and demographic lines. As we dined one evening at Matza, which has been rebuilt, a centrist graduate student at Haifa University named Uzi Nisim told me that Palestinian terrorists "will have the power to hit us, to hurt us, once [the IDF] withdraws from Jenin and elsewhere on the West Bank." Ami Pedahzur, of Haifa University, who is a leftist, agreed. He said, "There is widespread recognition in Israel that this is the only way to stop terrorism." I later heard the same thing from a South African couple, relatively new immigrants to Israel who are active in a variety of human-rights endeavors. "Just the other day," the husband told me, "even my wife said, 'Thank God we have Sharon. Otherwise I wouldn't feel safe going out.'"

Nevertheless, few Israelis believe that the current situation will lead to any improvement in Israeli-Palestinian relations over the long run. Dennis Zinn, the defense correspondent for Israel's Channel 1, told me, "Yes, there is a drop-off [in suicide bombings]. When you have bombs coming down on your heads, you can't carry out planning and suicide attacks. But that doesn't take away their motivation. It only increases it."

Given the relative ease and the strategic and tactical attraction of suicide bombing, it is perhaps no wonder that after a five-day visit to Israel last fall, Louis Anemone, the security chief of the New York Metropolitan Transit Authority, concluded that New Yorkers—and, by implication, other Americans—face the same threat. "This stuff is going to be imported

attack against the U.S." In fact, Palestinians had tried a suicide attack in New York four years before 9/11; their plans to bomb a Brooklyn subway station were foiled only because an informant told the police. When they were arrested, the terrorists were probably less than a day away from attacking: according to law-enforcement authorities, five bombs had been primed. "I wouldn't call them sophisticated," Howard Safir, the commissioner of police at the time, commented, "but they certainly were very dangerous." That suicide bombers don't need to be sophisticated is precisely what makes them so dangerous. All that's required is a willingness to kill and a willingness to die.

According to the Rand Corporation's chronology of worldwide terrorism, which begins in 1968 (the year acknowledged as marking the advent of modern international terrorism, whereby terrorists attack other countries or foreign targets in their own country), nearly two thirds of the 144 suicide bombings recorded have occurred in the past two years. No society, least of all the United States, can regard itself as immune from this threat. Israeli Foreign Minister Benjamin Netanyahu emphasized this point when he addressed the U.S. Congress nine days after 9/11. So did Dan Schueftan, the Israeli strategist, when I asked him if he thought suicide terrorism would come to America in a form similar to that seen in Israel this past year. He said, "It is an interesting comment that the terrorists make: we will finish defeating the Jews because they love life so much. Their goal is to bring misery and grief to people who have an arrogance of power. Who has this? The United States and Israel. Europe will suffer too. I don't think that it will happen in the U.S. on the magnitude we have seen it here, but I have no doubt that it will occur. We had the same discussion back in 1968, when El Al aircraft were hijacked and people said this is your problem, not ours."

The United States, of course, is not Israel. However much we may want to harden our hearts and our targets, the challenge goes far beyond fortifying a single national airline or corralling the enemy into a territory ringed by walls and barbed-wire fences that can be intensively monitored by our armed forces. But we can take precautions based on Israel's experience, and be confident that we are substantially reducing the threat of suicide terrorism here.

The police, the military, and intelligence agencies can take steps that work from the outside in, beginning far in time and distance from a potential attack and ending at the moment and the site of an actual attack. Although the importance of these steps is widely recognized, they have been implemented only unevenly across the United States.

- Understand the terrorists' operational environment. Know their *modus operandi* and targeting patterns. Suicide bombers are rarely lone outlaws; they are preceded by long logistical trails. Focus not just on suspected bombers but on the infrastructure required to launch and sustain suicide-bombing campaigns. This is the essential spadework. It will be for naught, however, if concerted efforts are not made to circulate this information quickly and systematically among federal, state, and local authorities.

- Develop strong, confidence-building ties with the communities from which terrorists are most likely to come, and mount communications campaigns to eradicate support from these communities. The most effective and useful intelligence comes from places where terrorists conceal themselves and seek to establish and hide their infrastructure. Law-enforcement officers should actively encourage and cultivate cooperation in a nonthreatening way.

- Encourage businesses from which terrorists can obtain bomb-making components to alert authorities if they notice large purchases of, for example, ammonium nitrate fertilizer; pipes, batteries, and wires; or chemicals commonly used to fabricate explosives. Information about customers who simply inquire about any of these materials can also be extremely useful to the police.

- Force terrorists to pay more attention to their own organizational security than to planning and carrying out attacks. The greatest benefit is in disrupting pre-attack operations. Given the highly fluid, international threat the United States faces, counterterrorism units, dedicated to identifying and targeting the intelligence-gathering and reconnaissance activities of terrorist organizations, should be established here within existing law-enforcement agencies. These units should be especially aware of places where organizations frequently recruit new members and the bombers themselves, such as community centers, social clubs, schools, and religious institutions.

- Make sure ordinary materials don't become shrapnel. Some steps to build up physical defenses were taken after 9/11—reinforcing park benches, erecting Jersey barriers around vulnerable buildings, and the like. More are needed, such as ensuring that windows on buses and subway cars are shatterproof, and that seats and other accoutrements are not easily dislodged or splintered. Israel has had to learn to examine every element of its public infrastructure. Israeli buses and bus shelters are austere for a reason.

- Teach law-enforcement personnel what to do at the moment of an attack or an attempt. Prevention comes first from the cop on the beat, who will be forced to make instant life-and-death decisions affecting those nearby. Rigorous training is needed for identifying a potential suicide bomber, confronting a suspect, and responding and securing the area around the attack site in the event of an explosion. Is the officer authorized to take action on sighting a suspected bomber, or must a supervisor or special unit be called first? Policies and procedures must be established. In the aftermath of a blast the police must determine whether emergency medical crews and firefighters may enter the site; concerns about a follow-up attack can dictate that first responders be held back until the area is secured. The ability to make such lightning determinations requires training—and, tragically, experience. We can learn from foreign countries with long experience of suicide bombings, such as Israel and Sri Lanka, and also from our own responses in the past to other types of terrorist attacks.

America's enemies are marshaling their resources to continue the struggle that crystallized on 9/11. Exactly what shape that struggle will take remains to be seen. But a recruitment video reportedly circulated by al Qaeda as recently as spring of last year may provide some important clues. The seven-minute tape, seized from an al Qaeda member by U.S. authorities, extols the virtues of martyrdom and solicits recruits to Osama bin Laden's cause. It depicts scenes of *jihadists* in combat, followed by the successive images of twenty-seven

Islamic Information.

The greatest military onslaught in history against a terrorist group crushed the infrastructure of al Qaeda in Afghanistan, depriving it of training camps, operational bases, and command-and-control headquarters; killing and wounding many of its leaders and fighters; and dispersing the survivors. Yet this group still actively seeks to rally its forces and attract recruits. Ayman Zawahiri, bin Laden's chief lieutenant, laid out a list of terrorist principles in his book, *Knights Under the Prophet's Banner* (2001), prominent among them the need for al Qaeda to "move the battle to the enemy's ground to burn the hands of those who ignite fire in our countries." He also mentioned "the need to concentrate on the method of martyrdom operations as the most successful way of inflicting damage against the opponent and the least costly to the mujahideen in terms of casualties." That martyrdom is highlighted in the recruitment video strongly suggests that suicide attacks will continue to be a primary instrument in al Qaeda's war against—and perhaps in—the United States. Suleiman Abu Gheith, al Qaeda's chief spokesman, has said as much. In rhetoric disturbingly reminiscent of the way that Palestinian terrorists describe their inevitable triumph over Israel, Abu Gheith declared, "Those youths that destroyed Americans with their planes, they did a good deed. There are thousands more young followers who look forward to death like Americans look forward to living."

Bruce Hoffman is an authoritative analyst of terrorism and a recipient of the U.S. Intelligence Community Seal Medallion, the highest level of commendation given to a nongovernment employee. He is currently the director of the Washington, D.C., office of the RAND Corporation, where he heads the terrorism research unit, and he regularly advises both governments and businesses throughout the world. This reading is a chapter from his book *Inside Terrorism*.

Maura Conway, 2003

Terrorism and IT: Cyberterrorism and Terrorist Organisations Online*

Introduction

Analysts have been saying for some time now that the 'new terrorism' depends on the information revolution and its technologies.

> Indeed, terrorism has long been about 'information'—from the fact that trainees for suicide bombings are kept from listening to international media, through the ways that terrorists seek to create disasters that will consume the front pages, to the related debates about countermeasures that would limit freedom of the press, increase public surveillance and intelligence gathering, and heighten security over information and communications systems. Terrorist tactics focus attention on the importance of information and communications for the functioning of democratic institutions; debates about how terrorist threats undermine democratic practices may revolve around freedom of information issues (Arquilla *et al.* 1999, 72; see also Arquilla and Ronfeldt 2001).

Of course, the increase in information, communication, and communication technologies is not simply impacting terrorist groups. Information is the new lifeblood of the international system. World politics today transcends simple international relations, and much of the change has taken place as a result of the spread of information infrastructures (Luke 2001, 113). The information revolution is driving dramatic changes in political, diplomatic, military, economic, social, and cultural affairs. In the second half of the twentieth century, economically advanced countries made the shift into what has been termed the 'information society' or the 'information age.' The futurist Alvin Toffler (1980) has labeled this transition the 'Third Wave', suggesting that it will ultimately be as consequential as the two previous waves in human history: from hunter gatherer to agricultural societies, and from agricultural to industrial ones. The rapid expansion and diffusion of new International Communications Technologies (ICTs), particularly evident in the growth of the Internet, contribute to the set of phenomena collectively labeled globalization and cut across traditional temporal and spatial boundaries.

Every machine connected to the Internet is potentially a printing press, a broadcasting station, or a place of assembly. The ability to communicate words, images, and sounds, which underlies the power to persuade, inform, witness, debate, and discuss (not to mention

*This paper is a reworking of two previously published articles (see Conway 2002a and 2002b). The research on which the paper is based was supported by a grant from the Irish Research Council for the Humanities and Social Sciences (IRCHSS).

paring to harness—the power of the Internet to harass and attack their foes. In newspapers and magazines, in film and on television, 'cyberterrorism' is in the zeitgeist. The Internet is an ideal propaganda tool for terrorists: in the past they had to communicate through acts of violence and hope that those acts garnered sufficient attention to publicize the perpetrators' cause or explain their ideological justification. With the advent of the Internet, however, the same groups can disseminate their information undiluted by the media and untouched by government sensors. In 1999 it was reported that 12 of the 30 terrorist groups deemed Foreign Terrorist Organizations (FTOs) by the United States Department of State had their own Web sites (McGirk 1999).[1] Today, a majority of the 33 groups on the same list have an online presence (see Conway 2002a, Table 1)[2] But are terrorists who operate in cyberspace 'cyberterrorists'? The answer hinges on what constitutes cyberterrorism.

Defining and Redefining Cyberterrorism

There are a number of stumbling blocks to constructing a clear and concise definition of cyberterrorism. First, a majority of the discussion of cyberterrorism has been conducted in the popular media, where the focus is on ratings and readership figures rather than establishing good operational definitions of new terms. Second, the term is subject to chronic misuse and overuse and since 9–11, in particular, has become a buzzword that can mean radically different things to different people. In addition, it has become common when dealing with computers and the Internet to create new words by placing the handle *cyber*, *computer*, or *information* before another word. This may appear to denote a completely new phenomenon, but often it does not and confusion ensues. Finally, a major obstacle to creating a definition of cyberterrorism is the lack of an agreed-upon definition of terrorism (Embar-Seddon 2002, 1034). This does not mean that no acceptable definitions of cyberterrorism have been put forward. On the contrary, there are a number of well thought out definitions of the term available, and these are discussed below.[3] However, no single definition of cyberterrorism is agreed upon by all, in the same way that no single, globally accepted definition of classical political terrorism exists.

Barry Collin, a senior research fellow at the Institute for Security and Intelligence in California, coined the term 'cyberterrorism' in the 1980s. The concept is composed of two elements: cyberspace and terrorism. Cyberspace may be conceived of as "that place in which computer programs function and data moves" (Collin 1996). Terrorism is a less easily defined term. In fact, most scholarly texts devoted to the study of terrorism contain a section, chapter, or chapters devoted to a discussion of how difficult it is to define the term (see Gearty 1991; Guelke1998; Hoffman 1998; Schmid and Jongman 1988; Wardlaw, 1982). This paper will employ the definition of terrorism contained in Title 22 of the United States Code, Section 2656f(d). That statute contains the following definition: "The term 'terrorism' means premeditated, politically motivated violence perpetrated against noncombatant targets by sub-national groups or clandestine agents, usually intended to influence an audience."[4]

Combining these definitions results in the construction of a narrowly drawn working definition of cyberterrorism as follows: "cyberterrorism refers to premeditated, politically motivated attacks by sub-national groups or clandestine agents against information, computer systems, computer programs, and data that result in violence against non-combatant targets" (Denning 1999, 2 & 27; Pollitt, n.d.). By this definition, sending pornographic e-mails to minors, posting offensive content on the Internet, defacing Web pages, stealing credit card information, posting credit card numbers on the Internet, and clandestinely re-directing Internet traffic from one site to another do not constitute instances of cyberterrorism, contrary to what local government authorities and the press have stated (see Conway 2002c). Admittedly, terrorism is a notoriously difficult concept to define; however, the addition of computers to old-fashioned criminality it is not.

The inflation of the concept of terrorism may increase newspaper circulation, but is ultimately not in the public interest. Despite this, many have suggested adopting broader definitions of the term. In a 1997 article in the journal *Terrorism and Political Violence*, Matthew Devost, Brian Houghton and Neal Pollard defined 'information terrorism' as "the intentional abuse of a digital information system, network or component toward an end that supports or facilitates a terrorist campaign or action" (1997, 75). They conceive of information terrorism as "the nexus between criminal information system fraud or abuse, and the physical violence of terrorism" (1996, 10; 1997, 76). This allows for attacks that would not necessarily result in violence against humans—although they might incite fear—to be characterized as terrorist. But while there is no single accepted definition of terrorism, a majority of scholars agree that it has two integral components: the use of force or violence and a political motivation (Guelke 1998, 19; Schmid & Jongman 1988, 5). Indeed, most domestic laws define classical or political terrorism as requiring violence or the threat to or the taking of human life for political or ideological ends. Devost, Houghton and Pollard are aware of this, but wish to allow for the inclusion of pure information system abuse (that does not employ nor result in physical violence) as a possible new facet of terrorism nonetheless (1996, 10). Others have followed their lead.

Israel's former science minister, Michael Eitan, has deemed "sabotage over the Internet" as cyberterrorism (Sher 2000). And according to the Japanese government, cyberterrorism aims at "seriously affecting information systems of private companies and government ministries and agencies by gaining illegal access to their computer networks and destroying data" (FBIS 2002b). A report by the Moscow-based ITAR-TASS news agency states that in Russia cyberterrorism is perceived as "the use of computer technologies for terrorist purposes" (FBIS 2002a). In 1999, a report by the Center for the Study of Terrorism and Irregular Warfare (CSTIW) at the Naval Postgraduate School in Monterey, California defined cyberterrorism as the "unlawful destruction or disruption of digital property to intimidate or coerce people" (Daukantas 2001). "We shall define cyberterrorism as any act of terrorism... that uses information systems or computer technology either as a *weapon* or a *target*," stated a recent NATO brief, *Technology and Terrorism* (Mates 2001, 6). Yael Shahar, Web master at the International Policy Institute for Counter-Terrorism (ICT), located in Herzliya, Israel, differentiates between many different types of what he prefers to call 'information terrorism': 'electronic warfare' occurs when hardware is the target, 'psychological warfare' is the goal of inflammatory content, and it is only 'hacker warfare', according to Shahar, that degenerates into cyberterrorism (Hershman 2000).

hacktivism—and terrorism. Such unwarranted expansion of the concept of cyberterrorism runs contrary to the definitions outlined earlier. Advancing one step further, Johan J. Ingles-le Noble, writing in *Jane's Intelligence Review*, had this to say:

> Cyberterrorism is not only about damaging systems but also about intelligence gathering. The intense focus on 'shut-down-the-power-grid' scenarios and tight analogies with physically violent techniques ignore other more potentially effective uses of IT in terrorist warfare: intelligence-gathering, counter-intelligence and disinformation (1999, 6).

Ingles-le Noble's comments highlight the more potentially realistic and effective uses of the Internet by terrorist groups (i.e. intelligence-gathering, counter-intelligence, disinformation, etc.). However, he mistakenly labels these alternative uses 'cyberterrorism.' Consider the November 2000 electronic attack carried out from Pakistan against the American Israel Public Affairs Committee (AIPAC), a pro-Israeli lobbying group based in Washington, DC. The group's site was defaced with anti-Israeli commentary. The attacker also stole some 3,500 e-mail addresses and 700 credit card numbers, sent anti-Israeli diatribes to the addresses, and published the credit card data on the Internet. Dr. Nuker, the Pakistani hacker who claimed responsibility for the incident, said he was a founder of the Pakistani Hackerz Club, the aim of which was to "hack for the injustice going around the globe, especially with [*sic*] Muslims." But even had Dr. Nuker broken into AIPAC's headquarters and physically stolen the credit card information and e-mail addresses, this would not be considered an act of terrorism, but a criminal undertaking. It is only acting on the information obtained to perpetrate an attack in furtherance of some political aim that could be considered terrorist.

Ingles-le Noble further contends that "disinformation is easily spread; rumors get picked up by the media, aided by the occasional anonymous e-mail." That may be so, but spreading false information whether via word-of-mouth, the print or broadcast media, or some other medium, is oftentimes not even criminal, never mind terrorist. Why should things be any different in cyberspace? Ingles-le Noble (1999) himself recognizes that:

> There is undoubtedly a lot of exaggeration in this field. If your system goes down, it is a lot more interesting to say it was the work of a foreign government rather than admit it was due to an American teenage 'script-kiddy' tinkering with a badly written CGI script. If the power goes out, people light a candle and wait for it to return, but do not feel terrified. If their mobile phones switch off, society does not instantly feel under attack. If someone cracks a web site and changes the content, terror does not stalk the streets.

Nonetheless, there is widespread concern that a catastrophic cyberterrorist attack is imminent particularly in the wake of the events of 9–11. However, the bulk of the evidence to date shows that while terrorist groups are making widespread use of the Internet, so far they have not resorted to cyberterrorism, or shown the inclination to move heavily in that direction. Dramatic predictions to the contrary certainly make good copy, generate high ratings and sell many books and journals, but do not contribute to an intelligent, well-informed analysis of the threat of cyberterrorism.

Distinguishing Characteristics

When it comes to discussion of cyberterrorism, there are two basic areas in which clarification is needed. First, the confusion between cyberterrorism and cybercrime. Such confusion is partly caused by the lack of clear definitions of the two phenomena. A UN manual on IT-related crime recognizes that, even after several years of debate among experts on just what constitutes cybercrime and what cyberterrorism, "there is no internationally recognized definition of those terms" (Mates 2001). Second, it is useful to distinguish two different facets of terrorist use of information technology: terrorist use of computers as a facilitator of their activities, and terrorism involving computer technology as a weapon or target. Utilizing the definitions outlined above, it is possible to clarify both difficulties. Cybercrime and cyberterrorism are not coterminous. Cyberspace attacks must have a 'terrorist' component in order to be labeled cyberterrorism. The attacks must instill terror as commonly understood (that is, result in death and/or large-scale destruction), and they must have a political motivation. As regards the distinction between terrorist use of information technology (i.e. for the purposes of inter-group communication, propaganda, etc.) and terrorism involving computer technology as a weapon/target, only the latter may be defined as cyberterrorism. Terrorist 'use' of computers as a facilitator of their activities, whether for propaganda, communication, or other purposes, is simply that: 'use.'

Kent Anderson[5] has devised a three-tiered schema for categorizing fringe activity on the Internet, utilizing the terms 'Use,' 'Misuse,' and 'Offensive Use.' Anderson explains:

> Use is simply using the Internet/WWW to facilitate communications via e-mails and mailing lists, newsgroups and websites. In almost every case, this activity is simply free speech... Misuse is when the line is crossed from expression of ideas to acts that disrupt or otherwise compromise other sites. An example of misuse is Denial-of-Service (DoS) attacks against websites. In the physical world, most protests are allowed, however, [even] if the protests disrupt other functions of society such as train service or access to private property... The same should be true for online activity. Offensive use is the next level of activity where actual damage or theft occurs. The physical world analogy would be a riot where property is damaged or people are injured. An example of this type of activity online is the recent attack on systems belonging to the world economic forum, where personal information of high profile individuals was stolen (Weisenburger 2001, 2).

Combining Anderson's schema with the definition of cyberterrorism outlined above it is possible to construct a four-level scale of the uses of the Internet for political activism by unconventional actors, ranging from 'Use' at one end of the spectrum to 'Cyberterrorism' at the other (see Table 1). Unfortunately, such a schema has not generally been employed in the literature or in the legislative arena. This is particularly disquieting given that the vast majority of terrorist activity on the Internet is limited to 'Use.'

Use	Using the Internet to facilitate the expression of ideas and communication(s)	Internet users	E-mails, mailing lists, newsgroups, websites
Misuse	Using the Internet to disrupt or compromise Web sites or infrastructure	Hackers, Hacktivists	Denial-of-Service (DoS) attacks
Offensive Use	Using the Internet to cause damage or engage in theft	Crackers	Stealing data (e.g. credit card details)
Cyberterrorism	An attack carried out by terrorists either via the Internet or targeting the Internet that results in violence against persons or severe economic damage	Terrorists	A terrorist group using the Internet to carry out a major assault on the New York Stock Exchange

'Use' and 'Misuse': Some Empirical Observations

Researchers are still unclear whether the ability to communicate online worldwide has resulted in an increase or a decrease in terrorist acts. It is agreed, however, that online activities substantially improve the ability of such terrorist groups to raise funds, lure new faithful, and reach a mass audience (Arquilla *et al* 1999, p. 66; Piller 2001). The most popular terrorist sites draw tens of thousands of visitors each month.

Hizbollah,[6] a Lebanese-based Shi'ite Islamic group, established their collection of Web sites in 1995. They currently manage three such sites: one for the Central Press Office,[7] another to describe its attacks on Israeli targets,[8] and the last Al Manar TV for news and information.[9] All three may be viewed in either English or Arabic.[10] The Central Press Office site contains an introduction to the group, press cuttings and statements, political declarations, and speeches of the group's Secretary General. One may also access a photo gallery, video and audio clips. The information contained in these pages is updated regularly. In the event that one would like to find out more, contact information, in the form of an e-mail address, is provided. In a similar vein, Hamas' Web site presents political cartoons, streaming video clips and photomontages depicting the violent deaths of Palestinian children.[11] It has been claimed that the Armed Islamic Group (GIA), a fundamentalist sect warring with the Algerian government, posted a detailed bomb-making manual on their site.[12] The online home of the Tamil Tigers (LTTE), a liberation army in Sri Lanka best known for the 1991 assassination of former Indian Prime Minister Rajiv Gandhi, offers position papers, daily news, an online store—for sale are books and pamphlets, videos, audio tapes, CDs, a 2002 calendar, and the Tamil Eelam flag—and free e-mail services. Other terrorist sites host electronic bulletin boards, post tips on smuggling money to finance their operations, and provide automated registration for e-mail alerts.

Many terrorist group sites are hosted in the United States. For example, a Connecticut-based ISP was providing co-location and virtual hosting services for the

Hamas site in data centers located in Connecticut and Chicago (Lyman 2002). While sites such as that maintained by Hamas are likely to be subject to more intense scrutiny following the September attacks, similar Web sites were the subject of debate in the United States previous to the events of 11 September. In 1997 controversy erupted when it was revealed that the State University of New York (SUNY) at Binghamton was hosting the Web site of the Revolutionary Armed Forces of Colombia (FARC) and a Tupac Amaru (MRTA) solidarity site was operating out of the University of California at San Diego (UCSD). SUNY officials promptly shut down the FARC site. In San Diego it was decided to err on the side of free speech and the Tupac Amaru site remains in operation (Collier 1997).[13] Interestingly, the FARC site now also operates out of UCSD. It is not illegal to host such a site, even if a group is deemed an FTO by the United States Department of State, as long as a site is not seeking financial contributions nor providing financial support to the group. Other content is generally considered to be protected speech under the First Amendment of the Constitution of the United States (see also McCullagh 2002a & 2002b).

It's not all plain sailing for these 'netizens', however. Their homepages have been subject to intermittent DoS and other hack attacks and there have also been strikes against their Internet Service Providers (ISPs) that have resulted in more permanent difficulties. In 1997, for example, an e-mail bombing was conducted against the Institute for Global Communications (IGC),[14] a San Francisco-based ISP, hosting the Web pages of the *Euskal Herria* or *Basque Country Journal*, a publication edited by supporters of the Basque group Homeland and Liberty (ETA). The attacks against IGC commenced following the assassination by ETA of a popular town councilor in northern Spain. The protestors wanted the site pulled from the Internet. To accomplish this they bombarded IGC with thousands of spurious e-mails routed through hundreds of different mail relays, spammed IGC staff and customer accounts, clogged their Web page with bogus credit card orders, and threatened to employ the same tactics against other organizations using IGC services. IGC pulled the *Euskal Herria* site on 18 July 1997, but not before archiving a copy of the site enabling others to put up mirrors. Shortly thereafter, mirror sites appeared on half a dozen servers on three continents. Despite this, the protestors' e-mail action raised fears of a new era of censorship imposed by direct action from anonymous hacktivists. Furthermore, approximately one month after IGC pulled the controversial site off its servers, Scotland Yard's Anti-Terrorist Squad shut down Internet Freedom's U.K. Web site for hosting the journal. Scotland Yard claimed to be acting against terrorism (Denning 1999, 20–21).[15]

The so-called 'cyberwar' that raged between Israelis and Palestinians and their supporters in 2000 was a mere nuisance in comparison with such targeted and sustained campaigns. The Mideast 'cyberwar' began on November—about three weeks after Hizbollah seized three Israeli soldiers on patrol in the Sheba'a Farms area of south Lebanon and held them for ransom—when pro-Israeli hackers created a Web site to host FloodNet attacks. Within days, Hizbollah's site was flooded by millions of 'pings'—the cyber-equivalent of knocks on the door—and crashed. Hizbollah then tried reviving the site under slightly different spellings, but they too came under sustained attack. In all, six different Hizbollah sites, the Hamas site, and other Palestinian informational sites were victims of the FloodNet device (Gentile 2000a, 2000b; Hockstader 2000). Hizbollah's Central Press Office site came under attack once again when the group posted video clips of Israeli ground attacks on Palestinians in Gaza. Hizbollah then increased their server capacity in order to ward off further attacks (Gentile 2000a). These efforts notwithstanding,

Bahrain	140,200	21.36
Iran	420,000	0.63
Iraq	12,500	0.05
Israel	1,940,000	17.12
Jordan	212,000	3.99
Kuwait	200,000	9.47
Lebanon	300,000	8.38
Oman	120,000	4.42
Palestine	60,000	N/A
Qatar	75,000	9.75
Saudi Arabia	570,000	2.5
Syria	60,000	0.35
UAE	900,000	36.79
Yemen	17,000	0.09

Source: http://www.nua.ie

pro-Israeli hackers successfully hacked into the Hizbollah Web site a further time on 26 December. They posted pictures of the three Israeli soldiers who were abducted in early October and the slogan "Free Our Soldiers Now" on a screen full of blue and white Star of David flags (Hosein 2001).[16] In addition, a group called Hackers of Israel Unite allegedly crashed the Almanar TV site using one computer with a 56K modem, an ADSL line, and a popular tool called WinSmurf that enables one to conduct a mass pinging (Gentile 2000b).

Also in October 2000, a number of media outlets in the US and Europe were contacted by a group claiming that hackers had defaced a Hizbollah site. When journalists accessed the site they were greeted by the Israeli flag, Hebrew text and a tinny piano recording of "Hatikva," the Israeli national anthem. This prompted several news organisations to report that Hizbollah's Central Press Office site had been defaced by pro-Israeli hackers (Hockstader 2000; Piller 2001). Only later did it become apparent that the site at hisbolla.org (which is no longer operational) was a fraud that had been established by an unidentified individual or group using an address in Lebanon (Garrison & Grand 2001).

According to Hizbollah's then Webmaster, Ali Ayoub, "Our counterattack is just to remain on the Net" (Hosein 2001). The Palestinians and their supporters were not long in striking back, however. In a coordinated counterattack, the Web sites of the Israeli army, Foreign Ministry, prime minister and parliament, among others were hit (Hockstader 2000). On a single day, 29 December, 80 Israel-related sites were hacked and defaced by pro-Palestinian hackers. It is estimated that, in all, more than 246 Israeli-related sites were attacked between October 2000 and 1 January 2001 as compared with approximately 34 Palestinian-related sites that were hit in the same period (Hosein 2001). The success of the Palestinian counterattack—variously dubbed the 'e-jihad,' 'cyber-jihad,' or 'inter-fada'—

may be explained by the way in which the pro-Palestinian hackers systematically worked their way through sites with dot-il domain names. Palestinian-related sites are generally harder to find because, although in March 2000 dot-ps was delegated the country code Top Level Domain (ccTLD) for the Occupied Palestinian Territories, only one such domain is currently operational (gov.ps) (see Cisneros 2001),[17] and not many groups have such easily identifiable URLs as Hizbollah. In addition, there are approximately two million Internet hookups in Israel, which is considerably more than any other Middle Eastern country (see Table 2). The upshot of this is that the Israelis have a far greater online presence than the Palestinians and their supporters in the Arab world and are therefore more easily targeted.

(Inter)Networking and 9–11

In their recent work Rand's John Arquilla, David Ronfeldt, and Michele Zanini point to the emergence of new forms of terrorist organization attuned to the information age. They contend, "terrorists will continue to move from hierarchical toward information-age network designs. More effort will go into building arrays of transnationally internetted groups than into building stand alone groups" (Arquilla *et al* 1999, 41). This type of organizational structure is qualitatively different from traditional hierarchical designs. In the future, terrorists are likely to be organized to act in a more fully networked, decentralized, "all-channel" manner. Ideally, there is no single, central leadership, command or headquarters. Within the network as a whole there is little or no hierarchy and there may be multiple leaders depending upon the size of the group. In other words, there is no specific heart or head that can be targeted. To realize its potential, such a network must utilize the latest information and communications technologies. The Internet is becoming an integral component of such organizations, according to the Rand analysts (Arquilla *et al* 1999, 48–53; Arquilla & Ronfeldt 2001). The militias or patriot movement in the United States are known to have adopted inter-networked. forms of organization similar to those outlined above. While the anonymity of the Internet is seen as fuelling the conspiracies of the militias, for the groups themselves access to such new technologies is seen as a vital tool for recruitment and funding (in a similar way to terrorist organizations). The Internet has enabled the militias to spread their ideas worldwide. There are militias in Australia and Canada, and it has been suggested that the Far Right in Europe has adopted the idea of 'leaderless resistance' via the Internet (Mulloy 1999, 16). Activists within the patriot movement have repeatedly urged their compatriots, not only to organize themselves along networked lines, however, but also to opt out of other more pervasive networks that are viewed as dangerously perceptible to attack: "We need to set up our own cashless societies, our own barter networks, and unhook from the grid, to become self-sufficient, away from the power company, the gas company, and the water company" (Mulloy 1999, 324; see also Arquilla & Ronfeldt 2001). At the same time that the militias are unhooking from the grid, however, it is asserted that terrorist groups are more networked than ever before.

The adoption of such inter-networked forms of organization by terrorist groups has not been sufficiently researched. However, since the events of 9–11 a clearer picture has begun to emerge of the way in which the Internet might be used to support such organizational structures. The abilities of intelligence officials to eavesdrop on e-mail and phone calls was supposed to help prevent attacks such as those that occurred in New York and Washington from ever coming to successful fruition, but they did not. As a

Ronald Dick, head of the United States National Infrastructure Protection Center (NIPC),[18] told reporters that the hijackers had used the Net, and "used it well."

In the immediate aftermath of the attacks federal agents issued subpoenas and search warrants to just about every major Internet company, including America Online, Microsoft, Yahoo, Google, and many smaller providers. It is known that the hijackers booked at least nine of their airline tickets for the four doomed flights online at least two to three weeks prior to the attacks. They also used the Internet to find information about the aerial application of pesticides. Investigators are said to have in their possession hundreds of e-mails linked to the terrorists in English, Arabic and Urdu. The messages were sent within the United States and internationally. According to the FBI, a number of these messages include operational details of the attacks. Some of the hijackers used e-mail services that are largely anonymous—Hotmail, for example—and created multiple temporary accounts. A number of them are known to have used public terminals, in libraries and elsewhere, to gain access to the Net, whereas others used privately owned personal or laptop computers to do so (Cohen 2001; Fallis & Cha 2001, A24).

In two successive briefings, senior FBI officials stated that the agency had found no evidence that the hijackers used electronic encryption methods to communicate on the Internet. This has not prevented politicians and journalists repeating lurid rumors that the coded orders for the attacks were secretly hidden inside pornographic Web images (Cohen 2001; Lyman 2002), or from making claims that the attacks could have been prevented had Western governments been given the power to prevent Internet users from employing encryption in their communications (Cha 2001, E01).[19] Although many e-mail messages sent to and from key members of the hijack teams were uncovered and studied, none of them, according to the FBI, used encryption. Nor did they use steganography, a technique which allows an encrypted file to be hidden inside a larger file (such as a '.jpeg' or '.gif' image, or an '.mp3' music file). Evidence from questioning terrorists involved in previous attacks, both in America and on American interests abroad, and monitoring their messages reveals that they simply used code words to make their communications appear innocuous to eavesdroppers.

Arquilla, Ronfeldt, and Zanini have also pointed to the way in which difficulties coping with terrorism will increase if terrorists move beyond isolated attacks towards new approaches that emphasize campaigns based on swarming. They point out that while little analytic attention has been paid to swarming, it is likely to be a key mode of conflict in the information age (Arquilla *et al* 1999, 41). In their *Countering the New Terrorism*, Arquilla et al. describe this new technique thus:

> Swarming occurs when the dispersed nodes of a network of small (and perhaps some large) forces converge on a target from multiple directions. The overall aim is the sustainable pulsing of force or fire. Once in motion, swarm networks must be able to coalesce rapidly and stealthily on a target, then dissever and redisperse, immediately ready

to recombine for a new pulse. In other words, information age attacks may come in 'swarms' rather than the more traditional 'waves' (Arquilla *et al* 1999, 53–54).

This device points to the adaptable, flexible, and versatile nature of offensive networks. with regard to opportunities and challenges. The fact that the 9–11 hijackers employed a technique similar to the one described above has given the Rand analysts' work a far higher profile than might otherwise have been expected. Far from being innovative or under-utilized, however, swarming has been employed by hacktivists—including those acting in support of terrorist organizations—for some time. As Dorothy Denning has pointed out, cases such as that involving the *Euskal Herria Journal* and other similar incidents illustrate the power of such tools. Despite the ISPs willingness to host the site, IGC simply could not sustain the attack and remain in business. On the other hand, such cases also illustrate the power of the Internet as an organ of free speech: because venues for publication on the In-ternet are so rich and diverse and dispersed throughout the world, it is extremely difficult for hacktivists and governments alike to banish from the Net content they deem offensive using swarming or any other techniques (Denning 1999, 21).

The Internet and 9–11: The Aftermath

Authorities have been keeping a watchful eye on Web sites perceived as extremist for a number of years. In February 1998, Dale Watson, chief of the International Terrorism sec-tion of the FBI, informed a United States Senate committee that major terrorist groups used the Internet to spread propaganda and recruit new members (Gruner and Naik 2001; Liu 2001). Previous to 9–11, however, the authorities were not entitled to interfere with such sites for legal reasons. Since that time, the FBI have been involved in the official closure of what appears to be hundreds—if not thousands—of sites. An Indiana ISP pulled several radical Internet radio shows, including IRA radio, Al Lewis Live and Our Americas, in late September 2001 after the FBI contacted them and advised that their assets could be seized for promoting terrorism. The New York-based IRA Radio was accused of supporting the Real IRA. The site contained an archive of weekly radio programmes said to back the dis-sident Irish republicans (Cobain 2001). The archive of political interviews from the pro-gramme Al Lewis Live, hosted by iconoclastic actor/activist Lewis,[20] drew some 15,000 hits a day. Our Americas was a Spanish-language programme about rebels in Latin America (Kornblum 2001; Scheeres 2001).[21] Yahoo! has pulled dozens of sites in the *Jihad* Web Ring, a coalition of 55 *jihad*-related sites, while Lycos Europe established a 20-person team to monitor its Web sites for illegal activity and to remove terrorist-related content (Gruner and Naik 2001; Scheeres 2001).[22]

In August 2001, the Taliban outlawed the use of the Internet in Afghanistan, except at the fundamentalist group's headquarters. The Taliban, nevertheless, maintained a prom-inent home on the Internet despite United Nations sanctions, retaliatory hack attacks, and the vagaries of the United States bombing campaign. The unofficial Web site of Dharb-i-Mumin, an organization named by the United States on a list of terrorist groups, is still operational.[23] Another site, entitled 'Taliban Online,' contained information including in-structions on how to make financial donations, or donations of food and clothing, to the Af-ghan militia, but is no longer operational. In addition, a United States–based Web site

'How Can I Train Myself for Jihad.' A number of Azzam's affiliates were shut down after people complained to the ISPs hosting the sites (at least one, following a request from the FBI). The British company Swift Internet, which was the technical and billing contact for an Azzam site, is said to have received threatening e-mails accusing it of supporting a terrorist Web site. Swift has since distanced itself from the site by removing its name as a contact on public Internet records. Meanwhile, as often as the site is shut down, it is replaced by a substitute/mirror site under a different URL. Said the Azzam spokesperson: "One cannot shut down the Internet" (Gruner and Naik 2001).

At the present time American officials are said to be searching the Internet for the reappearance of an Arabic language Web site that they believe has been used by al-Qaida. Statements ostensibly made by al-Qaida and Taliban members have appeared on the site Alneda.com.[24] The site, which is registered in Singapore, appeared on Web servers in Malaysia and Texas in early June 2002, before American officials shut it down. The site is thought to have first appeared on the Net in early February 2002. It is expected to reappear under a numerical address in an effort to make it harder for American officials to track down. According to media accounts, the site contained audio and video clips of Osama bin Laden; pictures of al-Qaida suspects currently detained in Pakistan; a message claiming to be from al-Qaida spokesman Sualaiman Abu Ghaith, in which he warned of new attacks upon the United States; and a series of articles claiming that suicide bombings aimed at Americans are justifiable under Islamic law (Iqbal 2002; Kelley 2002). There has been media speculation that the site is being used to direct al-Qaida operational cells (AFP 2002). According to one report the site has carried low-level operational information: in February it published the names and home phone numbers of al-Qaida fighters captured by Pakistan following their escape from fighting in Afghanistan with the aim that sympathizers would contact their families and let them know they were alive (Eedle 2002). Click on Alneda.com today and the following appears: Hacked, Tracked, and NOW Owned by the USA. The site is described as "a mostly unmoderated discussion board relating to current world affairs surrounding Islamic Jihad [sic] and the U.S. led war on terrorism (plus other conflicts around the globe)." Not only does the domain name Alneda.com point to this site, but the URL Nukeafghanistan.com also points to this discussion board (see also McWilliams 2002).

New Legislative Measures

In February 2001, the UK updated its Terrorism Act to classify "the use of or threat of action that is designed to seriously interfere with or seriously disrupt an electronic system" as an act of terrorism (see Di Maio 2001; Mates 2001).[25] In fact, it will be up to police investigators to decide whether an action is to be regarded as terrorism. Online groups, human rights organizations, civil liberties campaigners, and others condemned this classification as absurd, pointing out that it placed hacktivism on a par with life-threatening acts of public intimidation (Weisenburger 2001, 9).[26] Notwithstanding, in the wake of the events of 9–11, U.S. legislators followed suit. Previous to 9–11, if one successfully infiltrated a federal computer network, one was considered a hacker. However, following the passage of the USA Patriot Act,[27] which authorized the granting of significant powers to law enforcement agencies to investigate and prosecute potential threats to national security, there is the potential for hackers to be labeled cyberterrorists and, if convicted, to face up to 20 years in prison (NIPC 2001; see also Middleton 2002 & Levin 2002, 984–985). Clearly, policymakers believe that actions taken in cyberspace are qualitatively different from those taken in the 'real' world.

It is not the Patriot Act, however, but the massive 500-page law establishing the U.S. Department of Homeland Security that has the most to say about terrorism and the Internet. The law establishing the new department envisions a far greater role for the United States' government in the securing of operating systems, hardware, and the Internet in the future. In November 2002, U.S. President Bush signed the bill creating the new department, setting in train a process that will result in the largest reshuffle of U.S. bureaucracy since 1948. At the signing ceremony, Bush said that the "department will gather and focus all our efforts to face the challenge of cyberterrorism" (as quoted in McCullagh 2002c). The Department of Homeland Security will merge five agencies that currently share responsibility for critical infrastructure protection in the United States: the FBI's National Infrastructure Protection Center (NIPC), the Defense Department's National Communications System, the Commerce Department's Critical Infrastructure Office, the Department of Energy's analysis center, and the Federal Computer Incident Response Center. The new law also creates a Directorate for Information Analysis and Infrastructure Protection whose task it will be to analyze vulnerabilities in systems including the Internet, telephone networks and other critical infrastructures, and orders the establishment of a "comprehensive national plan for securing the key resources and critical infrastructure of the United States" including information technology, financial networks, and satellites. Further, the law dictates a maximum sentence of life-imprisonment without parole for those who deliberately transmit a program, information, code, or command that impairs the performance of a computer or modifies its data without authorization, "if the offender knowingly or recklessly causes or attempts to cause death." In addition, the law allocates $500 million for research into new technologies, is charged with funding the creation of tools to help state and local law enforcement agencies thwart computer crime, and classifies certain activities as new computer crimes (Krebs 2002; McCullagh 2002c; Poulsen 2002).

Conclusion

In the space of thirty years, the Internet has metamorphosed from a U.S. Department of Defense command-and-control network consisting of less than one hundred computers to a network that criss-crosses the globe: today, the Internet is made up of tens of thousands of nodes (i.e. linkage points) with over 105 million hosts spanning more than 200 countries. With a current (February 2003) estimated population of regular users of over 605 million people, the Internet has become a near-ubiquitous presence in many world regions. That ubiquity is due in large part to the release in 1991 of the World Wide Web. In 1993 the Web consisted of a mere 130 sites, by century's end it boasted more than one billion. In the Western world, in particular, the Internet has been extensively integrated into the economy, the military, and

World Trade Center. The site allowed Internet users worldwide to appreciate what millions of tourists have delighted in since Minoru Yamasaki's architectural wonder was completed in 1973: the glorious 45-mile view from the top of the WTC towers. According to journalists, the caption on the site still read 'Real-Time Hudson River View from World Trade Center' (O'Toole 2001). In the square above was deep black nothingness. The terrorists hadn't taken down the Net, they had taken down the towers. "Whereas hacktivism is real and widespread, cyberterrorism exists only in theory. Terrorist groups are using the Internet, but they still prefer bombs to bytes as a means of inciting terror," wrote Dorothy Denning (2001) just weeks before the September attacks. Terrorist 'use' of the Internet has been largely ignored, however, in favor of the more headline-grabbing 'cyberterrorism.'

In conclusion, the bulk of the evidence to date shows that terrorist groups are making widespread use of the Internet, but so far they have not resorted to cyberterrorism, or shown the inclination to move heavily in this direction. In keeping with this reality, Richard Clarke, White House special adviser for Cyberspace Security, has said that he prefers not to use the term 'cyberterrorism,' instead, he favors the term 'information security' or 'cyberspace security,' since at this stage terrorists have only used the Internet for propaganda, communications, and fundraising (Wynne 2002). In a similar vein, Michael Vatis, former head of the U.S. National Infrastructure Protection Center (NIPC), has stated that "Terrorists are already using technology for sophisticated communications and fundraising activities. As yet we haven't seen computers being used by these groups as weapons to any significant degree, but this will probably happen in the future" (Veltman 2001). According to a 2001 study, 75% of Internet users worldwide agree, they believe that 'cyberterrorists' will "soon inflict massive casualties on innocent lives by attacking corporate and governmental computer networks." The survey, conducted in 19 major cities around the world, found that 45% of respondents agreed completely that "computer terrorism will be a growing problem," and another 35% agreed somewhat with the same statement (Poulsen 2001). The problem certainly can't shrink much, hovering as it does at zero cyberterrorism incidents per year. That's not to say that cyberterrorism cannot happen or will not happen, but that, contrary to popular perception, it has not happened yet.

Maura Conway is a Ph.D. candidate in the Department of Political Science at Trinity College Dublin, Ireland, and a teaching fellow at the University of St. Andrews, Scotland. Her research interests are in the area of terrorism and the Internet. She has published in *First Monday*, *Current History*, the *Journal of Information Warfare*, and elsewhere. Her research has been facilitated by a grant from the Irish Research Council for the Humanities and Social Sciences.

Notes

1. On May 3, 2002, the European Union updated its list of prohibited organizations. See http://ue.eu.intlpressData/en/misc/70413.pdf. The latest country to devise such a list is Canada. See http://www.sgc.gc.ca/publications/news/20020723_e.asp.
2. A comprehensive list of all terrorist Web sites is available on Barry Cromwell's 'Separatist, Para-Military, Military, Intelligence, and Political Organizations' site at http://www.cromwell-intl.com/security/netusers.html.
3. One of the most accessible sound bites on what defines cyberterrorism is that it is 'hacking with a body count' (Collin, quoted in Ballard *et al* 2002, 992).
4. This is also the definition employed in the U.S. State Department's annual report *Patterns of Global Terrorism*.
5. Anderson was formerly senior vice-president of IT Security and Investigations for information security firm Control Risks Group.
6. Also Hizballah, Hezbollah, Hezbullah, Hezbollah, etc., a.k.a Islamic Jihad, Revolutionary Justice Organisation, Organisation of the Oppressed on Earth, and Islamic Jihad for the Liberation of Palestine.
7. Online at http://www.hizbollah.org.
8. Accessible at http://www.moqawama.tv/.
9. Online at http://www.manartv.com.
10. In addition, see http://www.nasrollah.org the home page of Sayed Hassan Nasrallah, the General Secretary of Hizbollah, in Arabic, English, and French.
11. Accessible at http://www.palestine-info.co.uk/hamas/index.htm.
12. I have not, as yet, been able to locate the GIA site.
13. The Tupac Amaru Solidarity Page hosted by UCSD is at http://burn.ucsd.edu/~ats/mrta.htm. The official homepage of the MRTA (in Europe) may be accessed at http://www.voz-rebelde.de. The latter page is available in English, Spanish, Italian, Japanese, Turkish, and Serbo-Croat translations. The Tupac Amaru were on the United States list of FTOs until 2001 when they were removed.
14. Online at http://www.igc.org/igc/gateway/index.html.
15. For more information on the e-mail bombing and IGC's response to it see http://www.igc.apc.org.ehj/. Also the press release issued by Internet Freedom UK in response to the shutting of their operations by Scotland Yard: http://www.fitug.de/debate/9709/msg00018.html. The group's Web site is located at http://www.netfreedom.org.
16. In October 2000, a group claiming that hackers had defaced a Hizbollah site contacted a number of media outlets in the United States and Europe. When journalists accessed the site the Israeli flag, Hebrew text and a tinny piano recording of Hatikva, the Israeli national anthem, greeted them. This prompted several news organizations to report that Hizbollah's Central Press Office site had been defaced by pro-Israeli hackers (see Hockstader 2000; Puller 2001). Only later did it become apparent that the site at hizbolla.org (which is no longer operational) was a fraud that had been established by an unidentified individual or group using an address in Lebanon (see Garrison and Grand 2001, 7).
17. The official Web site of the Palestinian National Authority at http://www.pna.gov.ps/ was accessible at time of writing. I have experienced difficulties accessing this site in the past.
18. The Clinton administration spearheaded the first major U.S. effort to upgrade computer security in government and business against cybercrime. President Bill Clinton issued an order in May 1998 establishing the National Infrastructure Protection Center, a collaboration between law enforcement, military, and intelligence organizations to increase defenses against computer crime. The center also developed an information-sharing network with major industrial sectors.
19. In Britain, Foreign Secretary Jack Straw provoked a storm of protest by suggesting on the BBC that the media and civil liberties campaigners had paved the way for the terror attacks on America by advocating free speech and favoring publicly available encryption.
20. Formerly Grandpa on the 1960s hit TV show 'The Munsters'!

23. Online at http://dharo-1-mumm.ejo.net.
24. The site has also appeared at http://www.drasat.com.
25. The full text of the UK Terrorism Act 2001 is available online at http://www.legislation. hmso.gov.uk/acts/acts2000/20000011.htm.
26. Furthermore, ISPs in the UK may be legally required to monitor some customers' surfing habits if requested to do so by the police under the Regulation of Investigatory Powers Act 2000.
27. The Uniting and Strengthening America by Providing Appropriate Tools Required to Intercept and Obstruct Terrorism (USA PATRIOT) Act of 2001 was signed into law by U.S. President George Bush in October 2001. The law gives government investigators broad powers to track wireless phone calls, listen to voicemail, intercept e-mail messages and monitor computer use, among others. I cannot enter into a discussion of the Act here due to limitations of space. However, the full text of the Act is available at http://www.ins.usdoj.gov/fgraphics/lawsregs/ patriot.pdf (Section 1016 pertains to critical infrastructure protection). See also Johnson 2001; Matthews 2001.

References

Agence France Presse (AEP). 2002. 'Investigators Watching for Suspected al-Qaida Web Site.' *Agence France Presse* 23 June.

Arquilla, J. & D. Ronfledt. 2001. 'Networks, Netwars, and the Fight for the Future.' *First Monday* 6(10), at http://www.firstmonday.org/issues/issue6_10/ronfeldt/.

Arquilla, J, D. Ronfeldt & M. Zanini. 1999. 'Networks, Netwar and Information-Age Terrorism.' In Ian 0. Lesser, Bruce Hoffman, John Arquilla, David F. Ronfeldt, Michele Zanini & Brian Michael Jenkins, *Countering the New Terrorism*. Santa Monica, Calif.: Rand.

Ballard, J.D., J.G. Hornik, & D. McKenzie. 2002. 'Technological Facilitation of Terrorism: Definitional, Legal and Policy Issues.' *American Behavioral Scientist* 45(6): 989–1016.

Cha, A.E. 2001. 'To Attacks' Toll Add a Programmer's Grief.' *The Washington Post* 21 September: E01.

Cobain, I. 2001. 'FBI Closes Website Linked to Real IRA.' *The Times* (London) 8 October: 8.

Cohen, Adam. 2001. 'When Terror Hides Online.' *Time* 12 November.

Collin, B. 1996. 'The Future of Cyberterrorism.' Paper presented at the 11th Annual International Symposium on Criminal Justice Issues, University of Illinois at Chicago, at http://afgen.com/ terrorisml.html.

Collier, R. 1997. 'Terrorists Get Web Sites Courtesy of U.S. Universities.' *San Francisco Chronicle* 9 May, at http://burn.ucsd.edu/archives/ats-1/l997.Mav/0042.html.

Conway, M. 2002a. 'Reality Bytes: Cyberterrorism and Terrorist 'Use' of the Internet.' *First Monday* 7(11), at http://www.firstmonday.org/issues/issue7_11/conway/index.html.

Conway, M. 2002b. 'What is Cyberterrorism?' *Current History* 101(659): 436–442.

Conway, M. 2002c. 'Cyberterrorism' Paper presented at the conference on *War and Virtual War: The Challenge to Communities*, Mansfield College, Oxford, 16–18 July.

Daukantas, P. 2001. 'Professors Hash Out Emergency Response, Cyberterrorism Strategies.' *Government Computer News* 14 December, at http://www.gcn.com/vol1_no_1/daily-updates/ 17642-1.html.

Denning, D. 2001. 'Hacker Warriors: Rebels, Freedom Fighters, and Terrorists Turn to Cyberspace.' *Harvard International Review Summer*, at: http://www.hir.harvard.edu/archive/articles/pdf/ denning.html.

Denning, D. 1999. *Activism, Hacktivism, and Cyberterrorism: The Internet as a Tool for Influencing Foreign Policy*. Washington D.C.: Nautilus Institute, at http://www.nautilus.org/info~policy/ workshop/papers/denning.html.

Devost, M., B. Houghton & N. Pollard. 1997. 'Information Terrorism: Political Violence in the Information Age.' *Terrorism and Political Violence* 9(1): 72–83.

Devost, M., B. Houghton & N. Pollard. 1996. 'Information Terrorism: Can You Trust Your Toaster?' *The Terrorism Research Center*, at http://www.terrorism.com/terrorism/itpaper.html.

Di Maio, P. 2001. 'Hacktivism, Cyberterrorism or Online Democracy?' *The Information Warfare Site* (IWS) 19 March, at http://www.iwar.org.uk/hackers/resources/hacktivism-europe/internet-europe.htm

Eedle, P. 2002. 'Terrorism.Com.' *Guardian* (UK) 17 July, at http://www.guardian.co.uk/Print/0,3858,4462872,00.html.

Embar-Seddon, A. 2002. 'Cyberterrorism: Are We Under Siege?' *American Behavioral Scientist* 45(6): 1017–1043.

Fallis, D.S. & A.E. Cha. 2001. 'Agents Following Suspects' Lengthy Electronic Trail.' *The Washington Post* 4 October: A24.

Foreign Broadcast Information Service (EBIS). 2002a. 'Russia Cracks Down on 'Cyberterrorism.' *ITAR-TASS*, FBIS-SOV-2002-0208, 8 February.

Foreign Broadcast Information Service (FBIS). 2002b. 'Government Sets Up Anti-Cyberterrorism Homepage.' *Sankei Shimbun*, FBIS-EAS-2002-0410, 10 April.

Garrison, L. & M. Grand (Ed.s). 2001. *National Infrastructure Protection Center: Highlights*, at http://www.nipc.gov/publications/highlights/2001/highlight-01-02.htm.

Gearty, C.A. 1991. *Terror*. London: Faber & Faber.

Gentile, C.J. 2000a. 'Hacker War Rages in Holy Land.' *Wired* 8 November, at http://www.wired.com/news/politics/0,1283,40030,00.html.

Gentile, C.J. 2000b. 'Palestinian Crackers Share Bugs.' *Wired* 2 December, at http://www.wired.com/news/politics/0%2C1283%2C40449%2C00.html.

Gruner, S. & G. Naik. 2001. 'Extremist Sites Under Heightened Scrutiny.' *The Wall Street Journal Online* 8 October, at http://zdnet.com.com/2100-1106-530855.html?legacy=zdnn.

Guelke, A. 1998. *The Age of Terrorism and the International Political System*. London: IB Tauris Publishers.

Hershman, T. 2000. 'Cyberterrorism Is Real Threat, Say Experts at Conference.' *Israel.internet.com* 11 December.

Hockstader, L. 2000. 'Pings and E-Arrows Fly in Mideast Cyber-War.' *Washington Post* 27 October: A01.

Hoffman, B. 1998. *Inside Terrorism*. London: Indigo.

Hosein, H. 2001. 'Bytes Without the Blood in Mideast.' *MSNBC* 4 January.

Ingles-le Noble, J. 1999. 'Cyberterrorism Hype.' *Jane's Intelligence Review*, at http://www.iwar.org.uk/cyberterror/resources/janes/jir0525.htm.

Iqbal, A. 2002. 'Site Claims bin Laden's Message.' United Press International 20 February, at http://www.upi.com/view.cfm?StoryID=20022002-075528-9498r.

Johnson, B. 2001. 'Farewell Web Freedom?' *The Guardian* (UK) 22 October.

Kelley, J. 2002. 'Agents Pursue Terrorists Online.' *USA Today* 20 June, at http://www.usatoday.com/life/cyber/tech/2002/06/21/terrorweb.htm.

Kornblum, J. 2001. 'Radical Radio Shows Forced from the Net.' *USA Today* 25 October: 3D.

Krebs, B. 2002. 'Homeland Security Bill Heralds IT Changes.' *The Washington Post* 25 November, at http://www.washingtonpost.com/wp-dyn/articles/A54872-2002Nov14.html.

Levin, B. 2002. 'Cyberhate: A Legal and Historical Analysis of Extremists' Use of Computer Networks in America.' *American Behavioral Scientist* 45(6): 958–988.

Leyden, J. 2000. 'Palestinian Crackers Give Out Tools to Attack Israelis.' *The Register* (UK) December 4, at http://www.theregister.co.uk/content/6/15199.html.

Liu, M. 2001. 'Holy War on the Web.' *Newsweek* (International) 15 October: 62.

Luke, T.W. 2001. 'Cyberspace as Meta-Nation: The Net Effects of Online E-Publicanism.' *Alternatives* 26(2): 113–142.

Lyman, J. 2002. 'Terrorist Web Site Hosted by U.S. Firm.' *NewsFactor Network* 3 April, at http://www.newsfactor.com/perl/story/17079.html.

McCullagh, D. 2002a. 'University Bans Controversial Links.' *CNet News* 25 September, at http://news.com.com/2100-1023-959544.html?tag=fd_top.

McCullagh, D. 2002b. 'University Backs Down on Link Ban.' *CNet News* 8 October, at http://news.com.com/2100-1023-961297.html?tag=mainstry.

McCullagh, D. 2002c. 'Bush Signs Homeland Security Bill.' *CNET News* 25 November, at http://news.com.com/2102-1023-975305.html.

McGirk, T. 1999. 'Wired for Warfare.' *Time* (International) 11 October.

McWilliams, B. 2002. 'One Man's Info War on al-Qaida.' *Wired* 18 December, at http://www.wired.com/news/infostructure/0,1377,56896.00.html.

Middleton, J. 2002. 'U.S. Hackers Could Face Life Sentences.' *Vnunet.com* 28 February, at http://www.vnunet.com/News/1129590.

Mulloy, D.J. 1999. *Homegrown Revolutionaries: An American Militia Reader*. Norwich U.K.: Arthur Miller.

National Infrastructure Protection Center (NTPC). 2001. *NIPC Daily Report: 11 December*. Washington, DC: NIPC.

Piller, C. 2001. 'Terrorists Taking Up Cyberspace.' *Los Angeles Times* 8 February: Al.

O'Toole, F. 2001. 'Terrorists Hold Levers of Control of New Kind of War.' *The Irish Times* 16 September.

Pollitt, M. n.d. 'Cyberterrorism: Fact or Fancy?' at http://www.cs.georgetown.edu/~denning/infosec/pollitt.html.

Poulsen, K. 2001. 'Cyber Terror in the Air.' *SecurityFocus.com* 30 June.

Scheeres, J. 2001. 'Suppression Stifles Some Sites.' *Wired* 25 October, at http://www.wired.com/news/business/0,1367,47835,00.html.

Schmid, A. P. & Al. Jongruan. 1988. *Political Terrorism: A New Guide to Actors, Authors, Concepts, Databases, Theories and Literature*. Amsterdam: North-Holland.

Schwartz, J. 2000. 'When Point and Shoot Becomes Point and Click.' *New York Times* 12 November.

Sher, H. 2000. 'Cyberterror Should be International Crime—Israeli Minister.' *Newsbytes* 10 November.

Toffler, A. 1980. *The Third Wave*. London: Pan Books.

Veitman, C. 2001. 'Beating Cyber Crime.' *Daily Telegraph* 1 March: 12E.

Wardlaw, G. 1982. *Political Terrorism: Theory, Tactics, and Countermeasures*. Cambridge: Cambridge University Press.

Weisenberger, K. 2001. 'Hacktivists of the World, Divide.' *SecurityWatch.com* 23 April, at: http://www.securitywatch.com/TRE/04230l.html.

Wynne, J. 2002. 'White House Advisor Richard Clarke Briefs Senate Panel on Cybersecurity.' *Washington File* 14 February, at http://usinfo.state.gov/topical/global/ecom/02021401.htm.

Madeleine Gruen, 2003

White Ethnonationalist and Political Islamist Methods of Fundraising and Propaganda on the Internet

W hite ethnonationalists and political Islamists use the Internet for five primary purposes: propaganda, recruitment, indoctrination, fundraising, and psychological warfare. This essay explores three uses of the Internet by these groups: 1) methods of propaganda for the purpose of recruitment and the indoctrination of teenage and young-adult males, including the employment of decoy sites and the exploitation of target-population interests in music and computer games in order to present troublesome ideology; 2) sites sponsored by lone-wolf actors that are created with the intention of inspiring further leaderless resistance; and 3) principal methods of fundraising via the Internet: product sales, Web-based appeals for funds, and side businesses that may or may not be related to the primary missions of the group.

White ethnonationalist as well as political Islamist Web presence are of particular interest because of the parallels in ideology and tactics used to recruit, indoctrinate, and raise funds, and because white ethnonationalist groups have had a pioneering presence on the Internet, appearing in Web sites and chat forums as early as 1995. White-ethnonationalist information technology strategies have effectively afforded groups that traditionally operated domestically a transnational presence, richer and more varied funding opportunities, and a profitable conduit to their desired recruitment demographic. Political Islamist groups desire the same results from their Internet campaigns, and so elements of the models established by white ethnonationalists are becoming evident in the burgeoning Internet campaign of the political Islamists. Using white ethnonationalists as a barometer, future trends in political Islamist Web presence can be predicted.

In the United States, when problematic presence on the Web began to emerge in 1995, media coverage was scarce, highlighting the lack of concern on the part of the general public and security agencies. At that time, only 5 percent of the American voting public had access to the Internet[1] and the Clinton administration did not consider monitoring the Web a high priority despite conservative and right-wing sites outnumbering left-wing or liberal sites at a ratio of 10 to 1.[2] The sentiment at the time held that since such a small percentage of the voting public frequented the global computer network, its impact on national politics would be limited. From the beginning, problematic material was placed on the Web to indoctrinate and incite violent response, and the influence was compounded with the millions who signed on each subsequent year. In early 2001, Richard Baumhammers shot down six people, all members of minorities, in suburban Philadelphia, inspired by material on the Internet.[3] In 2002, Michael Kenneth Faust, who spent several hours a day on the Internet

Two of the target audiences for white-ethnonationalist and political-Islamist recruitment are disaffected, English-speaking teenage and young-adult males, and lone-wolf actors. Those groups' desires to attract these audiences is evident in emergent trends in group Web presence. One third of white-ethnonationalist and one quarter of political Islamist Web sites are devoted to, or contain content geared towards the indoctrination of male children and young adults between the approximate ages of eight and twenty-two.[5] Because of trends in terrorism and advantages to active groups, there is a proliferation of sites built by lone-wolf actors and sites sponsored by organized groups that encourage lone-wolf activism.

Almost every political Islamist group has an English-language Web presence, which is reflective of the fact that 40 percent of the total on-line population are English speakers.[6] Internet users in the Middle East, South Asia, and Africa, a potentially more sympathetic audience for political Islamist ideology, accounted for less than 5 percent of the world's users.[7] Only 500,000 Arabic-speaking people access the Internet from North America and Europe,[8] which indicates that the political Islamists use their English-language sites to influence, persuade, and in some cases, recruit from the West's native population.

How are potential recruits led to politically incorrect material if they are not actively in search of it? Expert propagandists have initiated several methods:

1. Capitalizing on young adults' musical interests. Sites most trafficked by university students are those through which music can be accessed.[9]
2. Capitalizing on the popularity of computer games with male teens and young adults; 92 percent of boys in the U.S. play video/electronic games.[10]
3. Assigning Web addresses similar to those of popular sites, which leads subjects to troublesome material when they intended to go to a legitimate site.
4. Building bogus sites meant to resemble legitimate documentary-style sites that profile historical figures or events, especially popular subjects of school papers. More than 70 percent of school-aged children and young adults do research for papers on-line.[11]
5. Building decoy sites for seemingly legitimate organizations. Sites bear no reference to the sponsoring group but feature the same ideology.
6. Mentioning group Web addresses in legitimate news articles.
7. Posting Web addresses on popular mainstream message boards frequented by teens and young adults.
8. Engaging target subjects in chat rooms unrelated to white-ethnonationalist or political Islamist interests.

Once the subject is exposed to the material, what factors will make him return to the Web site? He may be attracted to the "us" vs. "them" rhetoric prevalent on white-ethnonationalist and political Islamist Web sites, which blames others for the subject's problems. He may be vulnerable to the allure of a peer group that he cannot find in the physical world. The propaganda may provide structure and a target for his previously undirected rage. He may suffer from mental illness that renders him prone to the conspiratorial content on many sites. This suggestive material accentuates his "fear of the other," and can lead him down a path of faulty logic that suggests that the only way to achieve happiness, success, or the desired equivalent, is to eliminate the enemy.

Is mere exposure to seditious ideology via the Internet powerful enough to incite an actor to commit violence? While not equivalent to face-to-face indoctrination, a Web site with all its features is a vessel that can sufficiently contain the elements of a multifaceted propaganda campaign, powerful enough to compel certain individuals to commit acts of violence.

Propaganda in a Nutshell

All of the various elements of a successful propaganda campaign, as identified by the Institute for Propaganda Analysis,12 can be issued over Web sites and their Internet "radio" broadcasts, chat boards, newsgroups, and other components. These attributes are:

- "Name-Calling," which links a person or group to a negative name or symbol.
- "Glittering Generalities," which are words associated with virtuous ideals based on deep-set experience. Buzz words used as "Glittering Generalities" will differ according to the culture on which they are being imposed.
- "Transfer," which is the association of an idea with a symbol. This concept can either be positive or negative depending on the symbol to which the concept is transferred.
- "Testimonials," which are used to convince an individual or population of an idea by having that idea endorsed by someone of respected stature. Conversely, an idea that may otherwise be accepted by an individual or population can be made dubious by connection with someone loathed or not respected.
- "Plain Folks," a device used to influence a population wherein the concept is delivered by someone who appears to be an average person.
- "Bandwagon," which takes advantage of a person's instinct to follow the crowd. The propagandist directs his campaign on those who are already held together by common ties, whether nationality, religion, or hatred of a common enemy. Along the same lines, the Institute of Propaganda Analysis also identified a technique they called "Card-Stacking," in which the propagandist employs all the arts of deception, including lies, censorship, distortion, and dodging facts, in order to win support for himself or his cause.
- "Fear," used as a weapon to manipulate populations to follow the directives of the propagandist on the threat that if the will of the propagandist is not followed then the population will fall prey to their greatest fears. The propagandist also wants to instill the fear of dissent through intimidation, and the subject's desire to conform to the group prevents him from offering a dissenting opinion.

The cyberworld provides enough interaction between likeminded individuals to validate and solidify problematic worldviews, and it also enables the presence of all-important charismatic leadership. Contact is established between the problematic group and the target subjects through chat forums, e-mail lists, and trickery to get them onto group Web sites, keeping subjects trapped in an endless loop of similar sites where buzz words, symbols, and

Don Black: Innovative Propagandist

Don Black, former Grand Wizard of the Ku Klux Klan, taught himself computer skills while imprisoned for the planned invasion of Dominica for the purpose of establishing an all-white nation.[13] He is owner and operator of Stormfront.org, the first and the longest-operating white-ethnonationalist Web site, launched in 1995. Stormfront.org defines itself as a catch-all resource site for the white-ethnonationalist movement; with a library of writings by prominent racists, links to organized white-ethnonationalist groups, articles on eugenics and political ideologies, and a library of graphics and logos. Of the countless millions of Web sites, Stormfront.org is one of the most highly trafficked on the Net, with a ranking of 6,600.[14] To contrast, Tolerance.org, a site owned and operated by the Southern Poverty Law Center, whose mission is to promote tolerance and eliminate white-ethnonationalist groups, has a traffic rank of 60,000.[15] In other words, Stormfront would be in the top percentile of the most popular sites on the Web; more popular than the official site of international pop star Michael Jackson (ranked 39,219 in June 2003), or nycvisit.com, the official tourism Web site for the city of New York (ranked 29,879). This indicates that there are more people interested in the messages of hate than messages of tolerance or the exploration of culture.

In addition to the highly-successful Stormfront site, Black operates Martinlutherking.org, designed to resemble a documentary-style site, but rather than containing historical information it instead contains defaming material on the civil-rights leader. Black counts on the fact that of the more than 70 percent of school-aged children and young adults who do research for school papers on-line, many will not be able to determine the difference between Martinlutherking.org and a legitimate site.

In the past, Black registered Web addresses similar to those of major newspapers, which led subjects back to his Stormfront site rather than to the newspaper. For example, *The Philadelphia Inquirer's* Web address is phillynews.com. Black registered Philadelphiainquirer.com, which linked directly to the Stormfront site.

Black continues to set trends in deceit tactics, which are incorporated into and improved upon in the recruitment campaigns of white-ethnonationalist and political-Islamist organizations.

Music as a Lure

Teenagers are attracted by the lifestyle image that white-power music companies intend to portray; it is subversive, alternative, and uses a language that is common only to fans of the white-power genre. The vulnerable subject wants the acceptance of a peer group, and the indoctrinated members then proceed to shape the subject's worldviews. In a second example, a political Islamist group dips into a pool of moderate Muslims and eases them into accepting more extreme worldviews by utilizing methods borrowed from proven propaganda campaigns: assigning negative labels to their Jewish adversaries, presenting testimonials from peers, and eliminating expressions of dissent to give the illusion of unity of thought by a large group.

"White Power" or "Resistance" Music

The results of one survey of 2,760 14- to 16-year-olds in 10 different southeastern American cities showed that that they listened to music an average of 40 hours per week.[16] Numerous studies have determined that there is a correlation between teenagers with a preference for heavy-metal music, which is the standard genre of white-power music, and alienation and risk-taking behaviors during adolescence.[17] The white-ethnonationalist movement has used music as an outreach tool to attract impressionable young people for decades. Concerts were a favored recruiting venue, and in the late 1970s and early 1980s when Oi! music, a punk derivative, was at its peak, neo-Nazi recruiters targeted the genre's skinhead fans, thus transforming a previously non-racist social group into one almost entirely associated with the neo-Nazi movement.[18] Successful white-power record-company and musical-group Web sites are visually exuberant; the Internet, the bands, the music, and the lifestyle they depict, they can reach the broadest audience possible.

Resistance Records, the white-power music company owned by the National Alliance, nets approximately $1.3 million per year.[19] William Pierce, the author of *The Turner Diaries* and director of the National Alliance until his death in July 2002, bought the company with the intention of targeting young people who feel dispossessed. Resistance.com is a strategic site, on which every element is instrumental in the indoctrination process. The chart below lists the tactical elements of the site and describes the intended purpose for each.

Element	Function
Revisionist history	Acclimates subjects to group doctrines
"Radio"	Presents the voice of charismatic leadership; subjects receive doctrines in a more passive form
Catalog of merchandise	Products sold to raise money are also tools for indoctrination
Clothes	A uniform meant to emphasize the "one-people" mentality
Games	Acclimate players to the idea of violence toward "sub-humans," that is, racial minorities and Jews
Forum	Shapes worldviews and modifies behaviors
Symbols	Meant to induce subconscious associations

The white-ethnonationalist movement has mastered the skill of marrying a lifestyle to its cause, and on their white-power-band Web sites, they blend musical interests with ideology almost seamlessly.

Hizb ut-Tahrir (HT), a controversial proselytizing fundamentalist party with an estimated following of 10,000 worldwide,[20] is among the most pervasive and professionally presented political Islamist groups on the Internet. Their primary target population consists of university students, whom they traditionally approached on campuses; however, because the group has been outlawed in central Asian countries and in Germany, accused of terrorism and seditious activity, students in those regions have been warned against the group. Therefore, HT, like many other political Islamist organizations, has come to rely on the Internet to reach the student population. In total, the group has built approximately fifty Web sites. One site, Muslimstudent.org.uk, is replete with group ideology but bears no mention of the group's sponsorship. The commonplace name of the site is such that it can be easily found by Muslim students in the United Kingdom who are in search of a peer group or student activities.

In addition to its Web sites, HT infiltrates and subsequently dominates newsgroups intended for moderate Muslim students. One such e-group was for the fans of Soldiers of Allah (SOA), a hip hop/technopop band from Canoga Park, California. As of February 2003, the group had 1,000 members, most of whom were university students from North America, Central Asia, South Asia, and Europe. The SOA newsgroup was intended to be a forum for the discussion of music, social topics, and light politics, but between its founding in December 2001 and December 2002, the postings slowly shifted to become more militant in nature. A new group of users posted messages imbued with the ideology of the more radical Islamist groups. One post quoted Henry Ford denouncing Jews as an "organized, dangerous, largely secret and incredible [sic] powerful menace to America."[21] Other postings admonished newsgroup members to regard themselves solely as Muslims and not identify themselves by a nationality; that their loyalty should be sworn only to Allah and any Muslim pledging allegiance to a nation (especially the United States) is betraying the Brotherhood. Further, the postings imply that to be moderate is equivalent to being a nonbeliever and to be militant is equivalent to being a true Muslim. In November 2002, the rhetoric intensified and the authors of these postings began to identify themselves as members of HT. In early December 2002, SOA announced that they were appointing a moderator to manage their newsgroup in order to regulate the overwhelming number of messages flooding into and subsequently jamming members' mailboxes. From that point on HT dominated the discourse of the forum with politics and blatant recruitment efforts. While at first a few newsgroup members wrote dissenting responses to the fundamentalist dogma, eventually any voice of dissent or element of debate disappeared.

The Soldiers of Allah newsgroup was used as a device to attract young moderate Muslims who were fans of the music group. Rather than finding a forum to communicate with others with a common interest, fans were immersed in a forum for indoctrination.

Multimedia Devices Issued by Separatist Groups: Computer Games

Studies such as Anderson and Dill's[22] conclude that playing violent video games is positively related to aggressive behavior and delinquency. The relationship between aggression and game-play is stronger for men and individuals who are characteristically aggressive. The National Institute for Media and the Family found that 92 percent of boys play video/electronic games, and on average they preferred a fair amount of violence in the game; a 7 on a scale of 1 to 10.[23] The same study shows that repeated exposure to violent images will desensitize the subjects' responses to them, and they also conclude that players of violent video games act with increased aggression for half an hour after they play.

Ethnic Cleansing

The white-ethnonationalist groups have been exploiting the popularity of computer games with teens and young adults by programming, marketing, and selling their own, with such names as "Sieg Heil," "Concentration Camp," "Hang Leroy," "Kill 'Em All," "Niggerhunt," and "Racial Holy War." Until the National Alliance began to sell their computer game "Ethnic Cleansing" in early 2002, all the games were downloadable free of charge from Internet sites. The Group sells copies for $14.88, a price point not based on any business model, but formed from codes particular to the white-ethnonationalist movement. The numbers "14" and "88" appear everywhere in the groups' vernacular: the number 14 is emblematic of "the 14 words," which are "We must secure the existence of our people and a future for white children."[24] The number "88" is code for the phrase "Heil Hitler"—*H* is the 8th number of the alphabet, therefore 88 represents the initials *H.H.*[25]

The game is the National Alliance's #1 best-selling item. In the game, the player wanders urban streets shooting racial minorities until the final level is reached, the object of which is to kill Jews.

The game sets a precedent for groups with troublesome ideology—the idea that combat games are popular with pre-teen, teen, and young-adult males, and that the premise of the action of the game can influence behavior and worldviews. Billy Roper, Deputy Membership Coordinator for the National Alliance, said that "the goal is, with most of the things we do with Resistance Records, is not necessarily to earn a profit. Our primary goal is to get our message out there… to young white people who, for the most part, have been alienated by a culture that denies them a sense of identity, denies them a sense of culture."[26]

Special Force

On February 16, 2003, Hizbollah launched its own computer game, "Special Force." It is a "first person shooting game" with sophisticated graphics, designed to allow players to simulate the experience of military operations against Israeli soldiers in battles re-created from actual encounters in the south of Lebanon, "real battles that humiliated the Zionist enemy, giving it a lesson…." Another feature of the programming allows players to sharpen their marksmanship using Prime Minister Ariel Sharon of Israel as a target.

Top officials of Hizbollah, who made the decision to produce the game,[27] believe that resistance to the Israelis occurs not only through military operations, but through the

The programming of "Special Force" is more technically sophisticated than that of "Ethnic Cleansing." In this case, a political Islamist group has borrowed a concept from the white-ethnonationalist movement and improved upon it.

Kaboom!

"Kaboom! The Suicide Bombing Game" is an Internet-based game in which the player detonates himself on a crowded sidewalk. Points are awarded according to the number of men, women, and children who are killed or injured during one "attack." The creator of "Kaboom!" has explained that he meant to highlight the absurdity of suicide bombings, not advocate them.[28] Because the phrase "suicide bombing game" is used in the game's title it is clear that the game was not intended for training or indoctrination purposes as the term "suicide bombing" is offensive to group actors. However, the game has been recommended by World Church of the Creator on their message boards.

As the sophistication of the games increases, players will become more desensitized to the violent actions they portray, and the games will be more likely to be introduced into mainstream society through word-of-mouth recommendations.

Leaderless Resistance on the Internet

Reflective of trends in the physical theater, lone-wolf actors are appearing with more frequency on the Internet and are nearly impossible to track down because they can conceal their identities when registering a Web site or newsgroup. The sheer numbers of this sort of site, and the fact that they are easily posted on Web sites hosting public "communities," such as Geocities and Angelfire, are reasons why it has been difficult for watchdog groups to accurately calculate the number of troublesome sites.

Lone-wolf actors participate on the Internet by 1) building their own sites; 2) by monitoring their own newsgroups, which are most often one-way forums for them to express thoughts on current news events; 3) by frequently posting on various chat boards; or 4) via clandestine non-interactive participation. Lone-wolf sites are intended to incite further leaderless resistance, and they often feature more violent rhetoric than the sites of the group by which the actors were first indoctrinated.

White Aryan Resistance

Tom Metzger, director of White Aryan Resistance (WAR), was once considered the most dangerous and influential actor in the white-supremacist movement. However, his power diminished after the murder of an Ethiopian immigrant by skinheads who were recruited, organized, and trained by WAR.[29] Metzger praised the skinheads for doing their "civic duty." A civil suit brought against Metzger in connection with the murder found him liable for $12.5 million, and he consequently lost his home, his television-repair business, and his meeting hall.[30] WAR now operates only as a Web site, and Tom Metzger and his son John are WAR's only visible, above-ground members. Without a formally incorporated organization and without any material assets, it is now more difficult for prosecutors to bring criminal or civil action against Metzger, and even if prosecutors could succeed in building a case of criminal incitement, Metzger would be unable to pay the judgment. The Metzgers support themselves by selling neo-Nazi paraphernalia over the site.

The WAR site is an informational hub for leaderless resistance that sympathizers visit in anonymity. The central image on the homepage is a wolf with blood dripping from its fangs and swastikas for pupils. In a typical propaganda campaign, such a menacing image would be used to portray the enemy, but WAR exists for a cadre of supporters who perceive themselves as angry and voracious for their enemies' blood.

Through a personalized daily e-mail missive from Tom Metzger and a "24-hour Aryan Update" telephone hotline, tips on how to raise funds for the procurement of munitions are offered. He also gives detailed instructions on how to handle federal enforcement investigations and how to evade questioning from the same. Metzger extols the violent achievements of lone-wolf operatives, derides Jews and racial minorities, and advocates separatism at any cost.

Because his site operates as a one-way forum, it is unknown how influential Metzger is. However, the concept of leaderless resistance is advocated by many dissident groups as an effective measure to dodge surveillance by intelligence agencies. Sympathetic individuals have built countless thousands of Web sites that feature the same dogma as organized hate groups, but there are few sites like Metzger's that are one-stop menageries of white-ethnonationalist doctrines. Such experts as Peter Bergen[31] predict that leaderless resistance is the direction in which terrorism will head. If this is the case, then many more hubs, such as WAR, will crop up to fuel white-ethnonationalist and political-Islamist missions.

Fundraising

The Internet is a low-cost means for terrorist groups to reach a larger audience than has been historically possible, and perhaps provides contact with a higher-income demographic. It is a simple way for a group to solicit donations and raise funds while bearing minimal overhead costs. The Internet also provides a means for groups to dodge detection from state actors who are aggressively trying to cut funding.

Terrorist groups raise funds via the Internet in 5 primary methods:

- By making appeals via e-mail or directly on their Web sites,
- By selling goods through their Web sites,
- Through side businesses that are not identified as group-owned but are nevertheless associated,
- Through on-line organizations that resemble humanitarian charity groups,
- Through fraud, gambling, or on-line brokering.

Internet and Web-Based Appeals

Groups make appeals through 1) correspondence sent directly to sympathizers who have registered their e-mail addresses on the group's main Web site; 2) sending solicitations to

come in three forms: 1) general appeals for funds needed to sustain their operations; 2) fundraisers for legal representation for members who have been arrested; and 3) donations good toward "official membership," which entitles subjects to additional material, such as newsletter subscriptions.

Despite the talk of the formidable challenge to terrorist funding networks by state agencies, many political Islamist organizations appear unhampered and continue to make blatant appeals via e-mail and on Web sites.

Hamas has circulated appeal letters to newsgroups consisting of moderate Muslims and those who share their ideologies. Hizbollah supplies bank-account information to those who solicit them by e-mail and they post their bank account information directly on several of their Web sites.

On the first page of the English portion of their subscription satellite television station Web site, manartv.com, Hizbollah makes a direct appeal for the funding of the "sustenance of the Intifadah" and supplies all relevant bank-account information to do so. Account numbers are also listed on the site of the Islamic Centre of England (ICE), a group associated with Hizbollah. ICE offers several options for donating, including paying with a major credit card by e-mailing details or by giving card details by phone. There is no explanation on the site as to what purpose the monies are allocated. It may be clear to donors where their money is going, but because of heightened vigilance in the United Kingdom purposes are not stated on the site.

Side Businesses

Political Islamists and white ethnonationalists have created on-line businesses, which may or may not be directly related to their primary operations. The status of the businesses involve more legal complexities than is possible to explore here, but there are enough loopholes and a vast enough playing field that these groups are able avoid detection or regulation from state agencies. Because so little information is required to register a Web site one group can launch multiple sites under various pseudonyms, thereby making it next to impossible to link the sponsors of one site to another. Many business models for troublesome groups imitate Mafia structures that are designed so money cannot be traced.

Groups also recognize the legal advantages of registering their entire organization, or one arm of it, as a non-profit or charitable organization, making them immune to government scrutiny or taxation.

Web-Hosting Services

As legitimate Web-hosting services are under pressure from watchdog groups to drop white ethnonationalist Web sites, these groups have begun to launch their own services devoted to the principle of freedom of speech. 1st-amendment.net, owned and operated by the World Church of the Creator, is professional in appearance and bears no mention or subtle clue of group sponsorship, making it an appealing service to any company or organization with politically incorrect site content. The Ku Klux Klan's Web-hosting service, "White Power Hosting," failed quickly, probably because of its overt symbolism and references to the white-ethnonationalist movement throughout the site, which limited the scope of its business opportunities.

On-Line Brokering

According to the United Kingdom's Financial Services Authority, terrorist groups launder their money through on-line brokerage firms and other non-face-to-face media because it is difficult for these firms to know the identity of their clients. The FSA report cites on-line brokerage and spread-betting firms as particularly vulnerable to terrorist-group exploitation because they are currently under-regulated and do not perform thorough checks to corroborate the identities of their investors. Internationally, e-trade investment firms perform varying degrees of identity checks, depending on what is required of them by state regulators. For example, in Russia, e-commerce trade does not require licensing; therefore, there is no uniform regulation imposed on businesses that conduct financial transactions over the Internet, other than requiring that the client submit an electronic signature to seal the transaction, which is not binding proof of an individual's identity.

Solutions for Change

In 1995, there was only one problematic hate site on the Internet. In 1997, the Southern Poverty Law Center counted 163 troublesome sites, and 254 at the end of 1998. At the end of 2000, the Simon Wiesenthal Center estimated that more than 3,000 hate sites existed on the Web. Today estimates range from 5,000 to more than 300,000. For many reasons, it is very difficult to calculate an accurate number, but what is evident is the exponential rate of proliferation of problematic material on the Internet. The numbers may only be an indication of increased access and technical knowledge rather than an increase in supporters. More likely, however, is that the expansion is a reflection of the limited efforts to deter group propaganda and a testimony to the evolution of its effectiveness; traffic to many of the sites discussed in this essay has increased within the span of their existence, which likely indicates an increase in sympathizers who adhere to group ideology.

The solutions for control and change must be multilateral, to include both state and private agencies. They will perform in clandestine capacities to effect change from within problematic groups, and in public spheres to raise awareness and effect legal resolutions that will bring about the reduction of problematic material. As individual reasons for enlistment vary, agencies must be flexible in their campaigns to counter efforts made by problematic groups to recruit. The incentives for desertion must correspond to the rewards for joining a problematic group: a sense of empowerment, a focus for rage, a peer group, an alluring sub-culture, and a perceived solution for change.

1. Civil-society actors hack group sites and demand that hosting firms remove problematic sites. These measures may make cyber-operation for groups difficult, and hard for sympathizers to find their new Web location, perhaps causing attrition of support. However, group sites will always reappear unless the physical group is disrupted.

tors who are drawn to the boards are combative and spark further acrimonious discourse between adversarial factions. Discourse to foster the subtle reversal of problematic worldviews should be introduced by skilled actors who will not draw attention to themselves as dissenters.

3. Just as intelligence agencies have created competitive decoy groups to divide loyalties and draw followers away from problematic leadership, decoy Web sites should be launched that appear to be group sponsored but feature content crafted to gently persuade viewers to more moderate worldviews. This tactic will require the skill of agents conversant in language specific to the movements so as not to raise suspicion among sympathizers, who have been admonished to be aware of such tactics.

4. Public awareness of the problem must be elevated in order to help parents know the dangers of material available on the Internet. Just as there are awareness campaigns launched against drugs, drinking, and teenage pregnancy, there should be similar efforts made to counter the influence groups have on young people.

5. Educators must introduce instruction on the proper use of the Internet into the curriculum at an early grade, when research assignments begin. Lists of acceptable reference sources and guidelines to verify Net sources should be provided. When students are guided on how to evaluate sites as they begin their education, they will make more accurate assessments as they grow older.

6. Requirements to register a business on the Internet must involve more thorough identity-verification standards.

7. While legislation to regulate free expression on the Internet raises questionable challenge to the 1st amendment, laws to eliminate threats toward a specific target and incitement to illegal action should be enforced. Offending sites will most likely resume operation from servers outside of the United States in states with more lenient regulations. However, the removal of such sites from servers in the United States will not only relieve it from the burden of sponsorship of hateful propaganda, but may also facilitate the filtering of problematic material before it reaches the susceptible target demographic, if such regulation should ever be enacted.

By September 11th, 2001, al-Qaeda had been operating for nearly eight years. U.S. intelligence agencies were operating at an eight-year deficit because they were inadequately informed. Al-Qaeda continues to remain at a strategic advantage because they are more familiar with the playing field—agencies are required to play their adversaries' game on their terms. The propaganda, recruitment, indoctrination, and fundraising campaigns launched by white ethnonationalists and political Islamists on the Internet represent the same quandary. Groups have been able to operate freely within the medium for eight years and have become familiar and comfortable with the terrain. This essay has documented evidence of their cunning, which evolves as they become more adept at manipulating the technology. In the U.S., legislators are confined by the 1st amendment, which prohibits them from silencing even the most venomous rhetoric on the Internet. The best efforts made by civil-society actors and private watchdog agencies have been inconsequential against the tidal wave of troublesome Web sites, chat boards, and newsgroups, and wily group propagandists stay ahead by never becoming complacent. They innovate increasingly deceptive and effective measures to achieve their purpose.

In the U.S., state focus is on cyber-terror involving hacking and destruction of utility and information systems rather than on problematic propaganda. To state agencies, the threat of disrupting information infrastructures becomes a more immediate priority because of the potential for enormous monetary damages. However, the long-term effects of exposure to problematic propaganda on the Internet will be more costly to repair.

Madeleine Gruen earned her master's degree in Terrorism, Security, and Intelligence Studies from Knightsbridge University, Denmark. She is the publicity director at Columbia University Press.

Notes

1. Preston, June, U.S. *Group Reports Sharp Rise in Hate Sites*, Reuters, February 24, 1999.
2. Ibid.
3. Mandak, Joe, *Baumhammers Sentenced to Death, Plus, for Mass Shooting*, Associated Press, September 6, 2001.
4. Barton, Gina, *White Supremacist Arrested on Gun Charges*, Milwaukee Journal Sentinel, December 24, 2002.
5. Calculation from 60 White Ethnonationalist sites and 60 Political Islamist sites.
6. Globalnet.com
7. NUA.com
8. Ibid.
9. Pew Internet & American Life.
10. Anderson, Craig A. and Dill, Karen E., *Video Games and Aggressive Thoughts, Feelings, and Behavior in the Laboratory and in Life*, Journal of Personality and Social Psychology, April 2000 Vol. 78, No. 4, 772–790.
11. Pew Internet & American Life.
12. Institute of Propaganda Analysis, *Propaganda Analysis*, Columbia University Press, 1938.
13. McKelvey, Tara, *Father and Son Team on Hate Site*, USAToday.com, July 16, 2001.
14. Alexa.com, May 5, 2003.
15. Ibid.
16. Klein JD, Brown JD, Childers KW, Olivera J, Porter C, Dykers C. *Adolescents' Risky Behavior and Mass Media Use. Pediatrics.* 1993; 92:24–31.
17. *Impact of Music Lyrics and Music Videos on Children and Youth,* American Academy of Pediatrics, Volume 98, Number 6, December 1996, pgs. 1219–1221.
18. Simon, *What is Oi! and How Does it Relate to Punk?*, comnet.ca
19. Associated Press, *White Supremacist Recruits with Music*, July 16, 2001.
20. Stapleton, John and Karvelas, Patricia, *Terror Hits Home: Repercussions*, The Australian, November 8, 2002.
21. This quote comes from the transcript of a radio address from Kevin Alfred Strom, who is the host of the National Alliance's "American Dissident Voices." The transcript is periodically circulated to white ethnonationalist newsgroups, which may suggest that the author of the SOA posting also subscribes to a white ethnonationalist newsgroup.
22. Anderson, Craig A. and Dill, Karen E., *Video Games and Aggressive Thoughts, Feelings, and Behavior in the Laboratory and in Life*, Journal of Personality and Social Psychology, April 2000 Vol. 78, No. 4, 772–790.

26. Bundy, Jennifer, *National Alliance's Foray into Music/Video Worries Watchdog Group*, The Associated Press, July 9, 2001.
27. Chayban, Badih, *Hizbollah Rolls Out New Computer Game: Special Force Lets Players Use Sharon for Target Practice*, The Daily Star Online, February 17, 2003.
28. Interview with Future999 most recently found on www.newgrounds.com
29. Dees, Morris, *Taking Hate Groups to Court*, Trial, February 1995.
30. Ibid.
31. Bergen, Peter, interview with *The Scotsman*, October 15, 2002.

Cited Web Sites

Alexa—Web traffic ranking
   www.alexa.com

Stormfront
   www.stormfront.org
   www.martinlutherking.org

Soldiers of Allah, now called Muslim Studio
   www.soldiersofallah.com
   www.muslimstudio.com

Hizb ut-Tahrir
   www.khilafah.com
   www.muslimstudent.org.uk

Bound For Glory—White Resistance Band
   www.musicalterrorists.com

National Alliance
   www.resistance.com
   www.aryanwear.com
   www.ethniccleansing.net

Hizbollah
   www.specialforce.net
   www.ic-el.org
   www.e-jihad.net
   www.manartv.com

White Aryan Resistance
   www.resist.com

Princess Taliban
   www.princesstaliban.shorturl.com

White Power Hosting
   www.whitepowerhosting.com
   www.1st-amendment.net

Aryan Nations
   www.aryan-nations.org

John Ellis, 2003

Terrorism in the Genomic Age

Two stories were published with little fanfare in the spring of 2003. One, a Reuters dispatch, began as follows: "Scientists have completed the finished sequence of the human genome, or genetic blueprint of life, which holds the keys to transforming medicine and understanding disease. Less than three years after finishing the working draft of the three billion letters that make up human DNA and two years earlier than expected, an international consortium of scientists said on Monday (4/13/2003) the set of instructions on how humans develop and function is done."[1]

The other story, which appeared in the British weekly *The Economist*, reported that after intensive debate, The Institute for Genomic Research (TIGR) had decided to publish the anthrax genome on its website. The Bush Administration had contracted TIGR to produce a finished sequence of the anthrax genome as part of its overall effort to better understand the dimensions of the bio-terror threat. The Administration argued that publishing the anthrax genome might be detrimental to the national security interests of the United States. TIGR argued that publishing scientific research made for better scientific research.[2]

Neither story attracted much media attention, but both stories were emblematic of a profound shift in human affairs. One might call it the dawning of the Genomic Age. As Juan Enriquez, director of the Life Sciences Project at the Harvard Business School wrote in 1998, genomic science promises to "tell us about the past, who evolved from whom, and how." More important, when combined with nanotechnologies, genomic science gives mankind unprecedented power. "By understanding and being able to recreate and modify the instructions that make life, humans will soon be able to directly and deliberately influence their own evolution and that of other species."[3]

Enriquez and others have written at length on how genomics is altering and will eventually transform the global economy. Whole categories of business—including agriculture, pharmaceuticals, petrochemicals and energy—are already reconfiguring themselves to adapt to genomic science and what it implies. The immediate consequence has been a rush of corporate consolidation; a pooling of resources to help fund genomic research. It is likely that by the end of 2010, as few as seven companies will control virtually all of the value-added of agriculture; which is to say that they will own the patents to genetically modified seed that will grow into food that will be more pest-resistant, more nutritious and may well have pharmaceutical benefits as well. It is equally likely that by the end of 2010, as few as seven companies will control much of the value-added of the pharmaceutical business. And with each passing decade of this century, the difference between economic success and economic stagnation will be determined by who possesses genomic knowledge and who does not.[4]

The speed with which genomic knowledge is advancing is breath-taking. It cost a consortium of private interests, the United States and the United Kingdom roughly $5

complete genomic sequence of a new-born baby, stamped onto a compact disk, within two days of that child's birth, at a cost of $1000.00 per fully sequenced genome. Mom goes in, has a baby, and two days later walks out with a $1000 CD that will inform that child's medical care for the rest of his or her life. U.S. Genomics expects to be able to do this before the end of this decade.[5]

Vast (and cheap) computing power enables and turbo-charges this extraordinary advance of genomic knowledge. Countries around the world are beginning to grasp the revolutionary implications and are acting accordingly. Singapore has what might be called a genomic industrial policy. Australia has the same thing. And China, fearing it might fall behind not only the United States but its much smaller neighbors, has decided to build an entire city devoted to genomic research and development. The city is known as Genome City, and its construction is perhaps the highest priority of the Chinese government and its military. Work on the project goes 24 hours a day, 7 days a week. When it is all done, Genome City will employ and house over 50,000 people. Construction should be completed by the end of 2004.[6]

Changing the instruction sets that control the evolution of all living things will eventually be the most important business in the world. Changing the instruction sets that control the evolution of pathogens was the most secret business of two countries in the last two decades of the 20th Century. In the former Soviet Union, in direct violation of the 1972 Biological Weapons Convention, a huge team of Soviet scientists working at a facility known as the Biopreparat developed genetically altered anthrax, smallpox and plague. Working under the guidance of the Soviet military, the Biopreparat employed over 30,000 people and produced a vast arsenal of weaponized chemical and biological agents. The head of the Biopreparat, Dr. Ken Alibek, detailed the breadth and scope of the undertaking in a book[7] after he defected to the United States.

It is a terrifying book, not least because Alibek maintains that at least some of the work that was done at the Biopreparat facility carries on to this day. But it is especially terrifying for what it implies. All research into chemical and biological warfare, into virus and pathogen, is essentially "dual use." One must develop the weapon to develop the vaccine or antidote. As research and development of weaponized biological and chemical agents advances, the likelihood of a stable biological or chemical weapon increases. And as the research advances, the possibility of targeting these weapons becomes very real indeed.

The ability to target biological and chemical weapons was the focus of South Africa's top secret chemical and biological program known as Project Coast. Project Coast was created by the then white-minority government in the late 1980s. The idea was to develop a biological or chemical weapon that would kill blacks but not whites, in the event that revolutionary fervor amongst the vast black majority endangered the white population. Project Coast worked on other "ideas," such as anti-fertility drugs that would slow black population growth. But the "big idea," if one can call it that, was to find the genetic key that would enable one ethnic group to exterminate another ethnic group without putting itself at risk.[8]

Just as pharmaceuticals might be targeted at individuals, based on genetic makeup, bioweaponeers in both the Soviet Union and South Africa were exploring the possibility of targeting specific ethnic groups with biological agents. This possibility was given new momentum, in a back-handed way, in 1995, when the Aum Shinrikyo cult attacked the Tokyo subway system with Sarin gas. The attack killed 12 people and injured more than 5000 others.[9]

In his Harvard Business School case study, Juan Enriquez described what didn't happen and why: "One of the mysteries was why more people were not hurt (in the Tokyo subway attack). The crowded subway should have acted as a giant aerosol can and infected many more people. Part of the answer is that the technology used by the cult was second rate. Another part of the puzzle may be that 25% of Asians and 10% of Caucasians have an enzyme called paraoxonase in their blood that allows them to break down Sarin and other pollutants ten times faster than most people."[10]

The key finding, clearly, was that some people would die and some would not in a Sarin gas attack, depending in part on whether they did or did not have the paraoxonase enzyme. Thankfully, some of those who were inside the Tokyo subway system on that fateful day in March of 1995, did have the enzyme and so were injured but not killed in the attack. But for bioweaponeers, the larger point was that biological and chemical agents could indeed be targeted, albeit crudely, by ethnic type.

Ken Alibek and others believe that after the break-up of the Soviet Union, a not insignificant number of the scientists affiliated with the Biopreparat program were, in baseball terminology, picked up on waivers by rogue states, including Iran, Iraq and North Korea. Western intelligence agencies believe that prior to the U.S. invasion of Iraq, the regime of Saddam Hussein was especially active in the development of weaponized chemical and biological agents. It was largely for this reason that President Clinton authorized the U.S. missile attacks on Iraq in 1998 and that President Bush followed up with a full-scale invasion in 2003.[11]

Militarily, it makes sense for economically backward or stagnant states to invest heavily in bioweapons. As Enriquez points out in his HBS case study, "a UN study (conducted in 1969) estimated that the cost of using biological weapons against civilians was 1/2000 that of conventional weapons and 1/800 the cost of using nuclear weapons." As a simple of matter of return on investment, developing bioweapons offer the cheapest path to deadly peril.[12]

This is especially true now that secondary and tertiary states can access genomic information that is routinely published as a matter of scientific protocol. If they need to see a complete sequence of the anthrax genome, as noted at the start of this essay, they need only have scientists acting as cut-outs visit the website of The Institute for Genomic Research. A few such scientists thus piggy-back on the combined enterprise of the wealthiest nations on earth to extract exactly the information necessary to produce more deadly (which is to say, vaccine resistant) anthrax spores. Weaponize those spores, whether in an aerosoal can or in a warhead of some kind, and suddenly a secondary or tertiary state possesses a strategic weapon of frightening lethality.

Perhaps more frightening is the distinct possibility that a secondary or tertiary state would not want to be held accountable for the development and deployment of such a weapon and so, instead of using it, sells it to a terrorist organization that shares a common enemy (more than likely, that enemy would be the United States, the United Kingdom,

when political pressure to do *something* would be at its zenith.

It is exactly this possibility that drove the Bush Administration to adopt its policy of pre-emptive action. In his speech to the graduating class of 2002 at West Point, President Bush shifted the national security policy of the United States from containment to preemption to put secondary and tertiary states on notice that if they were caught trafficking in the business of weaponizing chemical and biological agents (and/or nuclear/radiological devices), they would be subject to the full force of U.S. military power.[13] The policy of preemption has sparked considerable controversy in the United States, but it addresses the new reality of warfare. Weaponized chemical and biological agents are inherently de-stabilizing and wreak havoc on conventional military strategy and tactics. Unconventional policies are necessary to confront a thoroughly unconventional threat.

In the near term, there are two key groups whose financial wherewithal and global reach make it possible if not likely that they will use genomic knowledge for destructive and destabilizing purposes. First among these are the drug cartels. The Columbian cartels alone oversee a cash flow business of roughly $25 billion, according to DEA and independent estimates. The margins on cocaine and heroin production and distribution are well into the 70% range. This gives the cartels extraordinary financial leverage. (Obviously, the $25 billion figure is an guesstimate. The U.S. Drug Enforcement Agency and other law enforcement/intelligence services don't have a complete audit of the Cartel cash machine.[14]

That leverage, when applied to genomic drug research, enables them to not only research and develop ever more potent (and addictive) narcotics, but to research and develop next generations of drugs like Ecstasy, Viagra and methamphetamine. It is important to remember that Ecstasy was a legal drug for a number of years before Congress finally passed legislation banning its sale and use. As genomic knowledge advances, the ability to build Ecstasy-like chemical compounds (that produce a much stronger high, but more benign "hangover") will advance with it.

The rewards for building such a drug will be even more enormous than the present returns on the sale of heroin and cocaine. Scientists could stand to make tens of millions of dollars for developing a drug that produces Ecstasy-like euphoria, Viagra-like sexual enhancement and methamphetamine-like alertness. It's even possible that passing a law to outlaw such a drug would not pass, if enough people could be convinced that the after-effects were negligible. Whatever happens, it is certain that the drug environment into which the present generation of children (the so-called "echo boom" generation, which is the largest generational cohort in American history) will be loaded with chemical compounds and narcotic substances of unprecedented potency and/or addictiveness. And that the major financial beneficiaries will be the already cash-heavy cartels of Columbia and Mexico.

The second group with the financial wherewithal and global reach who can be expected to seize upon genomic knowledge for destructive and destabilizing purpose are, of course, terrorist organizations, the leading edge of which (at least for the moment) is Osama bin Laden's Al Qaeda.[15] General Wayne Downing (USA-Rtd), who served as the director of President George W. Bush's Global War on Terror (and who was largely responsible for authoring the U.S. Strategy for Fighting Global Terrorism, told the *Washington Post* at the end of 2002 that the thing that leaped off the pages and discs of the recovered (from Afghanistan) Al Qaeda documents and C-drives was Al Qaeda's zeal for either building or acquiring weapons of mass destruction.[16]

It is very difficult for an organization like Al Qaeda to build a nuclear weapon. It requires the indulgence of a host state and considerable scientific sophistication. It is considerably less difficult for an organization like Al Qaeda to build a radiological weapon, but it is much more difficult without a stable and secure "host." Least difficult is the acquisition or purchase of genetically-altered biological weapons. The price tag is very high, but the black market for such products exists. And again, as genomic knowledge advances, the cost of relatively crude genetically-altered biological and chemical weaponry will decline accordingly.[17]

What distinguishes Al Qaeda and other elements of radical Islam (from, say, nation-states like North Korea or Iran) is their willingness to use such weapons. What makes that willingness even more terrifying is that they have already shown that they can deliver such weapons through the use of what might be called "human missiles." The media call them suicide bombers. They're not. They're delivery mechanisms for strategic weapons.

The willingness of Islamic and Palestinian "terrorists" to use themselves as detonation devices makes problematic even the most basic tactics of "homeland defense." A terrorist willing to die of genetically-altered and vaccine-resistant smallpox can kill literally hundreds of thousands of people. If he or she kills hundreds of thousands of people in lower Manhattan, then the global financial markets have a seizure. If the global financial markets have a seizure, the global economy goes into a tailspin. The attacks on the twin towers of the World Trade Center cost New York City roughly $83 billion, according to a study conducted by the city's leading management consulting firms.[18] A genetically-altered smallpox attack would probably cause the City's finances to collapse altogether. And that would be the least of such an attack's consequences.

Aside from the specific threat posed by drug cartels and terrorist organizations armed with destabilizing and destructive genomic knowledge, there is another, perhaps larger, issue raised by the Age of Genomics. That issue is the separation between those who have genomic knowledge and those who don't. Countries like the United States and China that will be at the forefront of molecular biology, nanotechnologies, next generation information technology and pervasive computing will be on the winning side of what one might call the genomic/digital divide. On the other side will be a host of Islamic and African countries that will be literally unable to compete in or contribute to (except as laborers) the global economy. They will be genomic losers. One side will be able to cure cancer. The other side will beg for the medicial expertise. One side will be able to feed its population a hundred times over. The other side will experience horrific famine. One side will enjoy extraordinary wealth. The other will experience abject poverty. The seeds of resentment sown, when added to an already enraged movement of radical Islamists, will likely prove to be a highly volatile mix.

The underlying reality of modern life in most Islamic nations today is relentlessly grim. Life expectancy is short, illiteracy is high, famine is common, economic stagnation and deprivation is the norm. Governments, many of which have enjoyed long-standing

solace and sweet revenge in its destruction. Genomics accentuates this separation to the ultimate degree; on one side are people capable of manipulating the evolution of all living things, on the other are people who have no power at all. Except, of course, the power to create and replicate catastrophic events.[19]

So what does all this suggest, in terms of policy?

First, it is of paramount concern that the United States and its allies do everything possible to enforce strict protocols and conventions with regards to the use of biological and chemical weapons. Any country that indulges in this kind of research, development or deployment must be subject to the harshest possible sanctions, including the possibility of armed intervention.

Second, it is critical that the United States and its allies do everything it can to enhance its capability of responding to bioterrorism. A recent study by the Partnership for Public Service found, according to a *New York Times* report, that "the (U.S.) government is likely to be overwhelmed in the event of a bioterrorism attack because of serious shortages in skilled medical and scientific personnel." Even if one allows considerable leeway for hyperbole (when was the last time a public service advocacy group thought the government was doing a bang-up job?), the fact remains that the anthrax mail attacks in the fall of 2001 did indeed reveal an almost woeful lack of preparedness for biological attack. While U.S. government preparedness has substantially improved since them, the shortage of skilled personnel remains a source of real worry in the event of another attack.[20]

Third, it is critical that molecular biologists and genomic scientists engage in a Manhattan Project–effort to create new scientific protocols that will specifically address the national security issues raised by genomic research and development. Since Hiroshima and Nagasaki, physicists have engaged with the government to control and contain the spread of nuclear weapons. As Henry Kelly, president of the Federation of American Scientists, recently argued in the *New York Times*, the time has come for genomic scientists and molecular biologists to do the same thing.[21]

Fourth and perhaps finally, genomic research must advance. As Henry Kelly wrote in the *New York Times*, "the difference between a lab for producing lifesaving vaccines and one capable of making deadly toxins is largely one of intent." The more genomic knowledge we have, the more ways we will have to combat pathogens, either through vaccine or antidote, the less likely it is that a genetically-altered pathogen will yield a catastrophic result. Our intent must be to act in the best interests of mankind. We must grow the food, fight the disease, enrich and elongate life. The Genomic Age will largely be defined on how well we measure up.[22]

John Ellis heads Ellis Kreamer Partners, a small media consultancy in New York City. He has also contributed to *Fast Company Magazine*, the *Wall Street Journal*, *Inside* magazine, and the *Boston Globe*. His work for the *Boston Globe* was nominated for the Pulitzer Prize in 1999. Mr. Ellis is a Senior Fellow at West Point's Combating Terrorism Center, where he writes and lectures on the intersection of terrorism and technology and the strategy of the media in covering terrorism.

Notes

1. http://www.msnbc.com/news/899806.asp?0cv=HA00.
2. http://www.economist.com/displaystory.cfm?story_id=1748489.
3. *Gene Research, the Mapping of Life and the Global Economy* is a Harvard Business School Case Study, N9-599-016, written by Juan Enriquez and is available at www.hbsp.harvard.edu.
4. For more on how genomics is transforming agriculture and pharmaceuticals, see http://harvardbusinessonline.hbsp.harvard.edu/b01/en/common/item_detail.jhtml?id=R00203.
5. The exact cost of the Human Genome Project is, at some level, unknowable, since knowledge begets knowledge and the cost of academic research is fungible. The U.S. government contributions are detailed at http://www.ornl.gov/TechResources/Human_Genome/project/budget.html. The ballpark number of $5 billion includes the contributions of the United Kingdom and private charitable trusts. For more on Eugene Chan and his work at U.S. Genomics, visit http://www.cio.com/archive/010103/37.html. The specifics about stamping out a CD of an infant's genome were taken from notes at the Genomic Sequencing and Analysis Conference in Boston, Massachusetts, in September of 2002. The author attended the conference.
6. This information was gleaned from interviews with Juan Enriquez of the Harvard Business School, who was given a tour of Genome City by Chinese Government Officials.
7. *Biohazard: The Chilling True Story of the Largest Covert Biological Weapons Program in the World—Told from the Inside by the Man Who Ran It.*
8. See the *Washington Post*, April 20 and 21, 2003.
9. http://www.cdc.gov/ncidod/EID/vol5no4/olson.htm.
10. Enriquez, HBS Case Study N9-599-016.
11. See *The Demon in the Freezer*, by Richard Preston as well as *Biohazard*, by Ken Alibek.
12. Enriquez, HBS Case Study N9-599-016.
13. http://www.jinsa.org/articles/print.html?documentid=1492.
14. For a good overview of the drug threat, see http://www.usdoj.gov/dea/pubs/intel/02046/02046.html.
15. See *Inside Al Qaeda*, by Rohan Gunaratna.
16. http://usembassy.state.gov/mumbai/wwwfns.pdf for National Strategy for Combating Terrorism. For Downing comments, see *Washington Post*, December 24, 2002.
17. *Washington Post*, April 20–21, 2003.
18. http://www.nycp.org/impactstudy/release.htm.
19. See the annual *Economist* survey of 2002 for updated statistics of relative wealth and poverty; http://www.theworldin.com/.
20. *New York Times*, July 5, 2003.
21. *New York Times* op-ed, July 2, 2003.
22. *New York Times* op-ed, July 2, 2003.

Countering the Terrorist Threat

Chapter 7

The Challenges of Terrorism

Terrorist actions pose some very dramatic and extraordinary challenges to a state and to its code of conduct.

After the September 11 attacks, writes Laura K. Donohue, "In the public realm, Congress became consumed by terrorist measures." Donohue carefully charts the rapid succession of actions taken by the government after 9-11 and explores what she calls the "counterterrorist spiral," a phenomenon common to liberal, democratic states, that captured the nation in the aftermath of the attacks. Donohue not only presents a detailed diary of measures taken, she explores the theory of why actions were taken and, on a deeper level, what the ramifications are for a liberal, democratic state faced with the challenge of balancing the delicate tension between keeping its citizens and their property secure while also preserving the premise of civil liberties. "The difficulty was that while these provisions sought to ensure greater security for Americans," said Donohue, "many of them made serious inroads into the individual rights of both citizens and non-citizens. The consequences are borne not just in the domestic realm, but in U.S. foreign relations."

At a time when a nation is under threat of terrorist actions, intelligence gathering is key. Bruce Hoffman looks at the nasty, brutish business of gathering intelligence about an enigmatic enemy who operates in unconventional ways. The struggles against Osama bin Laden and his minions will rely on good intelligence, writes Hoffman, "But the experiences of other countries, fighting similar conflicts against similar enemies, suggest that Americans still do not appreciate the enormously difficult—and morally complex—problem that the imperative to gather 'good intelligence' entails." Hoffman cites scenarios—both fictional and real—about those who have been responsible for information gathering in times of crises and the unsavory but perhaps necessary measures they have taken. They act in times when extraordinary circumstances require extraordinary measures and must operate under the premise that the innocent have more rights than the guilty. Hoffman quotes a fictional character who faces such a dilemma: "To succumb to humane considerations," the character concludes, "only leads to hopeless chaos."

In conventional international conflict, there is a code of behavior. But—as international law expert Anthony Clark Arend points out—the activities of terrorist groups muddy the waters dramatically on how this "just war"

311

standards apply in conflicts with nonstate actors? For example, an element of the theory of discrimination is that innocent civilians are not to be attacked or targeted. In conventional warfare, military personnel are clearly identifiable; terrorists are not. They are—in fact—civilians (albeit not innocent citizens). States have diplomatic channels to pursue peaceful settlement and nonviolent sanctions before resorting to the actions of war; yet terrorist groups do not have the same formal systems of communication for resolving differences. Arend examines a range of issues in just war theory and offers recommendations to preserve the theory of just war while responding to the challenges of terrorism.

Brad Roberts examines the dilemma states face in dealing with rogue nations that flout agreed norms of state behavior; that threaten to use force against those who resist their ambitions; and who seek to acquire means of mass destruction—nuclear, biological, or chemical (NBC) weapons. In dealing with these rogue states, when is a preemptive strike justified? "Given what is now known about Iraq's pre-war unconventional-weapons programs… it is clear that in just a few additional months of sanctions aimed at pressuring Saddam Hussein to withdraw his army from Kuwait, Iraq's nuclear program would have produced one or two weapons while its biological program could have geared up to a very substantial level of production and weaponization," writes Roberts. The author explains the crucial timing in a preemptive strike situation, yet he explores the act of a strike in the context of the just war tradition and outlines specific conditions that would produce a strong moral case for a U.S. preemption, as well as conditions for a weak case. As Roberts concludes, "there is a moral case for a preemption, but it is not quite as tidy as policy-makers might desire."

Laura K. Donohue, 2002

Fear Itself
Counterterrorism, Individual Rights, and U.S. Foreign Relations Post 9-11*

"The only thing we have to fear is fear itself—nameless, unreasoning, unjustified terror which paralyzes needed efforts to convert retreat into advance."
—Franklin D. Roosevelt, first inaugural address, 1933

So often has it already been asserted that it is almost cliché to state that September 11 shattered Americans' sense of security within the United States. Despite calls to return to "business as usual," by January 2002 the United States had not. The fear that choked the nation dominated the public—and for many, the private—discourse.

In the public realm, Congress became consumed by terrorist measures. Between September 11, 2001, and January 11, 2002, 98 percent of the official business conducted by the House of Representatives and 97 percent of [that in] the Senate related to terrorism.[1] Congress proposed more than 450 counterterrorist resolutions, bills, and amendments. (This compared with approximately 1,300 total in the course of U.S. history.) Within four months of the attacks, more than two dozen new measures became law. President Bush issued 12 Executive Orders and 10 Presidential Proclamations related to the attacks. Only a handful addressed the war in Afghanistan. Most dealt with the domestic realm, the consequences of September 11, and U.S. preparedness for future terrorist attack. The difficulty with many of these measures was that, while they sought to ensure greater security for Americans, they made serious inroads into individual rights. The consequences are borne not just in the domestic realm, but in U.S. foreign relations.

This chapter does three things. First, it looks at characteristics of liberal, democratic states and the terrorist challenge that led to what can be termed a "counterterrorist spiral"— one in which the United States became caught in the aftermath of the attacks. Second, the chapter briefly considers the breadth of measures proposed in Washington. Third, it considers four provisions that directly impact individual rights and threaten the domestic realm and American relations with other states: widespread detention and questioning, military tribunals, and capital punishment. It examines the arguments for and against these provisions. The paper concludes with a brief discussion of trends emerging in the Bush Administration's handling of the current threat and the effect of this on the domestic and

*Portions of this chapter were published as part of the review of military tribunals in "Bias, National Security, and Military Tribunals," *Criminology and Public Policy* (July 2002).

I. The Counterterrorist Spiral

The most basic obligation borne by a liberal, democratic state is to protect the life and property of the citizens. Significant acts of political terrorism levied within this context have two effects. First, they attack the root of liberal states' authority: the state's ability to protect the citizens is called into question. Second, they question the current government's ability to uphold its compact to exercise state powers in a manner that upholds its most fundamental responsibility.

As a result, the government must not just respond, but it must be seen to respond. And not just to terrorism in general, but to each significant attack. Following the 1974 Birmingham bombings, for example, Westminster introduced the Prevention of Terrorism (Temporary Provisions) Act. After the August 15, 1998, Real IRA [Irish Republican Army] bombing in Omagh, Northern Ireland, the United Kingdom adopted the Criminal Justice (Terrorism and Conspiracy) Act and the Republic of Ireland introduced the 1999 Criminal Justice Act.[3] Following the 1995 attack by Timothy McVeigh on the Murrah Federal Building in Oklahoma City, the U.S. Congress adopted the 1996 Antiterrorism and Effective Death Penalty Act. And within weeks of September 11, America witnessed, amongst other provisions, the adoption of Public Law 107-56, the "Uniting and Strengthening America by Providing Appropriate Tools Required to Intercept and Obstruct Terrorism (USA PATRIOT) Act of 2001."

Before the September 11 attacks, there was already a heightened state of concern in the United States about the prospect of political violence within American bounds. To some extent this related to previous attacks on U.S. embassies and military in Kenya, Tanzania, Yemen, and the Middle East. It reflected prior domestic attacks. And it underscored concern at the activities of groups that no longer wanted, as Brian Jenkins famously remarked in the 1970s, "A lot of people watching, not a lot of people dead"—but both a lot of people dead and a lot of people watching.[4] The concern arose not just from the threats posed, but the increasing capabilities of actors to harness advances in technology for destructive ends.

There were numerous indicators of this already heightened concern: for example, the crash of TWA 800 off of Long Island, New York, on July 17, 1996, was immediately viewed as a terrorist attack. Although an inquiry later determined that it was an accident, in the interim the White House Commission on Aviation Security, formed in response to the crash, proposed 30 recommendations to counter possible terrorist attacks on U.S. aircraft. The money trail was similarly telling: between 1994 and 2000 the United States doubled its annual expenditures on terrorism, bringing the total to more than $10 billion, with $11.3 billion proposed for 2001.[5] From nothing earmarked specifically for domestic preparedness in 1995, in 1997 the total grew to $130 million, by 2000 topping $1.5 billion.[6] Between 1998 and 2000 the legislature held over 80 sessions on terrorism, involving a wide range of committees. In the Senate the Appropriations, Armed Services, Commerce, Science and

Transportation, Environment and Public Works, Foreign Relations, Health, Education, Labor and Pensions, Judiciary Committee, and Select Committee on Intelligence all held hearings. In the House the Armed Security, Commerce, Government Reform, Intelligence, International Relations, Judiciary, Science, Transportation and Infrastructure, and Joint Economic Committee became engaged in the issue.

The proliferation of interest in and concern about terrorism gets at the nature of the threat: sub-state terrorism is a multi-pronged attack. Individuals, groups, networks, and state proxies can adopt various modes of attack. Moreover, it is not a single threat from one particular individual, group, or state. The entities entrusted with the life and property of the citizens must respond. This results in a burgeoning effect in the breadth of measures introduced in response.

Legislative initiatives that cross the gamut often bear social consequences as they become incorporated into state security functions. In the United Kingdom, for example, between 1920 and 1922 political violence claimed 428 lives in Northern Ireland. The 1922 Civil Authorities (Special Powers) Act, introduced to quell the violence, empowered the Civil Authority to impose curfew, close premises, roads, and transportation routes, detain and intern, and proscribe organizations. It gave the government the ability to censor newspapers and radio and to ban meetings, processions and gatherings, and the use of cars. The legislation altered the court system. It granted extensive powers of entry, search and seizure, and, in a Draconian catch-all phrase, empowered the Civil Authority "to take all such steps and issue all such orders as may be necessary for preserving the peace and maintaining order." This clause led to over 100 new regulations, the substance of which ranged from preventing gatherings and processions to outlawing wearing an Easter Lily. The U.S. past measures followed a similar path, with the substance ranging from international diplomatic and coercive measures to domestic criminal and non-criminal initiatives.[7]

In the immediate aftermath of an attack and over time the substance of these initiatives tends to become increasingly extreme. There is a relatively straightforward reason for this: with terrorism, there is a tendency to evoke a worst-case scenario. Such acts are surrounded by incomplete information. They are stealthy operations involving not clearly identifiable enemies. More extreme measures are needed to counter more extreme possible threats. Further, the horror of the event creates outrage. The very use of the word signifies a moral opprobrium, a rejection of the actors, aims, and action itself. Resultantly, there is strong pressure on policy-makers to introduce measures with a message. During President Bush's address to Congress following the September 11 attacks, prior to any inquiry into what had happened that allowed such an attack to take place, there was extended applause for increasing the powers available to law enforcement and enhancing intelligence capabilities. At a state level the pressure increased substantially on those who had previously proposed or drafted counterterrorist measures to introduce further provisions. Often measures previously considered Draconian become easily swept through legislatures caught up in the emotion of the most recent attack. The roving wiretap provisions, for instance, rejected during Congressional consideration of the 1996 Antiterrorism and Effective Death Penalty bill, quickly became incorporated into the USA PATRIOT bill.

With the tide of public sentiment driving concern in the elected chambers, pressure increases to support whatever measures are introduced. If you are against counterterrorist provisions, you are seen somehow as for terrorism. Between 1972 and 2000 this was a frequent charge in Westminster and prevented parties from actively voting against

sible security threat faced by the state and the population, will often introduce "temporary" counterterrorist measures. The difficulty with this is that in the face of terrorism, it can be extremely difficult to repeal temporary provisions. To withdraw them in the future may require the conclusion either that a level of violence commensurate with the recent, devastating acts is acceptable, or that terrorism is no longer a threat. The former is politically untenable—and, in light of the massive, September 11 attacks—unfathomable, and the second impossible to prove. Terrorism, in a liberal state, is always possible. As destructive technology develops, it will become increasingly difficult to repeal measures that were introduced to meet the exigencies of a less extreme situation. Moreover, many of the measures work. They are effective. And so security forces become reluctant to relinquish them. Often they seep into ordinary criminal usage, becoming more deeply entrenched in the security forces' response to threats. The measures become a baseline on which future measures become built, leading to a steady ratcheting effect wherein provisions simply expand.

The Bush Administration's handling of the "War on Terrorism" from September 11 to January 11 follows patterns common to liberal, democratic states. The concern raised is that some of the measures, while there are some strong arguments for them, bear serious consequences for the domestic realm and U.S. relations with other states.

II. Response to September 11, 2001

The United States immediately responded to the attacks on the Pentagon and the World Trade Center and the crash of United Flight 93 in Pennsylvania with a wide range of emergency measures.[8] Within 24 hours of the attacks the President issued a declaration of a major disaster in New York[9] and a state of emergency in Virginia.[10] On Friday, September 14, the President issued an Executive Order declaring a national emergency, which he extended in the Executive Order regarding Financial Transactions on September 24.[11] In the following eight weeks, the President issued dozens of Proclamations and Executive Orders and the Executive Branch engaged in a widespread antiterrorist campaign. Congress introduced 323 bills and resolutions and adopted 21 laws and resolutions relating to the attacks and the war against terrorism.[12] This pace of new measures in the second eight weeks dropped by almost half—but almost all of these continued to be focused on terrorism.

From the initial emergency, the country swiftly moved into the heart of the counter-terrorist spiral. This section will briefly touch on the breadth of measures introduced in the subsequent four months. They fall into eight categories: incident management, emergency powers and war measures, consequence management, public statements, security measures, investigation and prosecution, administrative or bureaucratic reorganization, and international relations.

The United States' first concern in dealing with the incident was to secure the sites of the attacks and to prepare for other, immediate, possible attacks. Every branch entrusted with the life and property of the citizens reacted. For instance, the Executive Branch called the military into action. The Department of Health and Human Services mobilized medical personnel and supplies. First responders in New York began to mount operations around the clock. The FAA grounded flights, closed airports, and diverted international flights. [Department of Transportation secretary] Norm Mineta issued orders limiting the movement of vessels in international waters. Amtrak suspended operations.

Second, the federal government introduced extensive emergency powers and war measures. The President declared states of emergency in New York, New Jersey, Virginia, and the United States.[13] On September 18, 2001, President Bush signed PL 107-40, the War Powers Resolution and Senate Joint Resolution 23 ("Authorization for Use of Military Force").[14] Two days after the U.S. military campaign commenced in Afghanistan, the President notified Congress. By October 2, the military had deployed 29,000 military personnel in two carrier battle groups as well as an amphibious ready group and several hundred military aircraft. Approximately 17,000 members of the Reserve were called to active duty[15] as well as several thousand National Guard operating under state authority.[16] Despite the existence of what became referred to as the "war" in Afghanistan, the Administration did not technically declare war. Nevertheless, military actions commenced and Congressional members introduced a number of traditional wartime measures. For instance, the Senate amended the Treasury and General Government Appropriations Act of 2002 to include war bonds. Under the name "Unity Bonds," the proceeds would go to recovery operations and the war against terrorism.[17] Other bills dealt with price gouging with respect to motor fuels, providing farm credit assistance for reservists, and providing retirement compensation to individuals engaged in active duty.[18] Still others sought to increase the penalty for air piracy.[19] One of the boldest would have required the United Nations to suspend membership of any country that the U.S. Secretary of State labels a state sponsor of terrorism.[20]

Third, in the area of consequence management, three types of responses emerged: measures dealing with the site of the attacks, compassion measures, and economic recovery. PL 107-38 almost immediately provided for $40 billion to be made available to emergency recovery and response agencies and national security activities.[21] More than 30 bills before Congress sought additional funding.[22] Compassion measures included presidential proclamations, such as "Honoring the Victims of the Incidents on Tuesday, September 11, 2001" (September 12, 2001), the "National Day of Prayer and Remembrance" (September 13, 2001), the "Flags to Half-Staff" (September 14, 2001), and "Citizenship Day and Constitution Week" (September 19, 2001). Memorial services were held at the Pentagon, in New York, at the National Emergency Training Center in Emmitsburg, Maryland, and in Pennsylvania.[23] Congressional measures rapidly piled up: 12 bills aimed at establishing a national day of remembrance, providing Capitol-flown flags to survivors and families of the deceased, granting citizenship posthumously, building monuments, creating national service projects in honor of the victims, and authorizing prayers in the Capitol and in schools.[24] Nineteen statutes, bills, and resolutions focused on acts of heroism. Others focused on financial support to victims, with PL 107-37 providing for expediting payment to emergency personnel killed or injured as a result of September 11.[25] Measures focused on support to victims' families[26] and alleviating the financial penalties for victims.[27] Others looked at children and the effect of terrorism on them.[28] One of the most creative compassion bills advocated the creation of a lifetime pass for free admission to federally-owned parks, to help in the emotional healing process.[29] More than 45 proposals (in the form of bills and resolutions) focused on economic recovery. Their substance ranged from bail-out for insurance companies, hiring workers who lost jobs as a result of the attacks, and tax

Fourth, various efforts to respond in the public arena were made. Some were more successful than others. Three main efforts mark this area: compassion and patriotism, gaining the moral high ground, and transmitting information. In the first area, public statements honored acts of heroism and encouraged citizens to rally around the flag.[33] A presidential proclamation required that all government flags fly at half-staff. Bills in Congress ranged from attempts to rename September 11 "Patriot Day"[34] to prohibiting any social security or other government payment to individuals or entities that prohibit the flag to be flown. The White House invited Islamic and Sikh leaders to Washington and launched the "Friendship through Education" program. It also ensured that high-level officials appeared on Al Jazeera television.[35] The Bush Administration provided $320 million to Afghan people (up from roughly $170 million in 2000).[36] In the moral realm, officials made repeated references to "the evil one" and "fighting the scourge of terrorism." The Administration and Congress tried to provide information to the public in the form of press briefings.

Not all of these efforts were entirely successful. For instance, the money appropriated to Afghanistan fell ludicrously short of providing enough resources for food and medicine to be delivered to victims of the war. Some of President Bush's statements had a devastating effect. The President almost immediately seized on the U.S. response as a "crusade." His determination to "smoke out" the enemy led many in Afghanistan and Pakistan to believe that the United States would use chemical and biological weapons in its hunt for Osama bin Laden. These and other statements were then used as proof that more people must join the *jihad* against the United States. In terms of providing information to the U.S. public, it quickly became clear that the Bush Administration and, indeed, Congress had difficulty knowing how to handle both the terrorist threat and the psychology of responding to terrorism. *Newsweek* captured this lack of competence at the height of the anthrax scare. A political cartoon depicted a man running around in a biological hazard suit shouting, "The sky is falling, the sky is falling!" As an onlooker responded that someone ought to call the Homeland Security Advisor, from the suit we read, "I AM the Homeland Security Advisor!"

Fifth, population control, transportation security, vital infrastructure protection, credible threat warnings, and immigration and border control constituted the security measures adopted in the four months following the attacks. A debate on the use of identity cards quickly followed widespread efforts to control the movement of people at all airports and, more specifically, in New York and Washington, DC. Transportation security stood second only to economic recovery in the number of initiatives introduced into Congress. Within eight weeks of the attack nearly 30 bills before Congress addressed airline security. On November 19 one of these became PL 107-71.[37] Other initiatives sought to impose strictures on crop dusters, introduce more widespread use of sky marshals and the national guard in airports, and place limits on flight training. Vital infrastructure protection initiatives included water sources and transportation routes, public transportation, agriculture, food supply, information networks,[38] health services—particularly in the event of an attack using weapons of mass destruction—and the transfer of explosives and hazardous material.[39] In an innovative but controversial change from how other liberal, democratic states have responded, U.S. federal and state officials began issuing "Credible threat warnings." For instance, on October 11, Governor Tom Ridge indefinitely extended a general warning. The State Department issued one in relation to travel to the Philippines, and Governor Gray Davis of California issued one in regard to bridges throughout the state. The federal government also considered and adopted numerous immigration and border control initiatives. The INS [Immigration and Naturalization Service] issued new orders. The Executive Branch initiated discussions with Mexico and Canada to make immigration more compatible. Eleven bills before Congress would have provided for greater military defense of the nation's borders, airports, and seaports.[40]

Sixth, in the area of investigation and prosecution, the federal government engaged in widespread detention and interrogation. It also adopted broader surveillance tools, instituted new financial strictures and rewards, altered the judicial system, and required greater information sharing between agencies. The House passed legislation requiring the CIA director to implement the changes recommended by the June 2000 National Commission on Terrorism.[41] It increased the "Most Wanted Terrorist" list to 30 people and provided about $30 million in reward money for the September 11 attacks, with an additional $1 million for anthrax cases. The investigation quickly became the most comprehensive in FBI history, with 4,000 out of 11,500 agents, and 7,000 out of 25,000 employees exclusively focused on terror.[42] The FBI arrested more than 20 individuals for anthrax hoaxes.[43] In October, 6 of the 28 groups included on the list of foreign terrorist organizations designated by the Secretary of State were linked to Osama bin Laden.[44] The USA PATRIOT Act prevented citizens from supporting any designated terrorist organization for which all financial assets became blocked. The Administration froze the assets of 47 groups and individuals both in the United States and overseas. Operation Green Quest, a multi-agency initiative staffed by the IRS, Secret Service, FBI, DOJ [Department of Justice], and Customs, began to focus on counterfeiting, credit card fraud, fraudulent import and export schemes, drug trafficking, and cash smuggling. Modeled after the scheme that implicated the mafia, the operation follows the money sources for suspected terrorist operations. On December 5, 2001, at the request of the Attorney General, the State Department designated 39 entities as terrorist organizations pursuant to the USA PATRIOT Act. An increased emphasis on information sharing led to initiatives such as President Bush's insistence that the directors of the FBI and CIA be present for the other agency's daily briefings with him. Some bills before Congress would have required electronic and other information to be shared between intelligence agencies. The next section of the article will go into more detail on extended detention and interrogation, expanded surveillance powers, and alterations to the judicial system.

Seventh, in an attempt to answer the question "who is in charge?" the Bush Administration and Congress introduced new bureaucratic nodes and reorganized the federal administrative structures handling the prevention, prosecution, and management of actual attacks. It is one of the characteristics of a liberal state's response to terrorism that the immediate assumption is that something was broken, which allowed the act to occur. Answering it with bureaucratic reorganization is one way to demonstrate to the population that the government is doing something to respond. The Intelligence Authorization Act for 2002 included a Commission on National Security Readiness to identify structural impediments to the effective collection, analysis, and sharing of information on national security threats, particularly terrorism. President Bush created a number of special counterterrorist advisory

fice of Homeland Security.[46] Run by Governor Tom Ridge and established at a Cabinet-level position, one of the first recommendations was to create a Foreign Terrorist Tracking Task Force, which was established by Homeland Security Presidential Directive 2 on October 29, 2001.[47] This task force combined information from the INS, FBI, and State, and became housed in the Attorney General's [AG's] office.

The Attorney General, John Ashcroft, centralized counterterrorist prosecution. He established 93 U.S. Attorney Antiterrorism Task Forces, (in every U.S. Attorney office in the United States) with the aim to improve information sharing between federal, state, and local law enforcement agencies and, in a capacity unprecedented in law enforcement, "to help craft strategy to prevent terrorism across the country." The Attorney General also created a Terrorism Task Force to head up the investigation into September 11. Assistant AG Michael Chertoff, head of the Criminal Division, will take the case, instead of individual U.S. Attorney's offices. In the Senate a bill was proposed to create a new Deputy AG for Terrorism. Ten bills before Congress dealt with the further creation of new structures.[48] There was also extensive discussion about whether the FBI should be dedicated solely to terrorism.

Eighth, the federal government also introduced a number of international measures aimed at creating economic (dis)incentives and garnering support for a global "war on terrorism." In the first area, the Bush Administration lifted sanctions on Pakistan and India, provided $100 million in funding to Pakistan, designated Indonesia as a beneficiary development country (modification of duty-free treatment), signed a free trade agreement (FTA) with Jordan, only the third ever signed by the United States,[49] and continued stringent import and export controls on suspected state sponsors of terrorism. The United States engaged in diplomatic exchanges, pressing for UN resolutions and public statements from other countries to support the war effort and to introduce more stringent domestic counterterrorist measures within the home country. The United States applied pressure to a number of countries to choke the financial flows to al Qaida and other cells and sought to impress on other states both the practical and moral aspect of the attacks on their citizens and U.S. citizens working in the World Trade Center towers.

Many of these measures, such as the war itself, had a significant impact on American relations with other states. I do not here, however, specifically address the war. Instead, I narrow in on the counterterrorist measures most directly impacting individual rights that transcend state boundaries and thus bear both domestic and international consequences. They come from the sixth category: investigation and prosecution. I suggest that while they derive from an understandable dynamic, and that while there are strong arguments for their use, there are stronger arguments against their operation.

III. Measures Impacting Individual Rights

Terrorism itself is antithetical to liberal democracy. It violates the right to life and property and bypasses due process of law. It seeks to accomplish its goal outside the democratic process.[50] It tries to replace reason with emotion, and in so doing assumes a desire to return to rationality.[51] Terrorism takes for granted that a cost-benefit analysis will favor meeting the demands of those engaged in violence. Although it is levied against the population in general, it tries to change the behavior of the leaders, the elite—and its very nature is therefore undemocratic. When an open society has been taken advantage of in this manner the immediate response is to close it.

This reaction gives rise to at least two areas of concern: incursions into the civil liberties of citizens and incursions into non-citizens' individual and human rights. The first results in tension between new measures and constitutional norms. It also may potentially impact domestic tranquility. The second introduces tension in relations with other states. New counterterrorist measures are often justified on the grounds that they apply to "non-citizens" and are therefore acceptable. Such measures are aided by the psychology resulting from an act of terrorism. Following a significant attack, citizens or subjects become deeply suspicious of individuals fitting the political, ethnic, ideological, or religious profile of the perpetrators. The result is random violence against the ethnic group, a tendency to scapegoat, and, frequently, the suspension of ordinary judicial processes.

We generally understand civil rights to arise from the concept of democratic government—the codification of individuals' right to participate in the political realm in order to advance one's own ideas. Often overlapping in common usage, civil liberties arise from the concept of liberalism, or limited government. They protect individuals' abilities to form and express preferences or convictions and to act upon them without limitation from government in the private sphere. Such designations blur together in consideration of freedom of thought, conscience, expression, movement, privacy, and autonomy in the management of one's personal affairs, voluntary association, and political participation.

Civil rights or civil liberties incorporate, but can be distinguished from, human rights, which provide a basic standard of treatment for all people, regardless of nationality. The Universal Declaration of Human Rights, agreed by the United Nations in 1948, includes 30 articles.[52] Some of the most important include equality; the right not to be discriminated against based on race, color, sex, religion, property, or birth; the right to life, liberty, and security; and the right not to be enslaved. It also includes the right not to be subjected to cruel, inhuman, or degrading treatment or punishment; to be treated as a person before the law and to receive equal protection under the law; to an effective remedy by the competent national tribunals for violations of rights granted by the state; and not to be subjected to arbitrary arrest, detention, or exile. Articles protect the right of individuals to obtain a fair and public hearing by an independent and impartial tribunal and the right to the presumption of innocence in a trial in which the individual is afforded "all the guarantees necessary for his defense."

This paper addresses three measures introduced by the United States in the wake of September 11 that violate civil rights and freedoms and human rights. The next section provides information related to the extended detention of non-citizens, the introduction of military tribunals, and the stated intent of the Bush Administration to seek the death penalty in its response to al Qaida. It evaluates the arguments for and against these provisions.

A. Detention and Questioning

Immediately following the attacks, the Bush Administration compiled a list from Immigration and Naturalization Service (INS) and State Department records, of all males aged

zation to determine "within a reasonable period of time" whether or not someone should be held or released on their own recognizance pending a trial.

The government subsequently questioned more than 5,000 non-citizens and held more than 1,200 for further interrogation. The Attorney General refused to release the names and location of those held for questioning. The FBI conducted over 500 searches.[53] Legislation passed by Congress expanded the federal government's powers to detain non-citizens. The USA PATRIOT Act not just allowed but required the detention of anyone the AG had reasonable grounds to believe was connected to terrorism or was a threat to national security. The statute did not specify a time period. Detention without trial could continue until the suspect was either deported or determined no longer to be a threat.[54] The legislation expanded the definition of "engage in terrorist activity" to committing, or inciting to commit a terrorist act, preparing or planning a terrorist act, gathering information on potential targets for a terrorist act, or soliciting funds for a terrorist activity or organization. It lifted the previous requirement that the individual knew, or could reasonably know, that the funds were going in furtherance of terrorist ends. Terrorist organizations included any organization so designated by the Secretary of State, a group of two or more individuals, whether organized or not, engaged in terrorist activity, and organizations engaged in charitable service if the military arm attached. This legislation retroactively applied the measures to all aliens or acts by aliens, regardless of when the act took place.

In a little-publicized but nonetheless extremely significant INS order issued a few weeks after the attack, the Attorney General became empowered to ignore immigration judges' rulings and hold non-citizens indefinitely. Additionally, on October 31, 2001, a Bureau of Prisons (BOP) regulation authorized the BOP and the Department of Justice (DOJ) to monitor communications between the individuals being held and their attorneys where the Attorney General determined that the individual was likely to use the communication to further acts of terrorism.[55] Those allowed to be monitored include individuals who have not been convicted of any offense, on certification by the Attorney General "that reasonable suspicion exists to believe that an inmate may use communications with attorneys or their agents to facilitate acts of terrorism." The certification could last up to one year and was not subject to judicial review. As of January 11, criminal charges had been brought against 60 people in federal custody, with another 563 held on minor immigration violations.

There are many arguments in favor of these measures and using extended detention to respond to the attacks. The most important was the need to interrupt possible ongoing al Qaida operations. Proponents argue that the attacks took the American security establishment by surprise. Extended detention bought time for the INS to scan the pool of non-citizens present in the United States and for intelligence agencies to gather more information. Additionally, by increasing the number of individuals fitting the profile of the supposed hijackers under federal control, the odds of finding individuals involved in the planning and execution of September 11 increased. The Attorney General claimed that the names of those incarcerated were withheld to protect the privacy of the innocent and to prevent al Qaida from obtaining accurate information on which operatives might be in U.S.

custody.[56] He justified the BOP order on the grounds that communication between prisoners and their attorneys may allow detainees to, at best, communicate with the terrorist organization and, at worst, provide enough contact to conduct further operations. Another argument frequently put forward at the time was that non-citizens did not deserve the same protections as citizens, and so what might not be appropriate for an American protected by the Constitution was perfectly acceptable for an alien. Finally, the Bush Administration offered the al Qaida training manual, recovered during a raid in England, which specified how to take advantage of the openness of American society. The manual taught how to take advantage of due process of law. Extraordinary measures were necessary to counter the special training in how to abuse the American legal and judicial system. They would interrupt al Qaida's strategy and throw the organization off guard.

Some of these arguments, such as interrupting possible ongoing operations and undermining al Qaida's strategy, provide strong arguments for the use of such measures. But there are also strong arguments on the other side. One of the most important is precisely that extended detention and questioning interrupted due process of law, undermining one of the central tenets of the American judicial system. Critics point to the fact that many were held incommunicado, and it was difficult to get information on where they had been taken.[57] In addition to the BOP order, the detainees were questioned without an attorney present, despite client-attorney privilege being seen as essential to effective legal representation and protected by international law. Critics claim that the Department of Justice did not demonstrate the need for new rules to protect against attorneys who may help to facilitate future or ongoing criminal activity. Under existing law, federal authorities could seek appropriate remedies under the well-established "crime-fraud" exception to attorney-client privilege. It was already possible to conduct closed door hearings before a federal judge, and, without the offending attorney present, the court could order monitoring of all communications if necessary. The judge could have removed a suspect attorney from the case. Moreover, the prosecutors were free to initiate criminal proceedings against offending attorneys. Such procedures ensured judicial review, protected legitimate attorney-client communications, and provided the appropriate powers for authorities to investigate and prevent criminal activity without obstruction.

Critics charge that the sweep equated to harassment of an ethnic minority. Of the more than 1,200, some of whom were held for months, only a handful were considered material witnesses, with others held on minor immigration violations. This suggested a violation of equal protection before the law and a discriminatory regime based on religion and ethnicity—violating two rights protected in the Universal Convention of Human Rights. It also sent a message that it was all right to discriminate based on ethnicity. Reports of physical abuse proliferated.[58] Security force members who refused to cooperate in the widespread ethnic profiling became subject to severe criticism.[59]

The concern was not just that the action would cause tension within the United States between the minority, Middle-Eastern Islamic community and others, but that such mistreatment played into the hands of those levying the attacks, making it possible that individuals previously not involved would become alienated from the American state. Critics pointed to the previous use of widespread detention for ethnic and political minorities, pointing out that they had become an embarrassment in American history.[60] They claim that what might seem reasonable at the time later may prove not to be.

The alien did not have to be charged specifically with terrorist activity.[61] The INS claimed prior to September 11 that it could detain such aliens on the basis of secret evidence presented in camera and *ex parte* to an immigration judge. The INS previously could deny entry to any alien it had reason to believe may engage in any unlawful activity, including terrorist activity or supporting terrorist activity in the United States, and to any member of a designated terrorist group.[62] Terrorist activity was defined broadly, to include virtually any use or threat to use a firearm with intent to endanger person or property (other than for mere personal monetary gain), and any provision of support for such activity.[63] Additionally, the Secretary of State already had broad, generally unreviewable authority under the 1996 Antiterrorism and Effective Death Penalty Act to designate "foreign terrorist organizations," making it illegal to materially support such groups.[64] Al Qaida was already on this list.

It is not just on domestic soil that the United States detained and questioned foreign nationals. At the time of writing, the United States had detained more than 500 people at Camp X-Ray in Guantanamo Bay, Cuba, and hundreds more in Afghanistan.[65] Pictures showing the detainees being shackled and forced on their knees with their eyes and mouths covered spurred a storm of international criticism.[66] On February 8, 2002, the Bush Administration announced that it would extend the Geneva Conventions to the Taliban but not to members of al Qaida, whom the Administration classified as "unlawful combatants." This announcement glossed over the conditions under which the United States questioned Taliban and al Qaida captives over the four previous months. To extend the Geneva Conventions, the Administration argued, would be to consider al Qaida a legitimate organization. The Attorney General stated that al Qaida did not represent soldiers of a legally constituted foreign government.[67] The Bush Administration indicated that, following interrogation, some detainees would be returned to their home countries with the assurance they would be brought to justice. The detainees derived from over 35 countries. International concern at the treatment of the detainees ranged from formal inquiries and public statements from foreign governments to discussion within the United Nations' auspices. UN Secretary-General Kofi Annan emphasized that the prisoners "should be treated" in accordance with established norms of law, internationally and otherwise. He added, "The U.S. is a nation of laws. There's been quite a lot of debate about the application of the Geneva Convention.... Whether they are prisoners of war or common prisoners, there are certain rights and certain standards which have to be respected."[68] Pressure began to mount from countries the United States could ill afford to alienate, such as Saudi Arabia, which had more than 100 nationals being held by the United States, and the United Kingdom, with five nationals under American detention. What makes the issue of detainees particularly concerning is that the two options currently on the table are to either hold them indefinitely or to subject them to military tribunal.

B. Military Tribunals

On November 13, 2001, President Bush issued the military order: "Detention, treatment, and trial of certain non-citizens in the war against terrorism." Claiming his authority as Commander in Chief, Bush cited the emergency and potential of terrorist groups to inflict mass casualties, death, and disruption in the United States. This order suspended the use of domestic criminal courts. It applied to non-citizens whom there was reason to believe were members of al Qaida, engaged in or threatening to engage in acts of international terrorism that targeted U.S. citizens, property, national security, economy, or foreign policy, or who had harbored such an individual. The order allowed for the detention and prosecution outside the United States by military tribunal (five uniformed officers), with rules of evidence relaxed to include evidence with "probative value to a reasonable person." The proceedings could be conducted in secret, with the death penalty inflicted by a two-thirds vote. The order eliminated any right of appeal.

An outcry erupted both overseas and within the United States. Charges that the Executive Branch had failed to consult its allies, attorneys in the Defense Department, Congress, and expert legal advisors proliferated. In the domestic realm, an unusual confluence of the right and left on the political spectrum emerged.[69] In Congress, HR 3468, the Lofgren-Harmon bill, sought to create Congressional oversight over the tribunals.[70] After consulting more widely, the Bush Administration "leaked" new rules in late December 2001 that were more in line with the Geneva Conventions. The new guidelines required the presumption of innocence and required that guilt be proven beyond reasonable doubt (instead of preponderance of evidence). The new rules required a two-thirds vote for guilty verdicts, except in the case of the death penalty, where a unanimous verdict became required. They created a three-judge appeals panel, and opened the trials to the public and press except when national security might be at stake. The rules appointed military defense lawyers, but allowed the defendants to choose civilian attorneys. They allowed for hearsay and material gathered without a warrant (such as papers seized during battles, intelligence intercepts concerning bin Laden, and video recordings).

As with detention, there are some strong arguments in favor of military tribunals. I will here briefly outline five. First, military tribunals represent an accepted mode of trial for individuals accused of war crimes. Proponents point to the Defense Department's predecessor, "the War Department, which conducted 2,668 military tribunals in Germany and Japan during and after WWII for foreign soldiers and civilians accused of war crimes."[71] For use of military tribunals in a domestic context, the Administration cited the 1942 *Ex parte Quirin*, when eight German saboteurs were tried and found guilty of offences against the United States. The state executed six.

Second, the claim could be made that ordinary courts are simply insufficient for prosecuting acts of international terrorism. Rules of evidence are cumbersome. Interrogation and searches conducted on the battlefield don't fit the Supreme Court's Miranda decision or the Fourth Amendment search-and-seizure rules. Special rules are necessary to protect sources and information—who collects it, how it is collected, and what the information itself may be. The publicity afforded by a regular trial would simply play into terrorists' hands. Individuals argue that there is the need for a swift result to demonstrate swift justice for the horrific attacks of September 11. A lengthy trial and appeals process, in this environment, is simply unacceptable.

laws of war.

Fourth, the recent failure of the Lockerbie trials, brought in response to the downing of Pan Am 103 in 1988, demonstrates that an international court or tribunal would be ineffective. Tried by Scottish judges in a neutral country (the Netherlands), one of the two Libyans charged was found not guilty. The other initiated a lengthy appeals process. In the course of the prosecution the United Nations lifted its sanctions against Libya and the Libyan government renewed contact with the United States.

Fifth, the claim that it is better to let one guilty person go free than to have one innocent person incarcerated is reversed in the case of the possible mass destruction of human life. This deeply utilitarian argument demands that the protection of society outweighs the protection of individual rights, and it is one that has been codified in the past in the imposition of stricter penalties on crimes that threaten the very fabric of society. The military tribunals introduce a less lax regime that might be more likely to incarcerate an innocent person. But this risk is justified. Moreover, it is morally repugnant to let a "terrorist," who has engaged in an act both politically and morally offensive to society, go free.

Again, just as there are strong arguments for the use of military tribunals, there are also stronger arguments against them. First, the president did not have the power to introduce the tribunals. The Constitution clearly gives this power to Congress. The difficulty with appeal to the military tribunals in World War II and the 1942 German saboteur case is that Congress had specifically authorized the president, in its Articles of War, to establish military commissions to try spies, those harboring the enemy, and those violating the laws of war. Congress repealed this measure in 1956. Further, in 1942, Congress had declared war. But, in September 2001, Congress simply authorized military force against those "nations, organizations or individuals" responsible for the attacks. Further, the military order collapsed the distinction between the executive and judicial branches—a distinction rigorously protected by the Constitution as long as civilian courts continued to be open for business.

Second, there is nothing wrong with using the ordinary criminal system to try suspected terrorists. In the Southern District of New York, Mary Jo White, the federal prosecutor, obtained a 100 percent conviction rate for the 26 jihad conspirators accused of complicity in previous attacks both in the United States and against American personnel and property overseas. The trials demonstrated that the criminal system had adequate procedures for dealing with classified information. This was, precisely, the point of the Classified Information Procedures Act: to protect National Security.

Openness marked past terrorism trials. Those addressing the 1993 World Trade Center bombing, the attacks in Kenya and Tanzania, the "Unabomber," and the attack on the Murrah Federal Building in Oklahoma were conducted openly. Judges can order that witnesses' identities or key documents be held back from the discovery process. In most of the New York cases the jurors were anonymous. The prosecutors, defense attorneys, and even judges didn't know the jurors' names. The courts excused anyone afraid to serve and placed key witnesses in federal protection programs.[72]

The Bush Administration's decision to try Zacarias Moussaoui in a federal district court, rather than military tribunal, further demonstrates the salience of the domestic judicial system. He is charged with conspiring to murder people in the United States "resulting in the death of thousands of persons on September 11, 2001." If this, the most fundamental charge that can be levied against al Qaida, can be tried in a regular court, then so can charges of conspiracy to commit other crimes that have not yet become manifest. Vice President Dick Cheney's defense of the decision not to try Moussaoui by military tribunal was that the decision was "primarily based on an assessment of the case against Moussaoui, and that it can be handled through the normal criminal justice system without compromising sources or methods of intelligence.... And there's a good, strong case against him."[73] But this suggests that if there is a strong case against someone, then they can be tried in a federal court. If it is a weak case, then someone becomes subject to the military tribunal.

Opponents to military tribunals note that publicity isn't a problem in the domestic court system. The trials in New York were not televised. Defendants who might try to turn the witness stand into an opportunity to put forward their doctrinal beliefs become subject to difficult cross-examination. Individuals who interrupt the proceedings can be sent to rooms with closed-circuit television. And as for the length of the trial, critics of military tribunals claim that there is actually a benefit to it. The New York trials were long—the longest stretching up to six months. But in that time the state built up a considerable amount of information about al Qaida. Moreover, the institution of trial by military officers stole the opportunity from the ordinary citizens, the primary target of attacks, to participate in the administration of justice.

Third, as with the new INS powers, opponents claim that the new, extraordinary powers are simply not warranted. They encompass unacceptably wide powers of jurisdiction and fail to establish minimum guarantees for human rights. The order allows for indefinite detention. It is far from clear on the right of defendants to know charges and evidence against them. It says nothing about access to families, visitors, or attorney. It includes an overly-broad number of triable offences. It is not limited to just those engaged in war crimes but "any and all offenses triable by military commission." Further, the order authorizes the trial of any non-citizen accused of "acts of international terrorism," without defining it. So the government gets to determine who is a terrorist—a deeply political term that can be used in any number of ways.

Opponents also argue that the principle of it being better to let one innocent person be incarcerated than to let one guilty person capable of mass destruction go free is not sound. In an age where technology allows for the massive infliction of loss of life and destruction of property, this argument could be extended to any number of crimes. It is a fundamental shift in the very basis of the U.S. legal system. One could also argue that the introduction of this extraordinary process is simply unacceptable. *Ex parte Milligan* arose out of the Civil War—a war that tore at the very existence of the United States. In its decision the U.S. Supreme Court overturned the conviction of a man found guilty by military tribunal of plotting insurrection in Indiana on behalf of the confederacy. The court wrote, "The Constitution of the United States is a law for rulers and people, equally in war and in peace, and covers with the shield of its protection all classes of men, at all times, and under all circumstances. No doctrine, involving more pernicious consequences, was ever invented by the wit of man than that any of its provisions can be suspended

mony before the Senate Judiciary Committee, the Attorney General, John Ashcroft, said, "foreign terrorists who commit war crimes against the United States… are not entitled to, and do not deserve, the protection of the American Constitution." With this in mind, one would be forgiven for asking, if it has already been determined that an individual is a terrorist, why bother with a trial at all? As Laurence Tribe, the noted professor of Constitutional Law at Harvard University, put it, "The more you use ad hoc procedures, the more it looks like you're structuring the procedure to bring about a certain result."[74] Quite apart from issues of internal legitimacy, this approach will simply anger American allies and drive non-allied nations further away.

Fifth, terrorist acts lead to extremely emotional atmospheres. Yet it is precisely when many people are crying out for revenge that particular care must be taken. There are many examples from U.S. history where this was of issue. I will here cite two. The execution of Mary Surratt, who was convicted by a military tribunal on the basis of shaky evidence and hung for President Lincoln's murder. A civil court that operated in a less heated environment later exonerated her son. The trial of General Tomoyuki Yamashita, the commander of Japanese forces in the Philippines, provides a second. Justices Frank Murphy and Wiley Rutledge filed dissents that detailed the tribunal's failure to provide a fair trial. Murphy wrote, "By this flexible method a victorious nation may convict and execute any and all leaders of a vanquished foe, depending on the prevailing degree of vengeance and the absence of any effective judicial review." General [Douglas] MacArthur pushed through the sentence without even waiting to read the decision of the Supreme Court in what was regarded as an effort to stave off calls to hang the Emperor of Japan.[75]

Sixth, opponents could point to the dramatic international impact of the use of the military tribunals. They set a low standard that may be adopted by other nations and used as a basis for repressing people, including American citizens, seeking to exercise basic freedoms. Within weeks of the attacks various world leaders had begun to capitalize on the U.S. "war on terrorism." Vladimir Putin, the Russian president, repeatedly used September 11 and the U.S. campaign to demand a free hand in response to Chechen rebels. In Guatemala, a new antiterror commission was staffed by ex-military officials, who intimidated and murdered human rights and Mayan Indian activists. And in Zimbabwe, President Robert Mugabe was even more opportunistic. Anyone who objected to the expropriation of white-owned land was considered a "terrorist." Mugabe's government proposed a new security bill that punishes terrorism and other vague offenses with the death penalty.[76]

The military tribunals violate international law. The Third Geneva Convention requires that no prisoner be tried by a court failing to offer "the essential guarantees of independence and impartiality." But the tribunals give the president final authority to select who is tried, who tries them, who is put to death—and who is on appeals boards. As Tribe has elsewhere commented, "All the rules about proof beyond reasonable doubt and other similar protections can look tremendous but not add up to anything if in the end there is no guarantee of an appeal outside the executive branch."[77] In brief, the tribunals provide the executive branch with too much power.

Just as shifts in foreign policy affect international perception of the United States, the tribunals will harm U.S. past and future credibility abroad. It is simply inconsistent with previous American opposition to similar orders issued by other countries. Throughout the 1990s the U.S. State Department's reports on human rights throughout the world criticized the use of secret arrests and military tribunals in Peru, Egypt, Nigeria, Russia, and elsewhere. More recently the U.S. government registered its discontent with Peru's treatment of Lori Berenson, charged with aiding and abetting Shining Path terrorists. The U.S. government demanded that she be given a second, civilian trial, after she had been found guilty in a military tribunal. If states don't themselves adopt a similar structure, the tribunals may well be seen internationally as illegitimate. In addition to the arguments above, the U.S. military only has a handful of attorneys that have any experience in conducting a capital trial. (The last such case was in 1996.[78]) The military expressed concern that American officers who conduct tribunals may be found guilty of war crimes internationally.

Moreover, American soldiers may find themselves subject to similar procedures in other countries. As one military legal expert put it, "If the U.S. government is going to pull the wool out from under the Geneva Conventions, that is going to be serious for our soldiers."[79] It is not clear that designating the Taliban as protected under the Geneva Conventions but removing the suspected al Qaida operatives from its protection will address this concern. Members of al Qaida all have nationalities, and their home states may well decide that the United States, in refusing to treat their nationals under the auspices of the Geneva Conventions, has abrogated from the treaty.

C. Death Penalty

The order governing military courts included capital punishment in its auspices. In the rules leaked in late December [2001] the infliction of the penalty would require the unanimous agreement of the panel of military officers presiding over the trial.

I will here outline three central arguments for the use of the death penalty for terrorism. First, capital punishment fits the crime. This argument particularly resonates in the American context, where claims that the supreme crime requires the supreme punishment proliferate. Terrorist acts are not just murder, but a threat to society and the *politas*. Traditionally, the most serious crimes are treason and acts of war—acts that terrorism mimics if not commits. Moreover, the mass killing of innocents or noncombatants is not just a crime against this society or state, but a crime against civilization. Proponents argue that it is a just punishment: an eye for an eye, and a tooth for a tooth.[80] A life sentence, or a lesser punishment, would simply be inadequate. The United States uses the death penalty for "lesser crimes," which would make it inconsistent not to apply to the most heinous of all— mass attack on unarmed civilians.

Proponents claim further that the punishment is appropriate because terrorists can't be reformed.[81] Additionally, where the act of terrorism is irrational and plays strongly on emotion, capital punishment restores rationality.[82] Supporters point to safeguards in the system and say they are ample to prevent the execution of the wrong person.[83] They suggest that the perpetrator actually gets a better end than the victim: the guilty has the opportunity to prepare, whereas the victim, possibly in extended pain, doesn't have the opportunity to make peace.[84] For those who fear death, it is seen as appropriate to counter terror with terror. And the public does not want to see this form of punishment abolished.[85]

hope of reprieve—something that should not be nurtured. And its elimination would provide terrorists an overwhelming advantage over the population and the security forces.[89] It would lead to an increase in public anxiety.[90]

Third, maintaining capital punishment sends important messages. It creates a social stigma against use of violence for political ends.[91] And it plays an important role in retribution as a way of holding individuals responsible.[92] As for those actively seeking death and becoming martyrs through their execution, they would be martyrs anyway. They have already taken on the state. And neither they nor their supporters accept the legitimacy of the legal order anyway. By eliminating capital punishment the order will not be suddenly more acceptable. Finally, while civilization may be moving toward abolition, it can't be hastened through legislation.[93] To reach this stage, such violence would no longer exist. So as long as there is terrorism, there will be the necessity of having capital punishment.

Again, there are stronger arguments against use of the death penalty for, specifically, terrorism. First is the claim that it is not a deterrent.[94] Numerous studies have reached this conclusion for ordinary crime. The 1953 Royal Commission on Capital Punishment, Amnesty International report on Canada (where the murder rate per thousand fell after abolition), and 1988 United Nations Committee on Crime Prevention and Control provide some examples. In the United Kingdom and Ireland, during consideration of whether to eliminate the death penalty, one often-cited source was Albert Pierpoint, Britain's official hangman for more than 25 years. Pierpoint was responsible for more than 400 deaths, many of which related to political crimes regarding Ireland. He later wrote in his autobiography, "I do not now believe that any one of the hundreds of executions I carried out has in any way acted as a deterrent against future murder. Capital punishment, in my view, achieved nothing except revenge."[95]

One could argue that the argument is even more pronounced for terrorism, where most terrorist organizations teach that individuals may well die. If individuals were deterred by death, they would not be engaged in terrorist action. One need only think of groups like the PKK, where the average lifespan of a fighter is 18 months, or the IRA, where members are told that within two years they either will be dead or in prison. Many activists, such as those in Hammas or Hizb'allah may actually seek death to thereby demonstrate complete commitment to the cause. Moreover, death serves to heighten publicity for the cause and, most importantly, to create martyrs. As Che Guevara lay in final repose in Bolivia and Bobby Sands became memorialized on walls throughout Northern Ireland, the dead heroes assume a mystical, religious quality—a sense magnified when tried in military courts, as warriors, as the weak David taking on Goliath. As one TD [Teachta Dála, member of parliament] in Ireland put it in the Irish Parliament,

> Let us consider for a moment the mind of the terrorist. It is fair to say that in many cases down through the years terrorism has thrived on publicity. On going back over our history and our fight for freedom, one can see the manner in which the death penalty was used by our freedom fighters to build the code of martyrdom, the concept of heroism.

The ultimate deterrent of capital punishment was used to highlight the cause of the freedom fighter.[96]

In numerous cultures a great respect develops for martyrs and the families of martyrs, making the death penalty not only not a deterrent, but something to be sought. This is especially true for movements making extensive use of suicide bombers.

Second, with capital punishment there is the danger of miscarriage of justice that cannot be rectified.[97] Evolution in theory governing criminal law suggests that the proper aim of punishment is rehabilitation. Rehabilitation may counter social and economic structures and even psychological tendencies that give rise to violence. But capital punishment, by its very nature, is not reformative. It is hard to be rehabilitated when you are dead. Moreover, no matter how stringent a structure has been created, human judgment remains fallible.[98] And so the wrong people may be sent to the gallows—an occurrence made more likely by the emotive atmosphere that surrounds acts of terror.[99]

The release of the Birmingham Six vividly drew this point. Six Irish men served 16 years for wrongful conviction for the 1974 IRA pub bombing in Birmingham that left 21 people dead.[100] In 1991 the appeal court overturned their convictions, determining that evidence had been suppressed and falsified and incriminating statements extracted by physical force. In the case of the Guildford Four, seven people died in IRA pub bombings in Guildford, Surrey.[101] The British judicial system incarcerated four men for 15 years. They were released in 1989.[102] As he left the Old Bailey, Gerald Conlon, one of the Guildford Four, thanked God that capital punishment had not existed at the time of his arrest; otherwise the Secretary of State would have had to make his apology in a graveyard.[103] Such miscarriages of justice become even more likely when the evidentiary and other rules are softened, as is typical of counterterrorism and present in the introduction of military tribunals.

Civilization writ-large, and particularly, the United States' closest allies, are moving toward abolition.[104] The list of liberal, democratic states that have abolished it steadily expands: Holland (1870), Belgium (1863), Norway (1905), Denmark (1930), Sweden (1921), Italy (1948), Finland (1949), Portugal (1867),[105] the United Kingdom (1957), and Ireland (1990). Abolition is seen as progressive, and revenge has become distinguished as an outmoded concept.[106] The death penalty contradicts right to life, which has been recognized in numerous international and domestic instruments as an inalienable right.

Some argue further that life imprisonment presents a greater punishment than the fear of death.[107] Life imprisonment re-institutes reason, in place of the irrationality of either the act of terror or the further taking of human life.[108]

With the growing international norm against the use of the death penalty, its continued use harms America's relations with other countries. The European Union has refused to extradite suspects to the United States unless it receives assurances that the death penalty will not be applied. Within months of his arrest, France condemned the trial of Zacarias Moussaoui, a French citizen accused of being the 20th hijacker in the September 11 attacks. Spain, which arrested eight people suspected of complicity in the attacks, refused to extradite them. The Finnish parliament similarly said it would refuse to extradite if threatened by the death penalty. The growing international norm may keep perpetrators from being held responsible for their actions. As one British newspaper, the *Observer*, put it, "The British Government's view, which *The Observer* shares, is that bin Laden, Omar,

IV. Conclusion

One characteristic of terrorism is that it evokes a wide set of reactions. It challenges a liberal, democratic state's ability to fulfill its most basic obligation: to protect the life and property of the citizens. In some instances terrorism goes further, attacking the legitimacy of the state's monopoly over administrative structures and coercive measures. Reason of state dictates that when such attacks threaten the life of the country, the obligation of the government to respond intensifies. September 11 was seen as more than terrorism—as an act of war levied on the territorial integrity of the United States. With reason of state widely touted in justification, the Bush Administration and Congress introduced extraordinary powers.

The problem with this claim is that national security becomes a broad justification for any number of actions taken on the basis of information not available to the public. In his December 2001 testimony to the Senate Judiciary Committee, the Attorney General stated, "I trust that Congress will respect the proper limits of Executive Branch consultation that I am duty-bound to uphold. I trust, as well, the Congress will respect this President's authority to wage war on terrorism and defend our nation and its citizens with all the power vested in him by the Constitution and entrusted to him by the American people."[110]

The Bush Administration asked the public to trust them. Yet liberal democracy is founded on the concept of limited government. Distrust, with good reason, underlies the constitutional underpinning of the United States. Despite carefully crafted limitations, the United States has, in its history, seen abuse of the powers that are granted to the state. Prior to the attacks, considerable powers were available that already impacted on individual rights. While terrorism demands a response from the state—it has been seen to have failed to perform its most basic obligation: the protection of the lives and property of the citizens—it also drives states to do things they otherwise wouldn't contemplate. As Roosevelt so eloquently stated, the only thing we have to fear is fear itself. People are afraid, and, driven by fear, the government has introduced shortcuts. But these are expensive shortcuts with long-term effects.

Perhaps the most serious risk is that in enacting these measures the government plays into the hands of those engaged in such actions. In a liberal state, the steady incursion into civil rights will increase domestic dissent. At risk is not just the alienation of American citizens, but the marginalization of ethnic minorities. Moreover, such measures risk initiating a backlash against the government from right-wing ideologues committed to less government interference and an increasing number of strictures on the power of the government. This becomes increasingly true as there is seepage into criminal law, and such measures become less and less exceptional while new ones steadily expand the power of the central authority.

Equally important, these measures risk fomenting international dissent, alienating citizens and elites in other countries, and breeding cynicism at American efforts to further the establishment of democratic regimes. Such a unilateral rejection of basic equal rights angers allies. The French Foreign Minister "scoffs at the 'hyperpuissance'; the German Foreign Minister huffs about being treated as 'satellites,'"[111] and the general tone of U.S.-European relations daily gathers an increasing chill. As the United States becomes increasingly ethnically diverse and less Euro-centric, the intangible links between ethnic and religious groups in America and overseas will become weaker. Simultaneously, with a GDP larger than the United States, European power may well increase. In 1998 Steve Walt cogently argued that trans-Atlantic relations will be placed under increasing stress.[112] Measures such as those highlighted in this paper go some way toward accelerating such a process.

The line between security and liberty is, indeed, a difficult one to draw. There are strong arguments for and against widespread detention and questioning, military courts, and capital punishment. But if September 11 was an attack against civilization, and not just against America, the United States should count on civilization to respond. Crimes committed in America could be tried on U.S. soil, where the average citizens, deeply affected by the horrific attacks of September 11, would have an opportunity to participate in the administration of justice. Those committed overseas could be subjected to UN tribunal or to an International Criminal Court, demonstrating U.S. commitment to universal individual rights. This is not a time for the United States—or the Administration—to be acting unilaterally or under a veil of secrecy. Such actions breed cynicism and suspicion, two conclusions America can ill afford its allies or enemies overseas to reach, as it faces the threat of global terror.

Laura K. Donohue is a visiting fellow at Stanford University's Center for International Security and Cooperation and an acting assistant professor in political science. Her research focuses on terrorism and counterterrorism in the United States, the United Kingdom, the Republic of Ireland, Israel, South Africa, Turkey, and elsewhere. She is the author of *Regulating Violence: Emergency Powers and Counter-Terrorist Law in the United Kingdom 1999–2000*.

Notes

1. These numbers reflect the percentage of all resolutions, bills, and amendments proposed in each house that related all or in part to terrorism, counterterrorism, or consequence management measures.
2. For purposes of this paper I consider terrorism therefore to be acts that involve the following elements: violence, fear, a broader audience, clear purpose, political power, perpetrated against noncombatants, and instrumental. In this paper I focus on sub-state terrorism perpetrated against the United States, United Kingdom, and Ireland.
3. 29 died in the attack. ("Omagh bomb claims 29th victim," BBC News, 18 March 1999. http://news.bbc.co.uk/hi/english/events/northern_ireland/focus/newsid_165000/165159.stm) The British legislation allowed for individuals suspected of complicity in terrorist operations to be convicted on the word of a senior police officer. Silence in the face of such accusation became seen as corroboration of such police evidence. The British statute also allowed for the government to seize a convicted person's assets and made it illegal to conspire within the UK to commit terrorist acts outside the country. Ireland announced the new measures 19 November 1999.
4. Perhaps the most oft-cited example was the 1996 attack by Aum Shinrikyo on the subway system in Tokyo. For further discussion of this attack see *Toxic Terror*, edited by Jonathan Tucker.

fense Against Weapons of Mass Destruction/Domestic Preparedness and Critical Infrastructure Protection, May 18, 2000, p. 45.

7. See Donohue, 2001.
8. For example, the State Department closed U.S. embassies in Tokyo, Bangkok, New Delhi, Jakarta, and Canberra and placed the other U.S. embassies worldwide on high alert. Employees evacuated the UN building in New York and federal buildings in Washington, DC. The Secret Service secured the President, Vice President, Speaker of the House, national security team, the Cabinet, and senior staff members. The CIA operations center moved. The National Security Agency sent all but essential personnel home.
9. http://www.whitehouse.gov/news/releases/2001/09/.
10. http://www.whitehouse.gov/news/releases/2001/09/.
11. September 14, 2001 http://www.whitehouse.gov/news/releases/2001/09/20010914-6.html; see also http://www.whitehouse.gov/news/releases/2001/09/20010924-1.html.
12. These numbers include public bills, amendments, and private bills. Of the total, approximately 40 originated in House committees, and approximately 130 in Senate committees.
13. http://www.whitehouse.gov/news/releases/2001/09/. Additional bills before Congress, H.R. 3086 and S. 1570, would provide the Secretary of Education with specific waiver authority to respond to conditions in a national emergency. On October 20, 2001, the President also introduced an Executive Order adding HHS to Defense capabilities in time of war (http://www.whitehouse.gov/news/releases/2001/10/).
14. PL 107-40 included two resolutions from each house of Congress: H.J.RES.64 and S.J.RES. 23. Two additional declarations of war, H.J.RES. 62 and H.J.RES. 63, were referred to the House International Relations Committee and received no further action.
15. Executive Order; Ordering the Ready Reserve of the Armed Forces to Active Duty And Delegating Certain Authorities to the Secretary of Defense And the Secretary of Transportation; September 12, 2001 http://www.whitehouse.gov/news/releases/2001/09/20010914-5.html.
16. http://www5.cnn.com/2001/US/10/01/inv.frozen.assets/index.html.
17. S.AMDT.1574 to H.R.2590 (Treasury and General Government Appropriations Act, 2002). See also H.R.2899, H.R.2900, H.R.3021, H.R.3111, S.1430, S.1431, and S.1432.
18. See H.RES.238, S.1519, and S.1531.
19. H.R.3074, H.R.3076.
20. H.Con.Res. 293. H.R.3049 would have provided for the removal of the Taliban in Afghanistan.
21. The Emergency Supplemental Appropriations Act for Recovery from and Response to Terrorist Attacks on the United States, FY 2001 President Authorizes Emergency Response Fund Transfer; Text of a Letter from the President to the Speaker of the House of Representatives; October 22, 2001.
22. H.R.2215, H.R.3129, H.R.3174, H.AMDT.318 to H.R.2586, S.RES.171, S.1546, S.AMDT. 1562 to H.R.2500.
23. Defense Department Pentagon memorial—October 11, 2001; New York Memorial Service; National Firefighters Memorial—at the National Emergency Training Center; Emmitsburg, Maryland October 7, 2001, Pennsylvania Memorial Service, http://www.whitehouse.gov/news/releases/2001/09.
24. H.CON.RES.230, H.CON.RES.235, H.J.RES.71, H.R.2897, H.R.2982, H.R.2991, H.R.3036, S.J.RES.25, S.1556, H.CON.RES.223, H.CON.RES.239.
25. H.R.2882 became Public Law No.:107-37.
26. H.CON.RES.228.
27. H.R.3175.
28. See for example H.R.3106, S.1539, and S.1623.
29. H.R.2976.

30. H.RES.241, H.R.2884, H.R.2902, H.R.2930, H.R.2938, H.R.2940, H.R.2945, H.R.2946, H.R.2947, H.R.2955, H.R.2961, H.R.2968, H.R.3007, H.R.3011, H.R.3041, H.R.3045, H.R.3055, H.R.3067, H.R.3073, H.R.3090, H.R.3112, H.R.3137, H.R.3140, H.R.3141, H.R.3143, H.R. 3157, H.R.3210, S.1433, S.1440, S.1446, S.1454, S.1487, S.1493, S.1499, S.1500, S.1505, S.1532, S.1541, S.1544, S.1552, S.1578, S.1583, S.1622, S.1624.

31. Only one bill before Congress (H.R. 2956) addressed rebuilding the actual structures attacked on September 11.

32. *New York Times*, February 7, 2002.

33. H.CON.RES.225.

34. H.J.RES.71 became Public Law No.: 107-89.

35. For instance, National Security Advisor Condoleezza Rice announced during an interview on Al Jazeera television: "I would like to say to the Arab and Muslim world the following. I would like to say that America is a country that respects religious difference. America is a country that has many people of different religions within it."

36. Prime Time News Conference; http://www.whitehouse.gov/news/releases/2001/10/20011011-7.html#status-war. See also http://www.whitehouse.gov/news/releases/2001/10/20011004.html announcing $320MM package and intent to distribute through UN agencies.

37. 71.S.1447 became Public Law No.: 107-71.

38. H.R.2925, H.R.3035, H.R.3178, H.R.3184, H.R.3198, S.1456, S.1480, S.1528, S.1550, S.1551, S.1593, S.1608.

39. H.R.3091, H.R.3123, S.1557, S.1569.

40. H.R.2960, H.R.3013, H.R.3077, H.AMDT.316 to H.R.2586, S.1214, S.1429, S.1518, S.1559, S.1588, S.1618, S.1627.

41. H.AMDT.365 to H.R.2883, H.R.3108, S.1448, S.1510.

42. Terror attacks bring profound changes in FBI focus October 28, 2001. Posted: 1:46 PM EST (1846 GMT) http://www5.cnn.com/2001/LAW/10/28/inv.attacks.fbifocus.ap/index.html.

43. Radio Address by the President to the Nation, The Oval Office, November 3, 2001; http://www.whitehouse.gov/news/releases/2001/11/2011103.html.

44. These include al Qaeda, Islamic Movement of Uzbekistan, Egyptian Islamic Jihad, Gama'a al-Islamiyya in Egypt, Harakat ul-Mujahidin in Pakistan, and Abu Sayyaf Group in the Philippines. Several Middle East terrorist groups remain on the list, including Hezbollah, Hamas and the Popular Front for the Liberation of Palestine. The Israeli extremist groups Kahane Chai and Kach have been merged into one group, under the name Kahane Chai. Baruch Goldstein, who opened fire on a Hebron mosque in 1994, killing 29 Muslims as they prayed, was linked to the group. The State Department dropped the Japanese Red Army and the Tupac Amaru Revolutionary Movement from the list. Designation lasts two years.

45. http://www.whitehouse.gov/news/releases/2001/10/20011023-26.html.

46. Laid out in an Executive Order of October 8, 2001 (http://www.whitehouse.gov/news/releases/2001/10/20011008-2.html). Organization and Operation of the Homeland Security laid out in Homeland Security Presidential Directive-1, October 29, 2001 (http://www. whitehouse.gov/news/releases/2001/10/20011030-1.html).

47. Foreign Terrorist Tracking Task Force; Homeland Security Presidential Directive-2; October 29, 2001.

48. H.R.3026, S.RES.165, S.1449, S.1462, S.1490, S.1529, S.1534, H.R.3078.

49. H.R.2603, signed into law Sept. 28, 2001 (http://www.whitehouse.gov/news/releases/2001/09/20010928-1.html). See also http://www.whitehouse.gov/news/releases/2001/09/20010928-12.html.

50. Alex P. Schmid and Albert J. Jongman, with the collaboration of Michael Stohl, *Political Terrorism: A New Guide to Actors, Authors, Concepts, Data Bases, Theories, and Literature* (New York: North-Holland Publishing Co.), 1998.

51. Ibid.

52. Universal Declaration of Human Rights, G.A. res. 217A (III), U.N. Doc. A/810 at 71 (1948).

53. Ashcroft's testimony before Congress, http://judiciary.senate.gov/tel20601f-ashcroft.htm.

54. Right of appeal existed to the United States Court of Appeals or District of Columbia Circuit Court.

58. For example, Hasnain Javid, a Pakistani student held for three days, claims to have been severely beaten by other inmates. The guards ignored his yells for help. Later he allegedly was stripped naked and again assaulted. Again, the guards ignored it. Mohamed Maddy, an Egyptian arrested October 3, claims to have been assaulted by the guards in the Metropolitan District Center. Osama Awadallah, a 21-year-old Jordanian student living in Southern California, says he was taken to the same detention center and beaten and kicked by guards who insulted Islam and forced him against a U.S. flag. Middle Eastern detainees in North Carolina claim to have been stripped naked and subjected to freezing temperatures by the guards. When they tried to convey this to people outside the prison, any phone calls were cut off (http://www.cnn.com/ 2001/US/10/24/inv.jail.death).

59. Interview by author of Chief Mark Kroeker of the Portland, Oregon, police department January 2002.

60. For example, during the Red Scare of the early 20th century the U.S. government picked up 6,000 people in 33 cities throughout the United States. Taken into custody because of their political affiliation, they were placed into "bull pens" and beaten into signing confessions. 566 people eventually were deported. These "Palmer Raids" became a blemish on American history. A second, well-known example followed the attack on Pearl Harbor. In 1942 the U.S. government interned more than 100,000 people of Japanese descent, more than two-thirds of whom were U.S. citizens deemed to be a threat to U.S. national security. In 1988 the government finally apologized and paid restitution to the Japanese internees. A third example is drawn from the Cold War. The McCarthy era saw the introduction of the McCarran-Walter act, which empowered the government to prevent noncitizens that adhered to proscribed ideas from living in the United States. In 1990 Congress withdrew the McCarran-Walter Act on political exclusion and deportation grounds. (Testimony of Professor David Cole on Civil Liberties and Proposed Anti-Terrorism legislation before the Subcommittee on the Constitution, Federalism and Property Rights of the Senate Judiciary Committee, October 3, 2001; http://judiciary.senate.gov/tel00301sc-cole.html.)

61. 8 U.S.C. § 1226, 8 C.F.R. § 241.

62. 8 U.S.C. § 1182(a)(3).

63. 8 U.S.C. § 1227(a)(4). [Pursuant to the Alien Terrorist Removal provisions in the 1996 Antiterrorism Act, the INS may use secret evidence to establish deportability on terrorist activity grounds.]

64. 8 U.S.C. § 1189, 18 U.S.C. § 2339B.

65. http://www.cnn.com/2002/US/02/04/ret.detainees.flights/index.html.

66. http://www.cnn.com/2002/WORLD/europe/02/08/ret.cuba.redcross/index.html.

67. http://www.cnn.com/2002/US/02/01/guantanamo.detainees/index.html.

68. http://www.cnn.com/2002/US/02/01/guantanamo.detainees/index.html.

69. Senator Edward Kennedy and conservative columnist William Safire agreed on this point, as did the Executive Directors of Amnesty International USA, Human Rights Watch, the International Human Rights Law Group, the International League for Human Rights, the Lawyers Committee for Human Rights, Minnesota Advocates for Human Rights, Physicians for Human Rights and the Robert F. Kennedy Memorial Center for Human Rights.

70. This legislation would authorize the use of military tribunals in response to the September 11 attacks but would limit their jurisdiction to foreign nationals captured overseas. The bill prohibits the suspension of habeas corpus without congressional authorization and requires further congressional action should the courts continue in operation past 2005.

71. *USA Today*, December 31, 2001, "Proposal Would Widen Defendants' Rights," by Toni Locy and Richard Willing.

72. The judge who presided at many of the trials, Kevin T. Duffy, does have 24-hour security that may well last the rest of his life, but this was a choice he made to oversee the trials.

73. January 6, 2002, Senator Joseph L. Lieberman, *The Houston Chronicle*.

74. Quoted in the *New York Times*, December 29, 2001, B7, "A Nation Challenged: Civil liberties; Draft Rules for Tribunals Ease Worries, but Not All," by Katharine Q. Seelye.

75. Stephen Ives Jr, "Vengeance Did Not Deliver Justice," *The Washington Post*, December 30, 2001.

76. "The Antiterror Bandwagon," December 28, 2001, *The New York Times*, A18, Editorial.

77. *The New York Times*, December 29, 2001, "A Nation Challenged: Civil Liberties; Draft Rules for Tribunals Ease Worries, but Not All" by Katharine Seelye, B7, col. 5.

78. Since 1961 there have been no federal executions arising from military cases. The last capital case, that of Jessie Quintanilla, convicted of murdering an executive officer and attempting to murder two other Marines at Camp Pendleton, was in 1996. (*Los Angeles Times*, December 29, 2001, "Response to Terror.")

79. Francis A. Boyle, expert on the law of war at the University of Illinois. *The New York Times*, December 26, 2001. "A Nation Challenged: The Justice System; Critics' Attack on Tribunals Turns to Law Among Nations," by William Glaberson.

80. Mr. Derrig, Dail Debates, 5 December 1951, Vol. 128, cols. 428–30.

81. See for instance the *Garda News*, quoted in the Dail Debates, 1 June 1990, Vol. 399(a), cols. 1224–1225.

82. Mr. Derrig, Minister for Lands, Dail Debates, 30 January 1952, Vol. 129, col. 138.

83. Mr. Derrig, Minister for Lands, Dail Debates, 30 January 1952, Vol. 129, col. 138.

84. General MacEoin, Dail Debates, 5 December 1951, Vol. 128, cols. 426–7. See also MacEoin, Dail Debates, 5 December 1963, Vol. 206, col. 769.

85. Mr. Derrig, Dail Debates, 5 December 1951, Vol. 128, cols. 429–30.

86. Mr. Derrig, Minister for Lands, Dail Debates, 30 January 1952, Vol. 129, col. 137.

87. Mr. Cogan, Dail Debates, 5 December 1951, Vol. 128, col. 413–4.

88. Mr. Derrig, Minister for Lands, Dail Debates, 30 January 1952, Vol. 129, col. 137–8; Mr. Cogan, Dail Debates, 5 December 1951, Vol. 128, col. 413–5.

89. Mr. Dogan, Dail Debates, 5 December 1951, Vol. 128, col. 415.

90. Mr. Derrig, Minister for Lands, Dail Debates, 30 January 1952, Vol. 129, col. 137; and 5 December 1951, Vol. 128, col. 430.

91. Mr. Charles Haughey, Minister of Justice, Dail Debates, 6 November 1963, Vol. 205, col. 1001.

92. Mr. Derrig, Minister for Lands, Dail Debates, 30 January 1952, Vol. 129, col. 139.

93. Mr. Derrig, Minister for Lands, Dail Debates, 30 January 1952, Vol. 129, col. 137.

94. Mr. Charles Haughey, Minister of Justice, Dail Debates, 6 November 1963, Vol. 205, col. 1001.

95. Quoted in Dail Debates, 1 June 1990, Vol. 399(a), col. 1222.

96. Mr. Flanagan, Dail Debates, 1 June 1990, Vol. 399(a), col. 1206.

97. Mr. Cogan, Dail Debates, 5 December 1951, Vol. 128, col. 413. See also Mr. Charles Haughey, Minister of Justice, Dail Debates, 6 November 1963, Vol. 205, col. 1001.

98. Mr. MacBridge, Dail Debates, 21 November 1951, Vol. 127, col. 1165.

99. Mr. Flanagan, Dail Debates, 1 June 1990. Vol. 399(a), cols. 1207–1208.

100. In 1991 British authorities released Hugh Callaghan, Paddy Joe Hill, Gerry Hunter, Richard McIlkenny, Billy Power, and Johnny Walker, who had spent over 16 years in jail. See http://www.oireachtas-debates.gov.ie/D.0402.199011010060.html, and http://www.parliament.the-stationery-office.co.uk/pa/cm199091/cmhansrd/1991-01-14/Orals-2.html.

101. "Blair's Apology to Guildford Four," *Guardian Unlimited*, 6 June 2000, http://www.innocent.org.uk/cases/guildford4/#thegrauniad.

102. Paul Hill, Gerry Conlon, Paddy Armstrong, and Carole Richardson.

103. Paraphrased in Dail Debates, 1 June 1990, Vol. 399(a), col. 1254. Paddy Hill, one of the Birmingham Six, made a similar point, that while his incarceration had been terrible, things could be worse—if capital punishment had been around, he wouldn't be there to complain. Ibid.

107. Mr. O. Flanagan, Dail Debates, 30 January 1952, Vol. 129, col. 142; General MacEoin, Dail Debates 5 December 1951, Vol. 128, col. 426.
108. See for instance Dr. Browne, Dail Debates, 7 November 1963, Vol. 205, col. 1096.
109. Editorial, *The Observer*, January 6, 2002, "Comment: U.S. Justice Would Be an Injustice: The UN Must Try Terrorists."
110. Ashcroft testimony to Senate Judiciary Committee, December 6, 2001.
111. Andrew Rawnsley, "How to Deal with the American Goliath," *The Observer*, Sunday, February 24, 2002.
112. Stephen Walt, "The Ties That Fray: Why Europe and America Are Approaching a Parting of the Ways," *The National Interest*, Winter 1998/99.

Bruce Hoffman, 2002

A Nasty Business

Intelligence is capital," Colonel Yves Godard liked to say. And Godard undeniably knew what he was talking about. He had fought both as a guerrilla in the French Resistance during World War II and against guerrillas in Indochina, as the commander of a covert special operations unit. As the chief of staff of the elite 10th Para Division, Godard was one of the architects of the French counterterrorist strategy that won the Battle of Algiers, in 1957. To him, information was the sine qua non for victory. It had to be zealously collected, meticulously analyzed, rapidly disseminated, and efficaciously acted on. Without it no antiterrorist operation could succeed. As the United States prosecutes its global war against terrorism, Godard's dictum has acquired new relevance. Indeed, as is now constantly said, success in the struggle against Osama bin Laden and his minions will depend on good intelligence. But the experiences of other countries, fighting similar conflicts against similar enemies, suggest that Americans still do not appreciate the enormously difficult—and morally complex—problem that the imperative to gather "good intelligence" entails.

The challenge that security forces and militaries the world over have faced in countering terrorism is how to obtain information about an enigmatic enemy who fights unconventionally and operates in a highly amenable environment where he typically is indistinguishable from the civilian populace. The differences between police officers and soldiers in training and approach, coupled with the fact that most military forces are generally uncomfortable with, and inadequately prepared for, counterterrorist operations, strengthens this challenge. Military forces in such unfamiliar settings must learn to acquire intelligence by methods markedly different from those to which they are accustomed. The most "actionable," and therefore effective, information in this environment is discerned not from orders of battle, visual satellite transmissions of opposing force positions, or intercepted signals but from human intelligence gathered mostly from the indigenous population. The police, specifically trained to interact with the public, typically have better access than the military to what are called human intelligence sources. Indeed, good police work depends on informers, undercover agents, and the apprehension and interrogation of terrorists and suspected terrorists, who provide the additional information critical to destroying terrorist organizations. Many today who argue reflexively and sanctimoniously that the United States should not "over-react" by over-militarizing the "war" against terrorism assert that such a conflict should be largely a police, not a military, endeavor. Although true, this line of argument usually overlooks the uncomfortable fact that, historically, "good" police work against terrorists has of necessity involved nasty and brutish means. Rarely have the importance of intelligence and the unpleasant ways in which it must often be obtained been better or more clearly elucidated than in the 1966 movie *The Battle of Algiers*. In an early scene in the film the main protagonist, the French paratroop commander, Lieutenant

want to understand how to fight terrorism. Indeed, the movie was required viewing for the graduate course I taught for five years on terrorism and the liberal state, which considered the difficulties democracies face in countering terrorism. The seminar at which the movie was shown regularly provoked the most intense and passionate discussions of the semester. To anyone who has seen *The Battle of Algiers*, this is not surprising. The late Pauline Kael, doyenne of American film critics, seemed still enraptured seven years after its original release when she described *The Battle of Algiers* in a 900-word review as "an epic in the form of a 'created documentary'"; "the one great revolutionary 'sell' of modern times"; and the "most impassioned, most astute call to revolution ever." The best reviews, however, have come from terrorists—members of the IRA; the Tamil Tigers, in Sri Lanka; and 1960s African-American revolutionaries—who have assiduously studied it. At a time when the U.S. Army has enlisted Hollywood screenwriters to help plot scenarios of future terrorist attacks, learning about the difficulties of fighting terrorism from a movie that terrorists themselves have studied doesn't seem far-fetched.

In fact, the film represents the apotheosis of cinema verite. That it has a verisimilitude unique among onscreen portrayals of terrorism is a tribute to its director, Gillo Pontecorvo, and its cast—many of whose members reprised the real-life roles they had played actually fighting for the liberation of their country, a decade before. Pontecorvo, too, had personal experience with the kinds of situations he filmed: during World War II he had commanded a partisan brigade in Milan. Indeed, the Italian filmmaker was so concerned about not giving audiences a false impression of authenticity that he inserted a clarification in the movie's opening frames: "This dramatic re-enactment of The Battle of Algiers contains NOT ONE FOOT of Newsreel or Documentary Film." The movie accordingly possesses an uncommon gravitas that immediately draws viewers into the story. Like many of the best films, it is about a search—in this case for the intelligence on which French paratroops deployed in Algiers depended to defeat and destroy the terrorists of the National Liberation Front (FLN). "To know them means we can eliminate them," Mathieu explains to his men in the scene referred to above. "For this we need information. The method: interrogation." In Mathieu's universe there is no question of ends not justifying means: the Paras need intelligence, and they will obtain it however they can. "To succumb to humane considerations," he concludes, "only leads to hopeless chaos."

The events depicted on celluloid closely parallel those of history. In 1957 the city of Algiers was the center of a life-and-death struggle between the FLN and the French authorities. On one side were the terrorists, embodied both on screen and in real life in Ali La Pointe, a petty thief turned terrorist cell leader; on the other stood the army, specifically the elite 10th Para Division, under General Jacques Massu, another commander on whom the Mathieu composite was based. Veterans of the war to preserve France's control of Indochina, Massu and his senior officers—Godard included—prided themselves on having acquired a thorough understanding of terrorism and revolutionary warfare, and how to counter both. Victory, they were convinced, would depend on the acquisition of intelligence. Their method was to build a meticulously detailed picture of the FLN's apparatus in

Algiers which would help the French home in on the terrorist campaign's masterminds Ali La Pointe and his bin Laden, Saadi Yacef (who played himself in the film). This approach, which is explicated in one of the film's most riveting scenes, resulted in what the Francophile British historian Alistair Horne, in his masterpiece on the conflict, *A Savage War of Peace*, called a "complex organigramme [that] began to take shape on a large blackboard, a kind of skeleton pyramid in which, as each fresh piece of information came from the interrogation centres, another [terrorist] name (and not always necessarily the right name) would be entered." That this system proved tactically effective there is no doubt. The problem was that it thoroughly depended on, and therefore actively encouraged, widespread human-rights abuses, including torture.

Massu and his men—like their celluloid counterparts—were not particularly concerned about this. They justified their means of obtaining intelligence with utilitarian, cost-benefit arguments. Extraordinary measures were legitimized by extraordinary circumstances. The exculpatory philosophy embraced by the French Paras is best summed up by Massu's uncompromising belief that "the innocent [that is, the next victims of terrorist attacks] deserve more protection than the guilty." The approach, however, at least strategically, was counterproductive. Its sheer brutality alienated the native Algerian Muslim community. Hitherto mostly passive or apathetic, that community was now driven into the arms of the FLN, swelling the organization's ranks and increasing its popular support. Public opinion in France was similarly outraged, weakening support for the continuing struggle and creating profound fissures in French civil-military relations. The army's achievement in the city was therefore bought at the cost of eventual political defeat. Five years after victory in Algiers the French withdrew from Algeria and granted the country its independence. But Massu remained forever unrepentant: he insisted that the ends justified the means used to destroy the FLN's urban insurrection. The battle was won, lives were saved, and the indiscriminate bombing campaign that had terrorized the city was ended. To Massu, that was all that mattered. To his mind, respect for the rule of law and the niceties of legal procedure were irrelevant given the crisis situation enveloping Algeria in 1957. As anachronistic as France's attempt to hold on to this last vestige of its colonial past may now appear, its jettisoning of such long-standing and cherished notions as habeas corpus and due process, enshrined in the ethos of the liberal state, underscores how the intelligence requirements of counterterrorism can suddenly take precedence over democratic ideals.

Although it is tempting to dismiss the French army's resort to torture in Algeria as the desperate excess of a moribund colonial power, the fundamental message that only information can effectively counter terrorism is timeless. Equally disturbing and instructive, however, are the lengths to which security and military forces need often resort to get that information. I learned this some years ago, on a research trip to Sri Lanka. The setting—a swank oceanfront hotel in Colombo, a refreshingly cool breeze coming off the ocean, a magnificent sunset on the horizon—could not have been further removed from the carnage and destruction that have afflicted that island country for the past eighteen years and have claimed the lives of more than 60,000 people. Arrayed against the democratically elected Sri Lankan government and its armed forces is perhaps the most ruthlessly efficient terrorist organization-cum-insurgent force in the world today: the Liberation Tigers of Tamil Eelam, known also by the acronym LTTE or simply as the Tamil Tigers. The Tigers are unique in the annals of terrorism and arguably eclipse even bin Laden's al Qaeda in professionalism, capability, and determination. They are believed to be the first nonstate group in

same tactics against the Sri Lankan navy. Moreover, the Tamil Tigers are believed to have developed their own embryonic air capability—designed to carry out attacks similar to those of September 11 (though with much smaller, noncommercial aircraft). The most feared Tiger unit, however, is the Black Tigers—the suicide cadre composed of the group's best-trained, most battle-hardened, and most zealous fighters. A partial list of their operations includes the assassination of the former Indian Prime Minister Rajiv Gandhi at a campaign stop in the Indian state of Tamil Nadu, in 1991; the assassination of Sri Lankan President Ranasinghe Premadasa, in 1993; the assassination of the presidential candidate Gamini Dissanayake, which also claimed the lives of fifty-four bystanders and injured about one hundred more, in 1994; the suicide truck bombing of the Central Bank of Sri Lanka, in 1996, which killed eighty-six people and wounded 1,400 others; and the attempt on the life of the current President of Sri Lanka, Chandrika Kumaratunga, in December of 1999. The powerful and much venerated leader of the LTTE is Velupillai Prabhakaran, who, like bin Laden, exercises a charismatic influence over his fighters. *The Battle of Algiers* is said to be one of Prabhakaran's favorite films.

I sat in that swank hotel drinking tea with a much decorated, battle-hardened Sri Lankan army officer charged with fighting the LTTE and protecting the lives of Colombo's citizens. I cannot use his real name, so I will call him Thomas. However, I had been told before our meeting, by the mutual friend—a former Sri Lankan intelligence officer who had also long fought the LTTE—who introduced us (and was present at our meeting), that Thomas had another name, one better known to his friends and enemies alike: Terminator. My friend explained how Thomas had acquired his sobriquet; it actually owed less to Arnold Schwarzenegger than to the merciless way in which he discharged his duties as an intelligence officer. This became clear to me during our conversation. "By going through the process of laws," Thomas patiently explained, as a parent or a teacher might speak to a bright yet uncomprehending child, "you cannot fight terrorism." Terrorism, he believed, could be fought only by thoroughly "terrorizing" the terrorists—that is, inflicting on them the same pain that they inflict on the innocent. Thomas had little confidence that I understood what he was saying. I was an academic, he said, with no actual experience of the life-and-death choices and the immense responsibility borne by those charged with protecting society from attack. Accordingly, he would give me an example of the split-second decisions he was called on to make. At the time, Colombo was on "code red" emergency status, because of intelligence that the LTTE was planning to embark on a campaign of bombing public gathering places and other civilian targets. Thomas's unit had apprehended three terrorists who, it suspected, had recently planted somewhere in the city a bomb that was then ticking away, the minutes counting down to catastrophe. The three men were brought before Thomas. He asked them where the bomb was. The terrorists—highly dedicated and steeled to resist interrogation—remained silent. Thomas asked the question again, advising them that if they did not tell him what he wanted to know, he would kill them. They were unmoved. So Thomas took his pistol from his gun belt, pointed it at the forehead of one of them, and shot him dead. The other two, he said, talked immediately; the bomb, which had been placed in a crowded railway station and set to explode during the evening rush hour, was found and defused, and countless lives were saved. On other occasions, Thomas said, similarly recalcitrant terrorists were brought before him. It was not surprising, he said, that they initially refused to talk; they were schooled to withstand harsh questioning and coercive pressure. No matter: a few drops of gasoline flicked into a plastic bag that is then placed over a terrorist's head and cinched tight around his neck with a web belt very quickly prompts a full explanation of the details of any planned attack.

I was looking pale and feeling a bit shaken as waiters in starched white jackets smartly cleared the china teapot and cups from the table, and Thomas rose to bid us goodbye and return to his work. He hadn't exulted in his explanations or revealed any joy or even a hint of pleasure in what he had to do. He had spoken throughout in a measured, somber, even reverential tone. He did not appear to be a sadist, or even manifestly homicidal. (And not a year has passed since our meeting when Thomas has failed to send me an unusually kind Christmas card.) In his view, as in Massu's, the innocent had more rights than the guilty. He, too, believed that extraordinary circumstances required extraordinary measures. Thomas didn't think I understood—or, more to the point, thought I never could understand. I am not fighting on the front lines of this battle; I don't have the responsibility for protecting society that he does. He was right: I couldn't possibly understand. But since September 11, and especially every morning after I read the "Portraits of Grief" page in *The New York Times*, I am constantly reminded of Thomas—of the difficulties of fighting terrorism and of the challenges of protecting not only the innocent but an entire society and way of life. I am never bidden to condone, much less advocate, torture. But as I look at the snapshots and the lives of the victims recounted each day, and think how it will take almost a year to profile the approximately 5,000 people who perished on September 11, I recall the ruthless enemy that America faces, and I wonder about the lengths to which we may yet have to go to vanquish him.

The moral question of lengths and the broader issue of ends versus means are, of course, neither new nor unique to rearguard colonial conflicts of the 1950s or to the unrelenting carnage that has more recently been inflicted on a beautiful tropical island in the Indian Ocean. They are arguably no different from the stark choices that eventually confront any society threatened by an enveloping violence unlike anything it has seen before. For a brief period in the early and middle 1970s Britain, for example, had something of this experience—which may be why, among other reasons, Prime Minister Tony Blair and his country today stand as America's staunchest ally. The sectarian terrorist violence in Northern Ireland was at its height and had for the first time spilled into England in a particularly vicious and indiscriminate way. The views of a British army intelligence officer at the time, quoted by the journalist Desmond Hamill in his book *Pig in the Middle* (1985), reflect those of Thomas and Massu.

> Naturally one worries—after all, one is inflicting pain and discomfort and indignity on other human beings… [but] society has got to find a way of protecting itself… and it can only do so if it has good information. If you have a close-knit society which doesn't give information then you've got to find ways of getting it. Now the softies of the world complain—but there is an awful lot of double talk about it. If there is to be discomfort and horror inflicted on a few, is this not preferred to the danger and horror being inflicted on perhaps a million people?

quiet over my encounter with Thomas and over the issues he raised—issues that have now acquired an unsettling relevance. My friend sought to lend some perspective from his country's long experience in fighting terrorism. "There are not good people and bad people," he told me, "only good circumstances and bad circumstances. Sometimes in bad circumstances good people have to do bad things. I have done bad things, but these were in bad circumstances. I have no doubt that this was the right thing to do." In the quest for timely, "actionable" intelligence will the United States, too, have to do bad things—by resorting to measures that we would never have contemplated in a less exigent situation?

An international expert on terrorism and political violence, **Bruce Hoffman** is the RAND Corporation's vice president of external affairs and director of its Washington, D.C., office. He is well known for *Inside Terrorism* (1998), which has been translated into foreign language editions in nine countries, and was the founding director of the Center for the Study of Terrorism and Political Violence at the University of St. Andrews in Scotland. In 1998, Hoffman was awarded the Santiago Grisolía Prize and the accompanying chair in violence studies by the Queen Sofia Center for the Study of Violence (Valencia, Spain). Even before the terrorist attacks on September 11, he was consulting with governments and businesses on terrorism and political violence.

Anthony Clark Arend, 1998

Terrorism and Just War Doctrine

W hen classic just war theory developed, the world consisted of a variety of political entities—kingdoms, principalities, empires, and the like. With the passage of time, however, the territorial state emerged as the primary political unit, and writers in this tradition began to apply just war doctrine exclusively to the behavior of states. Today, the vast corpus of just war writings deals with questions about the permissibility of the recourse to force *by states* (the principles of *ius ad bellum*) and the conduct of hostilities *by states* (the principles of *ius in bello*).[1]

Since the Second World War, however, the world has witnessed the emergence of a number of non-state actors on the international stage. Among these actors are terrorist groups. Over the last several decades, the Palestine Liberation Organization [PLO], the Hezbollah, the Irish Republican Army [IRA], the Abu Nidal Group, the Red Brigade, the Red Army, and numerous other groups have used force against a variety of state and non-state targets. Their activities have elicited forcible responses by states—the United States and Israel, in particular.[2] Yet because these groups are not states and operate quite differently from states, it is unclear just how the principles of contemporary just war doctrine would apply to states attempting to counter these terrorist groups.

My purpose here is to attempt to find out—that is, to apply contemporary just war doctrine to state efforts to respond to terrorist actions. Parts one and two will explore the traditional *ius ad bellum* and *ius in bello* principles in relation to terrorism, and part three will offer several recommendations for making just war doctrine more applicable to the terrorist threat.

Ius ad Bellum and Terrorism

Classic just war doctrine was most concerned about when a political entity could justly undertake the use of force.[3] Plato and Aristotle, Augustine and Aquinas, and others searched for specific criteria that could be used to determine when war was justly entered into, and modern just war theorists have continued to use and refine these criteria. Today, while there is no single set that all just war theorists use, six elements figure in most contemporary discussions of *ius ad bellum*; competent authority, just cause, right intention, last resort, probability of success, and proportionality.

1. Competent Authority

To be justly undertaken, a war or other use of force must be initiated by a legitimate authority. As Aquinas explained, "[a] private individual may not declare war...."[4] Instead, "since responsibility for public affairs is entrusted to the rul[ers], it is they who are charged

345

thority.[6] But just what criteria such a group would need to meet remains unclear.[7] It would also seem logical to conclude that *the United Nations* can be considered a competent authority, given the authority vested in it by states. As states ratified the United Nations Charter, they did so with the understanding that the Charter empowered the Security Council to authorize the use of force when the Council determined that there was a threat to the peace, breach of the peace, or act of aggression.[8]

When the concept of competent authority is applied to the use of force against terrorists, on the surface it seems to provide no particular difficulty. Clearly, states are the entities that respond to terrorists, and states are the competent authorities *par excellence*. On closer examination, however, the situation is a bit murkier. In recent discussions of competent authority, scholars have explored precisely who or what body within a state is empowered to authorize the use of force. Can the American president do so alone? Or must Congress, which under the Constitution has the authority to "declare war," be involved in the decision? Virtually all scholars would argue that when the United States is under direct attack, the president can use force without the consent of Congress. But beyond that, scholars and public officials differ considerably on the circumstances under which the president can use force without congressional approval.

This problem is especially acute with respect to terrorism and its unconventional methods of warfare. Terrorists do not generally wear military uniforms and engage in overt attacks across international borders. It is not to be expected that a terrorist group will march across the U.S.–Mexican border with flags flying. Instead, terrorists will attack military and diplomatic installations abroad, take hostages, and kill civilians. Under American constitutional law, it is not clear whether the president has the authority to respond forcibly without the consent of Congress. The War Powers Resolution provides that the president can introduce troops into hostilities only "pursuant to (1) a declaration of war, (2) specific statutory authorization, or (3) a national emergency created by attack upon the United States, its territories or possessions, or its armed forces."[9] It does not provide for the use of force in response to actions against U.S. nationals abroad. Yet, presidents have certainly asserted such a right. In 1985, for example, Ronald Reagan unilaterally authorized force to bring down an Egyptian aircraft carrying terrorists allegedly involved in the *Achille Lauro* hijacking.[10]

2. Just Cause

The second criterion, just cause, can be divided into (a) the substance of the cause and (b) comparative justice.

a. The Substance of the Cause. Every just war theorist—from the most ancient to the most recent—has asserted that for war to be properly undertaken, there must be a substantive just cause, some legitimate reason for going to war. A state cannot simply declare war. Underlying this concept is a critical element of just war doctrine: there is always a presumption against the recourse to force. As the National Conference of Catholic Bishops has observed, "just-war teaching has evolved... as an effort to prevent war; only if war cannot be rationally avoided, does the teaching then seek to restrict and reduce its horrors."[11] It does this, they explain, "by establishing a set of rigorous conditions which must be met if the decision to go to war is to be morally permissible."[12] Especially today, they continue, "such decision... requires extraordinarily strong reasons for overriding the presumption *in favor of peace and against war.*"[13]

But while just war theorists agree that there must be a just cause, they do not agree on exactly what qualifies as a substantive just cause. Augustine wrote in the broadest of terms, explaining that "those wars are generally defined as just which avenge some wrong, when a nation or a state is to be punished for having failed to make amends for the wrong done, or to restore what has been taken unjustly."[14] More recently, James Childress has refined this concept of substantive just cause by narrowing it to three circumstances: "to protect the innocent from unjust attack," "to restore rights wrongfully denied," and "to re-establish a just order."[15]

Regarding the first of these circumstances there is universal agreement. All just war theorists would assert that a state can use force in the event of an armed attack. Indeed, Article 51 of the United Nations Charter guarantees states a *legal* right to "individual or collective self-defense if an armed attack occurs."[16] But the precise meaning of "armed attack" is unclear, especially in regard to terrorism. When does a terrorist action constitute an armed attack? Must it occur in the territory of the aggrieved state? Must it be of a particular intensity? Would an isolated terrorist action amount to an armed attack, or would it have to be part of an ongoing effort? Would the *threat* of an armed attack be sufficient? In other words, could a state justly engage in preemptive or anticipatory self-defense?

More problems arise with the second category of Childress's understanding of substantive just cause, the use of force "to restore rights wrongfully denied." In general just war discussions, scholars would probably take this to mean that force can be used in the face of genocide or other massive human-rights violations. With respect to state actions, a government that engages in genocide or other systematic abuses of the rights of its citizens may be liable to forcible intervention. Indeed, a growing body of literature discusses circumstances under which a "humanitarian" intervention can be justly undertaken.[17] But how the concept of humanitarian intervention would translate to terrorist activity is uncertain. If terrorists were killing or torturing innocents on a massive scale or taking large numbers of people hostage, that action would probably be equivalent to genocide by a state. But what if a terrorist group were causing a group of people to live in great fear for their lives, without actually doing physical harm on a large scale—could such a "reign of terror" give rise to a just intervention? Could a state argue that the mere presence of some terrorist groups poses such a threat to the indigenous population that a forcible action would be justified?

Finally, there are also difficulties with Childress's third category, that force can be justly undertaken "to re-establish a just order." What is a "just order," and when would terrorists violate it? Over the past several years, non-state actors of a variety of sorts have caused a tremendous degree of instability in states. In Lebanon, Somalia, the former Yugoslavia, Liberia, and Sierra Leone, for example, such actors have prevented the centralized government from exercising effective control over large portions of the state's territory. Would such a cast justify intervention? Could it be argued that force is necessary "to preserve," in the words of the U.S. Catholic bishops, "conditions necessary for decent human existence"?[18]

ficiently 'right' in a dispute, and are the values at stake critical enough to override the presumption against war?"[19] In other words, for a state to use force, its "just cause" should be better than its opponent's and must be worth the "violence, destruction, suffering, and death"[20] caused by war.

Here I will take the first aspect of the bishops' definition of comparative justice—which side is sufficiently "right"?—to reflect a proper understanding of that concept. The latter aspect—is the just cause worth the evil to be produced in the war?—can, I believe, be subsumed under the concept of proportionality and will be discussed later.

To apply the requirement of comparative justice to terrorism may seem at first to produce an extremely undesirable result. Typically, terrorist groups are motivated by legitimate causes. The Irish Republican Army has fought against the British for its "unjust occupation" of Northern Ireland. For years, the PLO challenged Israeli possession of the West Bank, the Golan Heights, and other territories. An observer might be inclined to conclude that comparative justice was indeed on the side of these groups. But terrorism introduces another factor into the calculation. What is abhorrent about terrorism is not the cause for which it is acting but the nature of the act. While certain terrorist groups may indeed have legitimate reasons for desiring change in the status quo, the methods of terrorism are in and of themselves impermissible. Targeting innocent civilians and other non-combatants, taking hostages, killing and torturing prisoners of war—these are completely unacceptable violations of the concept of *ius in bello*.

This aspect of terrorism introduces an important challenge to just war doctrine. How can we evaluate the comparative-justice requirement when the methods of one party are clearly unjust from the perspective of *ius in bello*?

3. Right Intention

Aristotle, one of the earliest proponents of the notion of the just war, explained that the ultimate purpose of war must be to establish peace. Just wars are to be fought out of a desire for charity and peace.[21] The purpose is not to obliterate an enemy but to end the aberrant behavior that has breached the peace. As Augustine noted, "the desire to hurt, the cruelty of vendetta, the stern and implacable spirit, arrogance in victory, the thirst for power, and all that is similar, all these are justly condemned in war."[22] Accordingly, revenge, hatred, and the demonization of the enemy have no place in a just war.[23]

This requirement of *ius ad bellum* is one of the most difficult in a conventional war.[24] It is a rare war in which the enemy is not portrayed as evil and the notion of revenge is not present—think of the American propaganda about the Germans and the Japanese during the Second World War. And for terrorist actions, the problem is even greater. Given the tactics of terrorist groups and their often fanatic ideology, it is quite easy to vilify them beyond reason. Moreover, because their deeds engender international outrage, the desire for punishment or revenge sometimes seems to be the main motivation for forcible response.

4. Last Resort

Hostilities should commence only after peaceful alternatives have been explored. There is, however, some disagreement among just war commentators as to how much effort should be expended on exploring these other methods of dispute resolution. The American bishops, for example, state that "all peaceful alternatives must have been exhausted,"[25] while William V. O'Brien notes that "all reasonable efforts to avoid it [war] while protecting the just cause should be tried."[26] The latter approach, requiring all "reasonable" efforts at avoidance, seems to make the most sense. In any conflict, an observer could always argue that there was "one more" alternative that had not been explored.

But even if we understand this criterion as requiring that we exhaust all reasonably peaceful remedies, terrorism raises special difficulties. In conventional international conflict, there are established diplomatic channels and international organizations that have states as parties. Such institutions provide clear methods for pursuing peaceful settlement and non-violent sanctions. Before the Gulf War, for example, the United States and its allies pursued traditional diplomacy and various multilateral methods available through the United Nations. Such methods are not formally available with terrorist groups. They do not have diplomatic missions in the traditional sense and are normally not members of international organizations, and they are not readily susceptible to economic sanctions and other non-violent pressures. As a consequence, it is unclear how a state could reasonably be said to have exhausted peaceful methods of dispute resolution in dealing with terrorists. Furthermore, efforts to establish any form of official contact may be seen as granting a legitimacy to the terrorist group that would help its cause. Israel's reluctance to negotiate with the PLO stemmed in part from this fear.

5. Probability of Success

A state should engage in the use of force only if the action is likely to succeed. As the American bishops note, the purpose of this requirement "is to prevent irrational resort to force or hopeless resistance when the outcome of either will clearly be disproportionate or futile."[27] But, they continue, "the determination includes a recognition that at times defense of key values, even against great odds, may be a 'proportionate' witness."[28]

But how is success defined when this criterion is applied to terrorism? In a standard war, success means the aggression is ended, or the territory is returned, or the status quo ante is reestablished. But does success against terrorism mean the ending of a particular series of terrorist acts? The capture or death of all the terrorists? Because of the tenacity of terrorists, success can often be elusive. How many years should a state fight against a PLO or an IRA?

6. Proportionality

While this criterion is also present in *ius in bello* calculations, as a *ius ad bellum* category proportionality means that "the damage to be inflicted and the costs incurred by war must be proportionate to the good expected by taking up arms."[29] Are the just causes sufficient to outweigh the injustices of war? Needless to say, this can be a perplexing calculation. It is difficult to anticipate the full consequences of a war. The tragedy far outstretches the

could be contended that force against them would have less significant long-term consequences than force against a state. Second, it also seems logical to assume that the type of force used against terrorists is likely to be less destructive than the force necessary to combat state actions.

Ius in Bello and Terrorism

Once a state has properly undertaken to use force, once it has satisfied the requirements of *ius ad bellum*, the conflict must then meet the *ius in bello* requirements in order to be considered just.[31] Over the years, two *in bello* criteria have emerged: proportionality and discrimination.

1. Proportionality

Here the requirement is that the means used in war be proportionate to the ends to be achieved. This means two things. First, any given use of force must be proportionate to the military end sought in that particular case. For example, if the military objective in a battle can be achieved by destroying the communications center of a particular unit, then only the amount of force necessary to accomplish that task should be used. Anything beyond that would be considered disproportionate and, thus, impermissible. Second, proportionality means that, as William V. O'Brien puts it, a military action "must be proportionate in the context of the grand strategic and moral ends of the war."[32] In his book on Israeli's conflict with the PLO, O'Brien notes that "an action might be justified in purely military terms at the tactical or strategic level, but not justified as part of a total pattern of behavior when viewed from the standpoint of the grand strategic ends of the war."[33] Specific uses of force must be proportionate not only in context but also to the overall goals of the general conflict.

Proportionality seems more difficult to apply at the tactical level of terrorism than at the grand strategic level. This is because at the specific case level, proportionality has frequently been understood to mean that the response to a specific terrorist act must be at roughly the same level of force as the act itself.[34] Oscar Schachter, for example, has observed that from a legal perspective, "the U.N. Security Council in several cases, most involving Israel, has judged proportionality by comparing the response on a quantitative basis to the single attack which preceded it."[35] This approach has been called "tit-for-tat proportionality."[36] The difficulty with it is that it could lead to a vicious cycle of terrorist acts and equivalent responses without any real progress toward ending the series of acts.

When the problem of terrorism is viewed through the lens of the broader goals, however, another approach to proportionality becomes plausible. This is what has been called the "eye-for-a-tooth" approach or "deterrent proportionality."[37] As O'Brien has explained, "counter-terror measures should be proportionate to the purposes of counter-terror and defense, viewed in the total context of hostilities as well as the broader political-military strategic context."[38] Accordingly, "the referent of proportionality" is "the overall pattern of past and projected acts."[39] Under this approach, a state responding to a terrorist act would be able to use force not just proportionate to that single act but proportionate to the terrorists' accumulated past acts and anticipated future acts. This approach makes a great deal of sense in light of the peculiar problem of terrorism; yet it is not universally accepted.

2. Discrimination

The principle of discrimination "prohibits direct intentional attacks on noncombatants and nonmilitary targets."[40] Needless to say, all these terms—"direct intentional attack," "noncombatants," and "nonmilitary targets"—have inspired debate.[41] This is especially true with regard to nuclear-weapons use and targeting.[42] Leaving aside these general debates, let us consider difficulties that the principle of discrimination presents for counterterrorism efforts.

A basic element of discrimination is that innocent civilians are not to be attacked or targeted. In a conventional war, military personnel are clearly identifiable. They wear uniforms, use military vehicles, and stay in military installations. Terrorists are not nearly so easy to identify. They do not necessarily wear uniforms or live in military compounds. They are, in fact, civilians. But they are not innocent civilians. Hence, one of the greatest difficulties is figuring out exactly who the guilty parties are. The matter becomes even more complicated because terrorists frequently use innocent civilians and normally immune targets—such as hospitals and churches—as covers. A terrorist group may have its headquarters in the middle of a crowded city, where innocent people go about their daily activities. How can any targeting policy that complies with the requirement of discrimination be established in such conditions?

Terrorism and Just War: Recommendations

Given the particular difficulties that terrorism poses for contemporary just war doctrine, I would like to make some recommendations regarding application of the *ius ad bellum* and *ius in bello* principles. These recommendations seek to preserve the spirit of just war thinking while responding to the specific challenges that terrorism presents.

The Principles of *Ius ad Bellum*

1. Competent Authority. The real question here is whether under domestic constitutional arrangements it should be easier to use force against terrorists than to engage in conventional war. My recommendation is that more freedom should be given to the executive of a state—the president of the United States in particular—to respond to terrorism. Short, quick actions against terrorist targets should be permitted. Without this type of accommodation, it could be very difficult to intervene in a timely fashion to prevent future terrorism.

2. Just Cause. First, regarding *substantive just cause*:

Under traditional just war doctrine, *self-defense* is the most obvious just cause. But how this applies to terrorism is somewhat unclear. I suggest that terrorist actions be regarded as an armed attack, engendering the right of self-defense, under the following circumstances.[43] First, a terrorist attack against targets within a particular state should be considered tantamount to an armed attack. If, for example, terrorists blew up New York's

regarded as an attack upon that state. This is harder to specify. Certainly, an isolated action against a few citizens abroad is tragic, but does it amount to an armed attack that would engender the right of forcible response? My own sense is that only when such acts are of significant proportion should they be considered an armed attack. Of course, "significant" is open to varying interpretations; but I believe that this criterion can be a starting point.

Must a state experience an act of terrorism before using force, or can it act preemptively to prevent such an act? Many scholars hold that under contemporary international law, states maintain a right of *anticipatory self-defense*.[44] Traditionally, however, the right can be asserted only if the state (1) can show necessity and (2) responds proportionately. In other words, the state must first demonstrate that if it does not respond immediately an attack will occur, and its response must be proportionate to the threatened attack.

I believe that these same criteria can be applied to anticipatory self-defense to preempt terrorist actions. If a state can show that an armed attack, as defined above, is imminent, and if it responds proportionately, such actions should be considered permissible.

As for *terrorist "genocide"*: Most just war theorists would assert that if a state engages in genocide or similar massive violations of human rights, another state can intervene justly to prevent further human suffering. I strongly suggest that this concept of "humanitarian intervention" be applied to terrorist actions. If a terrorist group is involved in wide-scale killings and terrorizing, an outside state should be able to intervene justly even if it or its citizens are not directly affected. If, for example, a terrorist group in the Sudan is murdering hundreds of innocent civilians, the United States would have a substantive just cause to intervene.

Concerning the second category of just cause, *comparative justice*:

While it is clear that terrorists may indeed have just motivation for their actions, their methods are fundamentally unjust. I recommend that the methods employed by the terrorist be part of the comparative-justice calculation. Even if a group is pursuing a valid cause, if it uses indiscriminate killings, torture, hostage-taking, and other such abhorrent methods, those actions should tip the balance against the terrorists.

3. Right Intention. Any use of force—even for a just cause—tends to be accompanied with a vilification of the enemy and a desire for revenge. This tendency is especially strong in response to actions by terrorists. I believe, however, that the same strict standard of right intention must also be applied to terrorists. While it is always proper to acknowledge an evil deed as evil, terrorists are human beings who must be dealt with out of charity. The purpose of using force against them must be to end their abhorrent actions, not to exact revenge. While it is of course impossible to change the hearts of decisionmakers who respond to terrorists, at the very least just war theorists should condemn rhetoric that savors of revenge.

4. Last Resort. This *ius ad bellum* requirement poses a particular problem for counterterrorist actions because the normal diplomatic channels available to states do not exist for terrorist groups. While states understandably wish not to legitimize the terrorist group through negotiations, the presumption against the use of force requires a good-faith exploration of peaceful alternatives. I am not suggesting that compromises should be struck with terrorists that would be fundamentally unjust, or that states should engage in negotiations if to do so would enhance the terrorists' status. Rather, I am suggesting that states should not immediately assume that only forcible methods exist. They should make an effort to determine if any other methods would secure a just result. It may very well be that in virtually all cases, the problems of attempting to pursue such alternatives would greatly outweigh the cost of forcible action. Nonetheless, the examination of these non-forcible options should still be undertaken. It is a fundamental tenet of just war thinking that force is not to be chosen without an exploration of other options.

5. Probability of Success.   Another difficulty with counterterror actions is how to define success. What would be a successful forcible action against terrorists? I recommend that success be defined as the elimination of the terrorist threat. This may not mean the capture of all members of a particular terrorist group, but rather the effective ending of the terrorist actions.

This goal is unlikely to be achieved by force alone, since force does not deal with the underlying causes of the terrorism—a desire for territory, a desire to participate in the political system, and the like. While states should not accede to terrorist "demands," they must give some consideration to addressing the underlying causes if they are to succeed in eradicating the terrorist threat.

The Principles of *Ius in Bello*

1. Proportionality.   Some would argue that each specific forcible response to terrorists must be directly proportionate to the proximate terrorist act. Given the nature of terrorism, however, I recommend adoption of the "deterrent proportionality" approach discussed above, according to which a state may respond in a manner proportionate to the accumulated past acts of the terrorists and their anticipated future acts. While this approach clearly introduces a greater element of subjectivity than the "tit-for-tat" approach, it is more suited to prevention of further terrorist actions.

2. Discrimination.   Once a determination has been made that it is permissible to use force to respond to terrorism, against what targets can a state act? This is a very difficult question, given the differences between terrorists and conventional warriors. In keeping with the importance of the principle of discrimination, I offer a couple of recommendations, aware that the precise targets will vary depending upon circumstances.[45] First, a clearly identifiable terrorist camp or training facility would be a legitimate target. Second, if the terrorists are being supported by another state, military assets in that state would be legitimate targets. Thus, if it were clearly established that Libya was providing a great deal of support to a particular terrorist group, Libyan weapons and military installations would be legitimate targets.

To conclude: While the nature of terrorists and terrorist actions raises a number of critical challenges for just war doctrine, that doctrine offers a great deal of guidance for counterterror operations. It is my hope that the observations presented here will help to illuminate this guidance.

ory. He is the author of several books and numerous articles. Among his recent publications is the book *Legal Rules and International Society* (1999).

Notes

1. Among the most important works on the just war tradition are: Paul Ramsey, *The Just War: Force and Political Responsibility* (1968); James Turner Johnson, *Ideology, Reason, and the Limitation of War* (1975); and *Just War Tradition and the Restraint of War: A Moral and Historical Inquiry* (1981); Michael Walzer, *Just and Unjust Wars* (1977); William V. O'Brien, *The Conduct of Just and Limited War* (1981) and, earlier, *War and/or Survival* (1969).
2. See Robert J. Beck and Anthony Clark Arend, "Don't Tread on Us: International Law and Forcible State Responses to Terrorism." *Wisconsin International Law Journal* 12 (1994): 153–219, for an examination of recent forcible responses to terrorism.
3. This is a point made by William V. O'Brien in *Law and Morality in Israel's War with the PLO* (1991), 275.
4. St. Thomas Aquinas, *Summa Theologies, Secunda Secundae*. 15 Q. 40 (Art. 1) cited in O'Brien, *The Conduct of Just and Limited War*, 17.
5. Ibid.
6. See National Conference of Catholic Bishops (NCCB), *The Challenge of Peace: God's Promise and Our Response* (1983), 28–29.
7. O'Brien, *The Conduct of Just and Limited War*, 18–19.
8. U.N. Charter, Arts. 39–51.
9. War Powers Resolution, sec. 2(c).
10. Beck and Arend, "Don't Tread on Us," 175–76.
11. NCCB, *The Challenge of Peace*, 27.
12. Ibid.
13. Ibid.
14. St. Augustine, Book LXLLIII, *Super Josue*, gu. X; cited in O'Brien, *The Conduct of Just and Limited War*, 20.
15. James A. Childress, "Just-War Criteria," in Thomas A. Shannon, ed., *War or Peace: The Search for New Answers*, 46; cited in O'Brien, *The Conduct of Just and Limited War*, 20.
16. U.N. Charter, Art. 51.
17. See, for example, Richard B. Lillich, ed., *Humanitarian Intervention and the United Nations* (1973); Natalino Ronzitti, *Rescuing Nationals Abroad Through Military Coercion and Intervention on the Grounds of Humanity* (1985); Fernando Teson, *Humanitarian Intervention* (1988).
18. NCCB, *The Challenge of Peace*, 28.
19. Ibid., 29.
20. Ibid.
21. As Professor O'Brien observes, "right intention insists that charity and love exist even among enemies." O'Brien, *The Conduct of Just and Limited War*, 34.
22. Augustine, *Contra Faustum* (LXXIV); cited in O'Brien, *The Conduct of Just and Limited War*, 33–34.
23. See John Foster Dulles, *War, Peace and Change* (1939), for a fascinating discussion of this dilemma.
24. See O'Brien, *The Conduct of Just and Limited War*, 34–35.
25. NCCB, *The Challenge of Peace*, 30.

26. O'Brien, *Law and Morality in Israel's War with the PLO*, 280.
27. NCCB, *The Challenge of Peace*, 30.
28. Ibid.
29. Ibid, 31.
30. See Anthony Clark Arend and Robert J. Beck, *International Law and the Use of Force* (London: Routledge, 1993).
31. NCCB, *The Challenge of Peace*, 31.
32. O'Brien, *Law and Morality in Israel's War with the PLO*, 281.
33. Ibid.
34. See Beck and Arend, "Don't Tread on Us," 206–9, for a discussion of different legal interpretations of proportionality.
35. Oscar Schachter, "The Extra-Territorial Use of Force Against Terrorist Bases," *Houston Journal of International Law* 11:215, 315 (emphasis added).
36. Beck and Arend, "Don't Tread on Us," 207.
37. Ibid.
38. William V. O'Brien, "Reprisal, Deterrence and Self-Defense in Counterterror Operations," *Virginia Journal of International Law*, 30: 462, 477.
39. Ibid., 472.
40. O'Brien, *The Conduct of Just and Limited War*, 42.
41. Ibid.
42. See NCCB, *The Challenge of Peace*, 31–34.
43. This draws upon recommendations that Robert Beck and I presented in "Don't Tread on Us," 216–19.
44. See Beck and Arend, *International Law and the Use of Force*, 71–79, for a discussion of anticipatory self-defense under international law.
45. These recommendations also draw upon Beck and Arend, "Don't Tread on Us," 218–19.

In May 1996, Secretary of Defense William J. Perry declared that new chemical-weapons facility in the desert of Libya "will not be allowed to begin production," implying that the United States would use military force to secure this promise.[1] Would such an action seem right, not only to Americans but to citizens and opinion-makers in other countries? Would it *be* right, which is to say defensible in moral terms?

The long-running debate over what to do about Libya's chemical-weapons program is symptomatic of a larger problem: what to do—if anything—about the emergence of a number of states that flout agreed norms of state behavior, both domestic and international; that use and threaten to use force to coerce those who resist their ambitions; and that seek to acquire arsenals of nuclear, biological, or chemical (NBC) weapons to abet these purposes. These are the "rogue" or "backlash" states identified in 1994 by then National Security Advisor Anthony Lake.[2] Perry's statement about Libya reflects the view of many, inside and outside the U.S. government, that preemptive military strikes on the mass-destruction weaponry of such states are essential both for the security of their neighbors and for the interests of the international community.

When policy-makers in Washington and other capitals debate whether or not, or how, to strike preemptively, the choices are highly contentious. Both action and inaction set precedents with long-term consequences. Doing what national-interest calculations call for is not always doing what is right by the hearts and minds of the American people or its friends and allies.

What does moral reflection contribute to the policy debate about preemption? In particular, what does the just war tradition instruct about the value of the different choices?[3] Can there be a moral case—indeed, a moral imperative—for preemption, in addition to a national-interest or legalistic case? In what follows I will offer some speculative answers to these questions. I will begin by reviewing the ethical considerations that typically shape the policy debate about preemption: (1) Is the action undertaken as a last resort? (2) Does it have a reasonable chance of success? (3) Will the action be proportional to the threat being removed? Each will be evaluated in light of the specific attributes of NBC threats. [I] will go on to explore two further considerations. First, self-defense: When and how can preemption be justified as an essential act of self-protection? And second, competent authority: What political legitimacy is needed to establish the authority to make preemptive strikes?

This review of criteria illuminates the various ways in which the specific NBC dimension of the targeted threat shapes ethical considerations associated with preemption. Two conclusions stand out from this review. One is that in some important places the just war tradition stops a bit short. Thus some further elaboration of the tradition seems warranted on the basis of the new strategic realities created by proliferators armed with weapons of mass destruction. The other conclusion is that tradition imposes some obligations on policy that are not typically appreciated in the policy world. An act of preemption cannot be deemed just simply if it meets the first three criteria stated above. The requirements posed by the self-defense and competent-authority criteria cannot be overlooked. Meeting those requirements, moreover, proves to be more complicated than might be expected, given certain attributes of the problem under discussion here.

This leads to a third and more general conclusion, one that is hardly surprising: A moral case for preemption is possible—even a moral imperative in some cases—but only under certain specific conditions. This [selection] evaluates a range of scenarios in which preemption may or may not be justified. It concludes with an assessment of the moral obligations that would follow a preemptive strike.

Why is it important for the policy-maker to think more fully through the moral context of preemption? It is not simply a matter of making preemption more palatable to an American public reluctant to use force for reasons of national interest. Rather, the answer has to do with the particular historical moment, defined by two factors. One is the emergence of the United States as "the world's only superpower"—as a state with unparalleled military power leading an international system in which most of the other states of the world participate as willing partners. The other is the ongoing diffusion of technologies and materials that can be used to produce nuclear, biological, and chemical weapons. If the United States fails to use its power in ways that others will accept as just, a terrible backlash could result. Cooperation could weaken, U.S. leadership could be delegitimized, and weapons could proliferate much more broadly. The future stability of international affairs and the moral framework of American action are thus inextricably intertwined.[4]

Three Prudential Considerations

Just war concepts are hardly new to the policy debate about when and how to use military force. The memoirs of public officials along with public statements of the moment reveal a good deal of concern and often debate about whether particular military actions will be just, and will be perceived as just by the American public and the international community. Policy-makers typically focus on three just war criteria: Can the proposed use of force be defended as a *last resort* effort, after all other means to manage the problem have been tried and failed? Is there a *reasonable chance of success*? And will the action have an effect *proportionate* to the problem it is aimed at solving? When the military act in question is a preemptive strike against the NBC arsenals of rogue states, these criteria require especially careful analysis, largely because the risks and possible consequences loom larger than in many other types of military action.

1. Last Resort

The last-resort criterion is generally understood to require that military action shall not be undertaken unless all other means have been tried and have failed; war-making, after all, should not be the first or preferred course of action in dealing with the war-mongering behavior of a potential aggressor. In fact, the moral requirement is a bit more subtle. Just war

erence for means other than war.

In the 1993 debate over preemptive military strikes against the nuclear assets of North Korea, Tokyo and Beijing were unpersuaded that this criterion had been met. Both believed that the United States was looking too readily to military solutions when the problem might still be susceptible to political and economic management. The Libyan chemical facility still fails to meet this criterion in the eyes of many countries; they are more impressed by the history of enmity between Washington and Muammar Qaddafi than by Washington's efforts to use other means at its disposal, such as a trade embargo or legal prosecution, to suppress the Libyan chemical-weapons program.

But the requirement that military action be taken only in last resort does not mean that military action must be forestalled until it cannot be successful (or can succeed only at far higher cost). In Bosnia, for example, the decision of the NATO [North Atlantic Treaty Organization] allies to use force only in last resort contributed to a widening of the war and a substantial increase in human suffering—the just war tradition would arguably have required a narrow interpretation of the "last resort" criterion and an earlier intervention.[6] Particularly when rogue regimes and weapons of mass destruction are a part of the threat calculus, the last-resort criterion should probably be subject to a quite narrow interpretation. Economic sanctions may take months or years to have an effect (and indeed, their likelihood of success is hotly debated). In contrast, weapons programs may quickly reach maturity once a confrontation begins to take shape. Given what is now known about Iraq's pre-war unconventional-weapons programs, for example, it is clear that in just a few additional months of sanctions aimed at pressuring Saddam Hussein to withdraw his army from Kuwait, Iraq's nuclear program would have produced one or two weapons while its biological program could have geared up to a very substantial level of production and weaponization. Moreover, where arsenals already exist, deferring a preemptive strike may induce an aggressor to disperse his weapons and give him the time to do so, greatly reducing the likelihood that preemption will eliminate them. In both scenarios, buying time could cost lives, literally hundreds of thousands of them.

2. Reasonable Chance of Success

This criterion requires that military actions not be undertaken unless they offer a meaningful prospect of eliminating the threat against which they are targeted. The just war tradition dictates that suffering be minimized. Again, the requirement is a bit more subtle than generally conceived. It requires not simply eliminating the threat but restoring a peace that has been disordered by the threat.

If a preemptive strike fails to eliminate an aggressor's nuclear weapons and motivates retaliation, those weapons may be unleashed, causing the loss of a great many lives. The North Korean case, for example, failed to meet the reasonable-chance-of-success criterion because there was little certainty of the number of nuclear weapons produced there, of their location in a massive network of underground storage and transfer facilities, and of North

Korea's capacity to use biological and chemical weapons to attack the South even if it were stripped of its nuclear weapons. The Libyan case presents similar considerations.

The difficulty presented by the reasonable-success criterion is magnified by the fact that many NBC assets are located in underground facilities that are very hard to attack successfully. In the case of the Libyan plant, for example, some administration statements have indicated that it might not be possible to destroy the plant without resort to nuclear weapons. This would undoubtedly raise questions of proportionality. Even if the United States acquires some reliable means other than nuclear weapons to destroy hardened underground facilities, gaining high-confidence intelligence about the location of such facilities or other weapons deployment sites may prove extremely difficult.

But "success" in this criterion need not mean perfect success. A preemptive strike that eliminates some but not all of an aggressor's NBC weapons could have a variety of benefits. It might induce greater caution and more conservative behavior by removing any doubt the aggressor might have entertained about the ability or will of the United States to meet his challenges. It might also leave the aggressor with so few weapons and delivery systems that they could readily be defeated by active and passive defensive measures, thus rendering his NBC weapons essentially irrelevant to any direct battlefield confrontation he might initiate.

3. Proportionality

The proportionality criterion is generally understood to require that the minimum necessary force be used. The just war tradition dictates that suffering be minimized, particularly the suffering of noncombatants, and military actions that cause more casualties than they prevent can hardly be deemed just. But once again, the precise requirements of the tradition are a bit more subtle. The proportionality criterion puts two obligations on those who would use force: regarding *ius in bello* (what it is right to do in using force), it requires that only minimum force consistent with the aim be used; and regarding *ius ad bellum* (when it is right to resort to force), it requires that the overall costs of action be less substantial than the costs of inaction. Will the good to be achieved by the resort to violence outweigh the damage to be done, both to individuals and to the community of nations?

With regard to *ius in bello*, it would seem at first glance that virtually any preemption of an aggressor's use of NBC weapons should pass the proportionality test—preventing the use of weapons of mass destruction should by definition save the lives of hundreds of thousands if not millions of people, in exchange for the much smaller number of lives that might be lost in the preemptive strike. The North Korean case failed to meet this test, however, because preemptive military action by the United States was seen as likely to precipitate a broader war on the Korean peninsula, one initiated by Pyongyang in response to U.S. actions. Even if stripped of its nuclear weapons, North Korea would possess a formidable capability to destroy South Korea's military and economic infrastructure and to hold Seoul hostage. In contrast, an attack on the Libyan chemical-weapons facility would be unlikely to pose these difficulties and could more easily meet the proportionality requirement.

With regard to *ius ad bellum*, the proportionality of preemption is clouded by a number of factors. Even if preemption successfully prevents the aggressor's use of those weapons, the cost of that thwarted aggression cannot be known—certainly not publicly proven. The United States would find itself in the position of tallying *actual* casualties

thing). The costs of this "use" of NBC weapons cannot readily be compared with the costs of preemptive military attack upon them. But such comparisons are necessary in the moral world. The potential coercive use of NBC arsenals does provide a moral basis for preemption, insofar at it is necessary to repel injury or to punish evil. From the perspective of the just war tradition, this moral claim is valid whether or not coercion has been openly backed by military threats. Appeasement, after all, has typically emboldened assertive leaders. Sometimes it has fueled acts of aggression that have produced many casualties and have been reversed only at high cost.

These three criteria draw on both *ius ad bellum* and *ius in bello* dimensions of the just war tradition. They present a substantial set of moral requirements for dealing with NBC-armed rogue states. But they are only the beginning of the story. They do not reflect a comprehensive reading of what that tradition requires of military action. They are in fact what one moral philosopher has termed "contingent prudential judgments."[7] Two prior criteria must be satisfied: the requirements that any use of force be in self-defense, and that any use of force be authorized by a competent authority.

Preemption and Self-Defense

Moral philosophy establishes that wars of self-defense are just, whereas wars of aggression are not. But there has long been a healthy debate about precisely what constitutes a war of self-defense. A scholar of just war in the mid-sixteenth century wrote, "There is a single and only just cause for commencing a war... namely, wrong received."[8] In our day Michael Walzer has argued, "Nothing but aggression can justify war.... There must actually have been a wrong, and it must actually have been received (or its receipt must be, as it were, only minutes away). Nothing else warrants the use of force in international society."[9] In the debate about preemption, the crucial issue is in those "minutes away": how proximate must the threat of the use of those weapons be? Does the just war tradition require waiting until the very last minute?

As James Turner Johnson has argued, much contemporary Catholic thought on war echoes this very circumscribed right to self-defense—"a defensive response to an attack still in progress."[10] Johnson attributes this way of thinking primarily to the Church's rejection of war as a viable instrument of order and peace under virtually any circumstances, and especially in the nuclear era.

A survey of other perspectives, both contemporary and historical, suggests that this circumscribed view is not universally held. Hugo Grotius wrote in 1625 that "the first just cause of war... is an injury, which even though not actually committed, threatens our persons or our property."[11] To safeguard against wars of aggression, Grotius emphasized that it was essential to be certain about the enemy's intent to attack. Elihu Root said in 1914 that international law did not require the aggrieved state to wait before using force in self-defense "until it is too late to protect itself."[12] Writing in 1977, Michael Walzer argued that "states can rightfully defend themselves against violence that is imminent but not actual."

However, Walzer rejects boastful ranting, arms races, and hostile acts short of war as legitimate bases of preemption, arguing that "injury must be 'offered' in some material sense as well."[13]

The United Nations Charter incorporates competing notions. In its Chapter 7, special rights are reserved for the Security Council to use force in response to threats to international peace and security; those threats are not specifically limited to instances of outright aggression. On the other hand, Article 51 of the Charter, which affirms the right of self-defense "if an armed attack occurs," is generally interpreted to forbid claims of self-defense *except* in cases of armed attack.[14]

International law restricts the right of states to resort to the offensive use of force in preemptive modes. As Johnson notes, "Under the controverted first-use/second-use distinction, aggression is defined as the first use of force regardless of circumstances, while defense becomes second use alone."[15]

This distinction is controverted for the simple reason that aggression does not usually begin, and injury is not usually "offered," when the first weapons are fired. Hot wars are usually but one phase of a competition of interest and power. In relations among states in an anarchic system, competition is inevitable. But it is usually pursued with "soft power," namely political and economic means, rather than the harder forms. War itself is frequently the culmination of a failure of other means to coerce, dissuade, or compel others. As Clausewitz noted, the aggressor is often peace-loving, and it is his resistant victim who causes war to erupt: "A conqueror is always a lover of peace (as Bonaparte always asserted of himself); he would like to make his entry into our state unopposed; in order to prevent this, we must choose war."[16]

War-Making Versus Preemption

Other than the mechanistic and unreliable use of the first-use/second-use distinction, what criteria can be used to distinguish illegitimate acts of war-making from legitimate acts of preemption? Walzer offers some useful commentary on this point:

> The line between between legitimate and illegitimate first strikes is not going to be drawn at the point of imminent attack but at the point of sufficient threat. That phrase is necessarily vague. I mean it to cover three things: a manifest intent to injure, a degree of active preparation that makes that intent a positive danger, and a general situation in which waiting, or doing anything other than fighting, greatly magnifies the risk.... Instead of previous signs of rapacity and ambition, current and particular signs are required; instead of an "augmentation of power," actual preparation for war; instead of the refusal of future securities, the intensification of present dangers.[17]

Walzer and others also emphasize the importance of illegal actions by the prospective aggressor, which is to say actions that abrogate specific legal undertakings of the state or that contravene accepted principles of international law.

The acquisition of weapons of mass destruction might fit many of these criteria quite well—these are actions that can confirm an intent to injure, create a positive danger, and raise the risks of waiting. Their dispersal in time of crisis would certainly signal preparation for war. But to acquire such weapons and to prepare for their use is not the same as what Walzer calls "actual preparation for war" or "the intensification of present dangers"—

Iraqi and North Korean nuclear-weapons programs do not exist in a historical vacuum. They are the expressions of evil, real-world political intentions whose character has been made plain over many years. Precisely for the same reason that we do not think about preemptive action against Britain and France, we can, without collapsing into the moral vulgarities of Realpolitik, consider proportionate and discriminate preemptive action against Iraq and North Korea.[18]

Rogue regimes have already established their aggressive intent—this is the essence of their characterization as "rogue" or "backlash." Their acquisition of NBC weapons is yet another confirmation of that intent. The moral obligation that falls upon them is to conform to established norms of interstate behavior. The moral obligation that falls on their potential victims is to protect themselves. But, given the particular nature of NBC weapons, such protection may be extremely costly if it must await the first blow with those weapons.

Threats to Peace and Order

Moreover, rogue regimes generally threaten not just the immediate sovereignty of their neighbors but the order that is the foundation of long-term sovereignty. They may pose threats to regional peace. For example, had Saddam Hussein been able to use his weapons of mass destruction to secure aggression with conventional weapons in the Middle East, and thus to emerge as a regional hegemon, there would have been significant repercussions for other states in the region—not only those whom he might seek to coerce to do his bidding, such as Egypt or Turkey, but those whom he might seek to defeat or destroy, such as Iran or Israel. In the Far East, were North Korea to prove successful in using its NBC capabilities to coerce the great powers into taking steps that compromised South Korea's safety and well-being, power relations in the region would undergo a period of deeply unsettling realignment, perhaps leading others in the region to acquire NBC weapons of their own.

Rogue regimes may also pose threats to the global order. If an NBC-armed rogue were able to challenge a major commitment or interest of one of the established nuclear powers, and thereby cause that power to back down and appease, others could draw the conclusion that the security guarantees of the great powers—and especially the United States—and the already limited promise of collective security are paper tigers. Similarly, the acquisition of weapons of mass destruction in contravention of existing legal undertakings, such as the Nuclear Non-Proliferation Treaty or the Biological and Toxin Weapons Convention, could lead to an unraveling of the international effort to control the proliferation of such weapons. That could prove highly damaging to international security. Many states have the capability to build NBC weapons but for the moment are uninterested in doing so. The actions of an NBC-armed rogue could lead to the wildfire-like building of mass destruction arsenals in regions in conflict and in regions now free of such weapons. Such far-reaching changes in the distribution of power and in the credibility of the major powers would be likely to erode sharply the international processes and institutions that for the moment at least are the foundation of international order. These changes could

norms antithetical to the interests of justice and peace.

To put it differently: in the international system that exists today, many small and medium-sized states depend upon international norms and collective mechanisms to compensate for their own modest capabilities to provide for their own security. Even the great powers experience a great deal of economic interdependence. Therefore, defending the stability of the system is in the national interest of many states. The world-order argument thus creates an additional moral justification for preemption. Protecting world order is long-term self-defense.

This way of thinking about the just-cause criterion contrasts with the narrow view of self-defense now in vogue. But it is in fact consistent with other elements of the just war traditions, elements that have been eclipsed by the emphasis on defense against aggression. Two other criteria have traditionally been used to define justifiable defensive wars: those aimed at the recovery of something wrongfully taken, and those aimed at the punishment of evil.[19] According to Johnson, in this way of thinking about just cause, just wars were those required to establish a just political and social order among states, "an order that was necessary for the presence of peace."[20] Such a view of war is well ingrained in the balance-of-power school of international politics. In the nineteenth century, for example, Britain viewed war as necessary to maintain a status quo in Europe that made possible the progress of liberty and thus increased the chances for zones of peace built on shared commercial and social interests.

This view of what can justify war predates the Industrial Revolution and the emergence in the twentieth century of total war, i.e., war that mobilizes all the resources of a society to defeat if not annihilate an enemy society similarly mobilized. Of course, wars of complete annihilation are not unknown in history, but technical and scientific sophistication has brought them to a new scale and immediacy. The view of war as a legitimate instrument of peace has lost favor in the Catholic Church not least because of this transformation of war, leading many to conclude that no war could pass the prudential tests cited above.[21]

Two Weaknesses in the Debate

This line of argument helps to expose the two basic weaknesses in the way the moral debate about the use of force draws upon the just war tradition. One relates to collective self-defense. Although the tradition posits the right of states to act in collective self-defense, the moral debate focuses almost exclusively on wars between two states—the aggressor and the aggrieved. In the international system of the late twentieth century, states coexist with multilateral institutions, transnational processes, global norms, and an international community. Aggression threatens interests far larger than those of the sovereignty of a given state. If aggression between states were permitted to return as a common mode of behavior, societies on every continent would pay a price. This suggests that in the moral calculation, the value of defeating an aggressive regime and thereby perhaps deterring similar ones must be added to the values of protecting the national sovereignty of individual states.

The second basic weakness relates to the nuclear revolution in international affairs. The moral debate on nuclear weapons is locked in a time now passed. In the memorable debate on the nuclear bomb in the early 1980s, the U.S. Catholic bishops by and large

peace secured in the Cold War and the victory that brought its end have much to do with nuclear weapons. The point here is that most of the moral philosophizing on matters nuclear is held hostage to this era now past—an era when nuclear war was a matter of East-West brinkmanship and global armageddon.

In the post–Cold War era, wars and threats by rogue states armed with nuclear weapons pose new questions. The particular issue from the point of view of this paper is that preemption entails the risk of nuclear confrontation—but not armageddon. If the preemptive strike is not successful in eliminating an aggressor's NBC weapons, and he opts to use them in reply, preemption would have unleashed a terrible chain of events. Wars such as this may or may not prove to be massively destructive, depending on the choices made by the aggressor and the character of the arsenals and delivery systems available to him, as well as the choices made by the United States about how to reply (and its defensive and offensive capabilities). No rogue has the nuclear capacity to annihilate a major power, although each major power has the capacity to annihilate a rogue. Limited nuclear wars of the kind long dismissed in the Cold War are now a matter requiring serious reflection. The United States must consider whether or how to use nuclear weapons in meeting the aggression of such states, not simply in deterrence or for national survival, but for larger purposes of international order. This new agenda permits no easy answers.

Some have seen an escape from the dilemmas of U.S. nuclear use in increased reliance on conventional rather than nuclear means to carry out attacks of strategic significance. The exceptional technical ability of the U.S. military to employ military force discriminately and to use conventional weaponry in precision strikes has fueled a perception that the United States has minimized, to the extent possible, the costs to noncombatants and the risks to anyone other than the soldiers and military infrastructure of the state being struck preemptively. This may make it easier to justify attacks on the NBC arsenals of rogue states.

The overwhelming military power in the hands of the United States does make it easier to threaten attacks. But reliance on overwhelming power and on military actions that impose essentially no cost in American lives raises proportionality questions of its own—questions that troubled senior U.S. policy-makers on the last day of Desert Storm as they considered the reported savagery of the "highway to death." Moreover, conventional preemption may not prevent an aggressor from using his unconventional weapons. The United States may then feel compelled to use its own nuclear weapons, whether for reasons of proportionality (so as not to suffer huge casualties in observing a nuclear taboo already broken by the aggressor) or for punishment (to establish the point that aggression with nuclear weapons is intolerable). In sum, conventional options are unlikely to eliminate nuclear dilemmas.

Preemption and Competent Authority

The second criterion for the just use of force that must be met *before* considerations of last resort, proportionality, and reasonable chance of success is that the decision to go to war must be made by a competent authority. The purpose of this requirement is to limit the right to make war to sovereign entities, thereby denying it to individuals or groups whose use of violence is not constrained by the dictates of international society and international law.

The competent-authority requirement is most easily met in wars between two sovereign nations. It is also met in wars of cooperative self-defense, albeit less directly. Moral philosophy permits states not only to act in self-defense but to make common cause in self-defense with others. Thus, under the rule that an attack on one is an attack on all, even a nation not directly attacked by an aggressor's first acts of war has a just cause to undertake military actions in reply.

But in the scenarios considered here, a particular difficulty emerges. Does the United States have the necessary authority to undertake preemptive strikes against rogue states that have not first made military attacks on it? This is one sense a trite questions: The United States is, after all, a sovereign entity. But in another sense it is more profound: if it is not the party immediately threatened by a rogue's NBC weapons, and if it is not in a formal alliance with such a party, by what means is its authority deemed legitimate? The cause may be just, but what makes it America's fight?

The United States faces a real dilemma in establishing its authority in this regard: if it arrogates to itself the right to determine when and how to strike at nations it considers outside the law, it may be judged as having put itself above the law. The United States finds itself, after all, in a peculiar historical moment. As the world's dominant military, economic, and political power, it has been cast in the role of primary defender of the global status quo—of the existing balance of global power and of the institutions it has labored to put in place to promote global stability, prosperity, and liberty. As the defender of the status quo, it has a special stake in turning back the aggressions and deterring the potential aggressions of rogue nations. The concern that the United States not put itself above the law is particularly evident among its closest allies, for their partnership with the United States is based on a belief in its benign use of power and on the legitimacy it enjoys within their societies as a steward of common interests. Both of these qualifications would be eroded by acts outside the law.

As A. J. Bacevich has argued: "Like Great Britain at the end of the nineteenth century, the United States at the end of the twentieth is a dominant world power with an interest above all in perpetuating that dominance. The existing order—the distribution of wealth and influence, the basic rules governing the game of world politics—suits us, and we are committed to its preservation."[23] To be sure, there are some fundamental differences between the system of today, in which the United States *is dominant*, and one *dominated by* the United States. Other nations have joined with it in building the current rules and institutions of order, and they remain free to seek an alternative order. Today, the vast majority of states side with the United States in its commitment to the status quo, so long as this permits them the opportunity to make evolutionary changes in ways that promote justice, peace, and prosperity. The genuine challengers to the status quo are few and far between, though many states aspire to improve their lot, which means not only gains in well-being or political status but also enhanced security. Because the so-called status quo has a certain promise of such goals, it is a status quo of unique and unprecedented character.

But this does not eliminate the moral issue for the United States as the primary beneficiary and defender of this status quo. How does it distinguish morally between preemptive

One answer might be for the United States to seek endorsement by the U.N. Security Council of a decision to strike preemptively. There could be many practical reasons not to consider such a move, not least the warning to the rogue state likely to be given by such an action, which might induce it to disperse its weapons and perhaps to use them before losing them. But the focus here is on establishing just authority. As Eugene Rostow has observed, it is not obligatory for a state exercising its right to self-defense to seek U.N. approval;[24] moreover, the Security Council has the legal authority to act not merely to uphold the right of self-defense but in reply to threats of whatever kind to international peace and security. But the Security Council lacks the moral authority to act as a sovereign. It lacks competent authority in two ways: absence of public accountability, and absence of a command-and-control system for the use of force.[25]

An alternative answer to the competent-authority dilemma might be to stimulate creation of a broad international coalition to carry out, and support, preemptive action. The moral benefit of this approach would be to attach American power and actions to a broad base of international sovereignty.

But this too poses problems. From a practical point of view, it is likely to prove very difficult to assemble such a coalition—preemption is a notoriously unpopular measure, and every hint that the United States might be considering a preemptive attack generates strong reactions among allies as well as potential adversaries. Moreover, it is not clear that this would solve the moral dilemma. As Walzer has argued, "when the world divides radically into those who bomb and those who are bombed, it becomes morally problematic even if the bombing in this or that instance is justifiable."[26]

A third approach would be to rely on unilateral action by the United States in the context of a strong moral argument. Such a case might build on its right to self-defense—after all, the United States seems to be a likely target of weapons possessed by leaders who believe the United States to be the primary defender of a corrupt status quo. It might also draw on the moral duty to help others. And the U.S. case would also have to draw on the obligations of a security guarantor that fall on it as a permanent member of the Security Council—after all, the NBC capabilities of the rogue pose a threat to the interests of international peace and stability.

In fact, the United States has begun to make this latter case. Anthony Lake's original characterization of the rogue-state problem was careful to look beyond the weapons programs of the named states to their flagrant disregard for basic norms of international society, including principally their regular reliance on violence to maintain domestic power and to coerce, if not invade and defeat, their neighbors. Lake thus was careful to frame a normative context for addressing the rogue-state problem that went beyond the national-interest arguments about military capability and power.[27]

This normative framework may provide an international context in which U.S. actions are legitimized. It seems unlikely to establish the United States as a competent authority in a moral sense, however, as the expression of this normative framework is a series of multilateral treaties and institutions that by definition distribute rights and authority through the international system. Unilateral action by the United States in support of those norms would be inconsistent with its commitment to the mechanisms that embody those norms. Moreover, so long as the United States finds itself isolated in making the case that certain states are rogues, any military actions based on this moral case will be open to the charge that they are merely national-interest actions hidden under the rubric of world-order interests. In fact, the Clinton administration's characterization of this set of states as rogues, and its subsequent policies to isolate them and undertake counterproliferation preparations for possible military action against their NBC weapons, are much criticized, not least by U.S. friends and allies abroad who see such actions as an effort to put the United States above or outside the law.[28]

The particular problem with this approach is that the United States sometimes acts in defense of interests that it but not others see as common, or in defense of norms that it asserts but others do not support. For example, in the mid-1980s the United States tried to make a moral case for preemptive attacks on Libya based on the latter's chemical-weapons production activities at Rabta, a case that was politically flawed by the fact that the United States was itself a possessor of chemical weapons and was at the time engaged in the production of such weapons. Even some U.S. allies questioned the moral basis of what appeared to be a punitive if not vengeful act. Similarly, in 1996 the U.S. case for preemption of Libyan chemical plants was weakened by the United States' own continued possession of chemical weapons and its reluctance to ratify the Chemical Weapons Convention. To be sure, there are fundamental differences between the "regimes" in Washington and Tripoli or Baghdad; but the isolation of the United States on these issues underscores how inconsequential those moral differences have proven to be politically.

This review suggests that there is no easy answer to the competent-authority requirement of the just war tradition in the current historical moment. Policy-makers will logically be drawn to the argument that if each approach is inadequate, the best approach is to do all three in combination. Making a clear normative argument, while also building a coalition and seeking a U.N. mandate, would help to satisfy many citizens that preemptive action meets the basic moral requirement of political legitimacy. But whether it would also satisfy moral philosophers is another question. This leads to a conclusion analogous to that in the discussion of self-defense: contemporary moral reasoning based on the just war tradition has not taken into account the moral requirements of a changing world.

Assessing the U.N.'s Authority

But within the tradition there are some touchstones for the path ahead. The emphasis should be on a critique of the moral authority of the Security Council. As noted above, such a critique rests on two key points: the absence of public accountability, and the absence of a command-and-control system for the use of force. Are these in fact the appropriate criteria by which to assess the competent authority of the U.N. to endorse preemptive action?

The Security Council does reflect a certain type of accountability. The Council is accountable to the principles that guide its actions, to the states that are its members, and thus indirectly to the citizens of those states. The indirect nature of its democratic credentials is analogous to that of the U.S. president in the days when he was put into office by the process of indirect election that was the Electoral College, before the electors were bound by the popular vote. The Council's capacity to use power is, moreover, subject to a number of

have the command-and-control system of a state. But it does have such a system appropriate to its particular role—a system that weaves together national command with multilateral institutions and processes. This too is subject to checks and balances. Its capacity to use force is thus limited to ad hoc circumstances, with the use of borrowed forces under charters granted by state members. The command and control flows from those who are directly responsible in the system.

Moreover, the U.N. embodies an agreed set of norms within the international community about behaviors within and among states that are either appropriate or inappropriate. To be sure, some states ignore the U.N. Charter (though ever fewer, as democracy takes hold in many parts of the world). And to be sure, there are fundamental political divisions within the organization. But it does reflect a consensus-based global normative structure. It is the only institution that aspires to represent the interests of the whole community of nations, and thus the only one with strong moral authority in purporting to defend those interests. Its most powerful members assume special obligations in their role as guarantors of international peace and security on the Security Council, though how they fulfill those duties—and how well they do so—is hotly contested.

The point here is not that the U.N. is sufficiently like a state to establish its sovereignty. Rather, it has a certain moral authority sufficient to the competent-authority requirement. The U.N. can provide the normative framework for actions by a state or group of states in defense of world-order interests. The U.N. is essential, not because it is supranational and "above" its member states, but because its normative attributes redress the competent-authority shortfall.

Invoking the U.N.'s Authority

But how is that authority invoked and operationalized? The moral authority of the U.N. would most clearly be engaged if the General Assembly, the Secretary General, and the Security Council unanimously agreed that a particular threat to world order was so egregious as to require preemptive military action. Such unanimity is of course highly unlikely. Political division implies that the U.N. will not reliably be able to act in times of crisis and will find it difficult to cope with questions of preemption. But the absence of unanimity is not necessarily a moral deficiency, as ethical issues are not determined in popularity contests.

On preemption, the Council possesses the authority to authorize such actions, given its special responsibilities, and the Charter legalizes the associated actions. But whether the competent-authority requirement also requires the assent of the Council for each and every act of preemption by a permanent member for world-order purposes is doubtful. In those cases where prior approval is sought from the Council, the moral requirement probably does not even necessitate an affirmative vote from the Council. To veto a just act is not to rob the act of its justness. General and broad reinforcement of this duty could help to bolster the moral case for specific acts of preemption.

Establishing the competent authority of a world-order defense argument would seem to require more than reliance on the Security Council, however. After all, many states see the Council itself as symptomatic of an *unjust* world order. The Council's authority is hotly contested by many who see it as an anachronism of a world war now a half century past, and as a body dominated by "the world's only superpower," whose use of power is unfettered and whose singular ability to mobilize the U.N. deprives the Security Council of a meaningful role beyond one that serves U.S. interests.[29] The moral authority of the Council can be buttressed only by addressing these concerns.

A footnote to this discussion of competent authority is in order. The competent-authority requirement is intended to bolster the role of sovereigns in international affairs. Under international law, sovereignty has become virtually sacrosanct. But while all states may be equal before the law, all sovereigns do not possess the same degree or type of sovereignty. This ambiguity may have been tenable at a time when the purpose of just war thinking was to codify war as a right of states, but it seems ever less acceptable. A dictator who holds power by the ruthless use of repression, torture, extortion, and murder cannot be equated morally with leaders somehow representing the will of the body politic. Why should he have equal legitimacy in waging war, especially if he is also making war on his own people? Sovereignty requires consent for its proper exercise. Such consent should be an increasingly important measure of sovereignty in an age in which widespread industrialization and technical innovation are putting massively destructive weapons and long-range delivery systems into the hands of more and more individuals or regimes whose grip on power derives from force, not popular will.

When Is Preemption Just?

There can, then, be no blanket reply to the question, Is there a moral case for preemption? Some acts of preemption will be deemed just, others unjust. For yet others, some elements of a moral case will be present, others absent.

The strongest moral case for U.S. preemption exists under the following conditions: (1) an aggressor has actually threatened to use his NBC weapons, has taken steps to ready the means to do so, and has specifically threatened the United States (including its territory, citizens, or military forces); (2) those NBC weapons have been built in violation of international law; (3) the aggressor's threatened actions invoke larger questions about the credibility of security guarantees or the balance of power within a region; (4) the president has secured the approval of the U.S. Congress; and (5) the United States has secured the backing of the U.N. Security Council and any relevant regional organization. The prudential tests of last resort, proportionality, and reasonable chance of success must also be met.

The weakest case for preemption exists when: (1) a state has made no NBC threats and has no prior behavior of aggression; (2) those weapons are permitted under international law (because the state is not a party to the relevant treaties); (3) the preemption is the culmination of a worsening bilateral relationship with the United States, driven by a loss of objectivity in Washington; and (4) U.S. actions have been condemned by the U.N. or opposed by the Security Council. Even if the intended strike meets all the prudential tests, it cannot be accepted as just under these conditions.

In the middle are a range of scenarios with mixed ethical configurations, drawing on the following factors: Threatened attacks on U.S. allies establish the same moral case as

plicit intentions as perceived in NBC weapons programs offer a less strong moral case, unless backed by other signals of aggressive intent.

This is not to argue that all acts of military preemption by the United States require approval by others if they are to be just. Rather, preemptions conceived by the United States as necessary to defend world-order interests, rather than those deemed necessary because of alliance guarantees or more discrete and specific national interests, require a normative framework that the United States alone cannot provide in its "unipolar moment."[30]

Moral Obligations Following Preemption

The just war tradition also imposes obligations in the aftermath of military action. One is the requirement to make a moral case for the action that has been undertaken. As Weigel has argued, "the presumption is always for peace, and the burden of moral reasoning lies with those who argue for the justness of a particular resort to war."[31]

Justice requires a clear explication of the moral reasoning that led to the chosen course of action. Especially in an era when many countries, both adversaries and allies, fear a hegemonic United States that puts itself above the law in defending its perceived national-security interests, it is incumbent upon the United States to establish that its actions are consistent not merely with the letter of the law but also with the spirit of justice and peace that underpins it. Making this case would help to heal the domestic divisions likely to be caused by preemptive military attack. It would also help to reassure those in other countries who might interpret U.S. preemption as signaling a more bellicose America more likely to intervene abroad.

Making the moral case for a world-order act means making the case to the world community, which of course encompass many different cultures and ethical traditions. A moral cast that draws only on the just war tradition of Westerners and Christians may be rejected by others as cultural imperialism. Moral philosophers face a critical challenge in building up a dialogue across cultures, one that gives them common terms of reference even if not common traditions. There are many obvious differences among cultures and ethical traditions, especially on questions of war. But because problems of war, peace, and justice are universal, there is good reason to believe that beneath the apparent cultural differences are some fundamental commonalities.[32]

A second moral obligation after a preemptive strike is to alleviate the suffering caused by U.S. actions. This may not be practical in cases where a regime that is antithetical to U.S. interests remains firmly entrenched, especially if it exploits the public-relations value of U.S.-inflicted casualties. But it may be practical where preemption leads to the collapse of the regime, or at least to the emergence of new political forces within the targeted country that would accept U.S. humanitarian assistance. Especially in those cases where preemption of nuclear attack leads to acts of retribution by the targeted country, perhaps with remaining nuclear or biological weapons, the United States will have a moral obligation beyond what it might normally feel to help minimize and redress human suffering.

A third requirement is to make a just settlement of the issues in dispute. If U.S. action is deemed necessary to recover something wrongfully taken or to punish evil, then its post-strike actions must work toward those ends.

Concluding Observations

In summary, there is a moral case for preemption, but it is not quite as tidy as policy-makers might desire. The just war tradition puts a number of obligations on policy. Preemption must meet the three basic prudential requirements (last resort, reasonable chance of success, proportionality). But it must first meet the requirements that the action be in self-defense and be authorized by competent authority. Not all contemplated acts of preemption are likely to meet all these criteria. It is not clear that every one must be met for an act to be just.

The latter two requirements (self-defense, competent authority) pose particular difficulties today. The current historical moment is characterized by the simultaneous appearance of two unprecedented factors: (1) broad international diffusion of the technical competence to inflict mass destruction, and (2) a unipolar international order in which the United States finds itself cast as the defender of a status quo. This implies not least that the United States must use its power in ways that others will accept as just; otherwise a terrible backlash could result.

The particular difficulties posed today are as follows. First, the self-defense requirement is too narrow in a world in which the security of so many depends upon the orderliness of the system; defending that order must have a moral quality analogous to that of defending the sovereignty of individual parts, but that quality is not well established in moral theory. Moreover, the self-defense requirement engages nuclear arguments rooted in an era now past. Addressing these problems requires returning to the nuclear debate, but in the light of current strategic realities, and then reconnecting moral debate to that part of the just war tradition that accepts war as an instrument of order under certain conditions.

Second, the competent-authority requirement is rooted in an era long past. Today policy-makers must cope with overlapping national and international institutions and sovereignties, and with world-order problems that transcend the interests of individual states. Addressing this problem requires formulating principles by which just war criteria can be satisfied by international institutions. The logical focal point is the U.N.—especially the Security Council. The potential moral legitimacy of actions endorsed by the U.N. is high, but its own weak legitimacy suggests how difficult this task will be.

Two final observations, the first on the disjunction between moral philosophy and international law on preemption. As noted earlier, international law has had the effect over time of progressively narrowing the legal recourse to war. Moral philosophy has not similarly constrained the just recourse to war. If law exists to serve justice, what is the authority of law that is inconsistent with moral reasoning? The law should permit what justice requires. Moreover, how does a nation that does not want to be above the law act in ways that moral reasoning requires? A world in which the only legal recourse to self-defense is in retaliation for an aggressor's first strike is a world that has legalized the coercive use of weapons arsenals and has made more likely the operational use of those weapons by those not constrained by moral reasoning or even the purposes of state. How tolerable is this when the weapons in question are weapons of mass destruction?

know what just wars are, but we are a lot less clear about just statecraft. We think we know that the order the United States seeks to defend and/or lead is a good one, but we are a lot less clear about the criteria and reasoning sufficient to this claim.

Moral philosophy could make a substantial contribution to the construction of a more just and peaceful world for the next century if it would direct more energy to such questions. At the very least, such a dialogue should help to clarify the moral duties that fall upon the United States in its special historical moment and help it to see more clearly when and how to use its power, and when not to.

An expert on the proliferation and control of weapons of mass destruction, **Brad Roberts** is an analyst at the Institute for Defense Analyses (Alexandria, Virginia) and an adjunct professor at George Washington University. He also acts as chairman of the research advisory council of the Chemical and Biological Arms Control Institute. Roberts is the author of *Weapons Proliferation in the 1990s* (1995).

Notes

1. Philip Shenon, "Perry, in Egypt, Warns Libya to Halt Chemical Weapons Plant," *New York Times*, April 4, 1996, 4.
2. W. Anthony Lake, "Confronting Backlash States," *Foreign Affairs* 73, no. 2 (1994). The author recognizes that Lake's views are not broadly accepted and that many question the right of the United States to deem others "rogues." But for lack of a better shorthand, the term is used here to refer to the category of states as defined.
3. For a summary discussion of the just war tradition, see chapter 1, "The Catholic Tradition of Moderate Realism," in George Weigel, *Tranquillitas Ordinis: The Present Failure and Future Promise of American Catholic Thought on War and Peace* (Oxford: Oxford University Press, 1987), 25–45. See also Michael Walzer, *Just and Unjust Wars*, 2d ed. (New York: Basic Books, 1992).
4. For a review of these themes, see Brad Roberts, "1995 and the End of the Post–Cold War Era," *Washington Quarterly* 18, no. 1 (Winter 1995).
5. Walzer, *Just and Unjust Wars*, xiv.
6. See Jane M. O. Sharp, "Appeasement, Intervention and the Future of Europe," and Ken Booth, "Military Intervention: Duty and Prudence," in Lawrence Freedman, ed., *Military Intervention in European Conflicts* (Oxford: Blackwell Publishers, 1994).
7. James Turner Johnson, "Just Cause Revisited," this volume, 26.
8. Francisco de Vitoria, *On the Law of War*, sec. 13.
9. Walzer, *Just and Unjust Wars*, 62.
10. Johnson, "Just Cause Revisited," 26.
11. Hugo Grotius, The Law of War and Peace, bk. 2, chap. 1, sec. 2. Elihu Root, "The Real Monroe Doctrine," *American Journal of International Law* 35 (1914): 427.
12. Walzer, *Just and Unjust War*, 74, 80.
13. Morton A. Kaplan and Nicholas deB. Katzenbach, "Resort to Force: War and Neutrality," In Richard A. Falk and Saul H. Mendlovitz, eds., *The Strategy of World Order*, vol. 2, *International Law* (New York: World Law Fund, 1966).

14. Johnson, "Just Cause Revisited," 25.
15. Clausewitz, On War, trans. Michael Howard and Peter Paret (Princeton, N.J.: Princeton University Press, 1976), 370.
16. Walzer, *Just and Unjust Wars*, 81.
17. George Weigel, "Just War After the Cold War," in *Idealism Without Illusions: U.S. Foreign Policy in the 1990s* (Washington, D.C.: Ethics and Public Policy Center, 1994), 155.
18. Ibid., 153.
19. Johnson, "Just Cause Revisited," 9.
20. Ibid., 19–24.
21. See Weigel, *Tranquillitas Ordinis*, 257–85.
22. A. J. Bacevich, "Just War in a New Era of Military Affairs," this volume, 74.
23. Eugene Rostow, "Competent Authority Revisited," This volume, 55.
24. Johnson, "Just Cause Revisited," 31.
25. Walzer, *Just and Unjust Wars*, xxi.
26. Lake, "Confronting Backlash States."
27. Michael Klare, *Rogue States and Nuclear Outlaws: America's Search for a New Foreign Policy* (New York: Hill and Wang, 1995).
28. See Rosemary Righter, *Utopia Lost: The United Nations and World Order* (New York: Twentieth Century Fund Press, 1995).
29. The term is Charles Krauthammer's, used to describe the United States as the dominant power in a world no longer bipolar, because of the collapse of the Soviet Union, but not yet multipolar. See Krauthammer, "The Unipolar Moment," *Foreign Affairs* 70, no. 1 (1991) 23–33.
30. Weigel, *Tranquillitas Ordinis*, 37.
31. John Kelsay, *Islam and War: A Study in Comparative Ethics* (Louisville, Ky.: Westminster/ John Knox Press, 1993).

Strategies and Approaches for Combating Terrorism

Four authors explore the September 11 tragedies as a cornerstone—on how the events of a single day can focus new light on America's stature in the world, and how the tragedies that occurred in the space of a few hours have caused a deep ripple effect in the nation's government and its policy-making efforts.

Richard K. Betts maps out the landscape, explaining why terror can be an effective means against a nation as powerful as the United States, why such tactics have impact despite a great imbalance of power. "American global primacy is one of the causes of this war," he writes. It is not just the way the nation and its moves are perceived by certain parties around the world: "Remaking the world in the Western image is what Americans assume to be just, natural, and desirable, indeed only a matter of time. But that presumption is precisely what energizes many terrorists' hatred," writes Betts. It is also the perception at home. But a nation's power does not make it invincible: "For many," he says, "primacy was confused with invulnerability." Betts discusses the tactics and countermeasures of this situation, when "intense political grievance and gross imbalance of power" became an explosive equation for terror.

James S. Robbins shows how, in the aftermath of the September 11 attacks, the United States countered the terror that al-Qaeda brought to U.S. shores—and how the goals these terrorists hoped to achieve were never fully realized. Robbins details "Bin Laden's War"—the background and the escalation of events that led to 9-11. The assault on the United States was "a tactical masterpiece," says Robbins. But it fell short of Osama bin Laden's ultimate goals, which became clear as the United States plotted its countermeasures and world opinion rang in during the days and weeks that followed the 9-11 tragedies. For one, as Robbins says, bin Laden underestimated his enemy, who he believed had "a reputation for strength but no staying power when it came to a hard fight." Instead, the attacks "aroused the wrath of the American people" who rallied behind the commander in chief—and Robbins makes reference to Pearl Harbor, to the waking of the proverbial sleeping giant. Rather than non-Americans around the world feeling indifferent to the attack, the reaction Robbins believes bin Laden expected, the attacks incited global outrage. Bin Laden also did not succeed in getting the Muslim world to rally around his cause, nor did he achieve the damage to the U.S. economy that Robbins feels he intended. "The war that Osama bin Laden planned to wage against the United States is over," writes Robbins, "and he has lost."

According to Richard Shultz, the failure of the intelligence community to prevent the September 11 attacks goes much deeper than the missed clues that might have led them to detect an impending threat. The author views the core of the problem as "a near decade-long reluctance to come to terms with the fact that international terrorists—most importantly al Qaeda—were undergoing a systematic transformation in terms of how they organize, deploy, and fight." Shultz details just how al-Qaeda is organized, with new information on the group and how the group operates, and he outlines the shift in thinking in national security policy, as championed by President Bush and Secretary of Defense Donald Rumsfeld, that will be necessary to fight this new war.

Barry R. Posen advocates for a grand strategy to combat terrorism. "The United States faces a long war against a small, elusive, and dangerous foe," he writes. Posen defines the adversary, the al-Qaeda network; he maps out the group's goals and structure and explains the depth of its motives: "It seeks to expel the most powerful state in history from a part of the world that has been central to U.S. foreign policy… and it intends to do so without a standing military…. It will seek to kill Americans so long as the United States does not give in to its demands," says Posen. The author advocates for a long-term, comprehensive strategy in dealing with the group. The effort he outlines will require discipline and determination; it will necessitate significant changes in U.S. national security; it will require tactics to deplete the resources of the group and the willingness to deal harshly with states who harbor them; and it will shape U.S. foreign policy, for "the United States will need friends, and thus must prioritize among its many foreign policy and defense policy initiatives," says Posen, to sustain a coalition for a protracted battle against a ruthless foe.

The chapter concludes with a reading by Wyn Q. Bowen who examines the role of deterrence in fighting terrorism. In working to craft a national and international response to terrorism, it is important to evaluate all options at hand and revisit concepts like deterrence that have been dismissed by some out of hand. Instead, Bowen argues, we must rethink our concepts of deterrence and apply these concepts in new ways. The key to this concept is understanding how nonstate actors such as al Qaeda calculate costs and benefits. Once the frame of reference is established, the counterterror government has several options with which to respond to the terrorist. Bowen examines options that range from punishment strategies, which may pose difficult questions for democratic countries given moral and ethical constraints, to denial, to deterrence and coercion.

Primacy: Tactical Advantages of Terror

> *In given conditions, action and reaction can be ridiculously out of proportion.... One can obtain results monstrously in excess of the effort.... Let's consider this auto smash-up.... The driver lost control at high speed while swiping at a wasp which had flown in through a window and was buzzing around his face.... The weight of a wasp is under half an ounce. Compared with a human being, the wasp's size is minute, its strength negligible. Its sole armament is a tiny syringe holding a drop of irritant, formic acid.... Nevertheless, that wasp killed four big men and converted a large, powerful car into a heap of scrap.*
>
> —Eric Frank Russell[1]

To grasp some implications of the new first priority in U.S. foreign policy, it is necessary to understand the connections among three things: the imbalance of power between terrorist groups and counterterrorist governments; the reasons that groups choose terror tactics; and the operational advantage of attack over defense in the interactions of terrorists and their opponents. On September 11, 2001, Americans were reminded that the overweening power that they had taken for granted over the past dozen years is not the same as omnipotence. What is less obvious but equally important is that the power is itself part of the cause of terrorist enmity and even a source of U.S. vulnerability.

There is no consensus on a definition of "terrorism," mainly because the term is so intensely pejorative.[2] When defined in terms of tactics, consistency falters, because most people can think of some "good" political cause that has used the tactics and whose purposes excuse them or at least warrant the group's designation as freedom fighters rather than terrorists. Israelis who call the Khobar Towers bombers of 1996 terrorists might reject that characterization for the Irgun, which did the same thing to the King David Hotel in 1946, or some Irish Americans would bridle at equating IRA bombings in Britain with Tamil Tiger bombings in Sri Lanka. Anticommunists labeled the Vietcong terrorists (because they engaged in combat out of uniform and assassinated local officials), but opponents of the Saigon government did not. Nevertheless, a functional definition is more sensible than one conditioned on the identity of the perpetrators. For this article, terrorism refers to the illegitimate, deliberate killing of civilians for purposes of punishment or coercion. This holds in abeyance the questions of whether deliberate killing of civilians can ever be legitimate or killing soldiers can be terrorism.

In any case, for all but the rare nihilistic psychopath, terror is a means, not an end in itself. Terror tactics are usually meant to serve a strategy of coercion.[3] They are a use of force designed to further some substantive aim. This is not always evident in the heat of rage felt by the victims of terror. Normal people find it hard to see instrumental reasoning behind an atrocity, especially when recognizing the political motives behind terrorism might seem to make its illegitimacy less extreme. Stripped of rhetoric, however, a war against terrorism must mean a war against political groups who choose terror as a tactic.

American global primacy is one of the causes of this war. It animates both the terrorists' purposes and their choice of tactics. To groups like al Qaeda, the United States is the enemy because American military power dominates their world, supports corrupt governments in their countries, and backs Israelis against Muslims; American cultural power insults their religion and pollutes their societies; and American economic power makes all these intrusions and desecrations possible. Japan, in contrast, is not high on al Qaeda's list of targets, because Japan's economic power does not make it a political, military, and cultural behemoth that penetrates their societies.

Political and cultural power makes the United States a target for those who blame it for their problems. At the same time, American economic and military power prevents them from resisting or retaliating against the United States on its own terms. To smite the only superpower requires unconventional modes of force and tactics that make the combat cost exchange ratio favorable to the attacker. This offers hope to the weak that they can work their will despite their overall deficit in power.

Primacy on the Cheap

The United States has enjoyed military and political primacy (or hegemony, unipolarity, or whatever term best connotes international dominance) for barely a dozen years. Those who focus on the economic dimension of international relations spoke of American hegemony much earlier, but observers of the strategic landscape never did. For those who focus on national security, the world before 1945 was multipolar, and the world of the cold war was bipolar. After 1945 the United States had exerted hegemony within the First World and for a while over the international economy. The strategic competition against the Second World, however, was seen as a titanic struggle between equal politicomilitary coalitions and a close-run thing until very near the end. Only the collapse of the Soviet pole, which coincided fortuitously with renewed relative strength of the American economy, marked the real arrival of U.S. global dominance.

The novelty of complete primacy may account for the thoughtless, indeed innocently arrogant way in which many Americans took its benefits for granted. Most who gave any thought to foreign policy came implicitly to regard the entire world after 1989 as they had regarded Western Europe and Japan during the past half-century: partners in principle but vassals in practice. The United States would lead the civilized community of nations in the expansion and consolidation of a liberal world order. Overwhelming military dominance was assumed to be secure and important across most of the domestic political spectrum.

Liberal multilateralists conflated U.S. primacy with political globalization, indeed, conflated ideological American nationalism with internationalist altruism.[4] They assumed that U.S. military power should be used to stabilize benighted countries and police international violence, albeit preferably camouflaged under the banner of institutions such as the

or the need to cater to the demands of others. When America acted strategically abroad, others would have to join on its terms or be left out of the action. The United States should choose battles, avoid entanglements in incompetent polities, and let unfortunates stew in their own juice. For both multilateralists and nationalists, the issue was whether the United States would decide to make an effort for world welfare, not whether a strategic challenge could threaten its truly vital interests. (Colloquial depreciation of the adjective notwithstanding, literally vital U.S. interests are those necessary to life.)

For many, primacy was confused with invulnerability. American experts warned regularly of the danger of catastrophic terrorism—and Osama bin Ladin explicitly declared war on the United States in his *fatwa* of February 1998. But the warnings did not register seriously in the consciousness of most people. Even some national security experts felt stunned when the attacks occurred on September 11. Before then, the American military wanted nothing to do with the mission of "homeland defense," cited the Posse Comitatus act to suggest that military operations within U.S. borders would be improper, and argued that homeland defense should be the responsibility of civilian agencies or the National Guard. The services preferred to define the active forces' mission as fighting and winning the nation's wars—as if wars were naturally something that happened abroad—and homeland defense involved no more than law enforcement, managing relief operations in natural disasters, or intercepting ballistic missiles outside U.S. airspace. Only in America could the nation's armed forces think of direct defense of national territory as a distraction.

Being Number One seemed cheap. The United States could cut the military burden on the economy by half after the cold war (from 6 percent to 3 percent of GNP) yet still spend almost five times more than the combined military budgets of all potential enemy states. And this did not count the contributions of rich U.S. allies.[5] Of course the margin in dollar terms does not translate into a comparable quantitative margin in manpower or equipment, but that does not mean that a purchasing power parity estimate would reduce the implied gap in combat capability. The overwhelming qualitative superiority of U.S. conventional forces cuts in the other direction. Washington was also able to plan, organize, and fight a major war in 1991 at negligible cost in blood or treasure. Financially, nearly 90 percent of the bills for the war against Iraq were paid by allies. With fewer than 200 American battle deaths, the cost in blood was far lower than almost anyone had imagined it could be. Less than a decade later, Washington waged another war, over Kosovo, that cost no U.S. combat casualties at all.

In the one case where costs in casualties exceeded the apparent interests at stake—Somalia in 1993—Washington quickly stood down from the fight. This became the reference point for vulnerability: the failure of an operation that was small, far from home, and elective. Where material interests required strategic engagement, as in the oil-rich Persian Gulf, U.S. strategy could avoid costs by exploiting its huge advantage in conventional capability. Where conventional dominance proved less exploitable, as in Somalia, material interests did not require strategic engagement. Where the United States could not operate militarily with impunity, it could choose not to operate.

Finally, power made it possible to let moral interests override material interests where some Americans felt an intense moral concern, even if in doing so they claimed, dubiously, that the moral and material stakes coincided. To some extent this happened in Kosovo, although the decision to launch that war apparently flowed from overoptimism about how quickly a little bombing would lead Belgrade to capitulate. Most notably, it happened in the Arab-Israeli conflict. For more than three decades after the 1967 Six Day War, the United States supported Israel diplomatically, economically, and militarily against the Arabs, despite the fact that doing so put it on the side of a tiny country of a few million people with no oil, against more than ten times as many Arabs who controlled over a third of the world's oil reserves.

This policy was not just an effect of primacy, since the U.S.–Israel alignment began in the cold war. The salience of the moral motive was indicated by the fact that U.S. policy proceeded despite the fact that it helped give Moscow a purchase in major Arab capitals such as Cairo, Damascus, and Baghdad. Luckily for the United States, however, the largest amounts of oil remained under the control of the conservative Arab states of the Gulf. In this sense the hegemony of the United States within the anticommunist world helped account for the policy. That margin of power also relieved Washington of the need to make hard choices about disciplining its client. For decades the United States opposed Israeli settlement of the West Bank, terming the settlements illegal; yet in all that time the United States never demanded that Israel refrain from colonizing the West Bank as a condition for receiving U.S. economic and military aid.[6] Washington continued to bankroll Israel at a higher per capita rate than any other country in the world, a level that has been indispensable to Israel, providing aid over the years that now totals well over $100 billion in today's dollars.[7] Although this policy enraged some Arabs and irritated the rest, U.S. power was great enough that such international political costs did not outweigh the domestic political costs of insisting on Israeli compliance with U.S. policy.

Of course, far more than subsidizing Israeli occupation of Palestinian land was involved in the enmity of Islamist terrorists toward the United States. Many of the other explanations, however, presuppose U.S. global primacy. When American power becomes the arbiter of conflicts around the world, it makes itself the target for groups who come out on the short end of those conflicts.

Primacy and Asymmetric Warfare

The irrational evil of terrorism seems most obvious to the powerful. They are accustomed to getting their way with conventional applications of force and are not as accustomed as the powerless to thinking of terror as the only form of force that might make their enemies do their will. This is why terrorism is the premier form of "asymmetric warfare," the Pentagon buzzword for the type of threats likely to confront the United States in the post–cold war world.[8] Murderous tactics may become instrumentally appealing by default—when one party in a conflict lacks other military options.

Resort to terror is not necessarily limited to those facing far more powerful enemies. It can happen in a conventional war between great powers that becomes a total war, when the process of escalation pits whole societies against each other and shears away civilized restraints. That is something seldom seen, and last seen over a half-century ago. One does not need to accept the tendentious position that allied strategic bombing in World War II would have killed hundreds of millions. In the 1950s, Strategic Air Command targeteers even went out of their way to plan "bonus" damage by moving aim points for military targets so that blasts would destroy adjacent towns as well.[10] In both World War II and planning for World War III, the rationale was less to kill civilians per se than to wreck the enemy economies—although that was also one of Osama bin Laden's rationales for the attacks on the World Trade Center.[11] In short, the instrumental appeal of strategic attacks on noncombatants may be easier to understand when one considers that states with legitimate purposes have sometimes resorted to such a strategy. Such a double standard, relaxing prohibitions against targeting noncombatants for the side with legitimate purposes (one's own side), occurs most readily when the enemy is at least a peer competitor threatening vital interests. When one's own primacy is taken for granted, it is easier to revert to a single standard that puts all deliberate attacks against civilians beyond the pale.

In contrast to World War II, most wars are limited—or at least limited for the stronger side when power is grossly imbalanced. In such cases, using terror to coerce is likely to seem the only potentially effective use of force for the weaker side, which faces a choice between surrender or savagery. Radical Muslim zealots cannot expel American power with conventional military means, so they substitute clandestine means of delivery against military targets (such as the Khobar Towers barracks in Saudi Arabia) or high-profile political targets (embassies in Kenya and Tanzania). More than once the line has been attributed to terrorists, "If you will let us lease one of your B-52s, we will use that instead of a truck bomb." The hijacking and conversion of U.S. airliners into kamikazes was the most dramatic means of asymmetric attack.

Kamikaze hijacking also reflects an impressive capacity for strategic judo, the turning of the West's strength against itself.[12] The flip-side of a primacy that diffuses its power throughout the world is that advanced elements of that power become more accessible to its enemies. Nineteen men from technologically backward societies did not have to rely on home-grown instruments to devastate the Pentagon and World Trade Center. They used computers and modern financial procedures with facility, and they forcibly appropriated the aviation technology of the West and used it as a weapon. They not only rebelled against the "soft power" of the United States, they trumped it by hijacking the country's hard power.[13] They also exploited the characteristics of U.S. society associated with soft power—the liberalism, openness, and respect for privacy that allowed them to go freely about the business of preparing the attacks without observation by the state security apparatus. When soft power met the clash of civilizations, it proved too soft.

Strategic judo is also apparent in the way in which U.S. retaliation may compromise its own purpose. The counteroffensive after September 11 was necessary, if only to demonstrate to marginally motivated terrorists that they could not hope to strike the United States for free. The war in Afghanistan, however, does contribute to polarization in the Muslim world and to mobilization of potential terrorist recruits. U.S. leaders can say that they are not waging a war against Islam until they are blue in the face, but this will not convince Muslims who already distrust the United States. Success in deposing the Taliban may help U.S. policy by encouraging a bandwagon effect that rallies governments and moderates among the Muslim populace, but there will probably be as many who see the U.S. retaliation as confirming al Qaeda's diagnosis of American evil. Victory in Afghanistan and follow-up operations to prevent al Qaeda from relocating bases of operation to other countries will hurt that organization's capacity to act. The number of young zealots willing to emulate the "martyrdom operation" of the nineteen on September 11, however, is not likely to decline.

Advantage of Attack

The academic field of security studies has some reason to be embarrassed after September 11. Having focused primarily on great powers and interstate conflict, literature on terrorism was comparatively sparse; most of the good books were by policy analysts rather than theorists.[14] Indeed, science fiction has etched out the operational logic of terrorism as well as political science. Eric Frank Russell's 1957 novel, from which the epigraph to this article comes, vividly illustrates both the strategic aspirations of terrorists and the offense-dominant character of their tactics. It describes the dispatch of a single agent to one of many planets in the Sirian enemy's empire to stir up fear, confusion, and panic through a series of small covert activities with tremendous ripple effects. Matched with deceptions to make the disruptions appear to be part of a campaign by a big phantom rebel organization, the agent's modest actions divert large numbers of enemy policy and military personnel, cause economic dislocations and social unrest, and soften the planet up for invasion. Wasp agents are infiltrated into numerous planets, multiplying the effects. As the agent's handlers tell him, "The pot is coming slowly but surely to the boil. Their fleets are being widely dispersed, there are vast troop movements from their overcrowded home-system to the outer planets of their empire. They're gradually being chivvied into a fix. They can't hold what they've got without spreading all over it. The wider they spread the thinner they get. The thinner they get, the easier it is to bite lumps out of them."[15]

Fortunately al Qaeda and its ilk are not as wildly effective as Russell's wasp. By degree, however, the phenomenon is quite similar. Comparatively limited initiatives prompt tremendous and costly defensive reactions. On September 11 a small number of men killed 3,000 people and destroyed a huge portion of prime commercial real estate, part of the military's national nerve center, and four expensive aircraft. The ripple effects, however, multiplied those costs. A major part of the U.S. economy—air travel—shut down completely for days after September 11. Increased security measures dramatically increased the overall costs of the air travel system thereafter. Normal law enforcement activities of the Federal Bureau of Investigation were radically curtailed as legions of agents were transferred to counterterror tasks. Anxiety about the vulnerability of nuclear power plants, major bridges and tunnels, embassies abroad, and other high-value targets prompted plans for big investments in fortification of a wide array of facilities. A retaliatory war in Afghanistan ran at a cost of a couple billion dollars a month beyond the regular defense budget for months. In one study, the attacks on the World Trade Center and the Pentagon were estimated to cost the U.S. economy 1.8 million jobs.[16]

Or consider the results of a handful of 34-cent letters containing anthrax, probably sent by a single person. Besides killing several people, they contaminated a large portion

the October anthrax attacks together probably cost the perpetrators less than a million dollars. If the cost of rebuilding and of defensive investments in reaction came to no more than $100 billion, the cost-exchange ratio would still be astronomically in favor of the attack over the defense.

Analysts in strategic studies did not fall down on the job completely before September 11. At least two old bodies of work help to illuminate the problem. One is the literature on guerrilla warfare and counterinsurgency, particularly prominent in the 1960s, and the other is the offense-defense theory that burgeoned in the 1980s. Both apply well to understanding patterns of engagement between terrorists and counterterrorists. Some of the axioms derived from the empirical cases in the counterinsurgency literature apply directly, and offense-defense theory applies indirectly.

Apart from the victims of guerrillas, few still identify irregular paramilitary warfare with terrorism (because the latter is illegitimate), but the two activities do overlap a great deal in their operational characteristics. Revolutionary or resistance movements in the pre-conventional phase of operations usually mix small-unit raids on isolated outposts of the government or occupying force with detonations and assassinations in urban areas to instill fear and discredit government power. The tactical logic of guerrilla operations resembles that in terrorist attacks: the weaker rebels use stealth and the cover of civilian society to concentrate their striking power against one among many of the stronger enemy's dispersed assets; they strike quickly and eliminate the target before the defender can move forces from other areas to respond; they melt back into civilian society to avoid detection and re-concentrate against another target. The government or occupier has far superior strength in terms of conventional military power, but cannot counterconcentrate in time because it has to defend all points, while the insurgent attacker can pick its targets at will.[17] The contest between insurgents and counterinsurgents is "tripartite," polarizing political alignments and gaining the support of *attentistes* or those in the middle. In today's principle counter-terror campaign, one might say that the yet-unmobilized Muslim elites and masses of the Third World—those who were not already actively committed either to supporting Islamist radicalism or to combating it—are the target group in the middle. As Samuel Huntington noted, "a revolutionary war is a war of attrition."[18] As I believe Stanley Hoffman once said, in rebellions the insurgents win as long as they do not lose, and the government loses as long as it does not win. If al Qaeda-like groups can stay in the field indefinitely, they win.

Offense-defense theory applied nuclear deterrence concepts to assessing the stability of conventional military confrontations and focused on what conditions tended to give the attack or the defense the advantage in war.[19] There were many problems in the specification and application of the theory having to do with unsettled conceptualization of the offense-defense balance, problematic standards for measuring it, and inconsistent applications to different levels of warfare and diplomacy.[20] Offense-defense theory, which flourished when driven by the urge to find ways to stabilize the NATO-Warsaw Pact balance in Europe, has had little to say directly about unconventional war or terrorism. It actually applies more clearly, however, to this lower level of strategic competition (as well as to the higher level of nuclear war) than to the middle level of conventional military power. This is because the exchange ratio between opposing conventional forces of roughly similar size is very difficult to estimate, given the complex composition of modern military forces and uncertainty about their qualitative comparisons; but the exchange ratio in both nuclear and guerrilla combat is quite lopsided in favor of the attacker. Counterinsurgency folklore held that the government defenders need something on the order of a ten-to-one advantage over the guerrillas if they were to drive them from the field.

There has been much confusion about exactly how to define the offense-defense balance, but the essential idea is that some combinations of military technology, organization, and doctrine are proportionally more advantageous to the attack or to the defense when the two clash. "Proportionally" means that available instruments and circumstances of engagement give either the attack or the defense more bang for the buck, more efficient power out of the same level of resources. The notion of an offense-defense balance as something conceptually distinct from the balance of power means, however, that it cannot be identified with which side wins a battle or a war. Indeed, the offense-defense balance can favor the defense, while the attacker still wins, because its overall margin of superiority in power was too great, despite the defense's more efficient use of power. (I am told that the Finns had a saying in the Winter War of 1939–40: "One Finn is worth ten Russians, but what happens when the eleventh Russian comes?") Thus, to say that the offense-defense balance favors the offensive terrorists today against the defensive counterterrorists does not mean that the terrorists will prevail. It does mean that terrorists can fight far above their weight, that in most instances each competent terrorist will have much greater individual impact than each good counterterrorist, that each dollar invested in a terrorist plot will have a bigger payoff than each dollar expended on counterterrorism, and that only small numbers of competent terrorists need survive and operate to keep the threat to American society uncomfortably high.

In the competition between terrorists on the attack and Americans on the defense, the disadvantage of the defense is evident in the number of high-value potential targets that need protection. The United States has "almost 600,000 bridges, 170,000 water systems, more than 2,800 power plants (104 of them nuclear), 190,000 miles of interstate pipelines for natural gas, 463 skyscrapers... nearly 20,000 miles of border, airports, stadiums, train tracks."[21] All these usually represented American strength; after September 11 they also represent vulnerability:

> Suddenly guards were being posted at water reservoirs, outside power plants, and at bridges and tunnels. Maps of oil and gas lines were removed from the Internet. In Boston, a ship carrying liquefied natural gas, an important source of fuel for heating New England homes, was forbidden from entering the harbor because local fire officials feared that if it were targeted by a terrorist the resulting explosion could lay low much of the city's densely populated waterfront. An attack by a knife-wielding lunatic on the driver of a Florida-bound Greyhound bus led to the immediate cessation of that national bus service.... Agricultural crop-dusting planes were grounded out of a concern that they could be used to spread chemical or biological agents.[22]

Truly energetic defense measures do not only cost money in personnel and equipment for fortification, inspection, and enforcement; they may require repealing some of the

nerability to single attacks. Tighter inspection of cargoes coming across the Canadian border, for example, wrecks the "just-in-time" parts supply system of Michigan auto manufacturers. Companies that have invested in technology and infrastructure premised on unimpeded movement "may see their expected savings and efficiencies go up in smoke. Outsourcing contracts will have to be revisited and inventories will have to be rebuilt."[24] How many safety measures will suffice in improving airline security without making flying so inconvenient that the air travel industry never recovers as a profit-making enterprise? A few more shoe-bomb incidents, and Thomas Friedman's proposal to start an airline called "Naked Air—where the only thing you wear is a seat belt" becomes almost as plausible as it is ridiculous.[25]

The offense-dominant character of terrorism is implicit in mass detentions of Arab young men after September 11, and proposals for military tribunals that would compromise normal due process and weaken standard criminal justice presumptions in favor of the accused. The traditional liberal axiom that it is better to let a hundred guilty people go free than to convict one innocent reflects confidence in the strength of society's defenses—confidence that whatever additional crimes may be committed by the guilty who go free will not grossly outweigh the injustice done to innocents convicted, that one criminal who slips through the net will not go on to kill hundreds or thousands of innocents. Fear of terrorists plotting mass murder reversed that presumption and makes unjust incarceration of some innocents appear like unintended but expected collateral damage in wartime combat.

Offense-defense theory helps to visualize the problem. It does not help to provide attractive solutions, as its proponents believed it did during the cold war. Then offense-defense theory was popular because it seemed to offer a way to stabilize the East-West military confrontation. Mutual deterrence from the superpowers' confidence in their counteroffensive capability could substitute for defense at the nuclear level, and both sides' confidence in their conventional defenses could dampen either one's incentives to attack at that level. Little of this applies to counterterrorism. Both deterrence and defense are weaker strategies against terrorists than they were against communists.

Deterrence is still relevant for dealing with state terrorism; Saddam Hussein or Kim Jong-Il may hold back from striking the United States for fear of retaliation. Deterrence offers less confidence for preventing state sponsorship of terrorism; it did not stop the Taliban from hosting Osama bin Laden. It offers even less for holding at bay transnational groups like al Qaeda, which may lack a return address against which retaliation can be visited, or whose millennialist aims and religious convictions make them unafraid of retaliation. Defense, in turn, is better than a losing game only because the inadequacy of deterrence leaves no alternative.[26] Large investments in defense will produce appreciable reductions in vulnerability, but will not minimize vulnerability.

Deterrence and defense overlap in practice. The U.S. counteroffensive in Afghanistan constitutes retaliation, punishing the Taliban for shielding al Qaeda and sending a warning to other potential state sponsors. It is also active defense, whittling down the ranks of potential perpetrators by killing and capturing members of the Islamist international brigades committed to jihad against the United States. At this writing, the retaliatory function has been performed more effectively than the defensive, as the Taliban regime has been destroyed, but significant numbers of Arab Afghans and al Qaeda members appear to have escaped, perhaps to plot another day.

Given the limited efficacy of deterrence for modern counterterrorism, it remains an open question how much of a strategic success we should judge the impressive victory in Afghanistan to be. Major investments in passive defenses (airline security, border inspections, surveillance and searches for better intelligence, fortification of embassies, and so forth) are necessary, but will reduce vulnerability at a cost substantially greater than the costs that competent terrorist organizations will have to bear to probe and occasionally circumvent them. The cost-exchange ratio for direct defense is probably worse than the legendary 10:1 ratio for successful counterinsurgency, and certainly worse than the more than 3:1 ratio that Robert McNamara's analysts calculated for the advantage of offensive missile investments over antiballistic missile systems—an advantage that many then and since have thought warranted accepting a situation of mutual vulnerability to assured destruction.[27]

The less prepared we are to undertake appropriate programs and the more false starts and confusions that are likely, the worse the cost-exchange ratio will be in the short term. The public health system, law enforcement organizations, and state and local bureaucrats are still feeling their way on what, how, and in which sequence to boost efforts. The U.S. military will also have to overcome the natural and powerful effects of inertia and attachments to old self-conceptions and preferred programs and modes of operation. Impulses to repackage old priorities in the rhetoric of new needs will further dilute effectiveness of countermeasures.

Nevertheless, given low confidence that deterrence can prevent terrorist attacks, major improvements in defenses make sense.[28] This is especially true because the resource base from which the United States can draw is vastly larger than that available to transnational terrorists. Al Qaeda may be rich, but it does not have the treasury of a great power. Primacy has a soft underbelly, but it is far better to have primacy than to face it. Even at an unfavorable cost-exchange ratio, a number of defensive measures are a sensible investment, but only because our overwhelming advantage in resources means that we are not constrained to focus solely on the most efficient countermeasures.

At the same time, as long as terrorist groups remain potent and active, a serious war plan must exploit efficient strategies as well. Given the offense-dominant nature of terrorist operations, this means emphasis on counteroffensive operations. When terrorists or their support structures can be found and fixed, preemptive and preventive attacks will accomplish more against them, dollar for dollar, than the investment in passive defenses. Which is the more efficient use of resources: to kill or capture a cell of terrorists who might otherwise choose at any time to strike whichever set of targets on our side is unguarded, or to try to guard all potential targets? Here the dangers are that counteroffensive operations could prove counterproductive. This could easily happen if they degenerate into brutalities and breaches of laws of war that make counterterrorism begin to appear morally equivalent to its target, sapping political support and driving the uncommitted to the other side in the process of polarization that war makes inevitable. Whether counteroffensive operations gain more in eliminating perpetrators than they lose in alienating and mobilizing "swing voters" in the world of Muslim opinion depends on how successful the operations are in neutralizing

September 11 reminded those Americans with a rosy view that not all the world sees U.S. primacy as benign, that primacy does not guarantee security, and that security may now entail some retreats from the economic globalization that some had identified with American leadership. Primacy has two edges—dominance and provocation. Americans can enjoy the dominance but must recognize the risks it evokes. For terrorists who want to bring the United States down, U.S. strategic primacy is a formidable challenge, but one that can be overcome. On balance, Americans have overestimated the benefits of primacy, and terrorists have underestimated them.

For those who see a connection between American interventionism, cultural expansiveness, and support of Israel on one hand, and the rage of groups that turn to terrorism on the other, primacy may seem more trouble than it's worth, and the need to revise policies may seem more pressing. But most Americans have so far preferred the complacent and gluttonous form of primacy to the ascetic, blithely accepting steadily growing dependence on Persian Gulf oil that could be limited by compromises in lifestyle and unconventional energy policies. There have been no groundswells to get rid of SUVs, support the Palestinians, or refrain from promoting Western standards of democracy and human rights in societies where some elements see them as aggression.

There is little evidence that any appreciable number of Americans, elite or mass, see our primacy as provoking terrorism. Rather, most see it as a condition we can choose at will to exploit or not. So U.S. foreign policy has exercised primacy in a muscular way in byways of the post-cold war world when intervention seemed cheap, but not when doing good deeds threatened to be costly. Power has allowed Washington to play simultaneously the roles of mediator and partisan supporter in the Arab-Israeli conflict. For a dozen years nothing, with the near exception of the Kosovo War, suggested that primacy could not get us out of whatever problems it generated.

How far the United States goes to adapt to the second edge of primacy probably depends on whether stunning damage is inflicted by terrorists again, or September 11 gradually fades into history. If al Qaeda and its ilk are crippled, and some years pass without more catastrophic attacks on U.S. home territory, scar tissue will harden on the soft underbelly, and the positive view of primacy will be reinforced. If the war against terrorism falters, however, and the exercise of power fails to prevent more big incidents, the consensus will crack. Then more extreme policy options will get more attention. Retrenchment and retreat will look more appealing to some, who may believe the words of Sheik Salman al-Awdah, a dissident Saudi religious scholar, who said, "If America just let well enough alone, and got out of their obligations overseas… no one would bother them."[29]

More likely, however, would be a more violent reaction. There is no reason to assume that terrorist enemies would let America off the hook if it retreated and would not remain as implacable as ever. Facing inability to suppress the threat through normal combat, covert action, and diplomatic pressure, many Americans would consider escalation to more ferocious strategies. In recent decades, the march of liberal legalism has delegitimized tactics and brutalities that once were accepted, but this delegitimation has occurred only in the context of fundamental security and dominance of the Western powers, not in a situation where they felt under supreme threat. In a situation of that sort, it is foolhardy to assume that American strategy would never turn to tactics like those used against Japanese and German civilians, or by the civilized French in the *sale guerre* in Algeria, or by the Russians in Chechnya in hopes of effectively eradicating terrorists despite astronomical damage to the civilian societies within which they lurk.

This possibility would highlight how terrorists have underestimated American primacy. There is much evidence that even in the age of unipolarity, opponents have mistakenly seen the United States as a paper tiger. For some reason—perhaps wishfully selective perception—they tend to see retreats from Vietnam, Beirut, and Somalia as typical weakness of American will, instead of considering decisive exercises of power in Panama, Kuwait, Kosovo, and now, Afghanistan.[30] As Osama bin Laden said in 1997, the United States left Somalia "after claiming that they were the largest power on earth. They left after some resistance from powerless, poor, unarmed people whose only weapon is the belief in Allah.... The Americans ran away."[31]

This apparently common view among those with an interest in pinning America's ears back ignores the difference between elective uses of force and desperate ones. The United States retreated where it ran into trouble helping others, not where it was saving itself. Unlike interventions of the 1990s in Africa, the Balkans, or Haiti, counterterrorism is not charity. With vital material interests involved, primacy unleashed may prove fearsomely potent.

Most likely America will see neither absolute victory nor abject failure in the war against terror. Then how long will a campaign of attrition last and stay popular? If the United States wants a strategy to cut the roots of terrorism, rather than just the branches, will American power be used effectively against the roots? Perhaps, but probably not. This depends of course on which of many possible root causes are at issue. Ironically, one problem is that American primacy itself is one of those roots.

A common assertion is that Third World poverty generates terrorism. While this must certainly be a contributing cause in many cases, there is little evidence that it is either a necessary or sufficient condition. Fundamentalist madrassas might not be full to overflowing if young Muslims had ample opportunities to make money, but the fifteen Saudis who hijacked the flights on September 11 were from one of the most affluent of Muslim countries. No U.S. policy could ever hope to make most incubators of terrorism less poor than Saudi Arabia. Iran, the biggest state sponsor of anti-American terrorism, is also better off than most Muslim countries. Poverty is endemic in the Third World, but terrorism is not.

Even if endemic poverty were the cause, the solution would not be obvious. Globalization generates stratification, creating winners and losers, as efficient societies with capitalist cultures move ahead and others fall behind, or as elite enclaves in some societies prosper while the masses stagnate. Moreover, even vastly increased U.S. development assistance would be spread thin if all poor countries are assumed to be incubators of terrorism. And what are the odds that U.S. intervention with economic aid would significantly reduce poverty? Successes in prompting dramatic economic development by outside assistance in the Third World have occurred, but they are the exception more than the rule.

The most virulent anti-American terrorist threats, however, do not emerge randomly in poor societies. They grow out of a few regions and are concentrated overwhelmingly in a few religiously motivated groups. These reflect political causes—ideological, nationalist,

likely to produce either peace or conventional war. Peace is probable if power is imbalanced but grievance is modest; the weaker party is likely to live with the grievance. In that situation, conventional use of force appears to offer no hope of victory, while the righteous indignation is not great enough to overcome normal inhibitions against murderous tactics. Conventional war is probable if grievance is intense but power is more evenly balanced, since successful use of respectable forms of force appears possible.[32] Under American primacy, candidates for terrorism suffer from grossly inferior power by definition. This should focus attention on the political causes of their grievance.

How are political root causes addressed? At other times in history we have succeeded in fostering congenial revolutions—especially in the end of the cold war, as the collapse of the Second World heralded an End of History of sorts.[33] The problem now, however, is the rebellion of anti-Western zealots against the secularist end of history. Remaking the world in the Western image is what Americans assume to be just, natural, and desirable, indeed only a matter of time. But that presumption is precisely what energizes many terrorists' hatred. Secular Western liberalism is not their salvation, but their scourge. Primacy could, paradoxically, remain both the solution and the problem for a long time.*

*The author thanks Robert Jervis for comments on the first draft.

Richard K. Betts is a specialist on national security policy and military strategy. He is the director of the Institute of War and Peace Studies at Columbia University and was a senior fellow and research associate at the Brookings Institution in Washington, D.C. Betts has served on the National Commission on Terrorism and the U.S. Senate Select Committee on Intelligence. He is author, editor, and coauthor of several books on the subject, including *The Irony of Vietnam: The System Worked* (1979), which won the Woodrow Wilson Prize.

Notes

1. William Wolf in Eric Frank Russell, *Wasp* (London: Victor Gollancz, 2000, originally published 1957), 7.
2. "The word has become a political label rather than an analytical concept." Martha Crenshaw, *Terrorism and International Cooperation* (New York: Institute for East-West Security Studies, 1989), 5.
3. For a survey of types, see Christopher C. Harmon, "Five Strategies of Terrorism," *Small Wars and Insurgencies* 12 (Autumn 2001).
4. Rationalization of national power as altruism resembles the thinking about benign Pax Britannica in the Crowe Memorandum: "... the national policy of the insular and naval State is so directed as to harmonize with the general desires and ideals common to all mankind, and more particularly... is closely identified with the primary and vital interests of a majority, or as many as possible, of the other nations.... England, more than any other non-insular Power, has a direct and positive interest in the maintenance of the independence of nations, and therefore must be the natural enemy of any country threatening the independence of others, and the natural

protector of the weaker communities." Eyre Crowe, "Memorandum on the Present State of British Relations with France and Germany," 1 January 1907, in G. P. Gooch and Harold Temperley, eds., *British Documents on the Origins of the War, 1898–1914*, vol. 3: *The Testing of the Entente, 1904–6* (London: His Majesty's Stationery Office, 1928), 402–403.

5. At the end of the twentieth century, the combined military budgets of China, Russia, Iraq, Yugoslavia (Serbia), North Korea, Iran, Libya, Cuba, Afghanistan, and Sudan added up to no more than $60 billion. *The Military Balance*, 1999–2000 (London: International Institute for Strategic Studies, 1999), 102, 112, 132, 133, 159, 186, 275.

6. Washington certainly did exert pressure on Israel at some times. The administration of Bush the Elder, for example, threatened to withhold loans for housing construction, but this was a marginal portion of total U.S. aid. There was never a threat to cut off the basic annual maintenance payment of several billion dollars to which Israel became accustomed decades ago.

7. The United States has also given aid to friendly Arab governments—huge amounts to Egypt and some to Jordan. This does not counterbalance the aid to Israel, however, in terms of effects on opinions of strongly anti-Israeli Arabs. Islamists see the regimes in Cairo and Amman as American toadies, complicit in betrayal of the Palestinians.

8. Theoretically, this was anticipated by Samuel P. Huntington in his 1962 analysis of the differences between symmetrical intergovernmental war and asymmetrical antigovernmental war. "Patterns of Violence in World Politics" in Huntington, ed., *Changing Patterns of Military Politics* (New York: Free Press of Glencoe, 1962), 19–21). Some of Huntington's analysis of insurrectionary warfare within states applies as well to transnational terrorism.

9. The Royal Air Force gave up on precision bombing early and focused deliberately on night bombing of German cities, while the Americans continued to try precision daylight bombing. Firestorms in Hamburg, Darmstadt, and Dresden, and less incendiary attacks on other cities, killed several hundred thousand German civilians. Over Japan, the United States quickly gave up attempts at precision bombing when weather made it impractical and deliberately resorted to an incendiary campaign that burned most Japanese cities to the ground and killed at least 300,000 civilians (and perhaps more than half a million) well before the nuclear attacks on Hiroshima and Nagasaki, which killed another 200,000. Michael S. Sherry, *The Rise of American Air Power: The Creation of Armageddon* (New Haven: Yale University Press, 1987), 260, 413–43.

10. The threat of deliberate nuclear escalation remained the bedrock of NATO doctrine throughout the cold war, but after the Kennedy administration, the flexible response doctrine made it conditional and included options for nuclear first-use that did not involve deliberate targeting of population centers. In the Eisenhower administration, however, all-out attack on the Soviet bloc's cities was integral to plans for defense of Western Europe against Soviet armored divisions.

11. In a videotape months after the attacks, bin Laden said, "These blessed strikes showed clearly that this arrogant power, America, rests on a powerful but precarious economy, which rapidly crumbled... the global economy based on usury, which America uses along with its military might to impose infidelity and humiliation on oppressed people, can easily crumble.... Hit the economy, which is the basis of military might. If their economy is finished, they will become too busy to enslave oppressed people.... America is in decline; the economic drain is continuing but more strikes are required and the youths must strike the key sectors of the American economy." Videotape excerpts quoted in "Bin Laden's Words: 'America Is in Decline,' the Leader of Al Qaeda Says," *New York Times*, 28 December 2001.

12. This is similar to the concept of political judo discussed in Samuel L. Popkin, "Pacification: Politics and the Village," *Asian Survey* 10 (August 1970); and Popkin, "Internal Conflicts—South Vietnam" in Kenneth N. Waltz and Steven Spiegel, eds., *Conflict in World Politics* (Cambridge, MA: Winthrop, 1971).

13. Soft power is "indirect or cooptive" and "can rest on the attraction of one's ideas or on the ability to set the political agenda in a way that shapes the preferences that others express." It "tends to be associated with intangible power resources such as culture, ideology, and institutions." Joseph S. Nye, Jr., "The Changing Nature of World Power," *Political Science Quarterly*, 105

(Cambridge: MIT Press, 1998).

15. Russell, *Wasp*, 64. The ripple effects include aspects of strategic judo. Creating a phony rebel organization leads the enemy security apparatus to turn on its own people. "If some Sirians could be given the full-time job of hunting down and garroting other Sirians, and if other Sirians could be given the full-time job of dodging or shooting down the garroters, then a distant and different life form would be saved a few unpleasant chores.... Doubtless the military would provide a personal bodyguard for every big wheel on Jaimec; that alone would pin down a regiment." Ibid., 26, 103.

16. Study by the Milken Institute discussed in "The Economics: Attacks May Cost 1.8 Million Jobs," *New York Times*, 13 January 2002.

17. Mao Tse-Tung's classic tracts are canonical background. For example, "Problems of Strategy in China's Revolutionary War" (especially chap. 5) in *Selected Works of Mao Tse-Tung* (Beijing: Foreign Languages Press, 1967), vol. i, and "Problems of Strategy in Guerrilla War Against Japan," in *Selected Works*, vol. ii (1967). Much of the Western analytical literature grew out of British experience in the Malayan Emergency and France's role in Indochina and Algeria. For example, Franklin Mark Osanka, ed., *Modern Guerrilla Warfare* (New York: Free Press, 1962); Gerard Chaliand, ed., *Guerrilla Strategies: An Historical Anthology from the Long March to Afghanistan* (Berkeley: University of California Press, 1982); Roger Triniquier, *Modern Warfare: A French View of Counterinsurgency*, Daniel Lee, trans. (New York: Praeger, 1964); David Galula, *Counterinsurgency Warfare: Theory and Practice* (New York: Praeger, 1964); Sir Robert Thompson, *Defeating Communist Insurgency* (New York: Praeger, 1966); Richard L. Clutterbuck, *The Long Long War: Counterinsurgency in Malaya and Vietnam* (New York: Praeger, 1966); George Armstrong Kelly, *Lost Soldiers: The French Army and Empire in Crisis, 1947–1962* (Cambridge: MIT Press, 1965), chaps. 5–7, 9–10; W. P. Davison, *Some Observations on Viet Cong Operations in the Villages* (Santa Monica, CA: RAND Corporation, 1968). See also Douglas S. Blaufarb, *The Counter-Insurgency Era: U.S. Doctrine and Performance, 1950 to the Present* (New York: Free Press, 1977); D. Michael Shafer, *Deadly Paradigms: The Failure of U.S. Counterinsurgency Policy* (Princeton: Princeton University Press, 1988); Timothy J. Lomperis, *From People's War to People's Rule: Insurgency, Intervention, and the Lessons of Vietnam* (Chapel Hill: University of North Carolina Press, 1996).

18. Huntington, "Patterns of Violence in World Politics," 20–27.

19. George Quester, *Offense and Defense in the International System*, 2nd ed. (New Brunswick, NJ: Transaction Books, 1988); Robert Jervis, "Cooperation Under the Security Dilemma," *World Politics* 30 (January 1978); Jack L. Snyder, *The Ideology of the Offensive: Military Decision Making and the Disasters of 1914* (Ithaca, NY: Cornell University Press, 1984); Stephen Van Evera, *Causes of War: Power and the Roots of Conflict* (Ithaca, NY: Cornell University Press, 1999), chaps. 6–8; Charles L. Glaser and Chaim Kaufmann, "What Is the Offense-Defense Balance and Can We Measure It?" *International Security* 22 (Spring 1998).

20. For critiques, see Jack S. Levy, "The Offensive/Defensive Balance of Military Technology," *International Studies Quarterly* 28 (June 1984); Scott D. Sagan, "1914 Revisited," *International Security* 11 (Fall 1986); Jonathan Shimshoni, "Technology, Military Advantage, and World War I: A Case for Military Entrepreneurship," *International Security* 15 (Winter 1990/91); Richard K. Betts, "Must War Find a Way?" *International Security* 24 (Fall 1999); Betts, "Conventional Deterrence: Predictive Uncertainty and Policy Confidence," *World Politics* 37 (January 1985).

21. Jerry Schwartz, Associated Press dispatch, 6 October 2001, quoted in Brian Reich, "Strength in the Face of Terror: A Comparison of United States and International Efforts to Provide Homeland Security" (unpublished paper, Columbia University, December 2001), 5.

22. Stephen E. Flynn, "The Unguarded Homeland" in James F. Hoge, Jr. and Gideon Rose, eds., *How Did This Happen? Terrorism and the New War* (New York: PublicAffairs, 2001), 185.
23. Ibid., 185–186.
24. Ibid., 193–194.
25. Thomas L. Friedman, "Naked Air," *New York Times*, 26 December 2001.
26. See Steven Simon and Daniel Benjamin, "America and the New Terrorism," *Survival* 42 (Spring 2000); 59, 66–69, 74.
27. Estimates in the 1960s indicated that even combining ABM systems with counterforce strikes and fallout shelters, the United States would have to counter each Soviet dollar spent on ICBMs with three U.S. dollars to protect 70 percent of the industry, assuming highly ABMs (.8 kill probability). To protect up to 80 percent of the population, far higher ratios would be necessary. Fred Kaplan, *The Wizards of Armageddon* (New York: Simon and Schuster, 1983), 321–324.
28. For an appropriate list of recommendations see *Countering the Changing Threat of International Terrorism*, Report of the National Commission on Terrorism, Pursuant to Public Law 277, 105th Congress (Washington, DC, June 2000). This report holds up very well in light of September 11.
29. Quoted in Douglas Jehl, "After Prison, a Saudi Sheik Tempers His Words," *New York Times*, 27 December 2001.
30. See data in the study by Barry M. Blechman and Tamara Cofman Wittes, "Defining Moment: The Threat and Use of Force in American Foreign Policy," *Political Science Quarterly* 114 (Spring 1999).
31. Quoted in Simon and Benjamin, "America and the New Terrorism," 69.
32. On why power imbalance is conducive to peace and parity to war, see Geoffrey Blainey, *The Causes of War*, 3rd. ed. (New York: Free Press, 1988), chap. 8.
33. Francis Fukuyama's thesis was widely misunderstood and caricatured. He noted that the Third World remained mired in history and that some developments could lead to restarting history. For the First World, the defeated Second World, and even some parts of the Third World, however, the triumph of Western liberalism could reasonably be seen by those who believe in its worth (as should Americans) as the final stage of evolution through fundamentally different forms of political and economic organization of societies. See Fukuyama, "The End of History?" *National Interest* no. 16 (Summer 1989); and Fukuyama, *The End of History and the Last Man* (New York: Free Press, 1992).

Some terrorism is ill-advised.
—Osama bin Laden

The September 11, 2001 al Qaeda assault on the United States was a tactical masterpiece. The terrorists achieved total surprise, damaged their intended targets greater than they had anticipated, and the attacks will be recorded in history as an epochal event. Yet, for all their tactical brilliance, the terror attacks were poorly suited to achieving al Qaeda's strategic goals. Placed in that context, they represented strategic overreach, a failure to understand the relationship between the techniques of terror and the objectives of warfighting.

Bin Laden's Grand Strategy

The key document for understanding bin Laden's strategic plan is his August 23, 1996 "Declaration of War Against the Americans Occupying the Land of the Two Holy Places."[1] In this lengthy document bin Laden spells out in detail both his objectives and his planned means of achieving them.

Bin Laden pursued four principal strategic goals. The first and most important of these was to expel the United States military from the Arabian peninsula. This was central to all other objectives in the region. Bin Laden states succinctly that "there is no more important duty than pushing the American enemy out of the Holy Land. No other priority, except Belief, could be considered before it."[2] U.S. forces had come to Saudi Arabia in August 1990 in response to Saddam Hussein's invasion of Kuwait. Bin Laden, the son of a wealthy and politically influential construction magnate, fresh from victory over the Soviet Union in Afghanistan, had offered the Saudi state the services of his army of Mujahedin, but King Fahd declined the offer. Bin Laden considered the mere presence of the "infidel armies of the American Crusaders" so close to the holy places of Islam a scandal. However, he was told this was a necessary defensive measure and would only be temporary.[3]

Six years later, U.S. forces remained in Saudi Arabia, which by then had become a base for the prosecution of the post war containment of Iraq; a "launching pad for aggression" according to bin Laden. He argued that the United Nations embargo and continued American military action inside Iraq had led to the deaths of millions of Iraqis.[4] The United States was also causing economic dislocations inside Saudi Arabia, and U.S. troops and civilian contractors brought with them harmful social influences.[5] The Saudi regime had become increasingly corrupted, straying from the dictates of the *Sharia*. Islamicist scholars, holy men and dissidents who questioned these developments were arrested or exiled, and bin Laden's Saudi citizenship was revoked in 1994 (he had fled the country three years earlier). "It is out of date and no longer acceptable to claim that the presence of the crusaders is necessity and only a temporary measure to protect the land of the Two Holy Places," bin Laden declared. "The regime has torn off its legitimacy."[6]

The second strategic goal was the overthrow of the corrupt Muslim (and particularly Arab) regimes, and the restoration of the "pious Caliphate." Bin Laden viewed the 1920 Treaty of Servés as the root of all evil in the region. This treaty had dismantled the Ottoman Empire and established the modern Arab state system.[7] According to bin Laden, the Zionist-Crusader alliance had broken up the region into small, bickering countries in order to control it. A united Arab-Muslim *Ummah* would command power far exceeding any of the modern states. "The existence of such a large country with its huge resources under the leadership of the forthcoming Islamic State, by Allah's Grace, represents a serious danger to the very existence of the Zionist State in Palestine."[8] Furthermore, bin Laden envisaged a pure Islamic state, guided by the *Sharia*, a Muslim utopia of virtue. The first step to creating this pan-Islamic superpower was removing the United States from the region. The rest would be elementary. "If the United States is beheaded," he claimed, "the Arab kingdoms will wither away."[9]

The third major strategic goal was the destruction of the state of Israel and the creation of a Palestinian homeland. Israel, the traditional nemesis of the Islamicists, was seen both as a creature of the United States, and a force that controlled American actions through the international Zionist conspiracy. America's close association with Israel increased the importance of the United States as a target. "Our duty is to fight whomever is in the trench of the Jews," bin Laden stated. "America and the American people are free, they have entered the trench, and they will get what is coming to them.... We swore that America will never dream of safety, until safety becomes a reality for us living in Palestine."[10]

Finally, bin Laden sought to punish the United States for its global acts of aggression against Muslims. Bin Laden believed that the United States had been the main instigator of violence against the Islamic world since the end of the Cold War, and sought thereby to keep Muslims from uniting. Almost every al Qaeda public statement refers to Muslims killed in various parts of the world, particularly in Palestine and Iraq. The United States was also the primary source of cultural contamination, which sought to extinguish Islam as a moral force.[11] This claim of physical and cultural "self-defense" became the primary rallying point and legitimizing factor of the struggle, and every subsequent action was characterized as a response to aggression. Bin Laden stated in 1996, "Terrorizing you, while you are carrying arms on our land, is a legitimate and morally demanded duty. It is a legitimate right well known to all humans and other creatures."[12] Self-defense was also the background of his infamous October 21, 2001 statement, "if killing the ones that kill our sons is terrorism, then let history witness that we are terrorists."[13]

The Need for Violence

Osama bin Laden saw himself and his movement as a revolutionary vanguard, a catalyst that would bring about a global Muslim resurgence. Violence was a fundamental aspect of his struggle. At a June 1998 special session of the World Islamic Alliance held in Kandahar, bin Laden, waving a Koran, stated forcefully, "You cannot defeat heretics with this book alone, you have to show them the fist!"[14] Violence was necessary, he argued, because the

tion of War explicitly stated the need for asymmetric engagement. The small Arab and Muslim conventional armies could not play a part in expelling the United States from their countries, they were too weak. Their task would come later, when it was time to rebel and overthrow the illegitimate regimes they served. Meanwhile, al Qaeda would begin unconventional warfare against the Crusaders. "Due to the imbalance of power between our armed forces and the enemy forces, a suitable means of fighting must be adopted, i.e., using fast-moving light forces that work under complete secrecy. In other words to initiate a guerrilla warfare, where the sons of the nation, and not the military forces, take part in it."[15] Bin Laden's war would seek to demoralize and exhaust the enemy through persistent, small-scale attacks, avoiding pitched battle and exposure to a massive conventional counter-assault. Al Qaeda would hold the initiative, set the terms of engagement, strike sharply and unexpectedly, then withdraw to safety while the enemy attempted to respond.

Bin Laden implemented this strategy in the years leading up to the 9/11 attacks. The bombings in Riyadh on November 13, 1995, at Khobar Towers, on June 25, 1996, at the American embassies in Kenya and Tanzania on August 7, 1998, and of the U.S.S. *Cole* on October 12, 2000, were all battles in bin Laden's anti-American campaign. In each of these attacks, bin Laden followed the precepts of guerrilla war. He did not seek a decisive engagement. He struck overseas, attacked government and military targets and avoided direct confrontation. U.S. responses were largely ineffective, at least in disrupting the al Qaeda network as a whole, or harming bin Laden personally. The most noteworthy attempt was the August 20, 1998 cruise missile attack on terrorist bases in Afghanistan and the al-Shifa pharmaceutical plant in Sudan. Less spectacular but more effective were the arrests of senior al Qaeda members in Europe and the United States.[16]

The cruise missile attack in particular helped convert bin Laden into a radical Muslim folk hero. Even before then, Muslims in Pakistan were naming their newborn sons Osama;[17] surviving the fury of the Americans made bin Laden a global celebrity. An analysis in the Egyptian opposition press observed, "What better proof that Bin Laden had hurt the United States and satisfied the desire of the Muslims than for Clinton himself to stand up and repeat the name of Bin Laden three times as he announced the strikes against Sudan and Afghanistan?... Had the United States not responded in this way, Bin Laden might not have become such a legendary hero."[18] Note that in his August 20, 1998 address to the nation the President referred to bin Laden and his network eight times, not three, and called him "perhaps the preeminent organizer and financier of international terrorism in the world today."

Bin Laden consistently denied any involvement with these or other acts of terror, while also acknowledging his admiration and support for those who committed them. For example, of the Riyadh and Khobar Towers bombings he said, "This was an incident on the basis of which Western propaganda masters are trying to prove me a terrorist. But this is a baseless allegation. I have denied this allegation several times and I still deny it." However, he noted that "challenging the authority of the United States will be a good deed in Islam in every respect.... It is the duty of every Muslim to struggle for its annihilation. It is up to you whether you consider it *jihad* or terrorism."[19]

During these years his network was growing, studying the United States, and learning lessons from their attacks. On February 23, 1998, he announced the formation of the World Islamic Front with representatives of extremist groups from Egypt, Pakistan and Bangladesh, in addition to his own. He did so in the form of a *fatwa* which restated briefly the charges leveled against the United States in the 1996 Declaration of War, and widened the scope of the struggle by stating that "the ruling to kill the Americans and their allies—civilians and military—is an individual duty for every Muslim who can do it in any country in which it is possible to do it."[20] Bin Laden's success, his growing reputation, and the ineffectiveness of U.S. responses fed his desire to escalate the conflict, take the war to the American homeland, and bring about a climactic battle with the infidel enemy. The germ of a plan may already have been present in 1998 when he stated, "In Iran [in 1980], U.S. planes collided with each other and were destroyed. In the future also the Americans will face destruction from collisions among themselves."[21]

Al Qaeda's 9/11 Operational Plan

The September 11, 2001 attacks were intended to accomplish the following:

- Demonstrate that the U.S. homeland can be attacked successfully
- Take revenge for the deaths of Muslims by killing Americans
- Publicize al Qaeda's cause
- Damage U.S. prestige
- Damage the U.S. economy (WTC attack)
- Strike and disrupt the U.S. military headquarters, and demoralize its troops (Pentagon attack)
- Decapitate the U.S. leadership (White House attack)
- Generate a fearful, terrorized, alienated U.S. public
- Create harsh, widespread domestic U.S. crackdown and end freedom in America
- Deter future U.S. action through fear of follow-on attacks

The extent to which al Qaeda accomplished these objectives will be discussed below. The September 11, 2001 attacks were well planned, exploited numerous gaps in American domestic security, and were at least 75 percent successful (that is, three of four aircraft hit their intended targets—the hijackings per se were entirely successful).[22] The attacks were unexpected, visually horrifying, and caused more physical damage than the planners expected. Bin Laden, who said he was the most optimistic of all, had calculated that three or four floors would be hit in each World Trade Center tower, and the sections above might collapse as well. "This is all that we had hoped for," he said.[23] The total destruction of both towers was a grotesque windfall.

Bin Laden assumed that an attack of this magnitude would court a vigorous response, and had accounted for this in his operational plan. The impenetrable sanctuary of Afghanistan was the keystone of bin Laden's defensive strategy. His Declaration of War states "By the Grace of Allah, a safe base is now available in the high Hindukush Mountains in Khurasan; where the largest infidel military force of the world was destroyed. And the myth of the superpower was withered in front of the Mujahedin cries of *Allahu Akbar*."[24] He was familiar with the country, had fought there during the Soviet occupation, had friends, and protected bin Laden in the aftermath of the 1998 Embassy attacks. The Taliban rebuffed overtures by the U.S. for bin Laden's extradition, stating that he was their guest and it would be a violation of the rules of hospitality to surrender him. They suggested the U.S. produce evidence for a trial to be held under the auspices of Islamic law, but neither evidence nor trial was forthcoming. The assassination of anti-Taliban Afghan resistance fighter Ahmed Shah Massoud on September 9, 2001 has been credited to bin Laden perhaps as payment in advance to the Taliban for their support during the expected 9/11 response, or a pre-emptive measure to deny the United States a potential ally inside the country.[26]

Bin Laden and the Taliban also felt they could rely on the continued support of Pakistan. The Pakistani regime was instrumental in creating the Taliban movement, and Pakistani military intelligence (SIS) gave logistics, intelligence and manpower support to the Taliban during their rise to power and afterwards. Furthermore, relations between Washington and Islamabad had soured since the end of the Soviet war in Afghanistan, particularly when the United States imposed sanctions to protest Pakistani nuclear tests in May of 1998, and after the October 1999 military coup which brought to power General Pervez Musharraf. A friendly Pakistan would guarantee Afghanistan's eastern flank and the critical mountain sanctuaries bin Laden had constructed in the 1980s and revisited and strengthened in the late 1990s.

Bin Laden also believed that the Muslim world would rally to his cause. He had stated in his Declaration of War, and again in his 1998 *fatwa*, that resistance to the Crusaders was a duty for all Muslims, a sacred obligation. Should the United States and its allies attempt to take concerted action against him, they would be answered by mass demonstrations. If the corrupt Muslim regimes attempted to crack down on the demonstrators, the people would rise up against them as well. Bin Laden may also have thought that the non-Muslim world would not support the United States, since they had criticized previous U.S. attacks, and might feel threatened by the possibility of sharing in the retribution should they get involved.

Bin Laden felt well prepared for an American military response. After the 1998 cruise missile attack bin Laden secured bombproof bunkers in Tora Bora, sacked most of his bodyguards, and made other improvements to his personal security system.[27] He was confident that he could survive an attack from the air, or U.S.-sponsored covert action. Ayman al-Zawahiri, bin Laden's chief aide, said, "we aren't afraid of bombardment, threats and acts of aggression. We suffered and survived Soviet bombings for 10 years in Afghanistan and we are ready for more sacrifices."[28] To prevent another spate of arrests outside Afghanistan, he retracted parts of his network to the mountain sanctuary in the weeks before the attacks were to take place.

Bin Laden also felt secure from an American ground offensive. He was a veteran of the 10-year guerrilla struggle with the Soviet Union, and the Soviet defeat in Afghanistan was his major formative experience. He was convinced that the Mujahedin not only defeated the Soviet military but also brought about the collapse of the entire Soviet Empire. "With insignificant capabilities, with a small number of RPG's, with a small number of antitank mines, with a small number of Kalashnikov rifles, they managed to crush the greatest empire known to mankind," he stated. "They crushed the greatest military machine."[29] An important event took place during a 1987 Soviet offensive against Mujahedin training camps in eastern Afghanistan, particularly the al-Ansar "Lion's Den" where bin Laden had taken refuge. He and 35 Arab fighters held off a large force for two weeks until the Soviets withdrew.[30] This story created the legend of "bin Laden the warrior," and fed his self-image and personal mythology as well. After the war, bin Laden consistently downplayed the contributions of others in defeating the Soviets, particularly the United States, which in his view played no consequential role whatsoever.

Not only could the United States be bested on the ground in Afghanistan, it would in fact be easier than defeating the Soviets. Bin Laden believed that the United States was a paper tiger, with a reputation for strength but no staying power when it came to a hard fight. His experience had shown that the United States was intensely casualty averse, and a dramatic body-bag-producing event would be sufficient to drive the Americans from the country. Bin Laden frequently cited the American withdrawals after successful attacks against U.S. forces in Beirut (1983) and Mogadishu (1993). In fact, bin Laden took personal credit for the latter: "It is true that my companions fought with Farah Adid's forces against the U.S. troops in Somalia.... You will be astonished that Farah Adid had only 300 soldiers while I had sent 250 Mujahedin.... In one explosion, one hundred Americans were killed, then 18 more were killed in fighting. One day our men shot down an American helicopter. The pilot got out. We caught him, tied his legs and dragged him through the streets. After that, 28,000 U.S. soldiers fled Somalia. The Americans are cowards."[31]

This then was bin Laden's vision of the course of the conflict. He and his associates in Afghanistan would be safe from diplomatic maneuvers, covert action, missile strikes, or air attacks. Should the United States invade Afghanistan, it would become embroiled in a Soviet-style guerrilla war, an endless, futile hunt in the mountains for the stealthy, experienced *jihadis*. The Muslim world would be in an uproar, and international opinion would be skeptical at best. The Americans would become demoralized after suffering only a few combat losses, and pull out. Meanwhile al Qaeda would pummel the U.S. with follow-on terror attacks inside the American homeland. Its people frantic, its economy in a downward spiral, its forces demoralized, the United States would be compelled to withdraw from the Middle East, bringing about the opportunity for the creation of the Caliphate and the destruction of the Zionist entity. Osama bin Laden would then take his rightful position at the head of the Muslim *Ummah*, and set about constructing his utopia.

Al Qaeda's Operational and Strategic Failure

The 9/11 attacks accomplished some of bin Laden's goals (see Table 1). They proved that the United States could be struck at home.[32] The objective of revenge was also satisfied, at least in part. The total casualties did not seem to satisfy al Qaeda sympathizers, who claim that they still have the right to kill four million Americans.[33] It is also worth noting that Muslims were among those killed on September 11.

Many of bin Laden's objectives had mixed, mainly negative outcomes. For example, al Qaeda did manage to publicize its cause, in a dramatic and unambiguous way that bin Laden praised as beneficial. "Those young men said in deeds, in New York and

(continued on page 399)

Effects of the 9/11 Attacks	
Demonstrate that the U.S. homeland can be attacked successfully	Accomplished
Take revenge for deaths of Muslims	Accomplished, in that Americans died—yet so did American Muslims
Publicize al Qaeda's cause	Mixed result, cause publicized but not in a positive light for the most part
Damage U.S. prestige	Mixed result, attack welcomed by those who already hated the U.S., generated sympathy elsewhere
Damage U.S. economy (WTC attack)	Mixed result, WTC successfully attacked, economic effects were temporary and did not affect U.S. military power
Strike and disrupt U.S. military HQ, demoralize military (Pentagon attack)	Mixed result, Pentagon successfully attacked, created brief disruption, generated total commitment among members of the military
Decapitate U.S. leadership (White House attack)	Failed, attack on White House not carried out; resulted in very motivated and capable leadership with clear mandate for unlimited action
Generate a fearful, terrorized, alienated U.S. public	Failed, public united behind leadership, motivation to seek retribution far outweighed fear of future attacks
Create harsh, widespread domestic U.S. crackdown and end freedom in America	Failed, limited domestic roundups approved by the public
Deter future U.S. action for fear of follow-on attacks	Failed, U.S. undeterred, in fact highly motivated, united, and eager to join battle immediately
Expected Responses and Their Effects	
Continued support from the Taliban	Taliban continued to support and protect al Qaeda
Continued support from Pakistan	Pakistan aligned with the U.S.
Muslim world united behind their cause, mass demonstrations and uprisings	Radical Muslim world united rhetorically, a few small demonstrations, no uprisings
Non-Muslim world opinion neutral; noting validity of Muslim complaints; mildly supportive	Non-Muslim world opinion rallied to U.S. side against terrorism and in favor of Afghan attack
U.S. air attacks on Afghanistan would be ineffective	Advanced munitions and vastly improved targeting capabilities produced unprecedented results
U.S. ground attacks on Afghanistan would be a graveyard for U.S. forces as it was for the Soviet Union	Innovative U.S. operation succeeded in overthrowing Taliban regime, destroying al Qaeda sanctuary
Casualty-averse U.S. military and public would not accept hard fighting	Motivated U.S. military and public accepts sacrifices in a clear just cause
Planned follow-on terror attacks would reinforce effects of initial strikes	Follow-on attacks disrupted; al Qaeda networks effectively broken up or muted

Washington, speeches that overshadowed all other speeches made everywhere else in the world.... This event made people think (about true Islam) which benefited Islam greatly."[34] Yet, the attention the attacks generated was more negative than positive. Likewise, U.S. prestige was damaged in areas where bin Laden might expect public approbation—spontaneous celebrations broke out in some parts of the world upon news of the attacks. But elsewhere, particularly in the western world, 9/11 brought forth an out-pouring of sympathy, and fostered a renewed respect for the United States. Actions that bin Laden thought would be greeted by global indifference, satisfaction, or at least under-standing, in fact generated disgust, fear and outrage. Bin Laden had brought perspective to the sometimes argumentative western allies, had shown them why they were allies to begin with. His brutality clarified their shared values. He reminded the civilized nations of the world what it means to be civilized. By early November 2001, the evident lack of global sympathy and support for his own cause led bin Laden to condemn the entire world in the form of the UN.[35]

The U.S. economy was a critical target of the 9/11 attacks. Al Qaeda had (correctly) pinpointed the economy as the U.S. center of gravity, the source of its national power, as well as of the "materialist way of life" for which he had contempt. Bin Laden and his fol-lowers had developed a fixation on the World Trade Center, and seemed to believe it was the centerpiece of the U.S. economy. (In fact, it was not even the headquarters of a single major corporation.) In October 2001, bin Laden discussed in detail the blows he had in-flicted on the U.S. economy, and claimed that the attack would cost $1 trillion "by the lowest estimate."[36] However, more than half of this was accounted for by losses on Wall Street, which regained its pre-9/11 value by December. Furthermore, it is unclear whether the brief economic contraction of the fall and winter of 2001 was caused by the attacks or was a natural turn of the business cycle that the attacks simply exacerbated. Regardless, the U.S. economy was diverse and robust enough to overcome the impact of 9/11, and it was clear by December that this objective had not been achieved in any lasting sense. In bin Laden's last verifiable statement to date, he appealed for more attacks on the economy.[37]

The Pentagon, "the biggest center of military power in the world," also held symbolic value for al Qaeda.[38] The Pentagon attack did some damage, but hardly enough to achieve the military objectives that bin Laden sought. Yet, striking at the heart of the DOD had a very important psychological impact. In his Declaration of War, bin Laden told the Secre-tary of Defense, "Your problem will be how to convince your troops to fight." One cannot overstate the motivational effect the blow at the Pentagon had on the men and women of the U.S. military. As an Air Force Lieutenant Colonel said bitterly on that day, "they hit the *home office*."[39] After this, there could hardly be a question of the desire of the armed forces of the United States to seek al Qaeda's annihilation.

Many desired outcomes resulted in unequivocal failures. The decapitation strike at the White House failed when the passengers of United Airlines Flight 93, alerted to what was happening over portable phones, acted spontaneously to save their own lives or at least disrupt the plans of the hijackers, and in so doing died heroically. But even had the plan been carried out, President Bush was not present at the White House at the time, and had the structure been destroyed he still would have been able to conduct the affairs of state and direct the U.S. response from several emergency command posts.

The greatest miscalculation, and the most significant shortcoming in the al Qaeda plan, was the belief that the attacks would demoralize the U.S. public, that they would

something he had already known but they perhaps had not—that the United States was at war with an implacable and dangerous foe who was targeting the American way of life and was willing to take any action, no matter how barbaric, to harm this country.

In January 2002, a bin Laden sympathizer compared the 9/11 attacks favorably to the 1941 Japanese surprise attack at Pearl Harbor, and claimed that al Qaeda "has inflicted the biggest psychological defeat of the Americans in their entire history."[41] This statement reveals the terrorists' obsession with technical capabilities over strategic goals. Al Qaeda did achieve surprise on the level of Pearl Harbor, but they also precisely replicated the U.S. national response of unity, anger, and desire for vengeance. Japanese Admiral Isoroku Yamamoto's comment is as aptly applied to 9/11; al Qaeda "awakened a sleeping giant and instilled in him a terrible resolve." Had bin Laden continued to wage his war overseas, hitting only military and government targets, he would not have engaged the American national will, or generated an overwhelming military response. The "Battles of New York and Washington," however, represent a classic case of strategic overreach. Bin Laden aroused the wrath of the American people, who handed their Commander in Chief the power to wage unlimited war on their behalf against al Qaeda. Any question of deterring the United States or other countries for fear of follow-on attacks was overwhelmed by the desire to strike back, to pursue the enemy regardless of cost or sacrifice, and to see justice done. Bin Laden was no longer facing a country distracted by internal political squabbles and lacking the leadership and national will to take the concerted action necessary to respond effectively to his provocations. He changed that himself on 9/11. It was indeed Pearl Harbor.

The magnitude of bin Laden's strategic miscalculation became apparent as the U.S. response developed in the weeks and months following the attacks. One bright note for bin Laden was that the Taliban stood by him, following exactly the same play book as 1998 (saying he was a guest who could not be handed over because of traditions of hospitality, asking for evidence that bin Laden was indeed behind the attacks, offering to have an Islamic trial if evidence was produced, and so forth). This of course did not sway the United States, and it placed the Taliban regime in the position of being accused of "harboring terrorists," thus becoming a legitimate target.

Pakistan surprised both bin Laden and the Taliban by withdrawing support and siding with the United States. Realist theory would have predicted this—there was very little to be gained for Pakistan by taking a stand in favor of overt terrorism and against the most powerful country in the world, especially given the motivation of the United States to carry out the mission. General Musharraf faced potential domestic disturbances and the possibility of a coup, but he was able to maintain control, fire high-ranking pro-Taliban members of his government (particularly in the ISI and the military) and mute potential internal disturbances. Bin Laden pleaded for the Pakistani people to rise up against Musharraf in November, but the response was insignificant.[42]

Likewise, there was no general uprising in the Islamic world to protest U.S. actions, or those of the "corrupt" Muslim governments. There was strong rhetorical support from many Muslim groups, but few demonstrations. The U.S. received valuable cooperation from several Muslim Central Asian states bordering Afghanistan. Most mainstream Islamic groups rushed to announce that bin Laden's strain of radical Islam was not representative of Muslim belief in general. It soon became clear that bin Laden was not the folk hero he thought he was. He had believed that a concerted attack on him and his cause would inflame the passions of the Muslim Street and create chaos. This reflects the same hubris that had primed bin Laden for overreach, the overweening self image that is frequently the fate of the authoritarian, messianic leader who closes himself off from the world and surrounds himself with worshippers. As noted above, the reaction of non-Muslim states was also not what bin Laden expected. U.S. allies rallied to the cause, and many of them sent troops or provided other support to augment U.S. fighting forces.

Bin Laden's trump card was his defensive bastion in Afghanistan, and it too proved not to live up to expectations. The U.S. air campaign became a test for new and improved weapons systems and capabilities, which were used in innovative ways. The Hellfire-armed Predator UAV is an example, as well as JDAMS munitions, ground spotters calling in air support from strategic bombers, even the employment of World War II-era bunker busters that were still in the inventory. Likewise, the ground campaign was not the war bin Laden had anticipated. Using a creative approach based on augmenting indigenous resistance forces with spearhead capabilities of Special Operations Forces, and later reinforced with conventional ground troops, the United States was able to seize the initiative and change the calculus of the battlefield. It is noteworthy that the United States engaged the enemy asymmetrically, while the Taliban relied on heavy forces and static positions instead of resorting to guerrilla war. This was a significantly different conflict from what bin Laden expected, or could even conceive.

Furthermore, bin Laden did not face the timid, casualty-averse enemy he had predicted. This was not Somalia, in which the American people had little understanding of why the United States was involved and what the sacrifice was for. In Afghanistan the public, the leadership, and the military were prepared to accept the casualties that might be necessary to prosecute the struggle. Bin Laden had, through his own actions, created this motivation. As it turned out, the United States and its allies suffered few casualties in the fall and winter of 2001, which is an indication both of Allied warfighting prowess and the inability of al Qaeda or the Taliban to mount a meaningful defense.

Finally, the expected al Qaeda follow-on attacks outside Afghanistan were not executed successfully. On October 10, 2001, an al Qaeda spokesman stated that "the battle will continue to be waged on [U.S.] territory until it leaves our lands." Four days later another spokesman warned that "the aircraft storm will not stop," and advised Muslims living in the United States not to travel by plane or live in tall buildings.[43] Bin Laden had to show his relevance by attacking shortly after the U.S. began to bomb Afghanistan October 7; the logic of violence as a means of communication demanded it. At least one attack was attempted, by shoe-bomber Richard Reid on December 22. However, the United States and its allies had moved effectively to break up the al Qaeda network still operating outside of Afghanistan and short-circuit any other attack plans. When major terror incidents failed to manifest themselves in the days and weeks following the commencement of hostilities in Afghanistan, it was clear that the original al Qaeda campaign plan was in terminal disarray.

cessful guerrilla struggle. Two basic asymmetries were involved, one of forces, and the other of perceptions and will. Bin Laden benefited in the years before 9/11 from the fact that the United States was not on a war footing. By taking terrorism to unprecedented extremes, he mobilized the American national will, and raised the U.S. level of commitment to his own or greater. In so doing, he lost his most important advantage. Furthermore, by overestimating his defensive capabilities and underestimating the offensive power of the United States, he found himself trapped in an indefensible position and unable to prosecute the follow-on attacks of his campaign plan.

As of this writing the War on Terrorism is ongoing, and bin Laden's fate unknown. The United States may face future attacks, perhaps even on the scale of 9/11 or greater. However, the critical imbalance in perceptions and commitment has been redressed, and future attackers will not benefit from the same lack of American awareness or resolve. Regardless of events yet to come, the war that Osama bin Laden had planned to wage against the United States is already over, and he has lost. It is no longer bin Laden's war, but America's.

James S. Robbins is a national security analyst and a frequent contributor to the *National Review Online*. He earned his Ph.D. from the Fletcher School of Law and Diplomacy.

Notes

1. "Declaration of War Against the Americans Occupying the Land of the Two Holy Places (Expel the Infidels from the Arab Peninsula)," *Al Quds Al Arabi*, August 23, 1996. *Al Quds Al Arabi* is a London-based Arabic newspaper with ties to al Qaeda. Hereafter cited as "1996 Declaration of War."
2. "1996 Declaration of War."
3. A good compendium of facts on Osama bin Laden and his intellectual and religious development can be found in John L. Esposito's *Unholy War: Terror in the Name of Islam*, New York: Oxford University Press (2002).
4. When asked about the alleged half-million Iraqi children who had died during the embargo, U.S. Secretary of State Madeleine Albright stated, "We think the price is worth it." ("Punishing Saddam," CBS News 60 Minutes, May 12, 1996.) Official statements of this nature were extremely harmful to the image of the United States in the Muslim world.
5. In an article by Abu-Ayman al-Hilali entitled "Highlights on the Political Thinking of Imam Bin Laden in Light of His Latest Speech" (*Al-Ansar* WWW-Text in Arabic 23 Jan 02 pp 22–29) he defines globalization as "the total invasion of the ideological, political, and economic tenets and values of the cultural existence of the Islamic nation."
6. "1996 Declaration of War."
7. The process of the creation of this system is ably chronicled in David Fromkin's *A Peace to End All Peace: The Fall of the Ottoman Empire and the Creation of the Modern Middle East*, New York: Avon Books (1989).
8. "1996 Declaration of War."

9. Interview with Osama bin Laden by Hamid Mir, Jalalabad, Afghanistan. Published in Islamabad *Pakistan* in Urdu, March 18, 1997.

10. Transcript of bin Laden interview, dated October 21, 2001, posted on May 23, 2002 on Qoqaz.net, text in English. Hereafter cited as October 21, 2001 bin Laden interview.

11. When asked if his struggle was a symptom of the "Clash of Civilizations," bin Laden said, "I say that there is no doubt in this." October 21, 2001 interview.

12. "1996 Declaration of War."

13. October 21, 2001 bin Laden interview.

14. Sanobar Shermatova, "Islamic Sword-Bearer," Moscow *Moskovskiye Novosti* in Russian, January 31, 1999, No 4 p 14.

15. "1996 Declaration of War."

16. Among them were Wahdi Al-Haj, an architect of the embassy bombings, arrested in Texas; Mamduh Muhammad Mahmud Salim, a financial and logistics adviser, arrested in Munich; and Khaled Fuaz, apprehended in London.

17. Rahimullah Yusufzai, "In the Way of Allah," Islamabad *The News* (Internet Version) in English June 15, 1998.

18. "Analysis: Why Bin-Laden Gained Popularity Among Ordinary Moslems," Cairo *Al-Sha'b* (Internet Version) in Arabic, September 27, 2001.

19. Interview With Osama bin Laden, Islamabad *Al-Akhbar* in Urdu, March 31, 1998, pp 1, 8.

20. "Jihad Against Jews and Crusaders," World Islamic Front Statement, February 23, 1998.

21. Interview With Osama bin Laden, March 31, 1998 (op. cit.).

22. Note that the claims of tactical brilliance and secrecy of the hijackers has been called into question by recent revelations of security lapses on their part. The factor most assisting them was the lack of awareness by the public of possible threats; thus, behavior that would seem suspicious post-9/11 and be reported was not taken seriously. See for example the bizarre behavior of 9/11 ringleader Mohammed Atta, "Face to Face With a Terrorist," ABC News, June 6, 2002.

23. Text of Osama bin Laden tape released by the Department of Defense, Dec 13, 2001.

24. "1996 Declaration of War."

25. Relations were so close that Mullah Omar took bin Laden's youngest daughter for one of his wives.

26. Massoud was killed by an exploding video camera carried by assassins posing as journalists. Note that bin Laden had never allowed those who interviewed him to bring their own cameras, and in cases where unanticipated cameras appeared bin Laden can be seen to be visibly nervous.

27. See for example, "Usama Bin Laden Moves Into Missile-Proof Bunkers," Karachi *Jasarat* in Urdu 24 Jul 99 pp 8, 7; and Jason Burke, "Bin Laden's Life Down On The Farm; Jason Burke Follows The Trail Through Afghanistan To The Hideaway Of America's Enemy," *The London Observer* (Internet version) July 4, 1999. Bin Laden allegedly had six doubles.

28. Rahimullah Yusufzai, "From the Horse's Mouth," Islamabad *The News* (Internet Version) in English, August 27, 1998. Jalaluddin Haqqani, who ran some of the training camps, said "Two Red Army air and ground attacks, artillery shelling and scores of air raids failed to destroy the Zhavara camps. What can 60 or 70 long-range Tomahawk cruise missiles do to a place as fortified as Zhavara?" Rahimullah Yusufzai, "Exporting Jehad?" Karachi *Newsline* in English, September 1998, pp. 36, 37, 39.

29. "Usamah Bin-Ladin, the Destruction of the Base," Interview with Usamah Bin-Ladin, Presented by Salah Najm, Conducted by Jamal Isma'il in an unspecified location in Afghanistan, Al-Jazirah Television, June 10, 1999.

30. "Usamah Bin-Ladin, the Destruction of the Base," op. cit.

31. Interview with Osama bin Laden by Hamid Mir; in Jalalabad, Islamabad *Pakistan* in Urdu, March 18, 1997. In the 1996 Declaration of War bin Laden states, "when tens of your solders were killed in minor battles and one American Pilot was dragged in the streets of Mogadishu you left the area carrying disappointment, humiliation, defeat and your dead with you…. It was a pleasure for the heart of every Muslim and a remedy to the chests of believing nations to see you defeated in the three Islamic cities of Beirut, Aden and Mogadishu."

35. Al-Jazirah Television in Arabic November 3, 2001, 1247 GMT.
36. October 21, 2001 bin Laden interview.
37. "It is important to hit the economy, which is the base of [U.S.] military power... If the economy is hit they will become preoccupied." Al-Jazirah Television in Arabic December 27, 2001.
38. October 21, 2001 bin Laden interview.
39. To the author, September 11, 2001.
40. October 21, 2001 bin Laden interview.
41. Abu-Ubayd al-Qurashi: "The Fourth Generation of Wars," *Al-Ansar* WWW-Text in Arabic, January 28, 2002.
42. Al-Jazirah Satellite Channel Television in Arabic November 1, 2001, 1357 GMT. Bin Laden also said "it is a duty on the brothers in Pakistan to make a strong serious move [against the government], for the victory of the religion of Allah, and the victory of the Prophet Muhammad." October 21, 2001 bin Laden interview.
43. Bin Laden stated that... "with the Grace of Allah, the battle has moved inside America. We will strive to keep it going—with Allah's permission—until victory is attained or until we meet Allah through martyrdom." October 21, 2001 bin Laden interview.

Richard H. Shultz and Andreas Vogt, 2002

The Real Intelligence Failure on 9/11 and the Case for a Doctrine of Striking First

*F*ollowing the 9/11 terrorist attack a number of media revelations asserted that it could have been prevented if only the intelligence community (IC) had acted on information in its possession regarding the impending attack. This article explains why and how the intelligence agencies failed on September 11th and assesses the need for and viability of preemptive military options for striking first to combat terrorism. First, it describes how the IC doggedly refused to regard terrorism as war through the 1990s. Second, the authors explain that an alternative perspective challenged this orthodoxy in the early 1990s, arguing that war was changing and entering its 4th generation. Third, based on new information about al Qaeda, the article addresses how al Qaeda organized for and executed its war, by delineating al Qaeda's organizational structure, ideology, linkages with other terrorist groups and supporting states, use of sanctuary, and financial base, and then detailing its targeting, weapons, and warfighting strategy. This assessment reveals how the al Qaeda network bears an unmistakable resemblance to 4th generation asymmetrical warfare and not to the 1990s profile portrayed by the IC. Finally, the authors demonstrate that President Bush has grasped 4th generation warfare by advocating preemptive strikes against terrorists.*

Introduction

Now that the Senate and House committees' bipartisan panel has opened its investigation of the September 11 surprise attack, the performance of the intelligence community (IC) has moved to center stage. The panel seeks to ascertain what the IC knew about the hijackers before September 11, and what it did with that information.

In the weeks preceding the opening session a number of media revelations pointed to the failure of both the FBI and CIA to put "two and two" together. First came the accounts this past May that the Bureau ignored a July 5, 2001, memo written by a Phoenix field agent warning that several Islamic radicals he had under surveillance were enrolled in aeronautical school and could be seeking to infiltrate our civil aviation system. For two weeks a relentless media wondered why the FBI had failed to act on this warning.

Then in early June the spotlight refocused on the CIA. *Newsweek* led the charge. Its June 4, 2002, cover story read "The 9/11 Terrorists the CIA Should Have Caught." The CIA allowed him to enter and leave the United States as he pleased…. [D]uring the year and nine months after the CIA identified them as terrorists, Alhazmi and Almihdhar lived openly in the United States, using their real names, obtaining driver's licenses, opening bank accounts and enrolling in flight schools—until the morning of September 11, when they walked aboard American Airlines Flight 77 and crashed it into the Pentagon.[1]

Astonishingly, says *Newsweek*, the CIA sat on these intelligence nuggets and "did not notify the FBI, which could have covertly tracked them to find out their mission."[2]

While it is imperative to discover whether a handful of intelligence nuggets could have prevented 9/11, we do not believe what occurred that day can be explained simply by missed warnings. The real intelligence failure has to do with how the IC, and the Clinton administration it served, did not understand and incorrectly assessed the transformation that terrorist organizations like al Qaeda were undergoing in the 1990s.

Indeed, significant differences can be seen between how the IC viewed this transformation before 9/11 and what we now know about al Qaeda, its alliances with other terrorist groups, and linkages with states that support it. These dissimilarities point to an astonishing failure of intelligence analysis. In two critical ways, the IC did not abide by the counsel of the ancient Chinese strategist Sun Tzu. Recall what he advised. First, study war: "War is a matter of vital importance to the state…. It is mandatory that it be thoroughly studied." Second, "Know the enemy."

Moreover, as we will contend later, the lessons from 9/11 necessitate a fundamental reevaluation and overhaul of U.S. policy for facing up to and combating terrorism. This is exactly what the White House has undertaken to do through the molding of a new national security doctrine that adds preemptive military options to the president's quiver. The emerging Bush doctrine radically changes a U.S. government mindset and two-decade-old defensive counterterrorism policy from conceding the initiative to the terrorists to seizing the initiative by striking first through offensive military operations. It is long overdue.

Turning a Blind Eye: Assessing Terrorism in the 1990s

Each year since the early 1980s the intelligence community has produced classified estimates of trends and developments in international terrorism. A declassified summary of these analytic products—*Patterns of Global Terrorism*—is released annually by the U.S. State Department's Office of the Coordinator for Counterterrorism. It is an instructive source for deducing how the IC assessed the evolution of the terrorist threat through the 1990s.

Other open source materials can likewise help us assemble an informed impression of the IC's pre-9/11 perspective on terrorism. These include IC testimony at congressional hearings, studies and reports by contractors that support the IC like RAND, and publications by serving intelligence officers such as the former deputy chief of CIA's Counterterrorism Center, Paul Pillar.[3] These sources tell us a great deal about how the intelligence community evaluated international terrorism as the 1990s drew to a close. Here are its principal deductions:

First, terrorism was not war. According to Pillar, terrorism "is not accurately represented by the metaphor of war. Unlike most wars, it has neither a fixed enemy nor the prospect of coming to closure, be it through a win or some other denouement."[4] Even after Usama bin Laden issued a declaration of war against America in 1998 when he called on his followers "to abide by Allah's order by killing Americans... anywhere, anytime, and wherever possible," the U.S. continued to abstain from regarding terrorism as war.

If terrorism was not war, then what was it? The U.S. Government defined it as a crime. And those who carried out such attacks—not the leaders who gave the orders to do so nor states who provided sanctuary and succor—were to be brought before American courts through extradition, rendition, or arrest. The U.S. established specific laws for prosecution and made "bring terrorists to justice for their crimes" the keystone of its policy for combating terrorism.

In terms of trends, the IC reported that terrorist incidents were down—though increasingly lethal and indiscriminate—and that the U.S. was the primary target. These developments were attributed to the growing number of radical religious groups—primarily militant Islamists—that wanted to kill as many Americans as possible. Such movements believed they were carrying out divine mandates that justified deadly and wholesale carnage. The IC also detected changes in how terrorist organizations were structured. In the 1980s they were organized hierarchically with a clear command and control structure.

Those who belonged to these groups were also considered professionals with well-defined political objectives. In the 1990s the IC noted that new terrorist organizations were emerging that were less cohesive, more diffuse, amorphous, and populated by amateurs. While fanatically motivated because of their religious and millenarian aims, the rank-in-file were the antithesis of 1980s' skilled practitioners. Those who carried out the 1993 World Trade Center bombing were illustrative. For the IC this was the gang that couldn't shoot straight.

Organizational devolution, in turn, negated the likelihood of an international terrorist network. Also working against global linkages and cooperative arrangements were political, philosophical, and spiritual differences among groups and states. Pillar put it this way:

> The fault lines are numerous. Ethnic, national, and socioeconomic differences have impeded efforts at unity, as have differing security perspectives. Sectarian differences are also significant—particularly, but not solely, the split between Sunni and Shia... The great ethnic, religious, and national divisions of the Muslim world are turning out to be stronger than all the calls to Islamic solidarity.[5]

Declining state support for terrorist groups likewise undercut the prospects for an international terrorist network. By the end of the 1990s seven states—Cuba, Libya, Iran, Iraq, North Korea, Sudan, and Syria—remained on the IC's state sponsorship list, but their involvement was said to be shrinking because these states had other more vital interests at stake. While Afghanistan was not officially listed as a state sponsor, late 1990s editions of *Patterns of Global Terrorism* expressed concern over the sanctuary that the Taliban provided to al Qaeda (to be discussed in more detail below).

the deadly 1998 East Africa embassy bombings. It still was not war, although the Clinton administration became somewhat more willing to go beyond the law enforcement approach and use limited cruise missile strikes against targets in Afghanistan and Sudan.

A New Form of Warfare

By the time the USS *Cole* was bombed in October 2000 Washington finally knew it was in a deadly struggle with al Qaeda, but it still shunned a military campaign to destroy it and the states that gave it help. In the words of Pillar, such an effort would be hopeless—"If there is a 'war' against terrorism, it is a war that cannot be won… terrorism cannot be defeated—only reduced, attenuated, and to some degree controlled."[6]

Beyond the refusal of the U.S. intelligence community, and for that matter the military establishment, to classify terrorism as warfare because it was not a serious enough danger, other reasons also contributed to this reluctance. Most important, terrorism was not war because it did not resemble modern war as the spooks and soldiers had known it, studied it, and practiced it. Therefore, *ipso facto*, it could not be war.

In the early 1990s an alternative perspective challenged this orthodoxy, arguing that war was undergoing big changes—transformation—and entering its 4th generation. The 1st generation—classical nation-state war—had been perfected by Napoleon. This was followed by industrial age war of attritions based on massive firepower. It reached its apogee in WWI. Maneuver warfare, introduced by the Germans in WWII and refined by the U.S. in the 1980s, marked the 3rd generation.

Among the first to propose that a new form of war was emerging was Martin van Creveld in his 1991 book *The Transformation of War*. Although considered a master military historian and author of two widely read earlier books—*Supplying War* and *Command in War*—most American strategic analysts and military professionals considered his new work too far out. The following forecast was flatly rejected as the musings of an eccentric intellectual:

> The modern paradigm for warfare, in which nation-states wage war for reasons of state, using formal militaries… [is] being eclipsed by a post-modern approach.… As war between states exits through one side of history's revolving door, low intensity conflict among different organizations will enter through the other.… National sovereignties are being undermined by organizations [non-state actors] that refuse to recognize the states' monopoly over armed violence.[7]

In 1991 the U.S. had just pulled off one of the most spectacular conventional land battles in modern military history. In 100 hours it rolled around and over an Iraqi army that many expected to put up a serious fight. In the afterglow of that feat, van Creveld's assertion that 3rd generation conventional maneuver warfare was in the final stages of abolishing itself required too great a leap of faith for most specialists to take seriously. A review of *The Transformation of War* prepared for the Office of the Undersecretary of Defense for Policy charged that van Creveld was not "a balanced strategic thinker," had "scant evidence for his view," and made "numerous unsubstantiated assertions."

Those few who embraced van Creveld's line of reasoning sought to understand how non-state actors, particularly terrorist organizations who were in the midst of their own transformation, were adapting to globalization, network-based organization, and information age technologies. How would these developments affect the terrorists' capacity to execute unconventional attacks—asymmetrical operations in the lexicon of the Pentagon—against the nation-states they targeted? How would terrorist groups cooperate among themselves and with state sponsors in order to operate and fight globally?

During the latter 1990s a picture began to emerge. Its architects included Charles Dunlap, an Air Force colonel who in 1996 published a highly provocative essay, "How We Lost the High-Tech War of 2007: A Warning from the Future."[8] It is a tale of how radical Islamic terrorists go to war with and defeat the U.S. using inconceivably barbaric and gruesome terrorist tactics. Few took Dunlap seriously.

Then there was Ralph Peters, yet another outspoken and controversial colonel. His 1990s essays in *Parameters: U.S. Army War College Quarterly* contended that future enemies would include tyrants, warlords, chieftains, ayatollahs, demagogues, gangsters, drug lords, and other thugs who would wage ferocious non-American-style warfare. No one in the Army had much time for Peters' grim and unlikely suppositions. In 1998 he retired but continued to write and speak.[9]

Another outspoken proponent of 4th generation warfare in the 1990s was Franklin "Chuck" Spinney, an analyst in the Pentagon's Office of Program Analysis and Evaluation. His web site is one stop shopping. Spinney is a brusque critic of the American military establishment he serves. He has charged that the Pentagon has lagged woefully behind the curve in developing the right military response for 4th generation warriors who have and will continue to target the U.S. Heavy firepower, attrition tactics, and long-range, high-altitude bombers are simply not the answers, he asserted.[10]

As the 1990s came to an end, the precepts that these eclectic oddball strategists believed terrorist groups would adopt as a part of what van Creveld had first called a "post-modern transformation of war" were as follows:

- Warfare will be highly irregular, unconventional, and decentralized in approach.
- Asymmetrical operations will be employed to bypass the superior military power of nation-states to attack and exploit political, economic, population, and symbolic targets. In doing so, terrorists groups backed by states will seek to demoralize the psyche of both government and its populace.
- Both the organization and operations of 4th generation warriors will be masked by deception, denial, stealth, and related techniques of intelligence tradecraft. They will wear no uniforms and will infiltrate and blend into the populations of the nation-states they seek to attack.
- Terrorist organizations and operations will be profoundly affected by information age technologies. The development of network-based terrorist organizations connected transnationally through cell phones, fax machines, e-mail, web sites, and the Internet will provide these non-state actors with global reach.

...the states they challenge. Their operations will be ...ited violence, unencumbered by compassion.

- ...ng terrorists and other non-state actors will be difficult for the armies of post-modern states. Terrorist organizations will have few, if any, targets that are vulnerable to modern conventional weapons systems. However, these conventional means are relevant against the state sponsors of terrorism.

Prior to the attack of September 11th the notion that a new kind of war based on these emerging principles would have a dramatic effect on how, when, and where terrorists were able to strike [was widely resisted]. Moreover, that those attacks could take place against targets in the great cities of America was considered nothing more than the unfounded reflections of a handful of strategic iconoclasts. The official U.S. government perspective on the evolution of terrorism in the 1990s was far from simpatico with these propositions.

What We Now Know: Al Qaeda Prepares for War

Since the attack of September 11th we have learned a great deal about al Qaeda. That information is used here to address two fundamental questions—how is al Qaeda organized for war and how does it carry it out? More specifically, we will scrutinize a vast amount of open source materials to: one, delineate al Qaeda's organizational structure, ideology, linkages with other terrorist groups and supporting states, Afghanistan sanctuary, and financial base; and two, detail its targeting, weapons, and warfighting strategy.

This assessment reveals how intimately the al Qaeda network bears an unmistakable resemblance to the template of 4th generation warfare and *not* to the 1990s profile portrayed by the intelligence community. Furthermore, it pinpoints the truest cause of the intelligence failure that took place on September 11th and the need for a new national security doctrine for fighting the war on terrorism.

I. The Al Qaeda Organization

Al Qaeda, as a terrorist group, is a child of 1990s globalization. As with international businesses, globalization had a transforming effect on how al Qaeda organized itself. Unlike hierarchically structured terrorist groups of the 1980s, Usama bin Laden (UBL) established a networked organization of small dispersed units that can deploy nimbly, anywhere, anytime. It is characterized by doctrine, configuration, strategy, and technology in sync with the information age.

During the 1990s, al Qaeda created an elaborate set of connections with several like-minded terrorist groups and terrorist-sponsoring states by, among other things, establishing cells across the globe in as many as 60 countries.

Before deconstructing the structural make-up of bin Laden's handiwork, it is essential to consider his message and how it has been exploited to assemble a multinational alliance among several extremist groups that may operate locally as well as transnationally.

A broad politico-religious appeal

Al Qaeda owes its global infrastructure to its broad appeal. Contrary to intelligence assessments of the 1990s that asserted its followers were exclusively Middle Eastern, Arab, and Sunni, post-9/11 evidence reveals otherwise. Its attraction is much wider, cutting across and linking groups that intelligence professionals like Pillar believed were so different that it "impeded efforts at unity." Recall his claim: "The great ethnic, religious, and national divisions of the Muslim world are turning out to be stronger than all the calls to Islamic solidarity."

Al Qaeda's wide-ranging politico-religious viewpoint attracted both militant Middle Eastern Islamic-oriented groups as well as broader pan-Islamic elements.[11] Al Qaeda exploits conditions that breed extremism. These include failing states characterized by excessive political and economic stagnation, rampant corruption, and brutal repression.

These developments are present in several regimes, including Egypt, Algeria, and Saudi Arabia, and each has experienced the rise of extremist Islamic groups who employ terrorist tactics. Al Qaeda calls for the use of force to overthrow these failed governments and to drive out Western influence. It is with terrorist organizations and individuals from these places that bin Laden has forged his most important alliances.

UBL also exploits other internal conflicts to recruit associates. These include arrangements with groups fighting regimes that are charged with repressing Muslim minorities (e.g., Bosnia, Kosovo, and India), as well as with movements fighting to establish independent states (e.g., Palestinians and Chechens). Finally, al Qaeda exploits the U.S. military presence and foreign policy initiatives in the Middle East, American relations with several of the failed Arab states just identified, and U.S. commitment to Israel.

These ideological themes can be found in UBL communiqués and declarations. Illustrative are the *fatwas*—religious decrees—he has issued. Take for example his 1996, "Declaration of War Against the Americans Occupying the Land of the Two Holy Places." The themes noted above saturate that diatribe. The same is true of his 1998 announcement of the formation of the "World Islamic Front for Jihad against the Jews and Crusaders."[12]

Since 9/11 there have been numerous reports that demonstrate how UBL's message resonates with a wide range of ethnic, religious, and national groups throughout the Muslim world. Al Qaeda uses them in the hope of fostering nothing short of an international Islamic jihad.

A globally networked organization

In a 1997 interview bin Laden described al Qaeda as "a product of globalization and a response to it."[13] It could simply not have operated in the 1980s as it did in the 1990s. Information age technologies and cyber networks allowed al Qaeda to recruit, communicate, establish cells and operatives, and attack targets globally.

Networked organizations share several basic features. First, communication and coordination within them are not formally specified but emerge and change according to the task at hand. Relationships are informal and marked by varying degrees of intensity according to the needs of the organization. Second, linkages to individuals and groups outside the main organization usually complement the internal network. Third, internal and external ties are facilitated by shared norms and values. Thus internal self-managing teams plan and execute operations, while external linkages with a complex association of contributing groups provide a constellation of support activities.[14]

Al Qaeda, which emerged in 1988 and expanded through the 1990s, adopted these features. Its basic internal network is organized vertically with bin Laden, the emir-general, at the top, followed by other al Qaeda leaders.[15] Horizontally, it is allied with numerous other terrorist groups.

Below bin Laden is the *shura majlis* or the consultative council. Four committees report to it. A military committee recruits fighters, runs training camps, and launches terrorist operations. It also oversees other clandestine functions including a special office for procuring, forging or altering identity documents such as passports and visas. A finance committee accrues the resources necessary to sustain al Qaeda. Justifying its actions by issuing rulings on *shari'a* law is the responsibility of the religious/legal committee. Finally, the media committee disseminates information in support of al Qaeda's political and military activities.

The al Qaeda leadership oversees a loosely tied network of cells that cannot be easily traced back to it. Each operates autonomously with its members not knowing the identity of other cells. Thus if one cell is compromised it will not betray others. The pattern that has emerged is of a web of cells around the world that provide the intelligence and manpower to execute terrorist attacks against the U.S. and other targets.

Due to its broad politico-religious dogma, al Qaeda has the capacity to infiltrate and operate out of Muslim communities that exist across the globe. It has established clandestine cells from New Zealand to India to the United States. In the Middle East, it receives the support of Islamic philanthropists and foundations to underwrite its organizational expansion.

Compartmentalization, secrecy, and deception differentiate al Qaeda from other globally networked organizations. These tools of intelligence tradecraft are drawn on to secure its network at all levels, including… cyberspace. Al Qaeda training manuals stress the importance of deception and denial methods. Ahmed Ressam, the al Qaeda operative who failed to bomb Los Angeles International Airport at the end of 1999, highlighted at his trial the extent to which these methods were stressed during training sessions at camps in Afghanistan.[16] It is unknown how al Qaeda became so adept at these professional spy procedures. Perhaps a state's intelligence service provided the instruction? If so, the likely suspects would include Iraq (which learned it from the KGB) or Iran.

To prepare the groundwork for the 1998 East Africa embassy bombings, several al Qaeda operatives were deployed as sleeper agents. For several years they burrowed into Kenyan and Tanzanian society. Then in August 1998 they struck. Western intelligence agencies now know there are other sleeper cells in Europe and North America waiting to be activated.[17]

The Mohammad Atta cells that carried out the attacks on the World Trade Center and Pentagon illustrate how al Qaeda operates. Using public data, Valdis Krebs has mapped a portion of that network centered on the 19 dead hijackers. His diagram discloses how compartmented and dispersed hijackers on the same team were from each other. Cell members were connected through the judicious use of transitory shortcuts in the network. Meetings were held to link up distant parts of the Atta cells to coordinate tasks and report progress.

After coordination was accomplished, the crossties went dormant until the need for their synchronization arose again.[18]

The hijack cells were integrated and synchronized for the operation by the Egyptian-born Atta. He came to al Qaeda through Egyptian Islamic Jihad, the group led by Ayman al-Zawahri, bin Laden's top lieutenant. Additionally, Khaled al-Midhar and Nawaq al-Hamzi, two other hijackers, were filmed at a January 2000 meeting in Kuala Lumpur with known al Qaeda operatives. Finally, several of the hijackers were trained at al Qaeda camps in Afghanistan.[19]

Within a week of the attacks, U.S. authorities concluded that the planning of the operation began as early as 1999, when some of the suspected 19 hijackers began to take flight training lessons in the U.S.[20] Furthermore, the 9/11 hijackers did not work alone. Other al Qaeda members and affiliates provided necessary skills and knowledge, and also served as conduits for transferring money.

The 9/11 hijackers were also linked to an underground network of Islamic militants in Europe that had grown over several years around al Qaeda.[21] Starting in 2000, European intelligence agencies began uncovering al Qaeda cells in Germany, Italy, France, the U.K., and Spain who were planning attacks on American targets. This was learned as a result of the arrest by United Arab Emirates police of Djamel Beghal, a French-Algerian Islamist, transiting through Dubai to France. While in French custody, Beghal confessed that he had received instructions from bin Laden's chief of operations, Abu Zubayda, to bomb U.S. targets in Europe.[22]

Training camps and sanctuary in Afghanistan

Landlocked Afghanistan provided al Qaeda with a unique political, security, and geographic shield. In return, al Qaeda forces fought alongside the Taliban, providing it with an important military capability, while bin Laden provided Taliban leaders with millions of dollars.

Hundreds of documents found in Afghanistan reveal an al Qaeda presence of several thousand. It established offices, communications facilities, guesthouses, training centers, and barracks. Training manuals, students' notebooks, ledgers, military records, communications and code books, and IBM desktop computers shed considerable light on al Qaeda's methods, preoccupations, and ambitions. Extensive interviews with Kabul residents present a picture of al Qaeda as a law unto itself.

At the same time, the evidence demonstrates that there was constant liaison between al Qaeda and the Taliban Ministries of Defense, Interior, and Suppression of Vice and Propagation of Virtue. "U.S. intelligence estimates suggest that between 1996 and 2001 some U.S. $100 million was given to the Taliban, effectively ensuring al Qaeda's organizational autonomy within Afghanistan and considerable influence within key ministries."[23]

Al Qaeda training camps, many of them dispersed in the rugged Afghan terrain in Afghanistan, played a vital role in the organization. The Meivand camp in the Rod Para Mountains is illustrative. Before it was destroyed, it could support the training of up to 700 fighters at any given time. Above ground, the camp consisted of more than 50 buildings, including a hospital. Below ground, a large cave complex, equipped with running water and electricity, was used for storage, housing, and security.[24]

This al Qaeda infrastructure also served the organization's global ambitions by drawing tens of thousands of radical Islamic militants to Afghanistan. While in the camps these individuals were assessed, recruited, and deployed for global operations. Others were assigned to the al Qaeda-led Arab and international brigades that fought alongside Taliban forces against the Northern Alliance. How many foreign Islamic militants received training in al Qaeda's camps in Afghanistan since the 1980s? Estimates range between 50,000 and as many as 100,000.

Documents unearthed in early January 2002 in the rubble of the Meivand camp portray an efficient operation that boasted to new terrorist recruits of its involvement in the 9/11 attacks. One of the instructors spoke about the planning of that attack, claiming that the airplanes that crashed in New York and Washington were part of a larger plan to hijack 25 airliners around the world.[25]

Linkages with other terrorist organizations

Al Qaeda has established both formal and informal affiliations—or linkages—with several Middle Eastern and Asian radical Islamist groups that employ terrorism against their own governments. For example, many of its members were drawn from two Egyptian organizations—the Islamic Group and Islamic Jihad. Two Algerian factions, the Armed Islamic Group and the Salafist Group for Preaching and Combat, likewise have strong ties with al Qaeda. In Yemen, where his family originated, bin Laden has formed bonds with Jaish Aden Abin al Islami. Finally, al Qaeda has allied a horde of smaller radical Islamist entities in northern Iraq, Saudi Arabia, Tunisia, Libya, Morocco, and elsewhere.[26]

In Asia, al Qaeda affiliates include three Islamist factions fighting in Kashmir, and the Moro Islamic Liberation Front and the Abu Sayaaf Group in the Philippines. With respect to the latter, evidence presented at the trial of terrorists involved in the first World Trade Center bombing (1993) show that these ties go back to the early 1990s.[27]

The federal trial in New York of those accused of plotting the 1998 bombings of the U.S. embassies in Kenya and Tanzania also revealed evidence of how al Qaeda established linkages with several radical Islamist groups, including the Egyptian Islamic Jihad and the Armed Islamic Group of Algeria. Court documents also describe the intimate relationship between al Qaeda and the Taliban.[28]

Perhaps the most interesting and controversial arrangement established by UBL was the one with Hizballah and its Iran patron. Recall that during the latter 1990s the U.S. intelligence community assumed that Sunni and Shia terrorist groups could never cooperate because of their sharply divergent interpretations of Islam. We now know that this supposition was flawed.

In 1995 and again in 1996, al Qaeda operatives are reported to have contacted Iran's Ministry of Intelligence and Security (MOIS) proposing to join forces against America.[29] "In June 1996, MOIS hosted a meeting of terrorist leaders in Tehran. Among those present were Imad Mugniyah, Hizballah's master terrorist planner, whose operations against the U.S. go back to the 1983 bombing of the Marine Corps barracks in Beirut, and senior aides to bin Laden. Subsequently, high-ranking al Qaeda officials met with Mugniyah on several occasions."[30]

During the trial of al Qaeda operatives, it was reported that a representative of bin Laden met with an official of the Iranian government prior to the bombings of the U.S. embassies in East Africa in order to establish an anti-U.S. alliance.[31] Ali Mohamed, who was convicted of conspiracy in those bombings, testified: "I arranged security for a meeting in the Sudan between Mughniyah, Hizballah's chief, and bin Laden... Hizballah provided explosives training for al Qaeda and al-Jihad," he added.[32]

According to the Director of Central Intelligence, George Tenet, "Iran continues to provide support—including arms transfers—to Palestinian rejectionist groups and Hizballah. Tehran has also failed to move decisively against al Qaeda members who have relocated to Iran from Afghanistan."[33]

Contradicting the intelligence community mantra of the 1990s—Sunni and Shia terrorist groups never cooperate—Tenet added: "while al Qaeda represents a broad-based Sunni worldwide extremist network, it would be a mistake to dismiss possible connections to either other groups or state sponsors—either Sunni or Shia. There is a convergence of common interest in hurting the U.S., its allies, and interests that make traditional thinking in this regard unacceptable."[34]

Evidently, collaboration against hated enemies takes precedence over denominational differences, as can be seen in the al Qaeda-Hizballah-Iran axis. Finally, related to the matter of Sunni-Shia solidarity is the widely reported linkage between Shia Iran and Hizballah and Sunni Palestinian groups to include Hamas and Islamic Jihad, as well as the secular Palestinian Authority.[35]

State support

Recall that during the 1990s the U.S. intelligence community reported that state support for terrorist groups, to include al Qaeda, was on the wane. This contention can be found in issue after issue of *Patterns of Global Terrorism* released by the State Department. As seen above, Afghanistan clearly contradicted that deduction. Al Qaeda had unprecedented and increasing access and support from the Taliban regime.

It likewise had a close association with Sudan, particularly in the first half of the 1990s, establishing a working relationship with the government in Khartoum. However, unlike the Taliban, intense diplomatic efforts on the part of the U.S. pressured the Sudanese to compel bin Laden to move his organization to Afghanistan. Nevertheless, the connection between Khartoum and bin Laden remained active up to 9/11.

Al Qaeda also maintained liaison with elements in the government of Yemen, as well as among different tribes, through the 1990s. And it was there that one of al Qaeda's most spectacular operations, the suicide attack on the USS *Cole*, took place in 2000.

In Pakistan, al Qaeda had strong ties with the notorious Inter-Service Intelligence Agency (ISI) since the 1980s. These linkages go back to the Soviet-Afghan War in which ISI was intimately involved with Mujaheddin factions and the non-Afghan Islamic militants. In the 1990s an ISI-al Qaeda-Taliban axis emerged that is believed to still exist—even after *Operation Enduring Freedom* started.[36] There was also, as was previously noted, a connection between al Qaeda and the regime in Iran. The extent of that linkage remains murky, especially in the aftermath of the September 11th attacks. Finally, there has been considerable speculation about ties between al Qaeda and Iraq. This issue has received a great deal of scrutiny by the Bush Administration since 9/11. Here is what we know.

Attention first focused on an April 2000 meeting in Prague between Mohammad Atta and Ahmed Khalil Ibrahim Samir al Ani, a senior Iraqi intelligence operative working under cover as a diplomat. The Czech government, which apparently videotaped the meeting, provided evidence to Washington confirming this fact and has never wavered on the matter.[37] However, what was discussed, if Prague knows, has not been revealed publicly.

This was followed by the revelations of various Iraqi defectors such as Sabah Khodada, a former army officer who served at a terrorist training camp run by the Mukhabarat, Saddam's intelligence service. According to Khodada, foreign personnel were trained in "assassinations, kidnapping, hijacking of airplanes, hijacking of buses, hijacking of trains and other kinds of operations related to terrorism." He also noted that the camp included a Boeing 707. Aspiring hijackers were "trained on how to get weapons inside the plane," and how to adapt to "situations where security will not allow you to get weapons into the plane."[38]

Next came the disclosure in *The New Yorker* (March 2002) about Ansar al-Islam, a radical Islamist group in Kurdish northern Iraq who has connections both to al Qaeda and Iraq's Mukhabarat.[39]

Finally, the civil/class action lawsuit filed on behalf of those seeking damages arising out of the September 11, 2001, terrorist attacks contains further details of Iraq-al Qaeda collaboration. It dates that linkage "to the early 1990s" when, following "the Gulf War, Iraqi agents traveled to the Sudan" to meet with bin Laden operatives. Over the next five years, "from 1991 to 1996," this led to "extensive interaction between al Qaeda and Iraq's intelligence officers." Then, in 1998, "two of bin Laden's senior military commanders met in Baghdad with Qusay Hussein, chief of Iraqi intelligence and son of Saddam." That meeting further cemented the relationship with "Iraq reportedly agreeing to supply al Qaeda with training, intelligence, weapons, and other support."[40]

The money trail

Bin Laden set up an elaborate financial network to ensure the financial well-being of al Qaeda and to support its operational and logistical requirements. Through this, UBL has invested in the future. For example, he has established an unknown number of "sleeper" cells awaiting orders to launch future attacks.[41]

The financial arm of al Qaeda appears to operate like a foundation. It has "high-ranking members selecting suitable applicants, such as a newly-established al Qaeda cell or a like-minded radical Islamist group, and providing financial assistance for terrorist activities."[42]

However, tracking the money is easier said than done. According to recent reports, al Qaeda's financial network experienced a "paradigm shift" well before 9/11. Knowledgeable of the vulnerability of its European bank accounts, al Qaeda apparently shifted its money into commodities more difficult to trace, like gold, diamonds, tanzanite, and sapphires.[43]

In addition to bin Laden's personal fortune, al Qaeda has turned to both legal and illegal activities to raise funds to underwrite its activities during the last decade.[44]

The former includes small business ventures, such as farms and fisheries, as well as larger construction, electronic appliances, and investment firms.

For example, Darkazanli, a Hamburg-based Import-Export Company, was the first private business to have its assets frozen due to suspected links with the 9/11 attacks. An executive order published in September 2001 describes it as a "front group" for al Qaeda and its CEO, Syrian-born Mamoun Darkazanli, as one of bin Laden's main financial lieutenants.[45] As Steven Emerson, an internationally recognized expert on terrorism and the militant Islamic infrastructure in the U.S., states: "Darkazanli offers a strategic paradigm for the manner in which a small, legitimate business with convenient European locations and inconspicuous business transactions, can be misused to launder money, purchase sensitive technical equipment, and facilitate the establishment—both in Europe and elsewhere—of business 'front' groups for al Qaeda."[46] Also worth noticing is the fact that the company's specialty in electronics was an ideal cover for procuring technical equipment for al Qaeda.

Other al Qaeda front companies started to emerge in the early 1990s. These included a Khartoum-based holding company, as well as construction, agriculture, investment, leather, and transportation companies. These business ventures transferred funds to al Qaeda operatives that carried out the East Africa U.S. embassy bombings.[47]

Funding—both wittingly and unwittingly—also comes from dozens of Islamic charities and mosques. A case in point is the Afghanistan-based Al-Wafa Humanitarian Organization. It is believed to have purchased equipment and weapons for al Qaeda. In 1999 the United Nations, under Resolution 1267, authorized the publication of a list of "persons and entities connected with Usama bin Laden." Al-Wafa was one of three charities included. The other two were the Al Rashid Trust and Makhtab Al-Khidamat/Al Kifah.[48]

Another charity that has come under scrutiny is the International Islamic Relief Organization (IIRO). It purportedly provided funds to al Qaeda's affiliate in the Philippines, Abu Sayyaf.[49] Established in 1978, the IIRO is headquartered in Saudi Arabia and has branches around the world. Canada's Security and Intelligence Service found that an IIRO official working there was assisting al Qaeda and UBL.[50]

Islamic charities linked to bin Laden are also located in the United States. Take the Chicago-based Benevolence International Foundation (BIF). The U.S. recently released evidence revealing that its Syrian-born executive-director, Enaam M. Arnaout, is a close associate and fundraiser for bin Laden. Those ties stretch back more than a decade and include assistance to al Qaeda operatives who were attempting to acquire chemical and nuclear weapons. The evidence is based on documents seized in the group's offices in Chicago and Bosnia and on a series of witnesses, including former al Qaeda members currently in U.S. custody.[51]

Drug money also found its way into al Qaeda coffers through the distribution of opium. Along with the Taliban, it produced thousands of metric tons of opium during the latter 1990s in a majority of the 31 Afghan provinces. It was then smuggled through neighboring Central Asian states.[52]

Al Qaeda also received cash from the well-heeled. Western intelligence agencies believe Arab businessmen paid bin Laden extortion money to avoid attacks on their interests throughout the Middle East.[53] Other wealthy individuals in various states such as Saudi Arabia gave willingly because they felt affinity and solidarity with the cause of UBL. These donors are believed to give millions of dollars every year.[54]

Finally, al Qaeda appears to have laundered its legal and illegal funds through long-established centers in the Middle East, Asia, Europe, and elsewhere. Global financial centers, including Frankfurt, London, and New York, have frozen more than $100 million in assets tied to al Qaeda, and investigations are currently under way in Malta, Italy, Panama, Singapore, South Africa, and elsewhere to determine whether al Qaeda laundered illicit capital through their financial institutions.[55]

II. Al Qaeda Targeting, Weapons, and Strategy

Since 9/11 we have learned a great deal about how al Qaeda plans and executes terrorist actions. This information has brought out in the open the organization's operational features and shed light on its intentions.

Selecting targets

In 1999 the Jordanian police arrested Khalil Deek in connection with a plot to bomb Amman's main airport on the eve of the millennium. In his possession they discovered a remarkable document that subsequently came to be referred to by Western intelligence agencies as the *Encyclopedia of Jihad*.[56] Consisting of eleven volumes and approximately 7,000 pages, it is considered a key manual for instructing al Qaeda operatives.

The manual paid particularly close attention to the selection of targets to assail and obliterate. They were categorized as follows. First, there were *symbolic targets* such as the Statue of Liberty in New York or the Eiffel Tower in Paris. In this case, the objective was not to kill large numbers, but to deliver a devastating psychological blow by demolishing a cultural icon. Next were *infrastructure targets*, including nuclear power stations, skyscrapers, ports, and train stations. While also having symbolic meaning, their destruction was intended to kill as many as possible. Finally, there were *human targets*—places where large numbers of people congregate or influential public figures. In the latter two cases the objective was to kill the unsuspecting and innocent.

In selecting targets al Qaeda surfed the Internet, collecting vital information posted on U.S. government websites. For example, terrorism vulnerability studies produced by the *U.S. General Accounting Office* were stored on the hard drive of one of al Qaeda's computers found in Afghanistan. These websites provided a rich menu of poorly secured targets. It is evident from this and other examples that al Qaeda was well aware of how official reports and assessments could be of great assistance in planning attacks on the United States. There is also evidence that it compiled information on U.S. nuclear power plants. All of these facts and figures were only a click away on the World Wide Web.

The debriefing of Abu Zubaydah provided additional confirmation that al Qaeda targetters were concentrating on bringing the group's war inside the borders of the United States. CIA Director Tenet said the same thing to the Senate Select Committee on Intelligence in February: "We know that terrorists have considered attacks in the U.S. against high-profile government or private facilities, famous landmarks, and U.S. infrastructure nodes such as airports, bridges, harbors, and dams. Al Qaeda also planned to strike against U.S. interests in Europe, the Middle East, Africa and Southeast Asia." He added that diplomatic and military facilities "are high-risk targets."[57]

Weapons

Al Qaeda weaponry range from standard issue small arms used by terrorists for decades, to plans for either acquiring or producing weapons of mass destruction. This was spelled out in the *Encyclopedia of Jihad*. It offered guidance on how to rig up a door lock to explode when the handle is turned, how to inject frozen food with biochemical agents to create mass panic, as well as how to bring down a plane with a missile. The latter drew on years of guerrilla fighting against the Soviets in the 1980s.

Among the most chilling pages of the manual were those that dealt with bioterrorism that spell out how to disperse lethal organisms and poisons ranging from botulism and viral infections to ricin and anthrax. It also called for maximizing public panic by poisoning medicine, hence jeopardizing treatment of affected individuals.

Another chapter of the *Encyclopedia of Jihad* concentrated on sabotage techniques. For example, one section illustrated how to turn cameras into a bomb. Ahmed Shah Masood, the leader of the Northern Alliance, the resistance organization fighting the Taliban, was assassinated in this way two days before the 9/11 attacks. In addition to analyzing how C4 and Semtex explosives can be used, the encyclopedia contains instructions on the ingredients needed to make bombs from innocuous substances bought in places like supermarkets and hardware stores.[58]

Since the Cold War ended, the acquisition of weapons of mass destruction (WMD) by non-state actors has received considerable attention. During a few distressing weeks last fall U.S. officials believed that this worst-case scenario was about to come true. In October 2001 intelligence warned that terrorists had obtained a 10-kiloton nuclear weapon from the Russian arsenal and planned to detonate it in New York City. The warning turned out to be a false alarm, but because nuclear weapons proliferation experts have suspected that several portable nuclear devices might be missing from the Russian stockpile since the mid-1990s, it was believable.[59]

Following the 9/11 attacks Taliban and al Qaeda access to Pakistan's nuclear arsenal and expertise also became a major worry. Intense media speculation ensued regarding the likelihood that Pakistani nuclear experts were assisting al Qaeda or, worse, that Pakistan's existing nuclear arsenal might fall into their hands.[60]

Documents found in Afghanistan make clear that bin Laden has made frequent attempts to buy nuclear weapons and to acquire the means to produce chemical and biological ones. But, thus far, U.S. forces in Afghanistan have uncovered none. What they did find were several primitive labs and a plethora of blueprints. The extent of al Qaeda's WMD efforts remains a mystery, and until they are discovered, WMD will loom large as a potential threat of catastrophic magnitude.

Information technology

Networked organizations cannot function without information age technology. At the center of al Qaeda's transformation into a post-modern terrorist organization was the Internet and global cellular communications. These cutting edge tools linked its globally deployed cells, nodes, and constituent groups. Through cyberspace bin Laden and his lieutenants planned, coordinated, and executed operations.

By using the Internet, al Qaeda was able to accelerate mobilization and amplify communication between members. As a result, the organization's flexibility was enhanced as tactics could be adjusted more routinely. Moreover, individuals or groups with common goals or agendas were able to form subgroups or cells, meet at a target location, conduct terrorist operations, and then promptly terminate their relationships and re-deploy.

The al Qaeda network's *modus operandi* functioned through websites, e-mail, and cellular communications. A window into this system was opened with the December 1999 arrest of fifteen terrorists in Jordan who intended to carry out attacks against U.S. and Israeli targets during the millennium celebrations. Found in their "safe house"—in addition to bomb-making materials, automatic weapons, and radio-controlled detonators—were computers, zip disks, and cell phones. From the hard drives of those laptops intelligence analysts extracted information about the intended operations, as well as files on bomb making and terrorist training camps in Afghanistan.[61]

Bin Laden's operatives used CD-ROM disks to store and disseminate information on recruiting, bomb making, weapons, and other operational particulars. The *Encyclopedia of Jihad* found in Jordan was on a CD-ROM. This was once considered the extent of al Qaeda's operational knowledge. However, a new volume discovered in Afghanistan, also on a CD-ROM, contained more precise formulas for chemical and biological weapons that can be made from ingredients readily available to the public. In a chapter called the "Science of Explosives," chemical formulas for biological weapons are laid out step-by-step.

Egyptian computer experts directed al Qaeda's communications system. They established a network that used e-mail, the web, and electronic bulletin boards to maximize information exchange between members. However, heading that effort was a Libyan, Abu Anas al-Liby. A member of al Qaeda for over a decade, his technical knowhow meant that he quickly became bin Laden's computer expert. He also played a key role in planning the bombing of the embassies in Nairobi and Dar-es-Salaam by traveling to Kenya to take surveillance pictures.

According to reporters who visited bin Laden's headquarters in the mountains of Afghanistan, he "uses satellite phone terminals to coordinate the activities of the group's dispersed operatives and has even devised countermeasures to ensure his safety while using such communication systems."[62] And even though the overthrow of the Taliban forced him to flee his once secure sanctuary, recent reports reveal he is still attempting to use the Internet. Signs of al Qaeda efforts to communicate and re-group online have also been detected.

Warfighting strategy and operations

The *Encyclopedia of Jihad* as well as other training documents found in Afghanistan point to the fact that al Qaeda has given considerable attention to the issues of warfighting strategy and operations. Several volumes in the *Encyclopedia* focused on these topics. They covered the principals of warfare, including battle organization, reconnaissance, infiltration, and ambushes. Examples of these operations are drawn from the Afghan War against the Soviets. Other topics included: how to spy; military intelligence; communications; secret observation; sabotage; and assassination. Al Qaeda also studied the strategy and operational approaches of the United States. Copies of various U.S. military manuals and documents were found in Afghan safe houses.[63]

In terms of doctrine, al Qaeda has grasped the principles of 4th generation warfare. It takes a nonlinear approach to the battlespace, and plans asymmetrical and unconventional attacks by dispersed small units. The war being waged by al Qaeda began with attempts to kill American troops in Yemen in 1992. This was followed by periodic major operations in 1993, 1995, 1996, 1998, and 2000. Since, there have been a number of other smaller attacks in different locations. Other operations have been prevented by good intelligence.

Bin Laden and his al Qaeda network seem "to have developed a swarm-like doctrine that features a campaign of episodic attacks by various nodes of his network—at locations sprawled across global time and space where he has advantages for seizing the initiative, stealthily."[64] Through this strategy they successfully have conducted 4th generation warfare against America.

It's War

On September 11th America suffered its second Pearl Harbor. But the attack that day was an even greater strategic surprise than the one on December 7, 1941. The strikes against the World Trade Center and Pentagon were, quite literally, bolts out of the blue. The U.S. intelligence community was caught fully off guard.

Without a doubt, September 11th was a colossal intelligence failure. However, the reasons for that debacle cannot be attributed just to a handful of what appear, with hindsight, to have been missed warnings. For example, much has been made of two messages intercepted by the National Security Agency on September 10th but not translated until September 12th. "The match is about to begin," said one, while the other declared, "Tomorrow is zero hour." What match? Zero hour for what and where? These telephone comments are too cryptic to be actionable intelligence.

Nor can 9/11 be attributed to a failure to take seriously threat scenarios spun out in government reports. Much has also been made of a 1999 Congressional Research Service forecast that "Suicide bomber(s) belonging to al Qaeda's Martyrdom Battalion could crashland an aircraft packed with high explosives into the Pentagon, the Central Intelligence Agency, or the White House." But the authors also speculated that the Liberation Tigers of Tamil Ealam could "become angered by President Clinton" and "react by dispatching a Tamil 'belt-bomb girl' to detonate a powerful semtex bomb after approaching the President in a crowd with a garland of flowers."[65]

These missed signals, correct or not, are emblematic of a deeper impediment. The real intelligence failure on September 11th has to do with a near decade-long reluctance by the intelligence community to come to terms with the fact that international terrorists—al Qaeda above all—were undergoing a systematic transformation in terms of how they organize, deploy, and fight.

Al Qaeda grasped the implications and opportunities globalization offered. However, to benefit from it necessitated the creation of a network-based terrorist organization that exploited the tools of the information age. And to secure its new global apparatus, al Qaeda employed the principles and methods of deception and denial typically found in intelligence tradecraft. In effect, UBL inspired a "revolution in terrorist affairs."

With this apparatus al Qaeda was ready for war. Beginning in 1996 it issued edicts to that effect. Its intentions were made crystal clear on February 22, 1998, when bin Laden endorsed a *fatwa* imploring his minions to "kill Americans—including civilians—anywhere in the world." Major terrorist operations followed and plenty of Americans fell.

But the U.S. intelligence community did not grasp the implications of al Qaeda's declarations and operations. It was in a war it did not understand or perhaps failed to recognize was even taking place. The same was true of the Clinton administration. Of course, there were exceptions like Richard Clark, the head of the National Security Council's Counterterrorism Strategy Group. He advocated a much more aggressive policy, to include the use of military force, against al Qaeda. But the Pentagon and State Department wanted nothing to do with such risky military options and fought bureaucratically to block them.

Even as al Qaeda upped the ante through bombings in East Africa, these actions were still not considered acts of war by the U.S. military services and intelligence agencies. International terrorism was a law enforcement matter; a crime to be solved and prosecuted. So ensconced was this mind-set that not even secret presidential instructions to use lethal means to kill bin Laden and his top al Qaeda lieutenants could foster new courses of action. The bureaucracy would not budge.

To be sure, operations were discussed *ad nauseam* and plans to attack frequently drawn up. But in the end, with the exception of the ineffectual August 20, 1998, cruise missile strikes against Afghanistan and Sudan, lethal measures were always nixed in the interagency process. Political, legal, and operational arguments advanced by the Pentagon, State Department, and CIA always persuaded risk adverse senior decision-makers, including the president, not to act forcefully.

Why? The answer has to do with the perceptions and impressions or, more accurately, misperceptions and misimpressions, that shaped and influenced policy choices. Over the 1990s these fostered the conviction that terrorism was neither a level-one national security challenge nor a form of warfare. In fact, those who saw it as such were demeaned as naive and extreme. There was no political will to use force aggressively and offensively because such actions were deemed unnecessary. The end result was September 11th.

The Bush Doctrine: Going on the Offensive

Over the last nine months, President Bush has chartered a new course for combating terrorism. To begin with, in all of his major speeches, he has labeled the attacks on the World Trade Center and Pentagon "an act of war" and told the American people "our nation is at war." Moreover, that war "must and will be waged on our watch."

In his remarks to the 2002 graduating class at West Point, the president explained that the September 11th horror illustrates a "new kind of war fought by a new kind of enemy."[66] Secretary of Defense Donald Rumsfeld has sounded the same warning in numerous public addresses and comments beginning in late September 2001 when he observed, "this war will be a war like none other our nation has faced... Our opponent is a global network of terrorist organizations and their state sponsors.... Even the vocabulary of this war will be different."[67]

Bush and Rumsfeld grasped 4th generation warfare. The following observations are elucidated in speech after speech. The enemy is a non-state actor—terrorist groups—whose capacity to operate has been greatly enhanced by globalization, organizational networking, and information-based technology. They are aided and abetted by states and also receive assistance from public and private organizations and individuals. Sanctuary provided by states allows terrorists like al Qaeda to secure their organizational and operational capabilities. They employ stealth and deception to attack in unconventional and asymmetrical ways. Operations are directed against political, cultural, and population targets with the goal of killing as many as possible.

Not everyone in the Bush administration sees it this way, a fact that was apparent in the internal debate over whether and how to fight in Afghanistan. It was likewise reflected in the initial limited and cautious approach devised by the senior military leadership and endorsed by the State Department. By late October 2001, the ineffectiveness of that strategy was apparent as the Taliban and al Qaeda dug in for the long haul. It took Rumsfeld and the civilian leadership in the Pentagon to devise a winning formula, and the president to put it in motion. It paid off. In December the Taliban fell and al Qaeda was on the run. Victory came by going on the offensive.

As one Taliban stronghold after another collapsed, Washington fell into another internal debate, this time over phase two of the war on terrorism. On the table was Iraq. A long time supporter of terrorism, it also is maniacal in its efforts to build nuclear, chemical, and biological weapons. Several officials in the Bush administration fear that Saddam Hussein not only wants these weapons of mass destruction for himself, but would also supply them to terrorists to use against the U.S., his primary enemy. Other appointees saw it differently.

Essentially, two camps fought it out. One, headed by Secretary of State Colin Powell and his senior associates, argued for a revised version of the Clinton policy of containment, this time through smart sanctions. Most of the economic controls would be lifted to help the Iraqi people, while Saddam's military would be kept in check. To work, serious diplomatic efforts were needed to shut down illegal trade that passed through Jordan, Turkey, Iran, and the Gulf Cooperation Council states. And WMD inspections had to be resuscitated.

In the Pentagon, much to the chagrin of the senior military chiefs who sided with Powell, Rumsfeld and his deputy, Paul Wolfowitz, wanted Saddam removed from power—regime change—through the use of military force. Vice President Cheney concurred. Containment was a nonstarter. It had not worked for Clinton and would not work for Bush. Moreover, the danger and unpredictability of a nuclear-armed Saddam was just too terrible a peril to allow to come to fruition. By February the interagency clash was over. The policy course for the second phase of the war was regime change. However, no sooner had this debate ended before another interagency squabble started over how to implement regime change.

These interagency mêlées exposed the need for an overarching strategic design—a *Bush doctrine*—for planning and executing the war on terrorism. Throughout the Cold War presidents attached their names to major foreign policy and national security initiatives. While there were differences among them, all of these doctrines were aligned with a security framework anchored by the defensive concepts of deterrence and containment.

In his West Point speech President Bush laid the foundation for a new national security doctrine, one that included offensive action. To fight the war on terrorism, he declared, the defensive constructs of deterrence and containment, while still necessary, were by no means sufficient for the new form of warfare confronting the United States:

> [N]ew threats also require new thinking. Deterrence—the promise of massive retaliation against nations—means nothing against shadowy terrorist networks with no nation or citizens to defend. Containment is not possible when unbalanced dictators with weapons of mass destruction can deliver those weapons on missiles or secretly provide them to terrorist allies. We cannot defend America and our friends by hoping for the best. We cannot put our faith in the word of tyrants, who solemnly sign non-proliferation treaties, and then systemically break them. If we wait for threats to fully materialize, we will have waited too long.[68]

Then the President transformed America's national security paradigm. He told the cadets that they will be part of a military that "must be ready to strike at a moment's notice in any dark corner of the world through *preemptive action* when necessary." [Emphasis added]

In light of the victory in Afghanistan and the fact that the ways of waging war had dramatically changed, adding preemption to America's quiver made strategic sense. Global terrorist networks and tyrannical regimes that support them cannot be relied upon to follow the same calculus that deterred or contained past adversaries. The "new war" demanded new means for fighting it. By declaring that "the war on terrorism will not be won on the defensive," the president reinterpreted the meaning of self-defense. He rejected armed attack as the basis or requirement for using force. Out of necessity, force must be used to preempt terrorists and those states that harbor and provide them with the means of war and terror.

Morally, the inclusion of preemptive operations in the concept of self-defense—or defensive intervention—is anchored in the *just war doctrine*. That doctrine places great importance on the state as the natural institution essential for man's security and development. So strong is the presumption in favor of self-defense that the *just war doctrine* does not confine itself exclusively to defensive measures and the legacy of the non-intervention rule grounded in the peace of Westphalia. Offensive operations are permitted to protect vital rights and interests unjustly threatened, not only injured by other states but also by non-state actors such as terrorist groups.

Preemption and defensive intervention radically changes a U.S. government mindset and a two-decade-old counterterrorism policy from conceding the initiative to seizing it through the use of offensive military options. In doing so, the president has triggered an intense debate inside the U.S. government and among national security specialists. Many find the very notion of preemption profoundly troubling, even as al Qaeda and its state supporters plot new ways to attack America.

"Striking first" likewise worries American opinion leaders. Witness the apprehension expressed by the editorial staff of *The New York Times*. "We are uncomfortable with the idea of Mr. Bush's giving himself carte blanche to make any military intervention he thinks necessary."[69]

However, it also is the case that bin Laden has gone into hiding and Saddam sleeps in different locations each night because they both feel the same uneasiness, distress, and fear that cause angst for Washington bureaucrats and media glitterati. Implementing the Bush doctrine will not only turn bin Laden's and Saddam's trepidations into reality but more important, should put the U.S. on a course to win the war on terrorism by ridding the world of al Qaeda, the Iraqi regime, and others who remain a part of this network of terror.

Richard H. Shultz is a professor of international politics and the director of the International Security Studies Program (ISSP) at the Fletcher School of Law and Diplomacy. He is coeditor and author of *Security Studies for the 21st Century* (1997), as well as the author of numerous other publications. He is currently writing a book on military-media relations.

Andreas Vogt is the program and research coordinator of the Fletcher School of Law and Diplomacy's International Security Studies Program (ISSP) while pursuing his Ph.D. in international relations as an H. B. Earhart Fellow. He also lectures at Tufts University and organizes and participates in international security-related conferences and simulations. He has served with NATO and with UN peacekeeping forces.

Notes

1. Michael Isikoff and Daniel Klaidman, "The 9/11 Terrorists the CIA Should Have Caught," *Newsweek* (4 June 2002); available from http://www.i-dineout.com/pages2002/newsweek6.2.02.html; Internet; accessed 4 May 2002.
2. Ibid.
3. Paul Pillar, *Terrorism and U.S. Foreign Policy* (Washington, D.C.: Brookings, 2001). Pillar served in a number of senior managerial and analytic positions at CIA prior to writing this book as a Federal Executive Fellow in the Foreign Policy Studies program of the Brookings Institution. He is currently National Intelligence Officer for the Near East and South Asia.
4. Ibid., 217.
5. Ibid., 53.
6. Ibid., 217–218.
7. Martin van Creveld, *The Transformation of War* (New York: Free Press 1991), 224.
8. Charles Dunlap, "How We Lost the High-Tech War of 2007: A Warning from the Future," *The Weekly Standard* (29 January 1996), 22–28.
9. Ralph Peters, *Fighting for the Future* (Mechanicsburg, PA: Stackpole Books 1999).
10. Spinney's Website, *Defense and the National Interest*; available from http://www.d-n-i.net/; Internet; accessed 10 June 2002.
11. Phil Hirschkorn, Rohan Gunaratna, Ed Blanche, and Stefan Leader, "Blowback," *Jane's Intelligence Review* 13/8 (1 August 2001); available from http://www.counterterror.net/janes1.html; Internet; accessed 6 May 2002.
12. World Islamic Front Statement, "Jihad Against Jews and Crusaders," 23 February 1998; available from http://www.library.cornell.edu/colldev/mideast/wif.htm; Internet; accessed 12 June 2002.
13. Foreign Policy Association, "In Focus—Al Qaeda"; available from http://www.fpa.org/newsletter_info2478/newsletter_info.htm; Internet; accessed 8 May 2002. See also Peter L. Bergen, *Holy War, Inc.: Inside The Secret World of Osama Bin Laden* (New York: The Free Press 2001), 222.
14. Michele Zanini and Sean J. A. Edwards, Chapter II: "The Networking of Terror in the Information Age," 31; available from http://www.rand.org/publications/MR/MR1382/MR1382.ch2.pdf; Internet; accessed 3 May 2002. This chapter draws on RAND research originally reported in Ian Lesser et al., *Countering the New Terrorism* (RAND, 1999).
15. Key figures include the Egyptian-born *Ayman al-Zawahiri*, the ideologist, and disciple of Palestinian scholar-guerrilla organizer Abdullah Azzam, who recruited thousands of Muslims to fight in Afghanistan. Zawahiri was founder of the Egyptian Islamic Jihad, which opposes the Egyptian Government through violent means. He helped forge the coalition of al-Jihad, al Qaeda, two Pakistani groups and another from Bangladesh in February 1998 to wage war on the U.S. *Mohammed Atef*, the military commander, was also born in Egypt. He headed al Qaeda's military committee and had primary responsibility for supervising training camps in Afghanistan and planning global operations. Among his first were attacks on U.S. troops by providing training to Somali tribes fighting them in 1993. *Abu Zubaydah*, the operations chief, was born in Saudi Arabia. Following the East African embassy bombings he appears to have replaced Atef as the primary contact for recruits and as the organizer of overseas operations.
16. "Trail of a Terrorist," *PBS-Frontline*, Transcript of Program #2004, Original airdate: 25 October 2001; available from http://www.pbs.org/wgbh/pages/frontline/shows/trail/etc/script.html; Internet; accessed 24 June 2002.
17. Hirschkorn et al (note 11).
18. Valdis E. Krebs, "Mapping Networks of Terrorist Cells," *Connections* 24/3 (2002) pp.43-52; available from http://www.orgnet.com/MappingTerroristNetworks.pdf; Internet; accessed 8 May 2002.
19. "The Investigation and the Evidence," *BBC News*, 5 October 2001; available from http://news.bbc.co.uk/hi/english/world/americas/newsid_1581000/1581063.stm.; Internet; accessed 10 June 2002.

20. Stuart Millar, Nick Hopkins, John Hooper, and Giles Foden, "Two Terrorists Were under Investigation by FBI," *The Guardian*, Monday 17 September 2001; available from http://www.guardian.co.uk/wtccrash/story/0,1300,553122,00.html; Internet; accessed 8 June 2002.

21. Craig Pyes, Patrick J. McDonnell, and William C. Rempel, "Hijacker Shuttled In and Out of U.S. on Visas Issued by Consulates," *Los Angeles Times*, 16 September 2001; available from http://www.webcom.com/hrin/magazine/la-atta.html; Internet; accessed 8 May 2002.

22. "Patterns of Global Terrorism—2001," U.S. Department of State, (Washington D.C., Office of the Coordinator for Counterterrorism, 21 May 2002); available from http://www.state.gov/s/ct/rls/pgtrpt/2001/html/10247.htm; Internet; accessed 15 June 2002.

23. Anthony Davis, "The Afghan Files: Al-Qaeda Documents from Kabul," *Jane's Intelligence Review* 14/1 (1 February 2002), 16.

24. In addition to [those in] Afghanistan, Indonesian intelligence claims international terrorists, including al Qaeda, have training camps on Sulawesi Island, Indonesia. Moreover, one of the leaders of the Egyptian Islamic Group has said that he spent several months at one of bin Laden's guerrilla training camps in Sudan. See Preston Mendenhall, "Chilling Lessons at Al-Qaida U.," *MSNBC*, 27 January 2001; available from http://www.msnbc.com/news/695030.asp; Internet; accessed 8 May 2002.

25. Ibid.

26. J. T. Caruso, United States Senate, Statement for the Record of Acting Assistant Director Counter Terrorism Division Federal Bureau of Investigation before the Subcommittee on International Operations and Terrorism Committee on Foreign Relations, *Al-Qaeda International* (Washington, D.C., 18 December 2001); available from http://www.fbi.gov/congress/congress01/caruso121801.htm; Internet; accessed 10 May 2002. See also Hirschkorn et al (note 11).

27. In the early 1990s, Ramzi Yousef was sent by bin Laden's officers to the Philippines to train Abu Sayyaf members. Yousef was convicted in September in New York City of a conspiracy to blow up 12 American jumbo jets in one day and convicted in 1997 as the "mastermind" of the 1993 World Trade Center bombing. See Dale Watson (Chief, International Terrorism Section, National Security Division, Federal Bureau of Investigation), United States Senate, Statement before the Senate Judiciary Committee Subcommittee on Technology, Terrorism, and Government Information, *Foreign Terrorists in America: Five Years after the World Trade Center* (Washington, D.C., 24 February 1998); available from http://www.fas.org/irp/congress/1998_hr/s980224w.htm; Internet; accessed 4 June 2002. See also Simon Reeve, *The New Jackals: Ramzi Yousef, Osama bin Laden and the Future of Terrorism* (Boston: Northeastern University Press 1999), 72–85.

28. See daily transcripts of the *USA v. Usama bin Laden et al* trial in the Southern District of New York.; available from http://cryptome.org/usa-v-ubl.zip; Internet; accessed 10 June 2002. See also EXECUTIVE ORDER 13129, *Subject: Blocking Property and Prohibiting Transactions With the Taliban* (Washington D.C., Office of External Relations, 4 July 1999); available from http://nodis.hq.nasa.gov/Library/Directives/NASA-WIDE/nasaeoas/eo13129.html; Internet; accessed 10 June 2002.

29. Yoni Fighel and Yael Shahar, "The Al-Qaida-Hizballah Connection," *The International Policy Institute for Counter-Terrorism*, 26 February 2002; available from http://www.ict.org.il/inter_ter/orgdet.cfm?orgid=74; Internet; accessed 15 May 2002.

30. *September 11 Class Action, 2002*; available from http://www.september11classaction.com/Havlish_Complaint.pdf; Internet; accessed 4 June 2002. According to FBI's Most Wanted Terrorist list, Mugniyah is the alleged head of the security apparatus for the terrorist organization, Lebanese Hizballah. He is thought to be in Lebanon. The list is available from http://www.fbi.gov/mostwant/terrorists/termugniyah.htm; Internet; accessed 4 June 2002.

31. *USA v. Usama bin Laden et al* (note 28).

32. See *United States of America v. Ali Mohamed*, United States District Court Southern District of New York, S (5) 98CR1023, 4 June 1999. See also *September 11 Class Action*, 2002 (note 30).

33. See testimony by George J. Tenet (Director of Central Intelligence), Senate Armed Services Committee, *Worldwide Threat—Converging Dangers in a Post 9/11 World*, (Washing-

ton D.C., 19 March 2002); available from http://www.cia.gov/cia/public_affairs/speeches/senate_select_hearing_03192002.html; Internet; accessed 15 June 2002.

34. Ibid.
35. Hirschkorn et al (note 11).
36. "Al Qaeda Prepares for War," *Jane's Intelligence Digest* (May 31, 2002).
37. "The Czech Interior Minister Stanislav Gross says that terrorist Mohammed Atta, a suspected pilot in the September attacks on the United States, did meet an Iraqi diplomat in Prague. Mr. Gross says this information comes from intelligence services and he says he cannot comment further on the matter. Mr. Gross was reacting to claims in the latest issue of the U.S. weekly *Newsweek*, which says Atta visited Prague but did not meet an Iraqi agent. See *Radio Prague—Print Version* (22 April 2002); available from http://www.radio.cz/print/en/news/27440.; Internet; accessed 13 June 2002.
38. "Gunning for Saddam: Interview with Sabah Khodada," *PBS-Frontline*, 8 November 2001; available from http://www.pbs.org/wgbh/pages/frontline/shows/gunning/; Internet; accessed 15 May 2002. Also see Chris Hedges, "Iraqi Defectors Detail Secret School for Terrorists," *New York Times Service*, Thursday 8 November 2001; available from http://www.sierratimes.com/cgi-bin/warroom/topic.cgi?forum=11&topic=38; Internet; accessed 10 May 2002.
39. Jeffrey Goldberg, "The Great Terror," *The New Yorker*, 25 March 2002; available from http://newyorker.com/fact/content/?020325fa_FACT1; Internet; accessed 20 April 2002.
40. *September 11 Class Action*, 2002 (note 30).
41. Trifin J. Roule, Jeremy Kinsell, and Brian Joyce, "Investigators Seek to Break Up Al-Qaeda's Financial Structure," *Jane's Intelligence Review* 13/11 (1 November 2001), 8–11.
42. Ibid.
43. Karen DeYoung and Douglas Farah, "Infighting Slows Hunt for Hidden Al Qaeda Assets; Funds Put in Untraceable Commodities," *The Washington Post*, 18 June 2002, p.1A.
44. Ibid.
45. See testimony by Steven Emerson, House Committee on Financial Services Subcommittee on Oversight and Investigations, PATRIOT Act Oversight: Investigating Patterns of Terrorist Fundraising, *Fund-Raising Methods and Procedures for International Terrorist Organizations* (Washington D.C., 12 February 2002): 13–14; available from http://financialservices.house.gov/media/pdf/021202se.pdf; Internet; accessed 15 June 2002.
46. Ibid.
47. Roule (note 41).
48. See UNITED NATIONS SANCTIONS ORDINANCE (Chapter 537); available from http://www.hksfc.org.hk/eng/licensing/html/intermediaries/003encl-2.pdf; Internet; accessed 12 June 2002.
49. Li Xueying, "The Asia Connection," *The Straits Times*; available from http://straitstimes.asia1.com.sg/mnt/html/webspecial/WTC/osama_asian.html; Internet; accessed 10 May 2002. See also note 26.
50. Emerson (note 45). For information about the IIRO, see its website, *The International Islamic Relief Organization, Saudi Arabia (IIRO)*; available from http://www.arab.net/iiro; Internet; accessed 10 June 2002.
51. Emerson (note 45).
52. See Ahmed Rashid, *Taliban* (New Haven: Yale University Press: 2001) 117–27. See also Véronique Maurus and Marc Roche, "L'homme le plus redouté des Etats-Unis, longtemps entraîné par la CIA…," *Le Monde*, 24 June 2002; available from http://www.lemonde.fr/article/0,5987,3216--221921-,00.html; Internet; accessed 14 June 2002. See also Roule (note 41).
53. Roule (note 41).
54. For information on the link between wealthy individuals and al Qaeda/bin Laden, see Robert O'Harrow Jr., David S. Hilzenrath, and Karen DeYoung, "Bin Laden's Money Takes Hidden Paths To Agents of Terror—Records Hint at Complex Financial Web," *The Washington Post*, Friday 21 September 2001, A13. See also John Mintz "Bin Laden's Finances Are Moving Target," *The Washington Post*, Friday 28 August 1998, A1. See also "The Money: Dry-

ing Up the Funds for Terror," *Council on Foreign Relations*; available from http://www.terrorismanswers.com/responses/money.html; Internet; accessed 10 June 2002.

55. See George W. Bush (President of the United States), "George W. Bush Delivers Remarks at the Treasury Department's Financial Crimes Enforcement Network (FINCEN)," (Washington D.C., FDCH Political Transcripts, 7 November 2001); available from http://financialservices.house.gov/media/pdf/021202se.pdf; Internet; accessed 15 June 2002. See also Roule (note 41).

56. Nick Fielding, "By the Book: ENCYCLOPAEDIA OF TERROR: Revealed: The Bloody Pages of Al-Qaeda's Killing Manual," available from http://www.la.utexas.edu/chenry/usme/aip01/msg00360.html; Internet; accessed 8 May 2002.

57. Kim Burger, "One Step Ahead," *Jane's Defence Weekly* 37/1 (20 February 2002), 21.

58. Fielding (note 56).

59. Massimo Calabresi and Romesh Ratnesar, "Can We Stop the Next Attack?," *Time.com*, Sunday 3 March 2002; available from http://www.time.com/time/nation/printout/0,8816,214064,00.html; Internet; accessed 10 May 2002.

60. "The general and the bomb," *Jane's Intelligence Digest* (2 November 2001), 1–4.

61. Zanini (note 14), 40.

62. Ibid., 36–37.

63. Fielding (note 56).

64. Ibid.

65. *The Sociology and Psychology of Terrorism: Who Becomes a Terrorist and Why?* (Washington, D.C.: Library of Congress Federal Research Division 1999), 13–14.

66. See Remarks by President Bush at 2002 Graduation Exercise of the United States Military Academy; available from http://www.whitehouse.gov/news/releases/2002/06/20020601-3.html; Internet; accessed 20 June 2002.

67. Donald Rumsfeld, "A New Kind of War," *The New York Times*, 27 September 2001, sec. I, p.1.

68. Bush (note 66).

69. "Striking First," *The New York Times*, 23 June 2002, sec. IV, p.12.

Barry R. Posen, 2001

The Struggle Against Terrorism: Grand Strategy, Strategy, and Tactics

Three to four thousand people, nearly all American citizens, perished in the aircraft hijackings and attacks on the World Trade Center and the Pentagon on September 11, 2001.[1] They were murdered for political reasons by a loosely integrated foreign terrorist political organization called al-Qaeda. Below I ask four questions related to these attacks: First, what is the nature of the threat posed by al-Qaeda? Second, what is an appropriate strategy for dealing with it? Third, how might the U.S. defense establishment have to change to fight this adversary? And fourth, what does the struggle against al-Qaeda mean for overall U.S. foreign policy?

The Adversary

Al-Qaeda is a network of like-minded individuals, apparently all Muslim but of many different nationalities, that links together groups in as many as sixty countries. Osama bin Laden, a wealthy Saudi who took part in the Afghan rebellion against the Soviet occupation (1979–89), developed this network. He inspires, finances, organizes, and trains many of its members. He seems to be in direct command of some but not all of them. Bin Laden and his associates share a fundamentalist interpretation of Islam, which they have opportunistically twisted into a political ideology of violent struggle. He and his principles enjoy some popular support in the Islamic world, though it is difficult to gauge its depth and breadth. Al-Qaeda wants the United States, indeed the West more generally, out of the Persian Gulf and the Middle East. In bin Laden's view, the United States helps to keep Muslim peoples in poverty and imposes upon them a Western culture deeply offensive to traditional Islam. He blames the United States for the continued suffering of the people of Iraq and for the Israeli occupation of the West Bank and the Gaza Strip. For him, Israel is a foreign element in the Middle East and should be destroyed. The U.S. military presence in Saudi Arabia is a desecration of the Islamic holy places and must end.[2] Once the United States exits the region, al-Qaeda hopes to overthrow the governments of Saudi Arabia and Egypt and replace them with fundamentalist, Taliban-like regimes. It is no wonder that the Saudi regime considered bin Laden so dangerous that it stripped him of his citizenship in 1994.

Al-Qaeda is an ambitious, ruthless, and technically proficient organization. The stark evidence is at hand. It has attacked the United States before, but not with such striking results.[3] For the September 11 attack, at least nineteen men, supported by perhaps a dozen others, plotted for years an action that at least some of them knew would result in their deaths. Each member of the conspiracy had numerous opportunities to defect. The terrorists piloting the four passenger jets understood the level of destruction they would exact. They carefully studied airport security and found the airports that seemed most vulnerable. Several of these men appear to have trained for years in U.S. flight schools to learn enough to pilot an aircraft into a building. The cockpits of the 757 and 767 are quite similar, which does not seem coincidental; a single experienced pilot could tutor all of the hijackers on the fine points of operating the aircraft. Between the two aircraft types, the conspirators could choose from a wide selection of flights. The 767s, the aircraft with the most fuel and hence the greatest destructive potential, were directed at the biggest target, the World Trade Center. The proximity of the departure airports to the targets permitted tactical "surprise." All four planes had small passenger complements relative to their capacity; this hardly seems coincidental given the hijackers' plan to take the aircraft with box-cutters. The hijackings of all four airliners were carefully synchronized. If this had been a Western commando raid, it would be considered nothing short of brilliant. Given the demonstrated motivation and organizational and technical skills of its members, al-Qaeda will likely attempt further large-scale attacks on the United States or its citizens and soldiers abroad, or both.

Al-Qaeda benefited from the direct support of Afghanistan, which had been governed in recent years by the fundamentalist Taliban religio-political movement. The Taliban ruled Afghanistan as a kind of crude police state. Not only was bin Laden protected by the regime, but his money and his forces were a pillar of its power. The Taliban had been asked before by the United States to expel bin Laden but always demurred. This base proved to be of great utility to bin Laden and to al-Qaeda. Individuals came from around the world to receive training in terrorist techniques and tactics.[4] Afghanistan is a large country, with rugged terrain and long and lawless borders, far from any Western base; it is hard to monitor, let alone attack—in other words, a perfect hideout. Without this bastion, bin Laden would probably have been on the run much of the time. Al-Qaeda also seems to have benefited from the tacit support of some other governments; persistent reports suggest that wealthy individuals in several Gulf states have contributed to the organization, with the knowledge though not the active cooperation of their governments. Saudi Arabia is often mentioned by name.[5]

As has often been pointed out, the United States and most developed, democratic countries are extremely vulnerable to terrorist attacks. These are open societies that have not policed their borders successfully. Drugs and illegal immigrants move into the United States with ease; cash, guns, and stolen cars move out. Dangerous activities occur in modern society every day. Aircraft take off and land; hazardous materials—flammable, explosive, or poisonous—move by truck, train, and ship. And in the United States, those with money and some patience can obtain explosives, firearms, and quantities of ammunition. Prosaic means can be employed against everyday targets to produce catastrophic results. One must nevertheless also be concerned about chemical, biological, or nuclear attacks. The ability to make chemical agents and biological poisons is more widespread than ever, though turning the basic ingredients into useful weapons and delivering them effectively on a large scale has thus far not proven easy for small clandestine groups.[6] Nuclear weapons are more difficult to obtain, but fears remain that some of the very large number manufactured during the Cold War, or some of those built by new nuclear states, could fall into the wrong hands. Alternatively, primitive nuclear weapons designs are widely available; getting the fissionable material to make a nuclear bomb is still difficult, but not all of this material is as secure as it should be. Thus the possibility of a major terrorist attack with biological, chemical, or nuclear weapons cannot be ruled out.

Most terrorists do not exploit the vulnerabilities of advanced industrial societies; law enforcement helps to make it difficult, though obviously not impossible. More important, most terrorist organizations do not wish to make the United States an implacable enemy. Many have limited political objectives, which the United States can hinder or help. Al-Qaeda clearly has more ambitious objectives than most terrorist organizations; it seeks to expel the most powerful state in history from a part of the world that has been central to U.S. foreign policy for more than half a century, and it intends to do so without a large standing military. Hence al-Qaeda has opted for large-scale murder to achieve its objectives, and it will seek to kill Americans so long as the United States does not give in to its demands.

What Is to Be Done?

Like any war, or even any large civil project, the war against al-Qaeda and other terrorist groups bent on mass destruction requires a strategy. A strategy lays out an interlinked chain of problems that must be solved to address the ultimate problem, the defeat of the adversary. Although the United States and its allies may never fully destroy al-Qaeda, or aligned organizations, or new organizations that emulate them, the antiterror coalition that the United States has built can aspire to reduce the terrorists to desperate groups of exhausted stragglers, with few resources and little hope of success. A strategy sets priorities and focuses available resources—money, time, political capital, and military power—on the main effort. Strategies have both a military and a diplomatic dimension. Within the military dimension, states may choose among offensive, defensive, and punitive operations. In this war, diplomacy will loom larger than military operations, and within the military dimension, defensive activities will loom larger than offensive and punitive ones. That said, without a militarily offensive component, this war cannot be won. Finally, this is a war of attrition, not a blitzkrieg. Al-Qaeda cannot be rounded up in a night's work. If the United States wishes to pursue a major effort against al-Qaeda, its supporters, and any future imitators, it must be prepared to accept significant costs and risks over an extended period. There will likely be an exchange of blows, in the United States and abroad. This war is necessary because bin Laden and others like him will continue to attack the United States so long as it asserts its power and influence in other parts of the world.

Sound strategy requires the establishment of priorities because resources are scarce. Resources must be ruthlessly concentrated against the main threat. There are two primary adversaries in this fight against terrorism: the extended al-Qaeda organization and the states that support it. Al-Qaeda is the principal terrorist organization that has attempted to engage in mass destruction attacks on the United States.[7] It has shown itself to be more capable and more politically ambitious than most. It is the imminent threat. Other terrorist organizations, however, must be kept under surveillance and attacked preemptively if they seem ready to strike the United States or its allies in mass attacks, or if they appear intent on aligning themselves with al-Qaeda.

Allies are essential for success in the war on terrorism, which helps to explain the determination of President George W. Bush and his administration to build a broad coalition. Bin Laden had training camps and bases in Afghanistan, but in other countries al-Qaeda's presence has been more shadowy. Wherever this organization takes root, it must be fought. But it will not always be necessary or possible for the United States to do the fighting. Allied military and police forces are more appropriate instruments to apprehend terrorists operating within their national borders than are U.S. forces. They have information that the United States may not have, and they know the territory and people better. The odds of finding the adversary and avoiding collateral damage increase to the extent that the "host" nation-state does the hard work. Moreover, host states can deal better politically with any collateral damage—that is, accidental destruction of civilian life and property. Much of the war will look a lot like conventional law enforcement by the governments of cooperative countries. Efforts must also be made to weaken terrorist organizations by attacking their infrastructure; both cooperative and clandestine methods can be used to deny these groups access to funds and matériel.

As noted earlier, al-Qaeda has found tacit and active support from nation-states. In the case of partial or tacit support, it may be assumed that there is some disagreement within the political leadership of the country in question about the wisdom of such a policy. The objective is to induce these states to change their practices through persuasion, bribery, or nonviolent coercion. Again, diplomacy looms large in this struggle. Nevertheless, the United States must be prepared to bypass national governments should they fail to cooperate. Given the utter ruthlessness of al-Qaeda, the United States cannot afford to allow it a sanctuary anywhere. From time to time, U.S. forces may simply need to attack al-Qaeda cells directly. This may be a job for special operations forces who would try to avoid contact with national armed forces. In any case, to deter national armed forces from getting in the way, or to foil them if they try, the United States must maintain a strong conventional military capability. Occasionally, it may be necessary to engage in conventional wars with such countries.

Some regimes may choose to support bin Laden's cause, like the Taliban did in Afghanistan. Where a regime has close relations with the terrorists, it is reasonable to treat the host nation as an ally of al-Qaeda and an enemy of the United States. The United States must be prepared to wage war against such states to destroy terrorist groups themselves, to prevent their reconstitution by eliminating the regimes that support them, and to deter other nation-states from supporting terrorism. The United States must make it clear that direct support of terrorists who try to kill large numbers of Americans is tantamount to participation in the attack. If a nation-state had directed a conventional weapon of war at the World Trade Center, U.S. forces would have retaliated immediately. Particularly in the age of weapons of mass destruction, the United States cannot allow any state to participate in catastrophic attacks on its homeland with impunity. More intensive defensive precautions can reduce but not eliminate U.S. vulnerability to mass destruction attacks, so deterrence must be the first line of defense. For these reasons, the Taliban regime in Afghanistan had to be destroyed.

Initially, the Bush administration hesitated to embrace the objective of ousting the Taliban regime.[8] The administration was more interested in bin Laden and al-Qaeda than in their hosts, and in his speech of September 20, President Bush gave the Taliban an opportunity to "hand over the terrorists" *or* "share their fate."[9] Even after the first five days of air strikes, in his press conference of October 11, President Bush gave the Taliban a "second chance" to turn over bin Laden and evict his organization from Afghanistan.[10] Given the difficulty of finding these terrorists, as well as the political complexities of waging war in Afghanistan, this was a reasonable offer, though in my judgment a harmful one from the point of view of deterrence of future attacks. Once the Taliban declined the opportunity to cooperate, the United States had no choice but to wage war on them to the extent that was militarily and politically practical, with the objective of driving them from power.[11]

Tactics: Forces and Methods

Any military campaign has defensive and offensive aspects. Because of its geographical position and great military potential, the United States is accustomed to being on the offensive, but in this campaign the defensive must assume equal or greater importance. Considerable time will be required to develop enough political and military pressure on al-Qaeda to suppress its ability to conduct operations. That organization will probably have the opportunity to attack the United States or its friends again. The United States must thus do all it can defensively to reduce the probability of additional attacks on the U.S. homeland, and to limit the damage should such attacks occur. The United States has been taught a costly but valuable lesson about the vulnerability of modern society to terrorism. Thus, even after al-Qaeda is destroyed, the United States will need to maintain its defenses. This means new vigilance in the most fragile corners of the transportation, energy, power, and communication systems and closer attention to the security of government buildings.

The mobilization of thousands of National Guardsmen and reservists after September 11 had the immediate purpose of enhancing U.S. territorial defenses—including more attentive airspace management, port surveillance, and airport security. This is only the beginning. A new or reoriented joint, multiservice command, staffed by active-duty regulars and reservists and dedicated exclusively to territorial defense, should be created to oversee this enduring mission.[12] Many additional military man-hours will likely be required on a sustained basis for territorial defense. Elements of the active armed forces, the Coast Guard, and the National Guard and Reserves may require redirection or expansion, or possibly both. The United States may need to ask its weekend warriors to serve more weekends, and indeed more weeks, each year.

Enhanced intelligence capabilities are necessary for both defense and offense. Students of terrorism and its close cousin, insurgency, invariably stress the critical importance of intelligence.[13] Intelligence must be gathered on terrorist groups overseas. Such intelligence will come not only from U.S. technical surveillance methods and spies but also from the daily hard work of national police forces abroad. The critical importance of intelligence is one of the main reasons why the United States needs the support of allies. U.S. law enforcement agencies will also have to redouble their efforts. Intelligence provides the data necessary for preventive and preemptive attacks by the national military or police forces of the countries in which the terrorist groups have taken refuge, or by U.S. forces. Even tardy warning of terrorist attacks as they get under way may provide a useful and life-saving margin of time. Intelligence from abroad must also be blended with intelligence gathered at home.

More sustained attention is necessary to the organization of the U.S. counterterrorism intelligence effort. Historically, the following has proven of great utility in all kinds of military endeavors: the staffing of a dedicated intelligence center with full-time, long-serving professionals with a deep knowledge of the adversary; the timely collection of intelligence from multiple sources in that center; the analysis of that data for specific information as well as patterns that reveal the adversary's presence or intentions; and the transmission of that data to those who can best use it for offensive or defensive purposes.[14] Anecdotal information suggests that the United States suffered shortcomings in this regard; data may have been present that could have permitted the early detection of the September 11 plot, but it was not fully exploited.[15] Formally, the Central Intelligence Agency's Counterterrorist Center (CTC) is responsible for "coordinating the counterterrorist efforts of the Intelligence Community," including "exploiting all source intelligence."[16] Nevertheless, this intelligence effort has been the subject of persistent criticism, in particular for weaknesses in interagency cooperation; failure to concentrate all potentially useful information in one place, especially information gathered by law enforcement agencies in the United States; and untimely analysis.[17] The CTC's mandate needs to be strengthened so that all useful information gathered by any intelligence or law enforcement agency is concentrated for analysis. The CTC will also require more money and staff.

Offensive action and offensive military capabilities are necessary components of a successful counterterror strategy. Offensive action is required to destroy regimes that align with terrorists; offensive capabilities allow the United States to threaten credibly other regimes that might consider supporting terrorists. Offensive action against terrorists is needed to eliminate them as threats. But even unsuccessful offensive actions, which force terrorist units or terrorist cells to stay perpetually on the move to avoid destruction, will help to reduce their capability. Constant surveillance makes it difficult for them to plan and organize. Constant pursuit makes it dangerous for them to rest. The threat of offensive action is critical to exhausting the terrorists, whether they are with units in the field in Afghanistan or hiding out in cities and empty quarters across the world. This threat will be credible only if the United States launches an offensive operation from time to time, large or small. Offensive action is also necessary to support U.S. diplomacy. Thus far, U.S. diplomats have stressed the concerns of existing and prospective allies that the United States might overreact with excessive and indiscriminate violence. It is disturbing that they believe that U.S. decisionmakers could be so stupid and brutal, but it is a good thing that they understand the deep emotion that drives U.S. purpose. The United States must threaten offensive war so that these allies understand the seriousness of U.S. intent. The more cooperation the United States gets from allies on the intelligence and policing front, the less necessary it becomes for the United States to behave unilaterally, militarily, and with the attendant risks of collateral damage and escalation. If the United States does not act militarily from time to time, this risk will lose its force as an incentive for U.S. allies. Periodically taking the offensive is also necessary to maintain morale at home. Given that al-Qaeda will continue to try to hit the United States and its friends, the public will probably want to see the United States "bring justice to our enemies."[18]

To take the offensive, the United States will need to exploit perishable intelligence on the existence and location of terrorist cells. Flexible, fast, and relatively discriminate forces are essential. The American people and the leaders of the American military must be prepared to accept the risk of significant U.S. casualties in small, hard-hitting raids. Even when other nations cooperate by providing intelligence, and would be willing to arrest or destroy terrorists in their midst, they may lack the capability and need augmentation from the United States. In any event, political decisionmakers in the United States and abroad who approve strikes on the basis of this information will have to come to terms with the risks to innocent civilians. Occasions will surely arise when there are trade-offs between effectiveness against the adversary and casualties to U.S. and allied forces, or to innocents caught in the crossfire. It will occasionally be necessary to err on the side of effectiveness. This is a tragic fact of war that will stress the persuasive skills of U.S. diplomats, as it did in the first weeks of the air campaign against Afghanistan.

The United States has large special operations forces well suited to the counterterror mission: small groups of highly trained individual fighters from all the services, supported by an array of specially designed and expertly piloted helicopters, aircraft, and small watercraft. (They also include experts at training and advising foreign soldiers.) These forces may be more effective and cause less collateral damage than cruise missiles or precision guided bombs in certain situations. In the past, U.S. decisionmakers have been reluctant to employ these forces because their missions involve a significant risk to the troops. Given the seriousness of the new war and the apparent commitment of the American people, such concerns are likely to diminish. These forces may require additional mobility assets—planes, helicopters, and other more exotic equipment. It may also be reasonable to expand the special operations forces by reorienting some active units such as the 82d Airborne Division and the 101st Air Assault (Helicopter) Division to this mission. The U.S. Marine Corps also deploys many units that could prove useful to the counterterror mission. Three separate reinforced battalions of marines are generally deployed afloat, on special assault ships loaded with helicopters and hovercraft, around the world at any one time. Though the marines judge these forces to be "special operations capable," it would be sensible to stress even further their special operations mission. Moreover, given that most U.S. Navy carrier air wings do not currently fill the hangar space available on existing carriers, it is reasonable to put a company of army or marine special operations troops and their associated helicopters on each one.[19] To permit speedy action, emergency basing and overflight rights around the world must be obtained in advance—yet another task for diplomacy.

The military will also need to augment its ability to gather tactical intelligence to support operations under way. Often the United States will have only a rough idea of where terrorist training camps, quasi regular units, or clandestine units are hiding. An enhanced ability to focus intelligence assets on key objectives is of great importance. Insofar as the adversary operates in small groups without much heavy equipment, the task will be difficult. For the last decade, the United States has experimented with unmanned aircraft, "intelligence drones." It needs to buy more drones, and soon. These devices have been used profitably to police Bosnia and Kosovo. They also played a role in the Kosovo war. Unlike satellites, intelligence drones are extremely flexible; they can focus on a small piece of terrain and remain overhead for several hours at a time. They are just machines, and by current standards not very expensive ones; the American people will not mind losing one every now and then to obtain critical information.[20]

Above all, the "war" against terrorism will require patience and sustained national will. It will take time for the United States and its allies build up a full intelligence picture of the adversary and enhance existing worldwide intelligence capabilities to better detect these elusive foes. As the United States pursues terrorist groups, they will fight back. They will resist locally when U.S. and other forces try to apprehend or destroy them. More important, the terrorists will try to mount additional attacks against the United States, against U.S. installations abroad, and against U.S. allies. Terrorists will attempt this anyway, but in seeking to destroy them, the United States may cause them to accelerate their attacks.

The U.S. security establishment will need to be innovative and adaptive, just as the adversary has proven to be.[21] The American people cannot go into this fight without understanding that they may suffer more pain before the problem recedes.

Finally, American leaders will have to fight political and bureaucratic inertia at home and abroad. Prior to September 11, the United States had a counterterror "administered policy." Administered policies prevail in democracies, where the political leadership regularly trades off initiatives that might be highly effective in one policy area against their costs measured in terms of other agendas, values, and policies. Bureaucracies struggle to maintain their autonomy and often fail to cooperate to achieve stated purposes. Change, when it comes, is incremental. Before September 11 the counterterror effort was like any other administered policy; although it enjoyed higher priority and more resources than it once did, it still competed for political, financial, and human resources on a relatively level playing field with many other policies. That approach was entirely reasonable to me, but has been proven wrong. War is different; in war other policies assume significantly lower priority. Because terrorists are elusive, it will be difficult to sustain the kind of focus that war requires. Failure to sustain that focus will allow al-Qaeda to remain quiet, lick any wounds it sustains in the first flush of U.S. anger and coalition solidarity, rebuild its cadres, and then strike again—harder and more effectively than before. While life must go on, a return to treating counterterrorism as an administered policy must await significant evidence of real success in destroying the al-Qaeda organization.

The Diplomacy of a Counterterror War and the Implications for U.S. Grand Strategy

Both enthusiastic allies and quiet back-channel assistance from around the world will be central to a successful counterterror campaign, but allies are not always easy to find. The United States has been spoiled by its Cold War success. Threatened neighbors of the Soviet Union quickly sought alignment with the United States. During Operation Desert Shield, Arab states in the way of Saddam Hussein's legions did not require much persuading to join the U.S. coalition; those farther away needed subsidies just to show up. The war against terrorism is more difficult. The major al-Qaeda terrorist action has been directed against the United States, though attacks both at home and abroad have caught many foreign nationals in the crossfire. States that have been the victims of tenuously related or unrelated terrorist groups have proven responsive to U.S. requests for help (e.g., Russia, India, and Israel). The United States also needs the assistance of states whose leaders believe that (1) they are not terrorist targets, (2) they can easily redirect terror toward others, or (3) their own citizens may sympathize with al-Qaeda.

The United States needs friends, and thus must prioritize among its many foreign policy and defense policy initiatives, because these initiatives have frequently antagonized other governments and peoples. All the governments whose help is required, whether they are democratic or not, must deal with their own publics. Therefore the United States must find ways to explain to their people why cooperation against these terrorists is in their interest. The United States clearly cannot afford to make every state in the world prosperous and happy. It cannot afford to end every conflict in favor of any ally the United States needs. Sometimes the United States will want the help of both parties to a regional conflict, and cannot reward one party at the expense of another. And it cannot afford to peremptorily abandon long-standing allies in a heartbeat. Such actions have their own costs and risks. But the United States must be much more disciplined in its choices, and much more attuned to the views of others, if it is to sustain this coalition over the long term.[22]

In the years since the Cold War ended, the United States has been immensely powerful, and relatively capricious. It has often acted against the interests of others in pursuit of modest gains, as it did in the case of NATO expansion, the Kosovo war, and the Bush administration's early insistence that national missile defenses would be built with or without Russian cooperation. All these policies had alternatives that could have achieved many of the goals of their U.S. advocates while leaving Russia and others less displeased. Similarly the United States has often failed to act out of fear of incurring modest costs: It has applied insufficient pressure on Israel to suppress its settlement policy in the West Bank and Gaza; has shown little creativity in trying to end the politically damaging low-grade war and leaky economic embargo of Iraq; and made no effort to help others inhibit the course of the Rwanda genocide. The American media have been content to cover international politics episodically and often superficially. The U.S. foreign and security policy record is not one of unalloyed failure.[23] It is, however, a record of indiscipline in which calculations of short-term domestic political gains or losses often dominated decisionmaking.

The post–Cold War world of easy preeminence, controlled low-cost wars, budgetary plenty, and choices avoided is over. In the past I argued that the United States failed to settle on a grand strategy to guide its international behavior after the demise of the Soviet Union.[24] Democrats and Republicans could agree on only one thing: The United States should remain the most powerful state in the world. Beyond that, a good many Democrats wanted to use this power to pursue liberal purposes: improving international organizations and institutions, strengthening international treaties, increasing the power of international law, and spreading democracy. Republicans seem to have wanted to use this power to consolidate U.S. superiority and to create still more power. Russia was viewed as perpetually on the verge of backsliding toward Soviet-style imperialism, and China was feared as a budding peer competitor; both needed containment. Neither political party energetically discussed its preferred policies with the American people. Neither was willing to ask the American people for serious sacrifices to pursue its preferred objectives, and neither had to do so. Sacrifice is now necessary if the United States is to sustain an activist foreign policy, and thus the reasons to pursue such a policy must be explained to and accepted by the American people. Otherwise, if the war on terrorism proves to be not only long but more costly than Americans hope, the temptation to retreat from the world stage will be strong.

Although the outlines are not clear, advocates of alternative U.S. grand strategies during the last decade now seem inclined to superimpose these strategies on the campaign against terror. Advocates of greater restraint in U.S. foreign policy, often unfairly dubbed "neo-isolationists," argue that the United States must retaliate strongly for the September 11 attacks if it is to deter future attacks. But they are uninterested in what comes after, because they believe that the United States should do less in the world. If the United States is less involved, it will be less of a target. If it is less often a target, it needs less assistance to defend itself and its interests. This approach to terror is internally consistent, but it definitely does not defend an active U.S. world role.

Liberal internationalists seem much more interested in the process by which the campaign against terrorism is conducted. The United Nations must be involved at every step. Resort to law must take precedence over tactical advantage. Terrorists must be treated like criminals, not enemies: Police should apprehend them; courts should try them. Military action should occur seldom if at all, and it should always be precise. A state that sponsors terrorism, such as Afghanistan, should be diplomatically isolated, condemned at the UN, subjected to an arms embargo, and economically sanctioned in any way that does not harm the general populace. The United States should join the international criminal court, and as a token of its good intentions sign most of the treaties it has eschewed. This approach preserves a world role for the United States but, given the determination of the adversary and the foibles of other countries, seems doomed to failure.

Primacists have also tried to direct this campaign. Perhaps the strangest advice is rumored to have come from Paul Wolfowitz, the U.S. deputy secretary of defense. He seems to believe that the time is ripe to deal with all of the United States' enemies and problems in the Middle East and Persian Gulf and further consolidate an already dominant U.S. power position. Wolfowitz is reported to have recommended action against Iraq, Syria, and Hezbollah bases in Lebanon.[25] Violent regimes and movements they are, and no strangers to terrorism, but none of them seems to be connected to al-Qaeda and its maximalist objectives and methods. Were this to change, Wolfowitz's inclinations would make more sense. But going after all of them now looks too much like a script written by al-Qaeda propagandists; such attacks would surely cause states whose cooperation the United States needs to see the campaign as anti-Arab and anti-Islam, and sit this war out. Such a multifront attack might produce the very rebellions in Saudi Arabia, the other Gulf states, and Egypt that the United States hopes to prevent. This proposed four-front war is especially odd given that the Bush administration campaigned on the proposition that the U.S. military was incapable of dealing with two nearly simultaneous major regional wars.

One grand strategy advocated over the last decade is broadly consistent with the requirements of an extended counterterror war. That strategy, termed "selective engagement," argues that the United States has an interest in stable, peaceful, and relatively open political and economic relations in the part of the world that contains important concentrations of economic and military resources: Eurasia. This is an interest that others share. In this strategy, U.S. power is meant to reassure the vulnerable and deter the ambitious. This is a big project that requires a careful setting of priorities. Yet its objectives are limited: The project seeks neither power for its own sake, nor the wholesale reform of other states' domestic constitutions, nor a transformation of international politics. The U.S. position in the Persian Gulf and the Middle East is a central element of this strategy. Al-Qaeda aims to challenge this position. Its leaders believe that if the United States left the region, they could take power in the Gulf and in Egypt. Were this to happen, one can easily imagine several possible dangers: a war between Iraq and Saudi Arabia as Saddam Hussein tries to strangle the fundamentalist Islamic baby in the cradle before its strangles him; war with Iran over security, religious, and nationalist issues; or war with Israel. Given the extreme destructiveness of the 1980–88 Iraq-Iran War (500,000 dead), which saw the use of chemical weapons and rocket attacks on cities—as well as the continued presence of chemical, biological, and nuclear weapons, and rocket delivery systems in the area—any of these possible wars could prove devastating for those in the region and harmful to those farther away. Moreover, any one of them would surely affect the production, distribution, and price of oil—still important to the global economy. Their political, military, and economic ripple effects would likely be felt globally, affecting other political relationships. The grand strategy of selective engagement does necessitate the campaign against al-Qaeda. The requirements of that campaign have already forced the Bush administration to act in ways that are more consistent with the strategy of selective engagement than they are with primacy.

The United States faces a long war against a small, elusive, and dangerous foe. That struggle must be pursued with discipline and determination if it is to be successful. The United States requires a strategy to guide its efforts, including the allocation of resources. That strategy must set priorities, because resources are scarce and this war will prove expensive. Significant changes in the U.S. national security establishment, including intelligence collection and analysis, military organization and equipment, and emergency preparedness, will prove essential. Finally, if the United States is to sustain both public and international support for the war on terrorism, it will need to resolve long-delayed questions about its future foreign and security policy through an extended discussion involving policymakers, policy analysts, and the American people.

Barry R. Posen is a professor of political science in the Security Studies Program at the Massachusetts Institute of Technology. His first book, *Sources of Military Doctrine: France, Britain and Germany Between the World Wars* (1986), won the American Political Science Association's Woodrow Wilson Foundation Book Award and Ohio State University's Edward J. Furniss Jr., Book Award. He has been an international affairs fellow with the Rockefeller Foundation and with the Council on Foreign Relations and is also the author of *Inadvertent Escalation: Conventional War and Nuclear Risks* (1992).

Notes

1. It is impossible at this time to offer a more precise figure. See Eric Lipton, "Numbers Vary in Tallies of the Victims," *New York Times*, October 25, 2001, pp. B1, B10.
2. United Kingdom, Foreign and Commonwealth Office (FCO), *Responsibility for the Terrorist Atrocities in the United States, 11 September 2001*, pp. 4–5, http://www/fco.gov.uk/news/keythemepages.asp. See also Kenneth Katzman, *Terrorism: Near Eastern Groups and State Sponsors, 2001*, Congressional Research Service, report for Congress, September 10, 2001, pp. 2, 9.
3. FCO, *Responsibility for the Terrorist Atrocities in the United States*, pp. 6–10, links al-Qaeda to the fight against U.S. special operations forces in Somalia in October 1993, to the bombing of the U.S. embassies in Kenya and Tanzania in August 1998, and to the attack on the USS *Cole* in October 2000, as well as to several thwarted operations. See also Katzman, *Terrorism*, pp. 10–11, which also links bin Ladin indirectly to the February 1993 World Trade Center bombing.
4. Ali A. Jalali, "Afghanistan: The Anatomy of an Ongoing Conflict," *Parameters*, Vol. 31, No. 1 (Spring 2001), p. 5, http://carlisle-www.army.mil/usawc/Parameters/o1spring;jalali.htm.
5. "Saudi Arabia: The Double-Act Wears Thin," *Economist*, September 29, 2001, pp. 22–23.
6. As of this writing, the anthrax poisonings in the United States do not contradict this statement. Until we know more, all we can conclude is that small amounts of lethal anthrax can be obtained and, through the mail, can hurt or kill small numbers of people.
7. The February 1993 bombing of the World Trade Center is not directly attributed to al-Qaeda, but Ramzi Yusef, convicted of masterminding that crime, reportedly collaborated with al-Qaeda to organize several unsuccessful terrorist efforts in Asia. Katzman, *Terrorism*, p. 10.
8. Indeed, as of late October 2001, both the U.S. Department of State and the U.K. Foreign and Commonwealth Office used elliptical language to discuss coalition war aims in Afghanistan.

Secretary of State Colin Powell could only bring himself to say, "There is, however, no place in a new Afghan government for the current leaders of the Taliban regime." See "Campaign against Terrorism," prepared statement for the House International Relations Committee, U.S. Department of State, October 24, 2001, p. 2, http://www.state.gov/secretary/rm/2001. The United Kingdom's statement of war aims suggests that "we require sufficient change in the leadership to ensure that Afghanistan's links to international terrorism are broken." Foreign and Commonwealth Office, "Defeating International Terrorism: Campaign Objectives," p. 1, http://www.fco.gov.uk/news/keythemehome.asp.

9. See "The President's Address," *Washington Post*, September 21, 2001, p. A24.

10. Patrick E. Tyler and Elisabeth Bumiller, " 'Just Bring Him In,' President Hints He Will Halt War If bin Laden Is Handed Over," *New York Times*, October 12, 2001, pp. A1, B5.

11. U.S. leaders wisely exercised some restraint; they did not put large ground forces into the country, who would have provided numerous targets for Afghan riflemen and the appearance of a mission of conquest. Nor did they use firepower indiscriminately, and by large-scale killing of Afghan civilians create the appearance of making war on all Muslims.

12. U.S. Department of Defense, *Quadrennial Defense Review Report*, September 30, 2001, p. 19, states that "DOD will review the establishment of a new unified combatant commander to help address complex inter-agency issues and provide a single military commander to focus military support." This is too tentative.

13. "Nearly all of the threatened or their experts agree that the key to an effective response to terrorism is good intelligence and that such intelligence is difficult to acquire." J. Bowyer Bell, *A Time of Terror: How Democratic Societies Respond to Revolutionary Violence* (New York: Basic Books, 1978), p. 134. Douglas S. Blaufarb draws similar lessons from the U.S. counter-insurgency effort in Vietnam: "Small, lightly armed units, pinpointed operations assisted by 'hunter-killer' squads, imaginative psychological warfare operations—and all of this based upon coordinated collection and exploitation of intelligence—should be the main reliance of the military side of the effort. The police, if they have or can be brought to develop the capability, should play a major role in the intelligence effort and in other programs requiring frequent contact with the public." Blaufarb, *The Counterinsurgency Era: U.S. Doctrine and Performance, 1950 to the Present* (New York: Free Press, 1977), p. 308.

14. The clearest historically grounded exposition of this argument is to be found in Patrick Beesly, *Very Special Intelligence* (New York: Ballantine, 1977), pp. 1–24, which details the formation of the Royal Navy's Operational Intelligence Center, to exploit all source intelligence for the antisubmarine warfare campaign early in World War II.

15. James Risen, "In Hindsight, C.I.A. Sees Flaws That Hindered Efforts on Terror," *New York Times*, October 7, 2001, pp. A1, B2. "In hindsight, it is becoming clear that the C.I.A., F.B.I. and other agencies had significant fragments of information that, under ideal circumstances, could have provided some warning if they had all been pieced together and shared rapidly."

16. "The War on Terrorism," DCI Counterterrorist Center, http://www.cia.gov/terrorism.ctc.html.

17. The National Commission on Terrorism, Ambassador L. Paul Bremer III, Maurice Sonnenberg, Richard K. Betts, Wayne A. Downing, Jane Harman, Fred C. Iklé, Juliette N. Kayyem, John F. Lewis, Jr., Gardner Peckham, and R. James Woolsey, *Countering the Changing Threat of International Terrorism,* report of the National Commission on Terrorism (Washington, D.C., June 5, 2000), http://www.fas.org/irp/threat/commission.htm; and James Kitfield, "CIA, FBI, and Pentagon Team to Fight Terrorism," September 18, 2000, GOVEXEC.com, http://www.govexec.com/dailyfed/0900/091900nt.htm.

18. This sentiment was expressed by President Bush in his address to a joint session of Congress on September 20, 2001: "Whether we bring our enemies to justice or bring justice to our enemies, justice will be done." See "The President's Address."

19. If U.S. Army special operations units are to be permanently deployed at sea, they will need to purchase new "marinized" versions of their current helicopters that are better able to fit below decks, communicate with navy vessels and aircraft, and withstand the corrosive effects of salt air.

20. The U.S. Air Force RQ-1A Predator costs about $8 million apiece. This is the price for a small production run; production on a larger scale would reduce the unit cost. The air force currently

has only thirteen Predators. Ted Nicholas and Rita Rossi, *Military Cost Handbook*, 22d ed. (Fountain Valley, Calif.: Data Search Associates, 2001), p. 4–2. See also Craig Hoyle, "U.S. Build-Up Highlights UAV shortage," *Jane's Defence Weekly*, October 10, 2001, p. 5.

21. For example, the Bush administration has appointed Governor Tom Ridge head of the new Office of Homeland Security to coordinate the activities of all the disparate governmental organizations that contribute to territorial defense; he controls nothing. It may instead prove necessary to organize a new Department of Territorial Security, to consolidate control over some or all of the following: air surveillance and defense units; the Coast Guard; the Border Patrol, counterterror elements of the FBI; and federal-level emergency medical response, humanitarian relief, and damage-repair capabilities.

22. Examples of the kinds of diplomatic choices that the United States faces abound. Russia can control its own nuclear materials and weapons and provide intelligence; Russia has been unhappy with NATO expansion and the Bush administration's national missile defense program. Saudi Arabia and the Gulf states have great air bases, all used by the United States during the Gulf War. These bases would prove useful if the counterterror campaign expands to Iraq. These countries find U.S. tolerance of Israeli settlement policies on the West Bank and Gaza to be a significant irritant. Though the UN oil-for-food program has enabled Iraq to feed and care for its people—and Saddam Hussein deserves the blame for their current misery—the continuation of Gulf War sanctions and the regular bombing of Iraq by U.S. and British warplanes help Saddam portray Iraq as the aggrieved party in the Arab world. Pakistan, a former close supporter of the Taliban, was alienated by the United States' cavalier treatment after the end of the Soviet occupation of Afghanistan. Pakistan was also, until recently, under economic sanctions enacted to show U.S. displeasure with its May 1998 nuclear weapons tests. Pakistan may have the most political influence over Pashtun tribes in Afghanistan whose cooperation will be needed to bring a stable government to that country.

23. Russia did not collapse; the nuclear weapons of the Soviet Union were gathered up and consolidated in Russia for safekeeping; the Balkan wars ended; and the great and middle powers of the world have not yet fallen into any new cold wars with one another. U.S. foreign policymakers get much of the credit.

24. Barry R. Posen and Andrew L. Ross, "Competing Visions for U.S. Grand Strategy," *International Security*, Vol. 21, No. 3 (Winter 1996/97), pp. 5–53.

25. Steven Mufson and Thomas E. Ricks, "Debate over Targets Highlights Difficulty of War on Terrorism," *Washington Post*, September 21, 2001, p. A25. The article depicts a policy fight between Secretary of State Colin Powell, the principal advocate of a policy focused on al-Qaeda, and Deputy Secretary of Defense Wolfowitz, "pushing for a broader range of targets, including Iraq."

Wyn Q. Bowen, 2002

Deterring Mass-Casualty Terrorism

W estern governments have become preoccupied with preventing mass-casualty terrorism. The American-led campaign against al Qaeda has shown that the preventive strategies most likely to succeed must focus on disrupting and destroying suspect groups and their capabilities. Indeed the emphasis of the Bush administration on preemption as a central pillar of emerging U.S. strategic doctrine indicates that this approach is the best way to deal with chemical, biological, radiological, nuclear, or enhanced high explosive (CBRNE) weapons. While active disruption and destruction constitute the most realistic options at hand, does this mean that deterrence has nothing to offer as an element of a broader, comprehensive strategy for preventing mass-casualty terrorism?

An Established Strategy

The object of deterrence is preventing real or potential enemies from initiating hostile acts. It differs from but is related to the concept of compellence—more often known as coercion—where the goal is getting an enemy to do something—to alter its behavior and an existing state of affairs. For example, air strikes by the United States against Libya in 1986 were intended in part to compel Colonel Qaddafi to stop sponsoring terrorist activity against American targets in Europe. The aim was changing Libyan policy, under which the regime sponsored terrorism, not preserving it.

A deterrent strategy can rely on one or both of two mechanisms. First, it can be based on threats to visit punishment on an enemy that significantly outweighs the gain of a particular course of action. This approach is traditionally viewed as targeting civilian assets and constituted the basis of the Cold War concept of mutual assured destruction.

Another approach is based on the concept of denial. Specific capabilities deter enemies from pursuing either a given objective or a conflict strategy. This is achieved by undermining their ability, or belief in their ability, to realize a desired outcome.

Deterrent strategies can include both punishment and denial mechanisms. For example, the United States appears to favor such an approach to deter unconventional weapons usage by a regime by combining denial capabilities like missile defenses with the threat of punishment. Both mechanisms may support a comprehensive strategy to prevent mass-casualty terrorism.

A credible deterrent posture requires the capability to deliver on the deterrent message, or at least the appearance of it. The deterrer must demonstrate the intent and resolve

The opinions, conclusions, and recommendations expressed or implied within are those of the author and do not necessarily reflect the views of the Joint Services Command and Staff College, the Ministry of Defence, or any other government agency.

to fulfill the message and effectively communicate this to an enemy, including which lines not to cross.

Deterrence also assumes that a target will be a cost-benefit calculator—a rational actor who evaluates options in terms of costs and benefits, including likely responses. But what is accepted as rational by one actor may not appear rational to another because of cultural factors or decisionmaking processes. This is a major consideration in the war on terrorism because of the asymmetric nature of the opposing sides in almost every respect. A preventive strategy in this context—deterrent or other—requires knowing enemy motives, worldview, resolve, capabilities (including conflict strategies and techniques), and vulnerabilities.

Measuring the failure of deterrence is straightforward because the action that the deterring party seeks to avoid occurs. However, measuring success is more difficult, as it cannot be proven that the strategy was pivotal, marginal, or irrelevant to why an enemy opted not to act. This can be significant when attempting to prevent mass-casualty terrorism.

What role might deterrence play preventing catastrophic terrorist attacks? How might such a strategy fit into broader counterterrorist policies? Should the aim be preventing actions that could create mass casualties or specific types of attack? Should the objective be preventing conflict escalation over a determined threshold (something that is hard to define) or buying time in order for preventive approaches to take effect?

Non-State Actors

Since deterrence is about preventing an enemy from acting in a particular way, success will depend on a target believing, or being made to believe, that the current state of affairs is preferable to the cost associated with a particular course of action, at least in the short term, if the purpose is buying time for other approaches. It follows that if an enemy is determined to act, deterrence could prove unworkable.

At first glance, this infeasibility appears to be the case in mass-casualty terrorism since the motives of nonstate actors to perpetrate such attacks are likely to be extreme and their level of resolve so high that deterrence is inapplicable. Indeed, groups that contemplate such activity have radical views derived from religious (al Qaeda) or apocalyptic beliefs (Aum Shinrikyo). Moreover, fanaticism is expressed in unrealizable goals, operates outside of commonly accepted political and moral norms, and remains impervious to negotiation and inducement.

For example, Osama bin Laden and members of al Qaeda claim to be acting in the name of Islam in pursuing objectives such as eliminating Israel and destroying America. Moreover, it s clear that many members of the al Qaeda network think in suicidal terms and are willing to endure significant costs and destruction in pursuit of their objectives.

In the mid-1990s, the Aum Shinrikyo sect in Japan sought to cause death, destruction, and chaos on such a large scale—through the use of chemical and biological weapons—that the resultant disorder and instability would cause the collapse of the political and social order.

It is vital to distinguish such radical terror groups from more traditional organizations such as the Irish Republican Army (IRA) and Basque Fatherland and Liberty (commonly known as ETA) that tend to attack people or places associated with relatively limited political goals. They exercise self-restraint and avoid undermining sympathy for their cause. In contrast to al Qaeda, they are open to negotiation and susceptible to inducements. As a result they will self deter when it comes to mass-casualty terrorism.

The real challenge in determining whether nonstate actors like al Qaeda are susceptible to deterrence logic involves penetrating their black boxes. This means understanding the frame of reference of actors, how it is evoked, options considered in decisionmaking, and the lens through which they will perceive deterrent messages.[1] Specifically, there must be emphasis on evaluating how specific groups or individuals calculate costs and benefits: Are they risk prone or risk averse? Do they think in terms of minimizing losses or maximizing gains? To what extent are they motivated by survival, security, recognition, wealth, power, or success? It will also be critical to assess the processes through which suspect organizations make decisions and avoid perceiving the capabilities and intentions of such actors as being like one's own. Addressing such questions will require concerted and targeted intelligence collection and analysis.

Inflicting Punishment

With regard to deterrence mechanisms, could punishment strategies deter in this context if directed against the leadership and members of terrorist groups? The key question is whether there are suitable high-value targets that could be threatened to make radicals such as bin Laden and his accomplices weigh the relative merits of various courses of action. Some argue that it is possible threaten such targets, including family and supporters, and cause even the most radical leaders to engage in cost-benefit analysis.[2] The question also arises over symbols of importance to specific terrorists that could be threatened as part of a deterrent strategy. For example, what would be the equivalent of the World Trade Center to bin Laden?

Such approaches are difficult to legitimize if pursued overtly by democratically elected governments because of political, legal, and ethical constraints. Even if threats were made covertly a target would probably doubt their credibility on the assumption that the deterrer is operating under such pressures. Moreover, it is important to assess the impact of such threats against the wider goal of reducing the danger posed by nonstate actors. It could be argued that such threats would increase and not reduce the terrorist danger by alienating the deterring party even further from the existing and potential target support base.

Denial

The heart of a denial-based approach involves demonstrating that the capability exists to ward off—or to minimize damage in the event of—an attack, thus mitigating the desired effects of the terrorists. While some requisite denial capabilities are applicable to all potential modes of attack, some are mode-specific.

Generic capabilities include using intelligence, diplomatic, military, and law enforcement means to locate and interdict nonstate actors before they act. For example, developing, bolstering, and refining the core elements of counterterrorist strategies could have a generic deterrent effect.

The main challenge is denial capabilities designed for specific modes of attack. In the realm of chemical, biological, and radiological threats, careful preparations for consequence management can have a dissuasive or preventive effect. Relevant capabilities include the demonstrated readiness of first responders to deal with chemical, biological, and radiological incidents. In part, this would entail knowledge of specific biological and chemical agents and possession of vaccines and other medical countermeasures.

In addition, deterrence can be achieved by demonstrating a strong capability for preventing or hindering the spread of materials and knowledge nonstate actors need to develop and produce chemical, biological, and radiological weapons. Relevant capabilities include export controls and detecting and interdicting suspect shipments. The aim is convincing an enemy that acquiring such weapons is not worth the time, resources, and effort required.

Moreover, there may exist some scope for deterring nonstate actors by developing forensic (biological and nuclear) attribution capabilities to underscore the threat of retribution. According to Jay Davis, if an enemy knows an event can be traced to the perpetrator, it can create "strong inhibitions in those that are not personally suicidal."[3]

A potential negative side effect of denial is the risk of it becoming a double-edged sword. Specifically, there is the danger that denying or deterring one line of attack will push an opponent to strike against less protected areas, possibly using different means—the balloon effect.[4] Other modes of attack could be less predictable and more dangerous. Was September 11 an example of this?

If the aim is buying time to frustrate an enemy who is strongly committed to alter the status quo, the consequences of succeeding may not always be foreseeable and positive. Indeed, short-term success could make a target more desperate. This is not to claim that developing a specific denial posture should be avoided. But it is essential to consider its negative effects.

Terms of Art

Mass Casualty. Any large number of casualties produced in a relatively short period of time, usually as the result of a single incident such as a military aircraft accident, hurricane, flood, earthquake, or armed attack that exceeds local logistic support capabilities.

Terrorism. The calculated use of unlawful violence or threat of unlawful violence to inculcate fear; intended to coerce or to intimidate governments or societies in the pursuit of goals that are generally political, religious, or ideological.

Weapons of Mass Destruction. Weapons that are capable of a high order of destruction and/or of being used in such a manner as to destroy large numbers of people. Weapons of mass destruction can be high explosives or nuclear, biological, chemical, and radiological weapons, but exclude the means of transporting or propelling the weapon where such means is a separable and divisible part of the weapon.

JFQ

Source: Joint Pub 1-02, *DOD Dictionary of Military and Associated Terms* (April 12, 2002).

Deterrence and Coercion

Beyond the terrorists themselves there is an added type of target for deterrence: regimes that provide refuge for them to operate. Here deterrence involves threats to punish regimes if they are found to be aiding groups by sponsoring, harboring, or merely tolerating them.

The campaign against the Taliban regime in Afghanistan was informative because it had a powerful deterrent effect, signalling that the United States has the intent, resolve, and ability to punish and depose regimes that may contemplate supporting terrorist networks. Prior to the events of September 11, it could be argued that the United States had not amply demonstrated that. Although al Qaeda posed a threat to U.S. security interests in Africa and the Middle East, it was not deemed sufficient to justify all-out military, economic, and diplomatic measures to destroy terrorist groups. The high profile but low-grade response of the Clinton administration to the bombings of U.S. embassies in Africa is evidence. However, attacks in New York and Washington radically altered the strategic calculus because they struck political and economic power centers of the United States. The campaign to unseat the Taliban has made deterrence more credible in the context of dissuading regimes from supporting terror groups.

As noted, there is a subtle distinction between the concepts of deterrence and coercion that can prompt confusion in application. Strictly speaking, threats or actions designed to stop a regime from supporting terrorists will be coercive because the aim is altering the status quo. The effort to coerce the Taliban into complying with American demands—namely, handing over al Qaeda members—failed, and the U.S-dominated coalition had to use force to impose a regime change in Kabul.

In sum, deterrence is about keeping things as they are and is only relevant to regimes not implicated in supporting terrorism but which might contemplate becoming involved. Thus, in the context of preventing mass-casualty terrorism, coercion and deterrence should be treated as related but different concepts.

Deterrence by denial is applicable when a target is a terrorist organization or network. However, because of extreme motives and resolve on the part of entities that have perpetrated or are likely to contemplate mass-casualty terrorism, this approach is a delaying option to buy time for other preventive approaches at best. A drawback is that deterring an attack in one area can force a nonstate enemy to change focus and strike at less protected areas with unpredictable and more heinous modes of attack.

When a target is a regime contemplating whether to support terrorists, deterrence by threat of punishment is most relevant. Allied action in the global war on terror should bolster both deterrence and coercion in the long term since it has indicated that the United States and its allies will act with determination against the perpetrators and would-be perpetrators of any mass-casualty attack.

Third, accurate and timely collection and analysis of intelligence is pivotal to countering the threat of CBRNE terrorism. The focus must be on the individuals, groups, networks, and states of greatest concern. Human intelligence will be key to understanding real and potential enemy motivation, resolve, culture, modus operandi, decisionmaking, resources, capabilities, locations, and conflict techniques. Such intelligence will be required for any preventive option. It will produce knowledge of how best to disrupt and destroy suspect groups and capabilities. In addition, it will also help in evaluating the susceptibility of such organizations—their leaders and other members—to deterrence logic.

Finally, because of the fanatical motives and resolve displayed by nonstate actors such as al Qaeda, many observers will simply dismiss deterrence as a preventive option out of hand. However, the activities associated with alternative approaches should contribute to a deterrent effect. Examples include preparing for consequence management, developing intelligence and military capabilities to disrupt and destroy terrorist networks, and demonstrating the resolve of ongoing military operations against al Qaeda.

Wyn Q. Bowen is a lecturer in the Defense Studies Department at King's College in London and coeditor of *Defense Studies*. He has served as a specialist adviser to the House of Commons Foreign Affairs Committee inquiring about weapons of mass destruction and as a UN weapons inspector in Iraq. He is currently researching asymmetrical conflicts and U.S. missile defense policy and programs.

Notes

1. Herbert Simon, quoted in Richard Lebow and Janice Stein, "Rational Deterrence Theory: I Think, Therefore I Deter," *World Politics*, vol. 41, no. 2 (January 1989), p. 214.
2. Gerald M. Steinberg, *Rediscovering Deterrence After September 11, 2001*, Jerusalem Center for Public Affairs, December 2001, http://www.jcpa.org/jl/vp467.htm.
3. Jay Davis, *The Grand Challenges of Counter-Terrorism, Center for Global Security Research*, Lawrence Livermore National Laboratory, 2001, http://cgsr.llnl.gov/future2001/davis.html.
4. See Anthony H. Cordesman, *Asymmetric Warfare Versus Counter-Terrorism: Rethinking CBRN and CIP Defense and Response* (Washington: Center for Strategic and International Studies, December 2001), p. 14.

Chapter 9

Organizing to Fight Terrorism

The effort of building the proper organization for fighting terrorism entails potential reform on many fronts: reform of government's structure, of national security capabilities, of intelligence practices, and of the policy-making process.

Martha Crenshaw explores how American counterterrorism policy is formed and points out that these policies are not simply a response to the threat of terrorism: they are a reflection of the domestic political process. The author introduces the different actors involved: the executive branch; Congress; and entities outside the government, such as interest groups and communities of "experts," business interests, victims and victims' families, and the media. The history of specific policy decisions is presented as an illustration of the complexity of the policy-forming process among actors with competing interests and diffuse authority. The author concludes that it is unlikely the process will change—and unlikely that counterterrorism policy will be based solely on an objective appraisal of the threat of terrorism without being filtered through the political lens.

Richard K. Betts explores prospects for reform in the intelligence community. September 11 brought on an immediate backlash—that the biggest intelligence system in the world could not prevent a group of fanatics from carrying out their devastating attacks, and the nation's intelligence services needed to be fixed. Betts delves into the matter more deeply. As he says, "The awful truth is that even the best intelligence systems will have big failures. The terrorists that intelligence must uncover and track are not inert objects; they are living, conniving strategists." He continues that to have a batting average of less than 1,000 seems terrible indeed, but a less-than-perfect average is the reality. The author looks at areas for change: more spending, stronger human intelligence, intelligence gathering on U.S. soil where the process comes under U.S. laws that protect civil liberties. And he delves into the history of intelligence—touching on the surprise attacks at Pearl Harbor—and uncovers a depressing historical pattern. He does not refute that the right reforms can better the nation's batting average, but he presents the reality and cautions that, "Reform will happen, and, on balance, should help. But for too many policymakers and pundits, reorganization is an alluring but illusory quick fix."

Jeffrey Norwitz presents us with the question that ultimately governs our response to terrorism: Should counterterror governments apply a judicial or military paradigm in fighting the global war on terrorism? Both approaches offer policy makers different tools and constraints with which to prosecute a counterterrorism campaign. Norwitz concludes that current judicial paradigms are lagging behind the current nature of the conflict and are inadequate to the challenge. This conclusion raises difficult questions for any democracy and what its citizens expect from their government. Nonetheless, the hard questions are exactly the ones that all citizens need to examine.

According to military expert Rob de Wijk, the events of September 11 "clarified the urgent need to refocus and restructure the way the United States and its allies think about and plan for a military campaign." This effort will require a new approach and new assets: developing irregular forces that are well-practiced in guerrilla tactics and asymmetrical retaliation; strengthening both special operations forces (SOF) and human intelligence (HUMINT), capabilities the author defines as being now scarce; abandoning some beliefs about traditional warfare; and sharpening the skills of coercive diplomacy, when dealing with states. Finally, de Wijk delves into the cultural aspect of this new war, of which a central component, he writes, "is the campaign to win the support of the populace of the opponent. In other words, the United States and its allies must also wage a battle for the hearts and minds of the people… in the Islamic world."

"The calculus of the war on terrorism is different from that of the previous wars," says David J. Rothkopf. Five grams of anthrax in an office tower ventilation system, a briefcase-sized nuclear device, or a dose of smallpox in an airport have the power to kill more people than were lost in a decade of fighting in Vietnam. Rothkopf proposes a resource in our midst to combat the odds: "scientists and doctors, venture capitalists and corporate project managers—the private-sector army that is the United States' not-so-secret weapon and best hope." According to Rothkopf, the marriage of the public-private forces is not new, and he details Tom Ridge's first steps toward the partnership and draws the root of the effort back to the Eisenhower administration's Small Business Act of 1958. But the author advises that the public-private coalition requires a new attitude, outlook, and structure; and the focus should be on efforts that require the federal government's participation, where threats to national security could lead to massive physical or economic devastation. These "regiments of geeks" are the unlikely warriors that can develop the software and analytical resources to track terrorists; the sensing systems to detect biological, chemical, and cyber threats; and the biometric devices that will be the next wave in security tools. As Rothkopf notes of these post-9/11 times, "The opportunity is strikingly clear: The United States can defeat terrorists by drawing on the very attributes that inflame its enemies."

Martha Crenshaw, 2001

Counterterrorism Policy and the Political Process

American counterterrorism policy is not just a response to the threat of terrorism, whether at home or abroad, but a reflection of the domestic political process. Perceptions of the threat of terrorism and determination and implementation of policy occur in the context of a policy debate involving government institutions, the media, interest groups, and the elite and mass publics. The issue of terrorism tends to appear prominently on the national policy agenda as a result of highly visible and symbolic attacks on Americans or American property. However, the threat is interpreted through a political lens created by the diffused structure of power within the American government.[1]

In general, focusing events, such as crises or disasters, trigger attention to a problem by attracting the attention of the news media and the public.[2] Such sudden and harmful events, rare by definition, come to the notice of the mass public and policy elites simultaneously. In the case of terrorism, focusing events frequently come in clusters, so that it is often difficult to trace a specific policy response to a single event. The reaction to the Oklahoma City bombing, for example, is linked to perceptions of the 1993 World Trade Center bombing and the 1995 Aum Shinrikyo sarin gas attack on the Tokyo subways. Under the Reagan administration, the 1986 military strike against Libya was a response not just to the La Belle disco bombing in Berlin but to earlier attacks such as the TWA and Achille Lauro hijackings and the shooting attacks at the Rome and Vienna airports in 1985. Thus, sequences of events rather than single disasters typically serve as policy catalysts.

As Robert Johnson has emphasized, in the United States threatening events are filtered through a political process that is characterized by lack of consensus among political elites.[3] The decision-making process is disaggregated and pluralistic, and power is diffused. Because not all issues can be dealt with simultaneously, political elites—the president, different agencies within the executive branch, Congress, the media, interest groups, and "experts" in academia and the consulting world—compete to set the national policy agenda. They compete to select certain problems for attention, interpret their meaning and significance, conceive of solutions, put them into practice, and evaluate their outcomes. Despite the secrecy inherent in formulating and implementing policy toward terrorism, issues are developed, interests formed, and policies legitimized through public debates.[4] Decision makers with different identities and preferences define and represent problems, or frame issues, in order to gain public support for their positions. Furthermore, the selection and implementation of policy depend on the particularistic interests of the actors or coalitions that assume the initiative as much as consistent policy doctrine or strategy based on a broad national consensus about what can and ought to be done. Lack of coordination and fragmentation of effort are often the result.

The Politics of the Executive Branch

The political process within the executive branch is characterized by progressive expansion of the number of agencies involved; overlapping lines of authority among them; expansion of jurisdictions to encompass new issues; parochialism; and competition. No agency in the executive branch of the government wants an issue on the agenda unless it has an efficient and acceptable solution for it. Thus, public policy problems such as terrorism are typically linked to proposed solutions that are in turn linked to specific institutions within the government. How an issue is defined will typically determine which government institution has jurisdiction over it and can thus take charge of policy solutions, often with corresponding budget increases. (Spending on antiterrorism programs jumped from $61.7 million to $205.3 million in the fiscal 1999 appropriations.[5] Overall spending on terrorism is generally estimated at $7 billion per year.)

As the definition of the threat of terrorism changes, so too does jurisdiction. If the image of an issue can be changed, then its institutional venue may change accordingly. Issues can be partitioned among agencies, or different institutions can have more or less authority at various stages or sequences of a decision. For example, if terrorism is defined as a crime, it is a problem for the Department of Justice and the nation's law enforcement agencies such as the Federal Bureau of Investigation (FBI). However, if it is defined as warfare or as a threat to national security, responsibility shifts accordingly. The Central Intelligence Agency (CIA) and the military become central to the process. Nevertheless, the FBI did not lose its role. In 1986, major legislation established extraterritorial jurisdiction for crimes committed against Americans abroad, which has led to prosecutions in the World Trade Center bombing and East Africa bombing cases, along with others. Definition of the threat of terrorism as "bioterrorism" in the 1990s brought a host of new agencies into the jurisdictional competition, including Health and Human Services (HHS) and its Centers for Disease Control. Previously, when the threat of "super terrorism" was interpreted as the danger of the acquisition of nuclear materials, the Department of Energy assumed a key role. In the 1990s, as the threat of terrorism came to be seen as a threat to the "homeland," not only did local and state governments enter the picture but the military was called on to provide "homeland defense." The Defense Authorization Act for Fiscal Year 1997 called on the Department of Defense (DOD) to train local "first responders" and to establish response teams to assist civilian authorities should there be a terrorist incident involving weapons of mass destruction (WMD).[6] The result was Joint Task Force Civil Support, established in 1999.[7]

Responsibility for dealing with terrorism is widely distributed, and lines of jurisdiction tend to be blurred and overlapping, with no clear institutional monopoly of the issue. The U.S. government tried to deal with this problem by establishing the "lead agency" concept. The Department of State is the lead agency for responding to international terrorism, while the FBI is the lead agency for domestic terrorism.[8] Nevertheless, the White House National Security Council (NSC) and the Department of State have traditionally competed for institutional control of the issue of international terrorism, and the FBI and the State Department sometimes clash. For example, Secretary of State Cyrus Vance resigned after his advice against a hostage rescue mission in Iran was overruled by the president and the NSC under National Security Adviser Zbigniew Brzezinski. Former Director of the Central

Intelligence Agency Stansfield Turner described the relationship between the NSC and executive branch agencies as it affected the rescue decision:

> The National Security Adviser and his staff often are frustrated because they have no direct authority to carry out the President's decisions. That's the task of the bureaucracy, which frequently resists outside direction, even from the President. Bureaucrats are even more likely to resist what they suspect are directives from the National Security Council staff. A result of these tensions is that the staff of the NSC often attempts to sidestep the bureaucracy and do as much as possible on its own.[9]

Turner and the CIA also resisted the NSC's proposals for covert operations against Iran, seeing the dispute as a case of "the professionalism of the experts keeping the political leadership from undertaking ventures that would be embarrassingly unsuccessful."[10]

Rivalries between the NSC and other executive branch agencies also emerged under the Clinton administration. In April 1998, as a result of having read the Richard Preston novel, *The Cobra Event*, the president held a meeting with a group of scientists and Cabinet members to discuss the threat of bioterrorism. The briefing impressed Clinton so much that he asked the experts to brief senior officials in DOD and HHS. On May 6 they delivered a follow-up report, calling for the stockpiling of vaccines (an idea that was soon dropped). *The Washington Post* reported with regard to the stockpiling proposal that "Some administration officials outside the White House expressed surprise at how fast the president and his National Security Council staff had moved on the initiative..., noting with some concern that it had not gone through the customary deliberative planning process."[11] Critics noted that not all scientific experts were disinterested; some stood to gain financially if the government invested large sums in developing technology against bioterrorism.

In the investigation of the October 2000 bombing of the destroyer U.S.S. *Cole* the State Department was said to be less than enthusiastic about the FBI's hard-line approach to Yemeni authorities.[12] While the FBI appealed to the president to demand that Yemen accept a central FBI role, the State Department countered by warning that the pressure would likely backfire.

Clinton's move to establish the position of a national coordinator for counterterrorism policy on the NSC staff also provoked opposition from within the executive branch. *The New York Times* reported that Clinton's May 1998 initiative "had provoked a bitter fight within the Administration, with the Departments of Defense and Justice opposing a key provision that critics feared would have created a terrorism czar within the White House."[13] As a result, Clinton created a national coordinator with limited staff and no direct budget authority. *The Washington Post* reported, "It is not clear how much real authority [Richard] Clarke will have.... The Defense Department successfully fought off proposals to give this coordinator a large staff and independent budget similar to those of the drug policy coordinator.... Clarke's appears to be essentially a staff job, reporting to National Security Adviser Samuel R. "Sandy" Berger."[14]

Moreover, agencies may reject jurisdiction and try to exclude issues from the agenda, especially if they think that they do not have a solution or that the new task is not appropriate to their mission or routine. The DOD, for example, appears divided and ambivalent about its new role in homeland defense. As early as July 1995, some Pentagon officials were calling for an expanded military role in counterterrorism, but this view did not appear to reflect an internal consensus. In a speech to the Council on Foreign Relations in New York in September 1998, Secretary of Defense William Cohen prominently mentioned terrorism.[15] His description of the military mission, however, was vague; he said that the administration hoped to consolidate the task of coordination into one lead federal agency, and that DOD would provide "active support" for that agency's operation. Falkenrath et al. argued that the DOD is not "fully committed to this mission."[16] The military see "homeland defense" as law enforcement, which the military supports only if ordered and when possible. Essentially, in their view, it is a diversion and misuse of defense dollars, and they would prefer that the entire domestic preparedness program be shifted to the Federal Emergency Management Agency (FEMA). The military's reluctance is confirmed by John Hillen, who sees DOD as dominated by interservice rivalries rather than leadership from the president or the secretary of defense: "Today the services are interested in neither the White House's new wars (peacekeeping, terrorism, organized crime, and the like) nor the Joint Staff's futuristic technological blueprint...."[17] The military really wants to fight wars that are like those of the past, only with upgraded equipment on all sides. In January 1999, press reports announcing Cohen's decision to seek presidential approval for a permanent DOD task force, with a senior officer, to plan for a chemical or biological attack on the U.S. quoted Deputy Defense Secretary John Hamre as saying "Frankly, we're not seeking this job."[18]

Similarly, FEMA did not want to take charge of the domestic preparedness program.[19] FEMA officials opted out on budgetary grounds, fearing that the program would be inadequately funded, and thus be a drain on already scarce resources, and that the agency would then be criticized for ineffective implementation of the program. Since they could not afford the solution, they did not want to take on the problem.

In 1998, the decision to retaliate against the Sudan and Afghanistan also revealed disarray within the executive branch, a state of confusion and contentiousness that threatened to eclipse terrorism as the issue at the forefront of public debate.[20] The FBI and the CIA were accused of failing to share complete information on threats in East Africa with the State Department.[21] Disagreement surfaced between Washington and bureaucracies in the field. The ambassador in Kenya in December 1997, and again in April and May 1998, asked unsuccessfully for support from the State Department Bureau of Diplomatic Security for the construction of a new and less vulnerable building. The decision to retaliate was controversial. Some analysts in the CIA and the State Department Bureau of Intelligence and Research remained unconvinced of the reliability of the evidence linking Osama bin Ladin's network to the pharmaceuticals plant in Khartoum and informed the news media of their doubts after the cruise missile strikes. The FBI and the Defense Intelligence Agency were excluded from the decision. Apparently Chairman of the Joint Chiefs of Staff General Shelton objected to the original targeting plan and succeeded in reducing the number of targets.

Congressional Politics

Congress frequently plays a critical role in shaping the counterterrorism policy agenda, without the constraint of necessarily having to present an integrated solution to the problem. Although the president typically has the most power to set the agenda, he depends on Congress to appropriate funds for the measures he proposes, and Congress can block issues or push forward others that the president has not chosen. Furthermore, executive branch agencies usually have their own channels of communication and influence with congressional committees. Congressional staffers and career bureaucrats often have extensive back-channel contacts. Individuals move back and forth between positions in Congress and in the executive branch. Thus, even if the president wants to keep an issue off the agenda or to minimize a problem, he may have to confront it because congressional actions have captured media and public attention. Confrontation is especially likely when the government is divided along partisan lines. The president cannot afford to appear to ignore a potential threat of terrorism, even if restraint might be the most appropriate and effective response. In the 1990s, the president and Congress often seemed to be engaged in a highly partisan politics of anticipatory blame avoidance.

Examples of congressional influence on critical policy decisions include President Reagan's decision to withdraw American troops from Lebanon in the aftermath of the 1983 bombing of the Marine barracks. Reagan was apparently dissuaded by congressional and military opposition encountered in the context of an upcoming campaign for reelection.[22] Initially Reagan resisted the idea of withdrawal, although the House Committee on Armed Services urged him to reconsider his policy and issued its own report critical of security at the Marine barracks. Reagan withheld the release of the DOD's Long Commission report for several days in order to limit the damage he feared it would create as a rallying point for opposition in Congress. Congressional responses from both Republicans and Democrats to Reagan's press conferences and speeches were lukewarm at best. Although the movement to reassess policy was largely bipartisan, House Speaker O'Neill assumed a prominent role in the debate, organizing the passage of resolutions calling for an end to the military presence in Lebanon, and Democratic presidential candidate Walter Mondale seized on withdrawal as a campaign issue. The State Department and the National Security Adviser opposed withdrawal, but DOD and the Joint Chiefs favored it. In early January, Reagan sent his national security adviser, secretary of defense, and the chairman of the Joint Chiefs of Staff to speak with leading House Republicans. Nevertheless, Minority Whip Trent Lott stated publicly that the Republicans had told them that they wanted the Marines out by March 1985. Still, in his State of the Union address in January 1984, Reagan persisted: "We must have the courage to give peace a chance. And we must not be driven from our objectives for peace in Lebanon by state-sponsored terrorism."[23] Within two weeks of the State of the Union address, Reagan announced the withdrawal.

An earlier instance of congressional influence over policy occurred during the Ford administration. Secretary of State Kissinger ordered the recall of the ambassador to Tanzania, Beverly Carter, when he learned that Carter had played an active role in facilitating negotiations for the release of American students held hostage in Zaire. Kissinger took strong exception to this violation of the official policy of no concessions and reportedly intended to end Carter's State Department career, although Carter had expected to be appointed ambassador to Denmark. However, when the Congressional Black Caucus intervened on Carter's behalf, generating negative publicity for the State Department, Kissinger relented.[24] It was also helpful to Carter's defense that he was a former journalist.

In the 1990s, as Richard Falkenrath points out, one source of the difficulties of the domestic preparedness program was "its origin in a series of discrete, uncoordinated legislative appropriations and administrative actions," the result of ad hoc initiatives rather than strategic concept.[25] In 1996, for example, Congress began "earmarking" specific counterterrorism projects, such as providing $10 million for counterterrorism technologies for the National Institute of Justice in the Fiscal Year 1997 Department of Justice budget. The FBI counterterrorism budget was also dramatically increased, largely as a result of the Oklahoma City bombing. Congress also instructed the Departments of Justice and Defense to prepare long-term plans for counterterrorism, and established an independent National Commission on Terrorism to investigate government policy. Lawmakers are also concerned about lack of congressional oversight of administration efforts.

Outside the Government

Actors outside the government also try to shape the public policy agenda. Interest groups and communities of "experts," sometimes associated with professional consulting firms, or think tanks, seek access to decision makers in order to promote favored issues. They often accumulate the scientific or technical information about the problem that then causes decision makers to recognize it. They can promote a specific conception of an issue, such as the idea of a new, more lethal and irresponsible terrorism in the 1990s.[26] They contribute the "talking heads" who appear regularly on television news programs such as CNN. They may also be influential in shaping policy solutions because of their expertise.

Among interest groups, in the area of terrorism, business interests may oppose economic sanctions against state sponsors. Interest groups devoted to protecting civil liberties are likely to oppose measures that restrict individual freedoms, such as expanding the power of the FBI or the use of passenger profiling at airports. The American Civil Liberties Union, for example, has frequently opposed legislative initiatives such as assigning responsibility for domestic preparedness to the military. Along with conservative Republicans, civil liberties interest groups blocked the wiretapping provisions of the 1996 bill.

The families of victims of terrorism, as well as victims themselves, such as the former hostages in Lebanon, have mobilized to influence policy. They have lobbied the State Department as well as the White House and Congress, and gone to the courts to press their claims against Iran and Libya. For example, the Victims of Pan Am Flight 103 organization established a political action committee, a legal committee, an investigation committee, and a press committee. They lobbied the State Department, published a newsletter, picketed Pan Am offices, and met with the president and Congress.[27] They were instrumental in the creation of a presidential Commission on Aviation Security and Terrorism to investigate the bombing. They played an influential role in the 1996 Iran-Libya Sanctions Act of 1996.[28] Their intervention led to major changes in airline procedures for handling disasters.

During the Iran hostage crisis, the families of the victims formed the Family Liaison Action Group, which, according to Gary Sick, "played a crucial role in public and government perceptions throughout the crisis."[29] Sick adds that President Carter promised the families that he would take no action that would endanger the lives of the hostages, although Brzezinski was pressing for a decisive response that would protect national honor.

The early development of counterterrorism policy was influenced by interactions between individual government agencies and specific interest groups. The debate over the Airport Security Act of 1973 shows how insider–outsider coalitions form.[30] The government players included Congress, the Departments of Transportation, State, and Justice, and the Federal Aviation Administration (FAA). The outside actors were the Air Line Pilots Association (ALPA), the Air Transport Association of America (ATAA), and the Airport

Operators Council International (AOCI). In the jurisdictional dispute between Justice and the FAA, the ATAA and AOCI preferred the FAA, while ALPA preferred Justice. In fact, Justice did not want jurisdiction. While the interest groups wanted the federal government to take responsibility for airport security measures, the Department of Transportation and the FAA wished to rely on local law enforcement.

All of these actors use the news media to articulate and disseminate their views not only to the public but to other elites. Government officials (or former officials) are the main source of information for reporters, as well as for Congress, sometimes openly and sometimes through strategic leaks. Leaks to the press can be a way of conducting internal battles as much as informing the public. The media's attraction to drama and spectacular events also makes it hard for the government to ignore an issue when policymakers assume that public opinion will track media attention. But the news media do not set the agenda, according to John Kingdon: "The media's tendency to give prominence to the most newsworthy or dramatic story actually diminishes their impact on governmental policy agendas because such stories tend to come toward the end of a policy-making process, rather than at the beginning."[31] The media tend to be responsive to issues already on the agenda, to accelerate or magnify them, rather than initiate attention. They report on what the government is doing or not doing.

Jeffrey D. Simon agrees.[32] He argues that the media image of crisis is due to the way presidents and their aides handle events; the press depends almost exclusively on authoritative official sources. Government officials set the tone through background briefings and off the record interviews as well as public speeches and press conferences. Presidents, not reporters, make hostage seizures into personal dramas. On the other hand, Brigitte Nacos argues that government policy is exceptionally sensitive to the news media and to public opinion, especially during hostage crises.[33] Yet the tone of general mass media coverage of U.S. counterterrorism policy is positive.[34]

Conclusions

It is unlikely that the politics of the domestic policy process will change. Thus, expectations for the future should be grounded in the assumption that the trends described in this article will continue. Terrorist attacks, especially spectacular incidents causing large numbers of casualties or targeting important national symbols, will contribute to putting the issue on the national policy agenda. They focus public attention on the threat of terrorism. However, policy will be developed within a general framework of diffusion of power. Multiple actors, inside and outside government, will compete to set the agenda and to determine policy through public debate, conducted largely in the news media. Each actor, whether an executive branch agency, Congress, or an interest group, wants to forge a national consensus behind its particular preference. Due to pressures from Congress, the president will not be able to set the agenda for counterterrorism policy with as much freedom as he can in other policy areas. Where the president dominates is in the rare use of military force, but these decisions may also be controversial within the executive branch. Implementation of policy decisions will also be affected by controversy, due to rivalries among agencies with operational responsibilities. Thus it will be difficult for any administration to develop a consistent policy based on an objective appraisal of the threat of terrorism to American national interests.

Martha Crenshaw is John E. Andrus professor of government at Wesleyan University, where she has taught international politics since 1974. She is the editor, with John Pimlott, of the *International Encyclopedia of Terrorism* and the author of countless articles and texts on the subject of political terrorism. Crenshaw currently serves on a task force concerning foreign policy toward the Islamic world at the Brookings Institution.

Notes

1. Despite its significance, little systematic attention has been paid to the politics of the counterterrorism policy process. William Farrell's early book, *The U.S. Government Response to Terrorism: In Search of an Effective Strategy* (Boulder, CO: Westview Press, 1982), analyzed the organizations behind counterterrorism policy. David Tucker, *Skirmished at the Edge of Empire: The United States and International Terrorism* (Westport, CT: Praeger, 1997), is also relevant, particularly Chapter 4 (pp. 109–132). Paul Pillar's *Terrorism and U.S. Foreign Policy* will also help fill this gap (Washington, DC: Brookings, 2001).

2. Thomas A Birkland, *After Disaster: Agenda Setting, Public Policy, and Focusing Events* (Washington, DC: Georgetown University Press, 1997).

3. Robert H. Johnson, *Improbable Dangers: U.S. Conceptions of Threat in the Cold War and After* (New York: St. Martin's, 1997), Chapter 2, "American Politics, Psychology, and the Exaggeration of Threat," pp. 31–48.

4. The classic work is John W. Kingdon, *Agendas, Alternatives, and Public Policies*, 2nd ed. (New York: Harper Collins, 1995). See also Frank R. Baumgartner and Bryan D. Jones, Agendas and Instability in American Politics (Chicago: University of Chicago Press, 1993) and Deborah A. Stone, *Policy Paradox: The Art of Political Decision Making* (New York: W. W. Norton, 1997).

5. See *Congressional Quarterly Weekly Report*, 16 January 1999, p. 151.

6. See Richard A. Falkenrath, "Problems of Preparedness: U.S. Readiness for a Domestic Terrorist Attack," *International Security* 25(4) (Spring 2001), pp. 147–186. See also Martha Crenshaw, "Threat Perception in Democracies: 'WMD' Terrorism in the U.S. Policy Debate," presented to the 22nd Annual Scientific Meeting of the International Society for Political Psychology, Amsterdam, 18–21 July 1999.

7. It has 82 members and an annual budget of $8.7 million, and is expected to increase to 121 people by 2003. It is based in Virginia, as part of the U.S. Joint Forces Command. In the event of a request from local or state government authorities, it would probably take direction from FEMA. See James Dao, "Looking Ahead to the Winter Olympics, a Terrorist Response Team Trains," *The New York Times*, 11 April 2001.

8. However, the Federal Emergency Management Agency (FEMA) has jurisdiction over "consequence management," which is in effect disaster response policy in the event of a domestic attack, especially one involving mass casualties.

9. In *Terrorism & Democracy* (Boston: Houghton Mifflin, 1991), p. 39.

10. Ibid., p. 81. Brzezinski set up an NSC committee to oversee covert actions because the CIA estimated that prospects for success were low. The CIA then vetoed the list of operations the NSC suggested, but Brzezinski was reluctant to take the dispute to the president.

11. 21 May 1998, p. A1.

12. See John F. Burns, "U.S. Aides Say the Yemenis Seem to Hinder Cole Inquiry," *The New York Times*, 1 November 2000.

13. 26 April 1998.

14. 23 May 1998, p. A3.

15. For the text of the speech, see http://www.defenselink.mil/news/Sep1998.

16. Richard A. Falkenrath, Robert D. Newman, and Bradley A. Thayer, *America's Achilles Heel: Nuclear, Biological, and Chemical Terrorism and Covert Attack* (Cambridge, MA: MIT Press,

1998), p. 263. See also Falkenrath, "Problems of Preparedness," p. 162, who says that the military see this role as a distraction from their core mission.

17. "Defense's Death Spiral," *Foreign Affairs* 78(4) (July-August 1999), p. 4.

18. *The New York Times*, 28 January 1999; also *The Hartford Courant*, with *Washington Post* by-line, 1 February 1999.

19. See Falkenrath, "Problems of Preparedness," p. 163.

20. On this subject, see James Risen, "To Bomb Sudan Plant, or Not: A Year Later, Debates Rankle," *The New York Times*, 27 October 1999, and Seymour Hersh, "The Missiles of August," *The New Yorker*, 12 October 1998, pp. 34–41.

21. See Report of the Accountability Review Boards: Bombings of the U.S. Embassies in Nairobi, Kenya and Dar Es Salaam, Tanzania on August 7, 1998, 11 January 1999. Available at (http://www.zgram.net/embassybombing.htm). See further details from the classified report in James Risen and Benjamin Weiser, "Before Bombings, Omens and Fears," *The New York Times*, 9 January 1999. According to this account, the Kenyan authorities arrested a group of suspects but the CIA station chief declined to interview them.

22. This section relies on research assistance by Karen Millard. See press reports such as Lou Cannon, "Political Pressure for Marine Pullout Likely to Increase," *Washington Post*, 29 December 1983; Martin Tolchin, "House Leaders Urge New Study of Beirut Policy," *The New York Times*, 3 January 1984; and John Goshko and Margaret Shapiro, "Shultz Asks for Support on Lebanon; Holds Hill Parleys as Pressure for Withdrawal Grows," *The Washington Post*, 27 January 1984.

23. See text in *The Washington Post*, 26 January 1984, p. A16.

24. See *The New York Times*, 14, 18, and 20 August 1975. Kate Whitman assisted with the research of this case.

25. Falkenrath, "Problems of Preparedness," p. 149.

26. For example, Ian O. Lesser et al., *Countering the New Terrorism* (Santa Monica, CA: Rand Corporation, 1999). The study was commissioned by the Air Force.

27. See Steven Emerson and Brian Duffy, *The Fall of Pan Am 103: Inside the Lockerbie Investigation* (New York: G. P. Putnams' Sons, 1990), especially pp. 221–225.

28. See Gideon Rose's account of the politics of the legislative process in his chapter on Libya in Richard N. Haass, ed., *Economic Sanctions and American Diplomacy* (New York: Council on Foreign Relations, 1998), pp. 129–156, especially pp. 142–144. See also Patrick Clawson's chapter on Iran, pp. 85–106.

29. See his chapter, "Taking vows: The domestication of policy-making in hostage incidents," in *Origins of Terrorism*, edited by Walter Reich (Washington, DC: Woodrow Wilson Center and Cambridge University Press, 1990), pp. 238–239.

30. Joel Rothman assisted with research on this debate. See U.S. Senate, Committee on Commerce, Subcommittee on Aviation, *The Anti-Hijacking Act of 1971*. Hearings. 92nd Cong., 2d sess., 1972.

31. Kingdon, *Agendas, Alternatives, and Public Policies*, p. 59.

32. *The Terrorist Trap: America's Experience with Terrorism* (Bloomington: Indiana University Press, 1994), especially Chapter 7, "Media Players," pp. 261–308.

33. *Terrorism and the Media* (New York: Columbia University Press, 1994).

34. Measured by references to international terrorism in the *Readers' Guide to Periodical Literature 1968–1998*. Database available upon request.

Richard K. Betts, 2002

Fixing Intelligence

The Limits of Prevention

As the dust from the attacks on the World Trade Center and the Pentagon was still settling, the chants began: The CIA was asleep at the switch! The intelligence system is broken! Reorganize top to bottom! The biggest intelligence system in the world, spending upward of $30 billion a year, could not prevent a group of fanatics from carrying out devastating terrorist attacks. Drastic change must be overdue. The new conventional wisdom was typified by Tim Weiner, writing in *The New York Times* on October 7: "What will the nation's intelligence services have to change to fight this war? The short answer is: almost everything."

Yes and no. A lot must, can, and will be done to shore up U.S. intelligence collection and analysis. Reforms that should have been made long ago will now go through. New ideas will get more attention and good ones will be adopted more readily than in normal times. There is no shortage of proposals and initiatives to shake the system up. There is, however, a shortage of perspective on the limitations that we can expect from improved performance. Some of the changes will substitute new problems for old ones. The only thing worse than business as usual would be naive assumptions about what reform can accomplish.

Paradoxically, the news is worse than the angriest critics think, because the intelligence community has worked much better than they assume. Contrary to the image left by the destruction of September 11, U.S. intelligence and associated services have generally done very well at protecting the country. In the aftermath of a catastrophe, great successes in thwarting previous terrorist attacks are too easily forgotten—successes such as the foiling of plots to bomb New York City's Lincoln and Holland tunnels in 1993, to bring down 11 American airliners in Asia in 1995, to mount attacks around the millennium on the West Coast and in Jordan, and to strike U.S. forces in the Middle East in the summer of 2001.

The awful truth is that even the best intelligence systems will have big failures. The terrorists that intelligence must uncover and track are not inert objects; they are living, conniving strategists. They, too, fail frequently and are sometimes caught before they can strike. But once in a while they will inevitably get through. Counterterrorism is a competitive game. Even Barry Bonds could be struck out at times by a minor-league pitcher, but when a strikeout means people die, a batting average of less than 1.000 looks very bad indeed.

It will be some time before the real story of the September 11 intelligence failure is known, and longer still before a reliable public account is available. Rather than recap the rumors and fragmentary evidence of exactly what intelligence did and did not do before September 11, at this point it is more appropriate to focus on the merits of proposals for reform and the larger question about what intelligence agencies can reasonably be expected to accomplish.

Spend a Lot to Get a Little

One way to improve intelligence is to raise the overall level of effort by throwing money at the problem. This means accepting additional waste, but that price is paid more easily in wartime than in peacetime. Unfortunately, although there have certainly been misallocations of effort in the past, there are no silver bullets that were left unused before September 11, no crucial area of intelligence that was neglected altogether and that a few well-targeted investments can conquer. There is no evidence, at least in public, that more spending on any particular program would have averted the September 11 attacks. The group that carried them out had formidable operational security, and the most critical deficiencies making their success possible were in airport security and in legal limitations on domestic surveillance. There are nevertheless several areas in which intelligence can be improved, areas in which previous efforts were extensive but spread too thinly or slowed down too much.

It will take large investments to make even marginal reductions in the probability of future disasters. Marginal improvements, however, can spell the difference between success and failure in some individual cases. If effective intelligence collection increases by only five percent a year, but the critical warning indicator of an attack turns up in that five percent, gaining a little information will yield a lot of protection. Streamlining intelligence operations and collection is a nice idea in principle but risky unless it is clear what is not needed. When threats are numerous and complex, it is easier to know what additional capabilities we want than to know what we can safely cut.

After the Cold War, intelligence resources went down as requirements went up (since the country faced a new set of high-priority issues and regions). At the end of the 1990s there was an uptick in the intelligence budget, but the system was still spread thinner over its targets than it had been when focused on the Soviet Union. Three weeks before September 11, the director of central intelligence (DCI), George Tenet, gave an interview to *Signal* magazine that now seems tragically prescient. He agonized about the prospect of a catastrophic intelligence failure: "Then the country will want to know why we didn't make those investments; why we didn't pay the price; why we didn't develop the capability."

The sluice gates for intelligence spending will open for a while. The challenge is not buying some essential element of capability that was ignored before but helping the system do more of everything and do it better. That will increase the odds that bits and pieces of critical information will be acquired and noticed rather than falling through the sieve.

Another way to improve intelligence is to do better at collecting important information. Here, what can be improved easily will help marginally, whereas what could help more than marginally cannot be improved easily. The National Security Agency (NSA), the National Imagery and Mapping Agency (NIMA), and associated organizations can increase "technical" collection—satellite and aerial reconnaissance, signals intelligence, communications monitoring—by buying more platforms, devices, and personnel to exploit them. But increasing useful human intelligence, which everyone agrees is the most critical ingredient for rooting out secretive terrorist groups, is not done easily or through quick infusions of money.

Technical collection is invaluable and has undoubtedly figured in previous counter-terrorist successes in ways that are not publicized. But obtaining this kind of information has been getting harder. For one thing, so much has been revealed over the years about U.S. technical collection capabilities that the targets now understand better what they have to evade. State sponsors of terrorism may know satellite overflight schedules and can schedule accordingly activities that might otherwise be observable. They can use more fiber-optic communications, which are much harder to tap than transmission over the airwaves. Competent terrorists know not to use cell phones for sensitive messages, and even small groups have access to impressive new encryption technologies.

Human intelligence is key because the essence of the terrorist threat is the capacity to conspire. The best way to intercept attacks is to penetrate the organizations, learn their plans, and identify perpetrators so they can be taken out of action. Better human intelligence means bolstering the CIA's Directorate of Operations (DO), the main traditional espionage organization of the U.S. government. The DO has been troubled and periodically disrupted ever since the evaporation of the Cold War consensus in the late stage of the Vietnam War provoked more oversight and criticism than spies find congenial. Personnel turnover, tattered esprit, and a growing culture of risk aversion have constrained the DO's effectiveness.

Some of the constraint was a reasonable price to pay to prevent excesses, especially in a post–Cold War world in which the DO was working for the country's interests rather than its survival. After the recent attacks, however, worries about excesses have receded, and measures will be found to make it easier for the clandestine service to operate. One simple reform, for example, would be to implement a recommendation made by the National Commission on Terrorism a year and a half ago: roll back the additional layer of cumbersome procedures instituted in 1995 for gaining approval to employ agents with "unsavory" records—procedures that have had a chilling effect on recruitment of the thugs appropriate for penetrating terrorist units.

Building up human intelligence networks worldwide is a long-term project. It inevitably spawns concern about waste (many such networks will never produce anything useful), deception (human sources are widely distrusted), and complicity with murderous characters (such as the Guatemalan officer who prompted the 1995 change in recruitment guidelines). These are prices that can be borne politically in the present atmosphere of crisis. If the sense of crisis abates, however, commitment to the long-term project could falter.

More and better spies will help, but no one should expect breakthroughs if we get them. It is close to impossible to penetrate small, disciplined, alien organizations like Osama bin Laden's al Qaeda, and especially hard to find reliable U.S. citizens who have even a remote chance of trying. Thus we usually rely on foreign agents of uncertain reliability. Despite our huge and educated population, the base of Americans on which to draw is small: there are very few genuinely bilingual, bicultural Americans capable of operating like natives in exotic reaches of the Middle East, Central and South Asia, or other places that shelter the bin Ladens of the world.

For similar reasons there have been limitations on our capacity to translate information that does get collected. The need is not just for people who have studied Arabic,

Pashto, Urdu, or Farsi, but for those who are truly fluent in those languages, and fluent in obscure dialects of them. Should U.S. intelligence trust recent, poorly educated immigrants for these jobs if they involve highly sensitive intercepts? How much will it matter if there are errors in translation, or willful mistranslations, that cannot be caught because there are no resources to cross-check the translators? Money can certainly help here, by paying more for better translators and, over the long term, promoting educational programs to broaden the base of recruits. For certain critical regions of the world, however, there are simply not enough potential recruits waiting in the wings to respond to a crash program.

Sharpened Analysis

Money can buy additional competent people to analyze collected information more readily than it can buy spies who can pass for members of the Taliban—especially if multiplying job slots are accompanied by enhanced opportunities for career development within intelligence agencies to make long service attractive for analysts. Pumping up the ranks of analysts can make a difference within the relatively short time span of a few years. The U.S. intelligence community has hundreds of analysts, but also hundreds of countries and issues to cover. On many subjects the coverage is now only one analyst deep—and when that one goes on vacation, or quits, the account may be handled out of the back pocket of a specialist on something else. We usually do not know in advance which of the numerous low-priority accounts might turn into the highest priority overnight (for example, Korea before June 1950, or Afghanistan before the Soviet invasion).

Hiring more analysts will be a good use of resources but could turn out to have a low payoff, and perhaps none at all, for much of what they do. Having half a dozen analysts on hand for some small country might be a good thing if that country turns out to be central to the campaign against terrorists, but those analysts need to be in place before we know we need them if they are to hit the ground running in a crisis. In most such cases, moreover, those analysts would serve their whole careers without producing anything that the U.S. government really needs, and no good analyst wants to be buried in an inactive account with peripheral significance.

One option is to make better use of an intelligence analyst reserve corps: people with other jobs who come in to read up on their accounts a couple of days each month to maintain currency, and who can be mobilized if a crisis involving their area erupts. There have been experiments with this system, but apparently without enough satisfaction to institutionalize it more broadly.

Of course, the quantity of analysts is less important than the quality of what they produce. Postmortems of intelligence failures usually reveal that very bright analysts failed to predict the disaster in question, despite their great knowledge of the situation, or that they had warned that an eruption could happen but without any idea of when. In fact, expertise can get in the way of anticipating a radical departure from the norm, because the depth of expert knowledge of why and how things have gone as they have day after day for years naturally inclines the analyst to estimate that developments will continue along the same trajectory. It is always a safer bet to predict that the situation tomorrow will be like it has been for the past dozen years than to say that it will change abruptly. And of course, in the vast majority of cases predictions of continuity are absolutely correct; the trick is to figure out which case will be the exception to a powerful rule.

A standard recommendation for reform—one made regularly by people discovering these problems for the first time—is to encourage "outside the box" analyses that challenge conventional wisdom and consider scenarios that appear low in probability but high in consequence. To some, this sort of intellectual shake-up might well have led the intelligence system, rather than Tom Clancy, to anticipate the kamikaze hijacking tactic of September 11.

All well and good. The problem, however, lies in figuring out what to do with the work this great analysis produces. There are always three dozen equally plausible dangers that are possible but improbable. Why should policymakers focus on any particular one of these hypothetical warnings or pay the costs of taking preventive action against all of them? One answer is to use such analysis to identify potential high-danger scenarios for which low-cost fixes are available. If President Bill Clinton had gotten a paper two years before September 11 that outlined the scenario for what ultimately happened, he probably would not have considered its probability high enough to warrant revolutionizing airport security, given all the obstacles: vested interests, opposition to particular measures, hassles for the traveling public. He might, however, have pushed for measures to allow checking the rosters of flight schools and investigating students who seemed uninterested in takeoffs and landings.

Another problem frequently noted is that the analytical corps has become fully absorbed in current intelligence, leaving no time for long-term research projects that look beyond the horizon. This, too, is something that more resources can solve. But as good a thing as more long-range analysis is, it is uncertain how productive it would be for the war on terrorism. The comparative advantage of the intelligence community over outside analysts is in bringing together secret information with knowledge from open sources. The more far-seeing a project, the less likely secret information is to play a role in the assessment. No one can match the analysts from the CIA, the Defense Intelligence Agency (DIA), or the NSA in estimating bin Laden's next moves, but it is not clear that they have a comparative advantage over Middle East experts in think tanks or universities when it comes to estimating worldwide trends in radical Islamist movements over the next decade. Such long-term research is an area in which better use of outside consultants and improved exploitation of academia could help most.

The War at Home

There is a world of difference between collecting intelligence abroad and doing so at home. Abroad, intelligence operations may break the laws of the countries in which they are undertaken. All domestic intelligence operations, however, must conform to U.S. law. The CIA can bribe foreign officials, burglarize offices of foreign political parties, bug defense ministries, tap the phones of diplomats, and do all sorts of things to gather information that the FBI could not do within the United States without getting a warrant from a court. Collection inside the United States is the area where loosened constraints would have done most to avert the September 11 attacks. But it is also the area in which great changes may make Americans fear that the costs exceed the benefits—indeed, that if civil liberties are compromised, "the terrorists will have won."

A Minnesota flight school reportedly alerted authorities a month before September 11 that one of its students, Zacarias Moussaoui, was learning to fly large jets but did not care about learning to take off or land. Moussaoui was arrested on immigration charges, and French intelligence warned U.S. officials that he was an extremist. FBI headquarters nevertheless decided against seeking a warrant for a wiretap or a search, reportedly because of complaints by the chief judge of the Foreign Intelligence Surveillance Court about other applications for wiretaps. After September 11, a search of Moussaoui's computer revealed that he had collected information about crop-dusting aircraft—a potential delivery system for chemical or biological weapons. U.S. officials came to suspect that Moussaoui was supposed to have been the fifth hijacker on United Airlines flight 93, which went down in Pennsylvania.

In hindsight, the hesitation to mount aggressive surveillance and searches in this case—hesitation linked to a highly developed set of legal safeguards rooted in the traditional American reverence for privacy—is exactly the sort of constraint that should have been loosened. High standards for protecting privacy are like strictures against risking collateral damage in combat operations: those norms take precedence more easily when the security interests at stake are not matters of your country's survival, but they become harder to justify when national security is on the line.

There have already been moves to facilitate more extensive clandestine surveillance, and there have been reactions against going too far. There will be substantial loosening of restraint on domestic intelligence collection, but how far it goes depends on the frequency and intensity of future terror attacks inside the United States. If there are no more that seem as serious as September 11, compromises of privacy will be limited. If there are two or three more dramatic attacks, all constraint may be swept away.

It is important to distinguish between two types of constraints on civil liberties. One is political censorship, like the suppression of dissent during World War I. There is no need or justification for this: counterterrorism does not benefit from suppression of free speech. The other type involves compromises of individual privacy, through secret surveillance, monitoring of communications, and searches. This is where pressing up to the constitutional limits offers the biggest payoff for counterterrorist intelligence. It also need not threaten individuals unnecessarily, so long as careful measures are instituted to keep secret the irrelevant but embarrassing information that may inadvertently be acquired as a by-product of monitoring. Similarly, popular but unpersuasive arguments have been advanced against the sort of national identification card common in other democratic countries. The U.S. Constitution does not confer the right to be unidentified to the government.

Even slightly more intrusive information-gathering will be controversial, but if it helps to avert future attacks, it will avert far more draconian blows against civil liberties. Moreover, Americans should remember that many solid, humane democracies—the United Kingdom, France, and others—have far more permissive rules for gathering information on people than the United States has had, and their citizens seem to live with these rules without great unease.

Red Tape and Reorganization

In a bureaucracy, reform means reorganization; reorganization means changing relationships of authority; and that means altering checks and balances. Five days after September 11, Tenet issued a directive that subsequently was leaked to the press. In it he proclaimed the wartime imperative to end business as usual, to cut through red tape and "give people the authority to do things they might not ordinarily be allowed to do.... If there is some bureaucratic hurdle, leap it.... We don't have time to have meetings about how to fix problems, just fix them." That refreshing activism will help push through needed changes. Some major reorganization of the intelligence community is inevitable. That was the response to Pearl Harbor, and even before the recent attacks many thought a major shake-up was overdue.

The current crisis presents the opportunity to override entrenched and outdated interests, to crack heads and force the sorts of consolidation and cooperation that have been inhibited by bureaucratic constipation. On balance, reorganization will help—but at a price: mistakes will increase, too. As Herbert Kaufman revealed in his classic 1997 book *Red Tape*, most administrative obstacles to efficiency do not come from mindless obstructionism. The sluggish procedures that frustrate one set of purposes have usually been instituted to safeguard other valid purposes. Red tape is the warp and woof of checks and balances. More muscular management will help some objectives and hurt others.

The crying need for intelligence reorganization is no recent discovery. It is a perennial lament, amplified every time intelligence stumbles. The community has undergone several major reorganizations and innumerable lesser ones over the past half-century. No one ever stays satisfied with reorganization because it never seems to do the trick—if the trick is to prevent intelligence failure. There is little reason to believe, therefore, that the next reform will do much better than previous ones.

Reorganizations usually prove to be three steps forward and two back, because the intelligence establishment is so vast and complex that the net impact of reshuffling may be indiscernible. After September 11, some observers complained that the intelligence community is too regionally oriented and should be organized more in terms of functional issues. Yet back in the 1980s, when William Casey became President Ronald Reagan's DCI and encountered the functional organization of the CIA's analytical directorate, he experienced the reverse frustration. Rather than deal with functional offices of economic, political, and strategic research, each with regional subunits, he shifted the structure to one of regional units with functional subunits. Perhaps it helped, but there is little evidence that it produced consistent improvement in analytical products. There is just as little evidence that moving back in the other direction will help any more.

What about a better fusion center for intelligence on counterterrorism, now touted by many as a vital reform? For years the DCI has had a Counter-Terrorism Center (CTC) that brings together assets from the CIA's directorates of operations and intelligence, the FBI, the DIA, the State Department, and other parts of the community. It has been widely criticized, but many believe its deficiencies came from insufficient resources—something reorganization alone will not cure. If the CTC's deficiencies were truly organizational, moreover, there is little reason to believe that a new fusion center would not simply replace those problems with different ones.

Some believe, finally, that the problem is the sheer complexity and bulk of the intelligence community; they call for it to be streamlined, turned into a leaner and meaner corps. Few such proposals specify what functions can be dispensed with in order to thin out the ranks, however. In truth, bureaucratization is both the U.S. intelligence community's great weakness and its great strength. The weakness is obvious, as in any large bureaucracy: various forms of sclerosis, inertia, pettiness, and paralysis drive out many vibrant people and deaden many who remain. The strength, however, is taken for granted: a coverage of issues that is impressively broad and sometimes deep. Bureaucratization makes it hard to extract the right information efficiently from the globs of it lying around in the system, but in a leaner and meaner system there will never be much lying around.

Some areas can certainly benefit from reorganization. One is the integration of information technologies, management systems, and information sharing. Much has been done within the intelligence community to exploit the potential of information technology in recent years, but it has been such a fast-developing sector of society and the economy in general that constant adaptation may be necessary for some time.

Another area of potential reorganization involves making the DCI's authority commensurate with his or her responsibility. This is a long-standing source of tension, because roughly 80 percent of the intelligence establishment (in terms of functions and resources) has always been located in the Defense Department, where primary lines of authority and loyalty run to the military services and to the secretary of defense. The latest manifestation of this problem was the increased priority given during the 1990s to the mission of support for military operations (SMO)—a priority levied not only on Pentagon intelligence agencies but on the CIA and others as well. Such a move was odd, given that military threats to the United States after the Cold War were lower than at any other time in the existence of the modern intelligence community, while a raft of new foreign policy involvements in various parts of the world were coming to the fore. But the SMO priority was the legacy of the Persian Gulf War and the problems in intelligence support felt by military commanders, combined with the Clinton administration's unwillingness to override strong military preferences.

Matching authority and responsibility is where the test of the most immediate reform initiative—or evidence of its confusion—will come. Early reports on the formation of the Office of Homeland Security indicated that the new director, Tom Ridge, will be responsible for coordinating all of the agencies in the intelligence community. This is odd, because that was precisely the function for which the office of Director of Central Intelligence was created in the National Security Act of 1947. The position of DCI was meant to centralize oversight of the dispersed intelligence activities of the military services, the State Department, and the new Central Intelligence Agency, and to coordinate planning and resource allocation among them.

As the community burgeoned over the years, adding huge organizations such as the NSA, the DIA, NIMA, and others, the DCI remained the official responsible for knitting their functions together. The DCI's ability to do so increased at times, but it was always limited by the authority of the secretary of defense over the Pentagon's intelligence agencies. Indeed, hardly anyone but professionals within the intelligence community understands that there is such a thing as a DCI. Not only the press, but presidents and government officials as well never refer to the DCI by that title; they always speak instead of the "Director of the CIA," as if that person were simply an agency head, forgetting the importance of the larger coordination responsibility.

Is Ridge to become the central coordinating official in practice that the DCI is supposed to be in principle? If so, why will he be better positioned to do the job than the DCI has been in the past? The DCI has always had an office next to the White House as well as at the CIA, and Ridge will have to spend most of his time on matters other than intelligence. A special review by a group under General Brent Scowcroft, the new head of the President's Foreign Intelligence Advisory Board, has reportedly recommended moving several of the big intelligence agencies out of the Defense Department, putting them under the administrative control of the DCI. That would certainly give the DCI more clout to back up the responsibility for coordination. Such a proposal is so revolutionary, however, that its chances of adoption seem slim.

The real problem of DCIs in doing their jobs has generally been that presidents have not cared enough about intelligence to make the DCI one of their top advisers. Assigning coordination responsibility to Ridge may work if the president pays more attention to him than has been paid to the DCI, but otherwise this is the sort of reform that could easily prove to be ephemeral or unworkable—yet advertised as necessary in the short term to proclaim that something significant is being done.

From Age-Old to New-Age Surprise

The issue for reform is whether any fixes at all can break a depressing historical pattern. After September 11, intelligence officials realized that fragmentary indicators of impending action by bin Laden's network had been recognized by the intelligence system but had not been sufficient to show what or where the action would be. A vague warning was reportedly issued, but not one that was a ringing alarm. This is, sadly, a very common occurrence.

What we know of intelligence in conventional warfare helps explain why powerful intelligence systems are often caught by surprise. The good news from history is that attackers often fail to win the wars that they start with stunning surprises: Germany was defeated after invading the Soviet Union, Japan after Pearl Harbor, North Korea after 1950, Argentina after taking the Falkland Islands, Iraq after swallowing Kuwait. The bad news is that those initial attacks almost always succeed in blindsiding the victims and inflicting terrible losses.

Once a war is underway, it becomes much harder to surprise the victim. The original surprise puts the victim on unambiguous notice. It shears away the many strong reasons that exist in peacetime to estimate that an adversary will not take the risk of attacking. It was easier for Japan to surprise the United States at Pearl Harbor than at Midway. But even in the midst of war, surprise attacks often succeed in doing real damage: recall the Battle of the Bulge or the Tet offensive. For Americans, September 11 was the Pearl Harbor of terrorism. The challenge now is to make the next attacks more like Midway than like Tet.

Surprise attacks often succeed despite the availability of warning indicators. This pattern leads many observers to blame derelict intelligence officials or irresponsible policymakers. The sad truth is that the fault lies more in natural organizational forces, and in the pure intractability of the problem, than in the skills of spies or statesmen.

After surprise attacks, intelligence postmortems usually discover indicators that existed in advance but that were obscured or contradicted by other evidence. Roberta Wohlstetter's classic study of Pearl Harbor identified this as the problem of signals (information hinting at the possibility of enemy attack) getting lost in a crescendo of "noise" (the voluminous clutter of irrelevant information that floods in, or other matters competing for attention). Other causes abound. Some have been partially overcome, such as technical limitations on timely communication, or organizational obstacles to sharing information. Others are deeply rooted in the complexity of threats, the ambiguity of partial warnings, and the ability of plotters to overcome obstacles, manipulate information, and deceive victims.

One reason surprise attacks can succeed is the "boy who cried wolf" problem, in which the very excellence of intelligence collection works against its success. There are often numerous false alarms before an attack, and they dull sensitivity to warnings of the attack that does occur. Sometimes the supposed false alarms were not false at all, but accurate warnings that prompted timely responses by the victim that in turn caused the attacker to cancel and reschedule the assault—thus generating a self-negating prophecy.

Attacks can also come as a surprise because of an overload of incomplete warnings, a particular problem for a superpower with world-spanning involvements. In the spring of 1950, for example, the CIA warned President Harry Truman that the North Koreans could attack at any time, but without indications of whether the attack was certain or when it would happen. "But this did not apply alone to Korea," Truman noted in his memoirs. The same reports also continually warned him of many other places in the world where communist forces had the capability to attack.

Intelligence may correctly warn of an enemy's intention to strike and may even anticipate the timing but still guess wrong about where or how the attack will occur. U.S. intelligence was warning in late November 1941 that a Japanese strike could be imminent but expected it in Southeast Asia. Pearl Harbor seemed an impractical target because it was too shallow for torpedo attacks. That had indeed been true, but shortly before December the Japanese had adjusted their torpedoes so they could run in the shallows. Before September 11, similarly, attacks by al Qaeda were expected, but elsewhere in the world, and not by the technical means of kamikaze hijacking.

The list of common reasons why attacks often come as a surprise goes on and on. The point is that intelligence can rarely be perfect and unambiguous, and there are always good reasons to misinterpret it. Some problems of the past have been fixed by the technically sophisticated system we have now, and some may be reduced by adjustments to the system. But some can never be eliminated, with the result being that future unpleasant surprises are a certainty.

Reorganization may be the proper response to failure, if only because the masters of intelligence do not know how else to improve performance. The underlying cause of mistakes in performance, however, does not lie in the structure and process of the intelligence system. It is intrinsic to the issues and targets with which intelligence has to cope: the crafty opponents who strategize against it, and the alien cultures that are not transparent to American minds.

Reform will happen and, on balance, should help. But for too many policymakers and pundits, reorganization is an alluring but illusory quick fix. Long-term improvements are vaguer and less certain, and they reek of the lamp. But if the United States is going to have markedly better intelligence in parts of the world where few Americans have lived, studied, or understood local mores and aspirations, it is going to have to overcome a cultural disease: thinking that American primacy makes it unnecessary for American education to foster broad and deep expertise on foreign, especially non-Western, societies. The United States is perhaps the only major country in the world where one can be considered well educated yet speak only the native tongue.

The disease has even infected the academic world, which should know better. American political science, for example, has driven area studies out of fashion. Some "good" departments have not a single Middle East specialist on their rosters, and hardly any at all have a specialist on South Asia—a region of more than a billion people, two nuclear-armed countries, and swarms of terrorists. Yet these same departments can afford a plethora of professors who conjure up spare models naively assumed to be of global application.

Reforms that can be undertaken now will make the intelligence community a little better. Making it much better, however, will ultimately require revising educational norms and restoring the prestige of public service. Both are lofty goals and tall orders, involving general changes in society and professions outside government. Even if achieved, moreover, such fundamental reform would not bear fruit until far in the future.

But this is not a counsel of despair. To say that there is a limit to how high the intelligence batting average will get is not to say that it cannot get significantly better. It does mean, however, that no strategy for a war against terror can bank on prevention. Better intelligence may give us several more big successes like those of the 1990s, but even a .900 average will eventually yield another big failure. That means that equal emphasis must go to measures for civil defense, medical readiness, and "consequence management," in order to blunt the effects of the attacks that do manage to get through. Efforts at prevention and preparation for their failure must go hand in hand.

Richard K. Betts is a specialist on national security policy and military strategy. He is director of the Institute of War and Peace Studies at Columbia University and was a senior fellow and research associate at the Brookings Institution in Washington, D.C. Betts has served on the National Commission on Terrorism and the U.S. Senate Select Committee on Intelligence. He is author, editor, and coauthor of several books on the subject, including *The Irony of Vietnam: The System Worked* (1979), which won the Woodrow Wilson Prize.

Jeffrey H. Norwitz, 2002

Combating Terrorism: With a Helmet or a Badge?

*W*ashington, DC—*In a surprise development that has the Justice Department spinning, Saudi dissident and wanted terrorist Osama bin Laden appeared today at Washington, DC, police headquarters accompanied by a team of defense lawyers. His attorneys told stunned police officials that bin Laden wished to surrender to law enforcement authorities. Bin Laden, who has been chased all over the world following his 1998 federal indictment for the dual embassy bombings in Africa as well as his alleged involvement in the 11 September 2001 terrorist attacks, said he'd been hiding in Iranian caves ever since the American military assaults on Afghanistan began. He decided to turn himself in rather than continue to evade U.S. special forces who "wanted him dead—not alive." His defense team refused to reveal how bin Laden, on the FBI's ten-most-wanted list, managed to make his way into the country undetected. They demanded safety for their client while he is in detention and, assuming that bin Laden would not be afforded bail, insisted on his right to a speedy trial. A Justice Department lawyer who requested anonymity told reporters that in the coming weeks, bin Laden's lawyers will probably move for full discovery of all evidence, testimony, witness identities, and details of the prosecution case. Additionally, anticipating that some of the evidence is classified, bin Laden's defense team may move that security clearances be given to them as well as their defendant so that he can assist in his own defense. Exercising due process provisions, bin Laden's defense team can be expected to force the prosecution to reveal sensitive criminal and intelligence leads or risk dismissal of charges. Furthermore, through the process of voir dire, designed to elicit information about prospective jurors so that attorneys can challenge members to find the most receptive audience, Justice lawyers are afraid that the defense will try to shape the jury with members who are amenable to bin Laden's cause.[1] In one nightmarish scenario that has the Attorney General scrambling, the accused terrorist and murderer of over 5,000 people may claim that it's impossible to receive a fair trial and challenge the justice system to relocate the trial where the population has no preconceived ideas about the 11 September attack, if that's even possible. If not, the defense has a good foundation for appealing any conviction, based on an inability to receive a fair trial. According to an experienced attorney with the Justice Department, "This case will bounce from one judicial stage to another until the concept of justice becomes secondary to procedure. A trial court is simply not suited for dealing with the sort of legal quandary posed by prosecuting such a defendant." Initial defense efforts to suppress evidence are already scheduled for pretrial motions next month.*

How prepared are we for such a development? Is this the way the American public expects terrorists to be handled? Is this the sort of "war" that President Bush envisioned—

a war of words, semantics, legal parsing of statutory phrases and constitutional rights granted to a murderous zealot who despises the very nation that grants him these rights? It's time to consider very carefully how this nation goes about waging war on terrorism. Is terrorism a crime to be fought with search warrants and jurisprudence, or is it an act of war, as President Bush has affirmed? If criminalists with a badge are the warriors, then the battlefield will look very much like this fictitious account.

The American public was galvanized by the events of 11 September. Military members mourned lost Pentagon comrades but became resolute, as instructed by the President, who said, "I have a message for our military: Be ready."[2] Meanwhile, our leaders in Washington demonstrated bipartisanship and genuine unity in the face of the largest terrorist attack ever on U.S. soil. Indeed, the word *war* became commonplace in media and government lexicon while citizens, political leaders, and the military became energized.

Curiously, as talk of military mobilization permeated the media, we heard of Herculean law enforcement efforts by thousands of federal, state, and local officers to gather physical evidence, execute search warrants, and run thousands of leads seeking to establish criminal culpability for the 11 September atrocity. This essay will examine old paradigms about terrorism and offer a perspective on how criminal approaches have not grasped the nature of this war.

Words Have Meaning

When viewed legally, terrorism will always be a crime regardless of whether the act is a murder, hijacking, kidnapping, or bombing. Within legal vernacular, terrorist crimes have "elements of the offense," each of which must be proven beyond a reasonable doubt; venue must be established to determine the appropriate court to hear the case; finally, if convicted, a defendant will be sentenced in accordance with precedent, and appeals can run their course as well. Viewed through a political lens, terrorism is a tool of non-state or state actors, driven by religious or political ideation designed to manipulate governments and politics through violence. Consequently, terrorism can be dealt with either as a crime or as an attack on the body politic. Since defeating terrorism is clearly in our national interest, all elements of power (diplomatic, economic, and military) ought to be employed.

In defining the nature of war, Clausewitz held that "war is not a mere act of policy but a continuation of political activity by other means." Terrorism is political activity, and the terrorist has chosen to make a political statement using violence. To further clarify what war is, consider Clausewitz's observation, "The political objective is the goal, war is the means of reaching it, and means can never be considered in isolation from their purpose."[3] In other words, war is a means toward a political end, and, correspondingly, terrorism is war.

Differing definitions confuse the question of whether terrorism is a crime or an act of war. The Defense Department defines terrorism as "the *calculated* use of violence or threat of violence to inculcate fear; intended to coerce or to intimidate governments or societies in the pursuit of goals that are generally political, religious, or ideological" (emphasis added).[4] In contrast, the Justice Department's definition includes "the *unlawful* use of force or violence against persons or property to intimidate or coerce a government, the civilian population, or any segment thereof, in furtherance of political objectives" (emphasis added).[5] Words mean something, and the differences are striking.

The Defense Department regards terrorism as a "calculated" act. The identity of the actor is irrelevant. It could just as well be an individual or a nation-state. Additionally, there is no suggestion of illegality—just that the act be purposeful as opposed to an accident, and intended to intimidate or coerce governance. Implicit in the Justice Department's definition of terrorism is the concept of illegality, which clearly empowers the department, via the FBI, to take the lead in a terrorist incident. Thereafter, the best forensic science and investigative resources are secured, enabling leads to be disseminated and results analyzed among countless law enforcement agencies. But consider for a moment the statutory guidelines, jurisdictional limitations, and laws of jurisprudence that must be adhered to in the legal rubric.

Because the objective of a criminal investigation is successful prosecution, all law enforcement effort must withstand judicial scrutiny at trial. Provisions of Articles IV, V, and VI of the U.S. Constitution, as well as the Bill of Rights, offer powerful protections against law enforcement excess, which, by extension, applies to international terrorists operating on our soil. Moreover, every decision made by investigators will be reviewed for compliance with legal precedent from countless prior decisions with mind-numbing attention to detail. Any procedural error—intentional or otherwise—will be cause for suppression of evidence or testimony. And what about differing legal structures between allied nations in countering terrorism? Evidence obtained by one nation's police may not meet the standards for admissibility into the court system of a partner nation. Likewise, will admissions of guilt be universally accepted in all courts regardless of which police conducted the questioning? Even if a conviction is obtained, the criminal justice system still will go over everything on appeal with the threat of a reversal of the first verdict. Is this the way we want to wage war on terrorists? Not according to the National Commission on Terrorism.

Federal Commission Findings

The National Commission on Terrorism was established by Congress in 1999 with the appointment of 10 commissioners (all eminently qualified), who, after a series of hearings and international visits, produced a report relative to new and emerging threats of international terrorism.[6] One of the commission's recommendations was to "pursue a more aggressive strategy against terrorism." Critical analysis was given to the question of whether terrorism should best be handled as a criminal matter, suggesting a new paradigm that would give the Defense Department a much greater leadership role in the event of a catastrophic terrorist attack. The members of the commission held that law enforcement tools were not adequate to address international terrorism. According to the commission:

> Law enforcement is designed to put individuals behind bars, but is not a particularly useful tool for addressing actions by states. The Pan Am 103 case demonstrates the advantages and limitations of the law enforcement approach to achieve national security objectives. The effort to seek extradition of the two intelligence operatives implicated most directly in the bombing gained international support for economic sanctions that a more political approach may have failed to achieve. The sanctions and the resulting isolation of Libya may have contributed to the reduction of Libya's terrorist activities. On the other hand, prosecuting and punishing the two low-level operatives for an act almost certainly directed by Qadafi is a hollow victory, particularly if the trial results in his implicit exoneration.

As it happened, only one of the Libyan defendants acting on behalf of the state intelligence service was convicted, and the other freed, without implication of Qadafi himself—a hollow victory indeed.[7]

In yet another example of apparent ineptitude of a police response to terrorism, research by the *Christian Science Monitor* disclosed that in the six months following 11 September, criminalists in the United States and Europe arrested nearly 1,400 people in connection with the attacks but charged only one. Moreover, no al-Qaeda cells have been uncovered in the United States.[8] Revelation of the 8 May 2002 Chicago arrest of New York–born Jose Padilla, aka Abdullah al Muhajir, for his part in planning a possible bombing attack on behalf of al-Qaeda is evidence of the value of militarily obtained intelligence employed to intercept a terrorist attack. Indeed, Padilla is being treated as an "enemy combatant" by the Justice Department and was sent to a military jail in South Carolina.[9]

While distinguishing terrorism as a crime or an act of war, Stephen Gale, a counterterrorism expert at the University of Pennsylvania, points out, "If you think someone is going to take out your electrical grid, in a criminal investigation you arrest him. In a war you shoot first and ask questions later."[10]

Michael Clarke, head of the Centre for Defense Studies at London University, observed, "Terrorism poses a fundamental challenge to the legal system. Terrorists often do nothing indictable till they commit the act. Ninety percent of the time sleepers are absolutely legal, so you can't do anything about them even if you know who they are. Terrorism challenges our categories of what is legal and what is illegal."[11]

The National Commission on Terrorism's findings highlighted unrecognized Pentagon organizational and resource strengths as they relate to terrorism.

> The U.S. Government's plans for a catastrophic terrorist attack on the United States do not employ the full range of the Department of Defense's (DoD's) capabilities for managing large operations. Additionally, the interagency coordination and cooperation required to integrate the DoD properly into counterterrorism planning has not been accomplished.
>
> The Department of Defense's ability to command and control vast resources for dangerous, unstructured situations is unmatched by any other department or agency. According to current plans, DoD is limited to supporting the agencies that are currently designated as having the lead in a terrorism crisis, the FBI and the Federal Emergency Management Agency (FEMA). But… when a catastrophe… is directly related to an armed conflict overseas, the President may want to designate DoD as a lead federal agency.

Missing from the commission's report, but of equal significance, is DoD's ability to compile worldwide intelligence from an array of sources unavailable to civilian law enforcement. Moreover, given the military intelligence community's system of satisfying diverse intelligence requirements, the infrastructure to do the same with terrorism is a DoD strength—and without the dilemma of testimonial scrutiny at a later time. Does that mean that military operations are free from legal constraint? Of course not.

Citizen-Soldiers

There is an ethos in America, rooted in our birth as a nation, that standing armies are a threat to governments, unless they are at war. Whig politics of the early American colonies held that when conflict is finished, so should be the standing army. Whigs believed that a standing military force in time of peace was a threat to liberty.[12] Evolution and compromise modified that dismal view of standing armies; however, the framers of the Constitution still wanted to limit the military's authority over the population, and our citizenry today holds that protection dear. Three documents with presidential or congressional authorship seek to ensure legal limits of military power.

The Posse Comitatus Act is codified in law under 18 U.S.C. 1385 and explicitly prohibits, unless with presidential intervention, using the armed forces to execute laws upon the citizenry.[13] Executive Order 12333, "United States Intelligence Activities," provides presidential endorsement to the limits of all intelligence activity, military and otherwise. The purpose of Executive Order 12333 is to balance constitutional protections against the need for timely and accurate information about the activities, capabilities, plans, and intentions of foreign powers, organizations, and persons.[14] Furthermore, Executive Order provides succinct, specific, and strong language relative to what Defense agencies may and may not do concerning intelligence activities. Lastly, Presidential Decision Directive 39, "U.S. Policy on Counterterrorism," lays out roles and missions for federal organizations, including the Department of Defense.[15]

As the bulwark to protect citizens against military abuse, these three documents provide a tremendous check and balance on what our armed forces can do domestically in performing homeland security missions. In contrast to fears of rampant military disregard for legal framework and citizens' rights, our courts are very attuned to permissible conduct, and so are today's military commanding officers and service personnel. The Pentagon has already embraced urban warfare in training and doctrine, resulting in exemplary skills for dealing with such a challenging environment.[16] But perhaps the strongest argument for trusting our armed forces with domestic security is the fact that they are citizen-soldiers, exemplifying the truest sense of volunteerism as envisioned by George Washington. If there are constitutional limits on the military's activity at home, what sort of guidelines exist for military operations on foreign soil?

The legalities of employing U.S. armed forces in foreign countries to battle terrorism are complex. Military operations abroad must complement, and be coordinated with, the strategic use of diplomatic and economic elements of national power. Likewise, if force is envisioned where casualties and property destruction are likely, the Law of Armed Conflict will limit military action to what is necessary, reasonable, and justified.[17]

Armed conflict is not the end of law. It is, in fact, the beginning of a different legal status as it relates to how belligerents behave. Two legal terms underscore the dimension for which the Law of Armed Conflict is codified: *jus ad bellum* is law that defines whether the conflict has a legal basis to happen in the first place; *jus in bello* is law that outlines what actions in war are legal in and of themselves. Clearly, war is not the absence of legal restraint, nor does war condone uncontrolled maniacal behavior. War crimes tribunals are evidence that the world will not stand for unconstrained military devastation. Any suggestion of unbridled American military vigilantes, ranging the globe on vendettas, is unsupportable.

American Perceptions

The American public has long held that terrorism was something that happened elsewhere. Former Secretary of State George Shultz theorized that our nation's threat was "99% overseas," and empirical data suggested this to be true.[18] In the 1970s and 1980s, international terrorist incidents varied annually from around 450 to more than 600 events. Occurrences lessened in the late 1980s; however, following the Gulf War, the number rose to over 560. By 1996, international terrorist incidents diminished to fewer than 300 a year.[19]

While the world experienced a statistical roller coaster of terrorist incidents, the number of domestic episodes remained startlingly low. America's premier law enforcement community of federal, state, and local authorities was praised for having halted terrorism at our borders, and with that apparent achievement, law enforcement also took on the responsibility of consequence response in the event of a rogue attack. FEMA seemed the likely candidate for coordination of national assets, while local and state agencies looked to FEMA for direction. Naturally, FEMA turned to the Army for resources, training, and actual response capability, seeing the Army as possessing the greatest capability for response to disaster, which, not surprisingly, replicated the mayhem of warfare. Meanwhile, many Americans developed an artificial sense that somehow our guardian oceans would keep harm from our shores, as historically was the case. Terrorism experts, however, warned that this sense of safety was fictional because of broadened economic globalization and ease of world travel; 11 September proved them correct.

Nevertheless, what worked in the past seemed adequate to ensure domestic tranquillity, especially in light of competing demands for scarce federal resources. The Pentagon was committed elsewhere, and terrorism remained the domain of law enforcement. Americans expected terrorism to remain an "overseas" dilemma, and the public expected police to be the key protector of the homeland.

What Is Our Experience?

How did our country come to deal with terrorism this way? Upon assuming office, President Reagan was deeply affected by the Carter administration's struggle against international terrorism and, as a result, was determined to deploy the traditional elements of national power to defeat the terrorist menace. Economic measures, diplomatic mechanisms, and military force were the tools that supported Reagan's strategy. During the early Reagan years, terrorism became synonymous with warfare, particularly after 241 Marines and other servicemen were killed in Beirut by a terrorist truck bomb on 23 October 1983.[20]

Despite early military victories such as airstrikes against Libya and the capture of Abu al-Abbas, who was responsible for the *Achille Lauro* hijacking, other driving factors undermined America's military assault on terrorism. Reagan's use of military force against terrorists was curtailed when it appeared we had traded weapons for hostages during the Iran-Contra scandal, thereafter diminishing our credibility with other nations as a consequence of our deal with Tehran. Accordingly, military strategies became almost impossible to execute because of reduced international support; as a consequence, American counterterrorist emphasis returned to law enforcement and a judicial approach. Military involvement in counterterrorism dwindled as criminalists took over. Yet one dilemma remained: the lack of intelligence haunted the battle against terrorism and indeed continues today.

Good intelligence is the cornerstone for dealing effectively with terrorism, and the U.S. intelligence community, heavily dependent on superb technical collection means, is almost omniscient. Unfortunately, terrorists don't tend to be vulnerable to technical collection, owing to their disparate cell-like nature and veiled operational profile, thwarting photographic and signals exploitation. Human intelligence collection is the most effective source but also the most difficult to obtain. Frequently, terrorist cells have familial foundations and are extremely difficult to penetrate. Unfortunately, American human intelligence collection capabilities were severely diminished during the 1970s and 1980s, when, responding to public outcry about the sometimes "dirty" nature of recruiting intelligence operatives, the CIA changed vetting practices, disallowing its agents to enlist sources with dubious backgrounds.[21] Furthermore, would intelligence agents be required to testify as to how they obtained information? For instance, would techniques of handling clandestine sources be subject to judicial scrutiny and rules of evidence admissibility? How could a legal case be prosecuted when "chain of custody," a judicial requirement to establish authenticity of evidence, cannot be demonstrated for bomb-making gear supplied by a double agent? If law enforcement officers captured terrorists, would the terrorists face their accuser and have the benefit of legal representation? Lastly, the rise of "leaderless resistance," a concept of independent action encouraging unitary but coordinated violence, has also severely limited American counterterrorist efforts.[22]

By 1990, with the fight against terrorism returned to the law enforcement world, the military went back about its business of fighting and winning the nation's wars and was relegated to a supporting role in counterterrorism. However, the paradigm of FBI primacy in the fight against terrorism took a new shift on 21 September 2001, when President Bush addressed Congress and the American people to explain a new war on terrorism. According to the President and congressional sentiment, the military seemed again to be the tool of choice.

Present Driving Forces

Just seven months before the terrorist attack of 11 September, the U.S. Commission on National Security/21st Century, popularly called the Hart-Rudman Commission after its chairpersons, issued its Phase III report, *Road Map for National Security: Imperative for Change*. In it, the commission made some startlingly prophetic observations about the preparedness of the United States to deal with a catastrophic terrorist attack. One of the key findings is related to "organizational realignment," in a subchapter of the same title. Therein is suggested the creation of the National Homeland Security Agency with cabinet-level status and direct responsibility to the president. The commission's findings included minimizing the Justice Department and FBI's leadership role in homeland defense and increasing Defense's profile across the range of mission tasks.[23]

Likewise, increased priority of homeland security is reflected in the Quadrennial Defense Review (QDR) Report, which lays out a Defense Department vision for future force structure and strategy. The QDR "restores the defense of the United States as the Department's primary mission."[24] Furthermore, the Pentagon acknowledges that preparing for homeland security will impact organization and structure of future forces and redefine expectations of reserve and active components. Indeed, the newly issued Unified Command Plan established Northern Command as a separate combatant command to provide a more coordinated approach for military support to homeland defense civil authorities.[25] As a road map for national military strategy, the QDR points out that "the U.S. military will be prepared to respond in a decisive manner to acts of international terrorism committed on U.S. territory or the territory of an ally." The Defense Department's vision for the future unequivocally includes the war on terrorism.

On War, Clausewitz's seminal work, states that war is successfully waged only when there is a synergy among the *government*, the *military*, and the *will of the people*. Support of all three is necessary for victory.[26] Likewise, Clausewitz observed that organized warfare between great powers has a construct that can be studied, albeit sometimes clouded by the fog and friction of battle. He also commented on the fortunes of a war against the likes of modern terrorists, suggesting that poor political understanding and a constrained military policy will play into the hands of an enemy that is without rules or moral limitations. As if predicting the difficulty of facing terrorism, Clausewitz observed, "Woe to the government, which, relying on half-hearted politics and a shackled military policy, meets a foe who, like the untamed elements, knows no law other than his own power."[27]

Colin Gray, professor of international politics and director of the Centre for Strategic Studies at the University of Reading, England, has supported the idea that terrorists are enemy soldiers and not criminals, but he pointed out, "If we redefine what the concept and legal idea of 'war' encompasses, then so also will we have to redefine who can wage it legitimately."[28] Indeed, the matter of militarily captured terrorists in Afghanistan challenged our concept of wartime prisoners and whether they could be questioned about terrorist activity. If interrogated as prisoners of war, must they be afforded self-incrimination protections? The American Bar Association, Task Force on Terrorism and the Law, concluded that the actions of 11 September 2001 were acts of war although, because noncombatant civilians were attacked, the perpetrators violated the law of armed conflict, forfeiting Hague Convention protections.[29] At the same time, Pentagon doctrine states that captured terrorists are not afforded prisoner-of-war protection because terrorists act outside the laws of war.[30] As we redefine notions about crime and war while rethinking strategies to fight terrorism, there are some key areas for consideration.

A New Paradigm Is Necessary

America must remove impediments, real and perceived, to Defense Department involvement in homeland security. First, we must reflect on the original purpose of the Posse Comitatus Act with a long view toward broadening the use of armed forces in traditional law enforcement roles. Only the military can truly deal with catastrophic events such as biological and chemical attack as well as radiological release and consequence management. Furthermore, the organic capability for superb military investigation, intelligence analysis, and fact-finding can be an invaluable augmentation of state and local authority during a calamity. This may need to include questioning of civilians and perhaps collection of information relevant to tracking terrorists. Furthermore, the possibility that this material may have evidentiary value cannot be discounted.

According to John R. Brinkerhoff, a retired Army officer and former FEMA associate director and senior career executive in the Office of the Secretary of Defense, the Posse Comitatus Act has been grossly misinterpreted as preventing the military services from acting as a national police force. Brinkerhoff pointed out that the Posse Comitatus Act was passed in 1878 when, reacting to Southern sheriffs and U.S. Marshals pressing Army troops into their service without Washington's approval, Congress voted to restrict the ability of U.S. Marshals and local constabulary to conscript military personnel into their posses.[31] In passing the Posse Comitatus Act, Congress conceded the use of military troops for police actions when authorized by the president or Congress. Brinkerhoff offered his opinion that an erroneous interpretation has resulted from a general Pentagon desire to avoid quagmires involving domestic unrest. He added that much of the twisting of the Posse Comitatus Act was by persons averse to any role for military forces in law enforcement, including the military itself.

It now appears that to fully engage our armed forces to defeat terrorism, we must rethink posse comitatus. It is not a rigid proscription of use of the military to enforce or execute laws. Rather, when so ordered by the president, the military can support civilian authorities in a wide array of enforcement missions for which it is uniquely trained and equipped. Why continue to craft strategies that require states to shoulder an additional burden owing to the Posse Comitatus Act since, when strictly construed, it is no obstacle to a partnership of the armed forces and civilian authority in domestic security? Rethinking policy and practice regarding posse comitatus should be a priority for the new Department of Homeland Security as it creates links to the Pentagon's Northern Command in the coming battle against terrorism, heretofore limited to the criminal justice system.[32]

The term *preemption* has drawn considerable attention, particularly in the President's rhetoric, and deserves consideration in the quiver of weapons against terrorism. In a criminal context, police can frustrate unlawful schemes only within a legally consistent framework of probable cause, elements of the offense, legally obtainable evidence, reasonable expectation of privacy, hearsay, and entrapment. Preemption, as envisaged by the Law of Armed Conflict, has none of these constraints and therefore finds fertile ground as a military option. Along these lines, Peter H. Liotta, Professor of Strategy at the U.S. Naval War College, stated that terrorists can be expected to practice chaos as a strategy. "We will practice preemption against those who seek to harm our vital interests and our way of life. Military forces will increasingly be in the business of shooting archers, and not just catching arrows. That is to say that we cannot just wait for chaos provocations to occur before we react."[33] According to Liotta, however, our execution of military options must be tempered by a clear understanding of the nature of the enemy and how, if misapplied, military force may play right into the hands of terrorists who will practice chaos as a strategy.

Conclusions

Considering the challenges and new risks that America is facing, "we are going to have to invent new ideas about what war is, and that will have far-reaching implications for the legal system," says Stephen Gale.[34] Another terrorist attack in the United States is inevitable.[35] The role for law enforcement in this fight against terrorism and via the Department of Homeland Security is undeniable; coordination and consolidation of federal enforcement agencies will be the challenge for the new cabinet appointee. Nevertheless, we must acknowledge the limitations of constabulary soldiers and courtroom battlefields, put aside the fingerprint powder and handcuffs, and instead tighten our helmet straps. This is after all, a war.

Jeffrey H. Norwitz has been in law enforcement for 28 years. Formerly an Army Captain in Military Police and a deputy sherriff in El Paso County, Colorado, he is now a civilian special agent with the Naval Criminal Investigation Service, where he has served tours in California, Washington, D.C., Rhode Island, Okinawa, Thailand, and Kuwait; as well as aboard submarines and surface combatants. He represents the Naval Criminal Investigative Service at the U.S. Naval War College, where he is a professor of National Security Decision Making. He holds a criminal justice undergraduate degree from Eastern Kentucky University and a master of arts degree in strategic studies from the Naval War College.

Notes

1. More information about voir dire can be found at www.jri-inc.com/voirdire.htm.
2. President George W. Bush, "Address to a Joint Session of Congress," 21 September 2001.
3. The late Michael I. Handel, a professor of strategy at the U.S. Naval War College, authored three books on Carl von Clausewitz. Handel established a matchless reputation as an expert on theories of war and Clausewitz in particular. Clausewitz is quoted in Handel's *Masters of War*, 3rd ed. (London: Frank Cass, 2001), p. 68.
4. Department of Defense Directive 2000.12, "DoD Antiterrorism/Force Protection (AT/FP) Program," 13 April 1999; www.dtic.mil/whs/directives/corres/text/d200012p.txt.
5. "Organization of the Department of Justice," Code of Federal Regulations, Title 28—Judicial Administration, (Washington, DC: U.S. General Services Administration, National Archives and Records Service, Office of the Federal Register, 1 July 2001), Chap. I, pp. 51–52; www.access.gpo.gov/nara/cfr/waisidx_01/28cfr0_01.html.
6. The members of the commission were L. Paul Bremer III, Maurice Sonnenberg, Richard K. Betts, Wayne A. Downing, Jane Harman, Fred C. Iklé, Juliette N. Kayyem, John F. Lewis Jr., Gardner Peckham, and R. James Woolsey. See the Report of the National Commission on Terrorism, *Countering the Changing Threat of International Terrorism* (Washington, DC: 1999); www.fas.org/irp/threat/commission.html.
7. Information about the Pan Am 103 trial and conviction is available at www.geocities.com/CapitolHill/5260/verdict.html.
8. Peter Ford, "Legal War on Terror Lacks Weapons," *Christian Science Monitor*, 27 Mar 2002; www.csmonitor.com/2002/0327/p01s04-woeu.htm.
9. Initial release of information on this case can be read at "Transcript of the Attorney General John Ashcroft Regarding the Transfer of Abdullah Al Muhajir (Born Jose Padilla) to the Department of Defense as an Enemy Combatant," 10 June 2002; www.usdoj.gov/ag/speeches/2002/061002agtranscripts.htm.
10. Stephen Gale, quoted in Peter Ford.
11. "Sleepers" are persons who quietly reside in a community and go unnoticed by intelligence or law enforcement but in fact have criminal or terrorist objectives and are waiting for an opportunity or higher direction to execute a planned mission. Sleeper agents are very difficult to detect and harder to prosecute due to the benign nature of their lives. See Michael Clark, quoted in Peter Ford.
12. In the 16th century, a British political faction known as Whigs drew upon certain ideas of Niccolo Machiavelli, believing that any army powerful enough to defend a state would also have the power to overthrow it. The danger, according to Machiavelli, was especially acute in time of peace, when the army's usefulness was finished. Therefore, the concept of standing armies was challenged by Machiavelli and by Whigs who found his philosophies attractive. This became central to their political thought and influenced early American colonial politics as well as the crafting of our Constitution and Bill of Rights.
13. An excellent treatment of posse comitatus is contained in Thomas R. Lujan, "Legal Aspects of Domestic Employment of the Army," *Parameters*, Autumn 1997; http://carlisle-www.

army.mil/usawc/Parameters/97autumn/lujan.htm. The Posse Comitatus Act itself is available at http://law2.house.gov/usc.htm.

14. Executive Order 12333, "United States Intelligence Activities, 1981," is available at www.nara.gov/fedreg/codific/eos/e12333.html.

15. Presidential Decision Directive 39, "U.S. Policy on Counterterrorism, 1995." This directive is classified Secret. A redacted version is available at www.fas.org/irp/offdocs/pdd39.htm.

16. One example of innovative training in the area of urban operations is the Center for Emerging Threats and Opportunities, a partnership of the Marine Corps and the Potomac Institute for Policy Studies dedicated to exploring innovative ways to deal with non-conventional threats to national security; www.defenselink.mil/news/Jul2001/p07232001_p143-01.html.

17. Yale Law School provides an extensive reference resource concerning the Law of Armed Conflict; www.yale.edu/lawweb/avalon/lawofwar/lawwar.htm.

18. George Shultz, quoted in Douglas Menarchik, "Organizing to Combat 21st Century Terrorism," in *The Terrorism Threat and U.S. Government Response*, ed. James M. Smith and William C. Thomas (Colorado: USAF Institute for National Security Studies, 2001), p. 222.

19. U.S. Department of State, *Patterns of Global Terrorism* (Washington, DC: 2001), as well as earlier annual reports; www.state.gov/s/ct/rls/pgtrpt/.

20. More information about the Marine barracks bombing is available at www.beirut-memorial.org/ <http://www.beirut-memorial.org/>.

21. An outstanding treatment of the challenges of human source intelligence and specifically the recruitment of questionable sources was authored by Admiral Stansfield Turner, U.S. Navy (ret.). The author reviewed his controversial tenure as Director of the CIA and the problems of operating a secret intelligence organization in a democratic society in *Secrecy and Democracy: The CIA in Transition* (Boston: Houghton Mifflin, 1985).

22. The concept of leaderless resistance was proposed by Ulius Louis Amoss in 1962. In 1983, Louis Beam expounded on Amoss' idea in a quarterly journal, *The Seditionist*, wherein he wrote an essay proposing the overthrow of the American government. Leaderless resistance is a system based on the cell organization but does not have any central control or direction. Under the leaderless resistance concept, all individuals and groups operate independently and never report to a central headquarters or single leader for direction or instruction. Beam's essay is available at www.louisbeam.com/leaderless.htm.

23. The commission's suggestion of a cabinet-level agency to deal with homeland security included some of the earliest deliberation reflected in the President's recent proposed Department of Homeland Security. See the United States Commission on National Security/21st Century, *Road Map for National Security: Imperative for Change* (Washington DC: 2001), pp. 10–29.

24. U.S. Department of Defense, *Quadrennial Defense Review Report* (Washington, DC: 2001). A copy and analysis of the QDR are available at www.comw.org/qdr/.

25. More information about Northern Command is available at www.defenselink.mil/specials/unifiedcommand/.

26. Handel, p. 102.

27. Ibid., p. 121.

28. Colin S. Gray, "Thinking Asymmetrically in Times of Terror," *Parameters*, Spring 2002, available at <http://carlisle-www.army.mil/usawc/parameters/02spring/gray.htm>.

29. American Bar Association. Task Force on Terrorism and the Law, "Report and Recommendations on Military Commissions," 4 January 2002; www.abanet.org/leadership/military.pdf.

30. Joint doctrine states, "*By definition, terrorists do not meet the four requirements necessary for combatant status* (wear uniforms or other distinctive insignia, carry arms openly, be under command of a person responsible for group actions, and conduct their operations in accordance with laws of war).... For this reason, *captured terrorists are not afforded the protection from criminal prosecution attendant to prisoner of war status*" (emphasis in original). See Joint Chiefs of Staff Publication 3-07.2, *Joint Tactics, Techniques and Procedures for Antiterrorism* (Washington, DC: 17 March 1998); www.fas.org/irp/doddir/dod/jp3_07_2.pdf.

31. An excellent treatment and analysis of posse comitatus and its history are found in John R. Brinkerhoff, "The Posse Comitatus Act and Homeland Security," *Journal of Homeland*

Security, February 2002; www.homelandsecurity.org/journal/Articles/displayarticle.asp?article=30.

32. The Department of Homeland Security is fully defined and discussed at www.whitehouse.gov/deptofhomeland/book.pdf.

33. Peter H. Liotta, Professor of Strategy at the U.S. Naval War College, wrote about the emergence of "adversaries who… will increasingly look for innovative ways to 'attack' without attacking directly the brick wall of American military predominance. The chaos strategist thus targets the American national security decision-making process and, potentially, the American people, rather than American military force, in order to prevail. Such a strategist seeks to induce decision paralysis." Liotta applied this concept to the war on terrorism and offered insightful analysis for American defense planners. See P. H. Liotta, "Chaos as Strategy," *Parameters*, Summer 2002; <http://carlisle-www.army.mil/usawc/parameters/02summer/liotta.htm>.

34. Stephen Gale, quoted in Peter Ford.

35. "In response to a senator's question about the gravity of the threat, one intelligence official said there is a '100 percent' chance of an attack should the United States strike Afghanistan." See Susan Schmidt and Bob Woodward, "FBI, CIA Warn Congress of More Attacks as Blair Details Case Against Bin Laden; Retaliation Feared if U.S. Strikes Afghanistan," *Washington Post*, 5 Oct 2001; www.washingtonpost.com/ac2/wp-dyn?pagename=article&node=&contentId=A8418-2001Oct4. According to a CBS News poll on 3 Apr 2002, 74% of questioned Americans thought that another terrorist attack was likely.

Rob de Wijk, 2001

The Limits of Military Power

Defense planning had only fleetingly dealt with the threat of apocalyptic terrorism prior to September 11. If the hastily revised U.S. quadrennial defense guidelines give any insight, the basis of defense planning will now shift from a threat-based model, analyzing whom the adversary might be, to capability-based planning, which focuses more on how an adversary might fight. Adopting this model is a great step forward, but the review itself offers little insight into the question of how an adversary might actually fight and what forces are needed to fight and win future wars.[1] The events of September 11 clarified the urgent need to refocus and restructure the way the United States and its allies think about and plan for a military campaign.

- The West's armed forces are fundamentally flawed. Conceptually, the focus is still on conventional warfare, but the new wars will be unconventional.
- Contemporary concepts, such as limited collateral damage and proportionality, have little value when preparing for the new wars.
- How concepts such as coercive diplomacy and coercion can be used effectively is unclear.

In sum, the United States and its allies face significant practical as well as conceptual challenges. The September 11 attacks demonstrated that terrorism no longer can be considered a tactical or local challenge, requiring cooperation between the national intelligence services and the police. The new terrorism is a strategic or international challenge, requiring international cooperation between intelligence services and armed forces. Meeting the challenge requires a new approach as well as new assets.

'Savage Warfare'

Western armed forces demonstrated their superiority clearly during the Persian Gulf War in 1991 when, after the extensive use of airpower, U.S. ground forces gained a decisive victory over Iraq within 100 hours. In contrast to conventional warfare, which relies on technological capabilities—manned arms and standoff weaponry—to engage the enemy, terrorists fight unconventionally. Technology plays a supporting role at best, for personal protection, communications, and targeting. In the final analysis, however, successes depend on old-fashioned fighting skills and the use of knives or small-caliber arms in search-and-destroy operations. In conventional warfare, armies take and hold ground, air forces conduct strategic bombing operations and engage the enemy, and navies support land forces by conducting offshore attacks and cutting off lines of supply. This method of operation is the Western way of waging war. The new wars on terrorism, however, will have to deal with irregular forces that practice guerrilla tactics, instill panic, and retaliate asymmetrically—when, where, and how they choose.

Actually, referring to the military campaign now under way as the "new" war demonstrates little understanding of the history of warfare. In 1898, in *Lockhart's Advance through Tirah*, Capt. L. J. Shadwell wrote about "savage warfare" (that is, non-European warfare) "that differs from that of civilized people." Some areas in the world have not changed much since Shadwell's time.

> A frontier tribesman can live for days on the grain he carries with him, and other savages on a few dates; consequently no necessity exists for them to cover a line of communications. So nimble of foot, too, are they in their grass shoes, and so conversant with every goat-track in their mountains that they can retreat in any direction. This extraordinary mobility enables them to attack from any direction quite unexpectedly, and to disperse and disappear as rapidly as they came. For this reason, the rear of a European force is as much exposed to attack as its front or flanks.[2]

In Afghanistan today, the biggest change is that army boots or Nikes have replaced grass shoes. Furthermore, local fighters possess limited numbers of modern weapons systems, such as Stinger antiaircraft missiles, which were acquired during the 1980s when the United States considered Afghans to be freedom fighters who needed support in their struggle against Soviet occupation. The basic Afghani weapons platform is the pickup truck, which carries fighters armed with guns; in mountainous regions, the mule is still the most important mode of transportation.

In most Western countries, irregular warfare has always been considered "savage warfare," for which there is no preparation. Historically, the British and the Dutch, in particular, fought insurgents quite successfully in their colonies. With the loss of Indonesia in the 1950s, the Dutch lost not only all their experience in waging this kind of war but also their mental preparedness for such action.

The Dutch army is now preparing a new field manual on counterinsurgency and counterterrorism. In drafting the manual, the army's staff utilized the old manuals that General Johannes van Heutsz used during the early twentieth century when he was combating insurgents and terrorists in what is now the Republic of Indonesia. Van Heutsz also reorganized his conventional ground forces to confront the insurgents, creating small units of a dozen armed men to carry out search-and-destroy missions. This military action led to an episode that the Dutch do not want to repeat. Today, that army's counterinsurgency operations could be perceived as war crimes. Because no distinction could be made between combatants and noncombatants, the Dutch burnt down entire villages in order to eliminate fighters' bases. For this reason, U.S. Secretary of Defense Donald Rumsfeld argued that direct attacks on terrorists are useless; forces are required to "drain the swamp they live in."[3]

In addition to consulting van Heutsz's tactics, the Dutch used the British counterinsurgency manual, which is still considered the most detailed manual for this type of warfare. Of the former colonial powers, only the British have not given up their military skills; at the same time, British forces have maintained the mental preparedness needed to carry out counterinsurgency operations.

The West needs special forces to confront irregular fighters such as terrorists, and these forces are not available in large quantities. A distinction should be made between special operations forces (SOF), which are used for covert or clandestine action, and specialized forces, which carry out specialized overt missions. The most famous of all SOF, Great Britain's Special Air Service (SAS), conceived by Captain David Stirling, has existed since 1941. Most SOF—such as Australia's Special Air Service Regiment; Holland's Bijzondere Bijstands Eenheid (BBE); France's new joint Commandement des Operation Speciale (COS) units; Germany's Grenzschutsgruppe (GSG)-9; Israel's Sayeret Matkal/Unit 269; and the U.S. Army 1st Special Forces Operational Detachment, Delta Force, and Naval Special Warfare Development Group—were established in the 1970s as a direct response to terrorist incidents.

When radical supporters of Iran's revolution captured 53 staff members and guards at the U.S. embassy in Tehran in November 1979, however, the United States still had no standing counterterrorist task force. As a result, a rescue team had to be assembled from scratch, and it took six months of preparation before the rescue operation could be launched. Charged with rescuing the hostages was the newly created Delta Force, with the support of U.S. Navy and Air Force airlifts. The tragic end of this attempt is well known. Technical problems and tactical failures caused the operation's abortion, and it ended in disaster in April 1980. Nevertheless, after this failed rescue operation, U.S. SOF received more funding and better equipment and training. Consequently, SOF became an important foreign policy tool for U.S. policymakers.[4]

SOF specialize in clandestinely rescuing hostages. SOF's military tasks focus on infiltrations into enemy territory to carry out sabotage as well as search-and-destroy and rescue missions and forward air control. Western militaries have extremely limited true SOF capabilities, probably no more than 3,000–5,000 troops for all of NATO.

In addition, Western governments have specialized forces that carry out overt actions. The United States has approximately 45,000 such troops; its NATO allies have 20,000–30,000. The U.S. Army Ranger battalions, which specialize in seizing airfields, are among the better known of these units; another is the 82nd Airborne Division, the world's largest parachute force. These forces seize key targets and prepare the ground for the general-purpose forces that follow.

Nevertheless, new concepts such as swarming, netwar, and counternetwar also need to be developed. Deployed SOF and specialized forces must disperse and form a network that covers large areas. These forces must make use of advanced communications, including uplinks and downlinks with unmanned and manned aircraft and satellites to enable quick-response strikes against high-value targets. For the military, netwar requires a different mindset because, unlike traditional formations, it has less hierarchy and less emphasis on combined arms operations.

Even though NATO countries have more than three million individuals in their collective armed services, only a very small portion of them are SOF or specialized armed forces—too few to engage in sustained combat operations. Clearly, it is too late to increase this capability for the campaign in Afghanistan and other countries hosting terrorists. Even if a decision were made to create more of these units, only a small number of young people would be willing or able to join these forces; according to some estimates, less than 10 percent make it through the grueling selection process.

The status of the West's human intelligence (HUMINT) capabilities is similar. For data collection, the intelligence communities of the United States and its NATO allies focus primarily on satellite imagery, signals intelligence, and electronic intelligence. Satellite imagery guides both SOF and HUMINT to targets. Although satellite imagery obtains important strategic information, SOF and HUMINT are the best way to obtain tactical information on the ground, especially because terrorist groups make only limited use of cellular telephones and satellite communications. Since the U.S. Cruise missile attacks on his training camps in August 1998, Osama bin Laden no longer uses his satellite telephone, which had made him easy to detect. Instead, he issues "mission orders," instructing his lieutenants orally, in writing, or on videotape that television stations broadcast widely. Consequently, the United States and its allies have no choice but to infiltrate his network.

Tapping into this network is an enormous task, however, because the al Qaeda organization has bases and cells in 50–60 countries, including the United States and most European nations, where so-called sleeper agents live. The individuals who carried out the attacks on the World Trade Center and the Pentagon had been ordinary residents in the United States and other Western countries. Therefore, agents from Islamic states' intelligence communities must infiltrate networks and cells both inside and outside the Islamic world, while Western governments must at the same time recruit agents in the Islamic communities in their own countries. Consequently, effective use of HUMINT requires intensive cooperation among intelligence services worldwide.

Without sufficient HUMINT capabilities, as well as SOF and specialized forces that can effectively address unexpected threats and unconventional warfare—the only option open to the West's opponents—the United States and its allies will find the campaign on terrorism almost impossible. In its most basic form, asymmetrical warfare utilizes one side's comparative advantage against its enemy's relative weakness. Successful asymmetrical warfare exploits vulnerabilities—which are easy to determine—by using weapons and tactics in ways that are unplanned or unexpected. The weakness of Western societies is perceived as their desire to reduce collateral damage by emphasizing technological solutions, the need to maintain coalitions, and the need to adhere to the international rule of law. Moreover, Western industrialized societies are economically and socially vulnerable. Thus, dealing with these new threats requires groups of well-trained, well-equipped, and highly motivated individuals who can infiltrate and destroy terrorist networks.

At the tactical level, the opponent conducting asymmetrical warfare tries to change the course of action in order to prevent the achievement of political objectives. These tactics—including guerrilla warfare, hit-and-run attacks, sabotage, terrorism, and the capture of soldiers who are then shown on television—will confront allied ground forces in Afghanistan and other places that harbor terrorist training camps and headquarters.

At the strategic level, the opponent using asymmetrical tactics exploits the fears of the civilian population, thereby undermining the government, compromising its alliances, and affecting its economy. The September 11 attacks were only partly successful on this score. The fear of further attacks has led to uncertainty about the future among the populations of most Western nations and as a result their economies have fallen into recession. On the other hand, the attackers very likely miscalculated not only the resolve of the leadership and population of the United States but also most of the world's willingness to form and maintain coalitions to fight terrorism.

Direct military action against insurgents and terrorists requires both SOF and HUMINT gathering. Both assets are scarce, however, and not available in the quantities necessary to fight and win sustained wars. Moreover, deploying SOF is extremely risky, and effective engagement requires skills and techniques that come very close to war crimes. Therefore, the United States and its allies need to develop a new defense-planning concept.

The Limited Value of Contemporary Western Concepts

For historical and cultural reasons, the armed forces of Western countries have been disinclined to prepare for military action that was considered uncivilized. As a consequence, policymakers, the military, and the public are psychologically ill-prepared for this war. They have become used to concepts such as limited collateral damage, proportionality of response, and the absence of body bags. The current situation, however, calls for a willingness to abandon these ideas, at least partially, a sacrifice that may be difficult for some individuals and nations to make.

During his visit to Pakistan on October 5, British Prime Minister Tony Blair called for "proportionate strikes... [that should] not be directed against the Afghan people." These concepts have little value when carrying out military operations against insurgents and terrorists for a number of reasons.

- *Collateral damage.* Because asymmetrical fighters do not usually wear uniforms, combatants are indistinguishable from civilians. These fighters depend on the local civilian population for logistics and shelter in rural areas, and in urban areas the population is used as a shield. Moreover, because the Afghan population is loyal to tribes and clans, differentiating between combatants and noncombatants is almost impossible. Thus, the concept of limited collateral damage is almost useless in unconventional warfare, in which civilian casualties cannot be avoided.

- *Proportionality of response.* Proportionality refers to the size and character of the attack and the interests at stake. On September 11, the terrorists turned airliners into weapons of mass destruction. Indeed, for two conventional bombs to cause the death of more than 5,000 civilians is nearly impossible. Additionally, the United States must now defend its national security, leadership, and credibility. If one takes the concept of proportionality literally, retaliation with a few low-yield nuclear weapons would certainly be justifiable, because only nuclear weapons could cause the same amount of damage as the September 11 attacks. Keeping the fragile coalition with Islamic countries together requires less than a proportional response, however, rendering nuclear weapons a non-option.

- *Absence of body bags.* Because vital interests of the United States and its allies are at stake, the concept of an absence of body bags carries little value either. Both Blair and President George W. Bush have the popular political support to withstand the inevitable heavy human losses. General Joseph Ralston, NATO's supreme allied commander, warned, "We cannot be in the mindset of a zero-casualty operation."[5] Whether most European allies are also willing to pay this high price is doubtful. Initially, the Belgian and Dutch governments saw invoking Article 5 of the NATO treaty as a symbolic measure and a demonstration of transatlantic solidarity. Other governments agreed so that they would be consulted on U.S. decisions and have some influence on U.S. decisionmaking. Except for the United Kingdom, few European NATO allies acknowledged that the decision to invoke Article 5 implies sending their own troops to Southwest Asia.

Thus, combating insurgents and terrorists requires mental firmness, a quality evident in the United States and the United Kingdom today but uncertain in other allies. The traditional concepts of proportionality and limited collateral damage, however, do not have much value under the present circumstances.

Coercion and Coercive Diplomacy

Another obstacle to using military means effectively to combat the new threats that terrorism poses is the limited insight that academics, and therefore policymakers, offer into the theories of coercion and coercive diplomacy, as well as governments' lack of experience using them to achieve the desired outcome. Coercion is defined as the deliberate and purposeful use of economic and military power to influence the choices of one's adversaries; coercive diplomacy focuses on the latent use of the instruments of power to influence those choices. The studies on which these theories are based, however, do not have much relevance for policymakers today. The terrorist attacks on the United States demonstrate the need for policymakers and the military to reevaluate the concepts that underlie their approaches to balancing political ends and military means.

Most theories of coercion find their origin in the Cold War period, but preoccupation with deterrence has distorted the concept. Deterrence as a concept is useless for today's challenges because the world cannot deter individuals such as bin Laden and his lieutenants. Deterrence also does not work for failed states, many of which provide sanctuaries for insurgents and terrorists. Because negotiating with failed states and terrorists is impossible, both coercive diplomacy and coercion are meaningless. The only solution in those cases is direct action with SOF support, backed up by airpower.

The United States can only use coercive diplomacy and coercion against functioning states that actively support or shelter terrorists. For that reason, Vice President Dick Cheney's warning that the "full wrath" of the United States would be brought down against nations sheltering attackers is an indication of the administration's emerging strategy for combating terrorism.

The problem is the West's lack of experience with this approach. Many cases of coercion and coercive diplomacy have failed. For example, the Gulf War was an unprecedented success, but attempts to coerce Saddam Hussein to comply with United Nations (UN) resolutions during the 1990s failed. The humanitarian intervention in Somalia during the early 1990s resulted in failure. The success of Operation Allied Force in the war in Kosovo was limited because it took 78 days to convince Serbian president Slobodan Milosevic to accept a diplomatic solution based on the Rambouillet agreements signed in early 1999.

Existing theories are based primarily on studies that Thomas Schelling, Alexander George, and Robert Pape conducted,[6] yet even these "classics" do not apply to the circumstances that the West faces today. Schelling distinguishes between "brute force" and "compellence." Brute force is aimed at forcing a military solution; compellence is aimed at using the threat of force to influence an actor's choice.[7] According to Schelling, armed conflict can only be averted when the opponent refrains from taking action. This situation requires a deadline because, without a clear ultimatum, threats are hollow.[8] Accordingly, the United States gave Afghanistan's Taliban regime a deadline, which it rejected, to surrender bin Laden and his lieutenants.

For Schelling, coercive diplomacy involves not only undoing a particular action but also threatening the opponent with the use of force, which can bring about complete surrender. The crux of Schelling's approach is "risk strategy": by threatening the civilian population and presenting the prospect of terror, the actor expects the opponent's behavior to change. This notion made sense during the Cold War, when Schelling's book—in which he sought alternatives to the concept of deterrence—was published in 1966. A risk strategy is meaningless in the war against terrorism, however, because the coercers—the United States and its allies—must clearly indicate that the war is not against the Afghan people, but against terrorists and the regime supporting them. Thus there are no civilian populations (such as the Soviet people in the Cold War) to threaten in the effective use of coercion. Worse, excessive military force could split the fragile Islamic alliance that is cooperating with the United States in the war against terrorism. In other words, coercion might not only be ineffective, it might also backfire. For that reason, humanitarian aid for the civilian population accompanied the initial attacks on Afghanistan in early October 2001.

George's study of coercive diplomacy first appeared in 1971; a new edition was published in 1994, in which George tested his theory on more recent cases. George distinguishes between defensive "coercive diplomacy" and offensive "military strategy." Coercive diplomacy consists of using diplomatic means, reinforced with instruments of power. Coercion, in the form of threats or military interventions, must force an adversary to cease unacceptable activities.

George's main argument is that coercion and diplomacy go hand in hand with rewards for the opponent when complying with demands.[9] In the case of the Taliban, Bush and Blair have stated there is no room for compromise and that no rewards will be given for handing bin Laden over. Consequently, the Taliban had no incentive not to fight for its survival, forcing the United States and its allies to confront the prospect of a prolonged struggle and also undermining the fragile coalition forged between Western and Islamic states.

Schelling's and George's theories focus primarily on the latent use of instruments of power, whereas Pape's theory concerns their actual use. Pape posits that coercion is effective when it aims at the benefit side of the cost-benefit calculation that every actor makes. To be effective, the opposing side must consider the cost of surrendering to the demands of the intervening states to be lower than the cost of resistance. Pape argues that this outcome is possible when the actor withholds military success from the opponent, while offering a reward after the demands have been met. Both the Taliban as well as the U.S. and British governments have vital interests at stake; therefore, the Taliban's will to defend and the West's will to coerce are at maximum levels. Consequently, both sides are willing to pay a high price, and neither will give up easily.

Regarding military strategy, Pape focuses on strategic bombing, which can be decisive only in long wars of attrition. The overall superiority of materiel determines the success of this approach, which was Russia's strategy in Chechnya during the strategic bombing campaign in Grozny, a strategy most Western governments severely condemned as inhuman. Nevertheless, a military coalition may have no option but to use elements of an attrition strategy. Given the unavailability of other assets, the destruction of some training camps and underground facilities may require the use of low-yield tactical nuclear weapons or fuel-air explosives. Moreover, some U.S. strategists are reportedly beginning to consider using the threat of a limited nuclear strike as a method of deterring potential adversaries that support terrorist organizations from using chemical and biological weapons or of destroying the storage site of these weapons.[10] Thus, the use of nuclear weapons might actually be militarily useful in the war against terrorism, but potentially grave consequences—such as fracturing the coalition—prevent policymakers from using them.

Pape argues that deposing political regimes is not feasible "because leaders are hard to kill, governments are harder to overthrow, and even if the target government can be overthrown, the coercer can rarely guarantee that its replacement will be more forthcoming."[11] In other words, Blair's warning to the Taliban "to surrender terrorists or to surrender power"[12] does not have many successful historical precedents. The removal of Panama's President Manuel Noriega from power in 1989 is one of the few successful examples.

Pape concluded that the use of airpower can be successful when it denies the opponent the use of military capabilities. This approach requires a strategy of denial—that is, the destruction of key military targets, including headquarters and command and control centers, logistics, and staging areas. In the case of unconventional warfare, however, the number of high-value targets is extremely limited; therefore, there is little to bomb. Consequently, the only strategy that can be successful is a military strategy of control, which requires search-and-destroy missions using land forces such as SOF reinforced by specialized forces and airpower, but as argued earlier, the United States and its allies have very limited capabilities in these areas.

These studies are useful as a starting point for further academic research, but their work has limited utility for contemporary policymaking. Consequently, the September 11 incidents have prompted both policymakers and the military to rethink their basic concepts and to seek another approach to the old challenge of balancing political objectives and military means. For example, a mechanism of second-order change could be developed, aimed at mobilizing neighboring states against a target state. The Islamic Republic of Iran, which is strongly opposed to the Taliban regime, could play a crucial role by putting pressure on Afghanistan. Pressure from Iran would have the added advantage of involving an Islamic country and thus strengthening the coalition. Thus, reexamining old concepts and traditional approaches are essential to employing military means successfully in the campaign on terrorism.

The Battle for Hearts and Minds

A significant component of the new war—one that has been historically successful for both allies and adversaries of the United States—is the campaign to win the support of the populace of the opponent. In other words, the United States and its allies must also wage a battle for the hearts and minds of the people, in this case, in the Islamic world. This effort—using several approaches, including humanitarian aid and propaganda—must be made along with diplomatic measures and military operations. The humanitarian aid that accompanies the bombs being dropped in Afghanistan in the current fight demonstrates that the United States recognizes the importance of this campaign.

Israel serves as an example of the difficulties that a nation confronts in a war against terrorists and of the way the battle to win the hearts and minds of the population can accompany military measures. Terror persists in Israel, despite the fact that the country has military assets that are important for waging this type of war, including defense forces and intelligence services that are among the best in the world, policymakers and a public who are willing to take risks and to accept casualties, and widespread public support for the military even if mistakes are made. Yet the country cannot prevent or deter terrorist acts or attacks with rockets from southern Lebanon. Israel's experience shows that armed forces—trained, structured, and equipped for conventional war—are incapable of dealing with insurgents. Israel had no choice but to develop new tactics, employ different weapons systems, and use small task forces to carry out small-scale operations; but even this shift in modus operandi has not guaranteed success.

Bin Laden, who is accused of being the force behind the September 11 attacks, fights a battle similar to the Intifada but on a global scale. His objective seems to be to unite the Islamic world under a political-religious figure, or caliph, by removing pro-Western regimes, the state of Israel, and the U.S. presence from the Islamic world.

Israel's experience also shows that, at best, governments can only manage the problem of terrorism. Its solution requires offensive military action, heavy security measures to prevent radical elements from carrying out their attacks, and the building of coalitions with moderate political figures. Israel's experience with gaining the support of the civilian population is important. For example, when the security zone in southern Lebanon still existed, Israel carried out a counterinsurgency campaign within it while providing aid to the Lebanese population therein, including projects to rebuild infrastructure and programs to provide health care. On the other side of the coin, radical movements such as Hamas use nongovernmental organizations extensively for these purposes.

Bin Laden is popular because of his "good works" in the Islamic world, especially in Pakistan and Afghanistan. Indeed, in most Islamic countries, radical groups of fundamentalists have developed a social and cultural infrastructure to build an Islamic civil society and fill a vacuum that their countries' governments have neglected. For example, during the 1990s in Egypt, Jordan, the West Bank and Gaza, Afghanistan, and Pakistan, radical movements provided health care, education, and welfare for those nations' poor. After the 1992 earthquake in Cairo, these organizations were on the streets within hours, whereas the Egyptian government's relief efforts lagged behind. In fact, Qur'an study centers have become the single most important source for recruiting new members for the radical movements.

These types of campaigns waged by radical Islamic movements have very successfully undermined the legitimacy of governments and gained the support of the local civilian population. Consequently, the diplomatic and military actions of the United States and its allies should go hand in hand with a campaign for the hearts and minds in order to win the support of the Islamic world's population. In addition to food rations, U.S. aircraft have dropped leaflets and small transistor radios to enable the Afghans to receive Washington's message. Nevertheless, even a dual strategy of humanitarian aid and military intervention does not guarantee success. Other factors must be taken into account.

Clashing Civilizations

The major obstacle to success in the campaign against terrorism is not military, political, or diplomatic, but cultural. Because of strong anti-Western sentiments in the Islamic world, a coalition to counter terrorism is fragile by nature but critical to the success of military measures. The geostrategic changes that occurred in the 1990s have contributed to anti-Western feelings in large parts of the world. First, the West "won" the Cold War, with the United States remaining the sole superpower; and in international relations the "hegemon" is always met with distrust. Second, in 1998 the differences between the United States and non-Western nations countries became clearer as a result of a new version of interventionism.

The year 1998 seems to be a turning point in recent history. Events that took place in 1998 and 1999 indicated that the U.S. approach had once and for all shifted to a narrower and more selective foreign and national security policy of unilateralism and preservation of the nation's dominant position in the world. A number of events contributed to this image:

- In response to the bombings of the U.S. embassies in Kenya and Tanzania, the United States intervened unilaterally—and without a UN Security Council mandate—in Sudan and Afghanistan in August 1998. The U.S. goal was to strike a blow against bin Laden's alleged terrorist network.
- In December that same year, Operation Desert Fox took place, in which the United States and the United Kingdom carried out bombing raids against Iraq. The military action was meant as retribution for Saddam Hussein's obstruction of the UN Special Commission's inspections of Iraq's development of weapons of mass destruction. In 1999 and 2000, the bombings continued, albeit with limited intensity.
- In 1998, the U.S. government decided to increase its defense budget (which had undergone a period of decline) by 5.6 percent, a development that some nations viewed with apprehension.[13]
- In March 1999, Operation Allied Force—led by the United States and without a mandate by the UN Security Council—intervened in Kosovo to force Milosevic to end his terror against the Albanian Kosovars and to find a solution to the situation in Kosovo.
- In July 1999, the United States presented its national missile defense initiative, designed to protect the country against limited attacks by rogue states using ballistic missiles. This development demanded a review of the 1972 Anti-Ballistic Missile Treaty. With the U.S. Senate's refusal to ratify the Comprehensive Test Ban Treaty, a general prohibition on conducting nuclear tests was dropped.

As a result of these events, many non-Western countries began to perceive the United States as a superpower that wants to change the status quo and create a "new world order" according to its own views. Because of the fundamental difference between Western and non-Western ideas, Russia, China, and Islamic countries distrust interventions that are based on normative principles, such as democracy and humanitarianism. According to Chinese commentators, for example, interventions by the United States indicate that the West can impose its liberal values on the rest of the world without fear of confrontation with Russia.[14]

Only Western governments appeal to normative principles as a reason for intervention. The notion that these principles are universal and that sovereignty is secondary to human interest won ground in the 1990s. The concepts of democracy, respect for human rights, the free-market economy, pluralism, the rule of law, and social modernization are deeply rooted in Western culture and are the product of a civilization that developed over centuries. Universal pretensions and a feeling of superiority are not alien to Western culture.

In 1860 Isaac Taylor wrote about the "ultimate civilization." He dealt with the moral supremacy of Western civilization and considered other civilizations barbaric because they held polygamy, prostitution, slavery, and torture to be legal. After the fall of the Berlin Wall in 1989, many came to the conclusion that Western values, particularly democracy, had triumphed. In 1992 Francis Fukuyama even referred to the end of history, because liberal democracies had prevailed and the collapse of dictatorships was supposedly inevitable.[15] In September 2001, Italian prime minister Silvio Berlusconi praised Western civilization as superior to that of the Islamic world and urged Europe to "reconstitute itself on the basis of its Christian roots." In a briefing to journalists, he talked about the "superiority of our civilization, which consists of a value system that has given people widespread prosperity in those countries that embrace it and [that] guarantees respect and religion."[16] Other Western politicians and the Islamic world did not appreciate Berlusconi's frankness.

Beginning in 1990, Western countries believed that they had the evidence for their claim to universal acceptance of their principles because a steadily growing group of countries, including Russia, claimed that they had embraced Western values. Similar declarations by non-Western governments ultimately mean little. First, these governments can pay lip service for purely opportunistic reasons that may relate to other issues of importance to them, such as trade policy. Second, declarations of acceptance of these principles do not necessarily indicate that governments actually embrace them. Their unwillingness to accept the consequences of noncompliance with these principles at times or, in certain situations, their willingness to set aside sovereignty—for example, in the event of a humanitarian disaster—belie these claims. This notion is particularly true for countries, such as Russia and China, that have rebellious minorities, leading to internal unrest, and aspirations to remain great powers.

The British-Canadian scholar and journalist Michael Ignatieff appropriately posed the following question: Whose universal values are actually involved? He pointed out that the outlooks of Western countries, Islamic countries, and authoritarian regimes in East Asia have fundamental differences.[17] In Asia, authoritarian state and family structures dominate for the most part, and democracy and individual rights are secondary. In general, Islamic countries reject the Western concept of the separation of church and state. Apart from Ignatieff's observation, however, the claim of universal acceptance of Western values constitutes a threat in the eyes of many non-Western countries, if acceptance is accompanied by dismissal of the cornerstones of international law, such as sovereignty and noninterference in domestic affairs. These countries perceive even humanitarian interventions as a new form of imperialism that should not be endorsed without question.

The war against terrorism is a golden opportunity for Western nations to enter a new era of cooperation with Russia and China, which are equally concerned about terrorism. Indeed, bin Laden and the Islamic insurgents in Chechnya are linked. Furthermore, the Islamic insurgency in Xinjiang in eastern China has a connection with the Taliban regime and, most probably, bin Laden as well.

The biggest challenge, however, is the resurgence of Islam, which is a mainstream movement and not at all extremist. This resurgence is a product of modernity and of Muslims' attempt to deal with it by rejecting Western culture and influence, committing to Islam as the guide to life in the modern world. Fundamentalism, commonly misperceived as political Islam, is only one aspect of this resurgence, which began in the 1970s when Islamic symbols, beliefs, practices, and institutions won more support throughout the Islamic world. As a product of modernity, the core constituency of Islamic resurgence consists of middle-class students and intellectuals. Even the fundamentalists who carried out the September 11 attacks were well-educated, middle-class men.

Because the resurgence of Islam is fundamentally an anti-Western movement, building coalitions incorporating Islamic nations in the battle against terrorism is not easy. The coalition that was built in the aftermath of the September 11 attacks was primarily based on attitudes against bin Laden, who seeks to establish an undivided *umma* (community of believers) under a political-religious leader—thereby presenting a challenge to most regimes in the Islamic world. Nevertheless, most regimes and large parts of their populations share some of bin Laden's anti-Western sentiments. Consequently, the coalition is fragile and, at best, willing to give only passive support. Thus, many Islamic people will consider a military campaign that is carried out by Western forces as, to use bin Laden's words, "a Zionist Crusade." Unfortunately, a controversial 1996 assertion that conflicts between cultures will dominate future international relations remains germane in the new millennium.[18]

The war on terrorism could improve the West's relations with China and Russia, but, if handled unwisely, it could also lead to a confrontation with the Islamic world. The United States' nightmare scenario is that friendly regimes in the Islamic world will fall and anti-Western regimes willing to play the oil card and support terrorists will emerge. Thus, the immediate consequence of the war on terrorism could be both ineffectiveness and a struggle for energy resources so vital to the Western world.

Limiting Expectations

As the war against terrorism shifts into full gear, the United States and its allies must meet significant practical and conceptual challenges if the campaign is to be successful. A war against terrorists or insurgents can be manageable, at best, if certain approaches are adopted. In principle, the following options, which are not all mutually exclusive, are available to the United States and its allies, depending on the target of the campaign:

- Pursue a military strategy of control in failed states that terrorists use as sanctuaries. Control involves search-and-destroy missions by SOF, supported by specialized forces and airpower. This option requires the United States and its allies to expand the number of SOF and specialized forces significantly.
- Adopt a strategy of coercive diplomacy or coercion against unfriendly regimes to pressure these regimes to end their support of terrorist movements. If they do not comply with these demands, these regimes should be removed from power, which is easier said than done. This strategy requires new thinking about the optimum way to coerce regimes.
- Use HUMINT gathering methods extensively to infiltrate the terrorists' networks in friendly countries and then destroy the terrorist bases from within. This option also requires the United States and its allies to expand their HUMINT capabilities substantially and to embark on even closer cooperation with intelligence services in other countries.
- Wage a campaign to win the hearts and minds of the Islamic people. This option would enable the United States and its allies to gain the support of the populace and thereby drive a wedge between the population and the terrorists or insurgents.

Nevertheless, even if these options are adopted and prove successful at least in the short term, an overriding issue must be addressed in order to achieve long-term success. The primary obstacle to success in the war against terrorism is a cultural one. To some degree, the battle is a clash of civilizations. Political Islam is fundamentally anti-Western, thus the prospect for success is limited. Using military means may exacerbate the potential that this campaign will be cast as a clash of civilizations, ultimately making the problem of terrorism even worse.

Rob de Wijk is an expert on military aspects of security issues at the Clingendael Institute for International Relations (The Netherlands). He also is a professor of international relations at the Royal Military Academy and professor of strategic studies at Leiden University. A former head of the Defence Concepts Division of the Netherlands Ministry of Defence, he is also co-author of *NATO on the Brink of the New Millennium: The Battle for Consensus* (1998).

Notes

1. U.S. Department of Defense, *Quadrennial Defense Review Report*, September 30, 2001.
2. L. J. Shadwell, *Lockhart's Advance through Tirah* (London: W. Thacker & Co., 1898), pp. 100–105.
3. "Rumsfeld," *International Herald Tribune*, September 19, 2001, p. 6.
4. S. L. Marquis, *Unconventional Warfare: Rebuilding U.S. Special Operations Forces* (Washington, D.C.: Brookings Institution, 1997), p. 2.
5. "Rumsfeld," p. 6.
6. See Thomas A. Schelling, *Arms and Influence* (New Haven: Yale University Press, 1966); Alexander L. George and W. E. Simons, eds., *The Limits of Coercive Diplomacy* (Boulder, Colo.: Westview Press, 1994); Robert A. Pape, *Bombing to Win: Air Power and Coercion in War* (Ithaca, N.Y.: Cornell University Press, 1996). See also Lawrence Freedman, *Strategic Coercion* (Oxford: Oxford University Press, 1998); Colin S. Gray, *Modern Strategy* (Oxford: Oxford University Press, 1999); Richard N. Haass, *Intervention: The Use of American Military Force in the Post–Cold War World* (Washington, D.C.: Carnegie Endowment for International Peace, 1994); Michael O'Hanlon, *Saving Lives with Force: Military Criteria for Humanitarian Intervention* (Washington, D.C.: Brookings Institution, 1997); and B. R. Pirnie and W. E. Simons, *Soldiers for Peace* (Santa Monica, Calif.: RAND, 1996).
7. Schelling, *Arms and Influence*, pp. 2–3.
8. Ibid., pp. 69–91; see also Thomas Schelling, *The Strategy of Conflict* (New York and London: Oxford University Press, 1965).
9. George and Simons, *Limits of Coercive Diplomacy*, p. 7.
10. "U.S. Strategists Begin to Favor Threat to Use Nuclear Weapons," *International Herald Tribune*, October 6–7, 2001, p. 4.
11. Pape, *Bombing to Win*, p. 316.
12. Prime Minister Tony Blair, speech to the Labor Party Conference, London, October 2, 2001.
13. International Institute for Strategic Studies, "U.S. Military Spending," *Strategic Comments* 6, no. 4 (May 2000).
14. J. Teufel Dreyer, *The PLA and the Kosovo Conflict* (Carlisle, Penn.: U.S. Army War College, May 2000), p. 3.
15. F. Fukuyama, *The End of History and the Last Man* (New York: Free Press, 1992).
16. "Berlusconi Vaunts West's Superiority," *International Herald Tribune*, September 27, 2001.
17. M. Ignatieff, *Whose Universal Values? The Crisis in Human Rights* (The Hague: Paemium Erasmianum, 1999).
18. Samuel P. Huntington, *The Clash of Civilizations and the Remaking of World Order* (New York: Simon & Schuster, 1996).

David J. Rothkopf, 2002

Business Versus Terror

Only a new kind of alliance can win the war on terrorism. This alliance will not be one between nations nor will it be bound by a treaty. Instead, it will be unconventional, involve millions of disparate actors, and be guided by rules that will be constantly rewritten. It will be an alliance of a motley army of horizontal partnerships, with a nontraditional leadership structure. Its best troops will be regiments of geeks rather than the special forces that struck the first blows against the Taliban in Afghanistan. These pocket-protector brigades live on rations of cold pizza and coffee, not MREs (the military's "Meal, Ready-to-Eat"). They take orders not from generals or admirals but from markets and stockholders.

The members of this fighting force are scientists and doctors, venture capitalists and corporate project managers—the private-sector army that is the United States' not-so-secret weapon and best hope. These unlikely warriors will provide the software, systems, and analytical resources that will enable the United States to track terrorists. It is they who will develop the sensing systems to detect biological, chemical, and cyber threats. And it is they who will perfect the biometric devices, such as retinal scanners or thumb-print readers or facial-recognition technologies, that will be critical components of next-generation security systems and that will close the gaps Mohammed Atta and his associates revealed.

The Bush administration and terrorism experts know this group is critical. The enormous Pentagon acquisition apparatus has already begun to direct funds to new private-sector ventures that can satisfy immediate and longer-term tactical and strategic needs. Governor Tom Ridge, director of the Office of Homeland Security, has taken the first steps toward institutionalizing the public-private partnership that is absolutely critical to achieving U.S. domestic defense goals. Even smaller operations—such as the Central Intelligence Agency's venture fund In-Q-Tel, Inc. (a private nonprofit created in 1999 to invest in information technology deemed critical to the intelligence community)—have begun directing their comparatively limited resources to addressing the burgeoning, boggling array of threats that Americans now must contemplate.

Nonetheless, many in the Bush Administration acknowledge that these initial steps toward a more effective public-private sector cooperation are inadequate at best. As a result, a vital resource in defending the nation remains underutilized. According to *Fortune* magazine, the private sector will spend over $150 billion on homeland security–related expenses such as insurance, workplace security, logistics, and information technology— approximately four times the federal government's announced homeland security budget. And private-sector organizations operate America's transportation networks, power facilities, telecommunications and data networks, healthcare infrastructure, pharmaceutical companies, and most of the security services upon which U.S. critical infrastructures depend. But to date, these companies have been involved in very little of the coordinated planning, drilling exercises, threat evaluation, intelligence sharing, cooperative research, or any of the other steps a national defense strategy requires.

Most of the critical questions about how to achieve this public-private sector cooperation have yet to be asked. And even if we find the right answers, a cultural divide between government and business threatens this partnership. Bridging this divide is crucial because an important shift has taken place in U.S. national security. Once, it was almost entirely the province of the federal government to provide for that security by protecting the nation through overseas alliances, the five branches of the American military, intelligence assets, and other tools of U.S. policy. The war on terrorism, however, has changed all that. With an almost infinite number of threats and targets across the United States and in U.S.-owned facilities around the world, Washington cannot be solely responsible for homeland security. Just as winning this war requires international coalitions, intelligence sharing, and law-enforcement cooperation, so too does it require finding a new division of labor between the public and private sectors.

Soldiers of Fortune 500

The seeds of victory in the war against terrorism were planted long before the emergence of al Qaeda. During the Cold War, the Eisenhower administration—worried that traditional military-industrial partnerships were not producing the technologies essential to defeating the Soviets—created the Small Business Act of 1958, which allowed the predecessors of today's venture capitalists (VCs) to leverage their private capital on a three-to-one basis with funds borrowed from the government at below-market rates. (This leverage was increased to four-to-one in the late 1970s). Essentially, the government said, "If you're willing to put some money behind risky but promising ventures, we'll lend you three bucks for every one you put in. And we'll lend it to you for less than any bank would, because we think this investment is good for the country." This pledge mitigated the risk for investors and thus increased a pool of risk capital that could flow to entrepreneurial ventures.

The verdict is in: This government program has worked big time.

The subsequently growing pool of venture capital produced a number of success stories even before the tech boom of the late 1990s. Companies such as Minute Maid, Digital Equipment Corporation, Eastern Airlines, Federal Express, Apple Computer, and Genentech, Inc. provided the kinds of returns on investment that drew ever greater amounts of capital to the higher returns of venture investments. The connection to the government and, in particular, to the security establishment has been apparent in a number of instances since the very first days of this industry. Even Minute Maid was born from efforts during the Second World War to produce concentrated fruit juice for troops overseas.

The venture-capital boom of the 1990s provided yet more proof that the partnership between the security and venture-capital communities has had a circular, self-reinforcing quality. The Internet and many fundamental breakthroughs in computer and software development emerged from research-and-development (R&D) organizations within the defense establishment, such as the Defense Advanced Research and Projects Agency. Entrepreneurs, in turn, used funds from VCs to develop the companies that enhanced those technologies, which in turn enabled the creation of the commercial World Wide Web. Today, the military is upgrading its systems by using many of the software, switching and routing technologies, and content innovations developed by the private sector in its process of reinventing and spurring the worldwide growth of the Internet.

The success of this technological development cycle has produced not only an explosion in new technologies but also spectacular growth in the amount of money that is now available to entrepreneurs via VCs. During the last half of the 1990s, U.S. venture investment increased 20-fold, reaching a peak of $102.3 billion in 2000. By that year, over 5,000 companies had tapped this pool. Though the amounts fell dramatically in 2001 to approximately $38 billion, this sum of money is still vastly greater than many of the federal budget's most significant new technology development programs. For example, efforts to counter terrorism involving weapons of mass destruction only garnered $1.7 billion in the fiscal year 2002 budget. Furthermore, government R&D efforts are built to serve existing plans and are slowed and guided by ubiquitous, lumbering bureaucracies. These megaprojects are not the source of much of the out-of-the-box thinking that can come from smaller, less constrained operations. Consequently, it is not surprising that while the defense budget will continue to drive important new technologies, VC financing is still going to be a vital player in the R&D world for some time to come.

And it will be a very agile player. Since the boom of the late 1990s, the United States has moved away from the R&D model that drove most of its growth in the second half of the 20th century, wherein funds flowed from corporate budgets into owned-and-operated corporate laboratories like Bell Labs (where researchers developed telecommunications and information processing technologies such as the transistor that helped trigger the Information Revolution) or Xerox's Palo Alto Research Center (famous for developing technologies that led to the icon-driven operating systems common in today's Windows systems). Instead, the new model has entrepreneurial-minded technologists leaving the corporate nest, raising venture capital, test flying their ideas, and then, if they are successful, cashing out by selling those ideas back to large corporations. What has happened, in effect, is that the corporate world has outsourced many of its R&D functions by letting others take the risks.

Today, given the enormous demands for new technologies linked to fighting the war on terrorism and preserving homeland security, VCs are beginning to sense an opportunity. Once the nearly $38 billion earmarked for homeland security in Bush's fiscal year 2003 budget is divided among the 40 federal agencies involved in combating terrorism (not to mention the 50 states and thousands of localities lining up for cash), the amounts for technological development will be comparatively miniscule. Furthermore, the private sector is quickly realizing that impossibly huge demands are being placed on federal, state, and local authorities who must manage their existing "homeland security–related tasks"—such as patrolling borders, processing immigrants, policing streets, and administering the law in an environment where the number of credible and increasingly complex threats has grown in a very short period.

Consequently, the private sector has begun to take care of matters on its own. One example of how the invisible hand of the marketplace is more agile than the heavy hand of bureaucracy comes from the financial sector. Despite the destruction of 17 acres of lower Manhattan last September—including much of the critical infrastructure on that part of the island and the offices of many major players in the financial community—the markets themselves reopened within four days. The reason for this quick recovery was that in the wake of the first bombing of the World Trade Center in 1993, many institutions developed redundant back-office systems and emergency-response plans that were then implemented within hours of last year's attacks on the Twin Towers. Now, of course, many industries are seeing the merits of such an approach and are developing their own standards and systems for coping with such catastrophes.

Companies are not only concerned about physical security but also cybersecurity, and with good reason. According to the CERT Coordination Center (formerly known as the Computer Emergency Response Team) at Carnegie Mellon University's Software Engineering Institute, the number of security incidents on the Internet has increased at an alarming rate. Over 20,000 incidents were reported to CERT in 2000. That number increased to more than 52,000 in 2001. As such, corporations and the U.S. government find themselves sharing the same foxhole as they seek to defend the critical functions of the national infrastructure. One important initiative that has already emerged is the Critical Infrastructure Protection Board chaired by Richard Clarke, the nation's cybersecurity czar. Clarke has been among the government's most effective architects of public-private partnerships in part because he was the driving force behind the government's Y2K efforts. This precedent-setting project was based on the idea that the Y2K bug—which many feared could cause critical computer systems to fail when the calendar hit the year 2000—was a national threat that could not be addressed by the government acting alone.

This ongoing cooperation was easily translated into a response to the war on terrorism after September 11. At that time, business leaders with whom Clarke worked closely—such as Microsoft's Bill Gates and Oracle's Larry Ellison, not generally seen as highly cooperative with one another—announced plans to make security a higher priority at their companies. Gates even circulated a memo to Microsoft staff mandating the establishment of security-related issues as the company's top priority.

The Creative Edge

The culture of innovation that is prevalent in the United States has produced an overwhelming response from the private sector in the aftermath of last year's terrorist attacks. One Pentagon office, the Technical Support Working Group (created to help coordinate interaction with private-sector technology developers), received 12,405 proposals for new technologies in the war on terrorism between October 2001 and January 2002. Similar requests for proposals have in the past garnered 900 to 1,000 responses. At In-Q-Tel, Inc., applications for funding have gone from approximately 700 during the first 30 months of the organization's existence to over 1,000 during the last six. But the Technical Support Working Group funds only about $70 million in such projects a year. And In-Q-Tel, Inc., which is interested in a broad range of technologies—such as Internet search engines, analytical software, and security and privacy technologies—has only funded more than 20 ventures in its short lifetime and allocates only about $30 million a year for investment purposes. Clearly, more such programs are needed if the United States is to tap its rich technological resources. And in addition to providing more financing, the government must be willing to get over the "not-invented-here syndrome" and to share new technologies broadly across agencies.

Again, market forces come to the rescue. In this security-minded environment, demand for these new products is engendering enormous sales potential for innovators even if the government cannot or will not fund them. International Data Corporation, an industry consultant, projects that the global market for information security services will triple from today's levels to over $21 billion by 2005. Similarly, even where relatively new technologies such as biometrics are concerned, growing demand will produce money for new R&D. It is estimated that between 500,000 and 700,000 identity thefts—one of the fastest growing modern crimes—occurred in the United States in 2000. Consequently, the International Biometric Group expects biometric sales to grow from some $500 million this year to almost four times that by the end of 2005. Homeland-security experts have shown particular interest in advanced ID cards with biometric identifiers stored on smart chips. The debate at the federal level about the appropriateness of creating a U.S. national ID card continues. But a market-driven alliance between state motor vehicle administrators (through the American Association of Motor Vehicle Administrators), biometric companies, and manufacturers of sophisticated databases is likely to produce a de facto national ID card by adopting common information standards for driver's licenses.

Given that many bioterrorism experts consider the U.S. food supply to be especially vulnerable to terrorist attacks, there is also a high premium on new bioanalytical devices that can determine whether pathogens reside in food. Taking 30 minutes rather than hours to determine whether a food product has been spiked with a bacterium or some poisonous chemical can mean the difference between life and death for potentially large groups of consumers. To speed the process along, the Washington, D.C., law firm Buchanan Ingersoll has proposed creating an antibioterrorism technology development venture capital fund that would put government dollars in the hands of venture professionals to help locate the most promising technologies for identifying and containing potential biological attacks. The objective would be to accelerate the development of a competitive antibioterrorism industry so that the government could use the technologies while the companies could benefit from other sales of the products developed—much as what happened with the computer, biotech, and Internet development efforts that took place within and in partnership with the government.

Unleashing the Market

Just as it is impossible for government to win this war alone, so too is it impossible for businesses to do the same. Businesses can protect, to some degree, their own assets. They can develop useful new technologies. They can finance innovation and dissemination of cost-effective tools for identifying, reducing, or containing threats. But they cannot wage war overseas, cannot conduct international diplomacy, and most importantly, cannot create a national strategy where one is lacking. Finally, if their willingness to work with the federal government is not reciprocated (right now many companies that have called the federal government with homeland-security ideas have been met with "We're not ready yet" or "We're too overwhelmed") or the potential impact of their ideas is limited (because one government agency grabs them and puts a lid on them), all they can do is wait until another cataclysm drives home the message that the public-private coalition requires a new attitude, outlook, and structure.

The U.S. government can take a range of new approaches that will allow it to further harness the power of this army of gray flannel allies. For starters, lawmakers and regulators need to precisely codify the extent to which privacy rights should be modified to enhance security. Otherwise, corporations will be extremely reluctant to share their databases with the appropriate government agencies. For example, had there been a more effective system in place for sharing data among car rental companies, flight schools, airlines, credit card companies, and federal visa and state drivers' license records, U.S. authorities could have had a much easier time identifying and perhaps stopping the terrorist activities of September 2001. However, if the wrong individual ends up being harassed by the government because of a record a private company handed over, how long will it be before lawyers file suit against that company?

By the same token, corporations that cooperate with the government will require indemnification against potential lawsuits by individuals who suffer damages as a consequence of a terrorist attack that succeeds despite the company's best efforts, or worse, because of a failure of their systems and services. Imagine what would happen if it could be proved that 250 people on a plane died because a new piece of expensive technology did not sniff out a bomb on board. Again, instant lawsuits would follow.

Moreover, the U.S. government must be the insurer of last resort in the event of catastrophic attacks, unless we want to see a major rollback in the high-profile, economically important development efforts that also produce high-risk potential targets. Urban areas in major U.S. cities would suffer the greatest losses, as is evidenced by this year's decline in construction of high-rise buildings and megaprojects. Insurance companies would also be forced to raise rates to stratospheric levels in the absence of such protection, thereby undermining the ability of the market to play an optimal role in the partnership.

Another vital step is to clarify exactly what the federal government means by "homeland defense." Is it defense of borders? Defense of the population? Defense against all threats? The answers to these questions will be crucial to developing a clear federal strategy for homeland security. There will be pitfalls if the government offers too broad a definition or too ambitious a set of objectives. The government cannot possibly hope to defend every potential target in the United States from every potential threat. Consequently, the definition and strategy must focus on areas that absolutely require the federal government's participation—specifically, those areas in which threats to national security portend massive physical or economic devastation. Thus, the focus should be on weapons of mass destruction (nuclear, biological, and chemical), weapons of mass disruption (cyberattack and coordinated conventional attacks), and organizations with the inclination either to undertake such attacks or to wage extended war on U.S. citizens or assets. Further clarification in other areas that guide federal action is also necessary: The definition of "first responders" needs to be broadened to include certain public and private healthcare workers. The definition of intelligence must be broadened so that it includes open-source and other unclassified forms of information sharing.

Such information sharing won't work, however, unless all participants have access to the best intelligence available. Only a comparative few will have access to classified components of this information, but tens or hundreds of thousands will need unclassified versions of this data. Even that unclassified information will require the latest encryption technologies to prevent it from falling into the wrong hands. Rather than relying on the traditional, stove-piped approaches in which agencies communicate up and down their organizational charts but not with others in the government who have similar missions, the system needs to have a more decentralized architecture and should offer end-users raw data for their own interpretation. The key will be to harness the more than 1 million pages of new data that appear on the Internet each day. The failure to deliver that intelligence to those who need it will only produce insecurity, doubt, and failure.

In addition to disseminating intelligence, it is vital to foster the dissemination of innovation. While the term "incubator" (in which a company offers space, resources, back-office services, and sometimes management expertise to multiple start-ups simultaneously) lost its former appeal among the tech crowd following the industry's shake-out, the idea of offering government facilities, technology, and potential markets to would-be entrepreneurs will give the U.S. government more mileage for its money and will bring in clusters of talented, market-trained innovators that it might not otherwise be able to attract. Similarly, groups of scientists and technology specialists might donate a week or two a year to participate in simulations of crises that are designed to reassess capabilities and stimulate new strategic or technical thinking about solutions.

Finally, as September 11 recedes into memory, complacency might emerge in the private-sector and among local agencies. To preempt this possibility, private-sector firms with requisite expertise should publish objective evaluations of readiness. Such ratings would be controversial, but they would also motivate states, localities, and companies to optimize their efforts. No city would want to be ranked at the bottom of a "National Homeland Security Readiness Index" lest it deter investment and growth. Nor would political or business leaders want to be seen as falling behind their peers in terms of this critical measure. Creating information products that promote innovation and vigilance is essential to maintaining readiness.

Balance Sheets of Power

The calculus of the war on terrorism is different from that of previous wars. In an instant, the United States can lose more people than died in over a decade in Vietnam. Five grams of anthrax in the heating and ventilation system of an office tower or a mall can kill thousands. A single successful attack using a briefcase-sized nuclear device or a dose of smallpox in an airport could kill tens of thousands or many more. A single vial of hoof-and-mouth disease or bovine spongiform encephalopathy ("mad cow disease") spread around a feedlot in Texas could shut down U.S. beef exports to the world.

But the guards at the feedlot and the mall are rent-a-cops and have neither the training nor the intelligence support to identify or respond to terrorist threats. The sensors that could contain such attacks have yet to be deployed, due to liability issues and cost factors. To stop an attack from a weapon of mass destruction will require a marriage of good intelligence and solid police work, sensing technologies and effective drills, and public and private resources. The government cannot do it alone, and the private sector is not only ready to help but has already made great strides in that direction. The opportunity is strikingly clear: The United States can defeat terrorists by drawing on the very attributes that inflame its enemies. The World Trade Center was a monument to American enterprise, American capital, American technology, the hard work of the American people, U.S. reliance on the marketplace, and the role of the individual. The towers may be gone, but the forces they embodied remain and stand ready to wage war on those who brought the towers down—if only the American people and the U.S. government will let them.

David J. Rothkopf is CEO of Intellibridge Corporation, which offers knowledge management and intelligence service to global corporations and organizations, and a former deputy under secretary of commerce for International Trade Policy (1993–1996). He also currently serves as adjunct professor of International and Public Affairs at Columbia University.

Appendices

Background Information on Designated Foreign Terrorist Organizations

T *he following descriptive list constitutes the 33 terrorist groups that currently are des- ignated by the Secretary of State as Foreign Terrorist Organizations (FTOs), pursuant to section 219 of the Immigration and Nationality Act, as amended by the Antiterrorism and Effective Death Penalty Act of 1996. The designations carry legal consequences:*

- It is unlawful to provide funds or other material support to a designated FTO.
- Representatives and certain members of a designated FTO can be denied visas or excluded from the United States.
- U.S. financial institutions must block funds of designated FTOs and their agents and must report the blockage to the U.S. Department of the Treasury.

Abu Nidal Organization (ANO)

a.k.a. Fatah Revolutionary Council, Arab Revolutionary Brigades, Black September, and Revolutionary Organization of Socialist Muslims

Description

International terrorist organization led by Sabri al-Banna. Split from PLO in 1974. Made up of various functional committees, including political, military, and financial.

Activities

Has carried out terrorist attacks in 20 countries, killing or injuring almost 900 persons. Targets include the United States, the United Kingdom, France, Israel, moderate Pal- estinians, the PLO [Palestine Liberation Organization], and various Arab countries. Major attacks included the Rome and Vienna airports in December 1985, the Neve Shalom synagogue in Istanbul and the Pan Am Flight 73 hijacking in Karachi in Sep- tember 1986, and the City of Poros day-excursion ship attack in Greece in July 1988. Suspected of assassinating PLO deputy chief Abu Iyad and PLO security chief Abu Hul in Tunis in January 1991. ANO assassinated a Jordanian diplomat in Lebanon in January 1994 and has been linked to the killing of the PLO representative there. Has not attacked Western targets since the late 1980s.

Strength

Few hundred plus limited overseas support structure.

Location/Area of Operation

Al-Banna relocated to Iraq in December 1998, where the group maintains a presence. Has an operational presence in Lebanon including in several Palestinian refugee camps. Financial problems and internal disorganization have reduced the group's activities and capabilities. Authorities shut down the ANO's operations in Libya and Egypt in 1999. Has demonstrated ability to operate over wide area, including the Middle East, Asia, and Europe.

External Aid

Has received considerable support, including safe haven, training, logistic assistance, and financial aid from Iraq, Libya, and Syria (until 1987), in addition to close support for selected operations.

Abu Sayyaf Group (ASG)

Description

The ASG is the most violent of the Islamic separatist groups operating in the southern Philippines. Some ASG leaders have studied or worked in the Middle East and allegedly fought in Afghanistan during the Soviet war. The group split from the Moro National Liberation Front in the early 1990s under the leadership of Abdurajak Abubakar Janjalani, who was killed in a clash with Philippine police on 18 December 1998. His younger brother, Khadaffy Janjalani, has replaced him as the nominal leader of the group, which is composed of several semi-autonomous factions.

Activities

Engages in kidnappings for ransom, bombings, assassinations, and extortion. Although from time to time it claims that its motivation is to promote an independent Islamic state in western Mindanao and the Sulu Archipelago, areas in the southern Philippines heavily populated by Muslims, the ASG now appears to use terror mainly for financial profit. The group's first large-scale action was a raid on the town of Ipil in Mindanao in April 1995. In April of 2000, an ASG faction kidnapped 21 persons, including 10 foreign tourists, from a resort in Malaysia. Separately in 2000, the group abducted several foreign journalists, 3 Malaysians, and a U.S. citizen. On 27 May 2001, the ASG kidnapped three U.S. citizens and 17 Filipinos from a tourist resort in Palawan, Philippines. Several of the hostages, including one U.S. citizen, were murdered.

Strength

Believed to have a few hundred core fighters, but at least 1,000 individuals motivated by the prospect of receiving ransom payments for foreign hostages allegedly joined the group in 2000–2001.

Location/Area of Operation

The ASG was founded in Basilan Province, and mainly operates there and in the neighboring provinces of Sulu and Tawi-Tawi in the Sulu Archipelago. It also operates in the Zamboanga peninsula, and members occasionally travel to Manila and other parts of the country. The group expanded its operations in Malaysia in 2000 when it abducted foreigners from a tourist resort.

External Aid

Largely self-financing through ransom and extortion; may receive support from Islamic extremists in the Middle East and South Asia. Libya publicly paid millions of dollars for the release of the foreign hostages seized from Malaysia in 2000.

Al-Aqsa Martyrs Brigade

Description

The al-Aqsa Martyrs Brigade comprises an unknown number of small cells of Fatah-affiliated activists that emerged at the outset of the current *intifadah* to attack Israeli targets. It aims to drive the Israeli military and settlers from the West Bank, Gaza Strip, and Jerusalem and to establish a Palestinian state.

Activities

Al-Aqsa Martyrs Brigade has carried out shootings and suicide operations against Israeli military personnel and civilians and has killed Palestinians who it believed were collaborating with Israel. At least five U.S. citizens, four of them dual Israeli-U.S. citizens, were killed in these attacks. The group probably did not attack them because of their U.S. citizenship. In January 2002, the group claimed responsibility for the first suicide bombing carried out by a female.

Strength

Unknown.

Location/Area of Operation

Al-Aqsa operates mainly in the West Bank and has claimed attacks inside Israel and the Gaza Strip.

External Aid

Unknown.

Armed Islamic Group (GIA)

Description

An Islamic extremist group, the GIA aims to overthrow the secular Algerian regime and replace it with an Islamic state. The GIA began its violent activity in 1992 after Algiers voided the victory of the Islamic Salvation Front (FIS)—the largest Islamic opposition party—in the first round of legislative elections in December 1991.

Activities

Frequent attacks against civilians and government workers. Between 1992 and 1998 the GIA conducted a terrorist campaign of civilian massacres, sometimes wiping out entire villages in its area of operation. Since announcing its campaign against foreigners living in Algeria in 1993, the GIA has killed more than 100 expatriate men and women—mostly Europeans—in the country. The group uses assassinations and bombings, including car bombs, and it is known to favor kidnapping victims and slitting their throats. The GIA hijacked an Air France flight to Algiers in December 1994. In late 1999 a French court convicted several GIA members for conducting a series of bombings in France in 1995.

Strength

Precise numbers unknown; probably around 200.

Location/Area of Operation

Algeria

External Aid

Algerian expatriates, some of whom reside in Western Europe, provide some financial and logistic support. In addition, the Algerian Government has accused Iran and Sudan of supporting Algerian extremists.

'Asbat al-Ansar

Description

'Asbat al-Ansar—the Partisans' League—is a Lebanon-based, Sunni extremist group, composed primarily of Palestinians, which is associated with Usama bin Laden. The group follows an extremist interpretation of Islam that justifies violence against civilian targets to achieve political ends. Some of those goals include overthrowing the Lebanese Government and thwarting perceived anti-Islamic influences in the country.

Activities

'Asbat al-ansar has carried out several terrorist attacks in Lebanon since it first emerged in the early 1990s. The group carried out assassinations of Lebanese religious leaders and bombed several nightclubs, theaters, and liquor stores in the mid-1990s. The group raised its operational profile in 2000 with two dramatic attacks against Lebanese and international targets. The group was involved in clashes in northern Lebanon in late December 1999 and carried out a rocket-propelled grenade attack on the Russian Embassy in Beirut in January 2000.

Strength

The group commands about 300 fighters in Lebanon.

Location/Area of Operation

The group's primary base of operations is the 'Ayn al-Hilwah Palestinian refugee camp near Sidon in southern Lebanon.

External Aid

Probably receives money through international Sunni extremist networks and Bin Laden's al-Qaida network.

Aum Supreme Truth (Aum)

a.k.a. Aum Shinrikyo, Aleph

Description

A cult established in 1987 by Shoko Asahara, the Aum aimed to take over Japan and then the world. Approved as a religious entity in 1989 under Japanese law, the group ran candidates in a Japanese parliamentary election in 1990. Over time the cult began to emphasize the imminence of the end of the world and stated that the United States would initiate Armageddon by starting World War III with Japan. The Japanese Government revoked its recognition of the Aum as a religious organization in October

1995, but in 1997 a government panel decided not to invoke the Anti-Subversive Law against the group, which would have outlawed the cult. A 1999 law gave the Japanese Government authorization to continue police surveillance of the group due to concerns that Aum might launch future terrorist attacks. Under the leadership of Fumihiro Joyu the Aum changed its name to Aleph in January 2000 and claimed to have rejected the violent and apocalyptic teachings of its founder. (Joyu took formal control of the organization early in 2002 and remains its leader).

Activities

On 20 March 1995, Aum members simultaneously released the chemical nerve agent sarin on several Tokyo subway trains, killing 12 persons and injuring up to 6,000. The group was responsible for other mysterious chemical accidents in Japan in 1994. Its efforts to conduct attacks using biological agents have been unsuccessful. Japanese police arrested Asahara in May 1995, and he remained on trial facing charges in 13 crimes, including 7 counts of murder, at the end of 2001. Legal analysts say it will take several more years to conclude the trial. Since 1997 the cult [has] continued to recruit new members, engage in commercial enterprise, and acquire property, although it scaled back these activities significantly in 2001 in response to public outcry. The cult maintains an Internet home page. In July 2001, Russian authorities arrested a group of Russian Aum followers who had planned to set off bombs near the Imperial Palace in Tokyo as part of an operation to free Asahara from jail and then smuggle him to Russia.

Strength

The Aum's current membership is estimated at 1,500 to 2,000 persons. At the time of the Tokyo subway attack, the group claimed to have 9,000 members in Japan and up to 40,000 worldwide.

Location/Area of Operation

The Aum's principal membership is located only in Japan, but a residual branch comprising an unknown number of followers has surfaced in Russia.

External Aid

None.

Basque Fatherland and Liberty (ETA)

a.k.a. Euzkadi Ta Askatasuna

Description

Founded in 1959 with the aim of establishing an independent homeland based on Marxist principles in the northern Spanish Provinces of Vizcaya, Guipuzcoa, Alava, and Navarra, and the southwestern French Departments of Labourd, Basse-Navarra, and Soule.

Activities

Primarily involved in bombings and assassinations of Spanish Government officials, security and military forces, politicians, and judicial figures. ETA finances its activities through kidnappings, robberies, and extortion. The group has killed more than 800 persons and injured hundreds of others since it began lethal attacks in the early 1960s. In November 1999, ETA broke its "unilateral and indefinite" cease-fire and began an assassination and bombing campaign that has killed 38 individuals and wounded scores more by the end of 2001.

Strength
Unknown; may have hundreds of members, plus supporters.

Location/Area of Operation
Operates primarily in the Basque autonomous regions of northern Spain and south-western France, but also has bombed Spanish and French interests elsewhere.

External Aid
Has received training at various times in the past in Libya, Lebanon, and Nicaragua. Some ETA members allegedly have received sanctuary in Cuba while others reside in South America.

Al-Gama'a al-Islamiyya (Islamic Group, IG)

Description
Egypt's largest militant group, active since the late 1970s, appears to be loosely organized. Has an external wing with supporters in several countries worldwide. The group issued a cease-fire in March 1999, but its spiritual leader, Shaykh Umar Abd al-Rahman, sentenced to life in prison in January 1996 for his involvement in the 1993 World Trade Center bombing and incarcerated in the United States, rescinded his support for the cease-fire in June 2000. The Gama'a has not conducted an attack inside Egypt since August 1998. Senior member signed Usama Bin Laden's *fatwa* in February 1998 calling for attacks against U.S.. Unofficially split in two factions; one that supports the cease-fire led by Mustafa Hamza, and one led by Rifa'i Taha Musa, calling for a return to armed operations. Taha Musa in early 2001 published a book in which he attempted to justify terrorist attacks that would cause mass casualties. Musa disappeared several months thereafter, and there are conflicting reports as to his current whereabouts. Primary goal is to overthrow the Egyptian Government and replace it with an Islamic state, but disaffected IG members, such as those potentially inspired by Taha Musa or Abd al-Rahman, may be interested in carrying out attacks against U.S. and Israeli interests.

Activities
Group conducted armed attacks against Egyptian security and other government officials, Coptic Christians, and Egyptian opponents of Islamic extremism before the cease-fire. From 1993 until the cease-fire, al-Gama'a launched attacks on tourists in Egypt, most notably the attack in November 1997 at Luxor that killed 58 foreign tourists. Also claimed responsibility for the attempt in June 1995 to assassinate Egyptian President Hosni Mubarak in Addis Ababa, Ethiopia. The Gama'a has never specifically attacked a U.S. citizen or facility but has threatened U.S. interests.

Strength
Unknown. At its peak the IG probably commanded several thousand hard-core members and a like number of sympathizers. The 1999 cease-fire and security crackdowns following the attack in Luxor in 1997, and more recently security efforts following September 11, probably have resulted in a substantial decrease in the group's numbers.

Location/Area of Operation

Operates mainly in the al-Minya, Asyu't, Qina, and Sohaj Governorates of southern Egypt. Also appears to have support in Cairo, Alexandria, and other urban locations, particularly among unemployed graduates and students. Has a worldwide presence, including the United Kingdom, Afghanistan, Yemen, and Austria.

External Aid

Unknown. The Egyptian Government believes that Iran, Bin Laden, and Afghan militant groups support the organization. Also may obtain some funding through various Islamic nongovernmental organizations.

HAMAS (Islamic Resistance Movement)

Description

Formed in late 1987 as an outgrowth of the Palestinian branch of the Muslim Brotherhood. Various HAMAS elements have used both political and violent means, including terrorism, to pursue the goal of establishing an Islamic Palestinian state in place of Israel. Loosely structured, with some elements working clandestinely and others working openly through mosques and social service institutions to recruit members, raise money, organize activities, and distribute propaganda. HAMAS's strength is concentrated in the Gaza Strip and a few areas of the West Bank. Also has engaged in political activity, such as running candidates in West Bank Chamber of Commerce elections.

Activities

HAMAS activists, especially those in the Izz el-Din al-Qassam Brigades, have conducted many attacks—including large-scale suicide bombings—against Israeli civilian and military targets. In the early 1990s, they also targeted Fatah rivals and began a practice of targeting suspected Palestinian collaborators, which continues. Increased operational activity in 2001 during the *intifadah*, claiming numerous attacks against Israeli interests. Group has not targeted U.S. interests and continues to confine its attacks to Israelis inside Israel and the territories.

Strength

Unknown number of hard-core members; tens of thousands of supporters and sympathizers.

Location/Area of Operation

Primarily the West Bank, Gaza Strip, and Israel. In August 1999, Jordanian authorities closed the group's Political Bureau offices in Amman, arrested its leaders, and prohibited the group from operating on Jordanian territory. HAMAS leaders also present in other parts of the Middle East, including Syria, Lebanon, and Iran.

External Aid

Receives funding from Palestinian expatriates, Iran, and private benefactors in Saudi Arabia and other moderate Arab states. Some fund-raising and propaganda activity takes place in Western Europe and North America.

Harakat ul-Mujahidin (HUM) (Movement of Holy Warriors)

Description

The HUM is an Islamic militant group based in Pakistan that operates primarily in Kashmir. It is politically aligned with the radical political party, Jamiat-i Ulema-i Islam Fazlur Rehman faction (JUI-F). Long-time leader of the group, Fazlur Rehman Khalil, in mid-February 2000 stepped down as HUM emir, turning the reins over to the popular Kashmiri commander and his second-in-command, Farooq Kashmiri. Khalil, who has been linked to Bin Laden and signed his fatwa in February 1998 calling for attacks on U.S. and Western interests, assumed the position of HUM Secretary General. HUM operated terrorist training camps in eastern Afghanistan until Coalition airstrikes destroyed them during fall 2001.

Activities

Has conducted a number of operations against Indian troops and civilian targets in Kashmir. Linked to the Kashmiri militant group al-Faran that kidnapped five Western tourists in Kashmir in July 1995; one was killed in August 1995 and the other four reportedly were killed in December of the same year. The HUM is responsible for the hijacking of an Indian airliner on 24 December 1999, which resulted in the release of Masood Azhar—an important leader in the former Harakat ul-Ansar imprisoned by the Indians in 1994—and Ahmad Omar Sheikh, who was arrested for the abduction/murder in January–February 2002 of U.S. journalist Daniel Pearl.

Strength

Has several thousand armed supporters located in Azad Kashmir, Pakistan, and India's southern Kashmir and Doda regions. Supporters are mostly Pakistanis and Kashmiris and also include Afghans and Arab veterans of the Afghan war. Uses light and heavy machine-guns, assault rifles, mortars, explosives, and rockets. HUM lost a significant share of its membership in defections to the Jaish-e-Mohammed (JEM) in 2000.

Location/Area of Operation

Based in Muzaffarabad, Rawalpindi, and several other towns in Pakistan, but members conduct insurgent and terrorist activities primarily in Kashmir. The HUM trained its militants in Afghanistan and Pakistan.

External Aid

Collects donations from Saudi Arabia and other Gulf and Islamic states and from Pakistanis and Kashmiris. The HUM's financial collection methods also include soliciting donations from magazine ads and pamphlets. The sources and amount of HUM's military funding are unknown. In anticipation of asset seizures by the Pakistani Government, the HUM withdrew funds from bank accounts and invested in legal businesses, such as commodity trading, real estate, and production of consumer goods. Its fundraising in Pakistan has been constrained since the government clampdown on extremist groups and freezing of terrorist assets.

Hizballah (Party of God)

a.k.a. Islamic Jihad, Revolutionary Justice Organization, Organization of the Oppressed on Earth, and Islamic Jihad for the Liberation of Palestine

Description

Formed in 1982 in response to the Israeli invasion of Lebanon, this Lebanon-based radical Shi'a group takes its ideological inspiration from the Iranian revolution and the teachings of the Ayatollah Khomeini. The Majlis al-Shura, or Consultative Council, is the group's highest governing body and is led by Secretary General Hassan Nasrallah. Hizballah formally advocates ultimate establishment of Islamic rule in Lebanon and liberating all occupied Arab lands, including Jerusalem. It has expressed as a goal the elimination of Israel. Has expressed its unwillingness to work within the confines of Lebanon's established political system; however, this stance changed with the party's decision in 1992 to participate in parliamentary elections. Although closely allied with and often directed by Iran, the group may have conducted operations that were not approved by Tehran. While Hizballah does not share the Syrian regime's secular orientation, the group has been a strong tactical ally in helping Syria advance its political objectives in the region.

Activities

Known or suspected to have been involved in numerous anti-U.S. terrorist attacks, including the suicide truck bombings of the U.S. Embassy in Beirut April 1983, and U.S. Marine barracks in Beirut in October 1983, and the U.S. Embassy annex in Beirut in September 1984. Three members of Hizballah, 'Imad Mughniyah, Hasan Izz-al-Din, and Ali Atwa, are on the FBI's list of 22 Most Wanted Terrorists for the hijacking in 1985 of TWA Flight 847 during which a U.S. Navy diver was murdered. Elements of the group were responsible for the kidnapping and detention of U.S. and other Western hostages in Lebanon. The group also attacked the Israeli Embassy in Argentina in 1992 and is a suspect in the 1994 bombing of the Israeli cultural center in Buenos Aires. In fall 2000, it captured three Israeli soldiers in the Shabaa Farms and kidnapped an Israeli noncombatant whom it may have lured to Lebanon under false pretenses.

Strength

Several thousand supporters and a few hundred terrorist operatives.

Location/Area of Operation

Operates in the Bekaa Valley, Hermil, the southern suburbs of Beirut, and southern Lebanon. Has established cells in Europe, Africa, South America, North America, and Asia.

External Aid

Receives substantial amounts of financial, training, weapons, explosives, political, diplomatic, and organizational aid from Iran and received diplomatic, political, and logistical support from Syria.

Islamic Movement of Uzbekistan (IMU)

Description

Coalition of Islamic militants from Uzbekistan and other Central Asian states opposed to Uzbekistani President Islom Karimov's secular regime. Before the counterterrorism coalition began operations in Afghanistan in October, the IMU's primary goal was the establishment of an Islamic state in Uzbekistan. If IMU political and ideological leader Tohir Yoldashev survives the counterterrorism campaign and can regroup the organization, however, he might widen the IMU's targets to include all those he perceives as fighting Islam. The group's propaganda has always included anti-Western and anti-Israeli rhetoric.

Activities

The IMU primarily targeted Uzbekistani interests before October 2001 and is believed to have been responsible for five car bombs in Tashkent in February 1999. Militants also took foreigners hostage in 1999 and 2000, including four U.S. citizens who were mountain climbing in August 2000, and four Japanese geologists and eight Krygyzstani soldiers in August 1999. Since October, the Coalition has captured, killed, and dispersed many of the militants who remained in Afghanistan to fight with the Taliban and al-Qaida, severely degrading the IMU's ability to attack Uzbekistani or Coalition interests in the near term. IMU military leader Juma Namangani apparently was killed during an air strike in November. At year's end, Yoldashev remained at large.

Strength

Militants probably number under 2,000.

Location/Area of Operation

Militants are scattered throughout South Asia and Tajikistan. Area of operations includes Afghanistan, Iran, Kyrgyzstan, Pakistan, Tajikistan, and Uzbekistan.

External Aid

Support from other Islamic extremist groups and patrons in the Middle East and Central and South Asia. IMU leadership broadcasts statements over Iranian radio.

Jaish-e-Mohammed (JEM) (Army of Mohammed)

Description

The Jaish-e-Mohammed (JEM) is an Islamic extremist group based in Pakistan that was formed by Masood Azhar upon his release from prison in India in early 2000. The group's aim is to unite Kashmir with Pakistan. It is politically aligned with the radical political party, Jamiat-i Ulema-i Islam Fazlur Rehman faction (JUI-F). The United States announced the addition of JEM to the U.S. Treasury Department's Office of Foreign Asset Control's (OFAC) list—which includes organizations that are believed to support terrorist groups and have assets in U.S. jurisdiction that can be frozen or controlled—in October and the Foreign Terrorist Organization list in December. The group was banned and its assets were frozen by the Pakistani Government in January 2002.

Activities

The JEM's leader, Masood Azhar, was released from Indian imprisonment in December 1999 in exchange for 155 hijacked Indian Airline hostages. The 1994 HUA kidnappings by Omar Sheikh of U.S. and British nationals in New Delhi and the July 1995 HUA/AI Faran kidnappings of Westerners in Kashmir were two of several previous HUA efforts to free Azhar. The JEM on 1 October 2001 claimed responsibility for a suicide attack on the Jammu and Kashmir legislative assembly building in Srinagar that killed at least 31 persons, but later denied the claim. The Indian Government has publicly implicated the JEM, along with Lashkar-e-Tayyiba for the 13 December attack on the Indian Parliament that killed 9 and injured 18.

Strength

Has several hundred armed supporters located in Azad Kashmir, Pakistan, and in India's southern Kashmir and Doda regions, including a large cadre of former HUM members. Supporters are mostly Pakistanis and Kashmiris and also include Afghans and Arab veterans of the Afghan war. Uses light and heavy machine-guns, assault rifles, mortars, improvised explosive devices, and rocket grenades.

Location/Area of Operation

Based in Peshawar and Muzaffarabad, but members conduct terrorist activities primarily in Kashmir. The JEM maintained training camps in Afghanistan until the fall of 2001.

External Aid

Most of the JEM's cadre and material resources have been drawn from the militant groups Harakat ul-Jihad al-Islami (HUJI) and the Harakat ul-Mujahedin (HUM). The JEM had close ties to Afghan Arabs and the Taliban. Usama Bin Laden is suspected of giving funding to the JEM. The JEM also collects funds through donation requests in magazines and pamphlets. In anticipation of asset seizures by the Pakistani Government, the JEM withdrew funds from bank accounts and invested in legal businesses, such as commodity trading, real estate, and production of consumer goods.

Al-Jihad

a.k.a. Egyptian Islamic Jihad, Jihad Group, Islamic Jihad

Description

Egyptian Islamic extremist group active since the late 1970s. Merged with bin Laden's al-Qaida organization in June 2001, but may retain some capability to conduct independent operations. Continues to suffer setbacks worldwide, especially after 11 September attacks. Primary goals are to overthrow the Egyptian Government and replace it with an Islamic state and attack U.S. and Israeli interests in Egypt and abroad.

Activities

Specializes in armed attacks against high-level Egyptian Government personnel, including cabinet ministers, and car-bombings against official U.S. and Egyptian facilities. The original Jihad was responsible for the assassination in 1981 of Egyptian President Anwar Sadat. Claimed responsibility for the attempted assassinations of Interior Minister Hassan al-Alfi in August 1993 and Prime Minister Atef Sedky in November 1993. Has not conducted an attack inside Egypt since 1993 and has never targeted foreign tourists there. Responsible for Egyptian Embassy bombing in Islamabad in 1995; in 1998 attack against U.S. Embassy in Albania was thwarted.

Strength

Unknown, but probably has several hundred hard-core members.

Location/Area of Operation

Operates in the Cairo area, but most of its network is outside Egypt, including Yemen, Afghanistan, Pakistan, Lebanon, and the United Kingdom, and its activities have been centered outside Egypt for several years.

External Aid

Unknown. The Egyptian Government claims that Iran supports the Jihad. Its merger with al-Qaida also boosts Bin Laden's support for the group. Also may obtain some funding through various Islamic nongovernmental organizations, cover businesses, and criminal acts.

Kahane Chai (Kach)

Description

Stated goal is to restore the biblical state of Israel. Kach (founded by radical Israeli-American rabbi Meir Kahane) and its offshoot Kahane Chai, which means "Kahane Lives," (founded by Meir Kahane's son Binyamin following his father's assassination in the United States) were declared to be terrorist organizations in March 1994 by the Israeli Cabinet under the 1948 Terrorism Law. This followed the groups' statements in support of Dr. Baruch Goldstein's attack in February 1994 on the al-lbrahimi Mosque—Goldstein was affiliated with Kach—and their verbal attacks on the Israeli Government. Palestinian gunmen killed Binyamin Kahane and his wife in a drive-by shooting in December 2000 in the West Bank.

Activities

Organizes protests against the Israeli Government. Harasses and threatens Palestinians in Hebron and the West Bank. Has threatened to attack Arabs, Palestinians, and Israeli Government officials. Has vowed revenge for the death of Binyamin Kahane and his wife.

Strength

Unknown.

Location/Area of Operation

Israel and West Bank settlements, particularly Qiryat Arba' in Hebron.

External Aid

Receives support from sympathizers in the United States and Europe.

Kurdistan Workers' Party (PKK)

Description

Founded in 1974 as a Marxist-Leninist insurgent group primarily composed of Turkish Kurds. The group's goal has been to establish an independent Kurdish state in south-eastern Turkey, where the population is predominantly Kurdish. In the early 1990s, the PKK moved beyond rural-based insurgent activities to include urban terrorism. Turkish authorities captured Chairman Abdullah Ocalan in Kenya in early 1999; the Turkish State Security Court subsequently sentenced him to death. In August 1999, Ocalan announced a "peace initiative," ordering members to refrain from violence and requesting dialogue with Ankara on Kurdish issues. At a PKK Congress in January

2000, members supported Ocalan's initiative and claimed the group now would use only political means to achieve its new goal, improved rights for Kurds in Turkey.

Activities

Primary targets have been Turkish Government security forces in Turkey. Conducted attacks on Turkish diplomatic and commercial facilities in dozens of West European cities in 1993 and again in spring 1995. In an attempt to damage Turkey's tourist industry, the PKK bombed tourist sites and hotels and kidnapped foreign tourists in the early to mid-1990s.

Strength

Approximately 4,000 to 5,000, most of whom currently are located in northern Iraq. Has thousands of sympathizers in Turkey and Europe.

Location/Area of Operation

Operates in Turkey, Europe, and the Middle East.

External Aid

Has received safe haven and modest aid from Syria, Iraq, and Iran. Damascus generally upheld its September 2000 antiterror agreement with Ankara, pledging not to support the PKK.

Lashkar-e-Tayyiba (LT) (Army of the Righteous)

Description

The LT is the armed wing of the Pakistan-based religious organization, Markaz-ud-Dawa-wal-Irshad (MDI)—a Sunni anti-U.S. missionary organization formed in 1989. The LT is led by Abdul Wahid Kashmiri and is one of the three largest and best-trained groups fighting in Kashmir against India; it is not connected to a political party. The United States in October announced the addition of the LT to the U.S. Treasury Department's Office of Foreign Asset Control's (OFAC) list—which includes organizations that are believed to support terrorist groups and have assets in U.S. jurisdiction that can be frozen or controlled. The group was banned and its assets were frozen by the Pakistani Government in January 2002.

Activities

The LT has conducted a number of operations against Indian troops and civilian targets in Kashmir since 1993. The LT claimed responsibility for numerous attacks in 2001, including a January attack on Srinagar airport that killed five Indians along with six militants; an attack on a police station in Srinagar that killed at least eight officers and wounded several others; and an attack in April against Indian border security forces that left at least four dead. The Indian Government publicly implicated the LT along with JEM for the 13 December attack on the Indian Parliament building.

Strength

Has several members in Azad Kashmir, Pakistan, and in India's southern Kashmir and Doda regions. Almost all LT cadres are non-Kashmiris, mostly Pakistanis from madrassas across the country and Afghan veterans of the Afghan wars. Uses assault rifles, light and heavy machine-guns, mortars, explosives, and rocket propelled grenades.

Location/Area of Operation

Has been based in Muridke (near Lahore) and Muzaffarabad. The LT trains its militants in mobile training camps across Pakistan-administered Kashmir and had trained in Afghanistan until fall of 2001.

External Aid

Collects donations from the Pakistani community in the Persian Gulf and United Kingdom, Islamic NGOs [nongovernmental organizations], and Pakistani and Kashmiri businessmen. The LT also maintains a website (under the name of its parent organization Jamaat ud-Daawa), through which it solicits funds and provides information on the group's activities. The amount of LT funding is unknown. The LT maintains ties to religious/military groups around the world, ranging from the Philippines to the Middle East and Chechnya through the MDI fraternal network. In anticipation of asset seizures by the Pakistani Government, the LT withdrew funds from bank accounts and invested in legal businesses, such as commodity trading, real estate, and production of consumer goods.

Liberation Tigers of Tamil Eelam (LTTE)

Other known front organizations: World Tamil Association (WTA), World Tamil Movement (WTM), the Federation of Associations of Canadian Tamils (FACT), the Ellalan Force, and the Sangilian Force.

Description

Founded in 1976, the LTTE is the most powerful Tamil group in Sri Lanka and uses overt and illegal methods to raise funds, acquire weapons, and publicize its cause of establishing an independent Tamil state. The LTTE began its armed conflict with the Sri Lankan Government in 1983 and relies on a guerrilla strategy that includes the use of terrorist tactics.

Activities

The Tigers have integrated a battlefield insurgent strategy with a terrorist program that targets not only key personnel in the countryside but also senior Sri Lankan political and military leaders in Colombo and other urban centers. The Tigers are most notorious for their cadre of suicide bombers, the Black Tigers. Political assassinations and bombings are commonplace. The LTTE has refrained from targeting foreign diplomatic and commercial establishments.

Strength

Exact strength is unknown, but the LTTE is estimated to have 8,000 to 10,000 armed combatants in Sri Lanka, with a core of trained fighters of approximately 3,000 to 6,000. The LTTE also has a significant overseas support structure for fund-raising, weapons procurement, and propaganda activities.

Location/Area of Operations

The Tigers control most of the northern and eastern coastal areas of Sri Lanka but have conducted operations throughout the island. Headquartered in northern Sri Lanka, LTTE leader Velupillai Prabhakaran has established an extensive network of checkpoints and informants to keep track of any outsiders who enter the group's area of control.

External Aid

The LTTE's overt organizations support Tamil separatism by lobbying foreign governments and the United Nations. The LTTE also uses its international contacts to procure weapons, communications, and any other equipment and supplies it needs. The LTTE exploits large Tamil communities in North America, Europe, and Asia to obtain funds and supplies for its fighters in Sri Lanka often through false claims or even extortion.

Mujahedin-e Khalq Organization (MEK or MKO)

a.k.a. The National Liberation Army of Iran (NLA, the militant wing of the MEK), the People's Mujahidin of Iran (PMOI), National Council of Resistance (NCR), Muslim Iranian Student's Society (front organization used to garner financial support)

Description

The MEK philosophy mixes Marxism and Islam. Formed in the 1960s, the organization was expelled from Iran after the Islamic Revolution in 1979, and its primary support now comes from the Iraqi regime of Saddam Hussein. Its history is studded with anti-Western attacks as well as terrorist attacks on the interests of the clerical regime in Iran and abroad. The MEK now advocates a secular Iranian regime.

Activities

Worldwide campaign against the Iranian Government stresses propaganda and occasionally uses terrorist violence. During the 1970s the MEK killed several U.S. military personnel and U.S. civilians working on defense projects in Tehran. It supported the takeover in 1979 of the U.S. Embassy in Tehran. In 1981 the MEK planted bombs in the head office of the Islamic Republic Party and the Premier's office, killing some 70 high-ranking Iranian officials, including chief Justice Ayatollah Mohammad Beheshti, President Mohammad-Ali Rajaei, and Premier Mohammad-Javad Bahonar. In 1991, it assisted the government of Iraq in suppressing the Shia and Kurdish uprisings in northern and southern Iraq. In April 1992, it conducted attacks on Iranian Embassies in 13 different countries, demonstrating the group's ability to mount large-scale operations overseas. In recent years the MEK has targeted key military officers and assassinated the deputy chief of the Armed Forces General Staff in April 1999. In April 2000, the MEK attempted to assassinate the commander of the Nasr Headquarters—the interagency board responsible for coordinating policies on Iraq. The normal pace of anti-Iranian operations increased during the "Operation Great Bahman" in February 2000, when the group launched a dozen attacks against Iran. In 2000 and 2001, the MEK was involved regularly in mortar attacks and hit-and-run raids on Iranian military and law enforcement units and government buildings near the Iran-Iraq border. Since the end of the Iran-Iraq War the tactics along the border have garnered few military gains and have become commonplace. MEK insurgent activities in Tehran constitute the biggest security concern for the Iranian leadership. In February 2000, for example, the MEK attacked the leadership complex in Tehran that houses the offices of the Supreme Leader and President.

Strength

Several thousand fighters located on bases scattered throughout Iraq and armed with tanks, infantry fighting vehicles, and artillery. The MEK also has an overseas support structure. Most of the fighters are organized in the MEK's National Liberation Army (NLA).

Location/Area of Operation

In the 1980s the MEK's leaders were forced by Iranian security forces to flee to France. Since resettling in Iraq in 1987, the group has conducted internal security operations in support of the Government of Iraq. In the mid-1980s the group did not mount terrorist operations in Iran at a level similar to its activities in the 1970s, but by the 1990s the MEK had claimed credit for an increasing number of operations in Iran.

External Aid

Beyond support from Iraq, the MEK uses front organizations to solicit contributions from expatriate Iranian communities.

National Liberation Army (ELN)—Colombia

Description

Marxist insurgent group formed in 1965 by urban intellectuals inspired by Fidel Castro and Che Guevara. Began a dialogue with Colombian officials in 1999 following a campaign of mass kidnappings—each involving at least one U.S. citizen—to demonstrate its strength and continuing viability, and force the Pastrana administration to negotiate. Peace talks between Bogotá and the ELN, started in 1999, continued sporadically through 2001 until Bogotá broke them off in August, but resumed in Havana, Cuba, by year's end.

Activities

Kidnapping, hijacking, bombing, extortion, and guerrilla war. Modest conventional military capability. Annually conducts hundreds of kidnappings for ransom, often targeting foreign employees of large corporations, especially in the petroleum industry. Frequently assaults energy infrastructure and has inflicted major damage on pipelines and the electric distribution network.

Strength

Approximately 3,000–5,000 armed combatants and an unknown number of active supporters.

Location/Area of Operation

Mostly in rural and mountainous areas of north, northeast, and southwest Colombia, and Venezuela border regions.

External Aid

Cuba provides some medical care and political consultation.

The Palestine Islamic Jihad (PIJ)

Description

Originated among militant Palestinians in the Gaza Strip during the 1970s. PIJ-Shiqaqi faction, currently led by Ramadan Shallah in Damascus, is most active. Committed to the creation of an Islamic Palestinian state and the destruction of Israel through holy war. Also opposes moderate Arab governments that it believes have been tainted by Western secularism.

Activities

PIJ activists have conducted many attacks, including large-scale suicide bombings against Israeli civilian and military targets. The group increased its operational activity in 2001 during the *Intifadah* [Palestinian uprising], claiming numerous attacks against Israeli interests. The group has not targeted U.S. interests and continues to confine its attacks to Israelis inside Israel and the territories.

Strength

Unknown.

Location/Area of Operation

Primarily Israel, the West Bank, and Gaza Strip, and other parts of the Middle East, including Lebanon and Syria, where the leadership is based.

External Aid

Receives financial assistance from Iran and limited logistic support assistance from Syria.

Palestine Liberation Front (PLF)

Description

Broke away from the PFLP-GC in mid-1970s. Later split again into pro-PLO, pro-Syrian, and pro-Libyan factions. Pro-PLO faction led by Muhammad Abbas (Abu Abbas), who became member of PLO Executive Committee in 1984 but left it in 1991.

Activities

The Abu Abbas–led faction is known for aerial attacks against Israel. Abbas's group also was responsible for the attack in 1985 on the cruise ship Achille Lauro and the murder of U.S. citizen Leon Klinghoffer. A warrant for Abu Abbas's arrest is outstanding in Italy.

Strength

Unknown.

Location/Area of Operation

PLO faction based in Tunisia until *Achille Lauro* attack. Now based in Iraq.

External Aid

Receives support mainly from Iran. Has received support from Libya in the past.

Popular Front for the Liberation of Palestine (PFLP)

Description

Marxist-Leninist group founded in 1967 by George Habash as a member of the PLO. Joined the Alliance of Palestinian Forces (APF) to oppose the Declaration of Principles signed in 1993 and suspended participation in the PLO. Broke away from the APF, along with the DFLP, in 1996 over ideological differences. Took part in meetings with Arafat's Fatah party and PLO representatives in 1999 to discuss national unity and the reinvigoration of the PLO but continues to oppose current negotiations with Israel.

Activities

Committed numerous international terrorist attacks during the 1970s. Since 1978 has conducted attacks against Israeli or moderate Arab targets, including killing a settler and her son in December 1996. Stepped up operational activity in 2001, highlighted by the shooting death of Israeli Tourism Minister in October to retaliation for Israel's killing of PFLP leader in August.

Strength

Some 800.

Location/Area of Operation

Syria, Lebanon, Israel, West Bank, and Gaza.

External Aid

Receives safe haven and some logistical assistance from Syria.

Popular Front for the Liberation of Palestine—General Command (PFLP-GC)

Description

Split from the PFLP in 1968, claiming it wanted to focus more on fighting and less on politics. Opposed to Arafat's PLO. Led by Ahmad Jabril, a former captain in the Syrian Army. Closely tied to both Syria and Iran.

Activities

Carried out dozens of attacks in Europe and the Middle East during 1970s–80s. Known for cross-border terrorist attacks into Israel using unusual means, such as hot-air balloons and motorized hang gliders. Primary focus now on guerrilla operations in southern Lebanon, small-scale attacks in Israel, West Bank, and Gaza.

Strength

Several hundred.

Location/Area of Operation

Headquarters in Damascus with bases in Lebanon.

External Aid

Receives support from Syria and financial support from Iran.

Al-Qaida

Description

Established by Usama Bin Laden in the late 1980s to bring together Arabs who fought in Afghanistan against the Soviet Union. Helped finance, recruit, transport, and train Sunni Islamic extremists for the Afghan resistance. Current goal is to establish a pan-Islamic Caliphate throughout the world by working with allied Islamic extremist groups to overthrow regimes it deems "non-Islamic" and expelling Westerners and non-Muslims from Muslim countries. Issued statement under banner of "The World Islamic Front for Jihad Against the Jews and Crusaders" in February 1998, saying it was the duty of all Muslims to kill U.S. citizens—civilian or military—and their allies everywhere. Merged with Egyptian Islamic Jihad (Al-Jihad) in June 2001.

Activities

On 11 September 2001, 19 al-Qaida suicide attackers hijacked and crashed four U.S. commercial jets, two into the World Trade Center in New York City, one into the Pentagon near Washington, DC, and a fourth into a field in Shanksville, Pennsylvania, leaving about 3,000 individuals dead or missing. Directed the 12 October 2000 attack on the USS *Cole* in the port of Aden, Yemen, killing 17 U.S. Navy members, and injuring another 39. Conducted the bombings in August 1998 of the U.S. Embassies in Nairobi, Kenya, and Dar es Salaam, Tanzania, that killed at least 301 individuals and injured more than 5,000 others. Claims to have shot down U.S. helicopters and killed U.S. servicemen in Somalia in 1993 and to have conducted three bombings that targeted U.S. troops in Aden, Yemen, in December 1992.

Al-Qaida is linked to the following plans that were not carried out: to assassinate Pope John Paul II during his visit to Manila in late 1994, to kill President Clinton during a visit to the Philippines in early 1995, the midair bombing of a dozen U.S. trans-Pacific flights in 1995, and to set off a bomb at Los Angeles International Airport in 1999. Also plotted to carry out terrorist operations against U.S. and Israeli tourists visiting Jordan for millennial celebrations in late 1999. (Jordanian authorities thwarted the planned attacks and put 28 suspects on trial.) In December 2001, suspected al-Qaida associate Richard Colvin Reid attempted to ignite a shoe bomb on a transatlantic flight from Paris to Miami.

Strength

Al-Qaida may have several thousand members and associates. Also serves as a focal point or umbrella organization for a worldwide network that includes many Sunni Islamic extremist groups, some members of al-Gama'a al-Islamiyya, the Islamic Movement of Uzbekistan, and the Harakat ul-Mujahidin.

Location/Area of Operation

Al-Qaida has cells worldwide and is reinforced by its ties to Sunni extremist networks. Coalition attacks on Afghanistan since October 2001 have dismantled the Taliban— al-Qaida's protectors—and led to the capture, death, or dispersal of al-Qaida operatives. Some al-Qaida members at large probably will attempt to carry out future attacks against U.S. interests.

External Aid

Bin Laden, member of a billionaire family that owns the Bin Laden Group construction empire, is said to have inherited tens of millions of dollars that he uses to help finance the group. Al-Qaida also maintains moneymaking front businesses, solicits donations from like-minded supporters, and illicitly siphons funds from donations to Muslim charitable organizations. U.S. efforts to block al-Qaida funding has hampered al-Qaida's ability to obtain money.

Real IRA (RIRA)

a.k.a. True IRA

Description

Formed in early 1998 as clandestine armed wing of the 32-County Sovereignty Movement, a "political pressure group" dedicated to removing British forces from Northern Ireland and unifying Ireland. The 32-County Sovereignty Movement opposed Sinn Fein's adoption in September 1997 of the Mitchell principles of democracy and non-violence and opposed the amendment in December 1999 of Articles 2 and 3 of the Irish Constitution, which laid claim to Northern Ireland. Michael "Mickey" McKevitt, who left the IRA to protest its cease-fire, leads the group; Bernadette Sands-McKevitt, his wife, is a founder-member of the 32-County Sovereignty Movement, the political wing of the RIRA.

Activities

Bombings, assassinations, and robberies. Many Real IRA members are former IRA members who left that organization following the IRA cease-fire and bring to RIRA a wealth of experience in terrorist tactics and bombmaking. Targets include British military and police in Northern Ireland and Northern Ireland Protestant communities. RIRA is linked to and understood to be responsible for the car bomb attack in Omagh, Northern Ireland, on 15 August, 1998 that killed 29 and injured 220 persons. The group began to observe a cease-fire following Omagh but in 2000 and 2001 resumed attacks in Northern Ireland and on the UK mainland against targets such as M16 headquarters and the BBC.

Strength

100–200 activists plus possible limited support from IRA hard-liners dissatisfied with IRA cease-fire and other republican sympathizers. British and Irish authorities arrested at least 40 members in the spring and summer of 2001, including leader McKevitt, who is currently in prison in the Irish Republic awaiting trial for being a member of a terrorist organization and directing terrorist attacks.

Location/Area of Operation

Northern Ireland, Irish Republic, Great Britain.

External Aid

Suspected of receiving funds from sympathizers in the United States and of attempting to buy weapons from U.S. gun dealers. RIRA also is reported to have purchased sophisticated weapons from the Balkans. Three Irish nationals associated with RIRA were extradited from Slovenia to the UK and are awaiting trial on weapons procurement charges.

Revolutionary Armed Forces of Colombia (FARC)

Description

Established in 1964 as the military wing of the Colombian Communist Party, the FARC is Colombia's oldest, largest, most capable, and best-equipped Marxist insurgency. The FARC is governed by a secretariat, led by septuagenarian Manuel Marulanda, a.k.a. "Tirofijo," and six others, including senior military commander Jorge Briceno, a.k.a. "Mono Jojoy." Organized along military lines and includes several urban fronts. In 2001, the group continued a slow-moving peace negotiation process with the Pastrana Administration that has gained the group several concessions, including a demilitarized zone used as a venue for negotiations.

Activities

Bombings, murder, kidnapping, extortion, hijacking, as well as guerilla and conventional military action against Colombian political, military, and economic targets. In March 1999 the FARC executed three U.S. Indian rights activists on Venezuelan territory after it kidnapped them in Colombia. Foreign citizens often are targets of FARC kidnapping for ransom. Has well-documented ties to narcotics traffickers, principally through the provision of armed protection.

Strength

Approximately 9,000–12,000 armed combatants and an unknown number of supporters, mostly in rural areas.

Location/Area of Operation

Colombia with some activities—extortion, kidnapping, logistics, and R&R—in Venezuela, Panama, and Ecuador.

External Aid

Cuba provides some medical care and political consultation.

Revolutionary Nuclei

a.k.a. Revolutionary Cells

Description

Revolutionary Nuclei (RN) emerged from a broad range of antiestablishment and anti-U.S./NATO/EU leftist groups active in Greece between 1995 and 1998. The group is believed to be the successor to or offshoot of Greece's most prolific terrorist group, Revolutionary People's Struggle (ELA), which has not claimed an attack since January 1995. Indeed, RN appeared to fill the void left by ELA, particularly as lesser groups faded from the scene. RN's few communiqués show strong similarities in rhetoric, tone, and theme to ELA proclamations. RN has not claimed an attack since November 2000.

Activities

Beginning operations in January 1995, the group has claimed responsibility for some two dozen arson attacks and explosive low-level bombings targeting a range of U.S., Greek, and other European targets in Greece. In its most infamous and lethal attack to date, the group claimed responsibility for a bomb it detonated at the Intercontinental Hotel in April 1999 that resulted in the death of a Greek woman and injured a Greek man. Its modus operandi includes warning calls of impending attacks, attacks targeting property [and] individuals; use of rudimentary timing devices; and strikes during the late evening-early morning hours. RN last attacked U.S. interests in Greece in November 2000 with two separate bombings against the Athens offices of Citigroup and the studio of a Greek/American sculptor. The group also detonated an explosive device outside the Athens offices of Texaco in December 1999. Greek targets have included court and other government office buildings, private vehicles, and the offices of Greek firms involved in NATO-related defense contracts in Greece. Similarly, the group has attacked European interests in Athens, including Barclays Bank in December 1998 and November 2000.

Strength
Group membership is believed to be small, probably drawing from the Greek militant leftist or anarchist milieu.

Location/Area of Operation
Primary area of operation is in the Athens metropolitan area.

External Aid
Unknown, but believed to be self-sustaining.

Revolutionary Organization 17 November (17 November)

Description
Radical leftist group established in 1975 and named for the student uprising in Greece in November 1973 that protested the military regime. Anti-Greek establishment, anti-U.S., anti-Turkey, anti-NATO, and committed to the ouster of U.S. bases, removal of Turkish military presence from Cyprus, and severing of Greece's ties to NATO and the European Union (EU).

Activities
Initial attacks were assassinations of senior U.S. officials and Greek public figures. Added bombings in 1980s. Since 1990 has expanded targets to include EU facilities and foreign firms investing in Greece and has added improvised rocket attacks to its methods. Most recent attack claimed was the murder in June 2000 of British Defense Attaché Stephen Saunders.

Strength
Unknown, but presumed to be small.

Location/Area of Operation
Athens, Greece.

Revolutionary People's Liberation Party/Front (DHKP/C)
a.k.a. Devrimci So, Revolutionary Left, Dev Sol

Description
Originally formed in 1978 as Devrimci Sol, or Dev Sol, a splinter faction of the Turkish People's Liberation Party/Front. Renamed in 1994 after factional infighting, it espouses a Marxist ideology and is virulently anti-U.S. and anti-NATO [North At-

lantic Treaty Organization]. Finances its activities chiefly through armed robberies and extortion.

Activities

Since the late 1980s has concentrated attacks against current and retired Turkish security and military officials. Began a new campaign against foreign interests in 1990. Assassinated two U.S. military contractors and wounded a U.S. Air Force officer to protest the Gulf War. Launched rockets at U.S. Consulate in Istanbul in 1992. Assassinated prominent Turkish businessman and two others in early 1996, its first significant terrorist act as DHKP/C. Turkish authorities thwarted DHKP/C attempt in June 1999 to fire light antitank weapon at U.S. Consulate in Istanbul. Conducted its first suicide bombings, targeting Turkish police, in January and September 2001. Series of safehouse raids and arrests by Turkish police over last three years have weakened group significantly.

Strength

Unknown.

Location/Area of Operation

Conducts attacks in Turkey, primarily in Istanbul. Raises funds in Western Europe.

External Aid

Unknown.

The Salafist Group for Call and Combat (GSPC)

Description

The Salafist Group for Call and Combat (GSPC) splinter faction that began in 1996 has eclipsed the GIA since approximately 1998, and currently is assessed to be the most effective remaining armed group inside Algeria. In contrast to the GIA, the GSPC has gained popular support through its pledge to avoid civilian attacks inside Algeria (although, in fact, civilians have been attacked). Its adherents abroad appear to have largely co-opted the external networks of the GIA, active particularly throughout Europe, Africa, and the Middle East.

Activities

The GSPC continues to conduct operations aimed at government and military targets, primarily in rural areas. Such operations include false roadblocks and attacks against convoys transporting military, police, or other government personnel. According to press reporting, some GSPC members in Europe maintain contacts with other North African extremists sympathetic to al-Qaida, a number of whom were implicated in terrorist plots during 2001.

Strength

Unknown; probably several hundred to several thousand inside Algeria.

Location/Area of Operation

Algeria.

External Aid
Algerian expatriates and GSPC members abroad, many residing in Western Europe, provide financial and logistics support. In addition, the Algerian Government has accused Iran and Sudan of supporting Algerian extremists in years past.

Sendero Luminoso (Shining Path, or SL)

Description
Former university professor Abimael Guzman formed Sendero Luminoso in the late 1960s, and his teachings created the foundation of SL's militant Maoist doctrine. In the 1980s SL became one of the most ruthless terrorist groups in the Western Hemisphere; approximately 30,000 persons have died since Shining Path took up arms in 1980. Its stated goal is to destroy existing Peruvian institutions and replace them with a communist peasant revolutionary regime. It also opposes any influence by foreign governments, as well as by other Latin American guerrilla groups, especially the Tupac Amaru Revolutionary Movement (MRTA).

In 2001, the Peruvian National Police thwarted an SL attack against "an American objective," possibly the U.S. Embassy, when they arrested two Lima SL cell members. Additionally, Government authorities continued to arrest and prosecute active SL members, including, Ruller Mazombite, a.k.a. "Camarada Cayo," chief of the protection team of SL leader Macario Ala, a.k.a. "Artemio," and Evorcio Ascencios, a.k.a. "Camarada Canale," logistics chief of the Huallaga Regional Committee. Counterterrorist operations targeted pockets of terrorist activity in the Upper Huallaga River Valley and the Apurimac/Ene River Valley, where SL columns continued to conduct periodic attacks.

Activities
Conducted indiscriminate bombing campaigns and selective assassinations. Detonated explosives at diplomatic missions of several countries in Peru in 1990, including an attempt to car bomb the U.S. Embassy in December. Peruvian authorities continued operations against the SL in 2001 in the countryside, where the SL conducted periodic raids on villages.

Strength
Membership is unknown but estimated to be 200 armed militants. SL's strength has been vastly diminished by arrests and desertions.

Location/Area of Operation
Peru, with most activity in rural areas.

External Aid
None.

United Self-Defense Forces/Group of Colombia (AUC— Autodefensas Unidas de Colombia)

Description
The AUC—commonly referred to as the paramilitaries—is an umbrella organization formed in April 1997 to consolidate most local and regional paramilitary groups each

with the mission to protect economic interests and combat insurgents locally. The AUC—supported by economic elites, drug traffickers, and local communities lacking effective government security—claims its primary objective is to protect its sponsors from insurgents. The AUC now asserts itself as a regional and national counterinsurgent force. It is adequately equipped and armed and reportedly pays its members a monthly salary. AUC political leader Carlos Castaño has claimed 70 percent of the AUC's operational costs are financed with drug-related earnings, the rest from "donations" from its sponsors.

Activities

AUC operations vary from assassinating suspected insurgent supporters to engaging guerrilla combat units. Colombian National Combat operations generally consist of raids and ambushes directed against suspected insurgents. The AUC generally avoids engagements with government security forces and actions against U.S. personnel or interests.

Strength

Estimated 6,000 to 8,150, including former military and insurgent personnel.

Location/Area of Operation

AUC forces are strongest in the northwest in Antioquia, Córdoba, Sucre, and Bolivar Departments. Since 1999, the group demonstrated a growing presence in other northern and southwestern departments. Clashes between the AUC and the FARC insurgents in Putumayo in 2000 demonstrated the range of the AUC to contest insurgents throughout Colombia.

External Aid

None.

Appendix B

Significant Terrorist Incidents, 1961–2001

1961–1982

First U.S. Aircraft Hijacked, May 1, 1961: Puerto Rican–born Antuilo Ramierez Ortiz forced at gunpoint a National Airlines plane to fly to Havana Cuba, where he was given asylum.

Ambassador to Guatemala Assassinated, August 28, 1968: U.S. Ambassador to Guatemala John Gordon Mein was murdered by a rebel faction when gunmen forced his official car off the road in Guatemala City and raked the vehicle with gunfire.

Ambassador to Japan Attacked, July 30, 1969: U.S. Ambassador to Japan A. H. Meyer was attacked by a knife-wielding Japanese citizen.

Ambassador to Brazil Kidnapped, September 3, 1969: U.S. Ambassador to Brazil Charles Burke Elbrick was kidnapped by the Marxist revolutionary group MR-8.

U.S. Agency for International Development Adviser Kidnapped, July 31, 1970: In Montevideo, Uruguay, the Tupamaros terrorist group kidnapped USAID police adviser Dan Mitrione; his body was found on August 10.

"Bloody Friday," July 21, 1972: An Irish Republican Army (IRA) bomb attack killed 11 people and injured 130 in Belfast, Northern Ireland. Ten days later, three IRA car bomb attacks in the village of Claudy left six dead.

Munich Olympic Massacre, September 5, 1972: Eight Palestinian "Black September" terrorists seized 11 Israeli athletes in the Olympic Village in Munich, West Germany. In a bungled rescue attempt by West German authorities, nine of the hostages and five terrorists were killed.

Ambassador to Sudan Assassinated, March 2, 1973: U.S. Ambassador to Sudan Cleo A. Noel and other diplomats were assassinated at the Saudi Arabian Embassy in Khartoum by members of the Black September organization.

Consul General in Mexico Kidnapped, May 4, 1973: U.S. Consul General in Guadalajara Terrence Leonhardy was kidnapped by members of the People's Revolutionary Armed Forces.

Domestic Terrorism, January 27–29, 1975: Puerto Rican nationalists bombed a Wall Street bar, killing four and injuring 60; 2 days later, the Weather Underground claims responsibility for an explosion in a bathroom at the U.S. Department of State in Washington.

Entebbe Hostage Crisis, June 27, 1976: Members of the Baader-Meinhof Group and the Popular Front for the Liberation of Palestine (PFLP) seized an Air France airliner and its 258 passengers. They forced the plane to land in Uganda, where on July 3 Israeli commandos successfully rescued the passengers.

Assassination of Former Chilean Diplomat, September 21, 1976: In Washington, exiled Chilean Foreign Minister Orlando Letelier was killed by a car bomb.

Kidnapping of Italian Prime Minister, March 16, 1978: Premier Aldo Moro was seized by the Red Brigade and assassinated 55 days later.

Iran Hostage Crisis, November 4, 1979: After President Carter agreed to admit the Shah of Iran into the U.S., Iranian radicals seized the U.S. embassy in Tehran and took 66 American diplomats hostage. Thirteen hostages were soon released, but the remaining 53 were held until their release on January 20, 1981.

Grand Mosque Seizure, November 20, 1979: 200 Islamic terrorists seized the Grand Mosque in Mecca, Saudi Arabia, taking hundreds of pilgrims hostage. Saudi and French security forces retook the shrine after an intense battle in which some 250 people were killed and 600 wounded.

U.S. Installation Bombing, August 31, 1981: The Red Army exploded a bomb at the U.S. Air Force Base at Ramstein, West Germany.

Assassination of Egyptian President, October 6, 1981: Soldiers who were secretly members of the Takfir Wal-Hajira sect attacked and killed Egyptian President Anwar Sadat during a troop review.

Murder of Missionaries, December 4, 1981: Three American nuns and one lay missionary were found murdered outside San Salvador, El Salvador. They were believed to have been assassinated by a right-wing death squad.

Assassination of Lebanese Prime Minister, September 14, 1982: Premier Bashir Gemayel was assassinated by a car bomb parked outside his party's Beirut headquarters.

1983

Colombian Hostage-Taking, April 8, 1983: A U.S. citizen was seized by the Revolutionary Armed Forces of Colombia (FARC) and held for ransom.

Bombing of U.S. Embassy in Beirut, April 18, 1983: Sixty-three people, including the CIA's Middle East director, were killed, and 120 were injured in a 400-pound suicide truck-bomb attack on the U.S. Embassy in Beirut, Lebanon. The Islamic Jihad claimed responsibility.

Naval Officer Assassinated in El Salvador, May 25, 1983: A U.S. Navy officer was assassinated by the Farabundo Marti National Liberation Front.

North Korean Hit Squad, October 9, 1983: North Korean agents blew up a delegation from South Korea in Rangoon, Burma, killing 21 persons and injuring 48.

Bombing of Marine Barracks, Beirut, October 23, 1983: Simultaneous suicide truck-bomb attacks were made on American and French compounds in Beirut, Lebanon. A 12,000-pound bomb destroyed the U.S. compound, killing 242 Americans, while 58 French troops were killed when a 400-pound device destroyed a French base. Islamic Jihad claimed responsibility.

Naval Officer Assassinated in Greece, November 15, 1983: A U.S. Navy officer was shot by the November 17 terrorist group in Athens, Greece, while his car was stopped at a traffic light.

1984

Kidnapping of Embassy Official, March 16, 1984: The Islamic Jihad kidnapped and later murdered Political Officer William Buckley in Beirut, Lebanon. Other U.S. citizens not connected to the U.S. Government were seized over a succeeding 2-year period.

Hizballah Restaurant Bombing, April 12, 1984: Eighteen U.S. servicemen were killed, and 83 people were injured in a bomb attack on a restaurant near a U.S. Air Force Base in Torrejon, Spain. Responsibility was claimed by Hizballah.

Golden Temple Seizure, June 5, 1984: Sikh terrorists seized the Golden Temple in Amritsar, India. One hundred people died when Indian security forces retook the Sikh holy shrine.

Assassination of Prime Minister Gandhi, October 31, 1984: The Indian premier was shot to death by members of her security force.

1985

Kidnapping of U.S. Officials in Mexico, February 7, 1985: Under the orders of narcotrafficker Rafael Cero Quintero, Drug Enforcement Administration agent Enrique Camarena Salazar and his pilot were kidnapped, tortured, and executed.

TWA Hijacking, June 14, 1985: A Trans-World Airlines flight was hijacked en route to Rome from Athens by two Lebanese Hizballah terrorists and forced to fly to Beirut. The eight crew members and 145 passengers were held for 17 days, during which one American hostage, a U.S. Navy sailor, was murdered. After being flown twice to Algiers, the aircraft was returned to Beirut after Israel released 435 Lebanese and Palestinian prisoners.

Air India Bombing, June 23, 1985: A bomb destroyed an Air India Boeing 747 over the Atlantic, killing all 329 people aboard. Both Sikh and Kashmiri terrorists were blamed for the attack. Two cargo handlers were killed at Tokyo airport, Japan, when another Sikh bomb exploded in an Air Canada aircraft enroute to India.

Soviet Diplomats Kidnapped, September 30, 1985: In Beirut, Lebanon, Sunni terrorists kidnapped four Soviet diplomats. One was killed, but three were later released.

***Achille Lauro* Hijacking, October 7, 1985:** Four Palestinian Liberation Front terrorists seized the Italian cruise liner in the eastern Mediterranean Sea, taking more than 700 hostages. One U.S. passenger was murdered before the Egyptian Government offered the terrorists safe haven in return for the hostages' freedom.

Egyptian Airliner Hijacking, November 23, 1985: An EgyptAir airplane bound from Athens to Malta and carrying several U.S. citizens was hijacked by the Abu Nidal Group.

1986

Aircraft Bombing in Greece, March 30, 1986: A Palestinian splinter group detonated a bomb as TWA Flight 840 approached Athens Airport, killing four U.S. citizens.

Berlin Discotheque Bombing, April 5, 1986: Two U.S. soldiers were killed, and 79 American servicemen were injured in a Libyan bomb attack on a nightclub in West Berlin, West Germany. In retaliation, U.S military jets bombed targets in and around Tripoli and Benghazi.

Kimpo Airport Bombing, September 14, 1986: North Korean agents detonated an explosive device at Seoul's Kimpo Airport, killing five persons and injuring 29 others.

1987

Bus Attack, April 24, 1987: Sixteen U.S. servicemen riding in a Greek Air Force bus near Athens were injured in an apparent bombing attack, carried out by the revolutionary organization known as 17 November.

Downing of Airliner, November 29, 1987: North Korean agents planted a bomb aboard Korean Air Lines Flight 858, which subsequently crashed into the Indian Ocean.

Servicemen's Bar Attack, December 26, 1987: Catalan separatists bombed a Barcelona bar frequented by U.S. servicemen, resulting in the death of one U.S. citizen.

1988

Kidnapping of William Higgins, February 17, 1988: U.S. Marine Corps Lt. Col. W. Higgins was kidnapped and murdered by the Iranian-backed Hizballah group while serving with the United Nations Truce Supervisory Organization (UNTSO) in southern Lebanon.

Naples USO Attack, April 14, 1988: The Organization of Jihad Brigades exploded a car bomb outside a USO Club in Naples, Italy, killing one U.S. sailor.

Attack on U.S. Diplomat in Greece, June 28, 1988: The Defense Attache of the U.S. Embassy in Greece was killed when a car bomb was detonated outside his home in Athens.

Pan Am 103 Bombing, December 21, 1988: Pan American Airlines Flight 103 was blown up over Lockerbie, Scotland, by a bomb believed to have been placed on the aircraft in Frankfurt, West Germany, by Libyan terrorists. All 259 people on board were killed.

1989

Assassination of U.S. Army Officer, April 21, 1989: The New People's Army (NPA) assassinated Col. James Rowe in Manila. The NPA also assassinated two U.S. government defense contractors in September.

Assassination of German Bank Chairman, November 30, 1989: The Red Army assassinated Deutsche Bank Chairman Alfred Herrhausen in Frankfurt.

1990

U.S. Embassy Bombed in Peru, January 15, 1990: The Tupac Amaru Revolutionary Movement bombed the U.S. Embassy in Lima, Peru.

U.S. Soldiers Assassinated in the Philippines, May 13, 1990: The New People's Army (NPA) killed two U.S. Air Force personnel near Clark Air Force Base in the Philippines.

1991

Attempted Iraqi Attacks on U.S. Posts, January 18–19, 1991: Iraqi agents planted bombs at the U.S. Ambassador to Indonesia's home residence and at the USIS [U.S. Information Service] library in Manila.

1992

Kidnapping of U.S. Businessmen in the Philippines, January 17–21, 1992: A senior official of the corporation Philippine Geothermal was kidnapped in Manila by the Red Scorpion Group, and two U.S. businessmen were seized independently by the National Liberation Army and by Revolutionary Armed Forces of Colombia (FARC).

Bombing of the Israeli Embassy in Argentina, March 17, 1992: Hizballah claimed responsibility for a blast that leveled the Israeli Embassy in Buenos Aires, Argentina, causing the deaths of 29 and wounding 242.

1993

Kidnappings of U.S. Citizens in Colombia, January 31, 1993: Revolutionary Armed Forces of Colombia (FARC) terrorists kidnapped three U.S. missionaries.

World Trade Center Bombing, February 26, 1993: The World Trade Center in New York City was badly damaged when a car bomb planted by Islamic terrorists exploded in an underground garage. The bomb left six people dead and 1,000 injured. The men carrying out the attack were followers of Umar Abd al-Rahman, an Egyptian cleric who preached in the New York City area.

Attempted Assassination of President Bush by Iraqi Agents, April 14, 1993: The Iraqi intelligence service attempted to assassinate former U.S. President George Bush during a visit to Kuwait. In retaliation, the U.S. launched a cruise missile attack 2 months later on the Iraqi capital, Baghdad.

1994

Hebron Massacre, February 25, 1994: Jewish right-wing extremist and U.S. citizen Baruch Goldstein machine-gunned Moslem worshippers at a mosque in West Bank town of Hebron, killing 29 and wounding about 150.

FARC Hostage-Taking, September 23, 1994: FARC rebels kidnapped U.S. citizen Thomas Hargrove in Colombia.

Air France Hijacking, December 24, 1994: Members of the Armed Islamic Group seized an Air France Flight to Algeria. The four terrorists were killed during a rescue effort.

1995

Attack on U.S. Diplomats in Pakistan, March 8, 1995: Two unidentified gunmen killed two U.S. diplomats and wounded a third in Karachi, Pakistan.

Tokyo Subway Station Attack, March 20, 1995: Twelve persons were killed, and 5,700 were injured in a sarin nerve gas attack on a crowded subway station in the center of Tokyo, Japan. A similar attack occurred nearly simultaneously in the Yokohama subway system. The Aum Shinrikyo cult was blamed for the attacks.

Bombing of the Federal Building in Oklahoma City, April 19, 1995: Right-wing extremists Timothy McVeigh and Terry Nichols destroyed the Federal Building in Oklahoma City with a massive truck bomb that killed 166 and injured hundreds more in what was up to then the largest terrorist attack on American soil.

Kashmiri Hostage-Taking, July 4, 1995: In India, six foreigners, including two U.S. citizens, were taken hostage by Al-Faran, a Kashmiri separatist group. One non-U.S. hostage was later found beheaded.

Jerusalem Bus Attack, August 21, 1995: Hamas claimed responsibility for the detonation of a bomb that killed six and injured over 100 persons, including several U.S. citizens.

Attack on U.S. Embassy in Moscow, September 13, 1995: A rocket-propelled grenade was fired through the window of the U.S. Embassy in Moscow, ostensibly in retaliation for U.S. strikes on Serb positions in Bosnia.

Saudi Military Installation Attack, November 13, 1995: The Islamic Movement of Change planted a bomb in a Riyadh military compound that killed one U.S. citizen, several foreign national employees of the U.S. Government, and more than 40 others.

Egyptian Embassy Attack, November 19, 1995: A suicide bomber drove a vehicle into the Egyptian Embassy compound in Islamabad, Pakistan, killing at least 16 and injuring 60 persons. Three militant Islamic groups claimed responsibility.

1996

Papuan Hostage Abduction, January 8, 1996: In Indonesia, 200 Free Papua Movement (OPM) guerrillas abducted 26 individuals in the Lorenta nature preserve, Irian Jaya Province. Indonesian Special Forces members rescued the remaining nine hostages on May 15.

Kidnapping in Colombia, January 19, 1996: Revolutionary Armed Forces of Colombia (FARC) guerrillas kidnapped a U.S. citizen and demanded a $1 million ransom. The hostage was released on May 22.

Tamil Tigers Attack, January 31, 1996: Members of the Liberation Tigers of Tamil Eelam (LTTE) rammed an explosives-laden truck into the Central Bank in the heart of downtown Colombo, Sri Lanka, killing 90 civilians and injuring more than 1,400 others, including two citizens.

IRA Bombing, February 9, 1996: An Irish Republican Army (IRA) bomb detonated in London, killing two persons and wounding more than 100 others, including two U.S. citizens.

Athens Embassy Attack, February 15, 1996: Unidentified assailants fired a rocket at the U.S. embassy compound in Athens, causing minor damage to three diplomatic vehicles and some surrounding buildings. Circumstances of the attack suggested it was an operation carried out by the 17 November group.

ELN Kidnapping, February 16, 1996: Six alleged National Liberation Army (ELN) guerrillas kidnapped a U.S. citizen in Colombia. After 9 months, the hostage was released.

Hamas Bus Attack, February 26, 1996: In Jerusalem, a suicide bomber blew up a bus, killing 26 persons, including three U.S. citizens, and injuring some 80 persons, including three other U.S. citizens.

Dizengoff Center Bombing, March 4, 1996: Hamas and the Palestine Islamic Jihad (PIJ) both claimed responsibility for a bombing outside of Tel Aviv's largest shopping mall that killed 20 persons and injured 75 others, including two U.S. citizens.

West Bank Attack, May 13, 1996: Arab gunmen opened fire on a bus and a group of Yeshiva students near the Bet El settlement, killing a dual U.S.-Israeli citizen and wounding three Israelis. No one claimed responsibility for the attack, but Hamas was suspected.

USAID Worker Abduction, May 31, 1996: A gang of former Contra guerrillas kidnapped a U.S. employee of the Agency for International Development (USAID) who was assisting with election preparations in rural northern Nicaragua. She was released unharmed the next day after members of the international commission overseeing the preparations intervened.

Zekharya Attack, June 9, 1996: Unidentified gunmen opened fire on a car near Zekharya, killing a dual U.S./Israeli citizen and an Israeli. The Popular Front for the Liberation of Palestine (PFLP) is suspected.

Manchester Truck Bombing, June 15, 1996: An IRA truck bomb detonated at a Manchester shopping center, wounding 206 persons, including two German tourists, and caused extensive property damage.

Khobar Towers Bombing, June 25, 1996: A fuel truck carrying a bomb exploded outside the U.S. military's Khobar Towers housing facility in Dhahran, killing 19 U.S. military personnel and wounding 515 persons, including 240 U.S. personnel. Several groups claimed responsibility for the attack.

ETA Bombing, July 20, 1996: A bomb exploded at Tarragona International Airport in Reus, Spain, wounding 35 persons, including British and Irish tourists. The Basque Fatherland and Liberty (ETA) organization was suspected.

Bombing of Archbishop of Oran, August 1, 1996: A bomb exploded at the home of the French Archbishop of Oran, killing him and his chauffeur. The attack occurred after the Archbishop's meeting with the French Foreign Minister. The Algerian Armed Islamic Group (GIA) is suspected.

Sudanese Rebel Kidnapping, August 17, 1996: Sudan People's Liberation Army (SPLA) rebels kidnapped six missionaries in Mapourdit, including a U.S. citizen, an Italian, three Australians, and a Sudanese. The SPLA released the hostages 11 days later.

PUK Kidnapping, September 13, 1996: In Iraq, Patriotic Union of Kurdistan (PUK) militants kidnapped four French workers for Pharmaciens Sans Frontieres, a Canadian United Nations High Commissioner for Refugees (UNHCR) official, and two Iraqis.

Assassination of South Korean Consul, October 1, 1996: In Vladivostok, Russia, assailants attacked and killed a South Korean consul near his home. No one claimed responsibility, but South Korean authorities believed that the attack was carried out by professionals and that the assailants were North Koreans. North Korean officials denied the country's involvement in the attack.

Red Cross Worker Kidnappings, November 1, 1996: In Sudan, a breakaway group from the Sudanese People's Liberation Army (SPLA) kidnapped three International Committee of the Red Cross (ICRC) workers, including a U.S. citizen, an Australian, and a Kenyan. On December 9, the rebels released the hostages in exchange for ICRC supplies and a health survey for their camp.

Paris Subway Explosion, December 3, 1996: A bomb exploded aboard a Paris subway train as it arrived at the Port Royal station, killing two French nationals, a Moroccan, and a Canadian, and injuring 86 persons. Among those injured were one U.S. citizen and a Canadian. No one claimed responsibility for the attack, but Algerian extremists are suspected.

Abduction of U.S. Citizen by FARC, December 11, 1996: Five armed men claiming to be members of the Revolutionary Armed Forces of Colombia (FARC) kidnapped and later killed a U.S. geologist at a methane gas exploration site in La Guajira Department.

Tupac Amaru Seizure of Diplomats, December 17, 1996: Twenty-three members of the Tupac Amaru Revolutionary Movement (MRTA) took several hundred people hostage at a party given at the Japanese Ambassador's residence in Lima, Peru. Among the hostages were several U.S. officials, foreign ambassadors and other diplomats, Peruvian Government officials, and Japanese businessmen. The group demanded the release of all MRTA members in prison and safe passage for them and the hostage takers. The terrorists released most of the hostages in December but held 81 Peruvians and Japanese citizens for several months.

1997

Egyptian Letter Bombs, January 2–13, 1997: A series of letter bombs with Alexandria, Egypt, postmarks were discovered at Al-Hayat newspaper bureaus in Washington, New York City, London, and Riyadh, Saudi Arabia. Three similar devices, also postmarked in Egypt, were found at a prison facility in Leavenworth, Kansas. Bomb disposal experts defused all the devices, but one detonated at the Al-Hayat office in London, injuring two security guards and causing minor damage.

Tajik Hostage Abductions, February 4–17, 1997: Near Komsomolabad, Tajikistan, a paramilitary group led by Bakhrom Sodirov abducted four United Nations military observers. The victims included two Swiss, one Austrian, one Ukrainian, and their Tajik interpreter. The kidnappers demanded safe passage for their supporters from Afghanistan to Tajikistan. In four separate incidents occurring between Dushanbe and Garm, Bakhrom Sodirov and his group kidnapped two International Committee for the Red Cross members, four Russian journalists and their Tajik driver, four UNHCR [UN High Commission for Refugees] members, and the Tajik Security Minister, Saidamir Zukhurov.

Venezuelan Abduction, February 14, 1997: Six armed Colombian guerrillas kidnapped a U.S. oil engineer and his Venezuelan pilot in Apure, Venezuela. The kidnappers released the Venezuelan pilot on February 22. According to authorities, the FARC is responsible for the kidnapping.

Empire State Building Sniper Attack, February 23, 1997: A Palestinian gunman opened fire on tourists at an observation deck atop the Empire State Building in New York City, killing a Danish national and wounding visitors from the United States, Argentina, Switzerland, and France before turning the gun on himself. A handwritten note carried by the gunman claimed this was a punishment attack against the "enemies of Palestine."

ELN Kidnapping, February 24, 1997: National Liberation Army (ELN) guerrillas kidnapped a U.S. citizen employed by a Las Vegas gold corporation who was scouting a gold mining operation in Colombia. The ELN demanded a ransom of $2.5 million.

FARC Kidnapping, March 7, 1997: FARC guerrillas kidnapped a U.S. mining employee and his Colombian colleague who were searching for gold in Colombia. On November 16, the rebels released the two hostages after receiving a $50,000 ransom.

Hotel Nacional Bombing, July 12, 1997: A bomb exploded at the Hotel Nacional in Havana, injuring three persons and causing minor damage. A previously unknown group calling itself the Military Liberation Union claimed responsibility.

Israeli Shopping Mall Bombing, September 4, 1997: Three suicide bombers of Hamas detonated bombs in the Ben Yehuda shopping mall in Jerusalem, killing eight persons, including the bombers, and wounding nearly 200 others. A dual U.S./Israeli citizen was among the dead, and seven U.S. citizens were wounded.

OAS Abductions, October 23, 1997: In Colombia, ELN rebels kidnapped two foreign members of the Organization of American States (OAS) and a Colombian human rights official at a roadblock. The ELN claimed that the kidnapping was intended "to show the international community that the elections in Colombia are a farce."

Yemeni Kidnappings, October 30, 1997: Al-Sha'if tribesmen kidnapped a U.S. businessman near Sanaa. The tribesmen sought the release of two fellow tribesmen who were arrested on smuggling charges and several public works projects they claim the government promised them. They released the hostage on November 27.

Murder of U.S. Businessmen in Pakistan, November 12, 1997: Two unidentified gunmen shot to death four U.S. auditors from Union Texas Petroleum Corporation and their Pakistani driver after they drove away from the Sheraton Hotel in Karachi. The Islami Inqilabi Council, or Islamic Revolutionary Council, claimed responsibility in a call to the U.S. Consulate in Karachi. In a letter to Pakistani newspapers, the Aimal Khufia Action Committee also claimed responsibility.

Tourist Killings in Egypt, November 17, 1997: Al-Gama'at al-Islamiyya (IG) gunmen shot and killed 58 tourists and four Egyptians and wounded 26 others at the Hatshepsut Temple in the Valley of the Kings near Luxor. Thirty-four Swiss, eight Japanese, five Germans, four Britons, one French, one Colombian, a dual Bulgarian/British citizen, and four unidentified persons were among the dead. Twelve Swiss, two Japanese, two Germans, one French, and nine Egyptians were among the wounded.

1998

UN Observer Abductions, February 19, 1998: Armed supporters of late Georgian President Zviad Gamsakhurdia abducted four UN military observers from Sweden, Uruguay, and the Czech Republic.

FARC Abduction, March 21–23, 1998: FARC rebels kidnapped a U.S. citizen in Sabaneta, Colombia. FARC members also killed three persons, wounded 14, and kidnapped at least 27 others at a roadblock near Bogota. Four U.S. citizens and one Italian were among those kidnapped, as well as the acting president of the National Electoral Council (CNE) and his wife.

Somali Hostage-Takings, April 15, 1998: Somali militiamen abducted nine Red Cross and Red Crescent workers at an airstrip north of Mogadishu. The hostages included a U.S. citizen, a German, a Belgian, a French, a Norwegian, two Swiss, and one Somali. The gunmen were members of a subclan loyal to Ali Mahdi Mohammed, who controlled the northern section of the capital.

IRA Bombing, Banbridge, August 1, 1998: A 500-pound car bomb planted by the Real IRA exploded outside a shoe store in Banbridge, North Ireland, injuring 35 persons and damaging at least 200 homes.

U.S. Embassy Bombings in East Africa, August 7, 1998: A bomb exploded at the rear entrance of the U.S. embassy in Nairobi, Kenya, killing 12 U.S. citizens, 32 Foreign Service Nationals (FSNs), and 247 Kenyan citizens. About 5,000 Kenyans, six U.S. citizens, and 13 FSNs were injured. The U.S. embassy building sustained extensive structural damage. Almost simultaneously, a bomb detonated outside the U.S. embassy in Dar es Salaam, Tanzania, killing seven FSNs and three Tanzanian citizens, and injuring one U.S. citizen and 76 Tanzanians. The explosion caused major structural damage to the U.S. embassy facility. The U.S. Government held Usama Bin Laden responsible.

IRA Bombing, Omagh, August 15, 1998: A 500-pound car bomb planted by the Real IRA exploded outside a local courthouse in the central shopping district of Omagh, Northern Ireland, killing 29 persons and injuring over 330.

Colombian Pipeline Bombing, October 18, 1998: A National Liberation Army (ELN) planted bomb exploded on the Ocensa pipeline in Antioquia Department, killing approximately 71 persons and injuring at least 100 others. The pipeline is jointly owned by the Colombia State Oil Company Ecopetrol and a consortium, including U.S., French, British, and Canadian companies.

Armed Kidnapping in Colombia, November 15, 1998: Armed assailants followed a U.S. businessman and his family home in Cundinamarca Department and kidnapped his 11-year-old son after stealing money, jewelry, one automobile, and two cell phones. The kidnappers demanded $1 million in ransom. On January 21, 1999, the kidnappers released the boy.

1999

Angolan Aircraft Downing, January 2, 1999: A UN plane carrying one U.S. citizen, four Angolans, two Philippine nationals, and one Namibian was shot down, according to a UN official. No deaths or injuries were reported. Angolan authorities blamed the attack on

National Union for the Total Independence of Angola (UNITA) rebels. UNITA officials denied shooting down the plane.

Ugandan Rebel Attack, February 14, 1999: A pipe bomb exploded inside a bar, killing five persons and injuring 35 others. One Ethiopian and four Ugandan nationals died in the blast, and one U.S. citizen working for USAID, two Swiss nationals, one Pakistani, one Ethiopian, and 27 Ugandans were injured. Ugandan authorities blamed the attack on the Allied Democratic Forces (ADF).

Greek Embassy Seizure, February 16, 1999: Kurdish protesters stormed and occupied the Greek Embassy in Vienna, taking the Greek Ambassador and six other persons hostage. Several hours later the protesters released the hostages and left the embassy. The attack followed the Turkish Government's announcement of the successful capture of the Kurdistan Workers' Party (PKK) leader Abdullah Ocalan. Kurds also occupied Kenyan, Israeli, and other Greek diplomatic facilities in France, Holland, Switzerland, Britain, and Germany over the following days.

FARC Kidnappings, February 25, 1999: FARC kidnapped three U.S. citizens working for the Hawaii-based Pacific Cultural Conservancy International. On March 4, the bodies of the three victims were found in Venezuela.

Hutu Abductions, March 1, 1999: 150 armed Hutu rebels attacked three tourist camps in Uganda, killed four Ugandans, and abducted three U.S. citizens, six Britons, three New Zealanders, two Danish citizens, one Australian, and one Canadian national. Two of the U.S. citizens and six of the other hostages were subsequently killed by their abductors.

ELN Hostage-Taking, March 23, 1999: Armed guerrillas kidnapped a U.S. citizen in Boyaca, Colombia. The National Liberation Army (ELN) claimed responsibility and demanded $400,000 ransom. On July 20, ELN rebels released the hostage unharmed following a ransom payment of $48,000.

ELN Hostage-Taking, May 30, 1999: In Cali, Colombia, armed ELN militants attacked a church in the neighborhood of Ciudad Jardin, kidnapping 160 persons, including six U.S. citizens and one French national. The rebels released approximately 80 persons, including three U.S. citizens, later that day.

Shell Platform Bombing, June 27, 1999: In Port Harcourt, Nigeria, armed youths stormed a Shell oil platform, kidnapping one U.S. citizen, one Nigerian national, and one Australian citizen, and causing undetermined damage. A group calling itself "Enough is Enough in the Niger River" claimed responsibility. Further seizures of oil facilities followed.

AFRC Kidnappings, August 4, 1999: An Armed Forces Revolutionary Council (AFRC) faction kidnapped 33 UN representatives near Occra Hills, Sierra Leone. The hostages included one U.S. citizen, five British soldiers, one Canadian citizen, one representative from Ghana, one military officer from Russia, one officer from Kyrgyzstan, one officer from Zambia, one officer from Malaysia, a local Bishop, two UN officials, two local journalists, and 16 Sierra Leonean nationals.

Burmese Embassy Seizure, October 1, 1999: Burmese dissidents seized the Burmese Embassy in Bangkok, Thailand, taking 89 persons hostage, including one U.S. citizen.

PLA Kidnapping, December 23, 1999: Colombian People's Liberation Army (PLA) forces kidnapped a U.S. citizen in an unsuccessful ransoming effort.

Indian Airlines Airbus Hijacking, December 24, 1999: Five militants hijacked a flight bound from Kathmandu to New Delhi carrying 189 people. The plane and its passengers were released unharmed on December 31.

2000

Car Bombing in Spain, January 27, 2000: Police officials reported unidentified individuals set fire to a Citroen car dealership in Iturreta, causing damage to the building and destroying 12 vehicles. The attack bore the hallmark of the Basque Fatherland and Liberty (ETA).

RUF Attacks on UN Mission Personnel, May 1, 2000: On May 1 in Makeni, Sierra Leone, Revolutionary United Front (RUF) militants kidnapped at least 20 members of the United Nations Assistance Mission in Sierra Leone (UNAMSIL) and surrounded and opened fire on a UNAMSIL facility, according to press reports. The militants killed five UN soldiers in the attack. RUF militants kidnapped 300 UNAMSIL peacekeepers throughout the country, according to press reports. On May 15 in Foya, Liberia, the kidnappers released 139 hostages. On May 28, on the Liberia and Sierra Leone border, armed militants released unharmed the last of the UN peacekeepers. In Freetown, according to press reports, armed militants ambushed two military vehicles carrying four journalists. A Spaniard and one U.S. citizen were killed in a May 25 car bombing in Freetown for which the RUF was probably responsible. Suspected RUF rebels also kidnapped 21 Indian UN peacekeepers in Freetown on June 6. Additional attacks by RUF on foreign personnel followed.

Diplomatic Assassination in Greece, June 8, 2000: In Athens, Greece, two unidentified gunmen killed British Defense Attache Stephen Saunders in an ambush. The Revolutionary Organization 17 November claimed responsibility.

ELN Kidnapping, June 27, 2000: In Bogota, Colombia, ELN militants kidnapped a 5-year-old U.S. citizen and his Colombian mother, demanding an undisclosed ransom.

Kidnappings in Kyrgyzstan, August 12, 2000: In the Kara-Su Valley, the Islamic Movement of Uzbekistan took four U.S. citizens hostage. The Americans escaped on August 12.

Church Bombing in Tajikistan, October 1, 2000: Unidentified militants detonated two bombs in a Christian church in Dushanbe, killing seven persons and injuring 70 others. The church was founded by a Korean-born U.S. citizen, and most of those killed and wounded were Korean. No one claimed responsibility.

Helicopter Hijacking, October 12, 2000: In Sucumbios Province, Ecuador, a group of armed kidnappers led by former members of defunct Colombian terrorist organization the Popular Liberation Army (EPL) took hostage 10 employees of Spanish energy consortium REPSOL. Those kidnapped included five U.S. citizens, one Argentine, one Chilean, one New Zealander, and two French pilots who escaped 4 days later. On January 30, 2001, the kidnappers murdered American hostage Ronald Sander. The remaining hostages were released on February 23 following the payment of $13 million in ransom by the oil companies.

Attack on U.S.S. *Cole*, October 12, 2000: In Aden, Yemen, a small dingy carrying explosives rammed the destroyer U.S.S. *Cole*, killing 17 sailors and injuring 39 others. Supporters of Usama Bin Laden were suspected.

Manila Bombing, December 30, 2000: A bomb exploded in a plaza across the street from the U.S. embassy in Manila, injuring nine persons. The Moro Islamic Liberation Front was likely responsible.

2001

Srinagar Airport Attack, January 17, 2001: In India, six members of the Lashkar-e-Tayyba militant group were killed when they attempted to seize a local airport.

BBC Studios Bombing, March 4, 2001: A car bomb exploded at midnight outside of the British Broadcasting Corporation's main production studios in London.

ETA Bombing, March 9, 2001: Two policemen were killed by the explosion of a car bomb in Hernani, Spain.

Bus Stop Bombing, April 22, 2001: A member of Hamas detonated a bomb he was carrying near a bus stop in Kfar Siva, Israel, killing one person and injuring 60.

Tel-Aviv Nightclub Bombing, June 1, 2001: Hamas claimed responsibility for the bombing of a popular Israeli nightclub that caused over 140 casualties.

Hamas Restaurant Bombing, August 9, 2001: A Hamas-planted bomb detonated in a Jerusalem pizza restaurant, killing 15 people and wounding more than 90.

Terrorist Attacks on U.S. Homeland, September 11, 2001: Two hijacked airliners crashed into the twin towers of the World Trade Center. Soon thereafter, the Pentagon was struck by a third hijacked plane. A fourth hijacked plane, suspected to be bound for a high-profile target in Washington, crashed into a field in southern Pennsylvania. More than 5,000 U.S. citizens and other nationals were killed as a result of these acts. President Bush and Cabinet officials indicated that Usama Bin Laden was the prime suspect and that they considered the United States in a state of war with international terrorism. In the aftermath of the attacks, the United States formed the Global Coalition Against Terrorism.

Source: Office of the Historian, Bureau of Public Affairs, U.S. Department of State, September 28, 2001.

Acknowledgments

Foreword Copyright © 2002 by Barry R. McCaffrey.

Part 1 Defining the Threat

Chapter 1

Bruce Hoffman, "Defining Terrorism," *Inside Terrorism* (Columbia University Press, 1998). Copyright © 1998 by Bruce Hoffman. Reprinted by permission of Columbia University Press.

Paul R. Pillar, "The Dimensions of Terrorism and Counterterrorism," *Terrorism and U.S. Foreign Policy* (Brookings Institution Press, 2001). Copyright © 2001 by The Brookings Institution. Reprinted by permission.

Eqbal Ahmad and David Barsamian, *Terrorism: Theirs and Ours*, foreword and interview by David Barsamian (Seven Stories Press, 2001). Copyright © 2001 by David Barsamian. Reprinted by permission of Seven Stories Press and Open Media Books.

Chapter 2

Martha Crenshaw, "The Logic of Terrorism: Terrorist Behavior as a Product of Strategic Choice," in Walter Reich, ed., *Origins of Terrorism: Psychologies, Ideologies, Theologies, States of Mind* (Woodrow Wilson Center Press, 1998). Copyright © 1990, 1998 by The Woodrow Wilson International Center for Scholars. Reprinted by permission of The Johns Hopkins University Press.

Louise Richardson, "Global Rebels: Terrorist Organizations as Trans-National Actors," *Harvard International Review*, vol. 20, no. 4 (Fall 1998). Copyright © 1998 by *Harvard International Review*. Reprinted by permission.

Chapter 3

Copyright © 2004 by Russell D. Howard.

John Arquilla, David Ronfeldt, and Michele Zanini, "Networks, Netwar, and Information-Age Terrorism," in Ian O. Lesser, John Arquilla, Bruce Hoffman, David Ronfeldt, Michele Zanini and Brian Jenkins, *Countering the New Terrorism* (RAND Corporation, 1999), pp. 39–72, 80–81. Copyright © 1999 by The RAND Corporation. Reprinted by permission of The RAND Corporation, Santa Monica, CA.

Chapter 4

Chapter 5

Chapter 6

Part 2. Countering the Terrorist Threat

Chapter 7

Chapter 8

Wyn Q. Bowen, "Deterring Mass-Casualty Terrorism," *Joint Force Quarterly*, no. 31 (Summer 2002).

Chapter 9

Martha Crenshaw, "Counterterrorism Policy and the Political Process," *Studies in Conflict & Terrorism*, vol. 24 (2001). Copyright © 2001 by Taylor and Francis, Inc. Reprinted by permission of Taylor and Francis, Inc., www.routledge-ny.com.

Richard K. Betts, "Fixing Intelligence," *Foreign Affairs*, vol. 81, no. 1 (January/February 2002). Copyright © 2002 by The Council on Foreign Relations, Inc. Reprinted by permission.

Jeffrey H. Norwitz, "Combating Terrorism: With a Helmet or a Badge?" *Journal of Homeland Security* (August 2002). Copyright © 2002 by Jeffrey H. Norwitz. Reprinted by permission of the author.

Rob de Wijk, "The Limits of Military Power," *The Washington Quarterly*, vol. 25, no. 1 (Winter 2002). Copyright © 2001 by The Center for Strategic and International Studies and The Massachusetts Institute of Technology. Reprinted by permission of MIT Press Journals.

David J. Rothkopf, "Business Versus Terror," *Foreign Policy* (May/June 2002). Copyright © 2002 by The Carnegie Endowment for International Peace. Reprinted by permission of *Foreign Policy*; permission conveyed through Copyright Clearance Center, Inc.